𝔗𝔥𝔢 𝔑𝔢𝔴 𝔜𝔬𝔯𝔨 𝔗𝔦𝔪𝔢𝔰
Twentieth Century in Review

THE BALKANS

VOLUME II: 1950–2000

Other Titles in
The New York Times 20th Century in Review

The Cold War
The Gay Rights Movement
Political Censorship

Forthcoming
The Rise of the Global Economy
The Vietnam War

𝕿𝖍𝖊 𝕹𝖊𝖜 𝖄𝖔𝖗𝖐 𝕿𝖎𝖒𝖊𝖘
Twentieth Century in Review

THE BALKANS
VOLUME II: 1950–2000

Editor
Ana Siljak

Introduction by Roger Cohen

Series Editor
David Morrow

FITZROY DEARBORN PUBLISHERS
CHICAGO LONDON

For information write to:

FITZROY DEARBORN PUBLISHERS
919 North Michigan Avenue, Suite 760
Chicago IL 60611
USA

or

FITZROY DEARBORN PUBLISHERS
310 Regent Street
London W1B 3AX
England

British Library and Library of Congress Cataloging in Publication Data are available.

ISBN 1-57958-330-X

First published in the USA and UK 2001

Typeset by Print Means, Inc., New York, New York

Printed by Edwards Brothers, Ann Arbor, Michigan

Cover Design by Peter Aristedes, Chicago Advertising and Design, Chicago, Illinois

CONTENTS

VOLUME I
1875–1949

VOLUME II
1950–2000

PART VII

THE COLD WAR ERA, 1950–1988

November 3, 1950

LIBERALISM GAINS IN YUGOSLAV VIEWS

Effort to Establish It Within Framework of Communist State Is Under Way

By M. S. HANDLER
Special to The New York Times

LJUBLJANA, Yugoslavia, Nov. 2—Recent developments in Yugoslavia indicate that the fight to establish liberalism as a way of life within the framework of the Communist regime is under way.

The revolt against the anti-liberal spirit inherited from the years of close association with the Soviet Union prior to the rupture in June, 1948, has spread to high officials and party intellectuals. The compatability of liberalism with the requirements of a militant Communist state has become a subject of discussion and debate in private.

The Communists who argue the case are trying to determine the degree to which liberalism can exist within a Communist state without becoming a threat to such a state.

The new stirring within the Yugoslav Communist party has already manifested itself in concrete forms. The evidence includes the new legislation that the Government will submit to Parliament next spring reforming the criminal code, the law on misdemeanors and the law on court procedure.

Courts to Be Strengthened

A legal expert who is involved in the preparation of the new laws described them as a reinforcement of legality by strengthening the courts at the expense of the state administration.

The transfer of judicial powers from the state administration to the courts will increase the protection of citizens against the state and is considered a step in the direction of a more liberal relationship.

The intention of the commission drafting the new laws is to diminish the authority of the public prosecutor and to increase the participation of defending counsel. Inspired by the Soviet example the Yugoslavs had permitted the public prosecutor to supplant the judges as the principal figure in any court actions although the legislation now in effect does not provide for this.

An attempt will be made to restore the prosecutor to his proper functions. The resumption of something of his former role by defending counsel is calculated to guarantee a more equitable dispensing of justice.

Break With Soviet Practice

These readjustments in court procedure are intended to break with the authoritarian and fundamentally anti-liberal Soviet practice of permitting the public prosecutor to run the trials.

On an intellectual level the storm created within the party by a writer named Branko Chopitch is significant. Mr. Chopitch satirized the snobbishness and luxurious living of high officials much to the approval of many readers and to anger of many party persons. In effect, he pulled the plug from the wall that had pent up the strong urge among Yugoslav writers to write as they pleased.

The controversy took on such proportions that the party leaders, including Marshal Tito, finally took a hand and called M. Chopitch to order. M. Chopitch and his friends were told bluntly that while writers had received freedom to write as they pleased they could not deviate from the party line.

This decision was apparently reached for the purpose of urging moderation on the writers who were straining at the leash that had been holding them back from breaking away completely with the anti-liberal hangover of the pre-1948 association with the Soviet Union.

* * *

August 29, 1951

WEST TO GIVE TITO $50,000,000 IN AID

U. S., Britain and France Will Provide Sum for Economic Help, E. C. A. Announces

Special to The New York Times

WASHINGTON, Aug. 28—An agreement between the United States, Britain and France to provide $50,000,000 of economic assistance to Yugoslavia during the remainder of this year was announced today by the Economic Cooperation Administration.

The United States contribution under the tripartite agreement recently concluded at Paris will be $29,800,000. This brings to $179,800,000 the total amount of economic aid advanced in loans and grants by this Government to Yugoslavia since the regime of Premier Marshal Tito broke with Moscow.

The British Government is to provide $11,500,000 of economic aid under the three-power agreement, the agency said, The French contribution, reported to be about $6,000,000, was not specified in the announcement, presumably because it has yet to be ratified by the National Assembly.

"The three-nation program is designed to support the Yugoslav economy in its contributions to the security of the free world and the maintaining and strengthening of the standards of living of the Yugoslav people," the announcement said.

Although the aid program agreed on in Paris was supposed to cover a much longer period, the announcement said nothing about the months beyond December, 1951. It described the $50,000,000 allotment as "the first installment" on the aid program agreed to at Paris.

Estimates of economic assistance supplied Congressional committees by the agency in connection with the Administration's $8,500,000,000 mutual security program included a tentative figure of $60,000,000 for Yugoslavia from the United States. Since, then, the House of Representatives and two Senate committees cut economic aid estimates about 30 per cent.

"The new United States allotment will help Yugoslavia overcome shortages of raw materials and other supplies vital to her economic strength and the support of her military defense effort," the agency said. "The United States dollars will be used primarily for purchases of such essential items as cotton, coke and steel."

The funds allotted today were transferred to the agency by the President from money appropriated to him under the Mutual Defense Assistance Act. It would be replaced if and when Congress appropriates for the new foreign aid program now awaiting Senate action.

Prior to today's allotment of funds, the United States had advanced Yugoslavia $150,000,000 of economic aid, including $95,000,000 of grants and $55,000,000 of loans through the Export-Import Bank.

In addition to dollar aid, the Economic Cooperation Administration has been providing Yugoslavia with essential services such as defense order priority ratings for her orders in this country and in locating scarce supplies in other areas.

* * *

September 1, 1951

BELGRADE LOOSENS REINS ON ECONOMY

Plans Further Decentralizing, With Partial Return to Law of Supply and Demand

By M. S. HANDLER
Special to The New York Times

BELGRADE, Yugoslavia, Aug. 31—The Yugoslav Government has published its new economic plan, which its authors hope will prime the pump of the country's economic system. This system has been brought to a low point through repeated errors in planning and execution.

The new plan is embodied in a draft law containing 162 articles that fill thirty-four pages. Boris Kidric, chairman of the State Economic Council, has attempted to explain the new plan in a voluminous article that will appear shortly in the magazine Komunist, an official publication of the Yugoslav Communist party.

The new economic plan involves a further stage in the decentralization of industry and a reversion to a limited form of the law of supply and demand. The decentralization will diminish the planning authority of the Central Government and expand that of the producing industries.

The law of supply and demand will be permitted to operate to certain limits in the fields of the production and sale of the goods, and the establishment of wage levels.

In explaining the plan, M. Kidric said in his presentation article that the old financial and economic system had resulted in the strangling of the objective law of supply and demand, and the law of value, and in the creation of bureaucratic control. M. Kidric and his associates were the responsible authors of the old financial and economic system to which they attribute the present unsatisfactory state of Yugoslavia's national economy.

The confidence that Western economic experts have in the new plan is to be found in the fact that their governments, the United States, British and French, are studying the possibility of convincing some eighteen European and non-European governments that have extended between $170,000,000 and $190,000,000 in short and medium term commercial credits to Yugoslavia in the last three years to deter the interest payments until the end of 1953 as a contribution to the tripartite effort of strengthening Yugoslavia's economy.

The Americans took the initiative in proposing the deferment to the British and French at a recent London conference, where it was decided that Washington, London and Paris would underwrite Yugoslavia's current trade deficit until the end of 1953.

The Americans felt, and the British and French concurred, that if their Governments were to render effective economic assistance to Yugoslavia, it would be necessary for the Belgrade Government to be temporarily freed from claims that would amount to at least $25,000,000 for this year alone.

Scores Planning From Above

In explaining the new economic plan, M. Kidric said that the trouble with the existing economic system was that everything was planned from above while the producing enterprises "had practically nothing to plan." The Central Government issued the detailed basic plan and left only the operational details to the producers.

The chairman of the State Economic Council acknowledged that this state of affairs placed very narrow limits on the workers councils which had not developed as effectively as was hoped.

Under M. Kidric's new plan, the Central Government would establish only what he called the "basic proportion of production and distribution," and leave the rest of that planning to the producers. This will enable the workers' councils, among other things, to make their fullest contribution to the national welfare, he said.

This decentralization of planning is to be accompanied by reorganization of the financial system. Under present conditions, what is presumably profit is transferred from the producers to the state treasury, which distributes it. M. Kidric described this procedure as bureaucratic and leading to the exploitation of the working class.

To Retain Most of Profits

Under the new plan, most of the profits will be retained by the producing enterprises, and only a small portion will be turned over to the state treasury.

In his article, M. Kidric acknowledged that all "former capital investments had been planned regardless of whether they had been vitally necessary or had only secondary importance for our further economic developments." This will occur no longer under the new plan, he said.

M. Kidric explained that, in the future, the Central Government would plan only basic capital investments indispensable for the further economic development of the country, while other investments would be left to the producing enterprises.

In the section of his article dealing with the law of supply and demand and of value, M. Kidric acknowledged that, under the present system, consumer requirements had been disregarded in planning production and, because prices were set by the Government, the price structure had resulted in shortages of goods.

He acknowledged also that the system of wages and salaries had operated contrary to supply and demand, with bad results.

Under the new plan producing enterprises and commercial organizations will be able to set their own prices, while the Central Government will retain the right to fix prices for basic raw materials, semi-finished and certain finished goods.

M. Kidric said wages would be based on the net earnings of industrial enterprises, but that the basic wages would be set by the Central Government. Supplementary wages will be established by the industrial management boards within limits fixed by the Central Government. Wage scales will depend on the skills and education of the workers.

* * *

April 14, 1952

200,000 IN BUCHAREST FACE EXPULSION AS 'UNPRODUCTIVE'

By C. L. SULZBERGER
Special to The New York Times

PARIS, April 13—The Rumanian Communist Government has ordered the enforced evacuation of "unproductive people" from Bucharest, and mass deportations are under way in the once gay capital that formerly called itself "the Paris of the East."

According to reports filtering through the Iron Curtain, about 200,000 persons, or one-fifth of the city's present population, are scheduled to be expelled.

Removals began early last month on the basis of an official decree published in February that explained that measures were being taken "to provide space for working people" and to "improve the provisioning of the capital."

Communists to Get Space

It is said by émigré sources that the first beneficiaries of space thus artificially created will be Soviet military and civilian personnel, Communist party clubs and institutions, and Government officials.

As enforced evacuation progresses, persons permitted to remain in Bucharest will be shifted to other residences to clear entire buildings, or in some cases whole city blocks.

So far deportations have progressed at a relatively limited pace and at a rate of probably fewer than 1,000 a week. This is expected to be stepped up.

It is said that numerous wooden barracks are being built on the barren Baragan steppe not far from Bucharest as temporary shelter for this latest wave of displaced persons. Their ultimate destination does not appear to have been decided upon.

Theoretically a warning of twelve to forty-eight hours is given to those designated for deportation. However, as word has spread of implementation measures, thousands of families have packed suitcases with emergency clothing and provisions in case of sudden eviction by the state militia.

This move appears to have been prepared since last autumn, when officials began to make curious and unrecognizable marks on identification papers, ration books and other documents presented in accordance with the necessities of a controlled state system. Presumably those represented designations for future displacement.

Three broad categories of persons to be evacuated have been drawn up: (1) families of war criminals or of those sentenced to prison or of those who have managed to flee the country; (2) former military personnel, state officials, industrialists, landowners or business men whose concerns have been nationalized; (3) saboteurs, offenders sentenced under the common law and persons under 56 who have retired.

These categories are sufficiently loose to permit the inclusion of virtually anyone the regime desires to banish from the capital. The word "families" includes non-immediate relatives. Landowners refers to anyone once possessing twenty-five or more acres.

Clearly this move is designed to "communize" the society of Bucharest and follows the pattern of the similar enforced evacuation of Budapest carried out last year by the Hungarian authorities to the horror of the outside world.

Previously there had been mass deportations along Rumania's Yugoslav border of thousands of families of Slavic or German origin.

It is reported by refugees who have recently managed to escape from Bucharest that eventually the regime hopes to remove politically "unreliable" elements from all industrial towns, and that measures are already being taken to carry out this policy in the seaport of Constanta and the petroleum center of Ploesti.

* * *

April 15, 1952

TERROR IN BUCHAREST

In the once gay city of Bucharest tens of thousands of citizens now go about with terror and dark foreboding in their hearts. Am I one of the 200,000 "unproductive people," who are to be forcibly evicted from the city? each one asks himself. What will happen to me and my family? Will we be sent to slave labor on the Black Sea Canal or, even worse, to the Soviet Union, where the coal mines of Karaganda and the forests of Siberia can always use more helpless victims?

Already the deportations have started in Bucharest, though only on a "small" scale of a thousand or so a week, but no doubt the pace will soon quicken. Tens of thousands have already packed small handbags so as to be ready when the secret police knock on the door and order them into the waiting trucks. The space thus vacated will then be available for "productive people," Soviet soldiers and civilian officials, Communist party members, secret policemen and the like.

Such mass deportations and mass tragedies as are now in store for one-fifth of Bucharest's people are an old story in the Stalinist world. The recalcitrant peasants of the early Nineteen Thirties, the unfortunate victims of the great purges of the mid-Thirties, the Volga Germans in 1941, the Chechen-Ingush, Crimean Tartar and related minority groups in 1944 and 1945, all these and others have gone through the same terror. Last year the pattern was extended to the capital of Hungary, and the story sent chills of horror up men's spines everywhere. Now it is Bucharest's turn. Some say the conscience of the world has been dulled by the surfeit of mass horror worked these past two decades under both Fascist and Stalinist totalitarianism. We do not believe that is true. The free world understands the enormity of the crime now beginning in Bucharest. It should speak out against the perpetration of these outrages.

* * *

June 3, 1952

RED LEADER NAMED PREMIER OF RUMANIA

By The United Press

BUCHAREST, Rumania, June 2—The National Assembly proclaimed Gheorghe Gheorghiu-Dej as new Premier of Rumania today to succeed Dr. Petru Groza, who was named President of the republic.

M. Gheorghiu-Dej was named Premier by a unanimous vote. Dr. Groza, who had been Premier since March 6, 1945, was elected President of the Assembly, a post tantamount to President of the republic.

The Government changes followed a request from the former President, Dr. Constantin Parhon, that he be relieved of his functions so he could dedicate himself entirely to his scientific work.

The Assembly took no action regarding Mme. Ana Pauker.

[The Bucharest radio revealed last week that Mme. Pauker, Rumanian Foreign Minister, had been dropped from the Rumanian Politburo and the secretariat of the Communist party. This was taken as an indication she had fallen at least partly from favor in a big shake-up of the country's Communist hierarchy. A Rumanian news agency dispatch from Bucharest said Mme. Pauker was seated on the Ministers' bench with Dr. Gvoza at today's Assembly session.]

M. Gheorghiu-Dej, 51, is secretary-general of the Workers [Communist] party and up to now had been Vice Premier. The new Premier is the son of a worker and was himself a former railroad hand.

While still young, he became a leader of the Rumanian workers movement and played a leading role in the creation of the Rumanian Communist party.

He was jailed many times for his work in behalf of the party. "Dej" was the name of a prison in which he served time and he has since tacked the word to his name.

Dr. Parhon requested he be relieved of the Presidency today in a letter to the Assembly, and the Assembly approved his request. The former President is an academician noted for his work in endocrinology.

Move Held Open Rule by Reds

By HARRY SCHWARTZ

The elevation of Gheorghe Gheorghiu-Dej to the Premiership apparently represents the final step in the complete and open monopolization of power in Rumania by the Workers (Communists) party.

As Premier, Dr. Petra Groza was purely a figurehead. A former wealthy landowner, Dr. Groza was installed as Premier in a period when the Kremlin still wished to preserve the appearance that Rumania was not entirely ruled by the Communist party. His transfer to the Presidency represents his relegation to the background and means that there is felt to be no need for even the semblance of power to be held by any non-Communist in Rumania.

The fact that Mme. Ana Pauker was seen at the National Assembly meeting sitting in a prominent place indicates clearly that she has still not fallen entirely into the Communist limbo. She apparently still retains her post as Foreign Minister despite her demotion in the Communist party hierarchy.

The elevation of M. Gheorghiu-Dej means that the Premiership of Rumania is now held by the one remaining Communist leader who has any large popular following. M. Gheorghiu-Dej's popular following dates back to his pre-war record as a fighter for the rights of workers, particularly of railroad workers. United States Government officials last week speculated that he was essentially a figurehead and that actual power in the Communist party and in the Government of Rumania was held by Gen. Emil Bodnaras, who long has been believed to be the head of the faction contesting with Mme. Pauker's group for absolute power in the Rumanian party and state.

Associated Press, 1946

Gheorghe Gheorghiu-Dej

By putting M. Gheorghiu-Dej in the Premiership, the ruling Communist group may be hoping to mobilize whatever popular sentiment the party commands in favor of the regime and thus help to ease the resentment over last January's monetary reform, resentment that is believed to have caused the expulsion from the Politburo last week of Teohari Georgescu and Vasile Luca.

* * *

July 4, 1952

RUMANIA ADOPTS OWN 'N. E. P.' PLAN

Course Similar to That Taken by Soviet in 1920's Laid to 'Financial Shortcomings'

VIENNA, July 3 (UP)—Bucharest newspapers received here today reported that the Rumanian Communist regime had adopted a "New Economic Policy," similar to the one to which Russia took recourse during the Bolshevik economic crisis in the Nineteen Twenties.

The N. E. P., introduced by Lenin, was a deliberate throwback to capitalism after the failure of the first attempts to communize Soviet economy. It was abolished by Premier Stalin in 1928, when the first great Soviet five-year plan began.

The Bucharest daily Contemporanul quoted Gheorghe Gheorghiu-Dej, Rumanian Premier and Secretary General of the Communist party, as having said:

"Our people's democracy, following the experience of the construction of socialism in the U. S. S. R., organizes this economic bond [between farms and industry] by the application of the N. E. P. policy.

"Small-scale production cannot be socialized through the expropriation of small producers. Small-scale production must be maintained for a certain time."

The newspaper linked the adoption of the N. E. P. with the recent purge of Vasile Luca, former Finance Minister, and Teohari Georgescu, Minister of the Interior, and the rebuking of Foreign Minister Ana Pauker.

It attributed the situation to "shortcomings in the financial field, in collections and purchases, in the economic exchanges among towns and villages."

M. Luca has been charged with sabotaging the country's financial and price systems and Mme. Pauker with failing to organize properly collective farms and the collection of crops. M. Georgescu was said to have "supported" the "deviation" of the others.

Mme. Pauker was removed from the Politburo and party secretariat. Some quarters suspect she may be under arrest.

The newspaper said the activity of saboteurs had led to the tripling of farm food prices since 1947, "strengthening the hostile activities of profiteers and capitalist elements in the towns and villages."

"Failure to fulfill the collection and purchase plans also hindered the supply of rationed goods to workers in the towns," it added.

Opinions Deferred

United States Government officials expressed reserve yesterday about Vienna reports of an "N. E. P." policy in Rumania and suggested that conclusions must be deferred until the full text of Gheorghiu-Dej's statements were available for study. They pointed out that the essence of the N. E. P. policy adopted by Lenin in 1921 was the freedom given small traders, small farmers and small industrialists to gain profits through private enterprises. This resulted in the development of kulak farmers in the Soviet Union, whereas in Rumania Mme. Pauker, M. Luca, and M. Georgescu were punished allegedly because they had followed a policy favorable to the kulaks.

* * *

January 5, 1954

YUGOSLAV ASSAILS REDS' DISCIPLINE

Parliament President Djilas Asks Communists to End 'Sterile' Cell Meetings

BELGRADE, Yugoslavia, Jan. 4 (UP)—One of Yugoslavia's top Red leaders condemned the Yugoslav Communist party's operation today as outmoded and proposed that the present system of strict party discipline be dropped.

Milovan Djilas, one of the leading Yugoslav Communist disciplinarians, also questioned whether it ever had been necessary for Yugoslav Communists to adopt the disciplinary measures laid down by the party under Stalin. The Yugoslav Communists broke with the Soviet in 1948.

M. Djilas, President of the new National Parliament and a member of the Communist party Executive Committee, said his proposal was to make the party an association of "the real, true Communists."

The proposal was made in a 7,500-word article titled "League or Party" in the official party newspaper Borba, published today.

M. Djilas proposed the elimination of compulsory "cell" meetings through which the Communist party rank and file members were guided and disciplined.

He said "cell" meetings in Yuogoslavia had become "sterile" because they had nothing concrete to discuss. He said the present disciplinary system of compulsory cell meetings and "churchlike" insistence on dogma had been set up to cover the revolutionary stage of Communist development.

M. Djilas asserted that in Yugoslavia the revolution was over and the rule of the "exploiters" of Yugoslav workers had been swept away.

He said the Yugoslav Communist party no longer had the right or the duty to fight against enemies of the regime of President Tito. He said Yugoslavia's legal and administrative system could handle such problems.

The Parliamentary leader questioned whether the "Stalinist" system of party discipline ever had been necessary, even in the early days of Communist development in this country. He said he also questioned whether Marx or Lenin would have approved use of the "Stalinist" disciplinary system in Yugoslavia.

Cell meetings were a waste of Yugoslavia's best minds and self-sacrificing personalities, who could accomplish more elsewhere, M. Djilas declared.

He proposed the elimination of careerists and opportunists, reducing the party's size. Old-time party members, who during the period of war and revolution had shown they put ideals above themselves, would stay in the proposed new organization, M. Djilas said.

He reported that party membership, estimated at 770,000 at the 1953 party congress, had begun to decline. He said "almost nobody is anxious to join" the party.

*   *   *

January 18, 1954

YUGOSLAV REDS OUST DJILAS AFTER ACCUSATIONS BY TITO

Strip Vice President of Key Posts at Hearings on His Criticisms of the Party

By JACK RAYMOND
Special to The New York Times

BELGRADE, Yugoslavia, Jan. 17—Milovan Djilas was dropped from the Yugoslav Communist Central Committee today after President Tito had criticized his views as unduly influenced by the West.

The 42-year-old partisan fighter and Communist had been regarded as a potential successor to Marshal Tito.

President Tito disclosed that a purge of "enemies" would begin immediately. In previous times, he said "different" methods would have been used but now, "milder methods would be employed to attain the same end."

M. Djilas was stripped of all his posts in the Communist League and given solemn "final" warning that even his membership in the Communist organization was at stake pending his further conduct. It was reported unofficially that M. Djilas also had resigned as President of Parliament. He had been named to that post last month.

One of Yugoslavians four Vice Presidents, a job he apparently also may lose along with other important positions, M. Djilas was condemned by the Central Committee on the following charges. Holding ideas opposed to the party line, creating confusing and harmful effects to the Communist League and the interests of the country and creating a "base for splitting and liquidating" the Socialist Alliance, the country's mass political organization.

Urged Reform of Red Group

Is a series of articles published in Borba, official Communist newspaper, M. Djilas had called for reform of the Communist League. He had suggested that Communists were not necessary for bringing about socialism. In a magazine article he also assailed the conduct of the wives of the "inner circle" of leading Communists.

According to M. Djilas, the Communist bureaucracy in Yugoslavia was preventing the achievement of democracy. Demanding equal treatment of non-Communists even bourgeoisie, with Communists. M. Djilas ridiculed the persistent attacks on the "class enemy" as a shield for bureaucratic despotism.

In his speech to the Central Committee today M. Djilas disclosed he had been "frightened" by the possible victory of bureaucracy in Yugoslavia. "I saw something here that reminded me of the Russians," he said.

Depressed by Defenders

While not retracting the essence of anything he wrote, M. Djilas acknowledged he might have put things too strongly and not have been philosophically clear enough. He admitted his guilt in provoking a possible split in the Communist League. He was particularly depressed, he said by elements abroad that came to his defense.

M. Djilas denied that he could even go over to the "class enemy," but he conceded there had been danger of his leading an opposition to Marshal Tito. He renounced such an objective.

Apparently only one man stood by M. Djilas in three plenary sessions of the Central Committee over which Marshal Tito presided yesterday and today. His lone defender was Vladimir Dedijer, another veteran partisan and Communist who became famous for his authoritative biography of Marshal Tito.

According to the Belgrade radio M. Dedijer's peroration on behalf of M. Djilas was so "apologetic" and "confused" that even M. Djilas disavowed some of his defender's remarks.

Apologizes for Article

Of some interest was the Belgrade radio report that Col. Gen. Peko Dapcevic, Chief of Staff of the Yugoslav Army, was among the Djilas critics. It was supposed that the Djilas attack on the conduct of the wives of his colleagues had been written on behalf of General. Dapcevic's actress wife who, he said, had been snubbed in leading social circles. M. Djilas apologized yesterday for the article which is understood to have provoked the final action against him.

Edward Kardelj, Yugoslavia's first Vice President, disclosed that a few days ago M. Djilas had come to him and made the following statements: That Marshal Tito was protecting Communist bureaucrats, that Dr. Kardelj and Alexander Rankovic, also Vice Presidents, felt as he did but were toadying to Marshal Tito, that a Socialist leftist party was in the process of creation in Yugoslavia, and that new Socialist parties would arise in this country.

Later, Dr. Kardelj said, M. Djilas came to him again and renounced these views. Then according to Dr. Kardelj, M. Djilas saw President Tito and confessed that he had held these opinions.

The remarkable aspect of the crisis was that the Belgrade radio broadcast today recorded versions of the Central Committee's debate. The station granted virtually as much time to M. Djilas as to Marshal Tito.

M. Djilas conceded today his views had been influenced by Social Democracy in the West. In his opening address yesterday Marshal Tito accused M. Djilas of seeking to bring about Western democracy in Yugoslavia. President Tito rejected such a goal. Western forms, he declared, were "going backward." Referring to assertions that Yugoslavia had been developing closer to the Western type of democracy, Marshal Tito declared: "Yugoslavia did approach the West, but not in domestic matters, only in the foreign policy field."

Accusing M. Djilas of revisionism, Marshal Tito said: "The question of democracy at all costs is opportunism and not revolutionary dynamism."

The Yugoslav President said M. Djilas' views were a result of his going abroad. In addition to earlier trips M. Djilas last year traveled to Burma to attend the International Socialist Congress. Later in the year he attended the coronation of Queen Elizabeth II. He is reputed to be a close friend of Aneurin Bevan, British Laborite, whose host he was in Yugoslavia last summer.

Tito Sees Nation Harmed

BELGRADE, Jan. 17 (AP)—President Tito told an extraordinary session of the Central Committee of the Communist party today that the articles written by Milovan Djilas amounted to a call for elimination of party discipline and created "enormous harm not only to the party but to the unity of the country."

The unanimous decision to sack M. Djilas came in a resolution that said his articles had "caused confusion among the public and inflicted serious harm both to the Communists and to the interests of the country."

It also charged that M. Djilas "moved away from the Central Committee and from the whole of the League of Communists. He isolated himself personally from practical work and provided an ideological basis for shattering of the ideological and organizational unity of the Yugoslav League of Communists and indeed for its liquidation."

In his repentance, Djilas confessed "my attitude was wrong," but said his differences with his colleagues had been only technical and ideological, that he remained a "true Marxist."

He denied that he opposed Marshal Tito and his policies.

"Tito was and is a most powerful and energetic leader and not only a symbolic one," he said.

He said his article about Communist wives was merely "satirical."

* * *

February 16, 1954

YUGOSLAVIA SEEKS MORE ARMS WORK

Wants Additional U. S. Orders to Bolster Industry and Fill Role in West's Defense

Special to The New York Times

BELGRADE, Yugoslavia, Feb. 15—The Yugoslav Government is seeking additional "offshore" contracts from the United States Army to keep its war industry going. An additional motive is a desire to gain a place for Yugoslavia among the Western countries entrusted with orders for the manufacture of arms and munitions in the Western defense system.

This may again bring up Yugoslavia's policy toward the North Atlantic Treaty Organization, of which she is not a member. She has categorically refused to join the Western defense group despite encouragement from Greece and Turkey with which she is allied in a tripartite pact.

Yugoslavia would like to obtain contracts for the production of war items not only for her Balkan treaty partners but for other Western European Atlantic treaty members as well.

Another aspect in the Yugoslav desire for a role in United States offshore procurement of military goods is the decrease in Yugoslavia's expenditures in support of her national defense. This appears in keeping with trends in other European countries.

The Government draft social plan and budget for 1954 proposes an expenditure of 164,000,000,000 dinars ($547,000,000), a drop from 180,000,000,000 dinars last year.

Earlier Contract to Face Test

This comes to 18.67 per cent of the anticipated national revenue, compared with an equivalent estimate of 20.05 per cent last year.

Whether Yugoslavia will obtain more offshore contracts will depend to a large extent on the result of firing tests of munitions ordered by the United States Army last year. The tests are scheduled here shortly. The munitions were manufactured under the terms of a "guinea pig" procurement contract for $5,390,000 signed last June. Details of the initial contract never were disclosed.

Yugoslavs have been known to manufacture a bolt-operated rifle and submachine gun as well as the 82-mm. mortar and small-rocket launcher.

Production in Yugoslav war industries has nearly doubled since 1949, the first year following the break with the Cominform.

However, a point has been reached where the Government faces the problem of utilizing capacity in some metal manufacturing industries because the peacetime needs of the Yugoslav Army do not match the potential output.

*   *   *

April 28, 1954

RUMANIA SAID TO TRY 100 JEWISH LEADERS

The World Jewish Congress reported here yesterday that Rumania began last month a series of secret trials involving more than 100 Jewish leaders, several of whom have already been sentenced to long imprisonment.

Citing London reports from an "absolutely authentic" source. Congress officials at the local office, at 15 East Eighty-fourth Street, said that the first trial had resulted in life imprisonment sentences for A. L. Zissu, described as a leader of the Zionist movement during Nazi rule; Mishu Ben-evenisti, former president of the Rumanian Zionist organization, and Jean Cohen, chairman of the Rumanian section of the World Jewish Congress.

The reports from London were said to have declared that the charges by Communist officials in Rumania included "Zionist activities and propaganda," clandestine meetings, attempts at illegal immigration and contacts with the legation of Israel.

Last night Dr. Nahum Goldmann, president of the World Jewish Congress, said that the news of the trials would be received with "horror and indignation."

*   *   *

May 2, 1954

TITO FEATURES U. S. AID

Jets and Tanks Dominate May Day Military Display

Special to The New York Times

BELGRADE, Yugoslavia, May 1—Yugoslav-piloted American jet planes and Patton tanks were featured in the May Day parade this morning. The march-past lasted for one and a half hours before an estimated crowd of 150,000.

For the first time since the war there were no placard pictures of Marshal Tito carried by any of the marching units.

The Yugoslav President, dressed in his familiar gold-braided uniform, took the salute from a stand before the Parliament building where he was accompanied by leading members of the Government.

Although there were many cavalry units and much horse-drawn equipment, they were outnumbered by motorized outfits, the benefits of Western military aid being plainly visible.

*   *   *

August 10, 1954

3 BALKAN NATIONS SIGN 20-YEAR PACT FOR MILITARY AID

Treaty Commits Yugoslavia, Turkey and Greece to Act at Once on Aggression

LINK TO NATO IS IMPLIED

Political Unity Is Provided—Three Power Assembly Foreseen by Signatories

Dispatch of The Times, London

BLED, Yugoslavia, Aug. 9—A twenty-year pact pledging immediate military aid to each other was signed today by Yugoslavia, Greece and Turkey.

The pact, for alliance, political cooperation and mutual assistance, linked three well-trained armies with a total potential exceeding seventy divisions in one of the most sensitive sectors of the Western defensive system. Greece and Turkey are members of the North Atlantic Treaty Organization; Yugoslavia is not.

The signing took place in the long conference room of the Villa Bled, the Yugoslav Government's official residence, where the Foreign Ministers of the three countries and their staffs had worked on the final preparation of the treaty.

Vast murals depicting scenes from the Yugoslav partisans' wartime struggles run the whole length of its walls. It was against this background that Koca Popovic of Yugoslavia, Stephan Stefanopolos of Greece and Fuad Koprulu of Turkey stood, smiling, their arms linked in a symbol of friendship, for the benefit of a host of newsreel and press cameras.

Champagne Toasts Drunk

Afterward, there were handshakes and toasts in Yugoslav champagne to the success of the "treaty of alliance, political cooperation and mutual assistance," which has been born out of the initial pact of friendship to which the same three ministers placed their signatures in Ankara, Turkey, eighteen months ago.

The Foreign Ministers also announced the general principles on which they believed their Governments might form an inter-parliamentary Balkan consultative assembly on the lines discussed during President Tito's visit to Athens earlier this summer.

M. Koprulu stressed at a news conference later that this represented only an agreement in principle. This statement suggested that much more discussion would be required before an assembly could be brought into being.

An outline of the proposed assembly suggested an equal number of members to be nominated from each country by its national parliaments. It would meet in regular session at least once a year and would examine the means and forms of developing cooperation among the Balkan states.

It also would have the power to make recommendations to the three member Governments. However, such suggestions would have to receive majority votes in each national group in the assembly before they could be submitted to the Governments.

The Balkan treaty consists of fourteen articles. Article 2 and 6 deal with the mutual commitments of the three allies in their own geographical area and the possibilities of common action in the event of hostilities commanding Greek and Turkish obligations elsewhere in Europe.

Article 2 bears a close resemblance to Article 5 of the North Atlantic Treaty. It was fashioned along those lines as a result of misgivings expressed in Atlantic alliance circles lest Greece and Turkey undertake greater commitments in the Balkan alliance than they accepted under the North Atlantic Treaty.

In terms almost identical with those used in the North Atlantic Treaty articles, the new treaty says that the signatories are agreed that an aggression against one or more of them, in no matter which part of their territory, will be considered an aggression against them all.

It also says that in the exercise of the right of individuals or collective self-defense recognized by Article 51 of the United Nations Charter, they will assist the party or parties so attacked by taking immediately, individually and collectively, all the measures—including here the use of armed force—deemed necessary to effective defense action.

Article 6 limits the obligation of Yugoslavia to an agreement to confer with her allies in the event of an act of aggression elsewhere that appears to menace Balkan security or to invoke the fulfillment of Greek and Turkish responsibilities to other nations.

This article also requires the Balkan partners to confer in the event of any serious deterioration of the international situation, particularly if this occurs in a region where it might adversely affect Balkan security.

It also provides for conferences on the "measures" to be undertaken in the event of an armed attack upon any country to which one or other of them—in this case Greece and Turkey—has undertaken commitments up to the time of the signing of the new treaty.

In general, this article seems to mark an appreciable Yugoslav step toward a willingness for more active participation in or association with the Atlantic Alliance and West Europe's defensive arrangements generally.

Britain Hails New Accord

Special to The New York Times
LONDON, Aug. 9—The British Foreign Office gave warm approval today to signing of the Balkan defense pact.

"It is hoped that the alliance will be followed by the strengthening of Italo-Yugoslav relations," a Government statement said. Reference to Italian-Yugoslav relations was interpreted by diplomatic observers as reflecting the Government's feeling that it would have been preferable if the Trieste dispute, chief point of contention between the two countries, had been settled before the signing of the pact.

* * *

August 22, 1954

WOMEN IN GREECE DEMAND EQUALITY

Unite in Drive for Full Rights After Suffrage Victory—Aim at Diplomatic Service

ATHENS, Aug. 19 (Reuters)—Women's organizations in Greece have united to fight for full equality.

Although they won the right to vote in the 1952 national elections and there now is one woman member of Parliament, they have found that men still are reluctant to relinquish such strong-holds as the diplomatic service. As a member of the executive committee of the organization Women's Rights said:

"Greek men are reluctant to grant further rights to women, and we believe that they will have to be forced by one means or another to make concessions."

Mme. Niki Goulandri, secretary of the Women Scientists Association, decided to force the Government's hand recently by applying for admission to the examination for embassy attachés. An attractive 28-year-old brunette, Mme. Goulandri is a graduate of the school of political and economic sciences of Athens University.

Officials Astonished

She created a sensation among Foreign Ministry officials when she went to the registrar's department at the ministry to hand in her application. The secretary in charge, astounded, hurried off to seek advice from his superiors.

He returned to inform her that her application could be accepted but that she must attach all necessary documents. This was to include a "certificate of army service or exemption from service," which is essential before embarking on a diplomatic career in this country.

Ministry officials apparently thought this requirement would enable them to reject Mme. Goulandris' application, since there is no conscription of women in Greece and therefore no certificate of exemption. But she was determined to fight her case to the end.

"I shall even go to the State Council," she declared, "if the ministry refuses my application on such grounds. For I am certain that Greece's supreme administrative court will not accept an excuse that is based on the exemption of Greek women from conscription."

Since 1920, when Women's Rights was founded, Greek women have made much progress toward full equality. In 1930, they won the right to vote in municipal elections if they were 30 years or over and on condition that they could read and write. In 1949 they obtained equal rights in municipal elections, being allowed to vote at 21, even if they were illiterate.

Their most significant victory came in 1952 when they received full suffrage.

However, women still do not enjoy full equality of rights or pay. Mme. Maritsa Thanopoulou, secretary of Women's Rights, summed it up as follows:

"Women still do not get equal pay with men for equal work, and under the civil laws, a woman is subject to man's authority as regards both her husband and her children. Nor does Greek law admit women as witnesses, jurors, judges or notaries. Nor may they become diplomats."

Hopes have been raised by Parliament's recent ratification of the international convention of women's political rights, under which women must be accorded political equality.

*　*　*

August 27, 1954

8 ALBANIANS BARE CURBS UNDER REDS

Group That Fled Into Greece Say Majority of Countrymen Would Follow if They Could

By A. C. SEDGWICK
Special to The New York Times

ATHENS, Aug. 26—Eight Albanians who fled their homeland described today life in the smallest of the Soviet Union's satellites.

Since their escape the Albanians have been living in a Laurion refugee camp near Athens, where they are being prepared for resettlement in other countries by officials of the United States refugee program and the World Council of Churches.

Seven farmers and the wife of one came from the Albanian village of Kamenitsa. They had to go afoot for only two hours to reach the Greek frontier. They said that persons not knowing the border country would find escape more difficult.

The vast majority of Albanians would escape if it were easier to do so, they asserted. They added that they had been cordially received by the Greek military authorities.

One of eight, Ahmet Huska, 33 years of age, said that all commodities in Albania were rationed and that the average worker earned too little to buy more than a part of what he is allowed. He added that a black market flourished in Albania, carried on by officials of the Communist cooperatives who, he said, lived "like lords."

The ragged clothes in which the refugees arrived in Greece were shown to reporters and appeared to testify to the extreme poverty of a typical Albanian rural community.

Another member of the group, Estref Ali, 46, said he knew of some guerrilla activity in the mountains against the Communist regime but guessed that it was unorganized. According to him one of the latest manifestations of anti-Communist feeling was the placing of a bomb in the Soviet Embassy in Tirana.

Mr. Ali said the Albanian authorities imposed twenty to twenty-five year prison sentences on all persons caught listening to Western broadcasts but he added that none the less the people listened to the Voice of America.

Sali Huska, 44, stated that a Greek Communist headquarters existed in Albania and insisted he had seen many Russian soldiers in southern Albania. He asserted that Russians in Albania occupied high posts mainly in the Ministry of Interior, the police and the security forces.

He added that among the rank and file of workers one in six was likely to be a government spy. The absence of strikes, he said, resulted from the fact that all the workers were cowed.

Mrs. Enie Hussen, the one woman in the party, said "we women hate Communists perhaps more than our menfolk do." She complained that women, often undernourished, were put on forced road labor without pay. She said the people were allowed to worship publicly but were penalized if they did so.

*　*　*

December 31, 1954

COURT OPENS CASE OF 2 TITO EX-AIDES

Djilas and Dedijer Accused of Moves to Hurt Yugoslav 'Vital Interests' Abroad

By JACK RAYMOND
Special to The New York Times

BELGRADE, Yugoslavia, Dec. 30—Criminal prosecution proceedings were initiated today against Milovan Djilas and Vladimir Dedijer. The case arose from interviews they granted foreign correspondents in which they criticized tactics of the Communist leadership here.

M. Djilas, the former Vice President who was expelled from the Central Committee last January, and M. Dedijer, the biographer of President Tito who was suspended from the committee two days ago, were charged with having attempted to damage Yugoslavia's "most vital interests" abroad.

They were summoned separately at 2:30 P. M. to the District Court of Belgrade and permitted to go there unescorted. After four hours' interrogation, apparently the opening phase of the prosecution, they were permitted to return to their homes.

An announcement carried this evening by Tanjug, the official news agency, was as follows:

"The investigating judge of the District Court for the city of Belgrade at the proposal of the Public Prosecutor brought a decision to open criminal investigation against Djilas, a pensioner, and Dedijer, both of Belgrade, because of slanderous and hostile propaganda directed at damaging abroad the most vital interests of our country, a criminal act under Article 118 of the criminal code. The defendants, Djilas and Dedijer, have not been deprived of their freedom."

Article 118 provides punishment by imprisonment for persons found guilty of engaging in hostile propaganda.

After he had returned to his home, M. Djilas was reported to have said that the procedure today had been "very fair" and that he had stressed that he would defend himself as "a free person." The description of M. Djilas as a pensioner was a reference to the fact that he was drawing a Government pension as a former Minister.

Today's was the first official intimation that M. Djilas as well as M. Dedijer faced prosecution. An announcement had been made concerning M. Dedijer when Parliament withdrew his parliamentary immunity at the request of the Federal prosecutor. Heretofore Communists had distinguished between the Djilas and Dedijer cases, since M. Djilas no longer held any Government post, whereas M. Dedijer was still a member of Parliament. However, they were infuriated with both men.

The interviews that aroused Yugoslav leaders were granted by M. Dedijer to The Times of London, in which he confirmed that a Communist control board had sought to question him about his attitude toward M. Djilas; and by M. Djilas to The New York Times, in which he expanded on his allegations that

the Communist organization needed "democratization," views that led to his downfall last January.

There was no indication tonight when a trial might begin. According to Article Eight of the law on Yugoslav courts, "hearings in court shall as a rule be public."

However, Brana Jevremovic, the Federal prosecutor, pointed out in an interview yesterday that the law permitted exclusion of publicity for reasons that he said would be valid in other countries.

So far as official Yugoslav public opinion was concerned, both MM. Djilas and Dedijer stood condemned. Edvard Kardelj, acting President in the absence of Marshal Tito, who is on a state journey in the Far East, has declared: "Every honest man should spit in the face of these politicians."

The attack upon them by Col. Gen. Peko Dapcevic, chief of Staff of the Army and erstwhile intimate of M. Djilas, to the effect that they were "foreign agents" was followed this morning by a denunciatory letter in Borba, the official newspaper, signed by Mitra Mitrovic, M. Djilas' former wife, who is a leading Communist.

Both General Dapcevic and Mlle. Mitrovic were reported under the same cloud as M. Dedijer and it is known that Mlle. Mitrovic like M. Dedijer was called before a Communist control board. Her questioning before the control board had been reported "severe."

For the first time excerpts of the Djilas interview were carried today in both Borba and Politika. The excerpts were extensive and correctly translated.

* * *

January 25, 1955

DJILAS AND DEDIJER FOUND GUILTY; YUGOSLAV COURT SUSPENDS TERMS

By JACK RAYMOND
Special to The New York Times

BELGRADE, Yugoslavia, Tuesday, Jan 25—Milovan Djilas and Vladimir Dedijer have been convicted of having waged hostile propaganda against Yugoslavia.

After a secret sixteen-hour trial they received suspended sentences and were permitted to return to their homes at 12:20 A. M. today.

M. Djilas, ousted former Vice President, was sentenced to one and one-half years and placed on probation for three years. M. Dedijer, biographer of President Tito, received a six-month term and was placed on probation for two years.

[Reuters reported that the official Yugoslav news agency, Tanjug, said M. Djilas and M. Dedijer had been heard during the morning proceedings Monday, but Tanjug did not report any of their evidence. There was no indication of the nature of their defense.]

They had been charged in Belgrade District Court under Article 118 of the Yugoslav Criminal Code, which provides possible imprisonment upon conviction. They had been

GET SUSPENDED SENTENCES: Milovan Djilas, left, and Vladimir Dedijer, Yugoslav Communist leaders. They were convicted of spreading hostile propaganda against Yugoslavia.

accused of intent to "undermine the authority of the working people" of the Federal People's Republic of Yugoslavia.

Aleksander Atankovic, the prosecutor, said in his opening statement yesterday that the two men "gave slanderous statements to the correspondents of the foreign press." He said the statements had "wrongly interpreted the situation in the country."

In one interview M. Djilas had called for the creation of a new democratic Socialist party and asserted that the Communist party here was controlled by undemocratic elements. In another, M. Dedijer had confirmed that he had been called to account for his political attitude before a Communist control board in connection with M. Djilas' expulsion from the Central Committee last year.

M. Djilas, who had been regarded as a likely successor to Marshal Tito, was disgraced last January for having published articles appealing for "democratization" of the Communist League.

At first only members of the foreign press were barred from the trial on the ground that they were not trusted to report the trial fairly. After the indictment was read, members of the domestic press as well as other selected ticket-holders were excluded.

The president of the five-man court, on recommendation of the prosecutor, declared the trial secret because Yugoslavia's relations with foreign powers would be discussed.

The indictment was not published. The radio did not mention the trial throughout the day. The semi-official news agency Yugopress carried its version of the opening procedure this afternoon in a special bulletin. This evening the Belgrade press carried only a brief announcement that the trial had begun.

The opening session lasted from 8 A. M. to 4 P. M. yesterday when a one-hour recess was allowed, but the defendants did not leave the courtroom. The trial was resumed at 5 P. M.

At first the police refused to allow M. Dedijer's lawyer to pass into the courtroom, but relented when advised who he was. He was Ivo Politeo, a prominent Zagreb attorney who defended Marshal Tito at a famous trial in November, 1928, when the Communist leader was sentenced to five years' hard labor by the old regime on charges of engaging in Communist propaganda. M. Politeo also defended Aloysius Cardinal Stepinac, Roman Catholic primate of Yugoslavia, after the war.

A slightly built man of 75 with a small gray mustache, M. Politeo avoided press questions and went directly to the courtroom with his client. M. Djilas' lawyer is Veljko Kovacevic of Belgrade.

Yugopress in its report said when the trial began both M. Djilas and M. Dedijer had confirmed that they had been treated correctly since the charges against them originally were filed on Dec. 30. They were not imprisoned during the preliminary examination.

The prosecutor, according to Yugopress, placed in evidence quotations from the press that he said showed that MM. Djilas and Dedijer sought to foment "a great campaign of some foreign circles" to harm Yugoslavia's prestige, her constitutional institutions and her highest representatives.

The defendants were accused also, according to Yugopress, of seeking to make Yugoslavia's international position more difficult in order to "precipitate interference by those foreign circles in the interior affairs of Yugoslavia and in that way obtain foreign help for realization of their aims."

The prosecutor, Yugopress continued, said MM. Djilas and Dedijer had "accepted the offers of the foreign press representatives and had thus chosen a moment" designed to cause not only pressure on the foreign and domestic policy of Yugoslavia but "even political changes in the social and economic management of our country."

When foreign reporters appeared at the courthouse at 7 A. M., as instructed by court officials, they were refused tickets.

The president of the court, Lilivoje Seratlic, then issued the following statement:

"The foreign newspaper men have not received tickets because of their campaign until now in connection with this case and because we are not persuaded they will report truthfully about the trial."

When the correspondents entered the office of the president of the court for clarification of his statement, the court president angrily declared, "I have nothing for the foreign press and I have no time to talk to you."

* * *

May 27, 1955

KHRUSHCHEV APOLOGIZES TO TITO IN BELGRADE AND BIDS HIM RETURN

Says Beria Incited Break in '48, Misleading Soviet— Yugoslav Is Silent

By JACK RAYMOND
Special to The New York Times

BELGRADE, Yugoslavia, May 26—The Soviet Union openly appealed today to Yugoslavia to return to the Communist community from which she was ousted in June, 1948.

Associated Press Radiophoto

President Tito of Yugoslavia greets Soviet Premier Nikolai A. Bulganin, left, and Nikita S. Khrushchev, Communist party secretary, at airport after arrival of Soviet leaders.

At Zemun Airport, Nikita S. Khrushchev, Soviet Communist party secretary, urged reconciliation in the name of Lenin and in the interests of the international workers' movement.

Mr. Khrushchev had just arrived by plane at the head of a high-ranking delegation including Soviet Premier Nikolai A. Bulganin for negotiations with President Tito and his sides to re-establish "normal" relations between their two countries.

Immediately after handshaking and reviewing the honor guard, the Soviet party leader made his call for ideological collaboration.

He not only apologized for past "aggravations" to Yugoslavia; he attributed them to the "fabrication" of Lavrenti P. Beria, the former Soviet Minister of Internal Affairs, and Viktor S. Abakumov, one of his deputies, who were executed in 1953 and 1954, respectively.

Mr. Khrushchev mentioned neither Stalin nor Vyacheslav M. Molotov, Foreign Minister, who had signed the letters for the Soviet Communist party in the exchange with the Yugoslav party when the Soviet-Yugoslav feud began.

Marshal Tito, who had just smilingly greeted Mr. Khrushchev after the Soviet plane landed, stood impassively as the Soviet party chief spoke into a microphone set up at the airfield. He did not respond to the remarks of the chief of the Soviet delegation.

The marshal's red-and-gold-braided blue uniform contrasted with the rumpled gray business suit of the Soviet visitor. Putting on reading glasses, Mr. Khrushchev lost no time in establishing that he was here as a Communist rather than as a governmental representative.

By including "Comrade Tito" and "leaders of the Yugoslav Communist League" in his phrase of greeting, he indicated he did not accept the Yugoslav view that this would be a negotiation merely between Governments.

Mr. Khrushchev expressed his greeting in the name of the Central Committee of the Soviet Communist party as well as the Presidium of the Supreme Soviet, of which he is a member.

He recalled "bonds of old fraternal friendship and mutual struggle against common enemies," collaboration in war and the joint wartime liberation of Belgrade—"this ancient Slav city"—by the Soviet Army and Yugoslav partisans.

The Soviet Explanation

He explained as follows what happened seven years ago when Marshal Tito's party was read out of the Cominform, the association of Soviet-dominated East European Communist states:

"On our part, we ascribe without hesitation the aggravations to the provocative role that Beria, Abakumov and others—recently exposed enemies of the people—played in the relations between Yugoslavia and the Union of Soviet Socialist Republics.

"We studied assiduously the materials on which had been based the serious accusations and offenses directed at that time against the leaders of Yugoslavia. The facts show that these materials were fabricated by the enemies of the people, detestable agents of imperialism who by deceptive methods pushed their way into the ranks of our party."

When Mr. Khrushchev finished, Marshal Tito, who had stood at his elbow, showed neither by word nor expression his reaction. There was no applause from a large turnout of Yugoslav officials. The Marshal merely showed Mr. Khrushchev to the open car that was to lead the auto convoy to Belgrade.

Aside from the emphatic bid by Mr. Khrushchev, the high point of the day came shortly after the two-motored Soviet plane appeared almost exactly at 5 P. M., the scheduled time of arrival.

Vasily A. Valikov, Soviet Ambassador, ran up the portable staircase that was placed at the side of the plane when it rolled to a halt before the Zemun Airport building. Mr. Khrushchev, first out of the plane, came down the stairs, Marshal Tito advanced to receive him.

They met and shook hands in front of photographers, first eyeing each other curiously, then breaking into broad but silent grins, as if aware of the picture they made—the Communist leader of the Soviet Union, who had come to Belgrade to apologize, and the leader of Yugoslavia, who had defied the Kremlin and got away with it.

Finally Mr. Khrushchev broke the silence and addressed Marshal Tito in Russian. Their exchange was lost in the whirring of cameras, but one could hear Mr. Khrushchev's booming "khorosho" (fine) in apparent response to a query about the trip.

* * *

May 27, 1955

PAGEANT IN BELGRADE

Belgrade is an ancient city in which today the heroic modern architecture of Marshal Tito's planners mingles with the remains of the long history of Turkish, Slav and Habsburg struggle for control. Belgrade's walls have seen many strange events over the centuries but few if any more strange than yesterday's spectacle. The rulers of Russia led by Mr. Khrushchev came hat in hand and apologetic in speech to beg forgiveness and friendship of Marshal Tito and his cohorts. Even the usually impassive peasants who form a good percentage of the throngs in Belgrade's streets must have been moved to laughter by the spectacle.

Mr. Khrushchev ate crow yesterday, but not very gracefully. The 1948 break between Yugoslavia and the Soviet Union, he said, had been a "misinterpretation," the result of the scheming of the "enemies of the people." He named Lavrenti P. Beria, dead a year and a half now so he cannot rise to defend himself. But before a new Communist myth rises too far from the ground it is worth while to review the facts and reiterate the truth.

Who, for example, represented the Soviet Union at the Cominform meeting in June, 1948, which sent Marshal Tito into Communist purgatory? It was the late Andrei A. Zhdanov, still an honored Soviet figure, Deputy Premier Georgi M. Malenkov and Communist party secretary Mikhail Suslov. Was it not Premier Bulganin, now a member of the Khrushchev delegation, who called Tito "Judas" in September 1949, and assured the world that the Marshal would answer for his "bloody crimes"? Did any member of the present Soviet "collective leadership" rise to defend Tito all during the long years from 1948 to 1953, when Moscow used every weapon at its command to subvert Yugoslavia? Did Mr. Khrushchev say a word against this "misinterpretation" during all these years?

To ask such questions is to answer them, but one must grant a grain of truth—unintended by Mr. Khrushchev, to be sure—in this apologia. It was the "enemies of the people" who warred on Yugoslavia's independence from 1948. It was Stalin and his closest henchmen—Molotov, Malenkov, Bulganin, Mikoyan, Khrushchev, et al. They were and are the enemies of the people and of the people's freedom in Russia, in Yugoslavia and in all lands.

* * *

August 14, 1955

TITO TURNS THE TABLES ON HIS SATELLITE FOES

Following Russia's Example, They Now Want to Be Friends but Past Weighs Heavily on Their Minds

QUESTION IS: WILL IT LAST?

By JOHN MacCORMAC

VIENNA, Aug. 13—The most significant occurrence in East Europe since the visit of Soviet Premier Nikolai Bulganin and Communist party boss, Nikita Khrushchev, to Belgrade last May was undoubtedly Marshal Tito's public criticism in a speech at Karlovac a fortnight ago of Hungarian and Czechoslovakian Communist leaders for not following this conciliatory example.

This week there was another significant development when Hungary's Communist boss, Matyas Rakosi, tacitly admitted the justice of Tito's strictures and promised to do better in the future.

Tito had complained that in some Soviet satellites, particularly Hungary and Czechoslovakia, those who favored reconciliation with Yugoslavia were being put in jail. This, he declared, was probably because the leaders of those countries had so many black marks on their own records, having sentenced innocent men to death for alleged "Titoism" and dragged the name of Yugoslavia into their trials.

Rakosi, though he blamed the worsening of Hungaro-Yugoslav relations on the machinations of a former police chief of Hungary, Peter Gabor, took Tito's reproaches lying down. He promised that "we shall do everything possible to bring our relations into the best possible order." In Belgrade, Premier Bulganin and Mr. Khrushchev had publicly blamed the expulsion of Yugoslavia from the Cominform on the executed Russian M. V. D. head, Lavrenti P. Beria, although they had privately agreed with Tito that its author was Stalin.

Rakosi and Tito

Peter Gabor was sentenced two years ago to life imprisonment and cannot talk back, but it is no secret to Marshal Tito that Rakosi was as much responsible, in his more limited sphere, for Tito's banishment as was Stalin. The chief reason why Laszlo Rajk, then Hungary's Foreign Minister, was executed in 1949 was that he was alleged to have plotted with Tito to "overthrow people's democratic regimes" and to have planned Rakosi's assassination on Tito's orders. That was an accusation not lightly to be forgiven by a leader as proud of his communism as of his nationalism

What Tito complained about in his speech, however, was less that the Communist leaders of Hungary and Czechoslovakia had followed Stalin's line in 1949 than that they were following it still.

What was the purpose of this open reproach? Some observers have speculated that Tito means to renew the bid for hegemony among the satellites which he seemed to be making before his split with the Cominform. But Bulgaria and Albania are closer to home than Hungary and Czechoslovakia and more likely units for a local grouping in which Yugoslavia could hope to dominate.

To Test Sincerity

A well-known Yugoslav journalist commented to this correspondent that Tito's purpose was probably to test the sincerity of Soviet protestations in Belgrade that all Communist roads need not lead to Moscow.

Actually, the reconciliation between Tito and the Soviet empire began shortly after the death of Stalin and had already been demonstrated by many official acts before the Bulganin-Khrushchev visit to Belgrade. Early in 1953 frontier incidents between Yugoslavia and her neighbors, which by then had numbered 1,320, ceased and the flow of insults over the satellite radios against the "imperialist traitor and hangman of the Yugoslav people" died away. Diplomatic relations were resumed, the last satellite to do so being Poland last November. Trade relations were revived and so were cultural exchanges.

Rude Pravo, the Communist central organ in Czechoslovakia, one of the two satellites against which Tito levied his charges of unfriendliness, recently listed the steps Prague has taken to improve relations.

Other satellite leaders, particularly those of Rumania and Bulgaria, have also been able to record improvements in relations with a neighbor with whom only two years ago their commerce was limited largely to insults and rifle shots.

Far From Close

All this, however, has not yet brought them closer to Yugoslavia than they are, say, to Austria. Their relations, political and economic, are far from those which would have existed had Yugoslavia not been banished from the Cominform. Economically it is doubtful whether they can ever develop along the lines envisaged in 1948.

Then it was planned that Hungary should found her iron and steel industry on Yugoslav ore, and the proximity of Hungarian bauxite to the waterpower of northern Yugoslavia offered another promising combination. But now Yugoslavia is smelting her own iron ore and developing her own bauxite resources, which are second in Europe only to Hungary's. Those raw ores which she cannot manufacture herself she is exporting to the West.

But Yugoslavia has another article of export which cannot be in demand by the present leaders of the satellites, and that is Titoism. Tito's regime stands not only for political Titoism—that is, independence of Moscow—but for liberalized communism—concessions to farmers and consumers somewhat like those of the repudiated Malenkov "new course" in the Soviet Union.

Rakosi's Problem

Had Imre Nagy—father of Hungary's "new course"—remained Prime Minister of Hungary, he would have been

Low, world copyright by arrangement with The Manchester Guardian

"Eat-your-own words banquet at Tito's."

troubled by few inhibitions in extending the hand of friendship to Tito. But Rakosi will not only be haunted by the ghosts of Titoists but be conscious of the fact that Tito's domestic policies are a direct challenge to his own.

It has been noted by Western observers here, and undoubtedly also by Tito, that neither Hungary nor Czechoclovakia nor, for that matter, any other satellite has copied Moscow's example of cultivating friendliness with the West. Some half-hearted attempts to promote tourist traffic were nullified by the fantastically fictitious value at which the satellites rate their currencies. Although Western newspapermen have recently been pouring into Moscow they have been unable, with few exceptions, to obtain visas for the satellites.

All this would seem to indicate either that the satellite Governments for their own reasons fear any rapprochement with the West or that they believe Moscow's policy of friend-

liness is only a short-lived tactic. This is probably one of the things Tito would like to find out.

*   *   *

September 2, 1955

YUGOSLAVIA GETS SOVIET AID GRANT

Moscow Puts $84,000,000 Into Credits and Loans—Trade Volume Set

By CLIFTON DANIEL
Special to The New York Times
MOSCOW, Sept. 1—Loans totaling $84,000,000 have been granted to Yugoslavia by the Soviet Union.

News of the credits was given tonight when it was announced that a new trade agreement had been concluded between the two countries. The level of trade between the Soviet Union and Yugoslavia was fixed at $70,000,000 a year for the next three years.

The agreement was concluded by a Yugoslav trade delegation that has been in the Soviet Union for the last few days. The documents were signed tonight in the Great Kremlin Palace. Anastas I. Mikoyan, a first Deputy Premier, signed for the Soviet Union and Gen. Svetozar Vukmanovic-Tempo, chief of the Yugoslav delegation, signed for the Belgrade Government.

The agreement was one of the first concrete results of an understanding reached in June between the Moscow and Belgrade Governments. That understanding put an end to the disagreement that had existed between the two countries since 1948, when Yugoslavia was expelled from the Cominform, the Soviet-led bloc of European Communist parties.

The agreement was in part designed to compensate Yugoslavia for economic losses she suffered as a result of the stoppage of trade between her and the Soviet bloc countries after 1948. Negotiations for agreement started Aug. 23 and were finished today. All figures in the agreement were given in dollars but that, of course, does not mean payment will be made in United States currency.

Exchange to Be Both Ways

As reported by Tass, the official Soviet news agency, the agreement did not specify whether the trade would amount to an exchange of $70,000,000 each way, but that is usual in such agreements.

The two parties also agreed that in January next year they would sign a protocol for the mutual exchange of goods within the framework of the agreement. Yugoslavia it was said, will send bauxite (aluminum ore), lead, tobacco and hemp to the Soviet Union. In return, the Soviet Union will supply coke, oil and cotton.

It was also agreed the two countries would in the shortest possible time sign an agreement on technical cooperation. This accord would include an exchange of manufacturing licenses and technical documents. The exchange would be financed by a fund to which both parties would contribute.

As for long-term cooperation, the two parties undertake to draw up in January an agreement whereby Yugoslavia would receive over a period of three years credit from the Soviet Union amounting to $54,000,000.

Soviet Aid to Build Plants

This credit would be used in the Soviet Union for the purchase of raw materials and would pay for labor and equipment for the construction in Yugoslavia of a nitrate fertilizer plant of 220,000 tons annual capacity with the necessary electric power plant. The fund also would be used to build a phosphate plant of 250,000 tons annual capacity and to reconstruct three mines.

Also, the Soviet Union would give Yugoslavia a gold loan of $30,000,000 for use by the Yugoslav National Bank. This money presumably would be available for purchases outside the Soviet Union.

The loan would carry a 2 per cent interest and be repayable in ten years.

The Soviet and Yugoslav negotiators also agreed upon "possible cooperation in the field of the use of atomic energy for peaceful purposes," Tass stated.

This agreement represents the first substantial aid that Yugoslavia has had from the Soviet Union since the two patched up their old quarrel. Negotiations that led to reconciliation were conducted in Belgrade last May and June by Nikita S. Khrushchev Soviet Communist party First Secretary, and Nikolai A. Bulganin, Soviet Premier, with President Tito.

In the intervening years since the Cominform split, Yugoslavia has relied for economic aid mainly upon the United States, Britain and France—especially the United States.

Recently, however, there have been indications that United States aid would be trimmed back somewhat. Marshal Tito has referred to that fact in recent speeches.

Trade With East Discussed

Special to The New York Times

ZAGREB, Yugoslavia, Sept. 1—On the eve of the opening of her biggest post-war international fair, Yugoslavia has initiated a drive for trade with the Eastern Communist countries.

The managing board of the Federal Chamber for Foreign Trade met here last night. Borba, the official newspaper, said the study of trade with and possibilities of export to Eastern countries was stressed at the meeting.

At the fair grounds here, as workmen put the finishing touches on exhibits, it was evident that the Eastern bloc was exerting quite a bit of effort to impress the Yugoslavs with trade possibilities.

Headed by the Soviet Union, six Eastern European countries occupied four-fifths as much space as fifteen other foreign countries.

The United States was among nations least represented, with only two exhibitors. However, the exhibit put together by the United States Information Services was the Atoms-for-Peace display that already has been shown in other countries.

* * *

March 24, 1956

THE METEMPSYCHOSIS OF A CITY

By C. L. SULZBERGER

BUCHAREST, Rumania, March 23—Before the war this city had a lovable cheek to call itself the Paris of the East. It was proud of its finely dressed woman, its comfortable well-furnished houses, its pretentious restaurants, night clubs and sophistication. Everyone with claims to education spoke French. A Latinity of Rumania, its traditions and aspirations, was proclaimed. More than some Continental capitals,

Bucharest had its seamy side: astonishing corruption, beggars as well as barflies, hovels as well as mansions. But it was colorful and full of life. Above all, it was gay.

Today Bucharest might call itself the Moscow of the West. The city's face has not been lifted. Instead, by miraculous new methods of psychological town planning, its face was dropped. Some strange glandular injection had altered its composite personality. Maybe, as Communist propaganda claims, the people are happier. Such things can never be statistically computed. But the people don't *look* happier. And the gaiety has vanished.

This is now a drab and earnest capital, bedecked with Red placards exhorting Marxist man to fill his norm. The women once more intent upon frivolity, have been given equal rights, including the Muscovite privilege of shoveling snow. The same big houses are there with ornate facades staring out on avenues and parks. But, inside, tenants are stacked up like sardines, and hall-ways are redolent of cabbage. The old restaurants taken over by the state, cater more to mass production than the palate. A queer red substance called "Manchurian caviar" has ousted the Danubian sturgeon's eggs. Although the country boasts automotive assembly plants, their products must go elsewhere. Few cars skid through the slushy streets.

Today's Hotels

The old and somewhat ostentatious hotels fulfill their functional duty as shelters. But the Ambassador smells like a Turkish bath. The Athenée Palace, a cynosure of pre-war pleasure, entertains serious gentlemen in Russian-tailored suits with bell-bottom trousers; earnest women wearing woolen stockings; and anonymous characters standing about in leather coats and those visored caps once fashionable on golf links and now the Communist mode.

The hotel bar, once cluttered up with British intelligence agents and later by arrogant Nazi officers, is now about as lively as a crematorium. Filed behind the counter are costly bottles of weird gins and brandies manufactured in the popular democracies and drinkable only by their citizens. The bored individual who presides complains; "Nobody leaves a tip. They say 'What for? You get a salary from the state.' Yes. Three hundred thirty-five lei [fifty-six dollars] a month. And I have two children."

The former self of Bucharest is poignantly recognizable. Tall, dark peasants with saturnine faces, sheepskin coats and conical fur hats still stride through the melting snows while an indifferent eastern wind blows down the Calea Victoriei. But the city has been transmogrified. Its character has changed.

Essentially this was produced by deliberate extinction of the bourgeoisie. Bucharest, beneath the tinsel, was primarily a middle-class city with both the virtues and the faults that this implies. It derived its life blood from the lawyers, doctors, bankers, business men who lived in the comfortable homes that have now become shabby boarding houses. This class has been wiped out.

Second-Class Citizens

It furnished much of the death roster of the revolution's most violent phase of the unhappy press gangs who labored to dig the now abandoned and utterly useless Black Sea canal, of the cellmates in gloomy prisons. Its survivors, disorganized, disillusioned and distressed, are on the whole second-class citizens unable and unpermitted to adjust to the brashly confident new world about them. Their pitiful last belongings are sold for a song in commission shops. Their families are breaking up.

An extremely intelligent play which—beneath an unnecessary coating of propaganda—discusses this social change is now the talk of Bucharest. This describes the disintegration of a happy bourgeois household during the revolutionary decade. Three members are arrested; three make a political adjustment of becoming what we would call fellow-travelers; one commits suicide and one goes mad. A bewildered character asks the Communist schoolteacher who lives in a requisitioned room: "How can you be so categoric, violently loving some people, violently hating others?" Says she: "When you believe in something, then you are categoric." And the matriarch, a scientist, advises: "Don't lose hope. Parents are bringing up their children. Don't waste time on illusions."

There is a brutal reality about the new drab Bucharest that is difficult to compare with the carefree glitter of the days before the war. The people beneath their unstylish clothes, look much the same. Physically the bourgeoisie is not entirely dead. Its ghosts plod in and out of familiar doorways on unaccustomed schedules of unfamiliar tasks. Their eyes mirror no heaven.

*   *   *

October 25, 1956

A DOCILE RUMANIA WATCHES CRISES

Hope of Soviet Concessions Growing
After Events in Poland and Hungary

By WELLES HANGEN
Special to The New York Times

BUCHAREST, Rumania, Oct. 24—Docile Rumania, long a Moscow favorite in the world of communism, hopes to be rewarded for her good behavior during the crises in Poland and Hungary.

The mood of almost everyone here, from novelists to waiters, is compounded of three elements—cynicism, passivity and hope.

The cynicism is directed at the whole Communist doctrine, at party propaganda and at the regime's grandiose plans.

The passivity is the key to Rumania's acceptance of Soviet domination and plunder.

Hope for better days, for concessions from the Soviet Union and for liberalization of the regime has been rekindled by Polish and Hungarian events.

Although the Rumanian press and radio continue to exclude all news of disaffection in other Soviet satellites, many persons here are following the events closely. They listen to the Voice of America, the British Broadcasting Corporation and other Western radio outlets or simply tune in on the amazingly well-informed local grapevine.

Jamming Is Stepped Up

The Bucharest regime has reacted by intensifying its jamming of foreign news broadcasts. Even B.B.C. English-language transmissions concerning the situation in Poland and Hungary were heavily jammed today.

The Polish press is unavailable in Rumania, except to a few approved customers. The virtual ban on the Polish papers went into effect shortly after the Poznan riots in June.

These moves apparently reflect the regime's fear that the present situation is explosive enough to jolt Rumanians into similar action.

Gheorghe Gheorghiu-Dej, First Secretary of the Rumanian Workers (Communist) party, and other top leaders are currently visiting Yugoslavia. But their return, according to the best information here, will make no difference in Rumania's docility in the present crisis.

Rumania's Communist rulers are fully dependent on Moscow and especially on the two Soviet divisions quartered here.

M. Gheorghiu-Dej and his colleagues came to power through the Soviet Army. Unlike the Yugoslav or Polish Communists, they can make no claim to having led a successful partisan struggle for liberation.

Minority Problems Cited

Furthermore, the Rumanian leaders are confronted with thorny problems of the large Hungarian minority in Transylvania and lesser minorities of Serbs, Croats, Turks and Jews. The leaders cannot speak for a relatively homogeneous population of the kinds that have defied Soviet rule in Poland and Hungary.

The Rumanians have historically bowed before foreign conquerors. They have been dominated in whole or part by Rome, Byzantium, the Ottoman Empire, Austria-Hungary, Germany and Russia.

There is intense interest here in the situation in Poland and Hungary, but no discernible tension. Even the traditionally volatile university students are apparently quiescent. Soviet troops are no more in evidence than usual.

A prominent Rumanian novelist with whom this correspondent talked today asked with interest about the events in the rest of Europe and displayed surprising knowledge of what was going on. He was perfectly content, however, to await the outcome and gave no indication of wishing to participate in any movement to ease the Soviet grip on his homeland.

The same outlook is apparent among newspaper men, officials and the man-in-the-street with whom one talks. Officials answer all questions about the Polish and Hungarian situation with guarded references to each country's right to develop its own brand of communism.

Everyone, however, except perhaps the top leadership, is clearly hopeful that something better may come out of it for Rumania.

*   *   *

November 3, 1956

REGIME TIGHTENS BULGARIAN CURBS

Reds Evince Nervousness, but Strong Controls Bar Articulate Opposition

Dispatch of The Times, London

SOFIA, Bulgaria, Nov. 2—The Bulgarian Communist Government has taken strong security precautions. These are accompanied by appeals for "vigilance against enemy encroachments" and threats of crushing blows against any "counter-revolutionary" attempts.

Soldiers carrying machine guns are patroling the streets of the cities, and at night identity papers are being checked more thoroughly than hitherto.

It is not only in these precautions that the regime has shown its nervousness. An announcement yesterday said that bread rationing, imposed three weeks ago, would be ended Nov. 10. This is symptomatic of the Government's desire to avoid any risks and any cause for trouble.

A measure such as bread rationing, unpopular even during normal situations, could easily prove dangerous at a time when the Bulgarians are watching events in Poland and Hungary with anxious expectations.

But the ferment now gripping Eastern Europe in the search for a national road to socialism is not conspicuous in Bulgaria. Any hope among the ordinary people that the developments in Poland might be repeated in Bulgaria was frustrated by the realization that Bulgaria does not have "its own Gomulka" (a reference to Wladyslaw Gomulka, who returned to power in Poland last month as Communist party chief). The impact of recent events in Eastern Europe has left the Bulgarian people with feelings of sad resignation, admiration and perhaps envy.

In Bulgaria there are none of the pressures that erupted in Poland and Hungary. There are rumblings and discontent, but they are not voiced in the newspapers or public discussion. After a short spell of criticism following the Communist party Central Committee's condemnation of Vulko Chervenkov, then Premier, in April, the Communist leadership clamped down on its critics and silenced them completely.

The events in Hungary have given the Bulgarian regime an opportunity for self-congratulation over the "timely resistance given to the petit-bourgois looseness." Now, a Communist party newspaper said, it becomes even more clear how "mature and wise" the Central Committee was in dealing with "malicious insinuations against party policy" at that time.

An announcement that the Soviet Union is to lend Bulgaria the necessary wheat to see her through the next harvest has given an opportunity to Bulgarian Communists to renew their eulogies to the Soviet Union and to the "inseparable friendship" between the Bulgarian and Soviet peoples.

*   *   *

November 24, 1956

NAGY IS ABDUCTED BY SOVIET POLICE; SENT TO RUMANIA

PLEDGE IS IGNORED

Ex-Premier Seized in Budapest on Quitting Yugoslav Embassy

By ELIE ABEL
Special to The New York Times

BELGRADE, Yugoslavia, Nov. 23—The Yugoslav Communist press reported tonight that Soviet security police had kidnapped Imre Nagy, former Hungarian Premier, in front of the Yugoslav Embassy in Budapest.

Only yesterday the Budapest Government gave Belgrade a written assurance that Mr. Nagy and his associates would be safe from political reprisals when they left the embassy to return to their homes.

[A dispatch from Vienna said that Mr. Nagy apparently had been first taken to the Soviet Kommandatura in Budapest and held overnight Thursday. On Friday, according to this report, Mr. Nagy was taken to a meeting with Janos Kadar, Hungarian Premier, and then seized again by the Russians. He later was sent to Rumania at his own request, the Budapest radio said.]

Communists Score Action

Tonight both major Communist newspapers, Borba and Politika, stressed that Mr. Nagy had been seized by the Russians in violation of the Hungarian Government's safe-conduct agreement.

This was the second incident of the day that the Yugoslavs interpreted as a Russian slap in the face for President Tito. The first was an attack on the Yugoslav leader in Pravda, Soviet Communist organ. That has been unanswered here so far. Borba in tonight's edition published the text of the Pravda article.

The abduction of Mr. Nagy, whose safety also had been guaranteed by the Yugoslav Government, was expected to worsen the already troubled relations between Belgrade and Moscow.

Borba, in its front-page account of the abduction of Mr. Nagy, said that as the former Premier and his associates boarded a bus that was to take them to their homes, a Soviet officer jumped aboard.

One automobile filled with Soviet security police moved in front of the bus and another alongside it. The cars escorted the bus to the army headquarters.

Associated Press

Imre Nagy

Two members of the Yugoslav Embassy staff, who were along to make certain Mr. Nagy got home safely, immediately protested the Soviet intervention. The Borba dispatch said the Yugoslav diplomats had been thrown into the street in front of the Russian headquarters.

Their protest that the Russians had violated the formal Yugoslav-Hungarian agreement did not impress the Soviet officers, who said they were under orders to take over the bus and its passengers, Borba added.

The report quoted Andras Partos, Chief of the Hungarian Government's Information Office in Budapest as having said he had no knowledge of Mr. Nagy's whereabouts.

Mr. Nagy and his associates had been sheltered in the Yugoslav Embassy in Budapest since Nov. 4 when Soviet Army units reoccupied the city and installed Mr. Kadar as Premier. This morning the Yugoslav Foreign Ministry strongly protested the disappearance of the men.

Hungarian Envoy Summoned

Dobrivoje Vidic, Yugoslav Under Secretary of State for Foreign Affairs, called in the Hungarian Chargé d'Affaires and demanded to know why Mr. Nagy and his party had not been returned to their homes.

The group with Mr. Nagy included the widow and son of Laszlo Rajk, Titoist Foreign Minister who was executed seven years ago.

Others were Geza Losomci and Ferenc Donat, members of the Politburo when Mr. Nagy was in power, and their wives and children.

[Altogether, there were ten men, fifteen women and seventeen children in the group, Reuters said. None could be found at their homes Friday.]

M. Vidic told the Hungarian official that the political refugees left Yugoslav Embassy voluntarily yesterday afternoon in the bus provided for them by the Hungarian Minister of Interior, Ferenc Muennich.

He added that if the missing persons were not promptly returned to their homes, Belgrade "would not only consider this a flagrant violation of existing friendly relations between the two countries but also of the recognized standards of international law."

Although Hungary was the immediate target of Yugoslav condemnation today, the disappearance of Mr. Nagy was expected to be laid at Moscow's door before long.

Diplomats in Belgrade found it inconceivable that the Kadar Government should have promised Mr. Nagy personal security without explicit approval of its Soviet sponsors.

From President Tito down through the ranks of the Yugoslav Communist party and Government, Premier Kadar had up to now received sympathy and support. In Yugoslavia, at least he has not been regarded as a Quisling.

There are indications, however, that Belgrade may have put a limit to its tolerance. Unless Mr. Nagy and his associates are set free without delay and Mr. Kadar wins the support of the workers' councils across Hungary, the Yugoslav Communists are expected to wash their hands of the new Premier, albeit reluctantly.

M. Vidic is believed to have worked out the safe-conduct agreement personally with Mr. Kadar during an unannounced visit to Budapest earlier this week. By its terms the two Governments in effect became the co-guarantors of Mr. Nagy's safety.

Budapest Account Varies

By JOHN MacCORMAC
Special to The New York Times

VIENNA, Nov. 23—Ex-Premier Nagy of Hungary was not only arrested but deported as well by the Russians, according to information received here today.

He had left his refuge in the Yugoslav Embassy in Budapest yesterday after a promise of immunity from the Kadar Government. He was arrested today by Soviet troops while he was negotiating with his successor, Premier Kadar, in the Budapest Parliament for formation of a coalition Government and was taken to an unknown destination.

The Hungarian radio, over which Mr. Nagy was to have announced this afternoon the result of his negotiation with Premier Kadar, announced instead that Mr. Nagy and his companions "left Hungary today and have departed for Rumania." It said this was because the former Premier had "expressed the wish to live in a people's democratic country. [Rumania is totally under Soviet control.]

The radio version was not believed in Budapest. But whether Mr. Nagy was spirited away because he refused to accept Moscow's terms or because Moscow would not have him in the Hungarian Government at any price was not clear. A reliable source in Budapest reported that Mr. Nagy had reached an agreement with Premier Kadar when Soviet soldiers entered Parliament and seized him.

The official announcement by the Budapest radio said:

"Former Premier Nagy and some of his colleagues, as is known, found asylum on Nov. 4 in the Yugoslav Embassy in Budapest. Their stay there ended Nov. 22. Two weeks ago Nagy and his companions had sought permission from the Hungarian Government to leave the territory of the Hungarian Peoples Republic and betake themselves to the territory of another Socialist country.

"With the permission of the Government of the Rumanian Peoples Republic, Imre Nagy and his colleagues entered the Rumanian Peoples Republic on Nov. 23."

It was reported in Vienna that a spokesman for the Yugoslav Government said in Belgrade tonight that when the Yugoslav Government inquired today in Bucharest it had been informed that no one there knew of Mr. Nagy's arrival in Rumania.

Apparently, after Mr. Nagy was taken away in a Soviet armored car Thursday and kept overnight in the Russian headquarters, he was allowed to begin his negotiations with Premier Kadar at noon today.

*   *   *

October 18, 1961

ALBANIA SCORED BY SOVIET CHIEF

Khrushchev Charges Party Follows Stalinist Line, Opposing His Policy

Special to The New York Times

MOSCOW, Oct. 17—The Albanian Communists were accused by Premier Khrushchev today of following a Stalinist line condemned by the Soviet Union.

He told the twenty-second congress of the Soviet Communist party that Albania's leaders not only had failed to understand his de-Stalinization policy proclaimed in 1956, "but indeed began to oppose that policy."

Thus confirming that an ideological break existed between the Soviet Union and the little Communist Balkan country, Mr. Khrushchev declared:

"The policy [on de-Stalinization], elaborated by the twentieth congress of our party is a Leninist policy and we cannot make a concession on that fundamental point either to the Albanian leaders or to anyone else."

No Albanians at Congress

No Albanian delegation is present at the Soviet party congress. When the Albanian Embassy in Moscow was asked today whether a delegation had arrived, a spokesman replied: "Not yet."

When pressed whether a delegation was expected, he said: "We have no information of that kind at present."

Despite the political break between the parties, the Soviet Union and Albania are expected to maintain relations at a governmental level.

Albania thus joined Yugoslavia as the two Communist states isolated from the world Communist movement—but for different reasons.

Yugoslavia broke with the Stalin-dominated movement in 1948. After a period of attempted rapprochement after Stalin's death, Marshal Tito's liberalized policies were assailed as "revisionist" by the leadership of the Chinese-Soviet bloc.

The Yugoslavs also came in for their share of criticism in Mr. Khrushchev's speech today.

"The Yugoslavs, plainly affected by national narrow-mindedness, have turned away from the straight Marxist-Leninist road on to a winding path that has landed them in the bog of revisionism," the Soviet Premier said.

"Revisionist ideas pervade both the theory and practice of the Yugoslav leadership. We have criticized and will continue to criticize the entire revisionist attitude."

Hoxha's Stand a Factor

Albania's break with world Communism apparently stemmed from the Moscow conference of eighty-one Communist parties last December when Albania's leader, Gen. Enver Hoxha, was said to have opposed Mr. Khrushchev's general line of peaceful coexistence.

It now appears that General Hoxha was also opposing the Soviet Union's post-Stalinist domestic reforms.

"The Albanian leaders," Premier Khrushchev told the congress today "are not hiding the fact that they do not like our party's policy aimed at resolutely overcoming the harmful consequences of Stalin's cult of personality, at a sharp condemnation of misuse of power and at the re-establishment of Leninist principles of party and government life.

"Such a position of the Albanian leaders is explained by the fact that they themselves, to our regret and sorrow, are repeating methods that took place in our country in the period of the cult of personality."

The Soviet leader added that the Albanian Communists were "trying to pull our party back to conditions that are to their taste but will never again recur in our country."

Appeal for Return Made

Then he continued:

"If the Albanian leaders hold dear the interests of their people and the cause of building Socialism in Albania, if they really want friendship with the Soviet Communist party and with all fraternal parties, then they must abandon their erroneous views and return to a party of unity and close collaboration in the fraternal family of the Socialist community, a path of unity with the entire world Communist movement."

"As far as our party is concerned, it will continue, in accordance with its internationalist duty, to do all in its power to insure that Albania marches shoulder to shoulder with all Socialist countries."

It was still unclear what effect the rupture between the Soviet Union and Albania would have on Communist China. Peiping has been allied ideologically with Albania in demanding that Mr Khrushchev adopt more militant tactics toward the West.

As Mr. Khrushchev denounced Albania and Stalinism, the head of the Chinese Communist delegation, Premier Chou En-lai, listened grimly without joining in the applause. He sat with his right arm hanging over the back of his chair on the stage behind Mr. Khrushchev.

Effect on Chinese Tie

Premier Khrushchev's public attack upon Albania yesterday appears to open the door for possible further major Soviet conflict with the Chinese Communists. Such conflict would arise if Peiping refuses to desert the little country that has been its staunchest ally in the Communist bloc infighting of recent years and defends the Albanians against the Khrushchev denunciation.

Presumably the world will know in the next few days whether the Communist Chinese will go along with the Soviet leader on this issue or break with him. The answer could come when Prenner Chou En-lai, head of the Chinese Communist delegation, addresses the current party congress in Moscow. Another clue may come when it becomes known whether Peiping has let its people learn of the Khrushchev denunciation.

*   *   *

October 20, 1961

CHOU CHALLENGES KHRUSHCHEV MOVE AGAINST ALBANIA

Chinese Leader's Rebuke Causes a Sensation at Soviet Party Rally

---

By SEYMOUR TOPPING
Special to The New York Times

MOSCOW, Oct. 19—Premier Chou En-lai of Communist China openly contested today Premier Khrushchev's decision to banish Albania from the Communist bloc.

The Chinese Communist leader challenged and, by implication, rebuked Mr. Khrushchev from the 'speakers' rostrum on the third day of the twenty-second congress of the Soviet Communist party.

In his speech opening the congress, Mr. Khrushchev denounced the Communist rulers of Albania, who are supporters of Peiping's militant interpretation of Communist philosophy.

The Albanians were not among the eighty Communist and worker parties invited to the congress.

Denunciation Scored

In an obvious reference to Mr. Khrushchev's castigation of the Albanians, the Chinese Premier said, according to observers in the congress hall:

"If there are quarrels in the Socialist camp we consider that they should be settled through bilateral contacts and that a public denunciation does not contribute to the cohesion of the Socialist camp."

[Mr. Chou appeared to be calling on the Soviet party to abide by the policy statement adopted last November by eighty-one Communist parties. That statement demanded "defense of the unity of the world Communist movement" and "avoidance of any actions which may undermine that unity."]

Premier Chou introduced his speech of greetings to the congress by stating that his country was a friend of the Soviet Union and "all other countries in the Socialist camp, which extends from North Korea to the German Democratic Republic and from Vietnam to Albania."

Talk Causes Sensation

There was a scattering of applause from the 5,000 delegates but it quickly died away when it was observed that Mr. Khrushchev and other members of the Soviet Presidium on the stage were not applauding.

The remarks of the chief of the Chinese delegation included the customary expressions of friendship and cohesion with the Soviet Union. When Premier Chou left the rostrum he shook hands with Mr. Khrushchev.

His public opposition to Mr. Khrushchev on the Albanian issue caused a sensation. It represented the most open manifestation of the ideological dispute that has been waged privately for years between Moscow and Peiping.

In party conclaves, the Chinese Communists with the support of General of the Army Enver Hoxha, the Albanian Communist chief, have opposed Mr. Khrushchev's foreign policy as too soft toward the West. Mao Tse-tung, the chairman of the Chinese Communist party and General Hoxha have resented Mr. Khrushchev's program and his condemnation of the "cult of personality."

Malenkov Denounced

In speeches during today's sessions Mr. Khrushchev's deputies followed the example set on Tuesday by the Soviet Premier in castigating Lazar M. Kaganovich and Georgi A. Malenkov, two of the antiparty group expelled from the Soviet Presidium in 1957 for Stalinist practices.

Kirill T. Mazurov, First Secretary of the Byelorussian party organization, declared that the continued membership of Mr. Malenkov in the party was "impossible." The former Soviet Premier was demoted to running a power station after his ouster but he retained party membership.

There were some specialists on Soviet affairs here who expressed the view that Mr. Khrushchev had attempted to reassert his authority over the Communist bloc by making an example of Albania. His criticism of Albania was regarded here as an implicit criticism of Communist China.

Mr. Khrushchev chose a moment for his attack on Albania when Communist China is in a weak economic position at home and more eager than ever for Soviet economic aid. Peiping's economy has received a severe setback because of the devastation of its agriculture by drought and flood.

Premier Chou indicated in his speech that Communist China was not seeking an open break with the Soviet Union. The Premier reaffirmed his adherence to the declaration of the eighty-one Communist parties that met in Moscow last November.

The November meeting resulted in a manifesto that represented a compromise between the Soviet and Chinese views of the strategy to be pursued in the attainment of world communism. Mr. Khrushchev's thesis of "peaceful coexistence" with the Western nations was affirmed but the parties also decided to press more militantly in support of "national liberation movements" in Asia, Africa and Latin America.

Tass, the Soviet press agency which did not publish Premier Chou's remarks on Albania, quoted extensively from those passages in which he expressed support for the policy of "peaceful coexistence" and the November agreement.

U. S. Is Denounced

Premier Chou read a message of greetings from Chairman Mao. It said relations between the Soviet Union and Communist China "have been tried and tested and are eternal and inviolable."

Denouncing the United States as the "sworn enemy of peace," the Premier declared:

"We actively support the liberation struggle of oppressed nations and oppressed peoples; resolutely oppose the policy of aggression and war conducted by the imperialist circles headed by the United States."

Well-informed sources said that the Chinese leader might attempt to raise the Albanian question and other issues in a closed meeting of the party leaders after the end of the congress later this month.

The Chinese Communists would have an opportunity to press for firmer action by the Soviet Union in support of Peiping's ambitions in Asia and its efforts to replace Nationalist China in the United Nations.

Some observers here linked the renewal of the attack on the Soviet "anti-party group," which also had included Vyacheslav M. Molotov and Nikolai A. Bulganin and others, to the Albanian controversy.

As a matter of course, the "anti-party" group would have been covered in Mr. Khrushchev's speech Tuesday. It is traditional to review the period of party activity dating back to the last congress.

In this case, the review went back to the twentieth party congress in 1956 since the twenty-first congress in 1959 was an extraordinary one called for the presentation of the seven-year plan.

However, the extent to which Soviet party officials are dwelling on the sins of the "antiparty group" raised suspicions that broader implications were involved, possibly on an international scale. Former President Klimenti Y. Voroshilov was implicated Tuesday by M. Khrushchev in the "antiparty group" although he was sitting on the forty-one member Presidium of the congress.

Nikolai V. Podgorny the party chief of the Ukraine, today denounced Mr. Kaganovich as a "degenerate who long since has had nothing of a Communist left in him."

Mr. Podgorny indicated that Mr. Kaganovich might lose his party membership together with Mr. Malenkov when he declared: "We consider that Kaganovich's actions were incompatible with the title of Communist party member."

Mr. Kaganovich, who is 68 years old, headed the Ukraine party organization from 1925 to 1928 and from 1946 to 1947. One of Stalin's chief deputies, he was instrumental in bringing Mr. Khrushchev into the Moscow hierarchy.

Mr. Kaganovich has been variously reported as working as a factory director and as living in Moscow in retirement.

Mr. Podgorny accused Mr. Kaganovich of surrounding himself with unprincipled persons and of the persecution of devoted party officials.

* * *

October 30, 1961

KHRUSHCHEV BERATED

Albanians Retort That Soviet Premier is Anti-Marxist

VIENNA, Oct 29 (UPI)—Albanian worker and youth groups have denounced Premier Khrushchev as anti-Marxist and compared him to the late Secretary of State John Foster Dulles, A.T.A., the Albanian press agency, said today.

It said messages also had accused Mr. Khrushchev of plotting the overthrow of the legitimate leadership of Albania.

A message from a clothing cooperative said:

His speech recalls to us the Christmas messages the United States Presidents issue from the White House in which, while shedding crocodile tears about the destiny of the Albanian peoples, call for the overthrow of the peoples' power.

"Mr. Khrushchev will be as successful as Dulles and his accomplices."

* * *

April 8, 1963

YUGOSLAVIA ADOPTS NEW CONSTITUTION; TITO RULES FOR LIFE

By The Associated Press

BELGRADE, Yugoslavia, April 7—The Yugoslav Federal Parliament unanimously adopted a new Constitution today. It makes Marshal Tito President for life and secures Communist party control of the country.

The Constitution went into effect immediately.

The two houses of the Parliament separately adopted the Constitution. Then a joint session, televised throughout the country, was called and the new Constitution was formally announced and Parliament dissolved. Elections for the new Parliament have been scheduled for June.

President Tito attended the joint session. He has been the nation's leader since World War II and was elected President in 1953, when Yugoslavia became a federal people's republic. He will be 71 years old next month.

The new Constitution replaces one adopted in 1946, two years before the Moscow-Belgrade split.

New Name for Country

Under the new Constitution, the country will become "The Socialist Federal Republic of Yugoslavia." This is Yugoslavia's way of saying that it has advanced as far as the Soviet Union in Communist development and further than Moscow's satellites.

Russia now calls itself a Socialist republic, but most of the other Communist countries retain the designation "people's republic." In Marxist terms, a people's republic is the first step to Communism, a Socialist republic the second.

The new Constitution reaffirms Yugoslavia's brand of decentralized Socialism, which has brought ideological conflicts with the Soviet Union and Red China. Yugoslav industrial management remains within workers' councils in individual plants, without centralized control of the Soviet type.

It does not provide for the existence of other political parties. Only the Communists and the Communist-dominated Socialist Alliance of Working People are allowed.

Names Tito Specifically

President Tito has been named in the Constitution as President of the republic for an unlimited term. Future Presidents, who will be elected by the Parliament, will be limited to two consecutive four-year terms.

The major change is the appointment of a Premier under the President. The Premier will relieve the President of much routine work. . . . A Vice President will retain firm control.

He is the supreme chief of the army. He nominates the Premier and can propose his removal, with the consent of Parliament. He can preside over meetings of the Cabinet when he desires. He can veto any Cabinet decision. A Vice President will preside when necessary.

* * *

October 18, 1963

KENNEDY AND TITO HOLD 'FRANK' TALK; ASSESS REDS' RIFT

Day's Tribute for Yugoslav Chief Is Cordial but Swift— White House Picketed

By MAX FRANKEL
Special to The New York Times

WASHINGTON, Oct. 17—President Kennedy gave President Tito a cordial but swift day of tribute at the White House today that pleased the Yugoslav leader and protected the Democrats' political flanks.

The maverick Communist was taken through the entire routine of an official visit—from a 21-gun salute and ruffles and flourishes to champagne toasts over luncheon and a formal, hopeful communiqué—in less than six hours.

Associated Press

President Tito, left, makes a point across the conference table to President Kennedy. With them are Mijalko Todovoric, center, Yugoslav Vice President, and Veljko Micunovic, Yugoslav envoy to U.S. Talk covered many subjects.

Then helicopters carried him back to Williamsburg, Va., as quickly as they had delivered him this morning over the heads of jeering pickets and protesting members of Congress.

The crammed schedule also allowed two and a half hours of "frank discussion" between the two Presidents on East-West relations, the dispute between the Soviet Union and Communist China, the United Nations and Marshal Tito's impressions of Latin America. He visited Latin America before coming to the United States.

Grateful for U.S. Aid

The Yugoslav visitor expressed gratitude on several occasions for the $2.5 billion in American assistance extended since he was thrown out of the international Communist movement by Stalin in 1948.

President Kennedy, in turn, paid tribute to the Yugoslavs' "valiant struggle" for national independence.

The roar of the Presidential helicopters that carried the Yugoslav party may have drowned out the hostile jeers and chants of several hundred pickets who marched outside the White House grounds.

They had gathered from several cities to represent groups of Serbs, Croatians and other peoples now united in Yugoslavia. They carried signs and literature denouncing Marshal Tito as a tyrant, a murderer of priests and political opponents, and a "Trojan horse" for Communist aggressors.

There were also a few more expressions of opposition from members of Congress, who echoed Senator Barry Goldwater's charge that Mr. Kennedy was "dining with our enemy."

President Tito offered the customary return invitation for President Kennedy to visit Yugoslavia. He said later that his host had accepted, but without a commitment to a particular time.

Officials on both sides said this evening that the day had gone extremely well, and even the politically minded in the Administration thought Mr. Kennedy had deftly protected himself from partisan assault.

For one thing, President Kennedy appeared to have maneuvered things so that no photographer caught him in an excessively expansive mood with President Tito.

No one managed to catch them shaking hands or in any other pose that might be used against Mr. Kennedy in an election; even the customary rocking-chair scene was replaced by a formal photograph showing host and guest on opposite sides of a conference table.

Mr. Kennedy was noticeably reserved in his first moments with his guest on the south lawn of the White House. Then, in a cordial welcoming speech, Mr. Kennedy remarked pointedly that he was repaying the hospitality shown Americans—

including members of Congress—in Belgrade and that there could be friendly discourse despite differences in political philosophy.

At a luncheon before guests that included Senator Everett McKinley Dirksen, the Republican leader in the Senate, Mr. Kennedy noted that his predecessors, Presidents Truman and Eisenhower, had also believed strongly in the independence of Yugoslavia and had appreciated the "extraordinary" efforts made to maintain it.

International rather than domestic politics was the main preoccupation of both leaders. Both wished to demonstrate that independence of Moscow, even by a Government that is faithful to Communism, can bring it influence in Washington.

Red Alignments Assayed

In their formal talks, during which President Tito spoke in Serbo-Croat but waved off translations of President Kennedy's remarks, the two men were said to have covered the following points:

Marshal Tito expressed his belief that the rift in the Communist world was widening and that fairly rigid groupings of Communist states would develop around Moscow and Peking. He also expressed confidence that Premier Khrushchev was genuinely interested in further East-West negotiations and steps to reduce the risks of war.

President Kennedy questioned his visitor about his month-long tour through Brazil, Chile, Bolivia and Mexico and was told that Latin Americans were eager for United States aid and much less worried than in the past about "Yankee imperialism."

Marshal Tito found South Americans still groping for the right forms of political and economic development. He said he had had no contact with Communists in the Western hemisphere.

Both men agreed that there was no longer any need for outright economic aid to Yugoslavia and that loans and trade should be the basis of future relations. Mr. Kennedy was still unable to say with certainty, however, whether Congress would permit the restoration of "most-favored nation" status, giving Yugoslavia the lowest tariffs given to other sellers in the American market.

New Aid in Quake

Presumably President Kennedy praised Yugoslavia's recent displays of independence from the Communist bloc in the United Nations, and especially her willingness to pay for peace-keeping operations in the Congo.

Mr. Kennedy offered the Yugoslav leader additional aid for the victims of the Skoplje earthquake and Marshal Tito accepted with thanks. White House aides said they planned to provide surplus barracks now stored in France to house about 10,000 people.

For the 71-year-old Yugoslav leader, who rose from the ranks of wartime partisan fighters to defy the superpowers of East and West, the first few moments at the White House appeared to be the most moving ones.

Though the years of unchallenged leadership have added much weight to his husky build, his well-tanned face appeared taut as he stood with a wry smile through the salute and the playing of anthems.

His 39-year-old wife, Jovanka, a major in the partisan army in World War II, seemed even more touched. She wore a black suit with a high pink hat and pink gloves and carried red roses given her by President Kennedy's sister, Mrs. R. Sargent Shriver, who substituted as hostess for the vacationing Mrs. Kennedy.

The President took oblique notice of the criticism of his guest by stressing the importance of "understanding" among nations of different political systems. He twice expressed confidence that Americans would welcome Marshal Tito and treat him hospitably on his visits to California, New York and New Jersey during the next eight days.

* * *

October 18, 1963

NEW LINE IN BELGRADE

Yugoslavs See Need of Policy Shift To Meet Changes in Power Blocs

By DAVID BINDER
Special to The New York Times

BELGRADE, Yugoslavia, Oct. 17—President Tito, who has been practicing nonalignment in various forms for at least a decade, remarked the other day that "nonalignment" might be inadequate to describe the present and future of Yugoslavia's foreign policy.

He was echoing a line that he and his aides have been voicing with increasing persistence for the last five months, especially since the signing in August of the treaty for a partial nuclear test ban.

Ten years ago, when Yugoslavia was treated as a renegade by the whole Soviet bloc, and when Marshal Tito, who is now in the United States, was dealing gingerly with the Western powers in an effort to shore up his hard-pressed economy and military establishment, the phrase was "positive neutrality."

Marshal Tito's only friend in "nonalignment" at that time was Prime Minister Jawaharlal Nehru of India.

Since then the phrase has evolved through "nonadherence to blocs," "nonbloc policy" and "active coexistence." In the intervening years, Yugoslavia has emerged as the precursor and, to a large extent, the inspiration, of the strains of national independence within the Soviet bloc.

Soviet Grip Loosened

The Soviet Union has had to loosen its rigid control enough to allow the satellites a limited degree of independent action, the prime examples being Hungary and Poland.

Premier Khrushchev has given his blessing to Yugoslavia's policy of independent Marxism-Leninism and has urged his bloc partners to do likewise.

During his talks with President Tito on Brioni Island in August, the Soviet leader went so far as to say that he considered the division of major powers into blocs "a temporary phase."

This was precisely in line with the thinking of the Yugoslavs; Marshal Tito lost no time in echoing the remark during his visit to Brazil last month.

The Yugoslavs appear to believe that the developments they have openly sought at least since 1957, namely the dissolution of the great-power blocs, is now in sight. If that is the case, they conclude, "nonalignment" no longer takes in all the elements of the new situation of an independent Socialist country's foreign relations.

To be sure, with the East-West opposition still evident in the North Atlantic Treaty Organization and Warsaw Pact alliances, Marshal Tito must continue to play it down the middle.

That is why Marshal Tito's handshake with President Kennedy today, only six weeks after he bid farewell to Premier Khrushchev, is a significant demonstration of the continuing practice of Yugoslav nonalignment.

Trade Aims Reflect Policy

This policy is also manifest in the Yugoslav intention to take observer status in the Soviet bloc's Council for Mutual Economic Assistance or Comecon, while seeking precisely the same status in the European Economic Community.

The new look in Yugoslav foreign policy, whose outlines are only barely discernible, is based on an assumption, that the bloc alignments are gradually being replaced by a distribution of forces that is characterized as a division between reconcilables and irreconcilables.

In the judgment of the Tito Government, the irreconcilables are found mostly in Peking, although a few are identified as such in the United States, the Soviet Union, Czechoslovakia, France and East Germany.

Though reluctant to name them, the Yugoslavs might include in their list men like Senator Barry Goldwater, Republican of Arizona; President Antonin Novotny of Czechoslovakia and Walter Ulbricht, chairman of East Germany's Council of State.

The Belgrade officials find it is easier to identify the reconcilables publicly. They name among them Soviet Premier Khrushchev, President Kennedy and, of course, Marshal Tito, the most reconcilable of them all.

The Yugoslavs seem to believe that elements of independence are gaining strength every day in Eastern Europe as well as in the Western alliance.

*   *   *

BOOTLEG WRY HUMOR

Special to The New York Times

SOFIA, Bulgaria, Jan. 5—Communist Bulgaria passed a law last week making it a crime to tell political jokes, punishable by 15 days in jail.

One of the jokes going the rounds in Sofia after the law was passed relates the conversation of Ivan and Petur as follows:

"Petur, if they open the borders will you remain here?"

"No, Ivan, why should I stay all alone in Bulgaria?"

*   *   *

WORKER IN RUMANIA TAKES DAY TO CELEBRATE HIS ANNIVERSARY

By DAVID BINDER

Special to The New York Times

ONESTI, Rumania, Jan. 13—Benedikt Halcescu stayed home from work today to celebrate his 12th wedding anniversary.

So he was taking it easy in bedroom slippers and a sports shirt when the strangers arrived to see how a skilled worker lives in Rumania. His wife, Ophelia, wore a morning coat.

But they didn't seem to mind the intrusion and they proudly showed off their three-room apartment.

The floors were covered with factory-made rugs with bright peasant designs. The furniture, and there was a lot of it, was old-fashioned in style but solid and comfortable.

There were a piano and a television set in the living room and a tape recorder next door. Mr. Halcescu keeps his photographic equipment in the bathroom, where he does his own developing and printing. The kitchen has a refrigerator.

Work at Chemical Plant

The Halcescus earned all these things on their wages from the Borzesti chemical plant, where they work six days a week.

Mr. Halcescu, who is 36 years old, earns about 2,200 lei monthly ($366 at the official exchange rate of 6 lei to the dollar) as a technician. His pay is more than twice the Rumanian average.

The apartment, which houses two children and Mrs. Halcescu's mother as well, costs about 160 lei, or $26 a month. The major expense of this family, and most Rumanian families, is for food. The Halcescus spend about 800 lei, or $133 a month on food. It has been estimated that an unskilled worker with two children spends as much as 70 per cent of his income on food.

In a land where there is still much poverty, particularly among the peasantry, the Halcescus live well. They said they saved about 500 lei a month and that "later, much later," they might buy a car.

In Rumania, the cheapest East German car, called a Trabant, costs 30,000 lei, or about $5,000.

Mountain Trip Planned

In the summer, the Halcescus have taken their three-week vacation at Mamaia on the Black Sea coast. But this year they are planning to visit one of the Carpathian mountain resorts. On weekends they sometimes go to the nearby Red Lake for recreation.

Onesti is a modern, well-planned industrial city of about 45,000. It has grown up from a provincial marketing town of about 5,000 since the construction of the chemical works. The apartment blocks are without architectural beauty but are solid and comfortable.

Situated in the broad valley of the Trotus River, the city is surrounded by the pretty hills and villages of Moldavia.

But the new industrial class of people like the Halcescus seem to prefer staying in town, however ordinary the life might be.

Last month Mr. Halcescu joined the Rumanian Workers (Communist) party. He said that the party did not impinge much on his life and that he had to attend meetings only once a month.

"I don't spend much time on the party," he said.

*   *   *

February 17, 1964

PAPANDREOU PARTY WINS IN GREECE

By DAVID BINDER
Special to The New York Times

ATHENS, Monday, Feb. 17—George Papandreou's Center Union party won an overwhelming victory in the national election yesterday. With about 90 per cent of the ballots counted, the Center Union had 2,260,052 votes against 1,415,884 for the conservative party, the National Radical Union. The pro-Communist United Democratic Left party, which backed the Center Union in 24 of 55 districts, had 499,611. Panayotis Canellopoulos, National Radical Union leader, said in a statement conceding defeat that his party would "do everything in our power to assist the smooth working of parliamentary democracy." With a margin so far of 53 per cent against 35 per cent for the National Radical Union, Mr. Papandreou, who was 76 years old last week was assured of a working majority in the 300-member Parliament. This was a goal he failed to achieve in his narrow victory margin at the last election in November.

Mr. Papandreou claimed victory at 11:15 P.M. last night. "The results have justified my expectations," he declared.

During his latest electoral campaign he had predicted that the "victory" of November over the eight-year-old Government of Constantine Caramanlis would lead to the "triumph" of February.

Caramanlis Not on Ballot

The sweep of his conquest showed especially in the country districts of northern Greece, where the National Radical Union, the creation of Mr. Caramanlis, had previously been

United Press International Radiophoto

George Papandreou, leader of Center Union party, as he voted yesterday in Athens during Greek national election.

strongest. Early returns indicated that the Center Union had 60 per cent of the vote even in Mr. Caramanlis's home district of Serrai.

Mr. Caramanlis, who went into self-imposed exile in Paris shortly after the November defeat, was not a candidate in this election. Mr. Canellopoulos was Mr. Caramanlis's chief deputy.

The size of the Center Union victory margin also appeared to rule out the possibility of future charges by the National Radical Union that Mr. Papanderou had won through collusion with the United Democratic Left. Mr. Canellopoulos had waged a large part of his campaign on the implication of collusion.

There were many elements in the Papandreou victory. First, there was widespread discontent with the domestic economy under the National Radical Union. There was unemployment and many Greeks were emigrating to northern Europe to find work.

In addition, there was Mr. Papandreou's strategy. He charged "corruption" and "dictatorship" at every turn and apparently persuaded many voters that there was a "mess" in Athens under Mr. Caramanlis.

When Mr. Caramanlis resigned last June in a constitutional dispute with King Paul, it seemed that his position had never been stronger. He was planning for quick elections and a wave of popular approval to carry him to a new and stronger mandate.

But elections were not held until four months later. Meanwhile, Mr. Papandreou stumped the country, urging that it was time for a change. He also made and later kept some generous promises to cut taxes, settle debts and provide free education.

After winning the premiership in November, he governed for about 50 days, and then set the February election date. A caretaker Government led by Premier John Paraskevopoulos has been in power pending the election.

Andreas Papandreou, 45-year-old son of the party leader, won a seat in Parliament as Deputy in his father's native district of Achaea. He had been a United States citizen for 20 years and, from 1956 until his resignation last month, he was chairman of the economics department at the University of California in Berkeley. He resigned the position and resumed his Greek citizenship to run for election.

He will serve as one of his father's chief aides in economic planning.

*   *   *

March 7, 1964

GREEK KING DEAD; SON, 23, WILL REIGN

Special to The New York Times

ATHENS, March 6—King Paul of the Hellenes died today from post-operative complications.

Queen Frederika, his wife, was at his bedside at the Tatoi summer palace when the 62-year-old King died at 4:12 P. M. The death was certified by the King's physician, Dr. Thomas Doxiades.

The Queen, her eyes blood-shot from lack of sleep, wept bitterly as she kissed the King for the last time.

Three hours later, their only son, 23-year-old Crown Prince Constantine, was proclaimed King at the royal palace in Athens. It is not yet known whether he will take the title of Constantine XIII or Constantine II. His grandfather styled himself Constantine XII to symbolize Greece's link with the Byzantine Empire.

The last Byzantine emperor, known as Constantine XI Palaeologus, lost Constantinople in 1453 to the Turks.

Today, Constantine, who was named Regent Feb. 20, on the eve of a major operation on his father, was proclaimed King in the presence of Government officials, the hierarchy of the Greek Church, leading judges and military authorities and members of Parliament.

Taking the oath he said: "I swear in the name of the Holy Trinity to defend the established religion of the Greek peoples, to guard the Constitution and laws of the Greek nation and to preserve and protect the national independence and integrity of the Greek state."

King Paul had been ill with blood clots in the right leg and left lung since his operation two weeks ago for stomach ulcers. Kidney trouble set in three days ago.

Palace sources disclosed tonight that the King's physicians had told him a month ago that an operation was necessary immediately. Although in great pain, he refused, fearing that

Associated Press Cablephoto

King Constantine stands during ceremony at the royal palace in Athens proclaiming him King of the Hellenes. At far right are Archbishop Chrysostomos and Premier Papandreou. The King's sister, Princess Irene, is at the left.

an operation might cause anxiety because it would come just before the general elections of Feb. 16.

On Feb. 19, King Paul collapsed after Greece's new Center Union Government had been sworn in.

The King's body will be taken from the Tatoi summer palace, 16 miles north of Athens, to the royal palace in the capital tomorrow. Here the court staff will pay its last respects. On Sunday the body will be taken in solemn procession to Athens Cathedral to lie in state until the funeral.

Heads of State Informed

King Constantine formally advised all heads of state tonight of the news of his father's death. Many of them are expected to come to Athens for the funeral. An official announcement said the funeral would be held Thursday.

The Belgian and Danish kings and the Dutch queen were reported to have announced they would attend. The Duke of Edinburgh, husband of Queen Elizabeth of Britain, was also expected to attend. He was a cousin of King Paul.

President de Gaulle was reported to be planning to attend unless the funeral interfered with preparations for his state visit to Mexico, which is to begin March 15.

King Constantine asked Premier George Papandreou to continue as head of the Government. The Premier, who took office after the elections, had handed in his Cabinet's resignation as a matter of form.

The new King must repeat his path before Parliament within two months. Parliament is scheduled to convene on March 19.

Sister Next in Line

King Constantine's younger sister, 22-year-old Princess Irene, becomes heiress presumptive to the throne. She is the first woman ever to be next in line to the Greek throne. Her duties will involve deputizing for the King when he is abroad. She will remain Crown Princess until the King, who is engaged to marry 17-year-old Princess Anne-Marie of Denmark in January has an heir.

According to the Greek Constitution succession to the Greek crown goes in order of birth, precedence being given to males.

Prince Peter of Greece, a cousin of the late King, is second in the line of succession.

Princess Sophia, the 26-year-old elder sister of the new King, lost her rights to succession in 1962, when she was married to Prince Juan Carlos, son of the pretender to the Spanish throne.

King Constantine, who will be the world's youngest reigning monarch, pledged in a broadcast tonight to follow his father's teaching. He said:

"I succeed my father to the throne with the firm determination to follow his lofty example and to draw inspiration from his virtues while carrying out any Constitutional duties.

"I pledge to serve my country with wholehearted devotion and all my powers as a vigilant guardian of the free institutions of the democratic regime. My only thoughts and cares will always be the true and supreme interest of our fatherland."

* * *

July 6, 1964

RUMANIA PRESSES PURSUIT OF INDEPENDENT ECONOMY

Drive to Achieve National Renaissance Affecting All Planning Sectors

By DAVID BINDER
Special to The New York Times

BUCHAREST, Rumania, July 5—The pursuit of independence and a national renaissance by the Communist leadership of Rumania appears to be developing with the precision and confidence of a well-made symphony.

The leitmotif remains the determination of the Government of President Gheorghe Gheorghiu-Dej to expand the country's economy on Rumanian terms, regardless of the wishes of the neighboring Soviet Union and its East European allies.

Counterpoint is provided by the regime's efforts to assert independent policies in foreign affairs and to introduce liberalizing reforms internally.

The program has touched virtually every aspect of the national life and it seems to be carefully orchestrated.

The goal of the program is a Rumanian version of national Communism. Judging from conversations with ordinary people, most adult Rumanians are aware of this. A hitchhiking worker said: "Our Communism is becoming like [Yugoslav President] Tito's Communism."

Rumania's trade pattern is still oriented predominantly eastward. More than 60 per cent of her exchanges are with Communist countries. For that matter, Rumania still belongs to the Soviet-directed Council for Mutual Economic Aid, or Comecon, and to the Warsaw military pact.

There is no sign that she intends to get out of these organizations. Rumanians still talk about their membership in the "Socialist camp" with conviction.

Western observers who have studied Rumania's economy maintain that a Soviet-directed blockade would bring temporary disruption or even chaos.

Hardest hit would be coal supplies, certain chemicals and spare parts. But the observers say Rumania's wealth in oil, natural gas, wheat and corn would enable her to "weather" the blockade.

No one here seems to expect the Soviet Union to exert sanctions. But the possibility is not ruled out and the Government plainly intends to safeguard Rumania against eventual pressures.

More Room for Maneuvering

It is clear now that the Rumanian independence drive was made possible and continues to expand because of the split between the Soviet Union and Communist China. What

COMMUNISM WITH A RUMANIAN TOUCH: Despite traditional celebration of May Day, symbol of party's international scope, the regime of President Gheorghe Gheorghiu-Dej is encouraging a growing trend toward nationalism in foreign and economic affairs.

started in 1960 as an economic development has since acquired an increasingly political character.

The growing antagonism between the two Communist giants has provided greater and greater maneuvering room for the Gheorghiu-Dej leadership.

The implications for the rest of the Communist countries are enormous, and they have not been lost on such astute leaders as President Tito. It appears now that Mr. Gheorghiu-Dej has joined the Yugoslav leader in seeking the establishment of a Socialist family of separate but equal states and parties. The success of the Rumanian example so far would seem to strengthen the chances of such a development.

A new element in the Rumanian situation is that the whole population of 19 million has been encouraged to take part in the national revival.

The drive started last fall when, in a series of tours of the provinces, President Gheorghiu-Dej began explaining some of the elements of his policies, including the invitation to Western companies to help build up Rumanian industries.

Interference Condemned

The next major move came April 22 when the Central Committee of the Ruling Rumanian Workers (Communist) party adopted a declaration condemning all efforts by Moscow to interfere with the country's economic planning and foreign policy.

The special target was Comecon, through which the Soviet Union has attempted to curb Rumania's program to build heavy industry. The statement of independence was swiftly-circulated in lower party ranks.

In the last three weeks of May the declaration was put up for discussion in factories, agricultural collectives and Government offices all over Rumania. The effect was electrifying.

A factory physician arose and denounced what he called "defective" medical equipment shipped from the Soviet Union. He said it had caused "grave accidents" in hospitals.

At another factory a worker said Premier Khrushchev had been "more brutal" than Stalin because he broke off diplomatic relations with Albania in 1961. The worker added that Stalin at least maintained the Soviet Embassy in Belgrade after the 1948 break between Yugoslavia and the Soviet bloc.

Other workers termed Mr. Khrushchev a "fool." His famous shoe-thumping act at the United Nations in 1960 was recalled with derision.

In another meeting a Central Committee member remarked that when Mr. Krushchev visited in 1962 he refused to tour

Rumanian factories—he just pulled his hat down over his eyes and kept repeating: "Do you grow corn in quadrangles?"

The mockery voiced in these meetings extended to other Communist countries with which the Bucharest leadership has disagreed.

Help Is Refused

A worker remarked that East Germany and Czechoslovakia, both of which have labor shortages, had "asked Rumania to send them peasants because of our agricultural tradition." The worker added: "Rumania refused and we shall go on eating our butter while they go on eating their margarine—that is their tradition."

"In our factory meeting we wrote a letter to President Gheorghiu-Dej to thank him for refusing to bow to the Russians," a worker said.

It has been reliably reported that the several thousand Rumanians who have Soviet wives were forbidden to attend these meetings and that recently the wives have been asked to take Rumanian citizenship.

Apparently the meeting represented the first occasion on which the Rumanian Government had ever sought expressions of public opinion on its policies. While it was greatly heartened by the surge of patriotism, there is evidence that it was also worried by the stinging virulence of the anti-Soviet criticisms.

Since the beginning of June there have been no more meetings. The party-controlled press has avoided all mention of the anti-Russian manifestations.

Nevertheless, the chronology of events since the April 22 declaration by the party Central Committee shows clearly that the Rumanian Government is following its independence course with single-minded determination.

On May 18, in the midst of the public meetings at home, a top-level delegation headed by the planning chief, Georghe Gaston Marin, started trade talks in Washington.

On May 26, Chivu Stoica, a Politburo member, led a delegation to the Soviet Union for talks with Premier Khrushchev and other senior Russian leaders.

The aim of this mission was apparently to compensate for the United States visit, but Mr. Stoica obviously made no concessions, for on May 30 Moscow broadcast a sharp criticism of Rumanian economic planning. Mr. Stoica returned quietly to Bucharest June 9.

Soviet Attacks Policy

During the first week of June, Izvestia, the Soviet Government organ, published three articles again attacking Rumanian economic policy.

Then, on June 5, the Bucharest radio replied to the Soviet criticisms, engaging in polemics for the first time and restating Rumania's claims to sovereignty.

A week later, on June 13, the weekly review called Viata Economice published a blistering condemnation of a Soviet writer's proposal for establishment of a supernational industrial-agricultural region in the lower Danube valley, including a large sector of Rumania.

It said, "This is a plan for the violation of the territorial integrity of Rumania, for dismembering its national and state unity."

The extreme sharpness of the criticism, directed against an obscure Soviet economist named E. B. Valev, led observers in Bucharest to conclude that something much greater was at stake.

It is suggested now that the Soviet Union had threatened vital Rumanian interests and that the Viata Economice article used Professor Valev's proposal only as a pretext for rebuttal.

In any case, this latest Rumanian assertion of sovereignty appears to have been crowned with success. Last Friday Izvestia published an abject apology, stating that Mr. Valev's views were erroneous and that the Rumanian complaints were "legitimate."

So far the Viata Economice article has been the high point in the Rumanian independence program, but there may be more.

More Key Moves

The last three weeks have brought other less spectacular but significant moves.

Looking inward, the Rumanian leadership decided on a profound liberalization move. On June 16 it ordered the release of 2,500 political prisoners, bringing the total freed in the last two years to 10,350. The announcement said almost all the remaining prisoners would be amnestied next month.

On June 22 President Gheorghiu-Dej met President Tito near the Yugoslav frontier and announced the attainment of a "full mutual understanding" on their views of Rumania's position and external relations.

On June 25 the Bucharest Government announced a broad 10 per cent wage increase, which is to add 4.2 billion lei ($333 million at the official rate of 12 lei to the dollar) to workers' salaries over the next 18 months. Taxes are also to be cut.

Last week senior members of the Government and party leadership began fanning out on foreign visits, while new delegations from Western and Asian countries, including Communist China, appeared in Bucharest.

Deputy Premier Gogu Radulescu went to Milan, Italy, to confer with officials of the Fiat company. Already Fiat cars are starting to appear on Rumanian streets, which are still dominated by Russian Volgas and East German Wartburgs.

The Politburo member Nicolae Ceausescu, led a high-level group to Budapest for talks with the Hungarian Premier, Janos Kadar. This visit did not appear too successful. The final communiqué, published yesterday, said only that views had been exchanged in a "sincere" manner.

It was also announced that a Politburo member and First Deputy Premier, Gheorghe Apostol, would go to Vienna tomorrow. On July 26 Premier Ion Gheorghe Maurer will fly to Paris.

These moves are designed to expand Rumania's Western relations. But it appears that the Communist leadership also intends to seek new friends for a time when it might find itself under economic pressure from the Soviet Union.

The impact of the independence drive on Rumania's internal development has yet to be felt with full force.

This is still essentially a police-controlled state. In small villages like Iaz and Caciulata the power of the Government is demonstrated by blue-uniformed militiamen carrying automatic rifles.

Armed policemen at control posts all over the country halt travelers to make sure that they have permission to enter the district.

But Mr. Gheorghiu-Dej has chosen a course that must lead him away from this.

He has opened the door for Western books, plays and businessmen. He has invited Western tourists some of whom now stay in private homes. He has "rehabilitated" Rumanian writers who were banned earlier as bourgeois decadents. He has stirred latent feelings of national pride as no Rumanian has in decades.

In seeking and acquiring public support he has chosen to enlist a mass of people who have been more or less indifferent to Communism. To keep them behind him he will have to expand their liberties.

Big Celebration Set

The national renaissance will find its most forceful expression on Aug. 23, the day 20 years ago when the Hitler-protected Antonesou dictatorship was overthrown.

It is rumored that the Communist leadership intends to give former King Michael a measure of credit next month for helping get rid of the Fascist regime in 1944.

It is also rumored that Mr. Georghiu-Dej may declare "the victory of Socialism" in Rumania. This would be another slap at the Russians because it has been the practice for the Kremlin to decide when the "complete construction of Socialism" has been achieved in East European countries.

Regardless of the credibility of the rumors, the preparations now under way all over Rumania show that Aug. 23 will bring a demonstration of national pride and independence unparalleled in the postwar period.

*   *   *

March 25, 1965

NEW CHIEF BACKS RUMANIAN POLICY

Independent Role Affirmed by Ceausescu in Eulogy

By DAVID BINDER
Special to The New York Times
BUCHAREST, Rumania, March 24—Nicolae Ceausescu strongly reaffirmed Rumania's policy of national independence in his maiden speech today as head of the Workers' (Communist) party.

He spoke before an audience representing all shades of Communism and capitalism. The occasion was the state funeral of his predecessor, Gheorghe Gheorghiu-Dej, who died Friday of cancer.

Mr. Ceausescu, at 47 years the youngest Communist chieftain in power, demonstrated throughout his address that he was Mr. Gheorghiu-Dej's heir, that he was fully in charge and that the Rumanian leadership was united around him.

Of the four funeral orators, he alone was accorded the privilege of addressing the late leader as "Dear Comrade Gheorghiu."

His remarks on Rumanian foreign policy came at the end of his eulogy, when, raising his voice and gesturing with short choppy movements, he said:

"In keeping with the line laid down in the April, 1964, declaration worked out by the party with Comrade Gheorghiu-Dej at its head, Rumania bases her international relations on the unshakable principles of independence, sovereignty and equality of all peoples of mutual respect and noninterference in internal affairs. The promotion of these principles on a world plane is a requirement of the development of cooperation among peoples."

The reference in this passage was to the Rumanian Central Committee declaration addressed mainly to the Soviet Union and its followers a year ago advising them that henceforth Rumania would make up her own mind about her national interests.

Foreign Communists who attended the service included President Anastas I. Mikoyan of the Soviet Union, Premier Chou En-lai of China. Vice President Aleksandar Rankovich of Yugoslavia and Premier Todor Zhivkov of Bulgaria.

Mr. Mikoyan and Mr. Chou, whose nations are engaged in a sharp ideological dispute, stood near each other throughout the day but did not converse.

Mr. Ceausescu's remarks on independence were echoed by Premier Ion Gheorghe Maurer, who is considered his equal in power and influence here.

The other speakers were Gheorghe Apostol, First Deputy Premier—and Chivu Stoica, member of the party Politburo and Secretariat.

Mr. Stoica, 56, was elected President of the State Council, or titular head of state, by acclamation by 456 members of the Grand National Assembly tonight.

Representing the United States was Ambassador William Crawford. The Communist party of the United States sent one of its leaders, Gilbert Green.

*   *   *

April 16, 1965

SOFIA SAID TO FOIL PRO-PEKING PLOT

2 High Bulgarians Linked to Anti-Zhivkov Group

SOFIA, Bulgaria, April 15 (UPI)—Security policemen have thwarted a plot by high-ranking pro-Peking Communists to overthrow the Government of Premier Todor Zhivkov, informed sources said today.

The sources said the plot was disclosed April 7 when Ivan Todorov-Gorunya, a member of the Central Committee of the Bulgarian Communist party, vanished from his office. The sources said he had gone into hiding but had been tracked down and arrested.

That same day, the sources said, Gen. Tsvetko Anev, commandant of the Sofia military district, was found shot to death in his apartment. The sources said he had apparently committed suicide.

The sources said General Anev and Mr. Todorov-Gorunya were reported to have been in contact with other conspirators holding high Government, party and military posts.

There was no official confirmation of the reports, and the capital was calm.

While there was no sign that a behind-the-scenes power struggle might be in progress, many political rumors circulated through the city.

The sources said that the plotters had been discovered by Bulgarian security agents before they could make a real attempt to seize power. The conspiracy was said to have involved a number of high officials, but there was no report of whether arrests had been made.

The sources emphasized reports that a clandestine organization hostile to Mr. Zhivkov was being formed. Mr. Zhivkov is both Premier and head of the Communist party, and he has backed Moscow in the Chinese-Soviet dispute.

Factions Long an Issue

Special to The New York Times

BELGRADE, Yugoslavia, April 15—Bulgaria's Communist party has been troubled by factionalism for more than six years. In 1962 Premier Zhivkov disclosed that the leadership had ousted eight top members, including two former Premiers—Anton Yugov and Vulko Chervenkov. All had reputations as Stalinists.

Since then Mr. Zhivkov has been actively revamping the party at lower levels.

For a short time in 1958, Bulgaria imitated Communist China's "Great Leap Forward" policy on a small scale by establishing communes. These were disbanded as soon as the Soviet Union criticized them.

But sympathies with the militant policy of Peking have lingered in the Bulgarian party.

Mr. Todorov-Gorunya, 48 years old, was a guerrilla fighter during World War II. He was chairman of the Chief Directorate for Water Economy. General Anev is 50 years old.

*   *   *

July 2, 1966

TITO'S CHIEF AIDE IS OUSTED AS FOE OF PARTY POLICY

Vice President Rankovic Out—He Opposed Yugoslavia Economic Reform Plans

SUCCESSION NOW OPEN

Deposed Leader Accused of 'Struggle for Power' in State Security Service

By DAVID BINDER
Special to The New York Times

BELGRADE, Yugoslavia, July 1—Vice President Aleksandar Rankovic, who was second only to President Tito in the leadership of the ruling League of Communists, was ousted today from his top party jobs.

He was linked by Marshal Tito to a "factional group" based in the state security service and opposed to the party line. It was announced later that Mr. Rankovic had also resigned as Vice President of the republic.

His removal from the posts of secretary of the Central Committee for Organizational Affairs and as a member of the party's executive committee is considered by well-informed

Camera Press-Pix

STRIPPED OF POWER: Aleksandar Rankovic, who was a top Yugoslav leader.

sources to be a key move in pushing forward Yugoslavia's current economic reform. Mr. Rankovic was known to have opposed it.

Biggest Change Since 1954

The ouster, the greatest change in the Yugoslav leadership since the party dropped the Deputy Premier, Milovan Djilas, in 1954, throws open the question of succession to the 74-year-old President. Mr. Rankovic, who is 56, was widely considered for years the most likely man to follow Marshal Tito.

The scene of today's shift was Brioni Island, the President's favorite vacation retreat, where he had convened a plenary session of the party's 154-member Central Committee to deal with the "struggle for power" of Mr. Rankovic and his associates in the leadership of the secret police.

Mr. Rankovic was Interior Minister from 1946 to 1953, when he became Deputy Premier and head of the Government's committee for internal affairs. He was elected Vice President in 1963.

Also ousted from all posts was Svetislav Stefanovic, 55, a right hand man of Mr. Rankovic. Mr. Stefanovic directed the secret police until last year. Tanjug, the official press agency, said President Tito had disclosed that the party leadership had set up a special "technical commission to ascertain certain deformations in the work of our state security."

The findings of this commission were presented to the executive committee in a session on June 16, presumably with Mr. Rankovic attending.

The 19-member committee then appointed a six-man "party and state commission" led by Krste Crvenkovski, the Macedonian party chief, to investigate the secret police still further. This group, with representatives from all six Yugoslav constituent republics, submitted an interim report to the executive committee June 22 and its final report to the Central Committee this morning.

The commission told the Central Committee that Mr. Rankovic could no longer serve in leading positions because of his "political responsibility" for the deviations of the secret police and his one-man rule of it.

Later in the Brioni session, Mr. Rankovic and Mr. Stefanovic spoke, but their remarks were not immediately available.

Following "unanimous adoption" of all resolutions before it, the Central Committee elected Mijalko Todorovic, a leading figure behind the economic reform, to Mr. Rankovic's vacated post as a party secretary.

The executive committee also took in Milentije Popovic as a new member, and Dobrivoje Radosavljevic became a new member of the Central Committee.

A new 40-member commission was established to study questions of party reorganization and further work.

It was also suggested that the million-member party hold another congress soon to work out its remaining problems. The last congress was held only 18 months ago and it was not due to have another until 1968.

In a brief address on Brioni, President Tito remarked that the party discussed some elements of the problem for three days in March, 1962.

"On that occasion we established more or less generally what these various anomalies and deviations were, but we did not establish their sources," the President declared.

"It seems to me we made a mistake at that time in not having gone to the end.

"We have made the mistake of having left our state security, so to say, to fend for itself during the last 20 or more years of its existence, and it was in charge of Comrade Rankovic."

President Tito, who is General Secretary of the party, said the secret police had "played an enormous role in which, of course, a great part of the credit goes to Comrade Rankovic." Then he asked:

"But have we the right to forgive what has been happening since, when such an organization becomes deformed and when, because of various deformations, a system is created that weighs upon our whole society?"

"Of course we have not and cannot," he went on "Credit is one thing, but these are tremendous mistakes."

Describing the nature of the "distortions," he went on:

"What is involved here is a factional struggle of a group, the struggle for power. Otherwise how could these things have re-emerged in an even more violent and graver form after 1962 when we discussed them?"

"I speak about individuals who became aggressive, who established their power over the people, power over the League of Communists, power over our society. These unfavorable distortions have penetrated down to enterprises, factories, to various social organizations, everywhere."

Marshal Tito said "a signal matter is the issue—the recovery of our party, separation of internal security from the party."

Asserting that he did not want to go into details, he concluded:

"Mutual mistrust has been fomented from top to bottom. Does this not rather resemble Stalin's times? I think it does, rather."

Following this Mr. Crvenkovski read the 18-page report, which finished with proposals to expel Svetislav Stefanovic from all his party and Government posts and to accept Mr. Rankovic's "resignation of his functions."

The commission report charged the Rankovic-Stefanovic group with deliberately "bringing misinformation to the leadership" and with establishing a "large network of collaborators" that "very often interfered in the whole work of enterprises on investment and cadre policies."

The report accused the secret police of having used "contemporary technology" on a huge scale to "listen to and control individuals and institutions and a certain number of state and political functionaries."

It said the Rankovic-Stefanovic group had used "a few words of criticism" and "gossip" to discredit individuals and to obtain their replacement.

The group was also assailed as a "conservative opposition" that used its enormous powers to block "decisions of the forum of the League of Communists" and to achieve other "political aims."

Apparently the Tito leadership had attempted to reform the security service more than a year ago by appointing Milan Miskovic, a 48-year-old Croatian, as the new federal secretary for internal affairs to replace Mr. Stefanovic.

But the investigating commission found that Mr. Miskovic, who had previously held lesser posts in the security apparatus, had been "prevented from performing his duty and performing the necessary reorganization."

Mr. Rankovic and other leading Serbs in the party hierarchy were known to oppose the economic reform that began last July.

Since winter, the reform has been stalled on several key issues involving banking arrangements, investment policy and a law authorizing foreign companies to set up joint enterprises here.

Well informed party sources said last spring that Mr. Rankovic and some of his associates in the police apparatus had successfully blocked the drafting of the foreign investment law. They said he had also succeeded in pushing through legislation permitting the siphoning-off of funds designated for individual enterprise use to large Federal projects, mostly in Serbia.

His downfall comes as a blow to the Serbs who had seen in him their first opportunity since the war to have a man of their nationality leading the country.

Of the three Communists who had been the closest aides and confidants of Marshal Tito since 1937, when he became General Secretary, and who had served through the harsh war years, only Edvard Kardelj remains. His is now president of Parliament, but he will be taking another senior post. The other two were Mr. Rankovic and Mr. Djilas, who is now serving a nine-year prison term for his outspoken criticism of the regime.

* * *

October 16, 1966

SPITE FEUDS FILL YUGOSLAVIA'S COURTS

Special to The New York Times

BELGRADE, Yugoslavia, Oct. 14—Yugoslavs often complain of a personality characteristic in their neighbors that they call inat, which translates roughly as "spite."

It is a trait that some scholars view as unique to Yugoslavs, otherwise a people renowned for hospitality and heroism.

One finds countless examples of inat chronicled in the press.

Recently Milan Nikolic, a reporter for the weekly Svet, attempted to list some glaring cases.

He recounted the case of two neighbors in the village of Pomoravlje who had been suing each other for 30 years over insults began when one "gave a dirty look" to the other's pet dog.

Last year the second district court in Belgrade was presented with 9,000 suits over alleged slanders and insults. Mr. Nikolic said these cases consumed 5,200 working hours.

Often the cases involve tenants crowded in apartment buildings. In one building in the Street of the October Revolution tenants began 53 suits against each other.

Other causes of "spite" suits he listed included "a bent fence" and "a nasty look." Business enterprises are not immune and one court is handling a complaint of the Zastava Company of Knic over a debt of 10 dinars (less than 1 cent).

In the countryside spite also appears in such petty forms as the brother who sued his sister because she gathered fruit fallen from a tree he regarded as his own and the peasant who has not spoken to his wife for 20 years because one day he looked for a clean shirt and there was one.

More often rural spite assumes more violent forms such as the blood feud, still widely practiced in regions like Montenegro and the Sandzak. Even in the western regions such as Croatia spiteful violence erupts. Last year a peasant from near Osijek who had quarrelled with two neighbors 37 years before over some land suddenly felt a desire to avenge himself and killed both.

Ethnologist Gives Views

Dr. Mirko Barjaktarevic, professor of ethnology at Belgrade University, said in an interview he believed spite was a national trait.

He remarked that few languages had as many expressions for and about spite as Serbian and that at every turn one hears phrases like, "I'm going to teach him a lesson," and "I don't want to be made a fool of."

Professor Barjaktarevic said he thought spitefulness in Yugoslavia had had its origin in the feudal system imposed during the 500-year Turkish domination of the Balkans. Lacking their own courts, he explained, the South Slavs began the practice of settling grievances by themselves without recourse to law, and this led inevitably to spite.

* * *

October 23, 1966

FOREIGN AFFAIRS: SQUARING THE CIRCLE

By C. L. SULZBERGER

BELGRADE—Nowhere is paradox more appreciated than among the Yugoslavs who enjoy attempting the impossible and frequently suffer for it. They are now in the process of trying to achieve Marxist dreams by using capitalist incentives and a leavening of private enterprise while curbing the Communist party itself.

The regime wants both to foster and ration liberty, a contradiction that can only in the platonic sense be approached. Thus Yugoslavia is without question the freest state calling itself Communist. Yet a professor was recently convicted for challenging the regime's political base while Milovan Djilas, once second only to Tito, remains in prison for sponsoring an entirely new system.

A Double Voice

There has often appeared to be a double Titoist voice. At times it has sounded as pro-Russian and anti-American as before Belgrade's break with Moscow but Tito's actions are what must be watched. He maintains a careful balance between the superpowers and, indeed, sometimes seems to follow the Pascal formula of speaking truth softly and falsehood loudly.

Tito clearly considers his problem is to weld together a solid state from among the disparate and quarrelsome south Slav groups—Catholic Croats and Slovenes, Orthodox Serbs, Macedonians and Montenegrins, plus large Moslem and other minorities. The disintegrating effect of south Slav bickering was most strikingly shown in this country's collapse before Axis armies 25 years ago.

Growing Liberty

Tito desires sufficient central leadership to restrict centrifugal forces while at the same time encouraging the growth of liberty. This quest produced the political demise of two close lieutenants: Djilas who wanted too much freedom and Alexander Rankovic, former Interior Minister, who wanted too little.

Mihajlo Mihajlov, the young professor who has appealed his sentence, was convicted of falsely describing Yugoslav Socialism as "schizophrenic," but there is indeed a schizophrenic strain in this extraordinary land. Although Marshal Tito imprisoned Cardinal Stepinac, the Catholic Primate, he permitted me to visit him for an uninhibited interview in his cell. Djilas was allowed to publish in the official party journal articles urging the party's own demise. Mihajlov, although now threatened with punishment, agitated openly with the aid of well-known anti-Communist organizations.

This is the only Communist country where Parliament has rejected Government law projects. It has tolerated publication of oppositionist intellectual magazines. The press is restricted on internal criticism but reports objectively on world affairs and foreign publications are freely on sale. Titoist society has achieved an atmosphere of ease. With the exception of the famous Djilas case there are no longer any well-known incidences of political repression. Relations have been restored with the Vatican and travel restrictions removed in the name of "proletarian internationalism."

'Democratization'

At its latest conclave the Communist party began formal efforts to abolish its own centralized machinery and withdraw from control of state administration. It is committed to "democratization," including free choice of candidates for public office—but it still wants to insure enough central power to make audacious economic reforms work and to prevent quarrels among the various nationalities. This produces a search for the means to ration liberty by squaring the political circle. Edvard Kardelj, Tito's most influential remaining

companion, says the regime favors neither a single-party nor a multiparty system but "a nonparty system."

The party itself is less conventionally ideological than in other Communist nations and 93 per cent of its members have no links with the period when Moscow was Belgrade's inspiration. Even in the Central Committee dissent is now tolerated as a kind of loyal opposition. It was to protect this liberalization that Tito moved to purge Rankovic, previously considered his heir apparent because he was the most powerful Serb and Serbia is the largest Yugoslav component.

Kommunist, the party organ, confessed after the Rankovic purge that "the struggle for power has become more important than the struggle for ideology." Tito spoke of "a factional struggle" using tactics that "rather resemble Stalin's times." It is clear he wished to prevent the dominance of the secret police and also of the Serbs who controlled Rankovic's apparatus.

Control vs. Freedom

The pendulum continues to oscillate between individual freedom and central control. There are anarchic trends inherent among these vigorous peasant people and Tito wants to keep them from destroying themselves. At the same time he wants them to have the freedom for which they paid so heavily in World War II.

Before his death, he would like to institutionalize the Yugoslav revolution but that in itself is logically impossible. Revolutions are dynamic not static and an institutionalized revolution would be like a frozen waterfall.

* * *

November 3, 1966

SOVIET AND TITOISTS DENOUNCED BY MAO

VIENNA, Nov. 2 (Reuters)—Mao Tse-tung has accused the Soviet Union, Yugoslavia and their allies of working to restore capitalism and of crawling before the imperialists.

In a message to the current Albanian Workers (Communist) party congress, the Chinese Communist leader denounced what he called the revisionist and Titoist cliques, the renegades and the strikebreakers.

"They are lackeys and courtesans who prostrate themselves before the imperialists while you [the Albanians] are the revolutionary proletarians who dare to fight the imperialists and their allies," he said.

His message, quoted in full today by the Albanian news agency, said the struggle of the Vietnamese people against United States "aggressors" presaged a storm of revolution in Asia, Africa and Latin America that would surely deal "a crushing and decisive blow against the entire old world."

At yesterday's session of the congress. Enver Hoxha, the Albanian Communist leader, accused the Soviet Union of doublecrossing the Vietnamese people and giving a free hand to American aggression.

* * *

April 15, 1967

ELECTIONS CALLED BY GREEK PREMIER

---

*Parliament Dissolved After Attempts at Compromise in
Political Crisis Fail*

By RICHARD EDER

Special to The New York Times

ATHENS, April 14—Premier Panayotis Kanellopoulos dissolved Parliament today and ordered elections for May 28 after efforts to solve Greece's political crisis collapsed.

Thus, despite attempts to moderate the situation, including private appeals by King Constantine and the United States, the way was open for a political confrontation that, responsible political and diplomatic observers believe, will represent serious danger to Greece's democratic institutions.

Shortly after 2 P.M., the 64-year-old Premier, who heads the National Radical Union, a conservative party, came out of a Cabinet meeting and announced that, rather than present his 11-day-old Government to a Parliament where it could count on a bare third of the votes, he had decided to order dissolution and elections.

March Is Postponed

Tonight the Premier addressed the nation by radio. He warned against disorders and said that he intended to enforce the laws "with special strictness." He called upon the Opposition to act as "co-guarantor" of a peaceful electoral process.

Not long after his address, the left-wing sponsors of a march scheduled for Sunday announced that they were postponing it until after the elections to avoid giving the Government political ammunition. The march had been banned, but it was thought that an effort would be made to hold it anyway as an act of defiance.

Moderates in the Premier's party, including Mr. Kanellopoulos himself, had wanted to submit to a parliamentary vote before calling for dissolution, apparently believing that this would be less abrupt and, as a matter of style at least, somewhat more conciliatory toward the Opposition. However, they were overruled by more intransigent party leaders.

The Kanellopoulos Government will remain in office during the campaign and the elections. This is a highly controversial point, since there is a tradition here that party governments resign during an electoral period in favor of nonpolitical caretaker regimes. Even more controversial is the fact that the National Radical Union holds fewer seats in Parliament than its main rival, the Center Union of George Papandreou, the former Premier.

Opposition Critical

Because the National Radical Union, when it was in power four years ago under Konstantine Karamanlis, was accused of rigging elections, the Opposition was strongly critical when the King named it to form a minority government on April 3.

Associated Press

CALLS FOR ELECTIONS: Panayotis Kanellopoulos, who is Premier of Greece.

The King previously sought a coalition government in which both the National Radical Union and the Center Union would join to prepare the elections, but he was rebuffed by Mr. Papandreou who called for a nonpolitical caretaker government instead.

According to most accounts, the King believed that Mr. Kanellopoulos would get the parliamentary support of the small parties, and that this would allow parliament to pass a law establishing proportional representation before the elections were held.

Not only the King but a broad spectrum of political opinion here holds that the election of parliamentary deputies on a proportional basis would diminish the win-all, lose-all character of the elections, and thus blur the dangerous confrontation between the National Radical Union and the Center Union.

When it became evident that the small parties would not back the Premier, the King tried to persuade Mr. Kanellopoulos to form a coalition with them. The Premier refused.

A series of visits by the United States Ambassador, Phillips Talbot, to party leaders to urge moderation and some kind of agreement was also unavailing.

In fact, after Mr. Talbot saw Mr. Papandreou yesterday, word began to leak out that the 79-year-old leader had warned that if the King allowed the National Radical Union to run the elections, the Center Union's campaign would become an attack not only on its political rivals but on the King as well.

The argument of the Center Union is that the King has shown favoritism to the National Radical Union—whose supporters are the nation's most convinced royalists—and has become a political figure. In a statement tonight, Mr. Papandreou warned the King that he would have to bear full responsibility for any interference with the electoral process. Mr. Papandreou's son, Andreas, said that the elections would be the King's "final examination"—meaning his last chance.

This does not mean that the Center Union, a large, sprawling party whose members range from conservative to moderate left, has decided to try to depose the King. But many of those close to the King—army leaders, some extremist members of the National Radical Union and other court advisers—believe that this in fact is what the Center Union would do if it won the elections, as seems likely.

What is widely feared here is that the King may become convinced by his advisers that there is no other way to preserve the monarchy except to prevent a Center Union victory. This argument becomes, in effect, a plea for suspending the Constitution and establishing a dictatorship.

*   *   *

April 21, 1967

ARMY IS REPORTED RULING IN GREECE ON KING'S ORDER

Military Radio Asserts Step Was Taken to Keep Peace—Curbs Announced

By The Associated Press

LONDON, Friday, April 21—An army radio station in Athens said today that the military had taken control of Greece under a royal proclamation signed by King Constantine, Premier Panayotis Kanellopoulos and his Cabinet.

The broadcast, monitored in London, said the army took over at midnight last night to preserve public order.

Vehicles were ordered off city streets and the public was warned against hoarding food.

Monitors said the broadcast was made by the Athens army radio.

Telephone service to Athens was not obtainable. Early yesterday, Greek telecommunications personnel went on a 24-hour strike for higher pay.

First word of the army takeover did not make it clear which side in Greece's political crisis the army had taken. There was immediate speculation in London, however, that the army action was a move to strengthen 26-year-old King Constantine in his long struggle with the 80-year-old former Premier, George Papandreou, leader of the powerful Center Union party. Observers believed that if the army had taken over, it had done so to strengthen the King's position by disbanding political parties.

Origins of Crisis

The speculation seemed to be borne out by the army broadcast.

There was no immediate word on what had happened to the country's political leaders.

Mr. Papandreou and his son Andreas have been outspoken critics of the monarchy, accusing it of meddling in politics, while many of the top army officers are known partisans of the throne.

Greece's latest political crisis began last month when the interim Government of Premier Ioannis Paraskevopoulos resigned after three months in office.

King Constantine summoned a meeting of all parliamentary leaders to try to form a coalition Government, but the meeting was boycotted by the elder Papandreou, whose Center Union held 122 of the 300 seats in Parliament.

New Government Falls

King Constantine then asked the National Radical Union leader Panayotis Kanellopoulos, to form a Government pending new elections. Premier Kanellopoulos took over on April 3, but his Government was unable to function. Last Friday he dissolved Parliament and ordered elections for May 28.

His Government was to stay in power during the campaign and the elections. That announcement drew heavy criticism because, traditionally, the party Governments resign during an electoral period.

Political sources in Athens said earlier this week that the King probably would not give Mr. Papandreou the mandate to form a Government if his party won the election.

Army and Politicians Feud

The reported take-over by the army in Greece came just weeks before the May elections, in which George Papandreou's Center Union Party, unfriendly to King Constantine and the army, was expected to win a majority and with it the right to form a new Government.

The right wing of the National Union Party, along with the army, as well as court figures, had been seeking to persuade the King to suspend the Constitution and sanction a dictatorship.

Mr. Papandreou and his son, Andreas, a former American citizen and economics professor, have been outspoken critics of the monarchy. They have also been critical of the closeness to the throne of leading army elements. The younger Papandreou had been accused of complicity with members of the so-called Aspida clique, composed chiefly of army officers who share his leftist political views.

The Aspida plot has dominated the Greek political scene for the last two years. Only last Tuesday Lieut. Gen. Demetrios Georgiadis, the army's former chief in Cyprus, was arrested in connection with the Aspida plot, on charges of high treason.

The Aspida "plotters" have been accused of trying to overthrow the monarchy and set up a Socialist regime. Andreas Papandreou has been accused of being the political leader of Aspida. The accusation was part of the court-martial indictment against General Georgiadis.

The Aspida adherents are said to be military men opposed to the traditionalist supporters of the King within the army. Fifteen of them were sentenced last month to jail terms of two to 18 years.

The Aspida controversy caused the downfall, in July, 1965, of the Center Union Government of Premier Papandreou, when the Premier clashed with King Constantine over rumors of his son's involvement in the alleged conspiracy.

"Aspida" is an acrostic made up of the Greek initials for "officers, save the country, ideals, democracy, meritocracy." The Greek initials form a word meaning "shield."

The Aspida affair brought into the open a long-standing split between political factions over the role of the army. The center-leftist elements of the Center Union Party have been fearful that the army was being kept as a right-wing preserve to be used against them if they continued to win elections.

The core of the dispute between former Premier Papandreou and the King was the Premier's plan to purge the army of right-wing officers. His explanation was that the officers were disloyal to Constantine's regime. He also sought to replace the Defense Minister, Peter Garoufalias, who was opposed to the Premier's plan.

The King apparently doubted Mr. Papandreou's sincerity; he readily accepted the Premier's proffered resignation on July 15, 1965.

* * *

April 22, 1967

ARMY IN GREECE INSTALLS PREMIER AFTER TAKE-OVER

Supreme Court's Prosecutor Named in Apparent Effort to Bolster Monarchy

ATHENS REPORTED CALM

Some Politicians Arrested in Campaign to Counteract Influence of Papandreou

Special to The New York Times

WASHINGTON, April 21—Constantine V. Kollias, chief prosecutor of the Greek Supreme Court, was installed as Premier in Athens today after the swift military take-over of power last night.

The armed forces said they acted in the name of King Constantine.

The new Premier made a proclamation to the people tonight as martial law restrictions were gradually being eased. He conceded that the take-over was a "deviation from the Constitution" but said it was needed "for the salvation of the country."

Washington officials said the take-over reflected military apprehension that former Premier George Papandreou, who heads the Center Union, Greece's dominant party, would use the coming election campaign as a test of strength with the King.

Early in the day, there were reports of the arrest of Mr. Papandreou, his son, Andreas, former Premier Stefanos Stephanopoulos, a police chief named Arhondoulakis and King Constantine's personal secretary, Maj. Michael Arnaoutis.

Nothing official was learned of the fate of these political leaders, but there were reports that some of them might be released soon.

Elections No Solution

Premier Kollias, in his proclamation, said elections would not have provided a solution to the impasse and would have led to bloodshed and chaos. That is why the army stepped in, he said.

He said that the few "arsonists" and professional anarchists who had led the nation to "this abyss" would be "isolated." The basic task of the new Government, Premier Kollias said, is to restore social justice. He warned that he was determined to stamp out all opposition to his Government's mission, "from whatever source."

After the take-over, Gen. Gregory E. Spandidakis, chief of the army general staff, was named Deputy Premier and Defense Minister. Christos J. Apostolakos, a former member of Parliament, was named Minister of Labor.

Col. George Papadopoulos, an army officer, was named Minister to the Premier, and Evangelos Karabetsos, who resigned two months ago as chief of the Athens police, was appointed Minister of Public Order.

An artillery colonel, Nilolaos Makerezos, was reported to have been named Minister of Economic Coordination. Brigadier Stylianos Patakos was reported to have been named Interior Minister.

Reports from reliable sources said three Greek military officers appeared to have served as leaders in the take-over. They were identified as Col. George Papadopoulos, Brig. Gen. Stiliano Patakos, an armored-division veteran and a Colonel Skarmaliorakis of the Greek Air Force.

Official and unofficial informants were unable to say to what extent the take-over had had the support of 26-year-old King Constantine.

While the new Government appeared to be dominated by the heads of the armed forces, it was unclear whether they had prompted the move or had merely agreed to head the new regime.

A communications shutdown in Athens, already in effect because of a strike, was extended by the armed forces. Diplomatic informants here said the situation in Athens and other major Greek cities appeared to be calm. A military curfew was keeping the streets of Athens virtually empty.

According to European sources, the new Cabinet was sworn in at 7 P.M., Athens time, in the presence of King Constantine. The ceremony followed by 19 hours the Greek Army's announcement proclaiming a state of siege.

Two hours later telephone communications in Athens were restored, but there were no links with foreign countries.

After tanks had moved at midnight to strategic positions, their machine guns ready, military patrols arrested Premier Panayotis Kanellopoulos and most of his ministers at 3 A.M.

Mr. Kanellopoulos was said to have been taken away by force when he put up resistance to arrest by an army patrol under a captain.

The military forces were also said to have taken into custody several news correspondents including George Androulidakis of United Press International.

News of the take-over was broadcast over the Athens armed forces radio at 6:40 A.M.

According to European sources, the speaker asserted that King Constantine had signed a decree suspending 11 articles of the Constitution.

Under this decree, it was said, anyone could be summarily arrested and committed to trial by extraordinary courts martial. Meetings were banned and would be dissolved by force if necessary. Strikes were also banned.

House searches could be conducted without warrant at any time. Domestic news media and correspondence abroad were to be subjected to censorship. Political and press offenders will be tried by special courts-martial, the speaker announced.

The armed forces' radio said that dealers hiding food would be tried for sabotage.

In addition, the stock exchange was closed, bank deposits were frozen and the purchase of gold and of foreign exchange was banned.

Schools and universities were also suspended.

The United States Ambassador, Phillips Talbot, was understood to have had an audience with King Constantine.

From all available indications, American residents in Greece—numbering 10,000, of whom some 600 are civilian and military employes of the United States Government—were safe and well.

The State Department spokesman, Robert J. McCloskey, said that the situation remained fluid and that the department was following events closely.

From other Washington sources, who declined to be identified, it appeared that the Administration had been surprised by the swift military move.

In Government circles here, there had been an awareness of tension since the dissolution of Greece's Parliament on April 14 by the caretaker Government of Mr. Kanellopoulos.

Relations between the King and Mr. Papandreou had deteriorated steadily since July 15, 1965, when the King dramatically dismissed him in a showdown over control of the armed forces.

Since then, Greek political life has been overshadowed by the struggle. King Constantine has been backed by a majority of the armed forces and moderate and conservative political and economic elements. Mr. Papandreou has had left-of-center political backing.

Mr. Papandreou's determination to break the royal power was symbolized in his political slogan: "The King reigns, but the people rule." Mr. Papandreou is said to have been spurred on by his son Andreas, a former economics instructor at Harvard and other American universities.

The break between King Constantine and the elder Papandreou centered on charges that Andreas Papandreou had led a left-wing group of officers, known as Aspida, or Shield, which sought to replace right-wing military influences around the King.

Right-wing political leaders have accused both Papandreous of aiming to abolish the monarchy, to break off Greece's membership in the North Atlantic Treaty Organization and to transform it into a socialist state.

Regime's Aims Broadcast

LONDON, April 21 (Reuters)—The Athens army radio listed the main aims of the new Greek Government tonight, including among them the intention to distribute the national income justly among all classes.

The broadcast, monitored here, also pledged to "adhere to responsibilities to NATO and the Western alliance." Other aims included the following:

"To restore internal tranquility and order."

"To create the necessary prerequisites for the country's return to parliamentary rule on a wholesome basis."

"To abide firmly by the idea of peace and freedom according to the United Nations Charter."

"To consolidate the country's national defense and internal security."

"To develop the country's economy and develop the proper atmosphere for a free and conscientious press."

*   *   *

May 11, 1967

GREEK JUNTA ACTS TO PURGE BISHOPS AND RULE CHURCH

New Law Will Oust Primate—Treason Plot Charged to Andreas Papandreou

By RICHARD EDER
Special to The New York Times

ATHENS, May 10—The Greek military junta has enacted a law that gives it almost total power over the Greek Orthodox Church, removes the entire ruling panel of bishops and forces out of office the primate, Archbishop Chrysostomos of Athens.

The new law constitutes a drastic purge of the church and is a radical assertion of state supremacy even for Greece, where the Government has traditionally played an important role in regulating religious affairs. It will take effect in a few days unless King Constantine refuses to sign it.

The junta, which seized power in a coup d'état April 21, charged Andreas Papandreou today with conspiracy to commit high treason, which carries a maximum penalty of 20 years in prison.

Plot in Army Alleged

The charge against Mr. Papandreou is less serious than a charge of actually having committed treason, which carries the death penalty. Until today it was not known which charge would be made against him.

Interior Minister Stylianos Patakos said yesterday he did not believe Mr. Papandreou would be sentenced to death even if he was convicted of having committed high treason. The United States and British Governments, among others, have expressed concern over Mr. Papandreou's fate.

Mr. Papandreou, son of former Premier George Papandreou, is accused of involvement in an alleged plot in which a group of officers of center and center-left views sought to gain control of the army. He is to await trial in a civil prison in Athens.

Power Taken From Bishops

The junta restored constitutional guarantees of freedoms, assuring the privacy of mails and banning political execution, and moved to establish a firmer legal base for itself. It was also announced—perhaps facetiously—that barber shops would be set up at airports and border crossings where officials are barring the admission of foreigners with beards and long hair.

The church law adopted today dismisses the 12 bishops of the Synod, which is the executive body of the 67-member Assembly of Bishops. By widening a compulsory retirement statute that up to now had not applied to him, it will force out the ailing, 86-year-old Archbishop.

More important, the new law allows the Government to choose members of the Synod, a power previously exercised by the bishop's assembly. Finally, it takes from the assembly the power to name new bishops and assigns this to the Government-appointed Synod, which is reduced in number from 12 to 9 bishops.

A further control is provided by the fact that the Synod must name three candidates to each bishopric, with the final choice to be made by the Government through the King.

Asked why the Government was taking such a step, the Interior Minister, Brigadier Stylianos Patakos, said tonight that the Constitution allowed the Government to regulate the Synod.

"There were very many things wrong in the church," he added. "They were all fighting with each other."

The restoration of two of the guarantees that have been suspended since April 21 is related to a move by the junta to narrow the area of unconstitutionality in which it is operating.

The junta's extraordinary powers rested on a constitutional provision that authorized them only if Parliament were summoned within 10 days to ratify them. This step was not taken. Now the junta has decreed a Constitutional amendment eliminating the parliamentary requirement.

Amendment Unlawful

One difficulty with this is that it is unconstitutional to amend the Constitution by government decree: the approval of two consecutive parliaments is necessary.

FORCED TO RETIRE: Archbishop Chrysostomos of Athens, Greek Primate.

Another major flaw in the original royal decree establishing extraordinary powers was that the King never signed it. The junta does not admit this, although recently it has stopped denying it.

It is believed, however, that King Constantine may now approve the Constitutional amendment in exchange for obtaining restoration of the ban on political executions and interference with the mails.

The announcement yesterday that foreigners with beards and long hair, as well as those with less than $80 for maintenance, would be denied entry has cause widespread puzzlement here. As the order is worded, it could exclude such respectable beard-wearers as Archbishop Makarios, President of Cyprus.

Asked about this tonight, Interior Minister Patakos, author of the ban, said jokingly that "we will have to think about the Archbishop." He went on to say, however, that "neat, well-groomed beards would not be forbidden."

Haircuts May Be Given

He also announced that barber shops were being set up at the Athens airport and at border crossing points to cut the hair and beards of those who insisted upon entry. Since Brigadier Patakos often gives offhand, even flippant, answers to questions—although he is, for the moment, the most active spokesman for the junta—it could not be determined whether he was speaking entirely in earnest.

The tourist industry here has expressed alarm over the junta's ruling, however, and several travel agency executives said they would try to have it modified.

As a further step in its campaign to prune the bureaucracy and make it more efficient, the junta has announced that the tenure of civil servants was being suspended for six months. During that time, presumably, those considered inefficient or corrupt will be dismissed.

However, fears have been expressed that in the name of efficiency there will be a purge of government employes of even moderately liberal views.

The drastic action against the church hierarchy was not entirely unexpected. Circles close to the junta had warned that a major part of the campaign to reform the moral climate of Greece would center on reforms in the church, which retains many feudalistic vestiges, in the hope of making it more attractive to the nation's young people.

* * *

December 14, 1967

GREEK KING FLEES TO ROME WITH FAMILY AFTER FAILING TO OVERTHROW THE JUNTA

'VICEROY' IS NAMED

Civil War Is Averted—Premier, Deposed, Also in Flight

By SYDNEY GRUSON
Special to The New York Times

ATHENS, Thursday, Dec. 14—King Constantine fled Greece early today after trying unsuccessfully to overthrow the military junta that seized power last April.

[The King and his family arrived in Rome with Constantine V. Kollias, who had served as Premier under the junta.]

Even before the 27-year-old King's departure the junta declared him deposed. It appointed Lieut. Gen. George Zoitakis as "viceroy" to exercise royal authority. The Cabinet was reorganized, with Col. George Papadopoulos as Premier.

The news of the King's departure came as the climax of 24 turbulent hours.

Most Forces Back Junta

The King called on his army yesterday morning to rally to him and unseat Colonel Papadopoulos and the other members of the junta.

But, so far as could be judged here, at least the bulk of military power in Greece remained under the junta's orders during all the decisive hours.

The King issued his proclamation in a broadcast from the military base at Larissa, 140 miles northwest of the capital. Announcing his dismissal of the regime that seized control last spring, he said he was acting in the name of democracy. He voiced sympathy with the junta's anti-Communist aims, but saw a danger that a "totalitarian regime" would refuse to return power to the people.

'Moral Values' Stressed

"I ask the Greek people as a whole," he added, "to assist me in re-establishing in this country the moral values which

United Press International Cablephoto

King Constantine and Queen arriving in Rome last night.

were born in this land and from which all civilized people take their moral, social, economic and cultural development."

In reply, the Athens radio broadcast repeated statements of victory in crushing a "conspiratorial counterrevolution."

According to reports received here, the security forces in Athens started arresting right-wing civilian politicians in the first hours of the countercoup. Among those reported arrested were former Premier Panayotis Canellopoulos and Achilleus Caramanlis, brother of former Premier Constantine Caramanlis, in self-imposed exile in Paris.

Shortly before midnight, there was a swearing-in ceremony for General Zoitakis as "viceroy" and Colonel Papadopoulos as Premier and Defense Minister. Brig. Stylianos Patakos, a member of the group that carried out the junta's coup d'état last April 21, was named Deputy Premier as well as remaining Minister of the Interior. The rest of the Cabinet remained unchanged.

During the King's short-lived struggle with the junta, he, too, designated a new Premier—Petros Garoufalias, a former Defense Minister, who is in Paris. At the time, Mr. Garoufalias said he was willing to return to Greece and serve if the King was successful.

Mr. Kollias, who had received the Premiership last spring at the King's urging to broaden the military regime, was dismissed.

General Zoitakis was sworn in by Archbishop Ieronymos Kotsonis, the Orthodox Primate of Greece, in the Greek Army headquarters near the capital.

Oath Is Revised

New members of the Government took oaths of office—the traditional ones, revised to omit any pledge of loyalty to the King. The oaths, taken in the name of the Trinity, pledged faith to the "constitutional monarchy" and obedience to the Constitution and the laws of the state.

In an Athens broadcast, General Zoitakis declared that his first aim was "to protect the establishment of my regal kingdom." He said he would "do everything possible to establish tranquillity in Greece."

At the end of the ceremony, Colonel Papadopoulos turned to the Archbishop and said, "With your blessing, may God help this country." The Archbishop replied, "Amen."

For most of the day after the King's dramatic radio appeal, the only news available was that broadcast by the Government over the networks it controlled in Athens and in Salonika to the north.

The King's rallying call to his people and the army was countered swiftly by Colonel Papadopulous.

"A criminal conspiracy and an attempt at the abolition of the state and law and order erupted a few hours ago," the junta's broadcast said. "Common adventurers, moved by a stupid ambition and ignoring the interest of the nation, led astray and misled the King, forcing him to turn himself against the national revolution, against the calm and quiet of the people. The national revolutionary government is absolute master of the situation, and no anxiety is justified."

The junta added that the armed forces were determined to defend "at any cost" what it described as the "national uprising of April 21" and to impose the unity of the nation by arms if necessary.

Rumors Abound in Capital

The Government's broadcasts never gave the slightest indication that the junta had lost control of the situation. Yet Athens was full of rumors of armed forces loyal to the King marching on this city.

One that was heard consistently last night was that the King had given Colonel Papadopoulos an ultimatum that was to expire this morning. But in the morning Athens could hardly have been quieter.

There was a tank, as there had been throughout the day, in front of the buff-colored Parliament building on Constitution Square, another tank near the Hilton Hotel not far from the United States Embassy and a third near the post office.

Generals Said to Give Up

ATHENS, Thursday, Dec. 14 (Reuters)—A Government spokesman said last night that all the generals involved in an attempt to unseat the military junta had surrendered.

He said there had been no bloodshed or resistance. Communications were restored with the whole country except the island of Crete.

The government offered an amnesty to all those it said had been misled into trying to turn the armed forces against it.

U.S. Silent on Upheaval

Special to The New York Times

WASHINGTON, Dec. 14—The State Department declined to comment on the flight of King Constantine and the Greek royal family to Rome last night after a day of nervous watching while Greece hovered on the brink of civil war.

From early morning local time a special force of experts on Greek affairs had been assembled in the State Department operations center, adjoining the seventh-floor office of Secretary of State Dean Rusk. Similarly at the White House the National Security-Council's operations staff had been on duty watching developments.

Commercial communications from Athens were severed early in the day, and air traffic was halted at the airport. Diplomatic reports and broadcasts from the rival radio stations gave officials here a sketchy and ominous picture of the day's swift developments.

Military sources here said two American aircraft carriers—the Franklin D. Roosevelt and the Shangri-La—were maneuvering in the central Mediterranean but had made no move toward Greece.

Envoy Cites Royal Link

In informal conversations early in the day, the Greek Ambassador in Washington, Christian X. Palmas, emphasized that he represented the King to the President of the United States, and that his headquarters was designated the Royal Greek Embassy.

Ambassador Palmas is understood to have appealed to United States officials for American intervention on behalf of the King. He argued that the United States could not remain aloof since Washington had long been urging Greece to abandon dictatorial rule and return to democratic government. This, he was said to indicate, was what King Constantine was trying to do.

State Department officials said that Ambassador Palmas had been invited to confer with the Assistant Secretary of State, Lucius D. Battle, during the afternoon but had declined to make a formal appearance.

A Greek Embassy spokesman said that diplomatic communications with Athens had been cut off since morning. Officials explained that, lacking formal channels of communications with his capital, Mr. Palmas did not wish to make an official representation.

* * *

February 4, 1968

RUMANIA AVOIDS NEW SOVIET TREATY AS OLD PACT'S TERM ENDS

Special to The New York Times

MOSCOW, Feb. 3—The Soviet-Rumanian treaty of friendship, cooperation and mutual assistance reached the end of its 20-year term today, and no new treaty has been negotiated to take its place.

While the pact will not expire—extension for five years is automatic since neither party has renounced it—the failure to replace it well before expiration with a new treaty reaffirming friendship is a singular event in the Soviet Union's relations with its European allies.

All other members of the Warsaw Pact, the Communist military alliance, hastened to renew their treaties months or years before their expirations, and each signing was an ostentatious occasion to demonstrate loyalty to the alliance's senior partner.

With negotiations between Moscow and Bucharest in suspension after a visit by a Soviet delegation to the Rumanian capital last month, the 20th anniversary of the signing of the existing treaty is being marked here in a very low key.

No Big Observance Planned

The Soviet Government and Communist party are planning no events to mark tomorrow's anniversary of the signing in 1945. The Moscow city party organization has scheduled a meeting at a factory to which the Rumanian Ambassador has been invited, and some Moscow movie houses will show three days of Rumanian films.

Tass, the Soviet press agency, published today brief accounts of anniversary messages exchanged between the Soviet and Rumanian party and Government leaders. They extolled the old treaty and passed in silence over the question of its renewal.

According to informed sources, no substantive issues prevent the signing of a new treaty. These sources say that the clauses on issues on which the Soviet Union and Rumania differ could easily be worded so vaguely as to make them unobjectionable.

These clauses pertain particularly to the obligation of both parties to consult each other "on all important international questions," in the words of the present pact, and the singling out of West Germany, with which Rumania has made her political peace and re-established relations, as an aggressive threat.

The reasons for Bucharest's obduracy, these sources suggest, lies in Rumanian unwillingness to render what might be regarded as an automatic act of allegiance to the Soviet Union.

Rumanian sources think it likely that a new treaty will eventually be signed, and a Rumanian delegation might soon come here to continue negotiations.

But by the time it was signed, Rumania would have shown to the world that the time when the Soviet Union drafted a treaty and Rumania signed it had passed.

Despite the failure of the visit here last December by Nicolae Ceausescu, Rumania's Communist leader and chief of state, to resolve the major political differences between the two countries. Rumanian sources contend that the visit has had one important economic development.

They say that Soviet delays in delivering iron ore, which had begun to hamper Rumanian industry, have ceased.

At the same time, however, Rumanians point with glee to foreign trade statistics that show that Rumanian trade with the Soviet Union, while growing in volume, is continuing to shrink in relation to trade with capitalist countries.

As a result, perhaps, of the improvement in economic relations, Rumanian sources now say that Bucharest will take part in the consultative conference of Communist parties later this month in Budapest.

They emphasize, however, that Rumania will do so with the understanding that attendance would not commit her to join in a world Communist conference for which the Budapest meeting might call.

If Rumania takes part in the Budapest session, the Rumanian sources say, it will be to recall to the Soviet Union that Bucharest will oppose any attempt to re-establish central control over the Communist movement or to deepen the division in the movement by a formal denunciation of China.

* * *

April 27, 1968

RUMANIANS DENOUNCE GHEORGHIU-DEJ

BUCHAREST, April 26 (AP)—In a move resembling the denunciation of Stalin in the Soviet Union in 1956, Rumania's Communist leaders toppled the late strongman Gheorghe Gheorghiu-Dej today from his exalted position in Rumanian Communist history.

A commission of the Rumanian Central Committee implicated Mr. Gheorghiu-Dej in the trial and execution of Lucretiu Patrascanu, a former Justice Minister, in 1954.

In the same connection, Alexandru Draghici, a member of the party Presidium, and a former Interior Minister, was stripped of his functions in the party. His removal from the Cabinet, in which he is Deputy Premier, was recommended.

Mr. Gheorghiu-Dej was both President and party chief. He died in 1965. Nicolae Ceausescu now holds both posts.

Mr. Gheorghiu-Dej was the last undisputed Communist leader in Eastern Europe by the time of his death.

Committee Fixes Blame

Today a special commission set up to look into the Patrascanu trial reported to a plenary meeting of the Romanian Central Committee that Mr. Gheorghiu-Dej was behind the trial. Mr. Patrascanu was Justice Minister from 1944 to 1948 and was convicted of espionage.

The commission also charged Mr. Gheorghiu-Dej with direct responsibility in the killing in 1946 of Stefan Foris, the war-time Secretary General of the Rumanian Communist party. The late Ana Pauker, former Foreign Minister, was also implicated in the death.

The commission said Mr. Mr. Foris "was arrested in an abusive manner and, in the summer of 1946, without having been tried and sentenced, was killed according to a decision adopted by Mr. Gheorghiu-Dej, Teohari Georgescu, Ana Pauker and Vasile Luca."

Mr. Georgescu, once an Interior Minister and Deputy Premier, and Mr. Luca, once a Minister of Finance and a Deputy

Premier, were ousted from the Politburo in May, 1952, along with Mrs. Pauker.

The communiqué said the Central Committee would investigate "the responsibility of all those who took part in repressive measures of an illegal nature" and would mete out "party punishment" accordingly.

This indicated further action against Communist functionaries involved in such activities and possibly still holding positions of power.

Mr. Ceausescu's position appeared strengthened by the action against Mr. Gheorghiu-Dej, and against Mr. Draghici, who is reported to be an opponent of Mr. Ceausescu.

The commission also named a former secretary of the Central Committee, Iosif Chisinevshi as having a role in the Patrascanc trial. It said he "directly concerned himself with the preparation and unfolding of the trial, resorting to rude fakes and to transgression of the most elementary rules of law."

Mr. Chisinevshi was toppled from power in 1961.

The Central Committee statement said the party must give an increased role to the Parliament and Cabinet, "which have a great role for developing democracy."

"Nobody in the party or the state has the right to ignore laws," the communiqué said.

It called on Rumanians "to watch with utmost strictness the observance of the democratic rights and liberties guaranteed under the Constitution so that the abuses and arbitrary acts could never be repeated."

* * *

August 22, 1968

RUMANIA WARNS SOVIET

Ceausescu Adamant

By JOHN M. LEE
Special to The New York Times

BUCHAREST, Aug. 21—President Nicolae Ceausescu of Rumania warned the Soviet Union and its allies today that they would encounter armed resistance if they tried to invade his country.

Addressing a huge, cheering crowd in the center of Bucharest, Mr. Ceausescu ringingly condemned the Soviet action in Czechoslovakia and reaffirmed Rumanian support for the Czechoslovak people and the Czechoslovak Communist party.

He said "armed patriotic detachments" of workers, peasants and intellectuals were being formed to defend Rumanian independence.

"The entire Rumanian people will not allow anybody to violate the territory of our land," he declared.

Mr. Ceausescu reasserted the right of socialist nations to determine their development free of outside interference, and he called the invasion of Czechoslovakia "a great mistake and a grave danger to peace in Europe, to the fate of socialism in the world."

Tens of thousands of people gathered at midday in the Republic Palace Square after hearing radio reports of the urgent morning meeting of the Central Committee of the Rumanian Communist party, the State Council and the Council of Ministers. Party and Government leaders appeared on the balcony of the Central Committee headquarters when the meeting ended shortly after 1 o'clock.

A communiqué was read by Paul Niculescu-Mizil, secretary of the Central Committee of the Communist party, and President Ceausescu addressed a crowd that some observers estimated at nearly 100,000 people.

Placards proclaimed "Solidarity with Czechoslovakia" and "Long live the Rumanian Communist party." Crowds chanted, "Ceausescu, Ceausescu."

The communiqué expressed "profound anxiety" over the invasion and said "nothing can justify the perpetration of this action."

"Our entire people express their conviction," the communiqué continued, "that the only way of liquidating the grave consequences created by the armed intervention in Czechoslovakia is the speedy withdrawal of troops of the five countries and the insuring of the conditions for the Czechoslovak people to be able to solve itself its internal affairs without any outside interference."

The communiqué expressed also "full solidarity with the fraternal Czechoslovak people and with the Communist party of Czechoslovakia."

A special session of the Grand National Assembly was called for tomorrow.

In his address, Mr. Ceausescu told the emotion-ridden crowd, "Let us be ready, comrades, to defend at any moment our socialist homeland, Rumania."

He called on the populace to "give proof of full unity, act with calm and firmness."

National Unity Displayed

The Rumanian President called attention to the display of national unity apparent in the combined public appearance of party and Government leaders, and he said he spoke in their behalf. He pledged that the group would faithfully serve the people in defending revolutionary gains and independence.

"We are convinced," he said, "that no Communist could be found anywhere to approve this military action against Czechoslovakia, that all the Communists will raise their voices for the promotion of liberty, for the promotion of the Marxist-Leninist principles, so that the Czechoslovak people, so that any people should be able to build as they wish the socialist society."

Mr. Ceausescu said that the Rumanian party and Government delegation that visited Czechoslovakia last week had satisfied itself that the people were unanimously supporting party and state efforts "for putting right the negative state of affairs inherited from the past."

"There is no justification whatsoever and no reason can be accepted for admitting for even a single moment the idea of military intervention in the affairs of a fraternal socialist state," he added.

*   *   *

August 22, 1968

TITO DECRIES THE INVASION

Yugoslav Meets Aides

By PAUL HOFMANN
Special to The New York Times

BELGRADE, Yugoslavia, Thursday, Aug. 22—President Tito and the top Yugoslav Communist leadership, in a harsh statement early today, condemned the invasion of Czechoslovakia as an aggression.

"Involved is not only an attack on the Czechoslovak Republic," the party declaration said, "but a significant, historical point of rupture, bearing on the relationship among socialist countries in general, on the further development of socialism in the world and on the international workers' movement, as well as on peace in Europe and in the world."

The statement was issued on the island of Brioni, Marshal Tito's summer residence in the Adriatic, after a four-hour night meeting of the Presidium and Executive Committee of the Yugoslav League of Communists, the Communist party, at which the head of state presided.

Forty-six members of the two party bodies attended the meeting. The party statement also expressed the fear that the Czechoslovak crisis would "encourage reactionary forces and intensity the cold war." The party leadership called on Yugoslav Communists to close ranks and beware of provocations.

In a declaration yesterday, President Tito denounced the occupation of Czechoslovakia by Soviet and other Eastern European troops as "a great blow to socialist and progressive forces in the world."

Marshal Tito declared in a statement that he was "deeply concerned over the entry of foreign military units into Czechoslovakia." However, he urged his nation to remain calm.

The President's statement, published by the Yugoslav press agency, Tanyug, was issued from his summer home on Brioni.

The 76-year-old President had returned to Brioni from a visit to Prague Aug. 8 to Aug. 10, during which he had expressed his solidarity with Alexander Dubcek, First Secretary of the Czechoslovak Communist party. In Prague, he had received a hero's welcome and had been wildly cheered wherever he went.

Foreign sources in Belgrade suggested that Foreign Minister Jiri Hajek of Czechoslovakia, who had been vacationing on the Adriatic coast, had also conferred with Marshal Tito yesterday, but the report could not be confirmed.

Mr. Hajek arrived Tuesday in the resort of Opatija, on the Istrian Peninsula, and proceeded yesterday morning to the Dalmation city of Split. From Split he left by plane for an undisclosed destination.

Demonstrations Prohibited

Ota Sik, a Czechoslovak Deputy Premier in charge of economic affairs, was also reported to have been in Split this morning and to have left with Mr. Hajek.

A full meeting of the Central Committee of the Yugoslav party is scheduled to be held on Brioni Friday to discuss the Czechoslovak crisis.

Tanyug reported that its representative had asked the President whether he expected demonstrations in Yugoslavia as a result of the events in Czechoslovakia. Marshal Tito was quoted as having replied: "I think we must maintain calm and no demonstrations that might turn into provocations of various natures will be allowed."

Belgrade was calm as most of its residents seemed to be listening to transistor radios throughout this hot, sunny day. News broadcasts this morning brought the first word of the Czechoslovak invasion. The Yugoslav radio amply quoted Czechoslovak broadcasts protesting the intervention of foreign military forces, and Western news services on the developments, but offered no editorial comment.

Tourists Mill About

About 200 Czechoslovak tourists milled for hours outside their country's embassy. They were told by the embassy staff that no information was available beyond what the Yugoslav radio was broadcasting.

Some Czechoslovaks in the orderly crowd told a reporter: "Of course, we don't go back home now."

The morning's news came as a shock also to about 50,000 other Czechoslovaks vacationing in Yugoslavia, most of them on the Adriatic Coast.

In various Yugoslav resorts, Czechoslovak committees were established to assist stranded fellow citizens.

The Yugoslav radio announced that visas about to expire would be automatically extended for Czechoslovaks who wanted to stay.

*   *   *

October 30, 1968

FOREIGN AFFAIRS: ODD MAN IN

By C. L. SULZBERGER

VARNA, Bulgaria—Bulgaria is the Soviet Union's only remaining Balkan satellite. For Moscow has in fact lost control of much of the Southeast Europe it once held. Yugoslavia and Albania, while Communist, are no longer allied to the U.S.S.R. Rumania is a member of Russia's Warsaw Pact but so reluctant that it did not even participate in the recent occupation of Czechoslovakia. Hungary is not a Balkan but central European state.

No fundamental doubts perplex little Bulgaria, which swears by the U.S.S.R., emulates the zigzags of its ideological twists and even dispatched a few hundred troops (via the Black Sea and Russia) to take part in the operation on Czechoslovakia. Todor Zhivkov, this country's Communist boss, once told me when discussing the word "satellite": "Of course we are Russia's most confident ally. The question is how you define what a satellite is."

Thus Bulgaria is today the only active member of what Moscow now calls the "Socialist commonwealth," and here the point is that Bulgaria is not simply an ideological stooge; its entire historical tradition has been staunchly pro-Russian. Russia is not popular here because it is Communist, but Communism has always had a certain glamour because it was Russian.

After Bulgaria regained its independence from the Ottoman Turks late last century every officer in its army above the rank of lieutenant was Russian. At one time two Czarist generals served as Premier and War Minister. When something goes wrong the villagers say: "Uncle Ivan from Moscow will come up the river to help." During World War II, although allied to Hitler, the Bulgarians wouldn't declare war on Russia.

Faithful Mirror

With this background it is understandable that Bulgaria has shown little inclination to experiment with the kind of independent Communism initiated in Yugoslavia and later copied in some respects and with varying success elsewhere. From the moment that Communism first took power here at the end of 1944, when Soviet troops stormed westward along the Danube, political patterns have faithfully mirrored those delineated in the Kremlin.

As Soviet trends shifted, following Stalin's death, there was also some shift here. However, things moved slowly because the Bulgarians, having long been occupied by the Turks, developed an innate sense of caution. Although they share no common border with the U.S.S.R. as does Rumania, they are content to eschew ideological audacity and, of course, cherish none of the inherited bias of the traditionally Russophobe Rumanians.

Thus, as the present Kremlin rulers began a new anti-liberal phase and frowned on currents of economic decentralization, one could detect here a new tightening of party control over various aspects of society and an economic decentralization. The latter followed some gingerly and rather half-hearted toying with the innovations of non-Marxist economists.

So-called "democratization" is now on the decline. There is emphasis on "the central determination of the structure of the national economy." This background of what one might call willing satellization carries the Bulgarian Government over many embarrassing humps.

There was certainly no vast enthusiasm for joining in to hammer the Czechs, but the decision inspired little detectable grumbling. The United States had long been popularly liked and respected; yet it is easy to assemble anti-American demonstrations when this suits the mood of Soviet policy. And any Sofia regime can reckon on mass approval for criticism of the traditionally disliked Yugoslavs, of whom the Bulgarians have always been jealous and resentful.

Furthermore, internally, there is no doubt that despite ideological ups and downs, Communism has done a good deal for the average Bulgarian's living standard. There is now much more industry in this essentially backward land.

Conditions Have Improved

Its cities and roads have been developed. There is a surprisingly large number of automobiles. The modest aspirations of these people are being tangibly if gradually met and, although the traditionalist farmers don't like collectivization, Communism—meaning Russia—gets considerable credit advancing material conditions.

For these reasons Bulgaria remains and is content to remain the odd man in, Moscow's only Balkan satellite and loyally responsive to any Kremlin proddings no matter what Yugoslavia, Rumania or Albania choose to do. It is not for nothing that Zhivkov, in a moment of euphoria, once said: "We have been and we will continue to be with the Soviet Union for life and until death."

*   *   *

May 8, 1969

IN YUGOSLAV FILMS, REALITY IS NO INTRUDER

Directors Don't Shy From Depiction of Misery and Strife

Special to The New York Times

BELGRADE, Yugoslavia—Does the Communist system foster knife fights, phony elections, strikes, murderous jealousy, lynchings, swindling, drunkenness, theft, social alienation and the corruption of party officials?

Filmmakers who turn out bland "constructivist" social dramas in the Soviet Union, East Germany and Poland would appear to answer, "no."

For them, contemporary conflicts are something to be resolved through sagacious and engaged mediation of Christ-like party officials. Their films are generally a bore, even to their own movie reviewers.

But in the Socialist Federative Republic of Yugoslavia during the last four years, young filmmakers have come up with quite a different and exciting version of life in a Communist society, where people love and hate, kill and cheat, lie and go hungry.

Of Death and Doom

"There is no place for angels," says one of the miserable and brutal figures of Zivojin Pavlovic's "When I Am Dead and Pale," his prize-winning 1968 film about the feckless adventures of an unemployed orphan who ends up being shot to death in a factory outhouse.

"The crack of doom is coming soon / Let it come, it does not matter," sing the stubble-bearded gypsy musicians in the programmatic title song of Alexander Petrovic's poetic new film to be shown in English as, "It Rains in My Village."

The movie, which is likely to be regarded as Mr. Petrovic's masterpiece, is set in a seemingly placid village of the Srem plain near Belgrade. There, a dumbstruck maiden is raped by the innkeeper, who then couples her with the young swineherd. The boy stays with her until a pretty but loose Communist schoolteacher seduces him. He slays the first girl, but his highly religious father takes the blame.

After the father dies in prison, the villagers take revenge on the swineherd, who has become a drunkard, by lynching him on the bell ropes of their new church. At his funeral the schoolteacher-party secretary appears at the church door as the incarnation of the devil.

Filmmaker's View

The 40-year-old Petrovic, who won international acclaim with his "Feather Merchants," said in an interview: "I am not an accuser. I am trying to tell the truth."

Mr. Petrovic's depiction was too much for some Yugoslav party critics. One charged, "There is a limit in presenting inhumanity."

Yet Borba, the paper most closely associated with the ruling party, called Mr. Petrovic a "poet and dreamer" in whose films "the magic of folk idiom explodes with all its force."

The film's author said that he got to know Yugoslavia's village life in all its rawness while making documentaries some years ago, and that the experience had helped him to elicit realistic performances from his professional actors as well as his peasant extras.

Though he is not a Communist, he is deeply concerned with Socialist theory and practice. One might say the same of the other Yugoslav author-directors who have made such an impact on the international cinema world in the last few years: Zivojin Pavlovic, Purisa Djordjevic, Dusan Makavejev, Fadil Hadzic and Vladan Slijepcevic.

They have all been accused of making films showing only the grimmest aspects of Yugoslav life. Mr. Djordjevic, for example, has been revolutionizing the image of the Partisan warrior, always the glorious patriot-hero in earlier Yugoslav films. His tetrology, beginning with "Morning" and "Noon" deals also with political changes wrought by Stalinism.

The new directors reject the argument that they are trying to make things look worse than they are. They seek, said one director, to draw artistic material out of reality instead of providing a fictional justification for dictatorship.

Generally speaking, the Yugoslav press and progressive members of President Tito's party are taking much the same view of the country's problems. Thus the new filmmakers are not out of step, but are in the vanguard of political developments here.

To a visitor familiar with the land, the most striking element of the new films is that they are, in the first place, "Yugoslav," rather than "Serbian," "Croat" or "Slovenian," as is often the case in poetry, novels and painting. The themes

are valid for the entire country and, in the case of some, such as the Petrovic movies, are universal.

The Yugoslav public is responding warmly. "Happy Gypsies" drew 400,000 moviegoers in Belgrade alone— half the population of the capital. "It Rains in My Village" had an audience of 154,000 in two weeks.

"It is an authors' film," said Djordje Babic, an export manager for Yugoslavia Film. "We have a dozen directors who can do what they want and get the money to do it. Nor are there any stars—just popular actors."

Though they are not getting rich—Mr. Petrovic, for example, drives a banged-up Volkswagen and $25,000 a year is considered a high salary—they are in excellent spirits.

Mr. Babic cited the example of Veljko Bulajic, who was offered large sums to work in Hollywood. He came back to direct the Partisan war epic, "Battle on the Neretva," saying, "Here I can work in freedom—there I would be one under dozens of bosses."

Last year, said Mr. Babic, Yugoslav film exports earned over $1-million for the country, and with more than 25 productions under way this year, the revenue should be higher.

"The international acclaim helps," said Mr. Babic. "But what we need are steady customers."

* * *

January 31, 1971

TO UNDERSTAND GREECE, GO TO LIA

The Story of a Greek Village, as Told by a Native Son . . .

By NICHOLAS GAGE

My body walks the streets of the city, but look for my soul in the shadows of my village. —Greek folk song

Anyone who wants to analyze Greek politics today must visit not only Athens and Salonika and the other large cities, but the villages as well. At the least, he should try to know some of the many village natives who now live in the cities. The harsh life style and the isolation of Greece's villages strongly affected their inhabitants and account for many of the contradictory aspects of current Greek life.

Before World War II and the Greek civil war that followed, 75 per cent of all Greeks lived in villages. Although half of all Greeks now live in the cities, most of those over 25 years of age were born in villages, including the colonels who today rule Greece.

The villages did not produce only right-wing politicians. Many shades of political thought were to be found in the villages before World War II, including Communism, which the colonels cited in 1967 as the excuse for their take-over of the Government.

Greek villages, of course, differ in many ways, depending on their nearness to the sea, their location otherwise in the country, and the occupations of the inhabitants. But there are bonds which have united all villagers—bonds formed in the struggle to wrest food from the hard land and to survive political storms.

Lia, the village where I was born, is as typical as any. Its sleepy look gives no hint of its bloody history during the last 30 years, the period which saw modern Greece forged amid privation, torture and civil war. Lia is near the northern border of Epirus, the northwest division of Greece, on a steep slope just below the timberline of the Mourgana mountain range. At the summit of the range, two-thirds of a mile above the village, is the Albanian border. Lia is so high that the villagers can often look down at the rain clouds over the bottom land below.

The people who settled Lia once lived on that bottom land, but in the 15th century, after the Turks conquered Greece, they began to move back to the mountains to escape persecution. As the Turks continued to make forays, seizing young men and boys for their Janissary corps and the girls for their harems, the villagers moved to more and more inaccessible mountain slopes, farther and farther up until they reached the timberline and could go no higher. Today there are five villages up in these mountains each about a half hour's walk from the next, and when I was a child these villages represented the farthest boundaries of my world.

Lia is luckier than the villages to the east and the west because it is set in an indentation where the slope of the mountain falls more gently. Babouri, the next village to the west, is set on a narrow ledge against a cliff that rises straight up. At Lia the squat houses of natural stone are built on steps of land held back by thick stone walls, so that from a distance the village looks like a large amphitheater.

The man who first settled on this spot must have been an optimist, for he had carried a small olive tree up from the valley and tried to make it grow in that harsh soil. The tree did not survive for long but, according to the tales of Lia, it gave the village its name: the settlers who followed would say, "We are going near the olive tree [elia]."

Turkish raids were infrequent at these high altitudes, but now and then the representatives of the pasha of the region would come to collect taxes. On these occasions the young girls would be kept hidden in the houses and any woman who did venture out tied her kerchief so as to hide her face.

Life in Lia was devoted to one all-important task—scratching an existence from the inhospitable mountain soil. Everyone in a family had to work and to exploit every possibility. There were two flat pieces of land near Lia suitable for tilling—one on a plateau a distance above the village, another on the foothills an hour's walk below. These spots were parceled out among the families in the village and those with the largest plots of land had the greatest social status. The land was cultivated mostly by the women, who also carefully searched the ravines for scrub brush that might burn, and carried huge loads of it up the mountain on their backs. The crop that grew best was corn, which was ground up to make meal for bread. The primary diet was of vegetables and the coarse corn bread, with meat only on special occasions. Each family had some animals as well—a few sheep and goats—and young boys would take the stock to a pasture above the timberline every day.

Young girls shared the many tasks of their mothers—tending the crops, shearing the sheep, spinning wool, weaving cloth, cutting brushwood, cooking, cleaning the house. The boys, after the age of 8, joined their fathers in the family trade.

Three occupations were followed by most of the men of Lia; the most common was tinsmithing. The tinsmiths would set out on long journeys which would keep them away from their homes six months to a year or more. They traveled from town to town, stopping at each house to ask if pots needed cleaning, mending or replacing with the new ones they carried. Because everyone cooked over an open fire, cooking vessels were always scorched black. The tinkers scoured the outside of the huge pots with sand. Cleaning the inside was the work of the small boys. First sand and a little water would be put in the pots, then an animal skin; the boy would stand in the pot and, with an expert shuffling of his feet, scour it until it shone. It was as a tinsmith's helper that my father first earned a living. Many tinkers in Greece were notorious for conniving, stealing and sending their thin, hungry-looking children into houses to beg, but the tinkers of Lia prided themselves on their reputation for integrity.

The second trade in Lia was that of cooper, and coopers, too, left their homes for months and even years, traveling all over Greece to make giant casks of wood with a skill that can no longer be equaled. The third occupation was milling. The millers were the élite of the village because they did not have to leave their families, and they received 10 per cent of the grain they ground, selling the flour they did not need.

During the Turkish occupation, which lasted in Epirus from 1430 to 1912, the men wore a Turkish-style garb of black pantaloons gathered at the knee over black socks and pomponed shoes; a white shirt and a square, often embroidered, vest. Many wore the fez. The women wore long embroidered skirts in somber colors and heavy jackets, also embroidered. Today in homes in Lia there are cherished old photographs of relatives dressed in this manner. These pictures often have a ghostly quality because of the past practice of having absent loved ones grafted into the picture by the photographer.

The life of the itinerant tinsmiths and coopers was a difficult one and many families in Lia lived constantly with the pain of hunger. By the end of the 19th century, some men from our village were going farther and farther from home. In 1910 my father, who was then 17 and the youngest of six brothers, returned from a journey of cleaning and repairing pots and told his mother that he had heard there were jobs to be had in the factories of the United States. She pleaded with him not to go, but he borrowed $48 from relatives, set out walking and hitchhiking down to the port of Patras, and for $28.60 bought his ticket to the United States. After six months he had sent back the $48. He found that he could indeed make a better living across the ocean. By fashioning sieves in a factory during the day he was earning $4.10 a week and by setting pins in a bowling alley at night be earned $2.70 a week more.

Other men, too, traveled far abroad in search of more money. One of the most famous in our village was John Costas, who went to South Africa in 1894, fought on the side of the Boers and opened a restaurant which yielded a modest fortune. But none of these men ever considered settling in the foreign countries. They believed they were just on longer versions of the working trips that the men of Lia had made for centuries, and they lived in Spartan simplicity, saving money for the day they could return. John Costas, in spite of his wealth, returned to Lia in 1912 to fight in the Balkan wars, which ultimately freed his native village from the Turks.

In 1924 my father, by now 31, returned to Lia from the United States. He brought with him $2,100 for his family and he stayed five months. During that time he became engaged to my mother, who was 18, and then returned to Massachusetts, where he sold fruit and produce from a truck. Two years later he returned again and was married in the old church of St. Demetrios. He brought his bride to his mother's home and, a year later, a girl was born. When the baby was 3 months old, he went back to his work in the United States, leaving his family behind. In the next eight years he returned two more times and fathered two more girls.

A number of men from the village were now working in factories in America and sending their pay home. Some families were even able to send a son south to the teachers' academy at Ioannina, the capital of Epirus. Before this time the only education Lia children had was a few years in the village school before becoming old enough, at 8 or so, to be set to work.

Among the several men from Lia to make the journey to Ioannina were two brothers, Spyros and Prokopis Skevis. During their stay at the academy these two became Communists and brought their ideas back to the village. The ideology they had adopted was to have grave repercussions for our village and for all of Greece. Many villagers listened with respect and pride to what the newly educated young men had to say. Their words fell on fertile ground because by now Greece was under a harsh military dictatorship, the Metaxas regime, which lasted from 1936 to 1941.

In 1937 my father returned for another stay with his family and, within a year, a fourth daughter was born. The village women began to look upon my mother with the suspicion that she had in some way angered the fates and was being punished by having only daughters. When my father returned to the United States, where he was now the chef in a Staten Island restaurant, my mother was pregnant again. Five months later a son was born amid great rejoicing. No one could have guessed that the gods were preparing more wars for Greece and that when my father saw me for the first time I would be 10 years old.

On Oct. 28, 1940, Mussolini delivered to dictator Metaxas an ultimatum demanding that Italian troops be allowed to advance into Greece and got a one-word reply: "Ohi" (No). The Italian troops, without waiting for an answer, were

"My mother, my four sisters, my aunt Nitsa (second from left, rear), and myself, photographed in 1947, just before Communist guerrillas seized our village during the Greek civil war. My mother was executed by the Communists after arranging our escape. My sisters are all in the United States now. Aunt Nitsa still lives in Lia."

already advancing over the Albanian border into Epirus. They occupied the village of Lia, among others, and stayed for two weeks. The villagers recall the Italians as surprisingly amiable occupiers who did not persecute the towns-people. Greeks were rallying to the defense of the country, and, to the astonishment of the world, they drove the Italian Army—vastly superior both in numbers and arms—back into Albania. The Greeks pressed on and seemed about to take all of Albania when Hitler stepped in. In April, 1941, the Germans invaded Greece from all directions, beginning a bloody occupation which was to last three years.

Food now became even harder to find in Lia. Some villagers, especially women, adopted a punishing method of increasing the supply. They would set out by mule on the two-day journey over the mountains to Igoumenitsa on the Ionian Sea. There they would collect salt, loading it on their mules and on their own backs. Returning to the village they would climb over the summit of the mountain into Albania where they traded the salt to the landlocked Albanians for corn. This was done even in the middle of winter by women weak from hunger. One woman became lost in the snow while descending from the Albanian border in 1942. Her body was not found until spring.

The Germans set up their headquarters for northern Greece in Ioannina. Greek partisans flocked to the rugged country around Lia to set up guerrilla groups, rightists forming EDES, leftists and moderates EAM. As time passed, EAM became more and more left-wing and Communists like the Skevis brothers took control. The villagers of Lia were divided in their loyalties, although most of the town favored the left-wing EAM. Periodically one or the other partisan group would sweep into Lia, find out from its sympathizers who favored the opposite faction, round up the "collaborators," lock them up in the school and beat some of them. During a series of beatings administered by the EAM, one man was killed.

Finally, in the third year of the occupation, the Germans decided to move into the mountains to clean out the troublesome guerrilla bands. Word reached the village that the Germans were on their way, but we were told they were coming from the north, so everyone fled to the south, hiding in caves and ravines. One old grandmother refused to desert her home and was left behind.

The Germans came not from the north but from the south and they passed so close to the ravine where my sisters and I were hiding that we could hear their footsteps. A short time later they ran into three men from our village who had been away and had not been warned. The Germans shot the three and left their bodies in the road. The troops continued on to the village of Babouri. One woman in Babouri could speak some German, so the villagers decided to stay and appeal through her to the troops; food and drink were offered and the village was spared. When the Germans entered our deserted village they burned the school, three churches and half the homes. When the old grandmother cried out at seeing her home in flames, they threw her into the fire.

When the people of Lia returned to their village, those whose homes had been destroyed moved in with relatives and began to rebuild. Eighteen months later the Germans were driven out of Greece, but the bloodshed did not end with their retreat. Immediately after the war the country was in turmoil over the disarming of the resistance groups and the question of how much power EAM, now fully dominated by the Communists, should have in the postwar Government. There were bloody riots in the large cities until, finally, in 1946, a conservative Government took over and launched a drive against EAM. As a result, many members of EAM left the country for Albania and Yugoslavia, where they were trained and armed and sent back into Greece to fight. By 1947 these guerrilla units had taken control of many mountain areas of Greece.

In the fall of that year when word reached Lia and the other villages of the Mourgana range that these guerrillas were on their way, there was no panic. The people of Lia felt that the several village men, including the Skevis brothers, who were among the guerrillas would not allow their fellow villagers to be harmed. The only concern arose from rumors that the guerrillas were drafting all able-bodied men they came across, so the men of Lia left and went to the coastal areas where the Greek Army was in control.

When the guerrillas arrived they were furious to find a village inhabited only by women and children. The Skevis brothers had assured the band that the men of Lia would be eager to join Communist forces. The guerrillas settled in for a long stay, building fortifications, confiscating food and requiring the women to work for them. After some initial successes against Greek Army units, the fighting went badly for the Communists, and as the months went by they became angrier and more brutal. They began drafting young girls to fight. In many villages individuals suspected of opposing EAM policy were executed after public trials during which the relatives of the accused were forced to condemn them in order to save their own lives. Children were made to watch the executions of their parents. Bodies were often left in the village square for days. The EAM forces were becoming more and more like the Germans they had been fighting during the war.

When the guerrillas began conscripting girls 16 and over into the army, two of my sisters were among the eligible. The older poured boiling water on her feet so that when the soldiers came to get her she couldn't walk, and she vowed it was an accident. The other sister went, but fainted so often from hunger during training that the soldiers finally sent her back.

The Communists also began a practice which many villagers found even more hateful than the conscription of girls. It was called pedomasoma (gathering of children). At first this was a voluntary program. The Communists would call the villagers together and ask women to volunteer to send young children behind the Iron Curtain to be educated as Communists. The soldiers emphasized that the children would be well fed, and they displayed boxes of sweets that would immediately be given to any children who were sent forward. This method was not so successful as the Communists had hoped, so in 1948 they stopped asking and began demanding a certain number of young children from each family. At this point my mother and some other women began planning an escape.

The day before the planned escape, June 25, 1948, the guerrillas began to round up women for a work detail. The women of the village were often required to go into the battle zone to carry wounded, dig graves and do other chores for the troops. On this particular day, each family had to provide one out of every two of its women over 13 to go to the wheat fields and harvest and thresh grain for the soldiers. My three oldest sisters were over 13 so my family had to supply two women. My mother decided that she would go and take my 14-year-old sister, who looked too young to arouse lustful feelings in the soldiers. She told the rest of us that we were to go through with the escape as planned.

The next evening 20 people, adults and children, met at the southernmost house in the village as if for a social gathering. We children were instructed to play tag down below and then to hide in a nearby cave. The adults would come calling us and would finally join us in hiding. As soon as darkness fell, we would start walking down the mountain, across the hills and up the next range until we met the Greek Government forces.

The escape succeeded. We walked, most of us barefoot, all through the night, and just after dawn we found a unit of the Royalists, who led us three more miles to a road. There we waited until an army truck appeared. It was the first vehicle my sisters and I had ever seen, although we had seen many planes over our village during the air war between the Germans and the Allies. When the soldiers put us in the truck and it rumbled off, my sisters began to scream because they thought the earth was moving and the truck standing still.

That journey was the beginning of many for us—to refugee barracks of corrugated metal in Igoumenitsa on the Ionian Sea, where our section of the floor was separated from others by hanging sheets; then a two-day journey by boat to Athens where, thanks to the efforts of relatives and my father in Massachusetts, we were eventually placed on a refugee boat bound for America.

My mother was executed after our disappearance, along with my aunt and three other villagers accused of disloyalty to EAM. They were shot and their bodies thrown in a ravine above our home. Because we lived in one of the largest houses in the village, it had been taken by the Communists as a headquarters and they kept prisoners, including my mother, in the basement before execution. The bodies of other executed prisoners were stuffed into our well or buried in the front yard. The villagers have seldom gone near the house since then, and it is now falling in ruins.

The guerrillas executed five to 10 people in every occupied village whether there were any escape attempts or not. It was a last effort by the desperate Communists to frighten the villagers into total submission and to divide the populace by making residents testify against each other. By the fall of 1948, three months after our escape, the Greek Army drove the Communist units back into Albania. As they retreated, the Communists took with them every villager who could walk and every inhabitant of Lia, including my 14-year-old sister.

The EAM forces thought they were suffering only a temporary setback. They put their Greek captives into camps for "re-education" and believed that the children would form Communist armies of the future. Altogether they took more than 100,000 Greek civilians behind the Iron Curtain. (Today there are still villagers from Lia in Albania, Poland, Rumania, Russia and East Germany.) Within a year, my sister, by a number of ruses, got herself sent to the battlefield in Macedonia where the guerrillas were making a last-ditch effort, and she managed to cross over to the Greek Government forces. After a time she was reunited with the rest of us in the United States.

By the early nineteen-fifties, when the Communists realized that they would not have a second chance, they began to allow some of the refugees to return to Greece. Some who wanted to come back were not allowed in by the Greek Government, however, because it was feared that they had become too indoctrinated. Other Greeks who had supported the guerrillas did not dare to return for fear of what their fel-

low villagers would do to them. Half of the refugees still remain behind the Iron Curtain today.

After that fall of 1948, Lia was a ghost town. A few of the men of the village returned from the seacoast, but most found the sight of the village too painful, vacant as it was of their women and children, and they went to the cities, becoming a part of the postwar exodus from the villages. When the first of the refugees began to trickle back over the border in the early nineteen-fifties, the Greek Government offered them loans to rebuild their homes and villages. Some accepted, but many, including the young people, had had enough of struggling for a meager existence and they set out to seek their fortunes in Athens, or in the United States. My father helped about a hundred Greeks from Lia settle in Massachusetts.

Even today these Greeks and their families still think of themselves as Lia villagers, and in both Athens and Massachusetts there are active societies of Liotes which send money back to the village for rebuilding churches and houses. Every summer many of the expatriated villagers return on a sentimental journey, the greatest number arriving on July 20, the feast day of the Prophet Elias, patron of the village.

There are only 180 permanent residents of Lia left. Before World War II Lia was a bustling place of 1,200 people, who were served by three mills and worshiped in 11 churches, from small local chapels to the centuries-old Aghia Panaghia (Church of Our Lady). None of the mills are operating now, and only one church is being used regularly. Today the town's six children all study in one room of the large village school. The Government has turned the rest of the building into a trade school where young women from 16 villages in the area can learn cooking, sewing, embroidery and other crafts. But in Lia itself there are almost no young women. The majority of the villagers are over 60 years old.

Life in the village despite a number of improvements, is still primitive. Women till the rocky soil using methods of agriculture that date back to Biblical times. Indoor plumbing is still unknown. In 1959 a road was finally built connecting the village to the rest of the world; the most dramatic change in the village's daily life was created by the advent of electricity in 1965. Now the clanging of sheep's bells is drowned out by the bouzouki music from the radios. Many of the village women still carry their water from the springs, but some families now have pipes that bring the spring water to a sink in the yard.

Apart from these modern conveniences, the village looks much as I remember it during World War II. The houses are of gray natural stone, roofed with gray shingles and usually they have two rooms. Outside every house is a beehive-shaped fourno (oven) of baked mud and, at a discreet distance, an outhouse.

The road is the lifeline that supports the old people of Lia. It brings money from their relatives overseas, Government pensions and newspapers. The road begins in Filiates, a large town to the southwest of the Mourgana range, then climbs the mountains and traces a tortuous path from village to village, clinging to the top of cliffs, winding in and out like ribbon candy, often crumbling partly away and finally descending from the mountains and running all the way to Ioannina in the southeast.

Not many foreigners travel that road because Lia and its neighboring villages lie within the "forbidden zone" near the Albanian border. A permit must be got from Government officials in Athens, Ioannina or Igoumenitsa in order to pass by the sentries who stand at the two bridges over the river separating the area from the rest of Epirus, and usually only Greeks who can prove they have relatives in the villages are allowed to enter.

A visitor approaching Lia from Filiates will find not only breathtaking views but shrines and chapels built in memory of the dead, often by relatives who have made money in America. As the road enters Lia there is a blue sign which says in Greek: "Lia, population 180, altitude 660 meters above sea level." Immediately to the right, below the road, is the house my maternal grandfather owned. He and my grandmother were married when he was 14 and she was 13 and, after 73 years of marriage, they died in 1967 within a month of each other. Now his daughter, my aunt Nitsa, aged 68, and her husband, Andreas, live in the house.

Far up the slope to the left, in a magnificent setting, lies the now deserted church of St. Demetrios, surrounded by giant cypress trees. Attached to the church is a room where the bones of the dead are kept in boxes, and among them the bones of my mother. (The Greek Orthodox disinter their dead after three years and store the bones this way. The cellar of St. Demetrios is lined with human bones and, in the dark, the phosphorescence of the bones makes them glow with a ghastly light.) Even higher, above St. Demetrios, lie the ruins of our house.

The road makes a sharp inward turn, following the curve of the mountain, and when it turns outward again, one can look down upon the house of Gregory Venetis, a thin, hawk-nosed old man who in addition to being a tailor, is the president (i.e., mayor) of the village. He can usually be seen from the road, sitting on his porch sewing.

The road next passes the cafenion (combination outdoor cafe and grocery store) of Nicholas Barkas. In the old days, when the men returned briefly from their working journeys, they usually passed the time sitting in one of several cafenions; today the town can barely support the two it has, and Nicholas Barkas does not take it kindly when townspeople are seen at his competitor's cafenion more often than at his. Below the road at this point is the house of the gray-bearded priest, Father Nicholas, who was once a cooper. He now acts as the correspondent for the village and keeps in touch with the societies of villagers in Athens and in America, informing them of the town's needs.

At the next outward bend, the road bisects the village square called T'alonia, which means the place where wheat is threshed. Here the cafenion of George Venetis, brother of the village president, is shaded by giant plane trees. Across from the cafenion is the kiosk where villagers can buy cigarettes, newspapers, toothpaste, stamps, aspirin, candy and a bewilder-

ing variety of things. The concessions for such kiosks, which are found throughout Greece, are usually given to disabled veterans, and Leonidas Charamopoulos, who runs the kiosk in Lia, is no exception. Below the square is the church of the Holy Trinity, restored by the gifts of villagers who have left Lia. And below the church is the schoolhouse.

At the far edge of town is the house of my uncle, Fotios Gatzoyiannis, who is in his late 80's but still gets up at 4 every morning to hunt for wild boar and pheasant. When he was young my uncle killed a Turk for insulting his wife and if the Turks had not been driven out of Epirus he would still be in jail.

His wife died shortly after his release and he married a second time and fathered nine children. His second wife was executed by the Communists at the same time as my mother, and he lost a son and a granddaughter in the civil war as well.

My uncle Fotios strongly supports the junta, as do most of the old people left in Lia. They have accepted the junta's early statements that it had to seize power to save the country from Communism. Given the choice between Communism and the junta dictatorship, the old people of Lia remember the past too well to hesitate.

During a visit to the village in the spring of 1969 I had a long discussion with my Aunt Nitsa, my mother's sister, and her husband about the junta. I tried to explain to them my objections to life under the colonels—the lack of freedom, the arbitrary arrests, the censorship, the repression. They listened to me patiently as Greek peasants do to anyone they believe to be morphomenos—educated.

Then my aunt asked me two questions: "Who have the colonels killed?" And before I could answer, she added, "Who killed your mother?"

The memories of the civil war so dominate the minds of the old people of Lia that it is impossible to convince them that Greece was not threatened by Communism when the colonels staged their coup, that the colonels themselves have stopped trying to use such a line, and that they hold the country in dictatorship because of personal desires for power.

Even George Venetis, the owner of the main cafe in Lia who was imprisoned by the junta, still supports the regime. In the heat of debate with some fellow villagers in 1967, Venetis called one of the junta's administrators in Epirus a thief, and was jailed two months for it.

He is not happy about that episode, but he still believes that the junta saved Greece from the Communists, whom he despises as much as any man in Lia. During the Communist occupation of the village in the civil war, the guerrillas seized his 5-year-old daughter for the pedomasoma—and sent her to Russia. The daughter is now in Tashkent, the capital of the Soviet republic of Uzbekistan, and George Venetis has not seen her in 23 years.

While most of the old people in Lia support the junta, many of their fellow villagers who have moved to Athens and other cities, where the sentiment is overwhelmingly anti-junta, do not. But they, too, remember the civil war and they are not likely to risk bringing that holocaust back by participating in any violent uprising against the junta so long as life is at all tolerable in Greece.

In summer Lia often regains a semblance of its old life, especially on Elias's feast day, when flocks of returning Liotes climb to the mountain top for the services. Then everyone descends for a picnic on the flat pasture by the dam just above the village. Whole lambs are roasted and the village women carry huge trays of cheese and spinach pies. Gypsies, who travel from one village festival to another, play Greek folk songs and everyone dances the Tsamikos, the spirited dance native to Epirus.

In spite of these sporadic signs of life, Lia is dying. Its young people have left permanently—and in a few decades there will be few if any returnees on the feast day. Lia is one of hundreds of Greek villages suffering the same slow death. What Greece will be without these villages no one can say. For most Greeks born in the first half of this century, whether they live in Athens, Johannesburg, Stuttgart, New York or Rio de Janeiro, the villages were Greece. Village life shaped their character and their destiny. Most Greeks would not want to return to their native village to live, but none of them will ever forget it.

Nicholas Gage is a Times reporter. This article is adapted from his forth-coming book, "Portrait of Greece" (New York Times/American Heritage Press).

* * *

January 31, 1971

SERBS AND CROATS IN LANGUAGE SPLIT

Joint Dictionary Project Is Dropped—Began in '54

Special to The New York Times

BELGRADE, Yugoslavia, Jan. 30—A long-standing linguistic feud, colored by both traditional and contemporary political rivalries, has halted a cooperative project to produce an official dictionary of the Serbo-Croatian language, spoken by two out of three Yugoslavs.

The official organization of the Croatian intelligentsia, the Croatian Matica formally announced last week that it would no longer work together with its Serbian counterpart on the joint project.

The two Maticas, a word that literally means "queen bee" but translates figuratively as "motherland association," have already published two volumes of the common dictionary in both the Cyrillic alphabet used in Serbia and the Latin used in Croatia. A third volume, covering the letter O and P will be published in March but only in Cyrillic.

"It will be more useful to prepare a separate dictionary of the Croatian language," the statement said, blaming the Serbian Matica for making "further cooperation impossible."

The two organizations, founded in the 19th century, had agreed on the project in 1954 on the ground that Serbian and Croatian were basically variants of the same tongue, namely Serbo-Croatian.

Croatian Held Different

"Today," the Croatian announcement maintained, "no objective person can any longer take the view that the national language of the Serbs, Croats, Montenegrins and Moslems [in Bosnia-Herzegovina] is one and the same language."

Serbs, the statement added, have frustrated "any independent work on the Croatian language or any creative attitude of the Croatian people toward its own language" by refusing to recognize its "substantial and cultural integrity and individuality."

With the exception of the alphabet, the most common difference between Serbian and Croatian is the spelling and pronunciation of the letter "E", a hard sound in Serbian that is softened by the Croats. Thus "mleko" and "mlijeko" are the respective words for milk, and "belo" and "bijelo" both mean "white."

Some words are completely different, such as "voz" in Serbian and "vlak" in Croatian, both of which mean train. The Croatian word for dance—"ples"—came originally from Serbia, where people now say "igra."

The Serbs, who accuse the Croats of linguistic chauvinism, say they regret the ending of the project. They plan to continue with publication of the dictionary in the Cyrillic alphabet alone.

The dictionary furor is reminiscent of a similar quarrel in 1967, touched off again by the Croats' demands for separate status for their language. At that time the Communist party stepped into the fray, forcing both Serbs and Croats to recant, reprimanding extremists on both sides and even expelling one Croatian writer from the party.

* * *

February 10, 1971

CROATIAN NATIONALISM GETS NEW IMPETUS

By ALFRED FRIENDLY Jr.
Special to The New York Times

ZAGREB, Yugoslavia, Feb. 6—A strange alliance of Communists and Roman Catholics, politicians and intellectuals, has coalesced here to assert the rights of some 4.5 million Croats to guide their own destinies and control their own riches.

The impetus sprang from Yugoslavia's efforts to decentralize the federal administration and honor a 25-year-old pledge to put the competitive nationality groups on an equal footing.

The overriding and unresolved questions as to how this can be done are economic, but the tie that binds the Croats together now is a highly developed sense—perhaps even an exaggerated awareness—of their cultural and ethnic identity.

"We still feel menaced," said Jure Juras, a doctor of medicine and of philosophy, a Croatian nationalist and an active Catholic.

The Serbs Are Dominant

In a talk in his spartan office at the University of Zagreb, he recalled a Croatian past replete with suppression by Hungarians, Italians, Turks, Austrians and Germans. Until the creation of Yugoslavia in 1918, he noted, "we were never managed by the Serbs, and I hope the conflict with them will prove to be the shortest."

The refrain of private conversation and official statements here is similar: The dominant position of the 8.5 million Serbs, whose kingdom became the center of Yugoslavia and whose bureaucracy retained its hold even under President Tito's Communism, must be broken.

On the economic side, Croatia, in an effort that is the subject of tough debate at the very top of the communist party, wants to set up its own banks and not let the federal ones in Belgrade control the foreign currency earned by Croatian exports, Croatian workers abroad and Croatian tourist resorts on the Adriatic coast.

In cultural affairs, Croatian and Serbian intellectuals have renewed their combat over whether the Croatian form of Serbo-Croat, written in the Latin alphabet, is simply a variant of Serbian, which uses the Cyrillic alphabet. (The linguistic division reflects the fact that the Croats are largely Roman Catholic while the Serbs are largely Eastern Orthodox.)

When a similar quarrel erupted four years ago over Croatian claims to a unique linguistic heritage, the Communist party here stepped in to silence the exuberant literati. Now the party says nothing and its silence is interpreted as encouragement.

A Risk of Alienation

On the political front, an impressive assortment of Croatian organizations has made a fierce attack on the wording of the federal census questionnaire to be used in April. A line that permits people to identify themselves by the region where they live, Croats assert, is an effort to fragment their nationality group into subclusters of Dalmatians, Slavonians and others in Croatia who would end up being counted simply as "Yugoslavs."

In all these outbursts and in the coalition that makes them, Croats acknowledge the risk of alienating other Yugoslavs and reviving traditional fears of a separatist, Catholic and conservative Croatia—the kind of society that accepted Quisling rule under the Nazis and connived in repeated massacres of Serbs. If such fears are unavoidable, the Croats insist that they are also unjustified.

"The tendency to look on Croatian nationalism, Croatian culture and the Catholic Church as unhealthy is part of the old mechanism that always sought to put Croatia at a psychological disadvantage as a preliminary to suppression," Professor Juras insisted.

"At the moment there are no elements of friendship on the scene, but only elements of conflict, but once everything is completely settled this year, we will all have the same problems, and Croatians, freed of their defensive reflex, will be more disposed to internationality cooperation."

Slobodan Lang, a 25-year-old medical student and a leading campus Communist, noted that the "Croatian sort of romantic nationalism is not specific to Yugoslavia—it is a world trend.

"Why shouldn't we let ourselves express it?" he asked. "We can go through that stage even if it might mean a period of oversimplification."

* * *

June 2, 1971

CEAUSESCU GETS BIG PEKING WELCOME

Special to The New York Times

PEKING, June 1—Premier Chou En-lai welcomed President Nicolae Ceausescu of Rumania to China on a state visit today and praised Rumania for "opposing big-power chauvinism," an allusion to the policies of the Soviet Union.

Premier Chou told a banquet audience in the gilded Great Hall of the People that Rumania had defied "brute force" in safeguarding her independence and sovereignty.

Earlier the people of Peking, ordinarily garbed in somber attire, shed their blue tunics and trousers and in gay costumes turned out to welcome the Rumanian Communist party and Government delegation. Nearly half a million people with drums beating and cymbals clanging lined an eight-mile section of the route from the airport into the city and through Tienanmen Square to the state guest house.

Hundreds of thousands of smiling school girls wearing brightly colored skirts danced and waved colored paper flowers and streamers, shouting "Welcome" in unison as they held aloft their little red books of Mao Tse-tung's quotations. The skirts were an unfamiliar sight in Peking.

The extravagant welcome appeared to have been organized by the Chinese to express appreciation for the stubborn stand of neutrality that the Rumanians have taken in regard to the ideological conflict and border dispute between Moscow and Peking.

At the Soviet Communist party congress in April, President Ceausescu refused to join in the condemnation of the Chinese Communist party expressed by the Soviet party's General Secretary, Leonid I. Brezhnev. The Rumanians have insisted on maintaining cordial relations with the Chinese.

'Important Victories' Cited

Praising the Rumanians for "keeping the initiative in their own hands," Premier Chou declared: "The Rumanian people have won important victories in their struggle of opposing big-power chauvinism and building socialism. They have withstood foreign pressure, foiled imperialist control, interference and threats of aggression, and courageously defended their national independence and sovereignty."

In his reply at the glittering banquet, attended by more than 500 people including Prince Norodom Sihanouk, the exiled Cambodian leader, Mr. Ceausescu refrained from taking a militant line and pleaded for an end of the Chinese-Soviet conflict.

"Our party and state make every effort toward overcoming the difficulties existing at present in relations between socialist countries and between Communist parties and actively campaign for strengthening their cohesion in the fight against imperialism and reactionaries, for socialism and peace in the world," the Rumanian leader declared.

Premier Chou noted that Rumania had been one of the first countries to extend diplomatic recognition to the Royal Government of National Union of Cambodia, the exile regime headed by Prince Sihanouk.

The Soviet Union has not recognized the Sihanouk government, which has some guerrilla forces fighting in Cambodia with the Vietnamese Communists.

Premier Chou also attacked what he termed "United States imperialism, which he said was "finding things together and tougher" throughout the world.

The Ceausescu party is scheduled to remain in China for about one week before continuing on to North Korea and then North Vietnam.

* * *

June 14, 1971

CHINA'S NEW GUEST LIST

The two Eastern European countries that President Nixon has visited—and he received truly warm receptions in both countries—are Rumania and Yugoslavia.

It is more than coincidence that representatives of those same two nations—Rumanian President Nicolae Ceausescu and Yugoslav Foreign Minister Mirko Tepavac—have visited the Chinese People's Republic this month as official and honored guests of the Peking Government. Mr. Tepavac's visit is particularly noteworthy because it shows how radically Mao Tse-tung has turned away from the policy of a decade ago when frequent Chinese propaganda assaults on "Yugoslav revisionism" were used as the cover for ideological onslaughts against Khrushchev's Russia.

For domestic reasons, Chinese officials welcoming Messrs. Ceausescu and Tepavac have sought to portray Rumania and Yugoslavia as emulating China in being opposed to both the Soviet Union and the United States. But Mao and his colleagues undoubtedly know that both Bucharest and Belgrade look to Washington to support their relative independence from Moscow. No amount of anti-American rhetoric in Peking can disguise the fact that in Eastern Europe both China and the United States want to encourage growth of greater independence and true national sovereignty among nations which have been involuntarily subservient to Moscow since 1945.

* * *

July 8, 1971

RUMANIA COMBATS WESTERN INFLUENCES

VIENNA, July 7 (Reuters)—President Nicolae Ceausescu of Rumania today called for a war on bourgeois influences in Rumanian life.

In a nine-page directive that was unanimously endorsed by the Executive Committee of the Communist party's Central Committee, Mr. Ceausescu demanded an offensive against Western influences that could herald a purge of Rumanian culture.

He told the nation to combat "cosmopolitanism" and "parasitism," to show more respect for the role of the worker, to ban alcoholic drinks from establishments for youth, to strengthen propaganda in the schools, and to teach young people a working-class outlook.

The directive will probably come as a blow to younger Rumanians, who have been increasingly fascinated by Western culture in recent years. It may also spell the doom of American television programs such as "Dr. Kildare" and "The Untouchables," which have appeared regularly on television.

Mr. Ceausescu visited China last month and may have been impressed by the austere policies that have emerged there since the Cultural Revolution.

He said television should portray peasants more often, and the educational and socialist role of radio and television programs must be enhanced.

"Arts must serve the people, the homeland, the socialist society," he said.

The artistic community must fight cosmopolitan attitudes and must not borrow from the capitalist world, his decree said. Films, plays, operas, operettas and ballets that were inspired by the Rumanian people's fight for socialism must find more room in the national repertory, he said.

Movie theaters will limit the number of thrillers and adventure films and will ban films that cultivate violence and vulgarity or popularize a bourgeois way of life.

A principal target will be youth, especially parasites—a Communist term for drop-outs who live off their parents. The party must encourage them to work on building sites and public utility work, the President decreed.

Political training in colleges and schools will be intensified and the Ministry of Education was instructed to inject ideological training into curricula and to staff educational departments with party activists.

Mr. Ceausescu summoned, a meeting of the Central Committee this fall to discuss progress in the program.

* * *

July 15, 1971

BAN ON ARMS AID TO GREECE FAILS

House Unit Defeats Measure—Floor Fight Planned

By FELIX BELAIR Jr.
Special to The New York Times

WASHINGTON, July 14—A proposal to ban arms aid to Greece was narrowly defeated today in the House Foreign Affairs Committee.

The committee rejected by a 14-to-12 vote an amendment to the Administration's $3.3-billion foreign aid authorization bill. The amendment had been proposed by Representative Wayne L. Hays, Democrat of Ohio, who said he would carry his fight to the House floor when the measure came up for action there.

The committee's action came as Rodger P. Davies, Deputy Assistant Secretary of State for Near Eastern and South Asian Affairs, told a Senate Appropriations subcommittee that the strategic importance of Greece on the southern flank of North Atlantic alliance outweighed her suspension of constitutional government and civil rights.

After the House committee's vote, its subcommittee on Europe heard testimony from four witnesses denouncing the Greek military Government. It was termed a "fascist dictatorship based on torture and intimidation" that "will weaken the moral foundations of the NATO alliance."

No Economic Aid

The Hays amendment would prohibit all military aid to the Athens Government unless the President found the assistance "vitally required" in the national security interests of the United States. No economic aid for Greece is planned in the current fiscal year.

Recently declassified figures on the military aid allocations planned by the Nixon Administration for the fiscal year that began July 1 include $118-million for Greece. This total would include the sale of $60-million in new weapons on credit. Twenty million dollars would be in the form of a grant and the remaining $38-million in the form of "excess" equipment no longer required for United States defense purposes.

Mr. Davies told the Senate Appropriations Committee that "we shared the concern of many members of Congress over the question of constitutional government and attendant issues, such as civil rights."

"Since the coup in April of 1967, we saw some tangible signs of a return to more normal democratic forms and procedures and we hoped that these would continue at a pace which would result in a restoration of full constitutional government at an early time," he said.

"Some progress has been made, but our relations with Greece have been made difficult by the failure of the Greek authorities to move more rapidly in that direction," Mr. Davies said. "We have had to weigh this situation against Greece's dedication to NATO and her steadfast support of that organization in a geographic situation which places her against Warsaw Pact borders."

Mrs. Papandreou Testifies

Criticism of United States policy toward Greece was given before the House foreign affairs subcommittee by Mrs. Margaret C. Papandreou, the American-born wife of Andreas Papandreou, who is the son of the late Greek Premier, George Papandreou, and leader of the Pan-Hellenic Liberation Movement.

Mrs. Papandreou, who now lives with her husband in Toronto, asserted that the "coup of the colonels" had been engineered by the Central Intelligence Agency and the State Department and implemented by the National Security Council in February, 1967, because of the opposition of her husband and his Center Union party to a proposed partition of Cyprus between Greece and Turkey.

"The Americans could have foreclosed a military takeover," the witness said. "If they had made a clear declaration that any attempt to impose totalitarian rule in Greece would mean immediate withdrawal of all economic and military aid, the severing of diplomatic relations and serious problems with the NATO alliance, no coup would have been possible."

Mrs. Papandreou asked Representative Benjamin S. Rosenthal, Democrat of Queens and chairman of the subcommittee, to demand from the State Department copies of the report of the Human Rights Commission of the Council of Europe with its charges of torture of Greek men and women who "had their teeth smashed out." She said the report had been "classified" by the department.

The other witnesses who criticized Administration policy toward Greece were Sir Hugh Green, former director of the British Broadcasting Company and chairman of the European-Atlantic Action Committee on Greece; Maurice J. Goldbloom, executive secretary of the United States Committee for Democracy in Greece, and Representative John Brademas, Democrat of Indiana.

* * *

October 4, 1971

BURTON ELICITS TIPS FROM TITO FOR FILM

By JAMES FERON
Special to The New York Times

DUBROVNIK, Yugoslavia—Once again German Stukas are wheeling and diving over the Sutjeska River gorge in southwestern Yugoslavia, their guns seeking groups of armed men scattering into the steep forests.

The planes are World War II relics, serving now in a Yugoslav film of the Battle of Sutjeska. The "partisans" are Yugoslav soldiers, part of a detachment of 5,000 camped on location for three months.

The gorge contains the graves of more than 3,000 partisans. It is where the main body of wartime irregulars under

Josip Broz—code-named Tito—fought out of a trap to regroup and become the nucleus of the postwar government.

"Sutjeska" as the film is to be called, is the second such partisan battle to go before cameras here. "The Battle of Neretva" appeared a few years ago. It was an unsophisticated, heroic production that one Yugoslav here described as a "sort of national anthem."

Long Hours With Tito

This one appears to be different. For one thing, the central figure in "Sutjeska" is President Tito. Political figures have rarely been portrayed on the screen in any depth while they are still alive.

Richard Burton, who plays Tito and who has spent long hours talking with the Yugoslav President to establish the role, said the film seemed unusually right from the start.

"It began earlier this year with a call from the Yugoslav Embassy in London saying the Ambassador wanted to see me," Mr. Burton said.

"I told them I was about to leave town, so two men—not the Ambassador, he couldn't make it—rushed over and showed me two photographs. One was of Tito as a partisan in 1943 and one was of me in uniform, in an Army film, I think it was 'Where Eagles Dare.' Someone had superimposed a cap on me and there was a striking resemblance.

" 'I see, you want me to play Tito', I said. They said that, indeed, that was their wish. I asked them about a script, but they had none. 'How about a treatment?' but they didn't have that either. When did they intend to start shooting? In three weeks, they said. In fact, they did have some material but it was all in Serbo-Croatian."

Mr. Burton served his guest a drink, poured tea for himself and returned to a couch in the comfortable lounge of his yacht, the Kalizma, moored in a small harbor near here. It has been where he and his wife, Elizabeth Taylor, have lived between the occasional days of filming at the remote mountainous site.

"Anyway, we communicated back and forth and they finally came up with a script," the actor went on. "But there was nothing for me to play. It was just Tito giving orders. He was just a puppet. It had been written equivocally, so that he could not possibly be offended.

"I happened to know quite a bit about Tito. He seemed a uniquely interesting person. For one thing, he fought and won his position himself. He was the only Eastern European leader not to have been placed in that position by Stalin."

Looked for Material

Mr. Burton said he began to look for more material.

"I read of the British military mission that was sent in at Sutjeska to determine if it was really Tito who was carrying the war to the Germans," he went on. "One of the men was F. W. Deakin, now a professor at Oxford, and he's written a book. I read that and discovered, for example, that Tito spent most of the war unarmed. He carried a pistol but never used it as far as anyone knows."

The Yugoslavs, meanwhile, were fashioning Tito's role out of extracts of his speeches.

"They were not producing anything of the man, possibly to avoid offending him," Mr. Burton said. "Finally, I asked Wolf Mankowitz if he would do the script. He did, and in 10 days he'd changed the form of the Tito role."

Mr. Burton warmed to his description of Tito: "I went to Brioni [President Tito's residence] with Elizabeth for three days. We talked from midday until we went to bed and it was fascinating. He speaks English slowly but very accurately.

"He was obviously very worried about the whole idea of the film. He's very modest about his achievements. He's also a very sensitive man and I think he was afraid of being embarrassed. I wrote to him later saying he must realize that he would have a final veto on any part he found unsuitable, but I don't think he'll use it. I think he has confidence in me now."

Mr. Burton said he asked President Tito many questions, for example, how much did he weigh at the time?

"He replied that 'while there were not many scales around' he guessed he weighed about 54 kilos [118 pounds]," the actor said. "That's quite slim. My normal weight is 180 pounds, so I stopped drinking. I'm now down to 163."

Mr. Burton, at 5 feet 10 inches, is three or four inches taller than President Tito. The actor now looks fairly gaunt.

Mr. Burton said the Yugoslavs asked his wife if she would like a role. "She could have played the part of a woman doctor, a partisan, who was badly wounded in that battle, had both legs amputated and died later," he said. "It's a nice part, but nobody would believe Elizabeth being a partisan."

"President Tito's wife was a partisan, a great fighter, I understand. You can see very quickly that underneath her charm there is a very strong woman. But she did not participate in that battle, and the Yugoslavs are remaining remarkably faithful to the facts."

Mr. Burton remembered another question his wife had asked President Tito. "They got on very well, you know," he said. "He likes pretty women, to begin with. Anyway, at one point she said she had noticed all the pictures of Tito showed him to be quite neat. 'You were quite a dandy,' she said.

"He replied to that yes, he was, but since the partisans wore no badges of rank 'I thought I would at least be well groomed.' She asked him if it was not unusual for a soldier to be without a stubble. He said he went only one day without shaving, and that was when he was wounded.

"That's another story, one we've included in the picture. It seems his dog, Lux, was terrified one day of the dive bombing. Tito held the dog to comfort him and at that moment a piece of shrapnel hit them, killing the dog and wounding Tito. He said he would have been hit in the chest or stomach if it had not been for his dog."

*   *   *

December 17, 1971

CROATIAN CAPITAL IS QUIET AFTER 4 NIGHTS OF RIOTS STIRRED BY NATIONALIST RESENTMENT AGAINST BELGRADE

By DAVID BINDER

Special to The New York Times

ZAGREB, Yugoslavia, Dec. 16—The downtown streets of this provincial capital were relatively quiet this evening for the first time this week, following four nights of violent demonstrations by Croatian nationalists, most of them young students.

The demonstrations, held at Zagreb's Square of the Republic on behalf of ousted Croatian liberal Communist leaders and jailed student militants, were crushed by riot police who put more than 170 persons behind bars.

The unrest was an outburst of national feeling that had been growing for months in this republic of 4.3 million.

According to knowledgeable Croatians and foreign observers, the nationalist wave was fed as much by resentment at economic discrimination emanating from the central Government in Belgrade as by the fanaticism of some old-fashioned Croatian intellectuals.

Condemned by Tito

President Tito stepped into the affair at the beginning of the month, just as Zagreb University's 30,000 students were ending a boycott of lectures. They were protesting the economic policies of Belgrade, which is also the capital of Croatia's larger ethnic rival to the southeast, Serbia.

At a special session of his party leadership, the 79-year-old President, who is a native of Croatia, condemned the regional chiefs in Zagreb for losing control.

Last weekend, the regional party leaders resigned under fire. Among those who stepped down were Mrs. Savka Dabcevic-Kucar, head of the Croatian party; the president of the executive bureau in Zagreb, Pero Pirker; and Zagreb's representative in the party's federal executive committee, Mika Tripalo. These and others who followed them into political limbo were considered among Yugoslavia's most intelligent and progressive politicians.

Their departure provoked the street riots.

Zagreb's students, with a dozen of their leaders already under arrest, stormed the Square of the Republic repeatedly, shouting slogans against the Belgrade Government and demanding a national referendum on the ethnic issue.

Some called for a Croatian national state, others for a Croatian seat in the United Nations General Assembly.

To federally minded citizens, it was an echo of old sentiments that ended in the establishment of a puppet Croatian state under the Nazi occupation.

Zagreb's hospitals have more than 30 patients with head injuries tonight because of the riots. Mr. Tripalo himself and several nationalistic Catholic priests are said to be under house arrest.

The economic motives of the Croatians concern Yugoslavia's hard-currency earnings. Statistics show that Croatia brings in a disproportionate 43 per cent of the country's hard currency, mostly through tourism on the Adriatic coast. Yet the central Government, in Belgrade, allots only 8 per cent of the hard-currency income to Croatia for reinvestment.

Yet the standard of living here is noticeably higher than in Serbia or other less-developed parts of the country.

The Croatian states' rights cause is as much cultural as economic. This was proved in the current crisis by the extremist behavior of numerous Croatian intellectuals.

Starting in September, the Croatian homeland organization, Matice Hrvatske, began publishing inflammatory patriotic calls in its widely read weekly, Hrvatski Tjednik, with headlines such as "Definition of a Croatian" and the words of the long frowned-upon Croatian hymn, "Our Lovely Homeland." The periodical is now banned and the homeland group leaders have retired.

"It is a tragedy," said a young Croatian businessman tonight. "Our best leaders were sacrificed to stupid student extremism. Those leaders, Mika and Savka, lost control and maybe that is the lesson—when you lose control of something progressive, it can be the opposite of progressive."

*   *   *

December 23, 1971

IS YUGOSLAVIA IN DANGER?

There was a time when speculation about Yugoslavia's future centered around the question whether a unified country could survive the passing of President Tito. But even though he is still very much alive, the survival of a unified Yugoslavia today is in more serious doubt than at any time since World War II.

The reason is that a series of dramatic events has just taken place in Croatia, where the past month has seen a major student strike, a purge of Croatian Communist party leaders, four nights of violent anti-Belgrade demonstrations in Zagreb, the capital of Croatia, and now the "resignation" of Croatia's Premier. Behind the trauma of these developments lies a reborn sense of Croatian nationalism and separatism that endangers not only Yugoslavia's future, but peace in the Balkans and in fact the balance of power in the Eastern Mediterranean.

In retrospect, the surprise is not that historic Croatian nationalism has exploded again, but rather that Tito managed to keep it under relatively tight control for the past quarter of a century. One reason is that Tito himself is a Croatian; another is that Tito and his colleagues have always been well aware of the sensitive nature of the nationalities issue in Yugoslavia, with its highly diverse population. Tito has therefore tried to follow a policy of making maximum concessions to demands for local autonomy.

What has now happened is that the growing nationalist desire for complete local control of Croatia's destiny and resources has sparked demands and expectations going far beyond what even the most liberal and sensitive government in Belgrade could grant. The real issue now is not the division of Croatia's foreign exchange resources, but whether Croatia will remain a part of a unified Yugoslavia. If Croatia goes, the danger exists that Yugoslavia would vanish and be replaced by a half-dozen mutually hostile ministates, each dependent on outside forces for its survival.

The most alarming aspect of the disturbing Yugoslav developments is evidence that has mounted during the past year that the Soviet Union may be working clandestinely to promote the break-up of Yugoslavia. Earlier in the year, Croatian émigrés in Western Europe suddenly called for an independent Croatia to be created under Soviet protection. They also hinted that in return for such help a future Croatian state would be willing to provide Moscow with strategic air and naval bases that could alter the whole military equilibrium along NATO's southern flank.

If Moscow is indeed playing the same divisive game in Yugoslavia that it has successfully encouraged for its own purposes in Pakistan and in many other countries around the globe, the consequences could be exceedingly dangerous for European and even for world peace. But Tito could fall into Moscow's trap if he emphasizes repression rather than political means to reknit the now-frayed ties between Zagreb and Belgrade.

* * *

September 6, 1972

TITO THREATENS 'HOSTILE' GROUPS

Party Members as Well as Dissidents Are Attacked

By RAYMOND H. ANDERSON
Special to The New York Times

BELGRADE, Yugoslavia, Sept. 5—Yugoslavia's late summer respite, when officialdom puts aside all but the most urgent problems and disappears for vacation, has ended abruptly with a stern warning by President Tito that Communist ranks must be purged and tightened to combat dissidents, nationalists and a new class of wealth and privilege.

Speaking to shipyard workers in Rijeka, President Tito stressed that prison awaited anyone who "persists in hostile activity."

The 80-year-old leader, looking fit and brisk on television, spoke out amid uneasiness over nationalist sentiments in the country's six republics, relentlessly rising prices and debate over economic development policies.

Pressures are mounting for a new wave of price increases this fall, and President Tito clearly had the shipyard workers' concern in mind when he denounced an "amassing of wealth" by some people in Yugoslavia.

"Even among Communists there are extremely wealthy people, whose wealth does not amount merely to tens or hundreds of millions, but even to billions of old dinars," President Tito declared. "That much cannot be earned. This is an expropriation of the results of other people's work."

Villa-Building Is Cited

"I am not against someone's building a house or weekend cottage if he works honestly," President Tito continued in his address yesterday. "But there are people who are building houses and villas in several places in Yugoslavia."

President Tito referred to old dinars, as many Yugoslavs still do seven years after the currency reform. A million old dinars equaled about $600, and a billion about $600,000.

A generally impressive economic reform in Yugoslavia has created a consumer society with an abundance of private cars and household appliances. But a trade union official, Mustafa Pljakic, complained this week that a third of the country's workers still earned less than 1,400 new dinars, or about $84, a month.

Economic issues, especially the price problem, are to come under intensive debate this fall when the federal assembly returns from vacation.

In his speech, President Tito put under a cloud those who have prospered most in recent years. Declaring that the fault lay with Communists, he said:

"We must undertake effective measures, investigate where such wealth is coming from and deprive these people of what does not belong to them. This must be done in favor of the community and above all of the working class."

Party Purge Suggested

President Tito also condemned middlemen, merchants and holders of funds in foreign banks who "cheat our community and discredit our system."

The Yugoslav leader voiced dissatisfaction with the performance of the League of Communists, as the one-million-member party is known here, and called for a purge.

"There are people whose place is not in the League of Communists, who often inconvenience us, and it would be better for them to leave on their own." President Tito said. "But if they do not want to go we will be obliged to remove them."

On the nationalism issue, which flared dangerously last winter in Croatia and has been followed by arrests and trials. President Tito accused the "class enemy, the enemy of socialism" and suggested that the dissidents were to be found mainly among intellectuals and the petit bourgeoisie.

President Tito warned: "You know what has been done in other countries. People have been killed and there has been imprisonment and all kinds of things. We do not want this, but, by God, if someone persists in hostile activity we will be obliged to isolate him somewhere. You know where people are isolated. There is no other solution."

He scorned speculation about a crisis in Yugoslavia after he died or stepped down. "What have I been doing with you if everything is to fall apart after the departure of one man?" he asked. "This would mean that I have done nothing."

The World War II Partisan commander called on the hundreds of thousands of Partisan veterans "to fight for the unity of Yugoslavia in the class struggle against nationalism, against the class enemy."

The speech was blunt about the challenges confronting Yugoslavia, but otherwise the Yugoslav leader seemed strikingly relaxed and in good humor during his visit to Rijeka. He was seen on television in lively conversation with officials and escorts, holding a king size cigar and frequently waving and smiling at spectators, who applauded ceaselessly.

*   *   *

September 16, 1972

HIJACKERS HOLD PLANE IN SWEDEN, FORCING THE RELEASE OF CROATIANS

By United Press International

MALMO, Sweden, Saturday, Sept. 16—Three gunmen advocating Croatian independence from Yugoslavia hijacked an airliner yesterday and won from Sweden a promise to release seven Croatian prisoners.

But complications developed after Premier Olof Palme announced that he had agreed to release the prisoners to save the 83 passengers and four crew members aboard the plane, a DC-9 of the Scandanavia Airlines System.

One of the seven prisoners apparently refused to join the hijackers, and a dispute developed over how the prisoners would be exchanged for the passengers. In the end it was decided that 36 of the passengers would be freed in exchange for three of the six prisoners as a first step.

After the first prisoners and passengers were exchanged however, the hijackers refused to release the other passengers until they received one million kroner, about $200,000, and until the fuel tanks of the plane were filled.

The hijackers said they would blow up the plane with everyone aboard if the prisoners were not released. Both prisoners and hijackers are from Croatia in northwestern Yugoslavia, where separatist groups have been demanding independence.

After the threat, Mr. Palme called a lengthy emergency meeting of the Cabinet after which he announced that he would free the prisoners. He ordered the seven prisoners taken to Bulltofta Airport in Malmö and turned over to the hijackers in return for the hostages.

A helicopter carrying one prisoner from Goteborg landed at 1:30 A.M. (8:30 P.M. Friday, New York time) only a few hundred yards from the hijacked airliner. Another helicopter touched down 10 minutes later with two prisoners and the four others arrived shortly afterwards aboard an air force DC-3 transport.

The prisoners were taken under heavy police escort into the airport building where the Minister of Justice, Lennart Geijer, said he would ask them if they wanted to be exchanged for the hostages.

There were 90 persons aboard the twin-engine airliner, including the three hijackers and a crew of four, when the pilot radioed he was being forced at pistol point to go to Malmö. The plane was on its way from Goteborg to Stockholm.

However, while negotiations were under way for the exchange, the hijackers released three sick passengers and a Navy physician, Dr. Torbjoern Burman. Not long afterward two more passengers—an elderly man and a middle-aged woman—were also allowed to leave the aircraft.

The man was taken away in an ambulance and the woman sped off in a police car.

The hijackers—identified only by their surnames as Simmic, Bajic and Braunco—negotiated over the plane's radio with Mr. Geijer, who had rushed to the airport's control tower when he heard of the incident.

The hijackers initially set a deadline of 1 A.M. today (8 P.M. Friday, New York time) for the release of the prisoners and the Government's decision came well before that. However, the actual exchange was not to take place before 4 A.M.

The prisoners were being held at separate jails for a variety of crimes. Two were convicted of murdering the Yugoslav Ambassador, Vladimir Rolovic, in Stockholm last year.

Mr. Palme said the most of the plane's passengers were Swedes.

The hijackers told Mr. Geijer they wanted to see the prisoners released and walk to the airliner. When they were safely aboard the hostages would be released, they said.

They did not say where they planned to fly with the prisoners.

The airport was completely darkened. All spotlights were switched off and only the shadows of the policemen moving on the outskirts of the field could be seen.

In the airport departure lounge from 500 to 1,000 people, mostly charter passengers waiting to take off for vacation sites in southern Europe, milled around in hushed silence.

Scores of police armed with submachineguns were posted in the hall.

The national police chief, Carl Persson, took personal charge of the operations. A spokesman for the National Police Board said an "emergency hijacking plan" had been put into operation.

The airliner had taken off from Goteborg at 4:35 P.M. It landed safely at Bulltofta and taxied to an airstrip far from the airport building. Policemen in bulletproof vests and carrying submachineguns ringed the aircraft but took no action.

"It's all quiet around the aircraft," an airport official said. "Nobody is moving and the passengers and the crew are held at gunpoint aboard."

There are about 60,000 Yugoslav workers in Sweden of whom 10,000 to 15,000 are from Croatia. Some are members of the Ustashi movement, which wants Croatian independence from Yugoslavia.

The three hijackers were reported to have demanded the release of Andelko Brajkovic and Miro Banecik, Ustashi members serving life terms for the murder of the Yugoslav ambassador.

They also wanted the release of three Yugoslavs who barricaded themselves in the Yugoslav consulate in Goteborg two years ago and threatened to kill four hostages.

* * *

September 17, 1972

YUGOSLAVIA BANS SERBIAN JOURNAL

Quarterly Criticized Jailing of 'Nationalist' Professor

By RAYMOND H. ANDERSON
Special to The New York Times

BELGRADE, Yugoslavia, Sept. 16—The Serbian Philosophic Society's quarterly journal, Filosofija, ordinarily does not stir much excitement when it appears in its full circulation of only 1,500 copies. But a court ban imposed on the latest issue, which was accused of "false and alarming statements," has aroused more than usual interest in the journal, assuring attentive reading of copies that have eluded the authorities.

The official objection to the issue, the second of this year, involved an editorial and article challenging the conviction and imprisonment of Yugoslavs accused of "hostile propaganda" and of attempts to "disrupt the brotherhood and unity of the Yugoslav nationalities."

In particular, Filosofija raised questions about the sentencing two months ago of Prof. Mihajlo Djuric of the Belgrade University Law School to two years in prison on a variety of charges, including opposition to a decentralization of authority under amendments to the federal constitution. The amendments strengthen the country's six republics against central control from Belgrade.

The focus of the indictment against Professor Djuric was that he was a "greater Serbian nationalist," disturbed by an apparent erosion of Serbian rights in the Yugoslav federation.

Another Journal Banned

In Croatia, where anti-Serbian nationalism persists, an issue of Praxis, the journal of the Croatian Philosophic Society also has been banned for articles critical of the sentencing of Professor Djuric.

The ban on Filosofija was imposed last Friday by Judge Ljubomir Radovic of the Belgrade district court, in response to a recommendation by the prosecutor's office. The judgment declared that the issue of Filosofija contained "assertions that might alarm citizens and endanger law and order."

A few weeks earlier, the same judge had declined to ban a book, "Whither and How Far," by Ljubomir Momcilovic, accused of seeking to foment Serbian hostility against Croats by dealing with atrocities by the Ustashi—Croatian Fascists—during World War II. However, the judge's ruling in favor of "Whither and How Far" was overturned by a higher court.

As part of the Yugoslav leadership's earnest endeavor to curb nationalist strife, the incitement of "national, racial or religious hatred or discord" is a criminal offense punishable by up to 12 years in prison.

Philosophers Offend Officials

Political philosophers occasionally offend the authorities when they ponder and debate the challenges of a society of differing peoples, languages and religions and that society's own interpretation of Marxism.

Last Sunday, President Tito had harsh words for some philosophers, warning that they should either "go on pension or find a new line of employment."

Speaking at Kozara, the site of an epic Partisan battle during World War II, Marshal Tito said: "I would not like to generalize criticism of professors because many of them work very well. Many old professors have worked and still work well, especially in certain fields like medicine, exact sciences and so forth. But in the faculties of philosophy they often are philosophizing in all possible ways. Our Marxist philosophy is not much used there."

In the philosophizing in Filosofija, the editorial that aroused anger warned that recent trials had "created a dark and troubled political scene" in Yugoslavia.

"Opinions cannot be put into prison," the editorial said and suggested that the wrong offenders were being tried, quoting the proverb, "They hang the doves and let the hawks fly free."

Swiss Article Reprinted

Besides the editorial, the prosecutor also objected to an article by Dxbrica Cosic, a wartime Partisan commissar, and the reprinting from the Swiss paper, Neuer Züricher Zeitung, of an article that dealt with the banning of Praxis in July over criticism of the sentencing of Professor Djuric.

Mr. Cosic, a novelist as well as polemical writer, deplored not only the imprisonment of Professor Djuric but also the sentencing of two Hungarian-Yugoslavs in the province of Vojvodina for "hostile propaganda," including criticism of the Yugoslav leadership and foreign policy.

"Is it possible," Mr. Cosic wrote, "that our society and state have no more dangerous enemies than student revolutionaries and utopians, who want for their country more freedom, social justice and equality, more socialism than exists today? Is it possible that these aspirations represent a danger to the power of the working people?"

In the case of Professor Djuric, Mr. Cosic noted that the principal charge against him had involved criticism of amendments under discussion to strengthen the power of the republics.

* * *

December 5, 1972

BELGRADE'S VIEW OF U.S. TV IS DIM

Popular 'Peyton Place' Is Going Off Air in Spring

By RAYMOND H. ANDERSON
Special to The New York Times

BELGRADE, Yugoslavia, Dec. 3—Are the melodramatic intrigues and scandals of rich and poor in Peyton Place, the small mill town in New England, subversive to a Marxist, working-class Yugoslavia?

Television program directors in Yugoslavia have concluded that they are, especially when the country's leadership is trying to tighten Marxist ideology in all walks of life.

As a result, the long-running television series "Peyton Place"—"Gradic Pejton" to its devoted Yugoslav fans—is to be suspended on Belgrade television next spring after a run of more than two years.

"Peyton Place" has come under criticism for fostering "petit-bourgeois values" among its viewers. At the same time, other American television programs, as well as films, are being subjected to hard-eyed scrutiny.

'Mod Squad' Draws Fire

Discontent has been expressed, for example, over "The Mod Squad," the TV series about Pete, Link and Julie, the youthful and unconventional California police officers.

One critic of "Peyton Place" has been Fedor Sheshun who has written tongue-in-cheek weekly commentaries on the series in Radio and TV Review.

Discussing, in mocking tones, the decision to suspend "Peyton Place," Mr. Sheshun asked rhetorically in the latest issue: "What will happen after this? What will the younger and older generations do in their free time?"

One thing they may do is watch an apparently more ideologically acceptable British series, "The Forsyte Saga," making its appearance this week.

Other substitutes include programs about the partisans of World War II and a Saturday-night quiz show with questions like "In what sector of the front did the first post-liberation Yugoslav Air Force squadron engage in combat in 1945?"

In an editorial approving the decision to drop "Peyton Place" next spring, Radio and TV Review commented:

"Incidentally, we are somewhat puzzled by the logic of the decision. If "Peyton Place" is an incubator for spreading petit-bourgeois values, would it not have been more logical to terminate it at once?"

Audiences and Ads

It might be more logical, but it might also be more provocative to the viewers, who are following the series intently now to learn whether Lee Weber indeed murdered Anne Howard, who is Rodney's real father, and where did Allison go after she disappeared from the Peyton Place hospital?

Watching "Peyton Place" has become nearly a ritual for many of Yugoslavia's television owners. On Sundays auto traffic dwindles near 6:20 P.M., the starting time of the hour-and-a-half show. Advertisers crowd the hour and a half with commercials for soft drinks, deodorants, furniture and other consumer products.

The coming demise of "Peyton Place" is only one aspect of a campaign against bourgeois influences. United States Army-type insignia, once popular with teenagers, has been removed from stores. Fashion designers are promoting youthful styles patterned on World War II partisan uniforms.

* * *

February 22, 1974

YUGOSLAVS ADOPT 4TH CONSTITUTION

'Self-Management' Stress is Viewed as Utopian

By MALCOLM W. BROWNE
Special to The New York Times

BELGRADE, Yugoslavia, Feb. 21—Yugoslavia today adopted a new socialist Constitution regarded by many foreign economists and diplomats as little short of utopian.

The theme of most of its 40,000 words is "self-management"—a philosophy evolved here with the aim of directly carrying out Marxist ideals.

Regional and national legislative bodies are expected to be made up of delegates selected by "basic organizations of associated labor." The latter also decide, among other things, what proportion of income each political-economic unit will spend for its members' wages and what proportion will be invested.

Much of the new Constitution, Yugoslavia's fourth since World War II, reads like a detailed labor-relations agreement in which even working hours and vacations are specified (no more than 42 hours a week, with at least 18 days' vacation a year).

Booming cannons, wailing sirens and loudspeakers announced the new Constitution's advent to the people of Belgrade and the regional capitals. The city was festooned with flags.

The Constitution, which was adopted by the Federal Assembly, the national parliament, is similar to a draft published last June by the newspaper Borba, official Communist organ. Since then several deep disagreements in party thinking have been discernible.

Two-Chamber Assembly

One of the principal ones has centered on how much power central Communist organizations should retain over national life. A particularly visible part of the dispute has had to do with artists and writers, who have recently been under pressure to conform to socialist ideas.

The Federal Assembly also passed a new election law in keeping with the Constitution. The legislative system is to be changed, with Assembly elections to be completed before May 15, when the new Assembly will convene.

It will consist of two chambers instead of the present five. One to be elected directly, will consist of 30 delegates from each of the six republics and 20 from each of the two autonomous provinces. The other chamber will be chosen by the regional assemblies, which must also be elected.

The legislative representatives are expected to reach the federal chamber after having risen through a system of subordinate assemblies composed of delegates from the basic labor units.

Yugoslav law does not stipulate that candidates must be Communists, but in fact the League of Communists dominates political life and has said it will not permit Western-style parties.

No Return to Centralism

The main impetus toward the new Constitution has presumably emanated from President Tito, who has for some time been dissatisfied with the evident deterioration of party hegemony and with "liberalist" economic and political tendencies.

Part of this stems from the market economy, which comes closer to the Western free-market pattern than to anything in the Communist world. This has led President Tito and others to become suspicious of "consumerism" and other potentially antisocialist effects.

The President and his aides have said they do not want Yugoslavia pointed back toward the harsh centralism associated with Stalinism, but at the same time they want a general tightening up, particularly in light of the President's age.

Marshal Tito, who is 81 years old, will remain in office for life, but upon his passing, under the new Constitution, the presidency will be rotated among the nine members of the new Presidential Council.

Foreign economists have expressed skepticism that the self-management system will work if too rigorously applied. They suggest that the Constitution, taken literally, would mean that many effective administrators and technicians would have to step aside in favor of direct worker authority.

"But the Yugoslavs are pragmatic people, and no one here would like to see the country become a business failure," one of the economists said. "Socialism and practical business will just find a new balance, that's all."

Two luminaries from Latin America—Maj. Raul Castro, brother of the Cuban Premier, and Carlos Altamirano, exiled First Secretary of the Chilean Socialist party, attended a ceremony in the Federal Assembly.

*   *   *

June 15, 1974

IN A CYPRUS VILLAGE, AMITY AND ANTIPATHY

By STEVEN V. ROBERTS
Special to The New York Times

APHANIA, Cyprus—When the Greek Cypriotes of Aphania were boys, they used to go to the Turkish coffee house and watch the shadow plays. Now, when night comes, armed guards patrol the Turkish quarter. The boys do not go to the plays any more.

The Talk of Cyprus

This is one of the ways that life has changed in this farming village of about a thousand people, two-thirds of whom are ethnic Greek and one–third ethnic Turkish. Fighting erupted between the two groups all over Cyprus in 1964, and for 10 years the resentments have continued to smolder, like a forest fire that is contained but never extinguished.

In many mixed villages the ethnic Turks fled when the fighting started, leaving homes and belongings. They stayed in Aphania partly because the United Nations peacekeeping force cooled things down and partly because the two communities have always gotten along fairly well here.

In Nicosia, the capital, the communities are sharply polarized, prisoners of their own rhetoric and rigid public positions. In Aphania, on a personal level, some of the ties between the two groups remain intact, but others have snapped, frayed by a decade of fear, bigotry and propaganda.

Standing 12 miles east of Nicosia across the plains of central Cyprus, Aphania is a mixture of old and new. Grain is harvested by a modern combine but stored in big golden heaps in the center of town. Structures of dried mud and straw are gradually being replaced by brick and concrete.

On the main street a double house is rising—a dowry for two sisters who are not yet married.

Myrophora Papanastasi, wife of the town's retired Orthodox priest, sat on her porch, two grandchildren at her feet. Mrs. Papanastasi, a tiny, bright-eyed woman dressed in traditional black, is 70 years old, but her gnarled fingers nimbly wove a rug from scraps of cloth as she talked with a visitor.

"Whenever there was a Greek wedding," she recalled, as her son translated, "you'd see the Turkish girls come to our church, and we used to go to their weddings to see their customs. You didn't have invitation cards. The relatives of the bride and groom would go to the houses and give out candles—that amounted to an invitation."

Today there are few invitations. "Only if they are people you have known all your life, when their children get married, you get one," she said.

A Turkish Cypriote shepherd drives his flock past the door of the Papanastasi house every day and grazes it in the family's fields beyond. In return he gives milk and cheese. It has been that way for years.

But most relations between the two communities are limited to the unavoidable, and as in most of Cyprus—where the

Greeks are 80 per cent of the population of almost 700,000—Greeks tend to dominate. The Turks buy food at the Greek store, work for Greek farmers and pay their water bills through the Greek Muktar, or Mayor.

The Muktar, Panayotis Afantitis, brushed some wheat chaff from his shirt as he joined the conversation on the porch. The problem, he said, is that "outsiders" are stirring up the Turkish Cypriotes, urging them to post armed guards and fear their Greek neighbors.

"We know that the Turks of Aphania are good fellows—if they weren't we wouldn't cooperate with them," said the Muktar, his gold teeth flashing. "I am convinced that if the Turks are left alone, they can live together with Greeks."

Across the road, in the Turkish sector, the houses seem a bit older, the clothes a bit shabbier. The Greek Muktar drives a truck; the Turkish Muktar rides a bicycle.

The schoolmaster, Kenan Kani, sat in the classroom where he is the only teacher for 42 students. Schools, like religion—Eastern Orthodox and Islam—have always been separate in Cyprus, but today they seem to reinforce the divisions on the island. On the wall was a huge map of Turkey and numerous pictures of Kemal Ataturk, the Turkish national hero. It was hard to find anything about Cyprus.

Mr. Kani, who appeared to be in his early thirties, has taught here for three years but has never talked with an ethnic Greek. "They live on their side and we live on ours," he explained.

Just recently, he said, a Turkish farmer was stopped by a Greek policeman and ordered to pay a debt owed by the man's son or go to jail.

"The Turkish are sleeping tonight," said Mr. Kani in halting English, "but they don't know, day after day, because they are afraid. All the Government, all the police, all the soldiers—they're all together. They want to kill all Turks."

Asked about the attitudes of his students, he replied: "Every day the children are listening to the radio, reading the newspapers, and they are thinking. What is our future? As a Turk you are not sure in your life."

Down the dirt street, at the Turkish coffee house, several men sipped bottles of an American soft drink called Bubble-Up and talked about Government money for drought relief. The Greek Cypriotes got their share last year, they complained, but the Turks have just started to receive theirs.

"The Turks and Greeks are not friends and never will be friends," snapped a young farmer, Hassan Halil. "When you fall down, the Greek will put his foot on your neck."

The Turks came to Cyprus as conquerors and ruled the Greeks for 300 years. The ancient animosities run deep, kept alive by an unyielding spirit of vendetta. Incidents that took place 15 years ago are recalled in vivid detail and with emotion.

"We meet and talk like friends," explained Mrs. Papanastasi, "but they belong to one nationality and we belong to another. You can't trust them completely."

Cyprus was never a garden of brotherly love, but, if anything, the situation is deteriorating. The Greeks say the Turks are teaching their children to be fanatics, and the Turks say the Greeks are preaching domination.

* * *

July 16, 1974

ARMY TAKES OVER CYPRUS IN A COUP LED BY GREEKS; MAKARIOS'S FATE IN DOUBT

SUCCESSOR NAMED

U.N. Reports Meeting of Archbishop and British Officer

By LAWRENCE VAN GELDER

Cypriote troops led by Greek Army officers overthrew the Government of Cyprus yesterday.

There were conflicting reports of the fate of Archbishop Makarios, the 60-year-old President. According to dispatches early in the day, the Archbishop was killed in the coup, but later reports indicated that he might have taken refuge.

A broadcast in what was purported to be the voice of the President was monitored in Israel.

At the United Nations last night, a spokesman reported that Archbishop Makarios had met earlier in the day with a British district commander from the United Nations' peacekeeping force. The spokesman added that the Archbishop had requested a meeting today with Secretary General Waldheim's special representative on Cyprus.

Tanks Used in Capital

The rebels named as President Makarios's successor Nikos Giorgiades Sampson, a 38-year-old Greek Cypriote newspaper publisher and one-time terrorist. Cyprus, off the coast of Turkey, has been plagued by communal friction between the island's Greek majority and its Turkish minority.

Tanks, machine guns and explosives were used in Nicosia, the capital, according to news agency dispatches. Fighting was also reported in Limassol, the republic's second largest city, as well as in the towns of Larnaca and Famagusta.

Rebel forces, apparently opposed chiefly by members of the police tactical reserve, seized the broadcasting system. International communications channels were severed and the airport at Nicosia was closed

Foreign embassies appealed to their nationals to remain indoors. There were no immediate reports of death or injury among foreign tourists or residents.

Roads Are Jammed

Last night, sporadic gunfire still crackled through Nicosia. Ambulances raced through nearly deserted streets, and hundreds of motorists jammed roads outside the capital as they waited for the fighting to end. In Larnaca and Famagusta, the tactical police were reported to have surrendered.

Archbishop Makarios   Nikos Giorgiades Sampson

The New York Times/July 16, 1974

Government in Nicosia (1) was reported overthrown, and President was said to be alive in broadcast from Paphos (2). Turkish Premier, in Afyon (3), expressed worry. In Athens (4) diplomats feared consequences. Fighting was reported in towns with names underlined.

A pooled dispatch from news agency correspondents in Nicosia said Pantazis Pandelakis, head of the tactical police force, broadcast an appeal last night, urging his men to yield and to support the new president.

In the uprising, which began yesterday morning, the Cypriote army, known as the National Guard and numbering about 10,000, was led by about 650 Greek officers brought to Cyprus as training instructors. At one point, the Presidential palace was reported to be ablaze and surrounded by 10 tanks.

The United Nations peace-keeping force, of 2,329 soldiers, has been assigned to prevent civil strife in Cyprus since 1964. Reports last night said that these soldiers were not involved in the current fighting.

Although a rebel broadcast declared the uprising to be "strictly an internal affair," there were reports that both Greece and Turkey, which long have had special interests in the island, had alerted their armed forces.

The island lies 40 miles off the Turkish coast and 500 miles from the Greek mainland. Greek Cypriotes compose about 80 per cent, or 520,000 of the population, and Turkish Cypriotes about 18 per cent, or 117,000.

Enosis Long a Factor

"Enosis," the drive for union with Greece, has long been a factor in Cypriote politics. It was the rallying point for Greek Cypriote guerrillas who fought against British rule from 1955 to 1959. The island became an independent republic in 1960.

In 1959, Archbishop Makarios, head of the Cypriote Orthodox Church, was elected President of the future republic, and although he had once been in the forefront of the fight for enosis, he eventually settled for independence, a decision in which Turkish Government resistance was a factor.

At a Greek-Turkish conference in Zurich, Switzerland, in 1959, the two countries agreed on a prohibition of a total or partial union of Cyprus with any other country or the partition of Cyprus into two independent states. That agreement is incorporated into treaties among Cyprus, Greece, Turkey and Britain.

In London yesterday, the British Government called the latest events on Cyprus "potentially explosive" and urged Greece and Turkey to exercise restraint.

British in Consultations

In an address to the House of Commons, James Callaghan, the Foreign Secretary, said Britain had begun to implement treaty provisions calling for consultation among Britain, Greece and Turkey.

There was little reaction from the Greek Government, but diplomats in Athens were deeply concerned about Soviet reaction, the possibility of intervention by Turkey and the effect on the North Atlantic Treaty Organization of possible conflict between Greece and Turkey. Both Greece and Turkey are members.

Earlier this month Makarios, in a letter to President Phaidon Gizikis of Greece, asked for the recall of the 650 Greek officers assigned to the Cypriote National Guard.

President Makarios said the officers were aiding EOKA-B, an organization dedicated to overthrowing his Government and unifying Cyprus with Greece. The initials EOKA stand for National Organization for the Struggle of Freedom of Cyprus.

Archbishop Makarios, who had been a member of the original EOKA organization that fought against British colonial rule, mounted a campaign against it. There were reports that the start of the rebellion had been preceded by a police crackdown on suspected EOKA members and that more than 200 suspects had been held.

Mr. Sampson, who was reported named President yesterday, was a leading member of EOKA during its campaigns against the British. He adopted the name Sampson as a guerrilla name and later kept it as his family name.

A radio broadcast monitored in Rhodes said he had been sworn in by Biship Gennadios, who had been appointed to succeed Archbishop Makarios as the island's Orthodox primate.

Bishop Gennadios of Paphos last year accused the Archbishop of forsaking the cause of union with Greece for the more worldly advantages of the presidency. When the President refused to resign, Bishop Gennadios joined with two other bishops in ruling him unfrocked and reduced to the status of layman.

Although Mr. Sampson's newspapers favor union with Greece, he was reported to have said in a Nicosia radio broadcast yesterday. "Cyprus will continue to be independent and will respect the rights of other states."

Communal Talks Pledged

The rebels broadcast a communiqué pledging "the restoration of unity and peace to Cypriote Hellenism," intercommunal talks with the Turkish minority and free elections within a year.

The communiqué said President Makarios had been killed. But a radio station identifying itself as the Voice of Free Cyprus in the town of Paphos said the Archbishop was alive "and is the only President of Cyprus."

From Tel Aviv came a report that a voice purported to be that of President Makarios was later heard on the Paphos station, assuring the people of Cyprus that he was alive.

"I was the target for the Athens military junta," the President was quoted as having said. "But they have failed. The military coup by the junta will not succeed. The only thing they have managed to achieve so far was to take over the Cyprus Broadcasting Corporation."

The broadcast went on: "They have decided to destroy Cyprus and its people. But they will not succeed. They will have to face the determination of the people of Cyprus to resist and to fight."

The voice, said to quiver with emotion, concluded: "Together we will carry on the sacred resistance and win freedom. Long live freedom. Long live Cyprus."

According to The Associated Press, Dinos Moushoutas, the Cypriote consul general here, said he had heard a recording of the broadcast and was certain the voice was that of the President.

*   *   *

July 16, 1974

ATHENS JUNTA WAS OPEN IN DISLIKE OF ARCHBISHOP

By STEVEN V. ROBERTS
Special to The New York Times
ATHENS, July 15—The immediate chain of events that led to the coup in Cyprus today probably goes back to last November, when President George Papadopoulos of Greece was ousted by a group of military officers.

The new rulers in Athens—rigid nationalists and strong anti-Communists—did not hide their dislike of Archbishop Makarios, the President of Cyprus since independence in 1960.

The Archbishop always maintained that he shared the traditional desire of Greek Cypriotes for enosis, or union with the Greek motherland, but insisted that it was not a practical solution in the face of fierce opposition from ethnic Turks, who make up 18 per cent of the island's population of 650,000.

This attitude by the Archbishop smacked of treason to some right-wing Greek Cypriotes, who also worried about the President's close ties with Cyprus's large and influential Communist party.

This spring, Archbishop Makarios accused the Cypriote National Guard, which is commanded by 650 Greek officers on contract, of supplying arms and inspiration to a terrorist group fighting for enosis. Two weeks ago, the Archbishop ordered the removal of the officers from the island, a direct challenge to Greek authority in Cypriote affairs.

Greek-speaking people have lived on Cyprus for thousands of years. Because of the island's strategic position in the eastern Mediterranean, it was invaded by a number of conquerors who built an occasional castle, added a new accent to the ethnic strain of the populace, and passed on.

Cyprus was seized by the Turks in 1571 and incorporated into the Ottoman Empire. During more than 300 years of Turkish rule, the Orthodox Archbishop of Cyprus, the "Ethnarch," served as both the spiritual and temporal leader of the Greek Cypriotes.

Through the centuries the church kept alive the idea of enosis, and in 1821, the Archbishop and many leading churchmen were executed by the Turks for their activities. As Lawrence Durrell commented in his book "Bitter Lemons," "From this one could see just how deeply hidden, and in what depths of unconscious historical process, the roots of enosis lay hidden."

Or as one Cypriote official put it: "This island has lived for centuries with one dream—to unite with Greece."

The British leased the island in 1878 and incorporated it into the Commonwealth in 1925. In the nineteen-fifties, agitation for enosis erupted in a campaign of guerrilla warfare. The organization was called EOKA, and its leader was Gen. George Grivas, a Greek Cypriote and legendary guerrilla fighter from the days of the Greek civil war who commanded great loyalty among his countrymen.

Archbishop Makarios had been exiled by the British in 1956, but was allowed to return in 1959 as a hero. With the Turks opposing enosis, the Archbishop agreed to what has been called a "shotgun marriage"—Greek and Turkish Cypriotes joining in an independent state with the Archbishop as President.

When trouble broke out between the two communities in 1963, President Makarios invited in a contingent of Greek officers to command the National Guard, including General

Grivas. A United Nations peace-keeping force arrived in 1964, and controlled the fighting until 1967, when it flared again.

Enosis: 'A Feeling'

The Archbishop and his Government continued to proclaim their belief in enosis, as Cypriote independence took hold, but their commitment was clearly diminishing. As one official put it recently: "The idea of enosis is a feeling, it's nothing more than that. Everybody believes it cannot be achieved. We're better off being independent, but we can't say it publicly. Enosis is part of our tradition."

To those who believed in enosis, in the "megali idea," or "great idea" of a new Hellenic empire ruled from Athens, President Makarios was a traitor. In 1971 General Grivas slipped back into Cyprus and formed EOKA-B.

Several assassination attempts against the Archbishop failed, but EOKA was a continuing annoyance. Then in January General Grivas died of a heart attack, and President Makarios saw his chance to eradicate the movement. He offered amnesty to any EOKA member who would surrender and lay down his arms, but only several dozen agreed.

Meanwhile, anti-Makarios agitation was growing within the National Guard and its Greek officer corps. The strongman of the Greek junta that took over in November, Brig. Gen. Demetrios Ioannides, served in Cyprus in the nineteen-sixties and was known to despise the Archbishop.

As a virulent anti-Communist, General Ioannides was particularly upset with the Archbishop's alliance with the Cypriote Communists, his independent foreign policy and his frequent trips to Communist capitals.

Matters came to a head this spring. The Archbishop felt that some cadets appointed to officers' training school in the National Guard were disloyal to him. He demanded that the appointments be withdrawn, but Greek officers refused.

A large cache of arms was stolen from a National Guard training center, and the Archbishop declared that the theft had been engineered by Greek officers to supply EOKA-B. When the police started rounding up guerrillas and recovering the arms, the terrorist group replied with a week of violence last month that left six people dead—mainly well-known supporters of the Archbishop.

National Service Cut

President Makarios decided to move more firmly. He announced that the term of national service would be cut from 24 to 14 months, thus reducing reliance on Greek officers. And in a blunt letter to the Greek President, Lieut. Gen. Phaidon Gizikis, he requested that the officers be withdrawn.

In that letter, the Archbishop charged that the Greek Government, "has been following a policy calculated to abolish the Cyprus state." He said Greece had tried to turn the National Guard into "an internal occupation army."

"The root of the evil is very deep, reaching as far as Athens," Archbishop Makarios wrote to General Gizikis. "It is from there that the tree of evil, the bitter fruits of which the Greek Cypriote people are tasting today, is being fed and maintained and helped to grow and spread."

Suddenly Athens blossomed with posters and leaflets, calling the Archbishop a "power-hungry monk" who had committed "treason against the Greek nation." Such posters could not have appeared without official sanction.

To many diplomats Archbishop Makarios was the linchpin of Cyprus, the one man who could keep the troubled nation together. They have worried for a long time that the fanatical right-wingers would gamble on chaos.

"What I'm afraid of," one diplomat said a few weeks ago, "is the assassination of Makarios. They might just try to create an inferno, out of which they think they'll get their way."

*   *   *

July 16, 1974

TURKS SAY THEY WON'T ACCEPT ANY 'FAIT ACCOMPLI' ON CYPRUS

Special to The New York Times

ANKARA, Turkey, July 15—Turkish Government officials warned today that they would not "accept and fait accompli" on Cyprus and expressed concern for the Turkish community there.

Premier Bulent Ecevit, who had set out on a tour of provinces where opium poppies are cultivated, cut short his visit to return to the capital. After a three-and-a-half-hour emergency session of Turkey's National Security Council, Mr. Ecevit said that the council had no doubt that the coup constituted intervention in Cyprus by the Greek Government.

United Press International

On way to emergency cabinet session in Ankara, Turkey, from left: Premier Bulent Ecevit; Interior Minister Oguzhan Asilturk, rear; Gen. Semih Sancar, Chief of the General Staff, and Hasan Esat Isik, Defense Minister. Men at right are unidentified.

Before he returned to the capital, he interrupted a speech he was making in the province of Afyon to tell a gathering of about 5,000 poppy farmers of "the murder of Makarios."

It had been reported during the day that Presidential Makarios of Cyprus had been killed in a military take-over of his Government. "I am worried about this bloody coup on Cyprus," the Premier said, adding to journalists who went on the tour with him, "Every military measure has been taken."

"Interference with the rights of our brethren on Cyprus and any fait accompli there cannot be accepted," he said. He had gone on the tour to explain to poppy farmers and foreign journalists alike the decision of his Government to allow resumption of opium-poppy cultivation, despite the wishes of the United States.

In Istanbul, the Chief of the General Staff, Gen. Semih Sancar, told reporters that he had expected "such developments on the island" and hinted that the Turkish armed forces had been put in a state of "readiness."

And here in Ankara Defense Minister Hasan Esat Isik called in the British and United States charges d'affaires to say that Turkey would not "accept any fait accompli" on the troubled island.

"Turkey," Mr. Isik said, "will not allow violation of the Geneva agreement" covering the Turkish community on Cyprus.

"Although it is reported that the intervention on the island is the affair of the Greek community," Mr. Isik said, "the Cyprus question also has international aspects. The welfare of the Turkish community on the island is protected by international agreements. Therefore any infringement in any form of the Turkish community's rights cannot be tolerated by Turkey."

In answer to a question, he said that Turkey had a right to intervene in Cyprus under the "agreement of guarantee" signed in 1959.

*   *   *

July 20, 1974

TURKEY LANDS AN ARMED FORCE IN CYPRUS; DROPS PARATROOPERS INTO NICOSIA SECTOR

CLASHES REPORTED

Capital's Airport and Northern Port Are Bombed

By NAN ROBERTSON
Special to The New York Times

ANKARA, Turkey, Saturday, July 20—Premier Bulent Ecevit announced today that Turkey had invaded Cyprus by sea and air.

The attack came after intensive diplomatic activity involving officials of Turkey, Britain and the United States had broken down. The crisis grew out of the overthrow Monday of the elected Cypriote Government of Archbishop Makarios by the Greek-officered Cypriote National Guard.

The Turkish Premier, his voice trembling with emotion, announced the invasion after meeting with Under Secretary of State Joseph Sisco of the United States at 2 A.M. today Ankara time (7 P.M., Friday, New York time). Mr. Sisco had flown here from Athens last night to try to avert war.

Bombing Reported

[Turkish forces strafed and bombed the northern port of Kyrenia and dropped paratroopers into Turkish-Cypriote areas near Nicosia, the capital, Reuters reported.

[Turkish planes bombed Nicosia airport and a Cypriote National Guard camp south of the capital. Other Turkish jets dropped bombs and rockets on a camp of the small Greek army contingent in Cyprus on the western side of Nicosia.

[Machine-gun fire and explosions were heard from many directions around the capital, and Turkish Air Force planes flew overhead.

[The Cyprus radio broadcast an appeal to all Greek Cypriotes with weapons to resist the Turkish invaders, and the Turkish Cypriote radio said that a Greek Cypriote gunboat had been sunk off Kyrenia.

[In San Clemente, Calif, President Nixon conferred late last night with Secretary of State Kissinger as soon as he received news that Turkish troops had landed in Cyprus, Reuters reported. The Presidential press secretary, Ronald L. Ziegler, said that "we are following the situation" but made no other comment.]

[The Pentagon ordered the United States carrier Forrestal and other naval vessels toward Cyprus in case American citizens in the area needed to be evacuated, The Associated Press reported.]

Premier Ecevit said that the decision to intervene in Cyprus was made at a 30-minute cabinet meeting just before dawn. Mr. Ecevit told reporters: "I hope this action of ours will be good for humanity, the nation and all of Cyprus. We hope we will not be confronted there with any resistance, and we hope it will not turn into a bloody war."

U. S. Urged Negotiations

Mr. Sisco and Mr. Ecevit conferred for about two hours. A high Turkish Government official who attended the meeting said that the Under Secretary had proposed the continuation of negotiations about the status of the Island. Archbishop Makarios was overthrown and fled Cyprus after the coup by fervent supporters of Union of Cyprus with Greece.

The official said that the Premier had replied that Turkey did not have the time for prolonged negotiations. Turkey, with Greece and Britain, is a signatory and guarantor of a 1960 treaty that established Cyprus as an independent republic.

Mr. Ecevit had been under intense pressure from the Parliament and the Turkish press to invade Cyprus.

'We Were Forced'

He said outside his office this morning that "We were forced to make this decision" after Turkey had explored all the diplomatic means to solve the crisis.

In a statement broadcast by the Turkish radio at 6:30 A.M. Ankara time, the Premier said: "I am obliged to express my gratitude to all of our friends and allies, especially the United States and Britain, with whom we had close consultation. If these efforts gave no results certainly the responsible ones are not those states, who expressed good will and much effort."

Immediately after Mr. Ecevit's statement the state radio network began playing martial music. Almost simultaneously the leader of the Turkish Cypriot minority on the island went on the air to announce the invasion. His speech was heard in Turkey.

30 Ships Sent Out

The size of the invading forces was not known. But about 30 ships, mostly landing barges, left the Turkish port of Mersin, about 75 miles from Cyprus, yesterday.

Since 1967, during another crisis between Greece and Turkey over Cyprus, a division of 20,000 troops trained for amphibious landings has been based between Mersin and Iskenderun. Military experts estimated that the Turkish concentration in the area may have reached from 25,000 to 30,000 troops recently.

Martial Law Declared

Martial law was declared in coastal areas of Turkey: which include the cities of Adana, Izmir and Istanbul. It was also imposed here in the island capital city of Ankara, and in the region of Thrace, where Turkish and Greek troops have been massed on their common border.

This country, like Greece is a member of the North Atlantic Alliance, and Turkey is one of the alliance's most important members because of her location and the number of men under arms—about 400,000.

The vanguard of the Turkish force reportedly landed troops and tanks near Kyrenia on the northern coast of Cyprus. The Turkish Cypriote community radio broadcast was the first news here of the landing.

Twice in the last decade, in 1964 and 1967, Turkey and Greece have been on the verge of war over Cyprus, and troops have been placed on alert.

As of last night, high officials of the Ankara Government and informed diplomatic sources were saying that the situation was extremely volatile here and that they did not know from moment to moment which way Turkey would go.

Landings Reported

NICOSIA, Cyprus, July 20 (Reuters)—The British forces' broadcasting service here said that Turkish troops were landing around the northern port of Kyrenia.

At the same time planes of the Turkish Air Force flew over Nicsosia, the capital, and scattered shooting was reported breaking out around the city

Most of the activity appeared to center on the line that separates the Greek Cypriote majority from the Turkish Cypriote minority.

United Press International

Premier Bulent Ecevit announcing invasion in Ankara.

Sources in the city said most of the firing appeared to come from the Turkish side of the line.

In addition to the troops landing at Kyrenia. Turkish landing vessels were also reported off the city of Lapithos, just east of the location of the initial attack, and other vessels were reported to the west.

Turkish Statement

ANKARA, Turkey, Saturday, July 20 (AP)—Following is the text of the announcement by Premier Bulent Ecevit that Turkish military forces had begun landing in Cyprus early today:

The Turkish armed forces have begun landing in Cyprus from air and sea. May God render this undertaking beneficial for our nation, for all Cypriots and all of humanity. We believe we shall thus be doing a service of peace for humanity. I hope that there will be no shooting at our forces resulting in a bloody confrontation.

We are not going for war but to bring peace to the island, not only to the Turks but to the Greeks as well. We arrived at this decision under necessity after trying all political and diplomatic ways. I consider it best to express my gratitude to all allied, and friendly countries, especially to Britain and the United States, with which we recently had consultations, for their well-intentioned efforts to find a solution to the problem through diplomatic channels without resort to intervention.

Of course the burden of the failure of a diplomatic solution lies elsewhere, not with these well-intentioned countries. Once more I wish that this undertaking be beneficial to humanity, to our nation and to the Cypriotes. May God protect our from disasters.

*   *   *

July 24, 1974

GREEK MILITARY BIDS CIVILIANS TAKE OVER; CARAMANLIS RETURNS, IS SWORN AS PREMIER; REBEL WHO DEPOSED MAKARIOS IS REPLACED

JUNTA'S RULE ENDS

Ex-Premier to Head a Government of National Unity

By ALVIN SHUSTER
Special to The New York Times

ATHENS, Wednesday, July 24—The military rulers of Greece announced yesterday that they had decided to turn the nation back to civilian political leaders.

Constantine Caramanlis, the former conservative Premier who governed from 1955 to 1963 before his self-imposed exile in Paris, returned to Athens and was sworn in as head of a new government of national unity.

The announcement, which apparently meant the end of seven years of military dictatorship, touched off a wave of jubilation and cheering. Thousands of people gathered in Constitution Square and shouted "Tonight fascism dies!" and "No more blood!"

Thousands Line Streets

Thousands lined the streets, shouted and threw flowers as Mr. Caramanlis's limousine traveled from the Airport to the Parliament building.

"I am here to contribute with all my forces for the return of the country to normalcy," he said. "The Greek people are gifted people with many qualities."

[Washington reacted warily to the events in Athens, welcoming the apparent return to constitutional processes but noting that the civilians called in represented all shades of political opinion, including the left. In London, former King Constantine called on Prime Minister Harold Wilson.]

The junta's decision, a direct result of the Cyprus crisis, was announced after the military rulers had called former civilian leaders to a meeting and told them to take over the government.

At 7 P.M. yesterday the radio announced that "the armed forces have decided to turn over the government of the country to a political government."

The meeting was presided over by President Phaidon Gizikis, who led a coup in November against another group of officers. He pledged to keep the military in the background and allow the civilian politicians to govern.

United Press International

Constantine Caramanlis, right, arriving in Athens today.

Among those called to the meeting were political leaders who had been arrested, exiled and jailed under military rule.

Premier Present

They included Panayotis Caneliopoulos, the Premier over thrown by the 1967 military coup, and George Mavros, who was deported to a barren island last March for three months as an alleged national security risk.

President Gizikis and the commanders of the army, navy and air force, told the politicians that the military would return to barracks. They asked the civilian leaders to set aside their differences and form a new government to lead the country out of its economic and political problems.

One politician said Brig. Gen. Demetrios Ioannides, the strongman of the junta, would be ousted. There was no word of his whereabouts or his role in the decision.

Press Censorship Dropped

One result of the military abdication was the elimination of press censorship. One newspaper, Vradyni, which had been closed seven months for publishing too freely, appeared on the street with a large photograph of Mr. Caramanlis. The headline was: "He Is Coming."

The military rulers clearly had come to the conclusion that the problems of Greece were growing too momentous for them to handle. The crisis over Cyprus, which brought Greece close to war with Turkey, was regarded as a disaster, and economic problems nagged.

There was a dearth of talent within the civilian government backed by the military because of the refusal of many Greeks to take posts in a dictatorship. The last Premier, who resigned today, was Adamantios Androutsopoulos.

Rarely had a national mood shifted so suddenly.

There was gloom when a Greek-led coup against President Makarios of Cyprus led to a Turkish invasion of the island.

Athenians parading in the street yesterday after military rulers announced a return to civilian leadership.

Greece mobilized, and thousands of young men marched off for military duty amid worry over war with the North Atlantic Treaty allies.

Even the cease-fire agreement in Cyprus left the nation anxious. And, with the prospect of crucial talks later this week on the future of Cyprus and its ethnic Greek and Turkish communities, the government found itself without the ability to cope with a crisis.

"For the first time we can thank the Turks for something," said one young man in a huge crowd last night.

The decision to give up the reins of government was a sudden shift from the rhetoric of the last seven years in which the military pledged not to give up power until the "transformation of Greek society," condemned the old politicians for mishandling the nation's affairs and made vague promises to move toward democracy.

First came the military rule of George Papadopoulos, who led the coup in 1967. Then, last November, came the present government by a group of men unknown to the public, apparently directed by General Ioannides.

King Constantine, who attempted a countercoup in December, 1967, fled Greece, and in June, 1973, the junta abolished the monarchy and proclaimed a republic.

The future political system remained one of the unanswered questions today. The former King has kept in contact with the civilian politicians who are again assembling here.

Another question was how active the military would be in the background. President Gizikis plans to remain as President for an indefinite time by agreement with the civilian leaders.

Still another unknown was whether some of the military were unhappy with the decision to return power to the civilians. President Gizikis and his colleagues appear confident that they have full authority to proceed.

The meeting of military and civilian leaders began quietly at 2 P.M. yesterday in the white-and-yellow building where Parliament met before the 1967 coup.

According to those present, President Gizikis said the armed forces would yield control. General Ioannides had been dismissed, and the President himself would resign if they wished.

The politicians said they asked the President to continue in office for the time being.

Apart from Mr. Canellopoulos, the 72-year-old leader of the National Radical Union party, and Mr. Mavros, leader of the Center Union, the politicians included Stephanos Stephanopoulos, a former Premier; Evangelos Averoff-Tossizza, a former Foreign Minister; Petros Garoufalias, former Defense Minister; Spyros Markezinis, a former Premier; Xenophon Zolotas, former governor of the Bank of Greece; and George Athanasiadis-Novas, a former Premier.

President Gizikis was joined by Gen. Gregorios Bonanos, the commander of the armed forces; Gen. Andreas Galatsanos, army commander; Rear Adm. Petros Arapakis, Navy commander, and Air Marshal Alexandros Papanicolaou of the air force.

After three and one half hours, the politicians left the building with Mr. Canellopoulos at the wheel of his own car. Small crowds, uncertain of the events taking place, gathered

President Phaidon Gizikis presiding at meeting to turn the Greek Government over to civilians. Clockwise, from left: Xenophon Zolotas, former governor of the Bank of Greece; Evangelos Averoff-Tossizza, a former Foreign Minister; Panayotis Canellopoulos, Premier who was overthrown in 1967; Gen. Gregorios Bonanos, armed forces commander; President Gizikis; Air Marshal Alexandros Papasicalsou; George Athanasiadis-Nevas, another former Premier; George Mavres, leader of Center Union party; Rear Adm. Petros Arapakis, Navy commander; and Spyros Markezinis, a former Premier. The 3½-hour meeting was held where Parliament met before 1967.

on Queen Sophia Street, the broad avenue stretching from Constitution Square.

The former civilian leaders went into meetings of their own to work out details and returned at 8 P.M. for more talks that lasted well into the night.

Mr. Caramanlis is a Macedonian-born lawyer who has held a variety of cabinet posts since the end of World War II. As Premier after 1955, he founded his own conservative party, the National Radical Union.

While he and his party were in power, Greece passed through a period of economic prosperity. However in 1963 the National Radical Union was defeated at the polls, and Mr. Caramanlis left for Paris.

*   *   *

August 18, 1974

FIGHTING ERUPTS ON CYPRUS AGAIN

Turkish Armored Column Makes New Drive South
Below Cease-Fire Line

By HENRY GINIGER
Special to The New York Times

NICOSIA, Cyprus, Aug. 17—The cease-fire declared on Cyprus last night broke down today with a new thrust southward by Turkish forces.

After seizing the northern third of the island, Turkey's powerful invasion army appeared to be seeking to reach Turkish Cypriote communities elsewhere.

An armored column reached Pyroi, a Turkish Cypriote community 10 miles southeast of Nicosia on the road to the coastal city of Larnaca. This effectively cut one of the island's north-south highways and brought Turkish positions well south of the line that was assumed yesterday to be the southern limit of what would be Turkish-controlled Cyprus.

In Athens, American and Greek officials were assuming that the United States would be asked to vacate or at least reorganize some of its military installations in Greece. Anti-American feeling swept Greece and demonstrations against the United States continued in Athens.

An Appeal for Help

Another Turkish Cypriote community, Louroujina, also appeared to be a goal of the Turkish thrust after its inhabitants reportedly appealed to the Turks for help. The town lies four miles southwest of Pyroi and its capture would enable the Turkish forces to isolate Greek Cypriote National Guard units in Nicosia from those in the south.

Larnaca itself has a large Turkish community and up to at least two days ago several-hundred Turkish Cypriote men were being held by the Greek Cypriotes in a school. There was conjecture in diplomatic circles that the Turks might be seeking to seize more territory than they had originally planned to strengthen their bargaining position at a new peace conference.

Both sides protested against the breach of the cease-fire and the commander of the United Nations peacekeeping force, Maj. Gen. Prem Chand of India, expressed concern.

Up to the early afternoon, the United Nations spokesman, Rudolf Stagduhar, had been able to announce that the cease-fire that went into effect at 6 P.M. yesterday had generally held up except for some sporadic firing in the Nicosia area.

General Chand and a special representative of Secretary General Waldheim, Luis Weckmann Nuñoz, held a long conference with the President of Cyprus, Glafkos Clerides. It was presumed that they handed Mr. Clerides a message from the Secretary General about Greek Cypriote needs on the island.

Mr. Clerides has not yet completely rejected a proposal for a new Geneva peace conference, but neither has he specifically accepted one in the present bitter mood among Greek Cypriotes. Turkey first sent invasion forces to Cyprus on July 20, but the all-out offensive to divide the island apparently along a line from Famagusta in the east through Nicosia to Lefka in the west did not begin until the peace talks in Geneva broke down on Wednesday.

Greek Villages Deserted

In northern Cyprus, Turkish forces appeared to be settling in for a long stay. Refugees who were moved through the Turkish lines to Turkish Cypriote communities found that life was returning to normality but Greek villages remained deserted, their inhabitants having fled south as the Turks approached. Turkish soldiers were seen removing such items as stoves, refrigerators and washing machines from empty houses.

Just after the invasion of Cyprus by Turkey, the Greek Cypriote National Guard took up positions around the Turkish Cypriote communities and virtually cut them off. There was great tension among the Turkish Cypriotes as they awaited a Turkish offensive.

After a fierce four hour battle at Mia Milea on the northeast outskirts of Nicosia on Thursday, Turkish troops broke out to the east in a drive for Famagusta. The national guard fled before them.

The Turks arrived at Chatos, a town of 1,200 people, just before 2 P.M. For two hours before that, the 400 to 500 Greek Cypriote soldiers stationed near the town had attacked it with mortars and the 120 Turkish Cypriote defenders suffered seven dead. Few houses in the town have escaped damage, but here and in other communities Turkish Cypriotes who fled the Greeks are moving back.

According to Adnan Edelial, the deputy police chief in Chatos, some Turkish Cypriotes sought to take revenge on the Greeks by burning their deserted homes, but he said the Turkish Army had given orders to leave Greek property alone.

"We are Moslems," he said, "and the Koran says that if you do harm to people you will pay for it in the end, either you, or your sons, or your sons' sons."

As he spoke, the first rain in five months fell on the dry fields and dusty streets. "We say that when it rains, it shows that God loves the Turks," Mr. Edellal said. He added that the rains indicated that "the highest power is very pleased with what has happened."

"We will have peace," he said, "because Turkey will leave some of the army here. We want security and we can't have it without Turkish forces."

* * *

September 4, 1974

GREEKS SAID TO ACCEPT CYPRUS PARTITION

Leader of the Turkish Community Expects Early Negotiations

By JAMES F. CLARITY
Special to The New York Times

NICOSIA, Cyprus, Sept. 3—Rauf Denktash, head of the Turkish Cypriote administration, said today that Greece and the Greek Cypriote Government had privately conceded that Cyprus would be formally divided into two zones, one for the ethnic Greeks and the other for the Turkish community.

Mr. Denktash said the Greek concession came during contacts in the last week between Greece and Turkey and between the two Cypriote communities. A formal partition of Cyprus has been Turkey's demand since the Turks invaded the island on July 20. The Turkish insistence on partition has been the major obstacle to a political solution of the Cyprus crisis.

The remarks by Mr. Denktash on a partition appeared to be the first indication that progress was being made toward a political settlement.

Speaking in his office here, with an air of calm confidence, Mr. Denktash said he thought new negotiations could begin within two or three weeks. He said the talks would probably take place in "a Swiss city," with the two Cypriote communities, Greece, Turkey and Britain as participants, as in the two unsuccessful negotiating sessions in Geneva in July and August.

Greeks Apprehensive on Issue

Asked to say precisely where the talks would take place, Mr. Denktash smiled and said, "I have nothing against Geneva."

He declined to name the Greek officials who, he said, had acknowledged to him and to officials in Turkey that they relented on partition of Cyprus. He said the Greek leaders were reluctant to announce the compromise because of bitter opposition to such a move in Greece and among Greek Cypriotes here.

The 540,000 ethnic Greeks make up 80 per cent of the population of Cyprus, but 40 per cent of the island is now controlled by the Turkish Army.

The Greek Cypriote administration of President Glafkos Clerides is studying a plan for a federated state of Cyprus, with two separate and autonomous parts. Mr. Clerides had said in recent days that he had "an open mind on all possible solutions to the crisis, including partition."

The position of Greece and the Greek Cypriote Government has been that the Turkish Army must retreat from its present lines on the island before any negotiations can begin.

'Realities Are Realized'

Mr. Denktash said today that he had made no concessions to the Greek side in return for partition. The Turkish position has been that all issues would be negotiable once the Greeks had agreed to partition. The Turkish leader said that this policy had not changed.

Discussing the apparent new attitude of the Greeks on partition, Mr. Denktash said:

"People who come and go between us confirm that the realities are realized." "There is a realization," he added, "that a geographical base—a federated system based on two regions—is the answer."

The Turkish leader added that the leaderships in Athens and of the Greek community in Cyprus had "reasonably accommodated mentally to settle on these terms."

Acceptance of partition by the Greek leaders, Mr. Denktash said, is not the problem.

"The problem is public opinion," he said, and added: "There is not enough courage among the leadership to announce the concession and persuade the Greek public to accept it."

Mr. Denktash said that "pressure" had been exerted on both Cypriote communities in the last week to renew negotiations. The pressure, he said, came from the United Nations, the United States, Britain, the Soviet Union and others.

Mr. Denktash, who is nominal Vice President of Cyprus, refrained from personal criticism of President Clerides. He said he expected to meet Mr. Clerides on Friday for a discussion of "humanitarian" issues such as the plight of tens of thousands of Cypriotes who fled their homes during the fighting.

A meeting between the two leaders was scheduled for last night, but it was postponed at the request of Mr. Denktash. He said he had put off the meeting because he had learned that Greek Cypriotes committed "mass murder" of Turkish Cypriote civilians last month.

The Turkish community is outraged by the discovery of the bodies of dozens of shooting victims near a Turkish Cypriote village, he said, but the issue will not disrupt the Friday meeting unless additional atrocities are discovered.

* * *

December 9, 1974

GREEKS REJECT MONARCHY BY WIDE MARGIN OF VOTES

By STEVEN V. ROBERTS
Special to The New York Times

ATHENS, Monday, Dec. 9—Greece voted decisively yesterday to become a republic and eliminate the monarchy that was installed here 142 years ago.

The votes in the national referendum were about 2 to 1 in favor of "uncrowned democracy," as it was called on the ballot. This means that King Constantine, the sixth member of his dynasty to reign as King of the Hellenes, will be stripped of his title.

As the results were broadcast last night, thousands of Athenians converged on Constitution Square in the center of the city, staging one of those impromptu celebrations that are a staple of Greek life. Horns blared, candles flickered, flags waved, hands were shaken, smiles exchanged. Here and there, a child slept on a father's shoulder.

The slogans chanted by the crowd praised democracy and derided Constantine. One said, "The German will die tonight," a reference to the dynasty's ethnic origins.

With 92 per cent of the returns counted, the republic won 2,899,282 votes, or 68.8 per cent, and the monarchy won 1,318,827 votes, or 31.2 per cent. About 25 per cent of those eligible did not vote.

The 34-year-old Constantine, who has been living in exile for seven years, has expressed a desire to return to Greece, no matter what the outcome of the referendum. But late last night Premier Constantine Caramanlis issued a statement advising Constantine that it "would not be very wise" for him to return "before some time goes by." A Government spokesman added that Constantine's legal status was still being studied.

The vote yesterday marked the end of a transition period that began on July 23. The military junta then ruling Greece was facing war with Turkey over the Cyprus issue and summoned a civilian government of national unity to take power.

The new Greek Parliament, elected three weeks ago, will meet for the first time today. After selecting its officers and receiving the Government's program, it is expected to choose a provisional president of the republic, possibly by the end of the week.

For Mr. Caramanlis the result of the referendum solves some problems but creates others. The voters' overwhelming preference for a republic should help end the struggle over the monarchy that has troubled Greece for much of her modern history.

In his statement, Premier Caramanlis noted that the question of Greece's form of government has caused "acute party antagonism to the detriment of the interests of the nation." He called on all Greeks to respect the results of the referendum and added: "All must recognize that the uncertainty of the form of the government has been decisively eliminated."

Possibly Divisive Issue

At the same time, the choice of a president could produce new political strife. Now considered most likely to be named provisional president is Panayotis Canellopoulos, a widely respected figure who was Premier at the time of the military coup in 1967.

Premier Caramanlis has yet to express his own long-range governmental aims. At one time it was thought that he wanted to create a strong presidency along French lines and seek the post himself.

According to his aides, however, he now intends to propose reforms that would strengthen the Premier's office and would limit the president to ceremonial duties as head of state. After a new constitution is adopted, probably this spring, a permanent president will be chosen.

Almost every area of the country voted in favor of a republic, a result that surprised some analysts here. Many observers had said that the provinces were strongly monarchist and the big cities prorepublican, but in the age of television the differences between rural and urban Greece might be diminishing.

Constantine Broadcast Appeals

Constantine had said in several broadcasts, recorded from abroad, that he believed in democracy and would stay out of politics, but he clearly did not convince many voters.

A dressmaker in the port city of Piraeus expressed a common feeling earlier this week when she said: "We want a genuine democracy, not what our grandfathers had—fairytales about kings."

The woman vouched another important factor in the referendum—the feeling that the monarchy was an outdated and troublesome institution. Constantine apparently represents a past they would like to forget.

Constantine inherited the throne in 1964, 101 years after the House of Glucksburg—a German-Danish family—was selected by the great powers of Europe to rule Greece. A Bavarian dynasty had been installed in 1832, but its king had been forced to abdicate after a reign of 30 years.

Forced Premier Out

In 1965, Constantine fought bitterly with Premier George Papandreou, a progressive, outspoken Republican. The King forced the Premier to resign—an incident that many historians believe helped cause the military coup two years later.

After the 1967 coup, Constantine cooperated with the junta for about eight months. In December of 1967 he tried to organize a revolt within the army, but when the plan failed he fled into exile. For most of the next six years he lived quietly in Italy with his wife, Princess Anne-Marie of Denmark.

He refused to return to Greece but never spoke out until 1973.

In that year George Papadopoulos, then the leader of the junta, proclaimed a republic and staged a referendum to endorse his action. The voting was widely regarded as fraudulent and caused the Contantine to criticize the junta publicly. Shortly afterward he moved to England, where he now lives.

Following the 1973 vote Constantine was deprived of his state income and his properties in Greece by the military government. The government later announced, however, that it would pay $4-million to the former royal family for the seizure of 10,000 acres of the family's private estates.

After Mr, Caramanlis took power in July, he called a new vote to settle the monarchy issue.

* * *

November 21, 1975

U. N. CYPRUS VOTE ANGERS THE TURKS

Assembly Demands a Troop Pullout—Denktash Warns of Grave Repercussions

By KATHLEEN TELTSCH
Special to The New York Times

UNITED NATIONS, N. Y., Nov. 20—The General Assembly approved a Cyprus resolution tonight over bitter opposition from Turkey, raising the possibility that the Turkish Cypriots would set up a separate, independent state on the island.

Ilter Turkmen, the Turkish delegate, had warned the Assembly of grave "repercussions" to be expected after the 117-to-1 vote. He castigated the members for having declined yesterday to hear Rauf Denktash, the Turkish Cypriot leader.

After the vote, Mr. Denktash said outside the Assembly hall that he felt "at complete liberty to take whatever action is necessary to save the Turkish community from the state of statelessness in which it has lived."

The resolution demanded the withdrawal without further delay of the Turkish troops that invaded Cyprus in July 1974, called for the return of refugees to their homes and urged resumption of a fifth round of negotiations by Greek and Turkish Cypriot leaders under the auspices of Secretary General Kurt Waldheim to reach "a mutually acceptable agreement."

9 Nations Abstain

Nine nations, including the United States, abstained from the vote. The resolution was sponsored by seven nonaligned nations.

Assembly resolutions are recommendations only, but the text was notably firmer than one adopted last year which urged the withdrawal of foreign troops from Cyprus but did not "demand" it as the new resolution does. The current measure also urges the parties to refrain from any unilateral action to change the demographic structure of Cyprus; the Greek side has accused the Turks of such action.

Mr. Denktash declared that he was "saying nothing" when asked if the Turkish Cypriots would unilaterally declare a complete break with the government in Nicosia headed by President Makarios, the Greek Cypriot leader.

The Turkish Cypriots last February declared a separate Turkish federated state in the northern part of the island that was occupied in 1974 by 40,000 Turkish troops. Turkey invaded to protect the Turkish minority and prevent any move to unite the island with Greece.

Mr. Denktash has continued to propose that the long conflict between the two ethnic communities be resolved by a two-zone federation of Greek Cypriots and Turkish Cypriots under a weak central government. But during the last week of acrimonious debates, there have been hints that the Turkish Cypriots would choose independence if Mr. Denktash was not given a hearing or if an objectionable resolution was adopted by the Assembly.

Heard Only in Committee

Turkey, with some support from members of the Islamic Conference group, has tried to have the full General Assembly hear Mr. Denktash. But since he did not represent a government, the majority agreed instead that representatives of the two communities be heard in committee, as was done last week. The Turkish side was represented by Vedat Celik, minister of state in the Turkish federated state.

Mr. Denktash met in Washington today with Secretary of State Kissinger, and the Turkish Cypriot leader said that he had been urged to agree to resume negotiations toward a Cyprus settlement. "But with this mentality of the Greek Cypriot side, the world must know it would be very difficult for us to do so and no good would come out of such negotiations," he said.

The Turkish Cypriot leader said that he would insist that he be heard by the Security Council before it renews the mandate of the 3,200-member United Nations Peace Force on Cyprus, which expires Dec. 15.

The United States abstention was seen either as a move to maintain Washington's usefulness in helping to negotiate a settlement, or possibly as a reflection that the United States is to begin negotiations soon with Turkey concerning 26 American bases. The Ankara Government took over the bases in retaliation for a Congressional embargo on military aid to Turkey imposed after Turkish troops invaded Cyprus. The ban was eased more than a month ago.

*   *   *

January 4, 1976

YUGOSLAVIA'S NEW SYSTEM

By HELLA PICK

BELGRADE, Yugoslavia—The shops here are laden with food, and figure-conscious Yugoslavs can even buy Diet Coke. The manager of a new multi-story department store says he gets his merchandising ideas all the way from GUM in Moscow to Neiman-Marcus in Texas. The traffic jams are as solid as in many Western cities, with the car becoming a necessity.

These are just a few signs of Yugoslavia's startling economic transformation. It is way ahead of its neighbors in Eastern Europe, and the standard of living has risen dramatically. But Yugoslavia is also more vulnerable—badly exposed to the economic winds from the capitalist world in the West and to an economic squeeze from the Communist camp.

Inflation is high with unemployment rising. The balance of payments deficit is mounting. And though Yugoslavia's planners speak with optimism, there is no doubt of the underlying concern over the political and economic problem of preserving the country's unusual mix of Communist "self-management" married to what has become an open Western-style market economy. Ultimately, Yugoslavia's policy of nonalignment could be threatened.

Self-management in Yugoslavia is an attempt to regulate the economy and all other aspects of life by agreements between the various groups in society. Regional autonomy and decentralization right down to the level of the commune has fundamental political as well as economic objectives. It is an attempt to create national unity by recognizing Yugoslavia's diversity.

Very often there is conflict between economic imperatives calling for larger units and political demands for greater local autonomy. Self-management is one attempt to reconcile such conflict by agreement.

Self-management in practice is multitiered. There are plant councils on the factory floor. There are also councils that bring together the managers of several enterprises, and there are councils right at the top of the economic pyramid.

In each factory the councils appoint their managers after advertising vacancies in newspapers, although there is often political pressure to appoint certain people. Salaries and wages are fixed by the councils—but only with certain parameters. There is a national minimum wage, and there are agreements for wage ceilings reached by councils for whole industries: individual factories have to fix their wages within these ranges.

Though individual factory managers in consultation with plant councils can fix prices for their products, there is a Government price freeze on certain basic commodities and prices cannot be raised without permission.

Yugoslavia owes much of its remarkable economic progress to the creed of self-management by which it has lived since Stalin's break with Marshal Tito in 1948. This meant that Yugoslavia could break out from the stranglehold of a centrally planned closed economy like those that have bedeviled the other Communist countries of Europe.

Self-management arises from President Tito's recognition that Yugoslavia, with its diversity of peoples and its turbulent history, could be forged into one nation only if power is diffused and decentralization genuine.

In the mid-1960's, Yugoslav leadership also came to recognize that the country could only make a great economic leap forward if it opened itself up to the West, allowed Western know-how and ideas to come in, and Yugoslavs—if they wanted—to leave. Surplus workers from Yugoslavia were allowed to seek their fortunes in the labor-hungry markets of Western Europe.

Yugoslavia now has a Constitution in which the Federal Government has narrow residual power and its six republics and two provinces are largely autonomous. Even foreign economic policy decisions cannot be taken without the agreement of the republics. But the power base goes much further down.

Self-management is not just a system for the control of enterprise by workers. It means that the decision-making goes right down to the shop floor, the hospital ward, the university or the theater. People can buy their own apartments and own a vacation home. Peasants can farm up to 25 acres of their own land; private businessmen—restaurants, repair shops and the like—can operate provided they do not employ more than five people. They can buy currency for traveling abroad. Banks operate much as in the West. But by far the largest sector of the economy has no distinctive ownership and is self-managed with the workers (or doctors, actors or farmers) appointing their own managers. The principal unifying element is the Communist League of Yugoslavia, which itself has been decentralized but still has considerable guidance from the leadership.

In its practical application, self-management has gone through several phases and is still constantly evolving. Yugoslavs try to explain how it all operates, but usually end up by throwing up their arms and saying "Well, you can see for yourself that it works—just look at the goods in the shops, their quality as well as their quantity." It means that Yugoslavs spend a great deal of time at plant meetings rather than at the factory bench. But more and more meetings are held outside working hours, and one American researcher who has made a computer comparison asserts that Western businessmen spend just as much time at the conference table. He suggested that self-management might in any case be seen as an alternative use of resources to advertising.

Perhaps surprisingly, Western capital seems to live easily enough with Yugoslavia's corporate self-management. Yugoslavia for many years has been seeking out Western capital, but foreign companies cannot acquire more than 49 percent of any enterprise. Though they can advise the "self-management managers," foreign investors do not sit on the plant councils.

This has required psychological adjustments for multinational concerns. But it does not seem to deter them. The Dow Chemical Corporation, for example, is about to finalize a multimillion-dollar agreement for joint-venture chemical facilities in the republics of Croatia and Serbia. This will be a model for the kind of enterprise that President Tito is now actively encouraging.

One of the great drawbacks of self-management has been that prosperity has tended to become regionalized, with enterprises investing their profits within their own republics. Thus Croatia has become more and more industrialized, while Macedonia for example, has remained far behind. Yugoslavia's leaders have been urging more economic cross-fertilization.

But it is really the overall economic picture that is both a source of strength and of weakness to the country. It is a source of strength because Yugoslavia has produced a growing middle class with an overriding interest in the preservation of the country's political cohesion and economic progress.

Today's prosperity is nevertheless also a source of weakness because of its dependence on external economic factors. When outsiders ask whether Yugoslavia's political fabric and independence can survive the aging President Tito, Yugoslavs dismiss the question confidently.

But the effect of Western recession, combined with the Soviet Union's capacity for pulling economic levers, constitute genuine question marks.

The dependence on the West is considerable. There is the need for credit and technology as well as export markets. This year alone, Yugoslav exports to the West have declined by 25 percent. The recession in the West has also put a brake on Yugoslavia's hopes for closer trade links with the European Economic Community. Yugoslav officials are bitter over what they regard as the Common Market's failure to keep to a negotiated commitment to buy Yugoslav meat.

But perhaps the greatest source of concern for Yugoslavia's economic relations with the West lies in the shrinking foreign markets for Yugoslav labor. Since 1965 when Yugoslavia launched its economic program, full employment here has been sacrificed to technological advance. Until two years ago, Yugoslavia could reasonably assume that Western Europe would take up the slack.

Yugoslavs were allowed to leave the country freely and by 1974, as many as 960,000 Yugoslavs out of a labor force of about 5.5 million were working outside their own country. Besides taking pressure off their economy, they were sending back large sums of money from their earnings. This corrected Yugoslavia's balance of payments deficit. In the current year, however, there may be a deficit.

Because of the West's own recession, foreign employment opportunities have shrunk. Last year, for the first time since 1965, more Yugoslavs returned to their country than left it. So far this year migration seems to have been fairly evenly balanced, but the returning workers include far more unskilled than skilled. The skilled ones tend to stay behind in West Germany and elsewhere, where they are allowed to claim unemployment benefits.

Inside Yugoslavia, unemployment has risen, and though figures are imprecise at least half a million workers, representing about 12 percent of the labor force, is out of work. All this creates social and political problems.

Yugoslavia is trying to diversify its economic links as much as possible. It needs to import about two-thirds of its oil requirements. It divides its oil purchases fairly evenly between the Middle East and the Soviet Union, buying from both sources at world prices. It is competing for the lucrative markets of the oil-producing countries of the Middle East, but it also retains strong links with the Soviet Union and the other Communist countries.

Yugoslavia insists on selling at world prices rather than at prices fixed within the artificial system of the Eastern bloc, and with Western markets shrinking, the trend is towards larger exports to the East.

But Yugoslavia is apprehensive: It does not want to encourage a trend that could add to Russian economic leverage.

Until now, Yugoslavia has managed to avoid giving the Soviet Union an economic trump-card—and it has also prospered. The big question is whether it can continue to do so.

Hella Pick is a correspondent for The Manchester Guardian.

* * *

September 3, 1977

RIGHTS CAMPAIGN IN RUMANIA WILTS AFTER A VIGOROUS AND BOLD START

By MALCOLM W. BROWNE
Special to The New York Times

BUCHAREST, Rumania, Sept. 2—The Rumanian human-rights movement, which began this year with an optimism and vigor unusual in this country, appears to have been crushed.

The novelist Paul Goma, who became the most articulate spokesman and leader, has been silenced. So have been hundreds of others who, five months ago, were signing protest petitions, appealing for support from international organizations and even staging modest public demonstrations. President Nicolae Ceausescu has succeeded in eliminating visible dissent, and with only a relatively small amount of physical force and imprisonment.

Mr. Goma and some of his colleagues were arrested April 1 but remained behind bars for only five weeks. On May 8, 19,000 prisoners including some political prisoners, were released in a general amnesty. Since then, despite the physical freedom of most if not all dissidents none have had anything to say to outsiders.

Mr. Goma, put to work in the national library in Bucharest may be viewed from a distance by foreigners and at close range by the ubiquitous police as he goes to and from work. He and his wife and infant son are said by the authorities to have been given an apartment to replace the one from which they were evicted at the time of his arrest. Acquaintances of Mr. Goma say he has refused to speak with foreigners since his release. Other former dissidents have become equally reticent; none have even offered to explain why.

This correspondent sought to visit several at their homes. All had once been eager to talk about Rumania and their problems but this time they limited their response to peering through the peepholes in their apartment doors. The few telephones that remained connected after the Government's April sweep were not answered, nor were notes.

"The dissidents have been hidden away like the rubble of downtown Bucharest after the earthquake in March," a Rumanian said. The quake, which killed over 1,500 people, razed hundreds of buildings in the capital. Although the rubble has been removed, the great bare sites are concealed by red and white panels.

The Goma movement, as it came to be known, began with a petition signed by him and seven others that called on the Communist Government to implement the Constitution and laws more completely with respect to freedom of expression, among other things. At first the Government vacillated between repression and conciliation.

Mr. Goma and some others were briefly placed under house arrest, and most of the foreigners in Bucharest were under intensive surveillance. Later, however, the authorities began issuing large numbers of emigration visas to those among the dissidents and many others who wanted to leave.

It developed that most of the dissidents, but not Mr. Goma, did want to leave. Of the hundreds who criticized the autocratic regime by signing Mr. Goma's petition, many openly conceded that they had done so in hopes of being "punished" with expulsion. Those who received visas jokingly referred to them as Goma passports.

Jews wishing to emigrate to Israel gave voice to long-standing allegations of anti-Semitism. Germans and Hungarians complained to foreign diplomats and newsmen about their treatment. A few people even managed to unfurl protest banners in public places before being swept away by ever-watchful policemen.

As eager to be rid of them as the would be emigrants were to leave, the Government opened the gates much more widely than before. Among the beneficiaries have been some of the 400,000 ethnic Germans, some of them in enclaves that have existed here for five centuries or more. Most would leave if they could, informed sources say. To keep this potentially troublesome community mollified, officials made it known to West German diplomats that during 1977 some 10,000 ethnic Germans would be permitted to leave. So far this year 5,000 have gone, and the goal seems attainable.

Hungarian Exodus Up Sharply

Hungarian emigration from the former Hungarian province of Transylvania has also sharply increased, with many signers of the petition being allowed to move to Hungary.

Getting out of Rumania remains difficult for most people, however. The private car arriving at the frontier is likely to be held up for hours while hidden passengers, political contraband or other things are searched out. But within the country even nonpolitical dissenters have received surprisingly lenient treatment lately.

An example of the leniency arose in connection with a chain of resort hotels on the Black Sea coast that is customarily reserved for foreign tourists able to pay in hard currency. This year tourism was poor, so Rumanians were permitted to rent rooms at the huge Hotel Neptun, near the Bulgarian border. Then when foreign tourists unexpectedly sought accommodations, the Rumanians were unceremoniously evicted and proceeded to stage an impromptu demonstration. Though such demonstrations are illegal in Rumania, the Government, after dealing with the demonstrators, ousted the Minister of Tourism, Ion Cosma.

The lenient policy even extended to Mr. Goma, who, just prior to his arrest, was offered a chance to cooperate with the authorities. Twice he was called in for interviews with Cornel Burtica, one of the two or three most powerful leaders of the Communist Party. Unlike most other dissident artists and writers, Mr. Goma refused to cooperate.

"He was a fool," a writer said. "Here everyone must make his peace with the security service sooner or later. I have done so. At least you stay out of jail, and that is a very important kind of freedom for anyone, say what you will. Anyway, it is possible to work within our system. You just have to do it according to their rules."

*   *   *

December 8, 1977

RUMANIANS GET CALL FOR MORE AUSTERITY

Ceausescu Defers Higher Living Standards Until Industry Achieves Further Growth

By DAVID A. ANDELMAN
Special to The New York Times

BUCHAREST, Rumania, Dec. 7—President Nicolae Ceausescu asked today for eight more years of austerity and sacrifices to raise Rumania to the ranks of the developed countries.

In a four-hour keynote speech to the national conference of the Communist Party, Mr. Ceausescu, who serves as the party's Secretary General, affirmed that the nation's principal effort would continue to be directed at building up industry and that consumers would have to wait for substantial improvements in living standards.

The speech, interrupted 40 times by applause, chants and cheers from the 3,000 delegates, was a remarkably frank exposition of Rumania's problems—a 10 percent drop in the grain crop, a lag in investment, difficulties in law and order, the need for tougher internal controls.

It was also a catalogue of the orthodox Communist measures that Mr. Ceausescu was prepared to take to solve these problems, allowing him late in the address the opportunity to affirm his position of independence from the Soviet Union by urging negotiations among all parties in the Middle East and

The New York Times/David A. Amdelman

At a public square in Lupeni, Rumania, a coal miner's wagon on a pedestal is a monument to labor. Miners in that area have been staging demonstrations, demanding better living and working conditions.

supporting the independent-minded Communist parties of Western Europe.

Party Autonomy Is Defended

"Communist parties should be allowed to define autonomous policies, with no outside interference," he said. "No party can be forced to follow certain patterns, but, at the same time, no party can impose its own way on others."

It was the Rumanian way that Mr. Ceausescu expounded in the flag-draped congress hall, a system that seemed aimed at tightening internal controls that are already the tightest in Eastern Europe. He said there was a need to assert tough police action to curb the rise in violent crime that has become a social problem since the release, in an amnesty seven months ago, of 30,000 criminal offenders. "All the necessary severity must be applied," he said.

But the controls will extend far beyond simple law enforcement. Earlier this year, the Central Committee abolished the central censoring organization in the expectation that newspapers, publishers and broadcasters will censor themselves. Mr. Ceausescu said today that the new system was designed to stiffen censorship.

"In this connection, we consider it necessary that in the future more workers and other working people directly involved in production should sit on the managing boards of publications and cultural institutions," he said. "This makes for more effective control over the editorial boards."

The motives for the new restrictions are not clear. As the Government prepares to marshal the nation's energies and demand more sacrifice for the final push toward full industrialization, it apparently wants to make certain it has full control over any possible avenues for the expression of dissent.

There was no doubt about Mr. Ceausescu's determination to pursue the economic program. While saying that investment had fallen more than $3 billion behind in the first two years of the present five-year plan (1976–80), he presented a supplementary program of yet higher goals for the final years.

Counties Among Poorest in Europe

By 1980, he said, he expects to see each of the nation's 40 counties, which include some of the poorest areas of Europe, to turn out at least $2 billion worth of industrial output. The additional program guarantees attainment of this target," he said, "providing for industrialization at a higher rate in the less developed areas."

Looking beyond the current plan, he said industrial output was scheduled to rise by 55 to 60 percent during the next five-year plan, so that by 1985 industry would contribute 70 percent of national income.

The President demanded special effort, too, from farmers, whose production of grain this year fell from last year's bumper crop of 20 million tons to 18 million. By 1980, Mr. Ceausescu said, there is to be a rise of one-third in this figure, largely because of wider use of irrigation.

These goals will be discussed by the party conference, a national gathering that has been held twice before—in 1967 and 1972—to assess midterm progress in fulfilling five-year plans. The goals are expected to be voted unanimously and resoundingly into law in the closing session on Friday, open as was today's meeting to foreign diplomats and correspondents.

Whether the workers and farmers themselves will respond quite so positively to the exhortations is another question. The party platform had little in it for the amenities of life. This lack in the past has fostered some dissatisfaction. Demonstrations by coal miners in the Jiu Valley and sporadic protests in industrial plants of Brasov and Bucharest appear to have undermined the consensus that Mr. Ceausescu has sought.

Today's presentation while pledging a cut in the work week from 48 to 44 hours over the next several years, as well as raises of 30 percent or more in base salaries and pledges of higher retail sales, did not seem to address most of the workers' complaints.

Instead Mr. Ceausescu, in calling for better quality of production as well as greater quantity, seemed to be telling the workers that if they wanted more and better goods, it was up to them to produce them, though not at the expense of heavy industry.

* * *

May 5, 1980

TITO DIES AT 87;
LAST OF WARTIME LEADERS

A Rotating Leadership Took Over in Belgrade During His Illness

By Reuters

BELGRADE, Yugoslavia, May 4—President Tito, Yugoslavia's leader since World War II, died today after a four-month illness, the official press agency Tanyug announced.

The wartime guerrilla chief, postwar rival of Stalin and leader of the third-world movement was three days short of his 88th birthday. He was the last of the major World War II leaders to die.

President Tito, whose left leg was amputated in January, died at a medical center at Ljubljana, capital of the Slovenian Republic, at 3:05 P.M. (10:05 A.M. New York time), Tanyug reported.

Belgrade officials said that his funeral would be held at noon Thursday.

[In Washington, President Carter, calling Marshal Tito "a towering figure on the world stage," affirmed that the United States would do whatever was necessary to insure Yugoslavia's independence, territorial integrity and unity.]

As Marshal Tito lay dying, a rotating system of succession was put into operation. His prolonged illness gave the Yugoslavs time to prepare for his death and the problems that might arise.

Marshal Tito, who in 1974 was named President for Life, created two collective leadership bodies to take over after his death: the State Presidency, representing six republics and two autonomous provinces, and the Communist Party's Presidium.

Posts Are to Rotate Annually

The top posts in the bodies are to rotate annually among the republics and autonomous provinces, with the aim of averting rivalries and concentrations of power.

Vice President Lazar Kolisevski, 66, a Macedonian, becomes head of the collective State Presidency. Later this month, the post will be taken over by Cvijetin Mijatovic of Bosnia-Herzegovina.

Stevan Doronjski, a 60-year-old Serb from the autonomous province of Vojvodina, takes charge of the League of Communists. His successor will be chosen later this year.

The body of Marshal Tito will be brought to Belgrade by his personal Blue Train. There will be a brief ceremony in Ljubljana tomorrow morning and the train will halt for a short observance in Zagreb, capital of Croatia, on the way to Belgrade.

Yugoslav officials said President Tito would lie in state at Parliament from tomorrow night until the funeral.

Presidents and kings, prime ministers and high officials from more than 100 countries are expected to be present, the officials said.

The President will be buried near his Belgrade villa, on a forested hill in suburban Dedinje overlooking the city. The tomb is near the Museum of the Revolution, devoted to Marshal Tito and the Yugoslav Communist movement.

The announcement of his death came as Yugoslavs were ending a four-day May Day holiday. The Government proclaimed seven days of mourning.

President Tito entered the Ljubljana clinic in January and his left leg was amputated Jan. 20 because of a circulation problem. He seemed to make a spectacular recovery from the amputation and was photographed several days later in a chair smiling and talking with his two sons. In mid-February President Tito suffered a relapse and in following weeks he was close to death several times, suffering from kidney failure, internal bleeding, heart weakness, pneumonia and other ailments accompanying a failure of vital organs.

Early last week, Marshal Tito pulled out of a critical state of shock. Yesterday, his eight doctors reported that his condition was showing a continued slight improvement.

In two bulletins early today, the doctors reported there was a renewal of weakness and said that his condition was once again critical.

Radio and TV Play Funeral Music

Just before President Tito's death was announced, the Yugoslav radio and television interrupted their programs and began to broadcast funeral music.

A television announcer, his voice trembling, said simply: "President Tito has died."

The radio broadcast a traditional song: "Comrade Tito we swear to you not to deviate from your path," a reference to the Marxist policies he adopted after breaking with the Soviet bloc in 1948.

A proclamation by the party's Central Committee and the State Presidency recalled that Marshal Tito had led Yugoslavia for three and a half decades and described him as "the greatest historical figure of our time."

It spoke of his role as leader of the Partisans who had fought a bitter and protracted struggle against Germans, Italians and other occupation forces during World War II.

"The great heart of the President of our Socialist Federal Republic of Yugoslavia stopped beating at 15:05 in Ljubljana," the proclamation said.

"Deep sorrow and pain have shattered the working class, peoples and nationalities of our country, our every man, worker, soldier and war comrade, peasant, intellectual, every creator, pioneer, youth, girl and mother."

A Unifying Figure in Yugoslavia

The proclamation by the Central Committee and State Presidency stressed President Tito's role in binding together Yugoslavia's diverse and sometimes rival ethnic groups.

"He knew well that it is our destiny to be interlinked, that for centuries we fought against foreign invaders, that our feeling is that everybody must be master in his own house," the proclamation said.

Camera Press

Marshal Tito

"He resolutely struggled against nationalism and chauvinism, against domination and hegemony, against all manifestations of separatism."

Hegemony is a Yugoslav code word for control of a Communist country by the Soviet Union.

Since President Tito fell ill, Yugoslav leaders have pledged repeatedly to follow his policies of nonalignment abroad and workers' self-management at home.

The proclamation said that the unity and combat readiness of Yugoslavia's 270,000-member armed forces were "the guarantee of our freedom and independence and the preservation of our brotherhood and unity."

The armed forces have been in a low stage of alert since President Tito fell ill.

* * *

May 5, 1980

TITO: THE FIGHTER-SURVIVOR WHO UNIFIED A COUNTRY

By DAVID BINDER
Special to The New York Times

WASHINGTON, April 20—He was the metal worker from the village of Kumrovec, the drill sergeant from World War I, the Partisan commander from World War II and, finally, the father of his country: Josip Broz Tito.

An Appreciation

His 87 years spanned the collapse of the European monarchs—one of whom, Francis Joseph, he served as a soldier—and the rise of new governments and nations—one of which, the Federal Republic of Yugoslavia, he fostered.

Above all he was a fighter and a survivor, with a price on his head as an illegal Communist Party organizer in prewar Yugoslavia, a reward posted by Hitler for his capture dead or alive during World War II and anathema pronounced upon him by Stalin in 1948.

Marshal Tito dealt with many of the great and powerful—Churchill, de Gaulle, Khrushchev, Nehru, Nasser—and lived on to deal with their lesser successors. He was the last survivor of the generation of leaders that emerged from World War II.

No Heir Apparent in the Wings

His closest wartime comrades had fallen by the way: Edvard Kardelj died in 1979; Aleksandr Rankovic was dismissed from his posts 14 years ago and was living in sad retirement; Milovan Djilas, the classic dissident since 1954, was in a kind of internal exile in Belgrade. In the end there were no heirs apparent.

After the death of Mr. Kardelj a Yugoslav official who had fought in the war as a young man remarked: "After Tito we have to jump two generations for the next leaders. That is the problem."

Did President Tito live too long?

At a time when Soviet tanks were on the move in Afghanistan, raising uncertainties again along the perimeter of the Soviet bloc, few in Yugoslavia wanted him to go.

His legacy for the six Yugoslav republics, with their three religious faiths and their welter of languages, was the simple slogan of his Partisan brigades: Brotherhood and unity. This and the trust embodied in his arming of every able-bodied man in a country with a terrible history of ethnic rivalries was his prescription for continued independence.

In politics Marshal Tito was more innovator than inventor. The one-time mechanic for the Daimler auto factory in Vienna was a lifelong tinkerer. As a young man he had witnessed not only the collapse of the Austro-Hungarian Empire but also, first hand, the birth of the vigorous Soviet Union. In 1920 he returned from Russia to the newly created kingdom of Yugoslavia, a fragile entity foredoomed because one nationality, the Serbs, were in a position to dominate a nation of several nationalities.

Part Croat and part Slovene, Marshall Tito appears to have developed a vision in the mid-1920's of a Yugoslavia that could work and survive by virtue of giving each nationality and each region an equal stake. It was a vision of a socialist Yugoslavia, and in the next five decades he never lost sight of it.

In 1937 he took over the Yugoslav Communist Party, riddled by factionalism and decimated by Stalin's purges and immediately set out to put his ideas into practice. Finding "whole regions with no party organization," he made it a cardinal point to spread his own organization throughout the country. When the Germans invaded in 1941 his was the only political movement functioning in all the provinces and the only one to promote a "united Yugoslavia."

Streak of Independence

He had brought something more back from his years as an official of the Comintern in Moscow: the determination not to accept bribes or subsidies from the Russians and become their vassal. He also said that the party leadership should "be at home among the people to share the rough and the smooth with them." This made him more independent than the "Muscovite" European Communists who spent World War II in the Soviet capital. In this sense he had already begun to defy Soviet suzerainty 10 years before he defied Stalin.

Marshal Tito learned early that loneliness was the only real companion of power. His first wife abandoned him during a five-year prison term for Communist agitation and he left his second and third wives. He chose as party lieutenants men 10 to 15 years his junior, who called him Stari (Old Man) even when he was in his late 40's. He started the Communist uprising alone, with no help from the Russians or anyone else, when the old Yugoslavia was torn to pieces by German, Italian and Bulgarian invaders and by quislings. His Yugoslavia later stood alone against Stalin's monolithic "socialist camp."

The logic of the break with the Soviet bloc in 1948, and Yugoslavia's vulnerability by virtue of its small size and location, led Tito the tinkerer to seek new instruments for guaranteeing its external and internal security. Domestically he favored Mr. Kardelj's proposals of decentralization, the principle of "workers' self-management" and, ultimately, a market economy. Externally he sought conciliation with the West and reconciliation with the East. When neither East nor West would offer sufficient agreement, he developed the policy of nonalignment between the two great blocs and found support in the third world.

Apology, Acceptance, Emulation

Nonalignment abroad and self-management at home, innovations more than inventions, were introduced, essentially, to keep Yugoslavia going. In Marshal Tito's later years he had the satisfaction of winning apologies, acceptance and even a measure of emulation from his former enemies and critics in the Communist world.

He had his faults. He could be ruthless toward real or supposed foes, but he did not have a permanent vindictive streak. He surrounded himself with royal trappings and in many ways lived like a king for his last three decades, but he remained Comrade Tito to his subordinates and never lost the ability to talk with ordinary people. He was unintellectual, sometimes anti-intellectual, but he learned to tolerate great freedom in the arts.

Marshal Tito's countrymen sometimes called him the "first and only Yugoslav." Yet in the end he could be fairly certain that even if they considered themselves Serbs or Bosnians or

Macedonians at home, they would all become Yugoslavs if attacked.

* * *

May 5, 1980

CARTER CALLS TITO 'TOWERING FIGURE' AND SAYS U. S. WILL BACK YUGOSLAVS

By BERNARD GWERTZMAN
Special to The New York Times

WASHINGTON, May 4—President Carter, mourning the loss of President Tito, a man he called "a towering figure on the world stage," affirmed today that the United States would do whatever was necessary to insure Yugoslavia's independence, territorial integrity and unity.

The White House put off until tomorrow the announcement of the official delegation to the Tito funeral Thursday. Plans have been made for Vice President Mondale to head the group, but officials tonight would not rule out the possibility that Mr. Carter might lead it.

The funeral will provide an opportunity for the first high-level Soviet-American contacts since the freeze in relations instituted by the United States after the Soviet military intervention in Afghanistan in December. But it was uncertain whether either side would take advantage of the occasion for private talks or whether they would wait until the next occasion, ceremonies marking the 25th anniversary of the Austrian peace treaty in Vienna on May 15–16, which is to be attended by Foreign Minister Andrei A. Gromyko of the Soviet Union and Edmund S. Muskie, who is expected to be sworn in as Secretary of State by then.

Because Marshal Tito had been in critical health for months, his death came as no surprise and there was no sense of crisis in Washington. President Carter, who reviewed foreign policy with his top aides at Camp David yesterday and Friday, remained at the Maryland retreat on this warm sunny day and decided not to return to Washington until tomorrow morning, when he plans a brief meeting with Lord Carrington, the British Foreign Secretary, who arrived last night.

Administration officials said they felt the long period in which Marshal Tito was incapacitated had helped the new Yugoslav collective leadership take effective power without the pressured atmosphere that might have prevailed if he had died unexpectedly.

There was no sign, the officials said, of any overt interference from the Soviet Union in Yugoslav affairs, but they expected in coming months and years that Moscow might try to reassert influence in Yugoslavia.

"For more than three decades, under administrations of both parties," President Carter said, "it has been the policy of the United States to support the independence, territorial integrity and unity of Yugoslavia.

"I reaffirm today that America will continue its long-standing policy of support for Yugoslavia and do what it must to provide that support."

The implication in the statement was that the United States would use military force to counter any Soviet attack on Yugoslavia, but the Yugoslavs have stressed privately that although they welcome affirmations of support, they do not want any specific pledges of military backing because they want now, more than ever before, to stress that Yugoslavia is a nonaligned country.

Mr. Carter also said that the United States "will not tolerate terrorist actions directed against Yugoslavia or its representatives here." There are many émigré groups opposed to the Yugoslav Government, and some officials predicted they would try to step up their activity after Marshal Tito's death.

"We have confidence in the new Yugoslav leadership, duly established in accordance with the provisions of the Constitution of Yugoslavia, to lead the nation and its economy through this period," Mr. Carter said.

Of the former leader, Mr. Carter said:

"President Josip Broz Tito was a towering figure on the world stage. After leading his Partisan forces to a hard-fought victory during World War II, he founded and led the postwar Yugoslav state for nearly 35 years. During that period he and his people faced many challenges but met them with a resolute determination to maintain Yugoslavia's independence and unity and its own unique approach to domestic and foreign policies."

"He was the last surviving member of that group of statesmen who founded and led the Nonaligned Movement to its present prominence in world affairs. President Tito's position in the history of his era is assured for all times."

At Camp David, Mr. Carter met with Secretary of State-designate Edmund S. Muskie, Acting Secretary Warren M. Christopher, Defense Secretary Harold Brown, Zbigniew Brzezinski, the national security adviser, and other aides.

In an apparent effort to affirm the President's support for Mr. Muskie's insistence on being the leading foreign affairs spokesman, a White House statement said there was detailed discussion of Senator Muskie's role as Secretary "in advising the President on policy issues, in public presentation of the Administration's foreign policies, and in working closely with the Congress."

* * *

May 5, 1980

SOVIET TV EULOGIZES TITO WITHOUT MENTIONING RIFT

Special to The New York Times

MOSCOW, May 4—The death of President Tito of Yugoslavia was announced in solemn tones on Soviet television tonight. A news commentator paid tribute to Marshal Tito as a fighter for peace and socialism without mentioning his differences with the Soviet Union.

"The Soviet people deeply mourn the death of Tito, the outstanding leader of the Communists and workers of Yugoslavia and a leading figure of the international Communist and workers movement," said a commentator on the principal Soviet television news program, Vremya.

The news evidently came too late in the day for more extensive television coverage. Shortly before the program, the death was reported in a three-line notice by Tass, the official Soviet news agency.

Tito's Soviet Honors Cited

The television commentator noted that President Tito had been awarded the Soviet Union's Order of Lenin on his 80th birthday and the Order of the October Revolution on his 85th birthday in recognition of his World War II services and his contribution to "fraternal friendship and all-round cooperation" between Yugoslavia and the Soviet Union.

Marshal Tito, the commentator said, "was an active fighter for peace and for the solidarity of progressive forces in the struggle against imperialism and colonialism."

There have been few reports about Marshal Tito in the Soviet press in recent weeks beyond the medical bulletins issued by his doctors.

The most recent comment on what his death would signify politically came in a Tass commentary two weeks ago ridiculing a remark by a State Department official, who was said to have reiterated American readiness to help preserve Yugoslavia's independence.

"The question is: Who threatens that sovereign socialist country?" Tass said. "Fabrications about 'a Soviet threat' that allegedly hangs or might hang over Yugoslavia are a lie and an ill-intentioned lie at that. The Soviet Union has always proceeded and continues to proceed from the desire to strengthen and develop friendly relations with Yugoslavia on the basis of full equality, mutual respect and absolute noninterference in each other's affairs."

The tribute to President Tito on Soviet television was excerpted from a longer obituary that was transmitted later in the evening over Tass's Russian-language service. The obituary made no mention of Marshal Tito's rupture with Stalin and his subsequent disagreements with Moscow.

* * *

December 26, 1980

GREECE'S BIG PLUNGE: THE COMMON MARKET

By PAUL LEWIS
Special to The New York Times

ATHENS, Dec. 25—Greece will become the 10th member of the Common Market on New Year's Day, and the change promises to mark an important but painful turning point in the country's development and in the evolution of the market itself.

During the next five to eight years, Greece, with fewer than 10 million inhabitants, will gradually integrate its small economy with those of its richer and stronger northern neigh-

bors, phasing out all barriers to free circulation of goods, money and workers.

But for the Government of Prime Minister George Rallis and the nine present member countries, the political implications of Greek membership in the European Economic Community have always seemed more important than the economic ones. Linking Greece to Western Europe is a way of insuring the survival of parliamentary democracy in Athens.

Membership will firmly mark Greece as a member of the Western industrial world, though it remains poorer than its partners. It is also administratively backward and isolated in the eastern Mediterranean, hemmed in by the rest of the Balkans and a hostile Turkey.

'Coming Home to Greece'

"Europe will be coming home to Greece," said President Constantine Caramanlis, a strong supporter of Common Market membership. He spoke of the sense of cultural security that the market will bestow on Greece, whose citizens call it the cradle of Western civilization while at the same time worrying that it may be slipping into the Middle East.

For the other market members, admitting Greece marks a decisive change in the nature of their community. Long branded a "rich man's club," the Common Market is now irrevocably committed to taking in Europe's poorer nations.

Spain and Portugal have applied to join, and the "Community of 12" that appears almost certain to emerge in the next two or three years will be richer and more populous than the United States—if it holds together.

But as Greece prepares to join, there are growing fears that it is unprepared for the shocks and strains ahead and that Greeks may quickly become disillusioned. Five years ago, when Greece first applied to join, its prospective partners warned that "structural changes of considerable magnitude" would be needed in its inefficient, protected economy and its stultifying bureaucracy. Today, there is no sign of those changes. "There has been great irresponsibility," a leading Greek banker said.

Shock Treatment

The Government seems to be relying on the shock of entry to force industry, banking and the bureaucracy to become more efficient. "Greeks are best when they are under pressure," said the Minister of Economic Coordination, Ioannis Palaiokrassas, who added that membership would sweep away the "protectionist cobwebs" that shroud many aspects of Greek life.

Government spokesmen say that the terms Greece has negotiated will keep the pain within tolerable limits. Athens expects to receive at least $280 million in agricultural price supports and development aid, and the amount could reach $500 million by 1985.

Greek industry has been prepared in part for the shock of free trade with northern Europe by earlier reductions in tariffs. Hopes are high that Greece's proximity to rich markets in the Middle East and Africa will make it an attractive site for investment.

"There are risks, but they are worth taking," said Stamitas Mantazavinos, head of the Industry Federation.

Economic Problems Grow

But Greece is joining the market at the end of the period in which years of high economic growth virtually eliminated unemployment. The economy is stagnant. Prices are rising at the rate of 25 percent a year. Unemployment, still only 2.5 percent, is expected to move higher.

A recent opinion poll suggested less public commitment to membership than Government enthusiasm implies. Though 40 percent of those questioned were in favor and only 20 percent were opposed, 40 percent did not understand the issue.

With parliamentary elections due by next November, Andreas Papandreou's opposition Panhellenic Socialist Movement is already warning that Common Market membership will do Greece more harm than good. The party is promising to negotiate a looser connection.

"Greece is joining at a difficult moment, and the Common Market may become the scapegoat for its troubles," a Western European ambassador here warned.

If that happens, many diplomats and businessmen fear that Greek membership may not be the hoped-for first step toward a politically powerful Common Market stretching from Greenland to the eastern Mediterranean. They say it may instead become the first step toward a "two-speed" Europe, with the poorer southern countries linked loosely to the more prosperous economies of the north and continually resentful of their greater success.

*   *   *

April 4, 1981

BELGRADE SENDS TANKS TO REBELLIOUS REGION

By UPI

BELGRADE, Yugoslavia, April 3—Yugoslav tanks and troops took up positions today in a province in the south to put down anti-Government riots by Albanian separatists.

The Interior Ministry imposed a curfew in Pristina, capital of the Autonomous Province of Kosovo, and in four other towns after a police order yesterday banning all public gatherings.

Under the curfew, citizens in five districts were ordered to stay in their homes from 8 P.M. to 5 A.M. Dzavid Nimani, head of the local government, accused Albanian nationalists of seeking to "destabilize, break up and endanger the territorial integrity and independence of our country." He called on Communists to unite to quell the demonstrations.

Mountainous and Underdeveloped

Although the central Yugoslav Government is aiding Kosovo's economic development, promoting industrialization in the mountainous farm region, the province remains the most economically underdeveloped region in multi-national Yugoslavia, which is made up of six republics and two autonomous provinces.

Kosovo, in the south between Albania and the Yugoslav republics of Macedonia, Serbia and Montenegro, has 1.6 million people, a million of them ethnic Albanians who mainly hold to old traditions, including feuds.

The separatists want to unite with Albania, the small and self-isolated Communist country on the Adriatic. In Pristina, according to residents, stood guard at the radio and television building, the post office, at hospitals, the jail and other official buildings.

Pristina, a city of 130,000 people, with postwar modern buildings situated among traditional old Balkan huts, is about 160 miles south of Belgrade.

Soldiers and policemen armed with machine guns were reported in control of the streets in the capital and in nearby towns. Helicopters were on patrol.

Residents of the capital said that some rioters had used small children as shields against police gunfire during the violence. Thousands of people were reported to have rampaged through the city, smashing shop windows and factory machines. In Belgrade, a Government official said the rioting in Kosovo was "the worst such an outbreak of separatist demands" in Yugoslavia since the end of World War II, when the country was patched together again after dismemberment by Axis invaders.

The official, who asked that his name not be used, said the Government would use "all possible means" to put down the violence. Faced with their worst crisis since the death last May of President Tito, Yugoslavia's Government and Communist Party leaders issued a statement charging that the riots had been organized by groups outside Yugoslavia, "creating instability and endangering the territorial integrity of Yugoslavia."

The disorders began some days ago when students at the University of Pristina demonstrated to protest the food in their cafeteria and other issues.

*   *   *

April 6, 1981

BELGRADE SEES PERIL OF MINORITY UNREST

By MARVINE HOWE
Special to The New York Times

BELGRADE, April 5—Yugoslav Government and Communist Party leaders have voiced apprehension that other national minorities may stage anti-Government demonstrations following the rioting by Albanian nationalists in Kosovo Province.

Kosovo Province, which is inhabited largely by ethnic Albanians, is still under a state of emergency after last week's rioting in which two demonstrators were killed and many people wounded. Movements and public gatherings were restricted and journalists were discouraged from visiting the province.

Nevertheless, the official press agency reported that life was "almost normal" in the province, factories were back to work and production had resumed. Workers were said to be cleaning up the debris and repairing damage caused by the demonstrators.

It was also announced that a new hydroelectric power plant, which will produce 94.6 million kilowatt hours annually, began its operation yesterday. This announcement was clearly designed to show a return to normality as well as continued development of what is generally considered Yugoslavia's poorest province.

Indications of Calm

Last night a television film of Pristina, capital of Kosovo, which is located 190 miles southeast of Belgrade, showed indications that calm had returned. People were seen walking about normally, traffic had resumed and shops were open.

But tonight, the state television reported that "things were not yet normal" and warned the population to be watchful against "the enemy."

Another sign of continued tension in the region was the cancellation of a soccer match today in Pristina. Two ethnic Albanian teams that had been scheduled to play in games outside the province, also did not play.

Belgrade citizens spoke in hushed tones about "the riots," which were the most violent that anyone could recall in recent history. Not since the end of World War II had curfew been proclaimed and movement restricted, they said.

Leading Communists Concerned

The gravity of the events was emphasized by leading officials of the Yugoslav Communist Party. Dusan Dragosavac, secretary of the party's Presidium, described the dissident elements as "irredentist" and "nationalistic."

"There is a real danger now of other nationalisms manifesting themselves here and there in response to the revealed Albanian nationalism," Mr. Dragosavac declared in a meeting last night with Yugoslav editors and publishers.

This was a reference to Yugoslavia's complex multinational state, which is composed of six federated republics as well as two autonomous regions.

Kosovo Province is part of the republic of Serbia. Albanian nationalists there are known to want the status of a full republic. The authorities have always dismissed this idea because they feared the Albanian majority in Kosovo would then seek to secede and unite with Albania.

The same theme was echoed by the president of the Serbian republic, Dobrivoje Vidid, addressing party members here. He warned of the need for increased "vigilance" in view of possible agitation in other areas.

An editorial in the influential Yugoslav daily Borba, called the events "an attempt to attack Yugoslavia's unity and integrity." Newspapers and senior Government officials denounced "the enemy" and "hostile elements" but refrained from identifying any specific source behind the Kosovo troubles.

* * *

April 20, 1981

ROOTS OF YUGOSLAV RIOTS: VAGUE 'ENEMY' BLAMED

By MARVINE HOWE
Special to The New York Times

PRISTINA, Yugoslavia, April 19—Even in the cold, dreary rain, women of Albanian ancestry with white headscarfs and long floral print skirts or baggy trousers strolled along the main street pausing to admire the window displays of modern dress shops, furniture stores and supermarkets.

There was little evidence that this provincial capital had been the scene two weeks ago of the worst riots in Yugoslavia since World War II. The only signs were a few remaining smashed windows, police on patrol, army guards at public buildings and the nervousness of people when asked about the events.

A state of emergency remains in force but has been relaxed in Kosovo Province, which borders on Albania and has one and a half million inhabitants, most of Albanian ancestry.

A curfew has been lifted, grade school students have gone back to classes, and the university, where the troubles began, is to open tomorrow.

Journalists Visit Province

Yesterday and the day before, for the first time since the emergency was proclaimed on April 2, a group of more than 50 foreign correspondents went on an official tour of the province. The journalists were barred, however, from visiting the area on their own.

In interviews, local officials proudly recited the achievements in Kosovo since World War II. They gave an impressive picture of social, economic and political development. Nevertheless, they were unable to provide a convincing explanation for the cause of the rioting or why it was so widespread among the youth who have benefited most from the postwar developments here.

Nor were the authorities very clear about what they are going to do to prevent a recurrence of the violence. It was announced that 28 people had been arrested and would be brought to trial at a later date but that "the enemy" was still being sought. No one was very precise about who the "enemy" was, except to say that it included everyone opposed to Yugoslavia's nonaligned, independent, Communist policies.

The only solutions offered were more political indoctrination, material progress and social improvements. That has been official policy all along, but it has not prevented periodic outbursts of Albanian nationalism.

People Hesitant to Talk

The Government reported "unanimity" at the provincial level on the handling of the events. It said that there was no question of officials resigning "as in bourgeois regimes." The provincial committee is scheduled to meet soon to make a "critical assessment" of the situation.

People of Albanian ancestry questioned by reporters were reluctant to talk about the rioting, which began on March 11 with a student protest over conditions in the university. The unrest erupted again on March 26 and culminated in a major outburst of Albanian nationalism on April 1 and 2. In the end, there were at least nine people dead and 59 seriously injured, according to official sources.

Most of those questioned said they did not want to talk about the rioting, were not around at the time or simply did not know what it was all about. Several in their early 20's asked aggressively whether the journalists had the right to be here asking questions. A university student asked if he could send a letter abroad to tell what happened. They generally looked about anxiously as if fearing to be seen talking with a foreigner.

Serbs, members of the largest ethnic group in Yugoslavia although a minority in Kosovo, were less reluctant to talk about the disturbances but could not explain why they had occurred and were worried that they might break out again. Although Kosovo was the heart of the medieval Serbian kingdom, the 220,000 Serbs in the province are outnumbered by more than a million people of Albanian origin.

14th Century Serbian Exodus

The first exodus of Serbs from here took place when the Ottomon Turks invaded Serbia in the 14th century. Modern migrations occurred as Serbs sought a better life in the industrialized north of Yugoslavia.

In recent times, Serbs are said to have been selling their property and leaving because, as one put it, "We don't feel comfortable with Albanian nationalism."

"We don't understand what they want because they have more rights than we do," a Serbian civil servant in the Kosovo administration complained. "They have more rights than we do, preference in housing, jobs, even in student hostels."

The roots of Albanian discontent are not immediately visible to the visitor. The development of Pristina, a modest backwater when the Communists assumed power after World War II, has been spectacular. The skyline of this fast-growing modern capital is dominated by high apartment and office buildings as well as cranes engaged in construction projects.

A Palatial New Hotel

Beside the minarets of ancient mosques, rise a palatial new hotel, a social center, a theater, a multidomed library and a vast university, the third largest in the country.

In a three and half hour news conference, Mahmut Bakali, the top Communist Party official in Kosovo, talked about the "unparalleled results" achieved in the past 36 years under the leadership of Yugoslavia's Communists.

He told of new factories to process the province's mining and agricultural resources and efforts to produce more jobs and housing. Kosovo still has the lowest per capital income in Yugoslavia, about $800. But Mr. Bakali said that this is no reason "to deny what has been achieved in absolute terms, the creation of an economic base and necessary cadres." He predicted that economic growth in the province would be much faster from now on and that the gap with the rest of the country would decrease.

The university has undergone similar growth. Vice Chancellor Ali Turku said that it started out in 1970 with 7,661 students, more than half of them Serbians. Today, he said, the university has 47,284 students, nearly three quarters of them of Albanian descent. He said that finding jobs for graduates would be no problem in view of the province's rapid development.

Growth May Have Been Too Fast

However, some local officials of Albanian background suggested that the growth in Kosovo had been too fast. They said that people, particularly the young, were suffering cultural shock. "We thought it was sufficient to give them material progress and education but we have failed to give them an ideology," an official said.

The authorities said that old claims of "Serbian domination" were unjustified. They said that ethnic Albanians have gained access to key jobs at every level in the provincial administration, the ruling Communist Party and the economy.

"I am an Albanian and I can say we have complete independence except for a few trappings of a state like shooting off a cannon," a senior official in the provincial administration remarked. "We make our own decisions and run things without interference from the republic."

Mr. Bakali insisted that none of the demonstrators' grievances or claims were justified. He said that "a handful of hostile elements," mainly youngsters of Albanian origin, had incited the crowd with popular slogans and then turned the demonstration into a nationalist incident.

"It was an organized, well-conceived, nonspontaneous action," the Communist Party leader asserted. He declined to identify the "hostile forces" behind the demonstration except to repeat what officials in Belgrade have already said, that they included both leftists and rightists from here and abroad.

He said that perhaps the authorities had been at fault for having tolerated these nationalists. But he stressed that the Communist Party has excluded a score of members who took part in the demonstrations.

*   *   *

July 19, 1981

CROATIAN MOVEMENT LEADS TO CONVICTION OF 5 OVER BOMBINGS

By PETER KIHSS

Five men have been convicted and 10 others are awaiting trial as investigations of possible planned violence in the United States by demonstrators for Croatian independence from Yugoslavia continue in New York and other major cities in the United States.

Only one terrorist action has been claimed in the name of Croatians since the arrests last December of seven members of the Otpor organization, according to Stuart J. Baskin, an assistant United States attorney.

In that incident, a pipe bomb went off in the State Supreme Court building at 60 Centre Street in Manhattan on Jan. 23. No charge has been filed in that blast or a March 17, 1980, bombing of a Yugoslav bank at 500 Fifth Avenue.

Otpor has lawful political, social and cultural programs, dating to the mid-1970's, with chapters in the United States and Canada. It is estimated to have as many as 300 members.

Charges Superseded

The Federal Bureau of Investigation, the New York police, United States Attorney John S. Martin Jr. and a Federal grand jury here are conducting inquiries.

The pending indictment for conspiracy and racketeering was filed against 10 men June 30, superseding June 25 charges against nine of them and adding a Chicago electrician, Milan Bagaric.

Five defendants were arraigned here last Tuesday. Bail of $1 million each was continued for Ante Ljubas of Chicago, earlier called the group's No. 2 leader in the United States, and Ranko Primorac, reported to be its Los Angeles chief. Mr. Baskin told Federal Judge Vincent L. Broderick that both lacked roots in this country.

Mile Markic of Skokie, Ill., was held in $300,000 bail, and Miro Biosic of San Clemente, Calif., and Ivan Misetic of Skokie, were held in $200,000 each.

2 Due for Arraignment

Last December's arrests led to the conviction of five men for conspiracy to kill a political foe and to bomb buildings. Four were sentenced. They were Ivan Cale, head of a New York chapter, who received 35 years in prison; Franjo Ivic, who received a 30-year term, and Nedjelko Sovulj and Stipe Ivkosic, who were given 20 years each. Sentence is pending for the fifth man, Ante Caron. A sixth suspect, Peter Stambuk, was acquitted, and the prosecution is expected to move to dismiss the charge against his brother, Andrew Stambuk.

In the pending case, Mr. Bagaric and Mile Boban, owner of a San Francisco construction business, are due here for arraignment July 27. Each is free on $250,000 bail.

Earlier arraignments were held for Andjelko Jakic, a machine shop operator, of Mamaroneck, now free on $100,000 bail, and Vinko Logarusic of Cleveland, who was held in $100,000 bail. Extradition is to be sought for Drago Sudar of Etobicoke, Ontario, who is being held without bail in Canada.

The current indictment cites actions starting with an attempt to blow up a Pittsburgh building Jan. 4, 1977, and includes a plot to murder a San Francisco man.

* * *

October 19, 1981

GREEK SOCIALISTS WIN BIG VICTORY; PREMIER CONCEDES

By MARVINE HOWE
Special to The New York Times

ATHENS, Oct. 18—Greece's Socialist opposition won a major victory in parliamentary elections today, bringing an end to 35 years of pro-Western conservative rule.

Prime Minister George Rallis conceded defeat after early returns showed that the Panhellenic Socialist Movement of Andreas Papandreou had taken a commanding lead in most parts of the country.

"We will not lead the country into any adventure," Mr. Papandreou, the son of George Papandreou, a former Prime Minister of Greece, said in a victory speech.

The Socialist victory, achieved with strong backing in the countryside, could mean radical change in this country's foreign policy since the party's program expresses opposition to Greece's membership in the North Atlantic Treaty Organization and the European Economic Community and to the presence of American bases here.

Strong Majority Seen

Incomplete returns issued tonight by the Interior Ministry suggested that Mr. Papandreou's party, known as Pasok, would have a strong majority in the 300-seat Parliament, with 176 representatives compared to 109 for the conservative New Democracy Party.

The pro-Moscow Communist Party appeared to be a weak third with only 15 seats. If these results hold, the Communists' hopes of holding the balance of power would be dashed.

With about 40 percent of the vote counted, the Socialists had 47.73 percent of the vote, New Democracy, 35.66 percent, and the Communists, 11.33 percent. Abstentions were running at about 22.5 percent out of a total 6.8 million registered voters.

In his victory speech, Mr. Papandreou called for "reconciliation, cooperation of all the people in a government for all the people." He added, "Our policy is to bring prosperity to all the people, national pride and social justice." After his broadcast message to the nation, Mr. Papandreou went outside his home in suburban Athens, where thousands of cheering supporters had gathered to celebrate victory.

In downtown Athens, huge crowds poured out into the streets waving green Socialist banners and the national flag, chanting "Victory for Change!" and "Pasok and the People to Power!"

Prime Minister Rallis conceded only three hours after the polls closed. "A few days ago I predicted a New Democracy victory," he said.

"I'm afraid this prediction has proven totally unfounded: there has not been a victory for New Democracy but for the opposition," the outgoing Prime Minister soberly told the crowd of Greek and foreign reporters in the official press center.

"I hand over to Mr. Papandreou a strong Greece and hope it will continue to develop in tranquility, progress and peace." The Socialist victory is likely to reverse the results of the last elections in 1977, when the ruling New Democracy Party won 42 percent of the vote compared to 25 percent for the Socialists.

The vote was not really a protest action since even Socialist militants acknowledge that living standards have improved substantially under the long conservative rule. It was above all a desire for change, according to conversations with dozens of voters.

The Greek electorate did not appear interested in foreign policy—which was the center of New Democracy's campaign. Instead, Greeks voted for a change in personalities and a change in priorities, with greater emphasis on social change.

Mr. Papandreou, a 62-year-old former economics professor at the University of California at Berkeley, is married to an American, the former Margaret Chant of Elmhurst, Ill. He is not regarded as a hardened Marxist, as his enemies portray him, but more as a politician in the style of Eugene McCarthy.

Socialist Pledged Change

The Socialist leader waged a long and exhaustive campaign telling the voters what they wanted to hear, that he would bring them change in their everyday lives. He talked to them about higher pensions, a new school system, the end of tax frauds, hospitals and better health care, and a cleanup of bureaucracy and corruption.

The New Democracy Party had waged an aggressive campaign charging that the Socialists would lead the country to chaos and ruin, disrupting ties with the Western alliances and bringing bankruptcy with its costly array of social programs.

Mr. Rallis, an uninspired campaigner, succeeded in unifying his own party and absorbing the right wing National Front Party and liberals but clearly failed to reach the voting masses.

Now President Constantine Caramanlis will ask Mr. Papandreou, as leader of the majority party, to form a new Government. It is expected to be announced as early as Wednesday.

Calm Atmosphere Reported

The Greeks went to the polls in an atmosphere of calm in sharp contrast to the carnival gaiety of the monthlong campaign. People filed into schools and cafes, converted into polling stations.

No significant incidents were reported during polling time from sunrise to sunset. The weather was hot and sunny and many voted early so that they could go to the beach. Voting is compulsory, with exemptions for people who are over 70, are sick or are living more than 120 miles away from their place of registration.

At the polling stations, men and women voted in separate booths. Inside, there were two booths, one for the parliamentary elections and one to select 24 representatives to the European Parliament. Greece joined the European Economic Community in January.

Generally representatives of the three main parties were present as observers.

Voters presented their identity cards and were then given ballots of the 14 participating parties. Once in the isolated booth, the voter would choose one ballot and put it in an envelope and throw away the unused ballots in a large cardboard box.

The streets of Athens appeared strangely deserted during polling hours. It was said that about one million people left the Athens-Piraeus area to vote in their villages of origin.

U.S. Expects Good Relations

Special to The New York Times
WASHINGTON, Oct. 18—The State Department said tonight that the United States looked forward "to continued close relations" with Greece under its new Government.

"We believe a good bilateral relationship is in the interest of both Greece and the United States," said Susan Pittman, a department spokesman. "We want to have the best relationship with the Papandreou Government and we intend to do what we can to foster that."

* * *

October 20, 1981

WHO LOST WHAT IN GREECE

It may well be that local factors, notably a yearning for change, explain the election victory in Greece of a Socialist regime with a marked neutralist tinge. But there is more to it than that. Roughly half of Greece's voters chose a party advocating the closing of American bases and withdrawal from the military wing of NATO. That program evidently was no liability to Prime Minister-elect Andreas Papandreou. And defending military alignment with the West did not save Prime Minister George Rallis, whose New Democracy Party has ruled since 1974, when Athens rid itself of the "colonels."

So when due allowance is made for local factors, the Greek vote carries a wider message for Americans. This news follows the British Labor Party's embrace of neutralism and a surge in anti-nuclear sentiment among West Germany's Social Democrats. Newly Socialist France has moved closer to Washington's view of East-West fundamentals, but France remains the odd country out in NATO, clinging to its "independent" nuclear deterrent.

This fraying of the Atlantic consensus is not in the first instance Washington's fault, nor is it conceptually sound. All West Europeans now take for granted a peace guaranteed by a balance of terror; the unilateralists among them want to be spared the risks of harboring regional nuclear weapons while they sit under the American umbrella. Protests are shouted against NATO; the Soviet missiles aimed at Western Europe are mildly censured or condoned.

But President Reagan has helped to make himself an easy foil. His intentions on arms negotiations remain obscure. Does he really wish an illusory strategic supremacy? Who speaks for his team on foreign policy? Indeed, slogans aside, is there a policy for dealing with the Soviet Union? The uncertainty burdens Europeans who defend the allied consensus. Ask George Rallis.

His defeat by a declared skeptic in Athens may finally impel sharper articulation of American objectives. Mr. Papandreou, a Greek-born but American-bred economist, needs no instruction on the value of an American connection. He knows that if Greece again departs from NATO's military command, the beneficiary will be his nation's bitter rival, Turkey. He knows where those four American bases might move if he evicts them.

As election day neared, Mr. Papandreou muted his neutralism and spoke mainly about his plans for radical social reform. And his call for a referendum on Common Market membership requires the assent of President Caramanlis, as Greek voters well understood. So no drastic overnight shift in Greece's international position is likely. Nor is a military takeover imminent as long as Mr. Caramanlis—and Mr. Rallis—remain prominently on the scene.

There is time for talk. Greece isn't "lost." What should be lost is the complacent assumption that American policy is so manifestly sound that it needs no refinement or articulation.

* * *

October 26, 1981

FOR MARGARET PAPANDREOU, A 'QUIET RAGE' OF FEMINISM

By MARVINE HOWE
Special to The New York Times

ATHENS, Oct. 23—Margaret Papandreou believes her husband's new Socialist Government will mean a breakthrough for Greek women, who she says "have been largely suppressed through our capitalist system and our patriarchal mentality."

The American-born wife of Greece's new Prime Minister is a dedicated feminist, a Socialist and the guiding inspiration behind the Women's Union of Greece.

"Women's problems are the same in Greece as in most countries, though maybe to a greater degree," Mrs. Papandreou said in a recent interview. She emphasized the need to open more jobs to women, set up more child care centers, change the education system, revise family laws and legalize abortions.

Greece's new First Lady is tall and blond with the unpretentious charm of a Midwestern farm girl. She comes from

Susan Muhlhauser

Margaret Papandreou

Elmhurst, Ill., and studied journalism and public health at the University of Minnesota.

Papandreous Met in Minnesota

It was there that she met and married an economics professor, Andreas Papandreou, in 1951. He had left Greece in 1940 before the invasion of Mussolini's troops, and had gone to Harvard University, where he obtained a doctorate in economics in 1943.

Mr. Papandreou became an American citizen in 1944. He served in the United States Navy for two years before going to the University of Minnesota to teach. In 1955, the Papandreous moved to the University of California at Berkeley, where he served as chairman of the Department of Economics.

Their four children were born in America. George Jeffrey, 29 years old, has just been elected to Parliament from the district of Patras, where his father and grandfather ran before him. Gayle Sophia, 27, who has just finished her master's degree in economics in Sussex, England, recently married and expects to get a job soon. Nicholas, 25, is studying for a doctorate in Princeton and Andreas Jr., 23, is studying at the London School of Economics.

It was in 1959 that Andreas Papandreou decided to return to Greece, his wife recalls. Mr. Papandreou, who had gone back with Fulbright and Guggenheim grants, was asked by Prime Minister Constantine Caramanlis to set up the Center of Economic Research in Athens. He resumed his Greek citizenship, won a seat in Parliament and was given a Cabinet post in the 1964 Government headed by his father, Prime Minister George Papandreou.

Colonels Arrest Father and Son

The rapidly growing influence and Socialist ideas of Andreas Papandreou were said to be among the main factors that prompted the 1967 colonels' coup. Both father and son were arrested.

George was released six months later and died the next year. Andreas was charged with high treason, kept in solitary confinement for eight months, then released under a Christmas amnesty and expelled.

Andreas spent his seven years of exile as a professor of economics, first at Stockholm University, then York University in Toronto. During his exile, he organized the Pan Hellenic Liberation Movement, a coalition of groups opposed to military dictatorship.

Mr. Papandreou and his family returned to Greece in 1974 when the junta collapsed after the Turkish invasion of Cyprus. He then founded the Pan Hellenic Socialist Movement, called Pasok. It grew in seven years from a small group with 13 percent of the vote and 12 seats in Parliament to become the major political force in the country with 48 percent of the vote and 172 seats in last Sunday's election.

'Margaret Taught Us Everything'

His wife started to build up the women's movement in 1975. "Margaret taught us everything, how to make a modern organization," says Titina Pantazis, a young woman who has just been elected on the Socialist ticket as deputy to the European Parliament. "She is the brains behind the women's union and has been elected president several times, but always refuses, preferring the post of vice president."

Mrs. Papandreou says her main activity has been to mobilize women, wherever they are—in the marketplaces, beauty shops, hospitals and particularly in the villages. There are now chapters of the Women's Union all over Greece.

"But there's still a strong belief that women belong at home," she said.

More Women Candidates

She is pleased that there were more women running in the last election—205 compared with only 103 in 1977—but she is disappointed that there were not many more. And only 12 women—8 of them Socialists—were elected to the 300-seat Parliament, just two more than in the last Conservative-dominated legislature.

Mrs. Papandreou rarely appeared with her husband during the election campaign, preferring to take part in women's rallies. She went to Piraeus to show support for the actress Melina Mercouri, who later won a seat in Parliament and has been named Minister of Culture and Sciences.

Miss Mercouri arrived at the rally late with a dramatic flourish, wearing the party's green colors and stealing the show with slogans, "No to American Bases!" and "Out With NATO!" Mrs. Papandreou showed up quietly and on time. In a correct, if stilted, Greek she made a strong plea for women to vote Socialist.

"We've had enough of high prices and high cost of living of this archaic educational system, the lack of child care centers," she said. "We've had enough of living in areas where our relatives or friends die because of lack of doctors, of hospitals, of emergency treatment. We've had enough of Government bureaucracy and corruption, of getting improper and dangerous abortions."

'Second-Class Citizens'

She went on, "We've had enough of being second-class citizens, always pushed to the margin, never listened to, never given rightful positions in decision-making bodies."

Militant men in the Socialist ranks generally approve of Mrs. Papandreou's discretion and say she has played "an appropriate role," concentrating on the Women's Union.

In a recent interview with a Greek newspaper, Mrs. Papandreou said she had been interested in women's rights ever since her high school days, when she wanted to play on the school basketball team, but it accepted only boys.

"Since then, a quiet rage developed in me over the unfairness of the system," she said. Almost wistfully, she expressed the hope that one day she would be seen by Greeks as not only the wife of Andreas Papandreou but also as Margaret Papandreou, a woman with her own personality and political activities, particularly her work with women.

Several years ago, she began writing children's books with a message—in Greek "with some help." She has written "an antiimperialist book" and a "women's lib book" for children aged 5 to 8.

"Children's fairy tales are political," she says. "All the books we read as children talk of kings, princesses, poor and rich, strong and handsome men, pretty women made for the home. This is the children's version of the capitalist system's ideology."

*   *   *

November 8, 1981

BULGARIA IS ZEALOUSLY MARKING ITS 1,300 BIRTHDAY

By MARVINE HOWE
Special to The New York Times

There is a rush to finish construction by the end of the year on the National Palace of Culture, an arts center that will have an auditorium that seats more than 10,000 people and contains works by more than 100 of Bulgaria's best artists.

Last month at Plovdiv in the heart of ancient Thrace, the Government opened a magnificent, well-preserved Roman theater with marble seats for about 3,500 people. And this month, a vast stone and concrete memorial complex is scheduled to open at Kolarovgrad, formerly Shumen, an early capital and the cradle of Bulgarian history.

These events are part of a kind of national mobilization this year to mark the 13th centennial of the foundation of the Bulgarian nation.

"Our 1,300th birthday is not just a simple event," Todor Ribarov, Chief Secretary of the National Commission for the Commemorations, said in a recent interview, "but a process to stimulate creative activity, accelerate our general development and improve our individual social conscience."

23,000 Events This Year

Mr. Ribarov said that this year alone there would be some 23,000 events connected with the 13th centenary and that celebrations would continue until 1994.

A strong sense of nationalism and increased self-confidence are widespread in Bulgaria. That is apparent in the crowds of young and old who flock to movie theaters to see "Khan Asparukh," a 5-hour, 45-minute trilogy on the national hero and the founding of the Bulgarian nation in 681. It was then that Bulgar tribes migrating from the east crossed the Danube, subjugated the Slavs and settled permanently.

There was general satisfaction when Bulgarian women recently won most of the medals at the world sports rhythmic gymnastics championship in Munich, defeating the Soviet team. The victories were dedicated to the 13th centenary of the Bulgarian nation. Similarly, the Bulgarian Alpine expedition's success in climbing the Himalayan peak of Lhotze last spring became a patriotic achievement and was officially hailed as a "great victory attained in glorification of the 1,300th anniversary of Bulgarian statehood."

They Object to 'Satellite'

Bulgarians openly resent their country's prevalent image in the West as a carbon copy of the Soviet Union. They readily express gratitude for past and present assistance from the Soviet Union but object to the word "satellite."

"Special relations with the Soviet Union are both ancient and modern," said Georgi Iovkov, chief of the Foreign Ministry's press department. "They are very close, privileged relations between two socialist countries, two separate countries each with its own identity."

A Bulgarian journalist said, "The Soviet Union is like our big brother." He compared the relationship to that of the United States and England, pointing out that it was even closer because Russians helped the Bulgarians in their war for independence against the Ottoman Empire.

Bulgaria's President and Communist Party leader, Todor Zhivkov, gave a political dimension to the jubilee year in the main ceremony held here on Oct. 20, which was attended by top state and party officials, national dignitaries and foreign delegations from 100 countries, including the United States.

'Good Neighborly Relations'

"Bulgaria stretches out her hand," Mr. Zhivkov said. "She is ready to sign bilateral agreements with the Balkan countries, including a code of good neighborly relations and a renunciation of any territorial claims. We warmly support the idea of turning the Balkans into a nuclear-free zone." He went on to propose convening a meeting of Balkan leaders next year to discuss the issue.

The suggestions were not new. Mr. Zhivkov offered to sign treaties with his Balkan neighbors last March during the party congress, and Rumania has long advocated a Balkan nuclear-free zone. Analysts question the viability of such a proposal, because among Balkan countries only the NATO nations of Greece and Turkey are said to have nuclear weapons on their soil, not the Communist countries of Bulgaria, Rumania, Yugoslavia and Albania.

Nevertheless, the Bulgarian leader's proposal attracted attention for its timing, coming when antinuclear feelings are high in Western Europe and after the victory of the Socialists in Greece, who have called for a nuclear-free zone in the Balkans. The Bulgarian move appears to parallel that of the Soviet Union, which has encouraged the establishment of a nuclear-free zone in Scandinavia.

Zhivkov Firm but Flexible

Mr. Zhivkov has ruled this country with a firm hand but with enough flexibility that some Western diplomats believe he might win a free election. The Bulgarian leader, who was 70 years old on Sept. 7, suffered a personal tragedy earlier this year when his daughter Lyudmila, 39, who was widely seen as a possible successor, died of brain hemorrhage.

The crisis in Poland is viewed by Bulgarian officials as evidence that the Zhivkov regime, with its gradual but total collectivization of agriculture and its loosening of rigid controls in industry, has chosen the right path. There are no food shortages here now, and foreign debts have been kept to a minimum.

The Government-controlled press contains daily denunciations of abuses of the system but not of the system itself. In recent days the press has reported various cases of misappropriation of public property, particularly goods stolen from freight cars.

There have also been reports on the ineffective organization of labor in the building industry, a lack of financial control in some state enterprises and corruption in some agricultural and industrial concerns.

No Visible Opposition

Some Bulgarians are unhappy, of course, but there is no visible organized opposition and no work stoppages. Individuals sometimes privately express bitterness over restrictions on travel, the dearth of Western publications and the opportunism of certain party officials. There are numerous divided families, with people here trying to get authorization to leave to join relatives abroad who have defected.

The number of political prisoners is not made public but is not believed to be very large. Although the Bulgarian Constitution guarantees human rights, people can be jailed up to five years for "antistate agitation or propaganda" and as many as 12 years for belonging to "an organization whose activities are aimed at committing offenses against the state."

Progress is generally measured from 1956, when Mr. Zhivkov took control. According to official figures, the real income of Bulgarians more than tripled in the 1956–1980 period. In that span, the population increased from 7.6 million to 8.8 million.

The per-capita consumption of meat more than doubled in that period, and the number of college-trained specialists increased by more than five times and now stands at one in 10 Bulgarians. The number of hospital beds increased from 38,331 to 79,588.

For every 100 households in 1980, there were 77 television sets, 77 refrigerators, 71 electric washing machines and 29 cars; none of those items were listed in 1956.

*   *   *

November 15, 1981

YUGOSLAVIA IS SHOWING STRAIN AT ITS MANY SEAMS

By DAVID BINDER

BELGRADE—A Yugoslav Foreign Ministry official, musing aloud to a visitor from the United States, remarked recently: "On every single occasion your officials talk to us or make public statements they repeat the formula that your Government supports our territorial integrity, independence and unity. Are you trying to tell us something? Do you think we're falling apart?"

The Belgrade official was citing a fact, but it is also a fact that, 18 months after the death of President Josip Broz Tito, this quintessentially Balkan country seems to be undergoing a new kind of self-induced balkanization.

This week and, for that matter, most of this year, the republic is marking the "40th anniversary of the Yugoslav Revolution." By that, Yugoslavs mean the uprising led by Tito against Fascist invaders in the name of freedom, independence, socialism and "brotherhood and unity." Over four decades and at a considerable cost, the first three goals have been largely attained but, lately, brotherhood and unity seem to have deteriorated.

To be sure, Yugoslavia, which means "the land of the South Slavs," is an artificial creation, a country of seven languages and three major religions, not to mention lesser rivalries. Until Tito came along, the dominant thrust for unification came from Serbia, which envisioned a reprise of a medieval empire that once stretched to the farthest shores of Aegean Greece. The vision of Tito, half Croat and half Slovene by origin, was of a federal republic bound together by independence, Communism and a spirit of innovation. Yet the seeds of Yugoslavia's current difficulties were planted in large part by Tito himself.

The Albanian minority of 1.3 million, half the size of the population of neighboring Albania itself, rose up against the perceived discriminatory policies of Belgrade last spring, a little more than a year after Tito had generously and probably unwisely told them in their own Kosovo region, "This land is yours." The bloody rebellion has stirred smaller but also disturbing signs of restiveness among the Croat Roman Catholic clergy and the newly recognized Moslem nation in Bosnia-Herzegovina.

The economy, which boomed ahead for 15 years until 1980, has developed severe inflation. Prices for most consumer goods went up 50 percent in the past year, while some imported goods disappeared from the shelves. When the economic frailties began to appear, the Belgrade collective leadership finally realized that it had underestimated the impact of the rise in prices for imported oil.

Katherine Young/Sven Simon

Extended family in Kosovo, Yugoslavia.

A whole of many parts

Yugoslav republics	Population (1979)	Per capita income (1979, in U.S. dollars)
Bosnia and Herzegovina	4,178,000	$1,695
Montenegro	589,000	$1,555
Croatia	4,597,000	$3,038
Macedonia	1,863,000	$1,854
Slovenia	1,826,000	$4,855
Serbia	5,532,000	$2,329
(Autonomous Provinces)		
Vojvodina	2,009,000	$2,917
Kosovo	1,566,000	$750
Total	22,160,000	$2,430

Sources: Yugoslav Government; World Bank

The leadership has also discovered that while the system of decentralized and rotated political power imposed by Tito's testament functions well in a mechanical sense, it lacks spirit and, above all, the power to inspire.

Yearning for a Little Charisma

In an interview, Lazar Mojsov, who ran the ruling League of Communists for one year until the last week of October, acknowledged that in Tito's lifetime, there seemed to be two Yugoslavias, one of fantasy and one of ordinary realities, with the former frequently seeming to dominate the scene. While Tito was alive, he said, "It made certain Yugoslav leaders think they were 10 feet tall." Since Tito's death, the realities of inflation, selfishness and separatism have asserted themselves to the point where the fantasy Yugoslavia has receded into memory for many of the 22 million people living in a country the size of Wyoming. "Before, we had one man who said everything," remarked a Belgrade intellectual. "Now we have a whole lot of men who can't say anything. Hold on to power, that's all they can think of."

"The era of charismatic great leaders is gone," Mr. Mojsov declared, as if also speaking for the ages to come. Yet in conversations, ordinary Yugoslavs seem to yearn for at least a couple of leaders with a touch of charisma, if only to give the country a greater sense of purpose.

Mr. Mojsov admitted that Tito's requirement of constant rotation within the leadership, down to the communal government and party levels, had run into a fundamental obstacle. There are not enough Yugoslavs able or willing to fill the jobs. (Sixteen years ago, when Tito first introduced the idea of "rotacija" of officials, the psychiatric clinics filled up with men bearing the signs of Napoleon complexes, the late Belgrade psychoanalyst, Viktor Komarecki reported at the time.)

For Mr. Mojsov, who was probably better known as the opera-loving president of the United Nations General Assembly in 1977 than as Yugoslav leader this year, the latest rotation in the 23-member Presidium means he will devote more time to his tasks as head of the Central Committee's ideological commission. As if relishing his new field of concentration, he spoke of a future Yugoslavia in which his ruling party would have simply melted away, of "associations of labor" as Marx foresaw them, or perhaps of a Yugoslavia of 22 million individual parties, all working together because by that time, a new Yugoslav man would have been created.

But it is hard to find even one Yugoslav man these days. There are just a lot of Serbs, Bosnians, Albanians, Croats, Macedonians, Montenegrins, Magyars, Slovenians— Communists, atheists, Catholics, Orthodox Christians and Moslems—trying to make ends meet.

Ranko Petkovic, a ranking Belgrade foreign policy commentator, recently described the scene in the Balkan region as "not a powder keg, but not a zone of peace, either." Mr. Petkovic cited the continuing Greek-Turkish feud, accused neighboring Bulgaria of maintaining claims against huge chunks of Yugoslav territory and charged Albania with inciting unrest.

It may be, the American visitor suggested to the Yugoslav Foreign Ministry official, that the great powers will end up trying to hold Yugoslavia together in spite of itself to keep the Balkans from blowing up again. To which the official indignantly retorted: "Do you mean big powers getting involved here again?"

* * *

April 16, 1982

VISIT TO CHINA KEEPING RUMANIAN LEADER BUSY

By Reuters

PEKING, April 15—Nicolae Ceausescu, the Rumanian leader, conferred today with Hu Yaobang, the Chinese Communist Party chairman, on the third day of an official visit.

On Wednesday, Mr. Hu accompanied Mr. Ceausescu on a one-day trip to the Manchurian industrial center of Shenyang. There the Rumanian leader was accorded the unusual privilege of appearing on the rostrum at a mass rally before 10,000 people.

After today's meeting, the New China News Agency said Mr. Hu had discussed the international situation and the development of relations with Mr. Ceausescu and briefed him on China's internal affairs.

"They agreed that Chinese-Rumanian relations in the political, economic and other fields will continue to grow," the press agency added.

* * *

October 20, 1982

IN RUMANIA, 'PLOTS' AND HARD TIMES

By R.W. APPLE Jr.
Special to The New York Times

BUCHAREST, Rumania, Oct. 19—Despite moves by President Nicolae Ceausescu to maintain his tight control, Rumania remains gripped by an economic crisis that shows no sign of easing.

This spring Mr. Ceausescu ordered the dismissal, and in some cases the arrest, of Government officials on the ground that they had participated in a plot by a transcendental meditation movement to obtain Rumania's withdrawal from the Warsaw Pact, the Soviet bloc's military alliance.

One of those ousted was the Education Minister, Aneta Spornic, a friend of the President's wife, Elena, who holds almost as many positions as Mr. Ceausescu himself does.

In June, there was another shuffle, with the Prime Minister, Ilie Verdet, five Deputy Prime Ministers and the Minister of Foreign Trade all losing their jobs. Earlier this month, still more officials of the national and Bucharest city governments were dismissed.

Plot in Paris Is Foiled

Finally, it emerged during the summer that a Rumanian agent had been ordered to kill two Rumanian emigre writers in Paris. French security officials say the assassination plot was foiled with the help of the agent, who has since defected, but the Rumanians deny any knowledge of the affair.

Western diplomats have been unable to find any clear pattern in these developments, and they are mystified by the role attributed to the transcendental meditation movement, whose goal is personal and global peace.

Officially, most of the dismissed officials are accused of corruption and incompetence. The party leadership recently announced that it had received 1.8 million letters from citizens complaining of inefficiency and illegality.

But diplomats describe the official explanations, and indeed the dismissals themselves, as part of an attempt to demonstrate, in the words of one Western European envoy, that "there is nothing wrong with Ceausescu, nothing wrong with his policies and everything wrong with some of his subordinates."

Mr. Ceausescu has ruled Rumania, where political repression is as severe as anywhere in Eastern Europe, for almost 20 years. Its standard of living is among the lowest in Europe, but neither that nor the recent political turbulence seems to have shaken his position.

The Rumanian leader's picture still adorns a wall in every office, signs praising him still stand at 500-yard intervals along country roads, and he still permits not a murmur of dissent. But he is no longer taken seriously in other Warsaw Pact nations, and the Hungarian Communist Party newspaper has portrayed him as a charlatan who sneers at "those who want to speak to me of the standard of living, of the supply of food, of the building of roads."

The signs of economic crisis are everywhere in Rumania with the approach of a winter that many inhabitants expect to be the worst since World War II, despite an excellent grain crop.

Food is short, partly because much of the best produce goes for export, partly because imports are restricted. Flour, sugar, meat, tea, coffee and cooking oil are often unobtainable; eggs, plentiful 18 months ago, are now scarce.

To the Milk Store at 6 A.M.

A housewife, who must go to her neighborhood store by 6 A.M. to be sure of finding milk on the shelves, commented that "life consists mainly of standing in line these days." The result of long waits is often meager—wormy apples, spongy potatoes, dry cheese.

For almost a decade, Western economists assert, Mr. Ceausescu has neglected agricultural investment to concentrate on industrial expansion, thereby crippling a once-robust farm economy. In northern Rumania, horse-drawn carts are still the norm, and heavy work must be undertaken with primitive tools.

Most tractors and harvesting machines are outmoded and subject to frequent breakdowns. Reports circulating here say that troops and schoolchildren had to be drafted to provide sufficient manpower for the harvest this fall.

Rumanian cities at night live in a chilly gloom. Even the most luxurious hotels turn on only a few lights in their lobbies and keep the heat low to save energy. In the desperate search for hard currency, every device is used to extract the last possible dollar or mark from Western travelers; it is almost impossible, for example, to place a collect telephone call to the West.

The West German Institute of Economic Research said this summer that Rumania was in fact bankrupt. Rumanian officials ridiculed the assertion, contending that the only problem was "short-term liquidity."

Despite all of this, Mr. Ceausescu, determined to transform his country into an industrial power and to lessen its dependence on foreign suppliers, is pressing ahead with ambitious plans. Two nuclear reactors are under construction near the Black Sea port of Constanta, with 20 scheduled to be in operation by the end of the century.

Rumania has just begun to assemble jet transport planes from parts provided by the British Aircraft Corporation, and it is at work on a second auto factory. The first builds the Dacia, an adaptation of a Renault design; the second will turn out Rumanian Citroens.

Crude Oil Output Dropping

At the same time, Rumania, with its own crude oil production declining, is scouring the world for oil for its large refining industry, with a daily capacity of about 600,000 barrels, despite the slump in Western demand. It has been forced to turn to the Soviet Union for part of its supply, but hopes with the aid of a $101 million World Bank loan to get more crude oil from its own aging wells.

Mr. Ceausescu has made progress this year in coping with his most immediate headaches—Rumania's inability to meet payments on foreign indebtedness of some $11 billion.

In what some Rumanian officials described as a gamble, the International Monetary Fund agreed in June to resume lending to Rumania after a six-month hiatus. To gain this "second chance," the Government agreed to increase food and gasoline prices and to provide the kind of financial data that past secretiveness had denied to all outsiders, including the fund.

*   *   *

January 30, 1983

GREECE GIVES WIVES EQUAL VOICE IN THE HOME

By MARVINE HOWE
Special to The New York Times

ATHENS, Jan. 29—Legislation intended to give married women an equal voice with their husbands in all matters of family life was unanimously adopted this week by the Greek Parliament.

"This is only the start," Minister of Justice George Mangakis said Tuesday after Parliament passed the new Family Law, under which a man is no longer legally the head of the family with a final say on all matters.

"We have won the battle to get the bill passed," Mr. Mangakis said, "but now we need to put it into practice with concrete measures."

With the word "battle" he was alluding to the strong attack made on him by the conservative wing of the Greek Orthodox Church while the legislation was being considered. Bishop Augustino Kantiotis of Phlorina recently condemned the measure as "a disaster for the Greek family" and called for the Justice Minister's excommunication.

'Husband and Wife Must Decide'

But Archbishop Seraphim, the Primate of Greece, said that the new legislation was "honest," and accused the conservatives of hypocrisy in defending the old legal situation.

"Henceforth, under the new law, husband and wife must decide together all matters relating to their common family life," Mr. Mangakis said in an interview on the eve of the parliamentary debate. No longer, he said, would a married woman have to get her husband's permission to set up a business, take their children abroad or even choose a school for them.

He said the other main section of the law provided that, for the first time in Greece, divorce would be possible based on mutual consent. If there is no agreement, divorce would be allowed on the ground of incompatibility after four years' separation.

In case of separation, he said, the disfavored partner would be given at least one-third of the family wealth, unless it could be proved that he or she had made no contribution.

Protection for the Single Mother

Other provisions, he said, would allow a wife to keep her own name for legal questions and to choose whichever family name she wished. The Justice Minister said the law sought to protect the single mother, who would automatically and legally be the guardian of her children.

Children born out of wedlock, he went on, would be guaranteed equal rights under the new law with those whose parents are married. One amendment abolishes the institution of dowry, which has become a system of tax evasion. Under a law enacted by the colonels who ruled Greece from 1967 to 1974, dowries were taxed by only half as much as gifts or inheritance.

In the future, the Justice Minister said, the transfer of property can be made to son or daughter, with or without marriage, and will be taxed at the normal rate if it is over five million drachmas, the equivalent of $60,240.

The parliamentary debate on the new law continued through four sessions. The conservative opposition criticized the regulations on divorce, particularly the provision on divorce by mutual consent, and suggested that without consent the separation should be six years instead of four, with other conditions. The Communists were also critical about the division of property in case of separation.

'An Important Advance'

In the end, in a rare display of national unity, all the parties voted in favor of the law. Chryssanthi Laion-Antoniou, a lawyer who is an adviser to Prime Minister Andreas Papandreou on equality issues and who was one of the 15 lawyers and professors who drafted the legislation, said Mr. Papandreou's Government was the first in Greece to present a concrete program for women's rights, but she added that more was needed. She said there was a particular need for new labor laws and laws on family planning.

* * *

March 4, 1983

80,000 GREEKS RALLY AGAINST U.S. BASES

By MARVINE HOWE
Special to The New York Times

ATHENS, March 3—Despite blustery weather, thousands of people opposed to American military bases in Greece gathered in the main square here today for a rally organized by the ruling Socialists, the Communists and an independent group.

This marked the first time since the Government of Prime Minister Andreas Papandreou took office 16 months ago that his Socialists openly joined the Communists in supporting such a demonstration.

Some diplomats said they thought the decision stemmed from anger over Washington's recent proposal to double military aid to Turkey in 1984 while keeping assistance to Greece at 1983 levels. Greek anger was increased, it was noted, after President Reagan said he would consider increased aid to Greece if current talks on keeping the four bases succeeded.

Anti-American Banners Held

Banners brandished at the rally said "No to American Bases" and "No to American Pressures and Blackmail." Government members did not actually take part in the demonstration, held in Constitution Square, but the Socialist Mayor of Athens, Dimitris Beis, was among the speakers. A spokesman for the organizers said members of all major political parties except the conservative New Democracy, the principal opposition group, had taken part.

The conservative opposition leader, Evanghelos Averof, had criticized the Government for encouraging its supporters to take part in the rally while base talks were under way.

"The Government has the right to keep or remove the bases," he said. "What it cannot do is hold a demonstration against itself," The Government spokesman, Dimitris Maroudas, said Socialists had been "historically against the presence of foreign bases in our country." He said the Government was "negotiating to establish a schedule for their removal."

Good-Humored Crowd of 80,000

It was a generally good-humored crowd of about 80,000, mostly students, trade unionists and militants of left-wing parties. After speeches by the leaders of the three movements, the crowd approved a resolution calling for the removal of the bases.

The rally was organized with the support of the Socialist-led General Confederation of Labor and the National Students Union. Other rallies have been planned for later this month at Piraeus, Salonika, Patras and at Herakleion in Crete, where two of the bases are situated, according to a spokesman for the organizers, Stavros Kanellopoulas.

Mr. Kanellopoulas, who is a leader of the Communist-dominated Greek Committee for International Peace and Detente, said that his movement had formed a joint council with the Socialists' Movement for Peace, Democracy and National Independence and the independents. He said he hoped this cooperation would lead to a reunification of the three movements.

The Greek movement, which had been affiliated with the Moscowbacked World Peace Council, split after the Socialists came to power in 1981, with the Socialists forming their own movement.

* * *

March 6, 1983

GREECE REFUSES TO JOIN IN NATO MANEUVERS

Special to The New York Times

ATHENS, March 5—Since last month the military chiefs of staff of most member countries of the North Atlantic Treaty Organization have been exchanging messages on how to deal with a hypothetical threat to the alliance. But Greece has refused to join in this exercise as part of its continuing dispute with Turkey over the Aegean Sea area.

Greek NATO sources said the refusal came when the alliance decided to exclude the Greek island of Limnos from the "threatened area" because of Turkish objections to its militarization. The island is in the northeastern part of the Aegean just off the Turkish coast.

Last November Greece refused to participate for the same reason in five-nation maneuvers scheduled for the Aegean by NATO. The maneuvers, which were to have involved a mock defense of Limnos by land, air and naval forces of the United States, Britain, Italy, Turkey and Greece, were then canceled.

The Greek Government of Prime Minister Andreas Papandreou charged angrily at the time that by excluding Limnos from the exercise area NATO was in effect supporting Turkey's demands for demilitarizing the island.

Turkey Renewed Demands

Two weeks ago Turkey renewed its demands for demilitarization of Greece's eastern Aegean islands, saying this was specified by agreements reached between the two countries before World War II.

The demands were refused again in a statement by Dimitrios Maroudas, the Greek Government spokesman, who declared that Greece had a right to defend its sovereign territory.

These exchanges and Greece's refusal to engage in all NATO maneuvers underline its uncertain status in the alliance's military wing, to which it returned in 1980 after six years absence.

Greek Defense Ministry sources said, however, that there was no question of any Greek withdrawal from NATO. They pointed out that Greece had participated in other maneuvers in which its demands for operational control of the Aegean had not been compromised.

Upsetting NATO Planning

The sources said Greece would continue to upset NATO military planning until the alliance restored all the operational rights Greek forces had in the Aegean before leaving the military wing.

The Greek Government has declared that the 1980 agreement on Greece's reintegration into NATO's military wing specifically pledged that all such rights would be fully restored.

Gen. Bernard Rogers, the NATO commander, who negotiated the agreement, says the agreement envisaged Greece's reintegration first and the settlement of operational rights with Turkey later.

Greek-NATO differences date from 1974, when the new civilian Government, headed by Constantine Caramanlis, withdrew from the military wing in protest over what it denounced as the West's failure to prevent the Turkish invasion of Cyprus.

Defense of the Aegean

Up to that point Aegean defense fell under the NATO command in Izmir, Turkey, called the Sixth Tactical Air Force. It was headed by an American commander with three subordinates, two Turks and a Greek.

The Greek commander had operational control of the airspace from the west coast of Greece to a boundary line just off the west coast of Turkey. Therefore, in liaison with Athens, he controlled air defense within NATO over most of the Aegean. But after Greece's withdrawal in 1974, Izmir eventually fell under a Turkish commander, and NATO took over operational control of the area's airspace in alliance matters.

As for naval operational control, Greek jurisdiction also extended across the Aegean up to the Turkish west coast, a situation that ended when Greece withdrew.

NATO, as part of the 1980 agreement, has called on Greece to set up an alliance command at Larissa to parallel the command at Izmir under Turkey.

But on taking office in October 1981, Prime Minister Papandreou refused, arguing that to do so would imply an acceptance of Turkey's demand.

* * *

November 16, 1983

TURKS RECOGNIZE THE NEW NATION

By MARVINE HOWE

ANKARA, Turkey, Nov. 15—Turkey gave formal recognition tonight to the newly proclaimed Turkish Republic of Northern Cyprus and warned "all concerned governments" against taking a negative position toward the new nation.

Foreign Minister Ilter Turkmen expressed hope that the Greek Government would "act with common sense." He emphasized that his Government would have preferred a solution to the Cyprus problem through the United Nations-sponsored negotiations between the island's two ethnic groups "without arriving at the present state of affairs."

The Turkish Government appeared to have been caught by surprise by the timing of the decision but considered the declaration to have been inevitable. Turkey's ruling National Security Council held an emergency meeting with Prime Minister Bulent Ulusu and Foreign Minister Turkmen. At a news conference after the meeting, Mr. Turkmen announced Turkey's decision to recognize the newly proclaimed nation.

'Peaceful Settlement' Urged

"We must now turn our attention to the search for a peaceful settlement," Mr. Turkmen declared. "We hope that all concerned governments will contribute to efforts in that direction. The adoption of a negative attitude toward the newly established republic will only serve to eliminate the possibilities of agreement."

This was viewed as a warning, particularly to Greece, that Turkey was ready to give its full backing to the new nation. Turkey has kept a force of 20,000 troops on Cyprus since the 1974 invasion with the aim of protecting the ethnic Turkish minority. Mr. Turkmen declared tonight that the presence of Turkish forces there was "dependent on the will of the new republic" and that the existing defensive alliance would remain in force.

Mr. Turkmen received the Greek Ambassador twice today, at the ambassador's request, briefing him on developments in northern Cyprus and later notifying him of Ankara's decision to recognize the new government.

Western diplomatic sources here were stunned by the news of the establishment of the Turkish Cypriot republic. Diplomatic sources believed that Pakistan and Bangladesh, which have close associations with Turkey, would also recognize the Turkish Cypriot nation.

De Facto Nation Since 1974

Diplomats pointed out that northern Cyprus had already existed as a de facto nation since the 1974 Turkish military invasion and the ensuing population exchange and had now been declared independent in law.

In general they felt that the new nation could continue to function so long as it had Turkish economic, political and

Associated Press

Prime Minister Bulent Ulusu of Turkey talking to reporters yesterday in Ankara after learning that Turkish Cypriots had proclaimed independence.

military backing but that this did not mean international recognition or admission to the United Nations.

The Turkish Cypriot leader, Rauf Denktash, called on all Moslem nations last summer to recognize an independent Turkish Cypriot nation when the time came. Some Turkish sources believed that Saudi Arabia might recognize the new republic but they felt that most of the Arab countries would not want to jeopardize good relations with Greece.

Mr. Denktash has repeatedly threatened to take action for several years but each time has been discouraged by the Turkish Government, which has insisted on giving the United Nations-sponsored talks a chance.

Turkey in an Interim Period

Foreign Minister Turkmen declared that Turkish Cypriots could not be held responsible for the failure of nine years of negotiations and added that "Turkish Cypriots enjoy the right of self-determination as much as the Greek Cypriots."

Mr. Denktash chose this time to make his break from Greek Cyprus because Turkey is in what amounts to a period of interim rule, according to sources who met with the Turkish Cypriot leader recently.

The Turkish military rulers are to hand over the Government to the leader of the conservative Motherland Party, Turgut Ozal, within two weeks following Mr. Ozal's recent election victory. Turkey's President, Gen. Kenan Evren, met today with Mr. Ozal and the leaders of the two opposition parties and briefed them on the Cyprus developments.

Mr. Ozal refrained from commenting on the Cyprus situation except to quote a passage from his party's program that states, "We are respectful of and support the decisions to be taken by the Turkish Cypriot community concerning its own position."

Wide Support Voiced

The Turkish Cypriot cause is a popular one in this country and statements of support have come from all sectors of the Turkish political spectrum.

Former Prime Minister Bulent Ecevit, who ordered the 1974 military invasion of Cyprus, approved the Turkish Cypriots' decision, which he said was a consequence of Greek intransigence. He said he felt the move would provide the necessary momentum to find a solution through establishment of a federal republic in Cyprus.

The leader of the new Social Democracy Party, Cezmi Kartay, declared, "The declaration of independence of northern Cyprus is inevitable and a natural consequence of the behavior of the Greek Cypriot community against Turkish Cypriots' rights and security."

*   *   *

November 16, 1983

MAIN REACTION AT U.N. IS SURPRISE AND DISMAY

By RICHARD BERNSTEIN

UNITED NATIONS, N.Y., Nov. 15—The Turkish Cypriot declaration of independence was greeted with surprise and some dismay at the United Nations, where the Security Council was expected to hold an emergency session on the issue on Wednesday.

The Security Council met early this evening for informal, closed-door consultations on Cyprus and announced that it would meet against Wednesday. It was expected that a full meeting of the Council would await the arrival here of Cyprus's Foreign Minister, George Iacovou, who is expected in New York Wednesday.

A statement this morning by the United Nations press office said that Secretary General Javier Perez de Cuellar "deeply regrets the announcement" by the Turkish Cypriots. The statement said Mr. Perez de Cuellar considered that "this move is contrary to the resolutions of the Security Council on Cyprus" and "is bound to affect adversely the situation in Cyprus."

The United Nations has played a principal role in searching for peace on Cyprus since the island was divided in 1974.

During the summer, Mr. Perez de Cuellar spoke with both sides seeking some common ground between them for a solution. A United Nations Peacekeeping Force of more than 2,300 soldiers is on the island to prevent a renewal of hostilities between the Greek and Turkish areas.

A draft of a Security Council resolution was circulated by Britain today. It "deplores the declaration of the Turkish Cypriot authorities of the purported secession of part of the Republic of Cyprus." The resolution would call on all countries "not to recognize any Cypriot state other than the Republic of Cyprus."

Little Backing for Turkey

Diplomats and United Nations officials here said the Turkish Cypriot move was unlikely to receive much sympathy among member countries. "I doubt that more than four or five countries will recognize the Turkish secession," a member of the Secretariat said.

Since conflict between the Greek and Turkish areas on Cyprus broke out in the mid-1960's, the Security Council has recognized the existence of two groups on the island and encouraged negotiations between them. It has several times, however, refused to recognize the Turkish part of the island as a "federated state."

The Turkish Cypriot are represented here by Nail Atalay, whose offices are in the same building as the Turkish Mission to the United Nations. Mr. Atalay this morning gave notice of the Declaration of the Turkish Republic of Northern Cyprus in a letter addressed to Mr. Perez de Cuellar.

In the letter, Mr. Atalay identified himself as "Representative of the Turkish Republic of Northern Cyprus." A spokesman for the United Nations, however, said that, while Mr. Atalay is acknowledged as the representative of the Turkish Cypriots, he did not have official status here as an observer or as the representative of a country.

An official at the Turkish Cypriot office, Reshat Caglar, said in a telephone interview that the Turkish Cypriots had offices in London and Brussels but neither office had diplomatic status.

Asked whether the Turkish Cypriots had formal ties with any other international organizations, Mr. Caglar said that the United Nations High Commissioner for Refugees, who has offices in both parts of Cyprus, maintains close and direct contact on the island with the Turkish Cypriots.

*   *   *

November 17, 1983

GREEK CYPRIOT VOWS TO REVERSE MOVE PEACEABLY

By MARVINE HOWE

NICOSIA, Cyprus, Nov. 16—The President of Cyprus said today that his Government was determined to reverse, through peaceful means, Tuesday's declaration of independence by Turkish Cypriots.

The President, Spyros Kyprianou, said there were many "effective, peaceful" steps that could be taken. He cited Britain's actions in dealing with the former breakaway state of Rhodesia, implying that some form of economic blockade was under consideration.

Speaking at a news conference here, the Greek Cypriot leader said he planned to work out a specific course in consultation with Greece and Britain.

Greek Cypriot high school students in Nicosia yesterday protesting Turkish Cypriot declaration of independence.

To Athens, London and New York

Afterward, Mr. Kyprianou flew to Athens for talks with Prime Minister Andreas Papandreou, who is considered the main backer of the Greek Cypriot cause. Mr. Kyprianou said he hoped to meet with Prime Minister Margaret Thatcher in London on Thursday and then would proceed to New York, where he expects to consult at the United Nations with Secretary General Javier Perez de Cuellar.

Mr. Kyprianou repeated an earlier accusation that Turkey had "conspired" with the Turkish Cypriot leadership to establish an independent republic in the northern third of the island. On Tuesday in Ankara the Turkish Foreign Minister, Ilter Turkmen, said his Government was surprised by the Turkish Cypriot move and had not encouraged it but understood it.

Mr. Kyprianou said his Government had also been caught by surprise. "We were told by many governments that they had assurances from Ankara that the Turkish Cypriot threats to declare independence would not take place," he said.

"Our primary aim is to achieve a reversal of this decision," he said. "We intend to use effective, peaceful means to change what has happened."

Opposed to Any Partition

Asked whether he believed that a failure of his efforts would lead to a "double enosis"—a term referring to the union of the Turkish Cypriot side with Turkey and the Greek Cypriot side with Greece—the Greek Cypriot President declared: "We are against double enosis just as we are against any form of partition."

Meanwhile, in an unusual expression of unity, a delegation representing the four main Greek Cypriot political parties left for New York to lend support to the Cypriot position at the United Nations. Delegates included the leaders of the Socialist and rightwing opposition as well as the Communist Party and President Kyprianou's Centrist Party.

Among the Greek Cypriots there seemed to be confusion. Some citizens said they expected a political or military development in response to the declaration, while others recalled that nothing was done to forestall the Turkish invasion of Cyprus in 1974.

Rumor of Jet Fighters

A rumor Tuesday that Greece had sent 15 jet fighters to help Cyprus was quickly quashed when it was learned that the planes, from Jordan, had just stopped for refueling on their way to Greece.

About 2,000 high school students marched from central Freedom Square to the Presidential Palace at noon today shouting such nationalist slogans as "we will never accept partition." President Kyprianou thanked the young people for their support and promised to do everything to reverse the Turkish Cypriot move.

"We have huge support from many other nations," he said, pointing out that only Turkey had recognized the new "secessionist state."

* * *

January 23, 1984

YOUNG PEOPLE IN EAST EUROPE TURN INCREASINGLY TO CHURCH

By JAMES M. MARKHAM
Special to The New York Times

BUDAPEST—Across Eastern Europe, there are signs of a religious renewal.

The pattern is as uneven as the patchwork of Roman Catholic, Protestant and Orthodox faiths that crisscrosses the six junior partners of the Warsaw Pact, and it is colored by the struggles between the countries and various churches that occurred both before and after the imposition of Communism in the late 1940's.

Particularly in Hungary, Czechoslovakia, East Germany and Poland, clergymen and scholars say growing numbers of people are turning to—or turning back to—churches that, under Marxist theory, should be on the road to extinction. In cities in Bulgaria and Rumania, there are reports of increased churchgoing, but few signs of a major revival.

Not a Mass Movement

With the exception of Poland, where the Roman Catholic Church is the guardian of national aspirations, the movement of renewal is not a mass phenomenon. Rather, active Christians are normally a minority in societies that have become secularized through industrialization, Communist propaganda and persecution.

"Our churches are smaller," said the Rev. Heino Falcke, a Protestant pastor in the East German city of Erfurt. "But I believe that inside, they are stronger and their communities are livelier."

One aspect of the renewal is the involvement of young people who grew up under Communism.

"In the big cities, there is a new form of religion," said the Rev. Laszlo Luckacs, 47 years old, a Roman Catholic priest in Budapest. "Young people are converting, and others who were raised as Catholics are returning to the church. The young people are asking, 'Why are we living?' "

The new believers, who also include many adults and once-secular-minded intellectuals, are often gravitating to grass-roots groups or "basis communities" at the margins of the Catholic and Protestant Churches. In sessions held privately in homes, there is an emphasis on meditation, spontaneous prayer and Bible study—concerns that some conservative Catholic prelates regard as worrisomely "Protestant."

In Hungary and East Germany, the renewal is occurring in an atmosphere of relative economic plenty and wary tolerance by the state; in Poland, it is occurring in conditions of hardship and considerable church autonomy, and in Czechoslovakia, amid fierce state repression, particularly of the Roman Catholic Church.

Activists often insist that their quest is spiritual, not political. But in Hungary some militant Roman Catholics have gathered around the Rev. Gyorgy Bulanyi, a priest at odds with a timorous hierarchy, and proclaimed military service to be incompatible with the message of Jesus. In East Germany, the Protestant Churches shield a movement that questions the nuclear military policies of the Warsaw Pact and the Atlantic alliance.

"Christians should go into the church and not take over the state," said the silver-haired Father Bulanyi, who spent nine years in prison during a post-Stalinist crackdown on the Hungarian churches. "But Christ said, 'Thou shalt not kill.' We would rather sit in jail than kill another man."

Students of Eastern Europe say one thread connecting the different situations in the Warsaw Pact nations is the intellectual exhaustion of the Marxist state ideology, which in the 1950's was preached with the fervor of a religion.

"It is an empty shell," said Gerhard Simon, a West German authority on Eastern Europe. "This ideology is good for careerists, but not for people who are asking questions of existence."

In this spiritual vacuum, the changes of the Second Vatican Council, notably the decision that mass was to be said in the vernacular, gave an impulse to the Roman Catholic Churches in the late 1960's. In 1975, the signing of the Helsinki human rights agreement by 35 European nations committed the Warsaw Pact nations to greater religious freedom—pledges that were partly kept in Hungary and East Germany.

But the event that emboldened and galvanized many believers was the naming in 1978 of Karol Wojtyla, the Archbishop of Cracow, as the first Eastern European Pope. For Eastern European Roman Catholics—but for a surprising number of Protestants, too—the reign of Pope John Paul II has conveyed the comfort and inspiration of a weighty ally in Rome.

'Focal Point and a Stimulus'

"The Pope provided a focal point and a stimulus for something that was amorphous and rather generalized," said Michael Bourdeaux, a British scholar who specializes in religion in Eastern Europe. "Something approximating a religious revival had already been going on." Numerous Eastern European prelates involved in the renewal echoed his analysis.

The Pope's tumultuous visit to Poland in 1979 contributed importantly to the emergence a year later of the independent trade union Solidarity. In a telltale act, one of the first Solidarity demands to emerge from the blockaded Lenin Shipyard in Gdansk in August 1980 was that the Government should broadcast Sunday masses live on television and radio.

The 13-month Polish experiment in freedom before martial law was declared in December 1981—it has since been partly lifted—has several Eastern European Communist Parties unnerved and watching their churches for symptoms of what East German officials privately call "the Polish disease." But the crushing of Solidarity in Poland appears to have increased the already enormous popular support for the Roman Catholic Church there.

Since the Pope's second visit to Poland last June, anti-Government demonstrations have been tightly associated with the Polish church, which has given succor to artists, writers and thinkers who in other days were highly secular.

Churches in Poland now regularly hold art shows, and banned journalists have found work in a growing number of nominally Roman Catholic periodicals.

No End to Religion in Sight

Eastern European Communist Parties, with the exception of Albania's, appear to have abandoned the hope that religion—Marx's "opiate of the people"—will vanish in some foreseeable future. In Hungary and East Germany, the state has occasionally solicited the aid of the churches in grappling with problems that have slipped beyond its control—the breakdown of family life, divorce, drugs, suicide, alcoholism and juvenile delinquency.

Several governments, according to Western diplomats, seem to calculate that relaxed relations with the churches can help ease the pinch of unpopular economic measures and lessen the chances of overt discontent. Church leaders have generally seized these opportunities to enlarge their own autonomy.

In Bulgaria and Rumania, the Orthodox Church hierarchies have a long history of collaboration with the Communist authorities, particularly on foreign policy issues. In cities in the two countries, there are reports of increased churchgoing, but few signs of a major revival. Last year, Rumania eased the severe repression of its Roman Catholic minority, allowing Catholics to go to Rome and permitting two bishoprics that had long been empty to be filled.

Church autonomy is greatest in East Germany and Poland, but it is in Hungary that church-state cooperation has gone the furthest. Laszlo Cardinal Lekai and his bishops have in effect been told by the Government to bring the grass-roots movement of renewal under control.

"In Hungary, the Catholic bakers don't make bread just for the Catholics and the Communists don't just make bread for the Communists," said the Cardinal, 63 years old, in defending his philosophy of "small steps" during an interview at his stately residence at Esztergom near Budapest. "The Catholics and Communists together make a Hungarian bread."

Last June, Cardinal Lekai and the Bench of Bishops suspended Father Bulanyi, the grass-roots or "basis community" leader, from his right to celebrate mass on the ground that his theological teachings, with their emphasis on highly subjective religious experiences, contradicted Roman Catholic doctrine. At least eight other priests allied with Father Bulanyi have been removed from their parishes.

The Cardinal has tried to split the somewhat radical "Bulanyists" from another basis-community movement, gathered around priests once active in the Regnum Marianum society, a group that had been closely involved in religious education for young people. By some estimates, the two movements have 50,000 adherents in Hungary, and similar Protestant groups have a smaller following.

Deeply concerned, the Vatican has tried to mediate in the dispute, urging Father Bulanyi to remain obedient to his bishops but at the same time prodding Cardinal Lekai to harness the energy of the basis-community movement.

Opposes Conscientious Objectors

Cardinal Lekai has publicly attacked the Bulyani followers for preaching conscientious objection and avoidance of military service. "Self-defense is right," the Cardinal has said. "Strength is justified."

In an interview in his cramped Budapest apartment, Father Bulanyi responded that he would "not retreat one millimeter" from his rejection of military service. "That once a Hungarian bishop could say 'no' to the state—that's not our style," the priest said sarcastically. "Even under the Hapsburgs the bishops never said 'no.'"

The standoff between the Cardinal and Father Bulanyi looks as if it will continue for some time, and there seems little likelihood that the state, eager to maintain Hungary's liberal image abroad, will move against the priest.

Imre Miklos, the chairman of the State Office for Religious Affairs, said in an interview: "They want to make the world believe that we are worried by this movement. We are not worried, and we are only interested insofar as it is likely to disturb the calm of our society."

Last October, on a visit to Esztergom, Jozef Cardinal Glemp, the Polish Primate, expressed the hope that Pope John Paul II might soon visit Hungary—an event that could be expected to detonate an outpouring of popular enthusiasm. But neither Cardinal Lekai nor Mr. Miklos sounded enthusiastic about the idea.

Most scholars say they believe that the advent of an activist Polish Pope has been responsible for the startling emergence of an "underground" Roman Catholic Church in Czechoslovakia, where the regime of Gustav Husak has embarked on what one Vatican source called "an experiment with the complete atheization of a country."

In Czechoslovakia, priests are routinely interrogated and jailed, most bishoprics are vacant because the Government insists on imposing prelates unacceptable to Rome, and a state-supported movement of priests, Pacem in Terris, serves as a kind of fifth column within the church.

Vatican officials say that the Pope's 1982 document prohibiting priests from being members of political organizations was principally aimed at Pacem in Terris.

Thriving 'Underground' Church

Even so, protected by Frantisek Cardinal Tomasek, a thriving "underground" church has sprung up in the last few years and is particularly strong in Prague and other urban centers. Alexander Tomsky, an authority on the Czechoslovak church at Keston College in Britain, said the clandestine cells regularly turned out three illegal mimeographed journals that have a circulation of about 7,500 copies.

"The underground has spread so widely that it could even be regarded as the mainstream," said Mr. Tomsky, who noted that the movement was strongest in the Czech-speaking parts of the country rather than in traditionally Catholic Slovakia.

As in Hungary, followers of the clandestine church typically meet in private homes for prayer sessions and mass, sometimes conducted by priests who have been secretly ordained. Before the emergence of Solidarity led to the restriction of travel to Poland, Polish bishops—including Karol Wojtyla—ordained Czechoslovak priests clandestinely, according to several East European clergymen.

The one Eastern European nation where a revival is occurring mainly in the framework of Protestant Churches is East Germany. Since a 1978 meeting between Erich Honecker, the Communist party chief, and Protestant leaders, church-state relations have been the most relaxed in Eastern Europe, though not without tensions.

Last year, both church and state honored Martin Luther, the founder of Protestantism, by marking the 500th anniversary of his birth. The occasion afforded Protestant Churches an opportunity to display their organizational skills, pulling a total of 200,000 people to seven different congresses. To the astonishment of their organizers, church assemblies have also drawn huge crowds—100,000 people, for example, showed up for a Lutheran gathering in Dresden last July.

The movement of renewal in East Germany is more politically tinged than in any other Eastern European country except Poland. Young arms protesters have sought out the church not always out of religious motives, but because clergymen have increasingly spoken out against the arms race in East and West.

East German clergymen, however, stress that they accept the legitimacy of the Communist Government and "a church in socialism."

*   *   *

March 19, 1984

GREECE UNDER PAPANDREOU: LEFTIST BUT IN WESTERN CAMP

By R. W. APPLE Jr.
Special to The New York Times

LONDON, March 18—After 40 years of almost continuous right-wing domination, Greece has lurched sharply to the left under Andreas Papandreou and his Socialist party that came to power in 1981.

Under Mr. Papandreou, the country has adopted an aggressive foreign policy, clashing repeatedly with and criticizing the United States and its other partners in the North Atlantic Treaty Organization and in the European Economic Community.

While building new links with Eastern Europe, Mr. Papandreou has dissented from American condemnation of the shooting down of the South Korean airliner last September, has sought to create a nuclear-free zone in southeast Europe, has attacked the deployment of American cruise and Pershing missiles in Europe and has denounced United States policy in Central America.

Anti-American Image Created

A strong impression of anti-Americanism has been created—so strong, in fact, that some officials in Washington and other capitals have begun to fear that the Prime Minister intends to lead his country out of the Western alliance into a policy of neutralism. On occasion he has seemed to visualize himself as a Tito for the 1980's.

But a closer look suggests that Greece's independent path is unlikely to lead as far as neutralism. Indeed, a surprising consensus emerged from recent interviews in Greece with politicians of all parties, with academics, journalists, businessmen and union leaders, and with foreign diplomats: Whatever actions Mr. Papandreou may take or gestures he may make to appease the far left at home, whatever initiatives he may undertake to correct what he sees as foreign—and especially American—domination of Greek life in the last three decades, he has not left the Western European mainstream.

The proof, his supporters said, lies in the decision of Mr. Papandreou's Socialist Government to remain in the Common Market and to extend for five years the lease on American military bases here despite pledges during his 1981 electoral campaign to do the opposite.

The Slogan Is 'Change'

Yet the Government's slogan is "change."

The Prime Minister says he wants "to be the catalyst and creator of a new and different society." He talks repeatedly and confusingly about dialectics, "multidynamism," the "third road of Socialism."

He has also said that "capitalism rises up before us as a destructive power, not only of this planet but potentially of humanity itself."

"We are the only Government in Western Europe that marches together and strengthens peace movements," he proudly told officials of his party, the Panhellenic Socialist Movement, recently. On another occasion he accused the United States of trying to violate its defense agreements with Greece.

There is more than a little irony in the impression of anti-Americanism. Alone among present-day European heads of government, Mr. Papandreou has lived in the United States, where he spent 15 years as an economics professor. His wife, Margaret, who takes an active role in politics, is American-born.

Mr. Papandreou's comments have produced contradiction, contention, controversy and bitterness—not least within the vocal Greek community in the United States.

Nevertheless, Eleni Vlachou, a strong-willed editor and publisher who closed her newspapers and left Greece during the period of military dictatorship between 1967 and 1974 and who opposes the Papandreou Government, offered reassurance. "Tell them in America not to worry," she said.

'Token Presents' for the Left

"The Prime Minister," she went on, "is like a man who offers his wife a mink coat and can't afford it. He gives her a few bottles of perfume instead—small ones, cheap, not even French. That's what Papandreou is giving the Greek left—just a few little token presents."

The New York Times/Ingeborg Lippeman

Andreas Papandreou

There are some who dissent from this view, notably members of wealthy families or others who benefited from life under the authoritarian colonels. One aristocratic woman argued, for example, that "Papandreou is slowly but surely taking us behind the Iron Curtain, concentrating power in his hands and getting ready to deny us our basic civil liberties."

The opposition and even some Government supporters accuse Mr. Papandreou of being trigger-happy. On March 8, after an incident in which he charged that a Turkish destroyer had fired at a Greek destroyer, Mr. Papandreou called it "the worst provocation against Greece since the 1974 invasion of Cyprus" and threatened to recall his ambassador from Ankara. Less than 24 hours later the Government acknowledged that the destroyer, the Panthir, had been in no danger and hauled down the alarm signals.

His critics also worry, in the words of one businessman, that the Prime Minister's polemics will lead people "to believe that the United States is imperialist, even if for Papandreou it's largely tactical."

Communist Influence Feared

Journalists and others also express concern about the influence of Communists in the trade unions, in the civil service—made possible by widespread "purges" of right-wingers—and especially in the mass media, notably on the staff of Ethnos, the newspaper with the country's largest circulation, which often takes a pro-Soviet line.

Over recent months Ethnos has been arguing that the vision of George Orwell in "Nineteen Eighty-four" was of the future of the West, and particularly the United States, and not of the Soviet Union.

On Feb. 12, in a lead editorial after the death of Yuri V. Andropov, Ethnos called for a continuation of his political and economic policies. It said: "Without the achievement of this objective, not only will the passage to Communism remain an unfeasible dream, but the Soviet Union, and by extension the people's democracies, will be endangered.

After all, daily practice proves that confronting imperialism can not only be done with arms."

But many who might be expected to resent deeply the changes enacted by the Prime Minister are much more restrained in their comments. The scion of one of the legendary Greek shipowning families, who oversees many of the family's local interests, said that "even the right-wingers will eventually realize that the left's time had come in Greece, and they will be grateful one day that the leftist who came to power was Papandreou and not someone with much more malignant policies in mind."

Endless Political Arguments

Nor is there much of a whiff of totalitarianism, much of the chill conformity of Eastern Europe, about Greece. Not with its endless political arguments in smoky cafes over cups of muddy Greek coffee and glasses of milky ouzo with water; not with its small but noisy newspapers spanning the spectrum from Stalinism to monarchism; not with its people, as undisciplined in their driving as they are explosive in conversation.

Instead there is a sense of often frantic improvisation. Modern Greece has never completely found its niche in the world. Neither wholly European nor wholly Asian nor wholly Balkan, neither wholly developed nor wholly underdeveloped, it has, as a nation, "no cousins," as Mr. Papandreou says. The Government, his backers say, is desperately seeking that niche.

An important element in the tensions in Greek politics is the bleak contrast between yesterday and today, between the shimmering marble of the Parthenon and the grubby, traffic-clogged lanes of the Plaka, between the stirring ruins of ancient Olympia and the dirt streets of the Peloponnesian villages nearby.

In no other country of Europe is there such a chasm between magnificent past and mundane present. The Greeks not only notice it; it wounds them. Out of that pain grows a special Greek sense of pride hurt, of honor injured. It is so much a national characteristic that there is a special word for it—"filotimo," or love of honor—and it helps give Greek politics its special passion and turbulence.

Economic Policies Criticized

Most of Mr. Papandreou's critics appear more concerned with what they term the administrative incompetence of the Socialist regime and, ironically enough, in view of the Prime Minister's academic credentials, with what they consider the disastrous results of its economic policies, than with his activities in the foreign policy arena.

Mr. Papandreou's standing with the public has benefited from his talents as an orator, from his insistence that Greece has a role to play in the creation of a "credible pole to prevent escalation between the two superpowers" and from his skillful exploitation of widespread resentment here toward the policies of a series of American administrations, including that of President Reagan.

While Greeks remain extraordinarily friendly to individual Americans—more hospitable, perhaps, than the people of any other country—there is nonetheless a substantial popular

United Press International

A demonstration in Athens, last Dec. 4, denounced the nuclear arms race between the United States and the Soviet Union. Greece has adopted an aggressive foreign policy, clashing repeatedly with the U.S. and other NATO allies.

antipathy toward American governments for what is described as Washington's support for the military dictatorship and what is viewed here as American favoritism for Turkey in the protracted struggles over Cyprus and the Aegean islands.

Two Major Achievements Seen

In addition, the 65-year-old Prime Minister has succeeded in persuading most Greeks, who are passionately interested in politics while profoundly distrusting politicians of every stripe, that he is different.

"For all the shortcomings of this administration," said Leon Karapanyiotis, editor of the pro-Government newspaper Ta Nea, "Papandreou can claim two great achievements: he is utterly uncorrupt in a country where everyone is corrupt, and he has convinced the average Greek that he finally has a friend, instead of someone bent on exploiting him, in high office."

Mr. Papandreou lives, far less grandly than any other Prime Minister of a Common Market country, in an unpretentious house in the northern suburb of Kastri that once belonged to his father, George, who was Prime Minister in 1963. The living room is furnished with inexpensive furniture, there are plastic flowers on the coffee table, the door is opened by a man in a sports shirt and the maid addresses the Prime Minister's wife as Margaret.

The Prime Minister gives almost no interviews, except to Greek newspapers that are firmly behind him. But Mrs. Papandreou said in a conversation at their home that "anti-Americanism" in this country had been misunderstood.

U.S. 'Interference' Charged

Mrs. Papandreou is a tall woman who gives an impression of resoluteness. An old American friend describes her as "very tough, very ambitious and determined to be more Greek than the Greeks." She argued that when "Greeks shout 'Americans out!' at demonstrations, they are only saying that they want to run their own country, without the kind of interference that has been common." She herself has taken part in such demonstrations in recent months.

"At the best," she said, "the Americans did nothing to hinder the colonels, and the Greek people know it and resent it deeply."

Resentment over that episode in Greek history has been eased by the performance of the American Ambassador here, Monteagle Stearns, a career diplomat on his third assignment in Athens.

But even he has been able to do little about the conviction, shared by the right and the left, that the United States considers Turkey—Greece's long-time rival—a more reliable and a more strategically placed ally and therefore tilts toward it. As one of Mr. Papandreou's aides put it, "The cowboys look at the map and say, 'We gotta be nice to the Turks, because they're right next to the bad guys.' "

Congratulations From Reagan

Mr. Reagan sent Mr. Papandreou a warmly congratulatory message when he was elected, and the United States condemned the recent declaration of independence by the ethnic Turks on Cyprus—two gestures that went down well here.

The good will generated by them was offset, however, when President Reagan recommended a military aid package for Turkey that upset the 10-to-7 ratio between Turkish and Greek aid to which the Greeks thought they had Washington's firm commitment, and by NATO policy in regard to one of the smaller Greek islands.

The proposed change in the ratio, though tiny, represented "a signal of tremendous importance," Mr. Papandreou said. It meant, he declared, that the Reagan Administration approved of the regime in Ankara.

"Once again," said one of the Prime Minister's counselors, "relations between our two countries are very difficult, even though Greeks like the American way of life very much and almost everyone has relatives there. It is like a family feud: sad, very sad. But Reagan's policy is a policy of double-cross. Turkey wants more—more in Cyprus, more in the Aegean. To change that, we need American pressure on Turkey, and you don't put pressure on Turkey by increasing the amount of money you give."

Dispute Over an Island

An even more pressing issue than Cyprus, if that is possible in a country where sensitivity on the Cyprus question is so keen, is that of the island of Limnos, just off the Turkish coast. The Turks argue that the 1923 Treaty of Lausanne demilitarized it, while the Greeks say that the 1935 Treaty of Montreux supplanted the Lausanne accord and gave them the right to maintain the military installations now there.

Until the dispute is settled, Gen. Bernard W. Rogers, the American commander of NATO, has ordered that the island be omitted from all NATO exercises. In addition, the Greeks complain, he has suggested negotiations over a dispute as to where the air-control boundary between the two countries should lie, a matter that the Greeks consider to be nonnegotiable.

Fearful that NATO is unwittingly helping Turkey to whittle away at Greek sovereignty in most of the Aegean, the Papandreou Government has refused to take any part in NATO exercises, has refused to sign NATO communiques and even dissented from some and has blocked the establishment of the planned Seventh Allied Tactical Air Force Command at Larissa in east-central Greece.

Countering the Turkish 'Menace'

"You always say that we overestimate the Turkish menace," commented Yiannis Capsis, the No. 2 man in the Foreign Ministry, who negotiated the new bases agreement. He jumped up and slid back a curtain concealing a military map. "Well, look at this," he said. "Your faithful ally has 120,000 troops in Kurdistan facing the Soviet Union, but it has 60 percent of all its air force and ground troops and 100 percent of its navy in Thrace and Asia Minor facing Greece. We are forced to do the same thing."

To the degree that Mr. Papandreou has been restrained from fulfilling his more extreme campaign promises, many politicians in Greece say, some credit must go to Constantine Caramanlis, the 76-year-old President. Because the Prime Minister all but ignores Parliament, confident of his big majority there, Mr. Caramanlis is the only opposition politician with a chance to talk to and influence him.

According to officials close to Mr. Caramanlis, the President has told the Prime Minister that he would force a public showdown if any move were made to pull out of NATO or the Common Market or to tamper with the army. Mr. Caramanlis is said to have reminded Mr. Papandreou forcibly that he retains a considerable following in the country.

*   *   *

June 20, 1984

BULGARIA ACCUSED OF PLOT ON POPE

ROME, June 19 (AP) —An Italian prosecutor said today that Bulgaria, possibly with Soviet support, masterminded the 1981 plot to assassinate Pope John Paul II, apparently in an attempt to eliminate the Pope's support for the independent Polish labor union Solidarity.

"That's the conclusion of my investigation," the prosecutor, Antonio Albano, said in an interview.

Mr. Albano confirmed that his report on the Pope's shooting says that "there was a specific interest in killing the Pontiff—the social convulsions in Poland" caused by the rise of the now-outlawed Solidarity union.

Suggesting that the Soviet Union might have been behind the plot to kill the Pope, Mr. Albano said: "Do you think Bulgaria could do this sort of thing without Moscow's agreement? Do you think Bulgaria's decision to boycott the Olympic Games was made by Bulgaria alone? I don't think so. But of course this is my personal opinion."

Soviet Union Not Named

He confirmed that his report does not specifically mention any Soviet connection with the shooting of the Pope on May 13, 1981, in St. Peter's Square.

The prosecutor's report was first made public in an article in The New York Times by Claire Sterling. The report does not mention the Soviet Union by name, but, speaking of the turmoil in Poland, says that "some political figure of great power took note of this most grave situation and, mindful of the vital needs of the Eastern bloc, decided it was necessary to kill Pope Wojtyla."

The Italian Government has ordered an investigation into how the report was made public.

Mr. Albano said he submitted the 78-page report on his inquiry to Judge Ilario Martella, who is in charge of the state investigation into the shooting of the Pope by Mehmet Ali Agca, a Turkish national now serving life in prison.

Asks Trials for Seven

The report recommends that three Bulgarians and four other Turks be tried in connection with the attack on the Pope, Mr. Albano said, adding that he expected Judge Martella to decide on his recommendations next month.

The three Bulgarians Mr. Albano said should be brought to trial are Sergei Ivanov Antonov, former station manager of the Bulgarian airlines in Rome, and two former Bulgarian Embassy employees, Todor Aivazov and Zhelyo Kolev Vassilev.

All three face charges of complicity in the attack on the Pope. Among them, only Mr. Antonov is in custody. The others returned to Bulgaria.

On Monday, Judge Martella granted a defense request that Mr. Antonov be removed from jail for medical reasons and placed under house arrest. Mr. Antonov had been allowed to be placed under house arrest last December after 13 months in prison, but he was returned to jail in March.

The Turks Mr. Albano said should be tried are Bekir Celenk, in custody in Bulgaria; Omer Bagci, in jail in Italy; Oral Celik, whose whereabouts are unknown, and Musa Serdar Celebi, in jail in Italy. All four Turks have been charged with complicity in the attack on the Pope.

Bulgaria Denies Involvement

Bulgaria has denied any involvement in the shooting of the Pope and has charged that the allegations were part of a Western plot to discredit the Communist nation.

The prosecutor also dismissed as "a strange argument" a contention by critics that Mr. Agca had been pressured to implicate Bulgarians in the attack on the Pope. Mr. Albano said much of the information on which his report was based came from Mr. Agca. But he said Mr. Agca's information provided only "starting points" for the state inquiry.

The prosecutor said that his report was covered by judicial secrecy and that copies have been given only to the investigating magistrate and defense lawyers.

Soviet Criticizes Report

MOSCOW, June 19 (AP)—The Soviet Union said today that an Italian prosecutor's recommendation that a Bulgarian official be tried in the shooting of the Pope "disregards numerous distortions of the facts" by Mr. Agca.

"The reactionary forces are now feverishly pressing ahead for the opening of a trial of the Bulgarian citizen," the official Soviet press agency Tass said in reference to Mr. Antonov.

Tass said a report by Mr. Albano based on his investigation "recognizes as 'trustworthy' the evidence given" by Mr. Agca.

"But at the same time," the press agency said, the Italian prosecutor's report "totally disregards the numerous distortions of the facts and controversial statements made by the criminal."

* * *

February 8, 1985

TOLL IN BULGARIA'S TURKISH UNREST IS PUT AT 100

By HENRY KAMM

SOFIA, Bulgaria, Feb. 7—Security forces are reported to have killed as many as 100 ethnic Turks, during roundups to force them to adopt Bulgarian names.

A series of reports, which have reached foreign diplomats, come from reliable witnesses, and add up to 100 dead. The figure itself has not been confirmed.

The diplomats say members of the security forces have also been killed in clashes since early December. Many ethnic Turks, who number around 800,000 in this country of nine million, were said to have been injured, others arrested and some tortured.

President Kenan Evren of Turkey has expressed anguish in a letter to Todor Zhivkov, the Bulgarian leader, but has received no reply. Informally, Bulgarian officials say that there has been no violence and that the name changes are voluntary.

The first reports of unrest originated from organizations of repatriated ethnic Turks in Turkey. Subsequently, similar reports reached foreign embassies here. Foreigners attempting to visit ethnic Turkish areas have been turned back.

The Bulgarian actions, which follow years of gentler pressure on ethnic Turks to change their names, began in the mountainous ethnic Turkish region between Plovdiv and the Greek border.

Villagers were said to have been presented with forms already filled out with names often bearing no resemblance to their real names and were told to sign. In some places, people gathered for protests in the main square; elsewhere local government or party buildings were occupied.

As a consequence, troops were often called in, villagers were loaded on trucks to be taken to Government offices to sign, fights broke out and often the troops opened fire.

Serious incidents were reported from Kurdzhali and, on Dec. 26, from Momchilgrad. As many as 40 people were said to have been killed.

In January, the Government is said to have carried the campaign to the other major ethnic Turkish area, the eastern plains south of the Danube border with Rumania. Riots were reported from Shumen, Razgrad and Turgovishte. More than 30 dead were reported in one clash in late January.

Since 1965, Bulgaria has stopped specifying ethnicity in its census statistics, asserting that there are only Bulgarians. Gypsies are the other major group affected by the new policy.

The Turkish minority is a heritage of nearly five centuries of Ottoman rule. In the Turkish view, the minority has been discriminated against since Bulgaria gained independence in 1878.

The situation has been compounded since World War II by the political and military division of Europe, with Bulgaria a member of the Soviet-led Warsaw Pact, and Turkey a member of the North Atlantic Treaty Organization.

Although the ethnic Turks represent about 9 percent of Bulgaria's population, only one Turk sits on the 192-member Central Committee.

There are no ethnic Turks in the higher levels of the Bulgarian Government, and none holds high military rank. Turkish-language schools were abolished in the 1950's; occasional courses in Turkish culture were dropped in the 1970's.

*   *   *

April 12, 1985

ENVER HOXHA, MASTERMIND OF ALBANIA'S ISOLATION

By WOLFGANG SAXON

Enver Hoxha, the Albanian leader, who died in Tirana yesterday, kept his isolated mountain country rigidly cordoned off for four decades.

Historically preyed on since Greek and Roman times, Albania maintained its independence under his defiantly Stalinist leadership. But his policies also left Albania with few friends abroad as his Government broke with a succession of more powerful foreign benefactors and protectors.

Mr. Hoxha derived his absolute powers at home from his positions as First Secretary of the Albanian Workers (Communist) Party and Commander in Chief of the armed forces.

"Let everyone understand clearly, the walls of our fortress are of unshakeable granite rock," he wrote in one of the many volumes of memoirs, some containing reminiscences of Stalin, that he penned over the years. More than 40 volumes of speeches and reminiscences by Mr. Hoxha were published.

Resonant Passages

His writing contained resonant passages. In 1982, after asserting that "imperialists and their lackeys say that we have isolated ourselves from the 'civilized world,' " he added this ringing sentence:

"Both the bitter history of our country in the past and the reality of the 'world' that they advertise have convinced us that it is by no means a 'civilized world,' but a world in which the bigger and stronger oppress and flay the smaller and the weaker, in which money and corruption make the law, and injustice, perfidy and backstabbing triumph."

Albania was one of the first Communist countries to denounce the revisionism of Josip Broz Tito of Yugoslavia, siding with Stalin in 1948. Then, Mr. Hoxha cut his ties with the Soviet Union, too, at the height of Nikita S. Khrushchev's de-Stalinization campaign in 1961, about the time of the Chinese-Soviet split.

Mr. Hoxha began to rely on China for material support. True to the old Balkan saying that the enemy of my enemy is

Gamma-Liaison

Enver Hoxha, left, the Albanian leader who died yesterday in Tirana at age 76, with President Ramiz Alia, who is expected to succeed him, during a 1983 ceremony marking 100th anniversary of the death of Karl Marx.

my friend, Mr. Hoxha became a vocal, albeit increasingly irrelevant, supporter of Mao Zedong when he found himself isolated from the Soviet bloc.

Chill in Ties With China

But again Mr. Hoxha grew disillusioned. The thaw in Chinese-American relations chilled Albania's friendship with China, and their cordiality turned into a rift that, by 1982, stopped just short of a break.

Albania then nurtured tentative contacts with Greece and Turkey, though the Hoxha Government's treatment of ethnic minorities, particularly the ethnic Greeks, strained such efforts. In fact, Vietnam remained just about the only country with which Albania had a close, if hardly profitable, relationship.

Domestically, Mr. Hoxha's objective was to modernize and industrialize what was generally regarded as one of the most backward countries in Europe, although travelers from more developed lands have reported, in recent years, that Tirana, with its old cobblestone streets and sparse auto traffic, retained an almost 19th-century air.

Over the years, the Hoxha Government was given credit for eliminating illiteracy. But it also repressed religion, true to Mr. Hoxha's dictum that Albania had been made into "the world's first atheist state, whose only religion is Albanianism." Public observances of religion were prohibited.

Problems for Ethnic Greeks

Ethnic minorities among the nearly 3 million people of Albania were harassed to the extent that ethnic Greeks, for instance, were forced to change Greek-sounding names. Only recently, according to visitors, some teaching of Greek was allowed in the schools as Albania edged toward a more open policy toward Greece.

Through it all, Mr. Hoxha maintained his grip on the tiller, foiling plots, presiding over bloody purges and mass imprisonments of those opposing or not quick enough to heed official changes in course.

Soon after Albania announced in 1981 that Mehmet Shehu, the longtime Prime Minister, had committed suicide, there were unconfirmed reports that he had in fact been killed. But Mr. Hoxha, in a book published in 1982, affirmed that Mr. Shehu had committed suicide.

Accordingly, Western analysts gave attention to a sentence in an article that appeared last February in the Albanian party daily, Zeri i Popullit. In a translation distributed by the Albanian mission to the United Nations, Mr. Shehu was called a "secret agent of the Americans, Soviets and Yugoslavs" who "was liquidated because he met with the unbreakable unity of the party with the people."

Doubts About Slaying Remain

Members of the Albanian-American community in New York contended that the translation was misleading and that the Albanian verb translated as "was liquidated" had been used in a figurative sense, which did not mean that Mr. Shehu had been killed.

They noted that the article also said: "The story on Mehmet Shehu's case has been described at length in all its aspects in the already known book by Comrade Hoxha."

In addition to concentrating on internal security, the Hoxha Government, in its last years, took steps to open transportation ties with its neighbors, Greece and Yugoslavia, although relations with them were chill.

And by last year, there were other indications that Albania was becoming less isolated and was looking for new ties to other countries. In March 1984, it signed a more extensive trade pact with Italy, which also agreed to enlarge cultural ties.

Son of a Moslem Merchant

Enver Hoxha—the name is pronounced enn-VEHR HAW-dja—was born Oct. 16, 1908, in Gjinokaster, a market town in southern Albania. His father was a Moslem cloth merchant. He was educated on a scholarship at a French secondary school in Korce and, at age 22, he went to France to study at the University of Montpellier.

While in France, he wrote for the Communist newspaper L'Humanite. In 1934 he was appointed a secretary in the Albanian consulate in Brussels, where he took a law course and continued writing for the French daily.

Since his articles were critical of the Government of Albania—then a monarchy under King Zog—his consular appointment was canceled after two years, but he managed to return home and accept a job as a French teacher at his old school in Korce. His continuing attacks on the Government resulted in a brief jail term in early 1939.

Underground During Italian Rule

The Italian Army of Mussolini conquered Albania later that year, forcing out King Zog and placing Albania under the Italian crown. An Albanian puppet government, having joined the Axis in World War II, declared war on the Allies in 1940.

Mr. Hoxha, who had gone underground, became the founder and leader of the Albanian Communist Party in 1941. He was also editor of Zeri i Popullit, the party paper.

He first operated out of a Tirana tobacco shop that served as a front for his Communist activities. The Italians never caught him, but he had to take to the mountains, where he received assistance from Soviet officers who landed in Albania by parachute as well as from American and British liaison officers.

The former French teacher built a guerrilla force of 70,000 men that battled the Italians and later the Germans, who sought to back up their ally for about a year.

After Italy's surrender to the Allies in World War II, its forces withdrew from Albania and the Communist guerrillas proclaimed a provisional government in October 1944, with Enver Hoxha, by then holding the rank of general, as Prime Minister and Defense Minister. This government was recognized by the Western allies later in 1945 with the understanding that free elections would be held.

Single List of Candidates Offered

When the balloting took place, there was only a single list of candidates, sponsored by the Communists. A People's Republic was proclaimed in Albania in January 1946, and the United States and Britain revoked their recognition and blocked Albania from joining the United Nations until 1955.

The Yugoslav Communists, who had helped the Albanian guerrillas from the beginning, had a monetary and customs union with the new Albania. But Mr. Hoxha, fearful of Belgrade's supremacy, cut all ties with the Yugoslavs at the time of the Stalin-Tito break in 1948. He also renamed his ruling Communist Party the Workers Party.

In 1954, Mr. Hoxha turned over the premiership to Mehmet Shehu, but remained the overlord as party chief, changing his title from General Secretary to First Secretary.

After Albania's break with the Soviet Union in 1961, Mr. Hoxha prevailed in a number of power struggles and in an attempted military coup in 1974, involving his own Minister of Defense. The minister and several army officers were executed.

Half of Central Committee Killed

In fact, nearly half of the 31 members of the party's Central Committee of 1948 were put to death in the years that followed. More recently, economic difficulties led to renewed political strife and hundreds of officials were reportedly thrown into prisons for resisting such policy moves as the break with the Chinese, who had served as one of Albania's main supports in its quest for economic development.

General Hoxha, a tall and impressive-looking man, was married to Nexhmije Hoxha, a schoolteacher whom he had met in the wartime guerrilla movement. She became a member of the Central Committee and served after 1969 as director of the Institute for Marxist-Leninist Studies in Tirana.

*   *   *

April 14, 1985

NEW ALBANIAN LEADER: RAMIZ ALIA

By DAVID BINDER

WASHINGTON, April 13—Ramiz Alia, the 59-year-old Albanian President, was selected today as the nation's new leader of the ruling Communist Party, succeeding Enver Hoxha, who died Thursday at 76. Mr. Alia, whose selection by the party's Central Committee was reported by the Albanian radio, was apparently picked for the job three years ago by Mr. Hoxha. In addition to being President, Mr. Alia had performed many of Mr. Hoxha's tasks since the summer of 1983. This became necessary when Mr. Hoxha's health deteriorated to the point where he was unable to do more than appear at occasional functions.

Mr. Hoxha had headed the party since he founded it in 1941. Throughout his rule, he preserved a Stalinist system, leading Albania through ideological breaks with Moscow, in 1961, and with Peking, in 1976.

Alia Lauded Hoxha in Speeches

Mr. Hoxha's apparent designation of Mr. Alia as the ultimate successor became especially evident in the summer of 1984, when Mr. Alia began a series of visits to provincial capitals, making speeches along the way.

The year before, in commemorating Mr. Hoxha's 75th birthday, Mr. Alia had said in a speech:

"Our party has had the great luck to have at its head such a leader as Comrade Enver Hoxha, loyal disciple and follower of the deeds of Marx, Engels, Lenin and Stalin, a leader who is characterized by the political wisdom, the ability to be oriented in every situation, the farsightedness and courage to adopt correct decisions and at the proper time."

Before his elevation to the inner circle of the Albanian leadership in 1960, Mr. Alia held a key position on the Central Committee staff for two years, in charge of ideology.

It was a critical time, because Albania had begun to extricate itself from dependence on the Soviet Union and to seek closer ties with the Chinese Communists. Mr. Alia's task then was to help prepare party members for the swing in allegiance.

Birthplace Seems in Dispute

Ramiz Alia—the name is pronounced rah-MEEZ uh-LEE-yah—was born Oct. 18, 1925. In official Albanian listings, his birthplace is given as the northern city of Shkoder. But a former teacher, Arshi Pipa, who is now a professor of Romance languages at the University of Minnesota, said Mr. Alia was born in Yugoslavia, in the ethnic Albanian autonomous province of Kosovo, and moved to Shkoder with his parents as a child.

As a northern Albanian, Mr. Alia is considered a Gheg, a member of one of the nation's two dialect groups. Mr. Hoxha was a Tosk, a member of the southern group. With the exception of Mr. Alia, nearly all members of the Albanian leadership are Tosks.

Reuters

At age 30, he was a candidate member of the ruling Politburo.

Mr. Alia attended a French secondary school in Tirana during the late 1930's and was already politically active as a student. In World War II, he joined the Communist-led guerrillas in 1944, at the age of 19. As a member of the newly formed Seventh Shock Brigade, he took part in what were essentially guerrilla actions against the retreating German forces.

He finished the war as the political commissar of the Fifth Division, with the rank of lieutenant colonel.

His first position in the Communist Government that was set up in Albania at the end of World War II was that of youth leader, at the head of what is known in Albania as the Union of Working Youth. He held that job until 1955, except for a brief stint on the party's propaganda staff in 1948.

Stephen Peters, an American official of Albanian origin who met Mr. Alia at that time, recalled him as "tall for an Albanian, lean, very pleasant and extremely friendly."

A Cabinet Minister Three Years

Mr. Alia was named Education Minister in 1955 and, three years later, became a fulltime official of the Communist Party.

When the party changed its formal name to Albanian Workers Party in 1948, the year of the Soviet bloc's—and Albania's—break with Yugoslavia, Mr. Alia, then still the youth leader, was made a member of the Central Committee. In his climb through the party hierarchy, he became a candidate member of the ruling Politburo in 1956, at the age of 30.

Five years later, in September 1960, he was made a full-fledged member of the ruling group, as a full member of the Politburo and one of the national party secretaries under Mr. Hoxha, the First Secretary.

In 1982, after having served in the party's Secretariat for more than two decades, Mr. Alia became the nation's President, formally chairman of the Presidium of the People's Assembly, succeeding the aging Haxhi Lleshi, who had held the post since 1953.

Married Educator's Daughter

Mr. Alia is married to Semiramis Xhuvani, the daughter of an educator, Alexander Xhuvani, who had been head of the Elbasan Teachers College before World War II and later served in the Communist Government. Mr. Peters recalled Semiramis Xhuvani as a "delightful girl" who had been one of his pupils at the Elbasan college. He said that her father, of Albanian Orthodox faith, had told him that he was "broken-hearted" that his daughter planned to marry a Moslem and asked Mr. Peters what he could do about it.

"I told him, 'Nothing, things are changing,'" Mr. Peters recalled.

Semiramis Alia is now dean of Tirana University's Natural Science Faculty. It is not known in the West whether the Alias have children.

Mr. Alia's former teacher, Dr. Pipa, was asked this week about his memories of the new leader. Dr. Pipa recalled that as a pupil in the Tirana high school in 1943, Mr. Alia had been "a good student, but not very conspicuous—quiet and reserved."

Dr. Pipa had been a political prisoner in Albania and, on his release in 1956, called on Mr. Alia, then the Education Minister, to see about a job. Mr. Alia made him a high school teacher in Shkoder.

"He was kind to me," said Professor Pipa. "He did not raise problems of the past."

*   *   *

June 12, 1985

PRESS RUMANIA ON RIGHTS

By NINA SHEA

President Reagan has recommended renewal of Rumania's most-favored-nation status—that is, nondiscriminatory treatment on imports—for another year. Congress ought to hinge approval of his request on human rights improvements.

In Rumania, human rights take a beating: no dissent is allowed; no independent labor unions, citizens' groups, scientific and legal or other professional associations can function. Not even underground presses survive. Ruling by decree, the regime controls virtually all aspects of life, intruding deeply into personal family and religious matters.

Yet Washington is soft on this Stalinism. It rarely questions Rumania's human rights abuses; instead, it grants Rumania trade privileges and loudly praises its relatively independent foreign policy. This prompted a public protest by David Funderburk, who recently resigned as Ambassador to Bucharest and accused senior Administration officials of

overrating Bucharest's independence from Moscow while downplaying the harshness of its internal practices.

Rumania does not hesitate to use brutal tactics to suppress dissent. More frequently, it uses more subtle but no less efficient administrative sanctions. It punishes without the pretext of a trial, and coerces and co-opts citizens simply by administrative order. Such measures include exile, forced labor, dismissal from jobs, eviction, and denial of wages, food and medicine.

Rumania suppresses religion. It bans religious education for the young, regulates distribution of Bibles, requires licenses for places of worship and presses believers to work on Christmas and other religious holidays. It is demolishing historic churches and monasteries. Dissident Roman Catholic, Protestant and Rumanian Orthodox leaders have been imprisoned, even killed. While Rumania maintains diplomatic ties with Israel and permits steady emigration of Jews, a recent decline in that emigration and the appearance of anti-Semitic publications have evoked concern.

Many thousands of Rumanians have been denied the right to emigrate, including those seeking medical treatment abroad or family reunification. Merely requesting exit permission triggers such reprisals as employment demotion or dismissal, eviction and denial of essential goods and services. Ethnic Hungarians, the largest minority, are persecuted.

Conditions have been deteriorating alarmingly. With the media under direct Government control, a new decree requiring police registration of private typewriters further restricts information. In 1984, West Germany uncovered a Rumanian bombing plot against Radio Free Europe, the only independent source of broadcast news about Rumania in Rumania.

Most-favored-nation status provides important leverage that should be used to obtain significant concessions in human rights performance.

The Jackson-Vanik Amendment links trade status with rights guarantees, particularly the right to emigrate.

Since 1975, Rumania has gotten most-favored-nation treatment without having to conform to Jackson-Vanik standards. Presidents annually waive the provision and Congress acquiesces after holding perfunctory hearings—in 1984, the House did not even bother with this gesture.

Negotiations on enhancing the rights of Rumanians who choose not to emigrate ought to precede renewal of most-favored-nation status. The Administration should request specific reforms in diverse areas and establish a definite timetable, and should temporarily suspend favored status until the talks are satisfactorily completed. Congressional trade committees would do well to review Rumania's rights record in hearings, and press for reforms.

Few Americans advocate severing an important link with Eastern Europe. But Bucharest is unlikely to let that happen. President Nicolae Ceausescu personally sought trade benefits in 1975, and no doubt during his nation's current economic crisis still prizes them. Faced with past threats to most-favored-nation status, he agreed to demands to rescind an education tax on emigrants, to increase emigration and to free political prisoners. It serves American interests to press for improvements that will strengthen Rumanian pluralism and institutions.

Nina Shea, a lawyer, is program director of the International League for Human Rights.

*   *   *

September 15, 1985

THE 'BULGARIAN CONNECTION' IS STILL ON TRIAL

By CLAIRE STERLING

When the Papal shooting trial resumes in Rome this week after a summer recess, the court will start at last to hear independent testimony on the "Bulgarian connection." So far, it has heard mostly from the gunman, Mehmet Ali Agca, who has done his bewildering best to becloud the proceeding, in which four fellow Turks and three Bulgarians are charged with conspiracy to assassinate Pope John Paul II. Now 120 witnesses for the state and scores more for the defense will help determine the veracity of Mr. Agca's pre-trial confession, the basis of the charges.

That confession appears to have a life of its own. Mr. Agca, who was convicted of the 1981 attack on the Pope in St. Peter's Square, had told the authorities that the Soviet Union, Bulgaria and a Turkish right-wing group, the Gray Wolves, organized the plot. But in court, he has seemed bent on discrediting his confession by zigging and zagging over previous statements, spicing his testimony with apocalyptic pronouncements ("I am Jesus Christ! I am omnipotent, and I announce the end of the world!"). Nonetheless, the state is prepared to present circumstantial evidence supporting the Agca confession, including details of his alleged meetings with the Bulgarians, their offer of money and a getaway truck.

Mr. Agca has never defected from his basic contention of Bulgarian involvement, and whatever the self-inflicted damage to his credibility, the defense has yet to show how he could have known as much as he proved to know about the Bulgarians now on trial unless he worked with or for them. That hasn't discouraged alternative theories, all based on the assumption that Mr. Agca was coached under one or another of the following circumstances:

- Italian or American secret services hired right-wing Turkish gunmen to kill the Pope, then blame it on the Russians. This theory, the first reaction of the Soviet bloc, has gained little credence elsewhere.
- Turkish gunmen were hired by crooked international financiers including Roberto Calvi, late head of the bankrupt Banco Ambrosiano, to prevent the Pope from exposing their shady dealings. Afterward, Western secret services seized the occasion to invent a Bulgarian connection, using Mr. Agca, to embarrass the Soviet Union. This theory has been advanced by Soviet bloc press and some Western journalists.

- The Gray Wolves did it on their own out of visceral Islamic hatred for Christianity, then sought to implicate the Soviet bloc, thus striking enemies in both the East and West. According to some versions, Western intelligence agencies followed up by inventing a Bulgarian connection.

The last theory is the most plausible but, like the others, has serious flaws. Barring Western intelligence involvement—and so far no evidence of it has emerged—it fails to explain Mr. Agca's detailed knowledge of the Bulgarians and their movements.

Advocates of the theory would argue back that he might have either fabricated his account from news reports or gleaned information during his known visits to Bulgaria.

Some variations hold that Western intelligence agencies somehow persuaded Mr. Agca to implicate the Bulgarians and the Russians while he was imprisoned, possibly with the aid of Raffaele Cutolo, a head of the Neopolitan underworld, who was in the same prison. Mr. Cutolo once acted as intermediary for the intelligence services to negotiate the release of a politician kidnapped by the Red Brigade, and a close aide has testified that Mr. Cutolo got to Mr. Agca on behalf of those agencies. But an equally close associate has denied it, as does Mr. Cutolo. In any event, he was moved in April 1982 to solitary confinement in another prison; Mr. Agca, no longer within his reach, did not begin to confess until May and did not implicate the Bulgarians until six months later. Of course, none of this excludes the possibility that others may have talked with Mr. Agca, but so far there is no evidence of it.

If only because these scenarios are so weak, the Bulgarian connection has survived Mr. Agca's baffling efforts to smudge it over. He is thought by the Italian prosecutor, Antonio Marini, to be maneuvering to attract help for an escape or win his release.

In any case, he has become hopeless as the state's chief witness, and Dr. Marini must proceed without him.

Though nothing approaching conclusive evidence on the Bulgarians has emerged, the court has gathered much pertinent information. The case has rested on the allegation that the Bulgarian secret service controlled a Turkish arms and drugs syndicate that supposedly hired a Turkish gunman for the attack. So far, two Turkish crime bosses, Abuzer Ugurlu and Bekir Celenk—a defendant in absentia—have been mentioned in the trial and tied to the Bulgarian secret service and Gray Wolves.

There is no telling where the trail might lead in the coming month, but two summer developments suggest a break. In Turkey, where Mr. Celenk has been jailed on smuggling charges, the authorities have spoken of "several witnesses" who confirm Mr. Agca's contention that Mr. Celenk offered him three million Deutschmarks to kill the Pope. Another new witness, Yalcin Ozbey, is to make a appearance this week. Long a close associate of Mr. Agca, Mr. Ozbey has told interrogators that he learned first-hand of the Bulgarians' role in the plot from a Turkish accomplice of Mr. Agca.

*   *   *

October 6, 1985

RUMANIA LEADER PUTS HIS IMPRINT ON CAPITAL

By HENRY KAMM
Special to The New York Times

BUCHAREST, Rumania—More than 10 churches, including some of historical and architectural importance, at least three synagogues and many other buildings have been bulldozed or dynamited in the center of Bucharest to make way for new buildings to house offices of the Communist Party and the Government, a project ordered by President Nicolae Ceausescu.

Leading up to the grandiose buildings, there is to be a Boulevard of the Victory of Socialism, 295 feet wide and about a mile long. Huge public buildings will line the thoroughfare. Monuments, fountains and trees will adorn it.

"The idea of constructing a center for the capital, of course, belongs to Comrade Ceausescu," said Petre Vraciu, a chief architect at the Bucharest Planning Office. "The architecture will show the imprint of our period. It is an original attempt to represent its spirit in an architecture that is new, but also recalls the ancient tradition of Rumania."

Mr. Vraciu said he had no information on the identity or number of historical buildings that were being demolished. The Rumanian press has reported on the project without mentioning the losses it entails. Much of the demolition takes place behind newly erected fences and at night.

Photographs Forbidden

A reporter who was photographing a synagogue soon to be destroyed was threatened with arrest by guards, told it was forbidden to photograph the building and driven from the area.

Resident Westerners said that since last year, when the scope of the destruction became evident, many Rumanians had voiced to them their indignation on religious and esthetic grounds. There have also been complaints of evictions on a day's notice of people whose houses were condemned.

The decision to demolish the buildings was announced after work was under way, and was accompanied by no public discussion or explanation. The full scope of the project is not known, and many say they fear much more destruction is to come. They say important architectural monuments far from the center are also being destroyed.

They include the Vacaresti Monastery, an 18th-century complex that in the early days of Communism served as a secret-police prison. The 18th-century Cotroceni Church was razed last year. A 17th-century church was reported destroyed to make way for the well-known 16th-century church of the Mihai Voda Monastery, which is to be moved to its site after the demolition of its monastery buildings.

Churches in City Center

Churches destroyed in the center include the Alba Postuvanu, where the national hero Michael the Brave was crowned Prince of Walachia in 1594; the Old and New Spirea Churches, the Izvorul Tamaduirii Church, known for a miraculous spring, and the 18th-century Dormition Church.

Particular regret was occasioned by the destruction of the Brancovan Hospital, a 19th-century neo-classical building on a central square, Piata Unirii. Mr. Vraciu said it was "of no architectural value and insalubrious."

Reports of destructive remodeling of old city centers have also been received from the provinces. Some villages were reported to have been put on notice that they would be razed to create more arable land.

The projects, which contrast with a general policy of stark austerity in meeting citizens' basic needs, are ascribed by Rumanians and diplomats to Mr. Ceausescu's striving to place his personal stamp on all Rumania, in what is being officially called the "Ceausescu Epoch." Choirs, broadcasters and writers maintain an almost continuous chorus in praise of the President, 67 years old.

A great variety of his books, bearing such titles as "Militant Solidarity With All Democratic and Progressive Forces for a Better and Juster World," fill store shelves otherwise poorly supplied because of a paper shortage. Texts of his speeches published in the press are interspersed with such glosses as "Strong applause and shouts of enthusiasm; in long-lasting chorus shouts of 'Ceausescu and the people!' "

*   *   *

November 25, 1985

AIRPORT SECURITY TIGHT, GREEKS SAY

By RICHARD WITKIN

Greek authorities, shocked by the second hijacking of an airliner from Athens in five months despite a security crackdown after the first incident, said yesterday that they did not believe the weapons were smuggled aboard at the Greek airport.

The chief security official at the airport was quoted by United Press International as suggesting that the weapons used in the latest incident, which ended in the storming of the plane in Malta and about 50 deaths, might have been put on board in Cairo. The Egyptair plane had initially flown to Athens from the Egyptian capital.

Security at the Greek airport came in for worldwide criticism after the June 14 hijacking of a Trans World Airlines plane that took off from Athens with 153 people on board and ended up in Beirut. An American Navy diver was killed by the Arab hijackers and 39 American hostages were held for 17 days.

The State Department issued a travel advisory on June 18 advising American travelers to avoid the Athens airport. The advisory was lifted July 22 after stringent inspections by the International Air Transport Association and the Federal Aviation Administration that led to tough new security measures. Both agencies ultimately labeled the airport as one of the world's best-guarded terminals.

'Security Was Second to None'

On Sunday the Egyptair incident was already touching off new demands for more intensive scrutiny of flight operations at Athens, a crossroads on airways to and from the Middle East. Officials of the international pilots' union spoke of a possible brief boycott of Athens to bring pressure for even more thorough security improvements than were put in place after the T.W.A. hijacking.

But the authorities in Greece, where earlier criticism had produced widespread outrage, came to the defense of the upgraded security system and began an inquiry to reconstruct how the Egyptair hijacking had come about.

A senior police official, quoted by The Associated Press on condition that he not be identified, said, "We have started looking into the event, but it is still too early to draw any conclusions." He too expressed doubt that the weapons used in the hijacking had been brought aboard the Boeing 737 plane in Athens, adding, "The passengers go through two security checks, ours and the airline's."

The senior security official at the field, Vassilis Meraviliotakis, went further, according to U.P.I., saying: "Both the Trans World Airlines jet hijacked from Athens in June and the Egyptair jet hijacked from Athens Saturday had originated in Cairo. The United States, whose officials inspected Athens airport after the T.W.A. hijacking, publicly declared security was second to none. This leads us to believe that the weapons used by the hijackers may have been placed aboard the aircraft in Cairo and not in Athens."

Security Measures Listed

Later a Government spokesman issued a statement listing in detail the security measures to which those who boarded the Egyptair plane had been subjected. These included use of electronic devices for bodily checks of passengers at two points, once by Greek security police and once by Egyptair employees using the airline's own equipment.

In addition, the statement said, passenger luggage got a triple inspection, once at check-in, a second time by security police using manual and electronic search procedures, and finally a manual check by airline personnel.

In the furor over the T.W.A. incident last June, critics of the Athens Government emphasized that the Athens airport had built a reputation over many years as one of the most loosely guarded of all the world's major terminals.

The international transport association, which has 140 member airlines, submitted an initial list of security recommendations to Greek authorities back in 1980. The security survey was one of a series that covered about 40 airports over 10 years, according to David Kyd, a spokesman for the association.

Large Dollar Losses

"In the case of Athens," he recalled after the T.W.A. hijacking, "we sent somebody there this past May to check what they had done and they found nothing much had happened."

But the outcry over the T.W.A. incident, which not only embarrassed the Athens Government but led to huge dollar losses as travelers shunned the area, did bring concrete improvements.

Mr. Kyd said on July 16 that "virtually all" new measures recommended by a inspection team of five airline experts had been carried out. "This means," he said, "that checking of passengers and hand luggage, protection of a perimeter of the airport, and access to parking areas of aircraft, are now all up to satisfactory standards."

The issue now is whether the Egyptair incident was made possible by a loophole in the Athens system or whether the weapons were smuggled on board somewhere else.

Meantime, the F.A.A. confirmed that American airlines and airport officials had been put on alert last week against reported security threats. But it was a general alert and no direct link could be made to the Egyptair hijacking.

An agency spokesman, Fred Farrar, said: "We regularly advise U.S. carriers of security-threat conditions anywhere in the world. It's a security matter and we don't comment further."

*   *   *

December 8, 1985

GOING BACK: BULGARIA, 20 YEARS LATER

By DAVID BINDER

I returned with a certain uneasiness to Bulgaria, where I had served 20 years earlier as a correspondent. In part, my discomfort grew from memories of wretched hotel food, which invariably made me break out in boils, and the rather hostile attitude of Bulgarian officials functioning under a mandated policy of anti-Americanism. Primarily it was based on the fact that the People's Republic had issued a ukase barring me from the country for life. Twice.

The reason given for the action was a joke I had used in an article to illustrate the attitudes of Rumania toward neighboring states. The joke took a cut at Todor Zhivkov, then Bulgaria's Prime Minister. It appeared first in 1965 in the daily paper, prompting the initial ukase. When it appeared a second time, in this magazine, the Bulgarians reiterated the lifetime ban. I had not tested the ban until now, and although I had no trouble getting a visa, I was a bit hesitant.

Not surprisingly, I found many changes in Bulgaria, from the easy availability of food, clothing and housing to the smooth handling of foreign correspondents—for a fee—by a special state agency. The furnishings of the Sofia hotel where I stayed hinted that life was more comfortable now: the bathroom taps were metal instead of the leaky plastic of yore; the restaurant food did not induce boils; the Gamza burgundy was excellent.

Pleasantly situated in a broad valley, Sofia is described by Bulgarians as "the greenest city in Europe" and streets are lined with black locusts, maples, birches, elms and horse chestnuts. Looming to the south is Mt. Vitosha, the queen of the Rila range; to the north are the long spines of the Balkan Mountains.

The city was established as Serdica in the second century by the Roman Emperor Trajan on the site of an ancient Thracian settlement; elements of Roman fortifications have been carefully preserved to this day. The architecture of the capital is a congenial mixture of Viennese, Byzantine and Turkish styles, although a Parisian critic recently described the mustard-tinted former royal palace as "a French town hall."

With its screeching yellow streetcars, its cobblestoned avenues and tin-roofed shacks housing thousands of Gypsies, Sofia seems an appropriate setting for old-fashioned international intrigue, but scarcely the ideal spot for masterminding a far-flung plot to murder a Pope.

Nonetheless, that is what an Italian magistrate has charged. In 1982, Mehmet Ali Agca—the lone Turkish gunman seized after attempting to kill Pope John Paul II the previous year—swore that Sergei I. Antonov, chief of the Bulgarian airline office in Rome, and two other Bulgarians had directed the plot. Worse still was the suggestion by the Italian magistrate, Ilario Martella, that the assassins were acting as agents of the Bulgarian Government.

The Bulgarians promptly rejected the charges as preposterous. But even if the "Bulgarian connection" is proved false (the outcome of Agca's interminable trial is as unpredictable as Agca's testimony, which has included—among other assertions—his claim that he is Jesus Christ), the incident further tarnished the image of a country that has already been implicated in a number of cloak-and-dagger activities.

There was, for instance, the case in 1978 of the notorious umbrella killer who fired from his bumbershoot a minuscule platinum pellet containing a powerful poison into the leg of Georgi Markov, a dissident Bulgarian writer living in London. Mr. Markov, who had assailed President Todor Zhivkov in broadcasts transmitted by Radio Free Europe to his homeland, died four days later at age 49. His assassin was never found. Then there are the charges that Bulgaria's large export company, Kintex, is an international arms trafficker. Deputy Foreign Minister Lyuben Gotsev acknowledged to me in an interview that "there have been cases in which Kintex arms have been found in the hands of people who are, as you say, hostile to the United States"—people, according to American intelligence agents, such as Arab terrorists in Lebanon and Libya.

In addition, the United States Drug Enforcement Administration says that Bulgarian authorities harbor international dealers responsible for shipments of heroin and other narcotics from the Middle East to northern Europe.

Domestically, the Government is waging a remorseless campaign to force homogeneity on what has been a typically multi-ethnic Balkan salad of Turks, Moslem Pomaks, Gypsies, Armenians, a handful of Albanians, Greeks and Rumanians, not to mention several hundred thousand Macedonians.

In the recent drive to "Bulgarize" the Turkish minority, at least 200 civilians and soldiers were killed. (Amnesty International has reported the figure at 500.) The aim, as described by the Communist Politburo member Stanko Todorov, is to make Bulgaria a "single-nationality state"—something southeastern Europe has not known in its 3,000 years of recorded history.

Bulgarian authorities call criticism on any of these points part of an "anti-Bulgarian campaign." With a studied air of resignation, Deputy Foreign Minister Gotsev said that a clipping service had collected 4,033 articles from United States periodicals on Sergei Antonov—the Bulgarian now being held and tried in Italy—adding, "Antonov has not even been sentenced and yet we are called assassins, terrorists."

The Bulgarian official who has become the international spokesman on the Antonov case is Boyan Traikov, director of the Bulgarian Telegraph Agency. A tall, long-faced man, suave in a pink shirt, Mr. Traikov receives me in his vast office on Sofia's Lenin Boulevard and recites his lines smoothly, calling the Turk Agca a fantasist: "It is of purely formal significance that Agca, traveling from Turkey to Western Europe, has passed through Bulgaria. He has been here, seen the people, streets, hotels," seen enough, in essence, to be able to fabricate the "Bulgarian connection" scenario.

The campaign, he says, smiling under heavy eyebrows, "is not directed exactly toward Bulgaria, but toward the Soviet Union." He continues: "It fits the thinking in the West about Bulgaria as the most faithful, the most orthodox—they call us a satellite.

"We are not so important as to be the object of such great attention around the world. The campaign is aimed at the Soviet Union and the Socialist system. Like billiards, you hit one ball to hit another." His allusion to the "Bulgarian connection" thus embodies the supposition of its believers: that the Soviet K.G.B. ultimately pulled the wires in the plot to kill the Pope, while the Bulgarians served as mere marionettes.

At least on the surface it would seem this country, the size of Pennsylvania and with a population of nine million, is indeed Russia's most faithful ally. The capital boasts not only a statue of Czar Alexander II and the Alexander Nevsky Cathedral, erected in gratitude for the 1878 liberation of Bulgaria, but also a huge monument to the Soviet Army, a large statue of Lenin and numerous avenues named for Russian figures. No Soviet troops or rockets are based here, but the Russian Embassy has more than 500 personnel, according to Western diplomats, who believe still more Russians function as military and police advisers.

Sovietization of Bulgaria began immediately after Marshal Fyodor I. Tolbukhin's troops took over the country in 1944. Thrust into power under Soviet guns, the Bulgarian Communist Party, numbering fewer than 11,000 members, began the bloodiest of all Communist takeovers in Eastern Europe. In less than a year, it passed 2,138 death sentences. Late in 1945, Bulgaria's most famous Communist, Georgi Dimitrov, became the Party Secretary and Prime Minister. After a brief flirtation with Yugoslavia's Tito in 1947 and 1948, however, he was reduced to simply a political puppet of Stalin. He died in 1949 and was succeeded by his brother-in-law, Vulko Chervenkov, a Moscow-trained Stalinist.

In 1954, a year after Stalin's death, Bulgaria acquired what is known as a "home Communist," a party member whose political experience was Bulgarian, not Russian. This was Todor Zhivkov, a printer who, in the last years of World War II, had become political commissar of the partisan Chavdar Brigade that fought Bulgarian fascist government forces.

Mr. Zhivkov is now the senior governing Communist in Europe, having ruled as party secretary for 31 years, and having survived the years of Stalin, Khrushchev, Brezhnev, Andropov, Chernenko and nine months of Gorbachev—as well as a military coup attempt in 1965.

To be sure, Mr. Zhivkov has paid public dues with such remarks as, "The Soviet Union and Bulgaria breathe with the same lungs and the same blood flows in our veins," and such actions as sending a token force to aid in the Soviet-bloc invasion of Czechoslovakia in 1968 (neighboring Rumania did not).

But to suggest that Mr. Zhivkov's Bulgaria is an unwavering Soviet satellite may be to exaggerate. A year ago, Mr. Zhivkov's long-planned trip to Bonn was called off at the last minute by Mikhail S. Gorbachev. This annoyed the Bulgarian leader, who responded to the humiliation with a series of visits to and from the heads of state of Rumania, Japan, Finland and France, thus asserting a degree of independence from Moscow.

In October, Mr. Gorbachev visited Bulgaria, this time as Soviet party chief. In private talks, he let Mr. Zhivkov know that the Soviet Union was no longer going to accept the second-rate goods Bulgaria was dumping in the Soviet market, while selling higher-quality products to the West. Putting the squeeze on further, he said Moscow was cutting back on its shipments of subsidized oil to Bulgaria.

Western diplomats maintain that the Soviet Union has never treated Bulgaria as a valuable partner. "The Soviets don't consult, they don't even inform their own allies," one ambassador observed.

Certainly, the Russians contemplate Bulgaria with a mixture of suspicion and envy. This Slavic nation, which sided with Germany in two wars, has accepted the Soviet system and improved upon it, so that agriculture and some industries are more productive than in the motherland.

Meanwhile, the Russians have remonstrated in private with the Bulgarians about the antiminority campaign, pointing out that the tensions it has raised could have serious repercussions among Russia's own fast-growing Turkish population. The Soviet press has maintained a disapproving silence about the Bulgarian drive.

Certainly the push to "Bulgarize" the minorities is the most dramatic event within the country since Mr. Zhivkov's rise to power. The campaign, which, according to some Bulgarians, was conceived in a secret party directive in 1971, has been massive: Although 250,000 Bulgarian Macedonians were recorded in the 1946 census, by 1975 none were listed—nor were there any headings indicating other national minorities.

Not content simply to drop minority listings, over the last four years, the Government has forced some 5,000 ethnic Albanians, along with thousands of Gypsies and Armenians, to take Bulgarian names. The People's Socialist Republic of Albania has lodged a formal protest.

In August 1984, the push gathered force, in anticipation of a national census scheduled for this month—when the Government is expected to declare the country ethnically pure, with no hints of any cultural diversity.

Last December, the Government focused its efforts on Bulgaria's one million ethnic Turks, starting in the southern district of Kurdzhali. There was bloody resistance in Momchilgrad and the state militia, the military and the Zapasi, or special reserves, were called in. Dozens of people were killed. In early January, the drive was expanded to the north. Whole districts were sealed off to foreigners.

Armed forces typically would surround a village and then force the inhabitants, at gunpoint, to line up and sign name-change petitions. Stopped by a roadblock on the outskirts of Yablanovo, on the northern rim of the Balkan range, a foreigner questioned a soldier. Yes, said the young rifleman, Turks had been killed in the rural town, and so had some soldiers. In all, about 30 died, he said, brandishing his AK-47 and sputtering, "Rrra-tat-tat-tat."

The Government has closed all Turkish schools (there had been 1,199 Turkish schools in 1951) and the one Turkish newspaper, Yeni Isik; Turkish-language radio broadcasts have been taken off the air and fines imposed for speaking Turkish in public. Increasing numbers of Turks have fled to Rumania and Greece.

A good deal of historical revisionism has accompanied the campaign. In 1964, Todor Zhivkov proclaimed that "all possible opportunities had been created for the Turkish population to develop their culture and language." As late as last year, Bulgaria told a United Nations committee that it had national minorities. But in early March, Stanko Todorov of the Politburo declared in the Turkish village of Novachevo: "At the end of 1984 and the beginning of 1985, a process was carried out with a new force spontaneously and comprehensively restoring the Bulgarian names of our compatriots who had Turkish-Arabic names. This process was concluded in the whole country in two to three months. The workers considered their past, recognized their Bulgarian roots and their Bulgarian national belonging." Ethnic Turks, he boasted, were really descendants of Bulgarians who had been "forcibly Turkicized" under Ottoman rule.

Clearly, some are not willing to accept this new version of their past. An explosion rocked the railway station in Plovdiv in August 1984, but it was not until May 16 of this year that Kostadin Lyutov, the state prosecutor, acknowledged that a woman had been killed in the blast; he added that seven others were killed by an explosion on a train on March 9. Some observers suggest that the death toll might be as high as 30 from bombs in a supermarket, a tramway, a disco and a hotel.

Off the record, Bulgarian officials charge that ethnic Turks are responsible; publicly, the bombs have touched off an explosion of hatred. "Our Turks don't believe in God, they believe in whisky," a middle-ranking government official remarked with a sneer. Later, in an outdoor cafe facing

Sofia's Eagle Bridge, a 29-year-old graduate student told me vehemently that all Turks "deserve to be punished." Others trotted out rationalizations typical of such ethnocentricity: the minority populations were reproducing at a fast clip, while the Slavic population was stagnating. The fact that the original Bulgarians—the Bulgars—were a Turkic people did not stop their xenophobic responses.

Still, the Zhivkov Government is palpably nervous about the ethnic Turk issue.

What was it Boyan Traikov had said to me? "They think we are a totalitarian police state, that no bird can pass over without being seen, that telephone conversations are being tapped, foreigners followed. But there is no such system of control."

Nonetheless, as a passenger in the cars of Western diplomats, it was clear to me that many were followed by unmarked automobiles of the Dazjavna Sigurnost, the state security force. Telephone taps? One day I called the Turkish Embassy from the hotel and was told to come to the chancery on Boulevard Tolbukhin. Guarding the embassy, in addition to a policeman, was a muscular youth in a camouflage uniform with a broad leather holster, from which the grip of a ten-shot Skorpion machine pistol protruded. He was a member of the Zapasi, the special reserve unit deployed in suppressing the Turks. Neither the policeman nor the Zapasi trooper bothered me, but next morning at 7:05, my phone rang and, when I answered, a male voice, plainly Slavic, snarled: "Tolbukhin!" "Tolbukhin?" I inquired. "Yes," came the reply, and then the line went dead.

My uneasiness returned. This was a warning. Yet, several days later when I set out into the mountains to find some ethnic Turks no one seemed to be following.

The Turks were not hard to find, but they were frightened. A group of construction workers told me everyone in their village had been compelled to accept Bulgarian names last December. There had been resistance and one man had been killed, others had been taken away to a camp for political prisoners on Belene, an island in the Danube.

Whenever anyone passed on the road, the men fell silent. With a look of disgust, one proffered his new internal identity pass, with his new Bulgarian name. The workers' Bulgarian foreman had warned them not to talk to strangers, one explained, adding that if they were caught they could be put off the job.

Nonetheless, they ticked off their complaints and fears: mosques had been closed; perhaps ethnic Turks would be denied higher schooling; they were not getting the full wages due them. Why the campaign of repression? "Because they fear we Turks will demand a federated state," said one. Would he emigrate if he could? "I was born here and I'll die here."

Todor Zhivkov boasts of making Bulgaria "the Japan of the Balkans." It is an overreaching claim, but a returning traveler cannot fail to be impressed by the transformation of what had been, 20 years ago, essentially a peasant society.

Today, Bulgaria generates 25 percent of its electrical power in nuclear plants and is planning on 50 percent in the year 2000. There are traffic jams in city streets and shop windows are filled with consumer goods. Evidently, decades of diligence—Bulgarians are known as disciplined workers—are paying off in terms of improved living standards for many citizens. The average wage is about 250 leva a month ($240 at the official exchange rate), but there are usually two or more wage earners in a family.

Thus the extremely harsh winter of 1984–85, with its power outages and food shortages, came "as a bit of a shock," in the words of a middle-aged office worker. Bulgarian Socialism, with its mania for fulfilling plans, had not taken account of such vagaries as bad weather or other natural calamities. Prospects for this winter are grim, as well: already, every day there are power outages for two hours.

One young West German technician who travels around the country servicing advanced machine tools told me: "They are 15 to 20 years behind us and they will stay there because they have no way of developing their own products." He was scornful of the lack of incentive—Bulgarian electronics engineers earn little more than ordinary factory workers—but spoke admiringly of some enterprises that were "as clean as those in Stuttgart and working beautifully."

Bulgarian farming is relatively prosperous, with large and growing agro-industrial complexes specializing in the cultivation of grapes, fruits and vegetables and raising cattle. Gradually, Bulgarian agricultural products are penetrating Western markets, although it appears that the better wines are not exported.

Nearly 28 percent of the agricultural output comes from the 13 percent of the land the Government lends to farmers as private plots. One Sunday, I saw Bulgarians tilling these small plots in the fertile Struma River Valley, their backs bent in classic peasant posture as they hoed. But they had driven to the fields in their own cars, mostly Soviet Fiat-licensed Ladas, a new kind of mobility for farmers in the Balkans. Encouragement of private farming is also partly the work of Mr. Zhivkov.

Todor Zhivkov became party chief in 1954 by denouncing the "personality cult" of his predecessor, Vulko Chernenkov. But now there would seem to be a Zhivkov personality cult. Through his largesse, his hometown of Pravets, formerly a small farming village, is today a model town, with a new high school, hotel, computer factory and a state-of-the-art dairy farm. A bust of the most famous native son dominates the square in front of the town's Culture Palace, which also contains a museum tracing Mr. Zhivkov's life in photographs. His collected works, with titles like "Some New Views and Approaches Concerning the Framing and Implementation of the Techno-Scientific Policy," have reached Volume 29, and cover only the years of his rule to 1979.

The road to Pravets is Bulgaria's newest four-lane highway, and on a mountaintop overlooking the town is Bulgaria's new state guest house where, according to one visiting diplomat, Mr. Zhivkov entertained Finland's President Mauno Koivisto with a daring girlie show.

The leader, it would seem, bears little similarity to the man I saw briefly 20 years ago at a state funeral in Bucharest.

Russia's Anastas Mikoyan and China's Zhou Enlai and all the other Communist leaders chatted among themselves, laughing and making small talk—all, that is, but Todor Zhivkov, who sat alone on a chair against the wall. No one spoke to him and, having just been barred from his country, I decided not to myself.

For a brief period, some observers wondered whether a Zhivkov dynasty was in the offing. After his daughter, Lyudmila, graduated from university in 1966, he drew her into the party, and by 1975 she had become chairman of the state committee for culture; four years later, at age 36, she was elected to the Politburo. She died in 1981 in an automobile accident. Typical of the Balkan rumor mill that works overtime in the absence of a free press, talk spread that Lyudmila had been "poisoned by Soviet doctors" for advocating nationalism.

She is commemorated by the Lyudmila Zhivkova National Palace of Culture, Sofia's largest and perhaps ugliest building. It serves as a backdrop to a memorial dedicated four years ago to 13 centuries of nationhood.

Such nationalism is also apparent in the schools. One Western diplomat tells the story of his son, who was enrolled in a Bulgarian high school. One day, in a military course, an officer-teacher pointed to a map of Europe. "You are not here because of the NATO military threat," he said. "You're here for this!" He rolled down a map showing medieval Bulgaria encompassing large areas of present-day Greece, Yugoslavia and Albania. It is just such extreme nationalism, and the dream of restoring the medieval empire of "Greater Bulgaria," that brought woe and shrinkage upon the nation in the first place.

Yet, it would seem that most of the young Bulgarians I met do not share such nationalistic dreams. Like their contemporaries all over the world, they are interested in jeans and rock music; one spoke of his dream to become a country-western singer, in Bulgarian. The young people say "ciao" and "merci" instead of "dovizhdane" and "blagodarya." Some, like the sweet-faced young woman I saw at noon on a weekday in Sofia's Sveta Nedelya church, light votive candles in the chapels. Still, there is the puzzle: Why does the Zhivkov Government indulge in such an atavistic nationalist paroxysm, going so far as to force its citizens to change their names? Why does a country that aspires to enter the high-tech age risk international opprobrium by engaging in trafficking in drugs, arms and cloak-and-dagger intrigues?

At least part of the answer lies in Bulgarian history. In the Middle Ages, the Bulgars created an empire stretching from the Black Sea to the Aegean and, for a time in the 9th and 13th centuries, to the Adriatic. Modern Yugoslavia's capital of Belgrade was, for a time, a Bulgarian citadel. So was Greece's Salonika. But for five of the last six centuries, there was no Bulgaria, only the Ottoman Empire, and what the nation's greatest writer, Ivan Vazov, called the Turkish yoke. Freedom movements were growing when Bulgaria was liberated in 1878 by the troops of the Russian Czar. "The Bulgarians never liberated themselves," remarked a Macedonian from Yugoslavia, who is a keen observer of this country, "and

after the Russians liberated them, they only won one war, a short one in 1885."

"Bulgarian history is discontinuity," he said, adding that, "they chose the wrong side in three wars," suffering defeat in the Second Balkan War, and again in World Wars I and II, when Bulgaria sided with Germany.

Having made wrong choices at three critical junctures in the space of less than three decades, "there is no fixed reference point," observed the Macedonian. "For Bulgarians, who is to say the choices they make now are not wrong?"

David Binder, who served as The New York Times's East Europe correspondent from 1965 to 1967, is assistant news editor of The Times's Washington bureau.

*   *   *

December 15, 1985

WINTER AT THE DOOR, RUMANIA CLOSES DOWN EARLY

By PAUL LEWIS
Special to The New York Times

BUCHAREST, Rumania, Dec. 14—After a warm fall, winter is closing in on this city, creating a visible reflex of apprehension in the population.

Wrapped in furs and coats, people scurry through the gray, foggy streets searching for life's essentials. Lines assemble wherever the elusive quarry is found. A crowd waits at a store's side door for packets of butter. Another gathers outside a butcher shop an hour before it opens.

Strings of tinsel add a little Christmas glitter to sad shop windows, but inside it is cold and dark. Light and heat have been turned down to save energy, leaving most streets inky black by 6 in the evening. That is when the theaters now open their doors so everyone can get back early to bed. Restaurants close by 9. Last winter, Rumanians were told that a 40-watt electric bulb was enough to light a room. Now they must do with 25 watts.

Last year, Rumanians froze in the coldest winter of the century as oil and coal ran out. Rumanians know they will freeze again this winter.

Independence in Foreign Affairs

But the country that Secretary of State George P. Shultz is to visit Sunday on an East European tour, in addition to suffering from the inadequacies of Communist economic planning, is also a maverick within the Soviet bloc.

Under Nicolae Ceausescu, it has hewed an independent line in foreign policy, irritating the Soviet Union in small ways and, Western diplomats believe, creating a precedent for independent action inside the Soviet bloc.

Rumania is the only Soviet-bloc country maintaining diplomatic relations with Israel, China and Albania. Mr. Ceausescu denounced the Soviet-led invasion of Czechoslovakia in 1968 and distanced himself from the intervention in

Afghanistan. He allows no Soviet bases in Rumania and does not take part in joint Warsaw Pact maneuvers.

In the United Nations, Rumania is careful in most cases not to vote against important United States interests, even if its delegate has to leave the chamber. Radio Free Europe and the Voice of America can be heard throughout the country.

Emigration is less restrictive than in other Soviet-bloc countries. Last year, 20,000 people left, including 1,300 Jews and 14,000 ethnic Germans.

But Mr. Ceausescu compensates for this show of independence in foreign affairs by running one of the most repressive internal systems in the Soviet bloc.

There have been signs of protest—a miners' strike in the Jiu Valley, promptly suppressed, and a rumored military coup attempt in 1983. But generally not a tremor of dissent is noticeable.

Uniformed Police Conspicuous

The uniformed police seem more conspicuous than elsewhere in the Soviet bloc. The security police, though less visible, are also ubiquitous. Ion Mihai Pacepa, a deputy chief of Rumania's foreign intelligence service, who defected to the United States in 1978, said one in every 15 Rumanians was a police informer.

Unlike the Roman Catholic Church in Poland, the Rumanian Orthodox Church is loyal to the state and is not an alternative focus for nationalism.

For the last decade, the United States has rewarded Rumania for its show of independence by granting most-favored-nation treatment, meaning normal import tariffs on Rumanian goods entering the United States. The only other Soviet-bloc country receiving this privilege is Hungary.

Now a group of American legislators, worried about Rumania's human rights record, specifically the persecution of unauthorized Christian sects, is trying to deny most-favored-nation status. The issue is expected to be high on Secretary Shultz's agenda.

Nonapproved Sects Suffer

Sects such as the Nazarenes, Seventh-day Adventists and the Church of Jesus Christ of Latter-day Saints, which unlike other faiths are not officially sanctioned, have had their churches closed or demolished, been denied Bibles sent from abroad and suffered other persecution. The number of sectarians appears small and is probably no more than 3,000.

Some sects, such as a dissident Baptist group, have incurred official displeasure by breaking away from the 14 sanctioned faiths, which include Roman Catholic, Jews and the major Protestant denominations.

Another accusation by the United States relates to a thousand people who are still awaiting United States entry visas after getting Rumanian permission to leave. Because of their intention to emigrate, they have lost their civil rights in Rumania and are often forced to give up their apartments, are assigned to menial jobs and denied food ration cards.

United Press International

Under Nicolae Ceausescu, Rumania has hewed an independent line in foreign policy.

The Rumanian Government attributes the problem to American delays resulting from the system of national immigration quotas, which has kept some Rumanians waiting for more than two years. Since July, Rumania has stopped issuing passports to emigrants until they get their United States visas, thus allowing them to keep their jobs and accommodations.

Evidence of Special U.S. Ties

Rather than an occasion for recrimination, Rumanians see Mr. Shultz's visit as confirmation of their country's special ties to the United States and of its peculiar position in the Soviet bloc.

In a recent interview, an official proudly recalled the visits of President Richard M. Nixon and President Gerald R. Ford, those of United States Secretaries of State, and Mr. Ceausescu's four trips to the United States.

"This is a normal visit," the Rumanian said, "because we have a long deep relationship with the United States based on our own strong national identity."

That sense of identity seems to have much to do with the repressive aspects of life and with the Government's determination to press ahead with a policy of forced industrialization and strong central planning, despite the wretched results achieved.

Economically, Rumania starts with the advantage of being Eastern Europe's only sizable oil and gas producer besides having large deposits of coal.

Miscalculations by Planners

But the planners got their calculations wrong. Originally, they expected oil production to climb during the 1970's and pressed ahead with ambitious oil refineries, chemical, steel and aluminum plants, all of which consume large quantities of energy. But after peaking at 14.7 million metric tons in 1976, oil output dropped to 11.5 million in 1980 and has remained near that level since.

Coal production, though rising as a result of the exploitation of low-grade lignite, has fallen short of long-term projections. The rate of growth of natural gas, significant in the 1970's, slowed down in the early 1980's.

The result is an energy shortage as winter approaches. The press concedes that some factories are working at 20 to 30 percent capacity, worsening the shortage of goods and food.

These shortages have been made worse by Mr. Ceausescu's decision, in the name of national independence, to repay the foreign debt of $12 billion by 1990. In the last three years, the debt has been cut in half, at the cost of reducing imports and selling more to the West. Rumania trades more outside the Soviet bloc than any other Eastern European country, except possibly Hungary.

Energy Crisis Building Up

As the energy crisis built up for the second year, Western diplomats say, the Government's response took on a desperate air. In September, Mr. Ceausescu spoke of repatriating pensioners from the cities to the countryside. A new draft law requires everyone to work six days a year without pay and mandates a 50 percent pay cut for those failing to achieve output goals.

In October, Mr. Ceausescu dismissed three ministers, put the military in charge of power stations and called for a "militarized system of work."

At a time when the Soviet Union is starting to follow the example of some Eastern European countries and is experimenting with relaxation of economic controls, Rumania continues to follow an orthodox line.

Last month, Mr. Ceausescu told the Central Committee that any move toward private ownership or market economics was "in total contradiction with socialist principals, and we will never permit it to happen under any circumstances."

*   *   *

May 11, 1986

AT LAST, FOR GREECE AND ALBANIA, WORLD WAR II IS COMING TO A CLOSE

By HENRY KAMM
Special to The New York Times

ATHENS—Greece is preparing to put a formal end to a legal vestige of World War II by proclaiming that it no longer considers itself at war with Albania.

The proposed action, which, according to Foreign Minister Karolos Papoulias, may come this month, is strongly opposed by organizations here and abroad that say that much of southern Albania is Greek territory. The largest such group is in the United States, which became a refuge for most of the Greeks who fled when the region of Epirus was divided between Greece and Albania after World War I. Mr. Papoulias's informal announcement of the pending action last month was also condemned by the major opposition party, New Democracy. The conservatives accused the Socialist Government of failing to assure the rights of Albania's Greek minority in return for ending the state of war.

Albania, an Italian puppet nation after the invasion in 1939, joined Italy in declaring war in 1940. Greece responded with a decree of a state of belligerency, under which Athens took into custody as enemy property extensive real-estate holdings of ethnic Greeks living across the border. The decree remains valid, and relatives in Greece enjoy the use of the properties—mainly in the Athens and Salonika areas—whose owners or heirs remain north of the border.

War Over, Albania Says

Albania says that it is not responsible for what was done in its name by Italy and that Athens implicitly ended the state of war by signing postwar agreements restoring peace in Europe and opening diplomatic relations with Albania in 1971.

To prevent militantly Communist Albania, which has nationalized all private property, from claiming the "enemy" holdings, Greece is expected to include in its measure scrapping of the state of war a declaration that it will not surrender the properties of ethnic Greeks.

Those opposed to the action are urging the Government of Prime Minister Andreas Papandreou to extract from Albania, the Government of which is considered the most restrictive in Europe, improvements in human rights for the Greek minority in return for declaring peace. They are no longer pursuing earlier efforts for the recovery of northern Epirus by Greece.

Albania publishes no ethnic statistics, but some in Greece estimate that there are as many as 400,000 ethnic Greeks in a population of 2.7 million in 1981. Albanian authorities have told Greek officials that the number is 50,000 to 60,000.

The Papandreou Government, according to a Foreign Ministry official, believes that rather than exacting a quid pro quo, Greece should take advantage of Albania's tentative efforts to improve ties with some Western nations by the encouragement that an end of the state of belligerency might provide.

An official said progress had been made and could be measured by realities rather than formal agreements. In 1984, he said, a Greek rural guard strayed across the border while hunting and was shot dead. Recently a farmer made the same mistake while drunk and was sent home.

The official said cross-border family visits had increased, but Vlassis Socratides, general secretary of the association of northern Epirus groups in Greece, said that the visits remained limited to pro-Communists from both sides and that those coming from Albania have had to leave close family members behind as hostages for their return. The total number of such visitors, which has not been made public, is estimated at 2,000 to 3,000 a year from both sides.

Greeks Lecture in Albania

The official said two Greeks had lectured last year at an Albanian college in Gjirokaster on teaching Greek. Curbs on manifestations of national culture, including the language, are among the principal accusations that Albania is suppressing the minority.

The ethnic Greeks, like all other Albanians—who were about 70 percent Moslem before World War II—are affected by Albania's proclamation in 1967 that it had become the world's first atheist nation. All religious institutions, including Orthodox churches, a contributor to a sense of Greek ethnicity, were closed, and religious literature and teaching outlawed.

Pope John Paul II recently issued an appeal for religious freedom. "In Albania, the church has disappeared on the surface, but we know well that the church cannot disappear from people's hearts," the Pope said to a group of Albanian refugees in a parish church in Rome.

* * *

May 11, 1986

BULGARIA HAS MET THE ENEMY: IT'S ONLY ROCK-AND-ROLL

Special to The New York Times

SOFIA, Bulgaria—In the technical language of the report of the Central Committee to the recent Communist Party congress, it was called "denationalization of the musical environment." What it means is rock music, live and recorded, which is as popular in Bulgaria as it is elsewhere.

Having failed in a longstanding campaign to bring Bulgarian folk music back into vogue and to make new Communist and patriotic songs popular to fill the space now dominated by rock, the party congress raised the issue to the highest level.

In a document notable for its insistence on a return to Communist orthodoxy in a country that is thought never to have strayed from it, the policy-making congress included the issue in the "theses" that it proclaimed.

"The party, state and public bodies should take the necessary measures for overcoming drawbacks in the mass musical and artistic activities, against all manifestations of inferior taste and the denationalization of mass musical culture," the theses state. Such edicts are binding instructions to all organizations in this highly organized nation.

Passion for Western Music

Bulgaria has been trying for years, with a spectacular lack of success, to limit the public passion for Western popular music, as well as videotapes, which circulate widely.

Youth clubs and discotheques have been instructed to vary their programs with folk music and talks on traditional Bulgarian music. The club managers have obeyed by performing the dutiful exercises at the beginning of their evening's program, before the night's action begins to swing.

To limit the damage, a 9 P.M. curfew on schooldays has been imposed on adolescents up to 16 years of age, and their homeroom teachers have been made responsible for enforcing it. Teachers make the rounds carrying out spot checks. This has strengthened parent-teacher relations and often gives teachers a chance to join in watching the pirated videotapes that are shown in Bulgarian homes.

"The people who buy the tapes are not film critics or intellectuals," a party journalist lamented in a conversation. He was bemoaning the fact that most of the videos are not of what he considers edifying character and some are frankly pornographic.

Bulgarians said the videos were smuggled in by overland truck drivers, tourists and the many Arab students who are active on the Bulgarian black market.

'Nothing Can Be Done to Stop It'

"They are part of modern technology, and nothing can be done to stop it," the journalist said. Ironically, the principal theme of the congress, enunciated in the keynote address by Todor Zhivkov, the party leader, was the promotion of high technology for the benefit of Bulgaria.

The Central Committee report cast in a sinister light the many casual rock groups and gatherings to watch videotapes that have sprung up all over the country by linking them to crime.

It said, apparently defying the same report's injunction against what it called pompous language:

"The emergence of informal youth groups prompted by ideological and esthetic leanings of dubious nature and the sustained juvenile crime figures bring to a boil the issue of raising the standards of political and moral education of the working people and youth."

Broadcast Programs Criticized

The programs of the state-controlled television and radio, which some Bulgarians and most foreign residents consider infused with politics to the point of tedium, were criticized for being insufficiently political.

"The point is to raise their ideological, artistic and professional levels," the Central Committee said, "to politicize entertainment television and radio programs in a skillful way."

One way the party has found to present television of appropriate standards is to relay the full program of a Soviet television channel to Bulgarian viewers.

* * *

October 24, 1986

SERBS BEWAIL THEIR LOT IN THE YUGOSLAV FEDERATION

By DAVID BINDER
Special to The New York Times

BELGRADE—To listen to Serbs these days in this, their capital, which is also the capital of the multinational feder-ated state of Yugoslavia, is to hear a rising chorus of rancor about their lot.

In the cafes and restaurants, but also in Parliament, Serbian politicians, writers, academicians, housewives and handymen rail that their nation, which they consider the founder and chief defender of modern Yugoslavia, is getting the worst economic and political treatment of any of the country's six constituent republics and two autonomous provinces.

The main complaint is that alone among Yugoslav nation-alities, the Serbs—the largest group, with over 8 million of Yugoslavia's 23 million people—were denied their own state within the federation. The problem was that after World War II, the Communist Party saddled Serbia with two autonomous provinces, Vojvodina in the north, now with 150,000 ethnic Hungarians, and Kosovo in the south, now with about 1.7 million ethnic Albanians.

The problem was submerged as long as Yugoslavia retained a typically centralized Communist Government, but since the death of President Tito in 1980, Vojvodina and Kosovo have behaved more like the seventh and eighth Yugoslav republics, increasingly ignoring the wishes of the central Government and of Serbia.

Manifesto by Academy

Early in October, Belgrade was abuzz with descriptions of an unpublished 70-page manifesto by members of the Serbian Academy of Sciences containing allegations that Tito, of Croat origin, and his deputy, Edvard Kardelj, a Slovene, had conspired to "destroy Serbia," as one Serb familiar with the text said.

"Now, for the first time there is a Serbian separatist movement," said a Belgrade journalist. "It is the opposite of Serbia's former unitarist attitude toward Yugoslavia as a whole."

Yugoslavia has long been beset by separatist movements, traditionally in Croatia and more recently by the nearly two million ethnic Albanians of Kosovo, many of whom have been vociferously demanding a Kosovo republic for themselves.

The journalist went on to quote the late Vladimir Bakaric, an eminent Croatian Communist politician, as saying in 1971, just as separatism was growing in Croatia, "Yugoslavia can exist with a Croatian problem, but it cannot exist with a Serbian problem."

Called 'Narrow Serbia'

Many Serbs now speak of their part of Yugoslavia as "narrow Serbia," without Vojvodina and without the Ko-sovo region, which was the ancestral homeland of the Serbs and the place where their first dynasty was founded 800 years ago.

"Narrow Serbia is becoming like a beehive," said Vuk Draskovic, a Serbian novelist from the republic of Bosnia-Herzegovina, "because all the Serbs are coming home."

"Now we have internal emigration," he said. "Six hundred thousand Serbs have moved here from Bosnia-Herzegovina, 500,000 from Kosovo since World War II. Two hundred fifty thousand have moved from Croatia to Serbia since 1971."

Over the last several years, leading writers have also entered the fray with novels portraying Serbia's plight in the oral epic tradition. Among the leading examples are Milorad Pavic's "Khazar's Dictionary," Dobrica Cosic's "Sinner" and "Book About Milutin" by Danko Popovic.

Kosovo Serbs Petition

Since last spring, delegations from Serbian communities in Kosovo have been petitioning the Serbian leadership in Belgrade—mostly without success—to help them stay in their homes despite mounting pressure from the ethnic Albanian majority in the province to leave. One of the few Serbian leaders to give them a hearing has been Ivan Stam-bolic, the Premier of the Serbian Republic, but apparently he has been unable to provide much help.

In the first week of October, the Government disclosed that 5,000 refugees from neighboring Albania had found asylum in Yugoslavia, mostly staying with their ethnic kin in Kosovo. What galled Serbs here was the disclosure that a number of the Albanian refugees had been given money and then land that had belonged to Serbs who felt they had had to flee Kosovo for their lives. Some of these Albanians had kept Albanian citizenship and not even tried to become Yugoslav citizens.

Mr. Draskovic, whose novels "Knife" and "Prayer" have caused him to be banned from Bosnia-Herzegovina, said he had become so desperate that he had addressed an appeal to the Association of Hebrew Writers in Tel Aviv proposing a "blood brotherhood" between Serbs and Jews. "We Serbs are a lost unhappy tribe of Israel," he remarked.

Told of this, another Serbian writer said: "People who oth-erwise would be sensible and rational, are becoming nation-alists and irrational—the best writers and painters."

*   *   *

November 30, 1986

THE CULT OF CEAUSESCU

BY DAVID BINDER

The first question people ask when they hear that you have just spent an hour with Nicolae Ceausescu is, "How did he look?" So it went with the hotel concierge, the restaurant waiter, the taxi driver, the travel-agency clerk and foreign dip-lomats in Bucharest. The implication of the question, and much of what is said in the police state that is Rumania deals in implications and inferences, was whether President Ceausescu

Rumanian Embassy

Ceausescu greets construction workers. Despite a weak economy, his reign is being commemorated with gigantic building projects.

has long to live. A year ago, he had been out of action for weeks, the rumor being that he had prostate cancer. But now, the 68-year-old leader seemed, to the nondiagnostic eye, more or less fit.

I had asked to see Ceausescu in March, just 20 years after he barred me from Rumania while I was serving as Balkan correspondent of The New York Times. The reason for the ban, suggested but never made explicit, was an article I had written, based on many interviews, saying that Ceausescu, then in power for one year, appeared to be scarcely known in the Rumanian countryside. Ten years later, I was readmitted, returning again in 1979 and 1983. In the interim, the Rumanian President had become a kind of a Communist king, due in large part to the systematic development over the last dozen years of a cult of personality that has equaled, or even surpassed, those of Russia's Stalin, China's Mao and Yugoslavia's Tito. In guarded moments, Rumanians refer to him as "Mao-Cescu."

Ceausescu is probably the most powerful ruler in the history of the Rumanians, a history he likes to trace back to the Geto-Dacians, who stopped an invasion by Persia's Darius in the reed banks of the Danube delta 2,500 years ago. With the placement of scores of his family members in high positions, there is even the framework now for a dynasty.

To his subjects, Ceausescu is all-knowing and omnipresent. The first half of the state television's single, two-hour

weeknight program is customarily devoted to his activities and accomplishments, as are the front pages of the tightly controlled newspapers. Bookstores must devote a showcase to the 28 volumes of his speeches; news kiosks carry a smaller selection and music stores display records of his speeches. Painters and poets are required to produce works celebrating him. At the entrance to the Bucharest Fairground, a new triumphal arch bears the legend "The Golden Epoch— the Epoch of Nicolae Ceausescu."

The Ceausescu cult also requires that even high-ranking party officials are obliged to rise to their feet at party rallies and join in such ritual chants as, "Ceausescu—Rumania, our pride and esteem!"

Beyond the borders of Rumania, Nicolae Ceausescu is viewed more dispassionately. Mikhail S. Gorbachev, the new Soviet leader, who has shunned the semblances of a personality cult for himself, appears to have adopted a scornful stance toward Ceausescu and has not accorded him more than the minimal courtesies. Although the United States has developed closer ties on cultural, political and economic levels, there has been a certain disenchantment with Rumania's system of suffocating controls in its domestic policy.

One of Rumania's few distinctions has been its independent foreign policy. Over the last two decades there have been moments of daring defiance of Soviet-bloc policies: having good relations with China; maintaining ties with Israel after the 1967 war; refusing to join in the 1968 invasion of Czechoslovakia; not boycotting the 1984 Olympics at Los Angeles. These actions undoubtedly annoyed Moscow, but they were tolerated, because they never constituted any real threat to Soviet national security. Now, with the Moscow-Peking split in a healing process and talks begun between Israel and some bloc countries, the uniqueness of Rumania's independent policy is fading. Rumania had also become more dependent on trade with the Soviet Union. "The Russians are not unhappy," a Rumanian foreign policy specialist observes, "to see a weak Rumania on their southwestern frontier."

Yet, despite a crumbling economy, Ceausescu is busily commemorating his reign with gigantic building projects. Already finished, though little used, is the Danube-Black Sea Canal. Under way in Bucharest is an unneeded $1.2 billion civic center that includes a state palace for the President, and a nationwide $1.8 billion irrigation system. Under consideration is a plan—frightening to environmentalists—to fill in much of the vast Danube delta wetlands to create new farmland. Construction is scheduled to begin next year on a parallel capital to Bucharest, at Tirgoviste, as there had been during the 16th-century reign of Michael the Brave, who first united all three Rumanian lands—Walachia, Transylvania and Moldavia.

In Tirgoviste's history museum, there is a new exhibition of "Rumanian" heroes. An enormous portrait of Ceausescu gazes down on the busts of Rumanian rulers. Among the venerated is Vlad Dracula, the 15th-century prince whose cruelties gave rise to the Dracula vampire legend. Flanking the entranceway are huge bronze busts of Decebal, the Dacian king, and Trajan, the Roman emperor who defeated Decebal at great cost in the second century.

Could it be that Ceausescu is casting himself not only as a Rumanian emperor but as a Roman one as well? After all, he carried a jeweled royal mace at his 1974 induction as President.

"Roman emperor!" the guide snorted. "No, he already thinks he is a god." "What do you mean?" "In the newspapers, they have already printed poems about Ceausescu describing him as a 'demigod.'"

Although he claims Dracula as part of his political lineage, it appears that Ceausescu has not allowed torture or killing to be part of his style of governance. But in its 1986 report on Rumania, the Helsinki Watch, which monitors human rights, speaks of "totalitarian control as repressive as any in Eastern Europe."

To visit Ceausescu as a journalist requires that written questions be submitted. These are then processed by Agerpres, the state press agency, the Ministry of Foreign Affairs and by the President's personal advisers. Over a period of seven months, four sets of questions were submitted, revised and eventually agreed upon. An interview was set for the week of Sept. 29.

I arrived in good time, then waited three days before receiving word that Ceausescu would receive me at 9:30 A.M. on Oct. 2. The setting would be the headquarters of the Central Committee, whose general secretary he is, rather than at his presidential seat in the former royal palace. An elaborate ritual ensued. A foreign ministry official picked me up at my hotel at 8:25 A.M., and we walked for seven minutes in a circuitous route to the headquarters. An army colonel met us at the doors; two protocol officials took us to the second floor, along a lengthy corridor, around a corner and down to the mezzanine level, where we were escorted into a 20-by-50-foot reception room dotted with potted palms. Three still photographers and a television cameraman stood by. All such Presidential activities are recorded and dutifully presented in the Rumanian press and on television. Ceausescu requests that his interviews with foreign reporters be published in full.

A compact man, about 5 feet 6 inches tall, Ceausescu entered, walking a bit stiffly. As I moved forward to shake hands with him, cameras clicked and whirred. Having reported on the absence of a Ceausescu cult two decades ago, it occurred to me, I was now participating in one. Before I could pull out a notebook, he shot a question at me: "What are your impressions of Rumania?" An interpreter translated. It did not seem to be the moment to talk about personality cults or meat and power shortages, so I replied, lamely, "There is a lot of construction going on." The President nodded with satisfaction before opening a small red folder containing my questions. As instructed, I said, "Let us proceed to the first question."

He spoke softly and carefully, pausing to ponder each question before proceeding. His responses added nothing to previous statements, but they did make plain where his interests lie, as evidenced in these excerpts:

Question. What was the most memorable event in your career?

Answer. I think its acme [was] when we turned Rumania from a backward agrarian country into a developed industrial-agrarian country.

Q. How would you characterize Rumania's relations with the U.S.A. And the U.S.S.R.?

A. Today, our relations with the Soviet Union are fine. And . . . so are the links between Rumania and the U. S. . . . . I believe things would be much better if the problem of the most-favored-nation clause [according Rumania preferential tariffs] did not arise every year. . . .

Q. How will Rumanian society develop in the coming years?

A. We plan that by 1990, Rumanian industry should compare with the world's technically and qualitatively most-developed ones. Likewise, we plan to take Rumanian agriculture to a high development level. We have endorsed a series of measures for the application of a new economic and financial mechanism, of the principles of self-management and self-administration. . . .

It was all quite extemporaneous, but a bit like interviewing a juke box: you push a button and a record starts playing back familiar songs.

At the end, Ceausescu permitted a few additional questions. When I asked how he had been drawn into the Communist movement, his face grew somber and he replied in measured tones:

"I had a very difficult life in the village. I came to the city to work, and . . . entered into a relationship with several revolutionaries when I was 12 or 13. I began to understand that another kind of living conditions could be created."

I also asked if I might see his native village, meet another Ceausescu, perhaps his younger brother, Ilie, and visit Tirgoviste. He spread his arms wide in a gesture of generosity and replied: "Poftim!"—"Be my guest."

We shook hands again and he marched out. It was an odd moment. It did not seem as if I had been in the presence of an emperor, much less a demigod, or even the object of a cult, more like a distracted corporate chief executive officer. Then I noticed the eyes of the Rumanian aides who had remained behind. They were glistening.

But of course, the Ceausescu cult was there for domestic consumption, not for people like me.

Exiting a few minutes later onto the Piata Gheorghe Gheorghiu-Dej, named for Ceausescu's predecessor and mentor, a striking figure suddenly appeared: a tall elderly man wearing white trousers, a red cravat and a black double-breasted blazer out of whose pocket spilled a huge orange-and-black checked silk handkerchief. On his head, a broad-brimmed black fedora, and in his hand a Malacca cane, which he flourished. He was a vision of the decadent past, when Bucharest was a legend throughout Europe, and beyond, for luxury and debauchery. He nodded slightly to the gawking pedestrians as he proceeded majestically on his way. I raised my camera to take his picture. The foreign ministry man lightly touched my elbow. "Please don't," he said. "He is crazy."

The encounter was but one of several reminders that the Ceausescu cult, despite its pervasiveness, coexists with other, perhaps more durable, Rumanian realities.

It is in the everyday life of the 23 million Rumanians that the iron shoe of the Ceausescu system pinches. Rumania exports large quantities of meat and vegetables to European countries while supplies at home remain critically short. An item as innocuous as black pepper is prized because it is one of thousands of consumer goods no longer imported in an austerity drive aimed at liquidating Rumania's $6.6 billion foreign debt. If you ask for sugar to go with your morning coffee in an A-category hotel, the waiter reaches into his pocket, withdraws a single packet of zahar and solemnly hands it to you.

In a country whose wells produce 12 million tons of oil annually, gasoline is periodically rationed. Here again, the Ceausescu shoe pinches. Based on what had long been a major oil industry, the present regime built a huge refining capacity. Now the global market for refined products has shrunk, but Rumania is still saddled with agreements to purchase Soviet oil at world prices and then turn it into gasoline that can only be sold abroad, and at a loss. A driver of the state-owned Maxi-Taxi enterprise complains bitterly: "They give me a quota of 15 liters [less than four gallons] of gas a day, which takes me about 150 kilometers [94 miles]. That's half a day's driving. What am I supposed to do?" What he and nearly all Rumanians do is to participate in a second economy, in which the standard currencies are United States dollars, American filtered cigarettes and Viennese ground coffee, and in which bartering is the medium of trade.

Some of the worst shortages are in the power sector. The gas supply is often so low that stove pilot lights go out. During the last two winters, Rumania was caught stealing power from a joint Yugoslav-Rumanian hydroelectric station, The nation's first nuclear power station was supposed to have come on line last year, now the talk is of 1989.

"Basically, the outlook is pretty grim," says an economist at a Western embassy in Bucharest. "People talk of a 20 to 30 percent drop in the living standard in the last three years. Ceausescu has ruled out any economic reform whatsoever." A colleague of his rejoins: "Given the green light, they could do very well. They've got the potential. The schools are good, the infrastructure good. But innovators are ignored. Initiative is stifled. They are sliding toward being an undeveloped country, reduced to dealing in commodities."

The question on the minds of ordinary Rumanians, foreign diplomats, journalists and scholars is whether Nicolae Ceausescu seeks to create a dynastic succession. The question takes on weight when one learns that at least 40 members of his extended family have been identified in positions of varying power in the party-state apparatus. The question narrows if one considers the role of his wife, Elena, a chemist by training, who began to appear in public 15 years ago in the role of First Lady. Now, at age 67, she is generally viewed as the second-most influential person in the leadership.

She is a key member of the executive committee of the Central Committee in charge of personnel policy, and the holder of numerous other high political posts.

In recent years, her birthday has been marked as a state occasion.

For a time, it was thought that the President's son Nicu was being groomed for succession. But though appointed to high posts in the party and put in charge of the national Communist Youth Union, he has preferred to indulge in fast cars, womanizing and drink. Of late, he has become increasingly inactive, and some Youth Union leaders have even dared to suggest that he be replaced.

The other Ceausescus, including daughter Zoia Elena, a director of the Mathematical Institute, and an adopted son Valentin, secretary of the Rumanian Institute of Nuclear Physics, keep a low profile, despite their Government positions. As do several Presidential brothers: Ion, deputy chief of the State Planning Commission; Florea, a retired journalist; Marin, a trade official, and Nicolae Andruta, a lieutenant general in the Ministry of the Interior.

Some specialists have surmised that Ceausescu placed so many of his and his wife's relatives in key positions to assure personal control of crucial sectors of the Communist power structure as much as to extend his dynasty. For the moment, the only Ceausescu deemed strong-willed enough to try to succeed the President in the event of his death would be his wife, Elena. But she is so widely disliked that, should she try, no one thinks she would last more than a few months.

The day after my interview with him, the President made good on his poftim. I was to meet my third family member, having encountered Mrs. Ceausescu in Washington in 1978.

A black Dacia car took me to meet brother Ilie, a lieutenant general in the Ministry of Defense, who is eight years younger than Nicolae, balder, and a charming host. His official position is chairman of the army's political administration, but his first love is military history.

I had just seen "Battle From the Shadows," a new Rumanian film about World War I, and had recently read about Vlad Dracula's military campaigns against the Turks. Was my impression that Rumanian strategy had long depended on ambushes an accurate one? Plainly delighted, the general commenced his response with the ambush of Darius I by the Dacians in 514 B.C. and concluded, two hours later, in the 20th century. It was a learned discourse, presented with great verve, rich details and gentle humor.

What did he talk about with his brother, the President? I asked.

"Everything," he replied. "No problems. We get together when possible. But each of us has very many activities. Even our wives don't get together."

I asked if I could snap his picture. He agreed but admonished me: "You may keep the photos of me on two conditions—one, that you don't publish them and, two, that you don't publish them together with photos of my brother."

The following morning, I drove westward to the village of the Ceausescu clan.

One sees the Ceausescu cult in full flower in Scornicesti, which now boasts paved streets, a new candy factory, a soccer stadium, stores with more goods in the windows than in comparable small villages, a discotheque and a stone monument opposite the modest ancestral Ceausescu cottage, which has been completely renovated.

The village has even acquired a second small Orthodox church, perched on a hillside next to the marble tombs of the President's parents. The new chapel prompted a Rumanian wit to dub the village "Scornicesti-les-deux-Eglises," as in the hometown of Charles de Gaulle, Colombey-les-deux-Eglises.

Nicolae Ceausescu was the third of 10 children, seven of them sons. Their father, Andruta, was known locally as a heavy drinker, which may explain why he named two of his sons Nicolae. The one who became President was sent from home in 1929, at age 11, to Pitesti, a nearby big city, where he was apprenticed to a shoemaker. Soon after, he moved to Bucharest.

In 1933, at age 15, he was arrested for leftist political activities and in 1936 was tried as a Communist and sentenced to several years in Doftana Prison. There he met older Communists, including Gheorghiu-Dej, who liked the precocious teen-ager, and took him under their wing. Party lore has it that he met Elena at the 1939 First of May celebration in Bucharest, where she was queen of the workers' parade. They married that year. He was arrested again in 1940, and spent the war years in various internment camps.

I departed Scornicesti still wondering about the dynasty theory. Perhaps, in traditional peasant fashion, Ceausescu was merely taking care of his extended family members. But that would still leave begging an explanation for the cult and the megalomania. Those of us who watched Gheorghiu-Dej in the early 1960's thought we were witnessing the beginning of his cult. Maybe Ceausescu got the idea from him. But it was Gheorghiu-Dej who promulgated Rumania's policy of independence from the Soviet Union in foreign affairs and economic relations; his successor has merely elaborated on it.

Rather, the Ceausescu stamp is evident in the creation of monster steel and aluminum industries that work at half capacity because there is no market for their products, in the gigantic irrigation scheme that lowers the water table and leaches the soil to the point of infertility, and in the law prohibiting abortions.

There may not be individual cruelty, as in the reign of Vlad Dracula, but there is institutionalized misery and despair. It touches the majority of the population, except the police, who are paid more than university professors to carry submachine guns and stand on every street in the capital and at road-control points every 10 miles or so in the countryside. Some Rumanians estimate that half the population is involved in the security apparatus in one way or another, if only as informers.

"When Ceausescu rides down Dorobantilor Road in his convoy of eight cars in the morning, the blue militia jeeps appear at the cross streets," a Bucharest woman recounts. "The militia lines the road, one posted every few yards. Plainclothesmen in black leather jackets appear among the trees, ready to shoo people into the doorways. Buses are drawn up to block against suicide drivers."

In all likelihood, this is part of Nicolae Ceausescu's response to a youth of rejection, privation and imprisonment. He implied as much during the interview, in response to a question about the most significant event in his life:

"I would say that one of the important moments was when, resolved to defy any act of repression and to serve the Rumanian people, I chose the path of the fight for the revolutionary transformation of Rumanian society."

David Binder is assistant news editor in the Washington bureau of The Times.

* * *

March 21, 1987

WIDE WALKOUTS IN YUGOSLAVIA PROTEST AUSTERITY WAGE PLAN

By HENRY KAMM
Special to The New York Times

BELGRADE, Yugoslavia, March 20—Throughout Yugoslavia since the beginning of this month, thousands of workers have walked off their jobs to protest severe wage restraints when the prices of most necessities are being raised.

The other day, Prime Minister Branko Mikulic found himself in a Slovenian restaurant whose waiters had gone on strike and refused to serve him.

Cotton industry workers at a labor meeting in Belgrade discussing a work stoppage to protest low wages.

The strikes appear to be spontaneous and uncoordinated, rarely affecting an entire company, and the strikers usually go back to work within a few hours. They have not been penalized. Nor is Yugoslavia the only Communist country experiencing protests over the prices of consumer goods. In Poland, the Government-sponsored labor federation that replaced the outlawed Solidarity movement has declared that expected increases in the price of food and fuel are unacceptable to Polish workers. Still, in number and geographic extent, this is the most acute period of labor unrest that Yugoslavia has experienced, and officials believe the end is not in sight. Unlike other Communist countries, Yugoslavia tolerates strikes, although they are illegal here too.

Apparently in reaction to the walkouts, the Government announced today that it would suspend several scheduled price increases. A statement issued through the official Tanyug press agency said the 90-day freeze on prices would affect food, consumer goods, tools, textiles and furniture. It will take effect within five days and will hold prices at the levels of Dec. 31.

In Yugoslavia, the number of strikes so far is 70, Deputy Information Minister Mirko Marinovic said in an interview. Unofficial reports put the number higher.

Half of Strikes in Croatia

More than 10,000 workers are officially reported to have taken part. About half of the walkouts have occurred in Croatia, one of Yugoslavia's most industrialized republics.

The unrest is putting heavy domestic pressure on the Government at a time when contrary pressures are developing from its foreign creditors. Yugoslavia owes nearly $20 billion to Western banks or governments; Belgrade itself facing nonpayment of large loans to Arab debtors.

Worried by an unpublished report by the International Monetary Fund that criticizes the Government's performance in enforcing economic austerity, 16 creditor governments are to meet at the end of the month in Paris to decide on Yugoslavia's request to reschedule part of the debt.

The outcome is uncertain, and even Belgrade's most influential supporter, the United States, is reported to be undecided on its stand. About 15 percent of Yugoslavia's debt is owed to American banks.

Mihailo Crnobrnja, the equivalent of minister for economic and social planning for the Serbian Republic, said the crisis was mostly political.

"Do we have the political foresight and stability, is the party sufficiently in command, to overcome this difficult period?" Mr. Crnobrnja said. "Can we 'survive' for a year until the results we seek start arriving?"

Half of Earnings Go for Food

He spoke before the announcement today that some price increases had been suspended—an announcement that suggested the Government's resolve might no longer be as firm as it had once seemed.

The average family spends an unusually high share of earnings for food, about 50 percent. Until the announcement today of the price freeze, a new round of significant increases was scheduled to go into effect on most staples. Rents, utilities and the minimal pleasures of life have been steadily increasing in cost.

Under continued high inflation—the rate was more than 90 percent last year—austerity wilted. Real wages rose by more than 10 percent last year. Inflation is now running at an annual rate of 130 percent, Mr. Marinovic said.

The gloomy outlook led Prime Minister Mikulic to demand and receive immediate approval for four "interventionary" laws to restrict incomes and public-sector spending. The strikes are being provoked by a law that virtually freezes wages in some sectors and bases them for the rest of the labor force on the levels of the last quarter of last year.

Curb to Last Until June 30

The restraints are to remain in effect until June 30. By that time, a permanent wage formula is to have been worked out firmly linking wages to productivity.

On Wednesday, in the face of the strikes, the Communist Party leadership affirmed its backing for the restraints. The party's main task, Mr. Crnobrnja said, is to educate the public to the fact that the aim of the measures is a lasting increase in the standard of living.

"We are now in a tunnel with light at the end," the planner said. "We are no longer in a maze without light.

"The problem is that the complexity of Yugoslavia's problems is so huge that you can't guarantee that the party leaders won't review their firmness. Events are not entirely under control."

*   *   *

April 25, 1987

YUGOSLAVIA POLICE AND 10,000 CLASH DURING A PROTEST OVER ETHNIC BIAS

By AP

BELGRADE, Yugoslavia, April 24—The police clashed briefly today with a crowd of about 10,000 in the ethnically tense province of Kosovo, Yugoslav news organizations said.

The incident occurred when thousands gathered outside the Hall of Culture in the city of Kosovo Polje.

The Communist Party chief of Serbia, Slobodan Milosevic, was on hand to listen to complaints that minorities had been harassed by the ethnic Albanian majority in Kosovo, the Yugoslav television reported.

Witnesses said about 300 delegates from the crowd of Serbs and Montenegrins were admitted to the hall to talk to Mr. Milosevic, but 10,000 to 15,000 people waiting outside also wanted to be at the talks.

Police Used Truncheons

The clash started at about 6:30 P.M., half an hour after Mr. Milosevic began to listen to the complaints, when police

officers trying to control the crowd pushed people away from the entrance and across the street, witnesses said.

The national press agency, Tanyug, said "a number of citizens threw stones at police." Witnesses said policemen used truncheons during the clash, which lasted about 10 minutes. [According to Reuters, Tanyug reported that several people were lightly injured.] Tanyug said Mr. Milosevic emerged at 7 P.M. and "was greeted with applause, shouts and chanting." Witnesses quoted him as telling the crowd that the police had no right to use truncheons so indiscriminately.

The crowd later sang the national anthem, "Hej Sloveni!" ("Hail Slavs!"), bringing the incident to a close, witnesses said. The anthem is said to be unpopular with Albanians.

History of Violence

Serbs and Montenegrins have long complained of harassment and acts of violence by Albanians in Kosovo, an autonomous province of the Serbian Republic within Yugoslavia.

In the spring of 1981, Kosovo was the scene of riots involving Albanian nationalists seeking greater autonomy. At least nine people were killed. The area, which has 1.7 million Albanians and a total of 200,000 Serbs and Montenegrins, has remained uneasy since.

Kosovo Polje, not far from Pristina, capital of Kosovo Province, is about 420 miles south of Belgrade.

*   *   *

May 27, 1987

GORBACHEV SPEAKS TO RUMANIANS ON 'OPENNESS' TO COOL RESPONSE

By HENRY KAMM
Special to The New York Times

BUCHAREST, Rumania, May 26—Mikhail S. Gorbachev explained his concepts of openness and restructuring today to a mass rally in the Communist country whose leader is believed to be the least interested in introducing such policies.

The handpicked crowd of 5,000 party faithful, following the example of the Rumanian leader, Nicolae Ceausescu, listened in silence to the Gorbachev passages alluding to his innovations in Soviet society.

Their lack of response was in sharp contrast to the effusiveness with which the listeners at the rally punctuated Mr. Ceausescu's speech with rousing ovations.

The Rumanian leader was interrupted by applause 30 times in 45 minutes at the rally. Eighteen times the crowd rose to its feet to applaud rhythmically, shouting the names of the two leaders in unison or such slogans as "Ceausescu—Peace!" and "Disarmament—Ceausescu!"

Mr. Gorbachev's words were greeted by applause 16 times, but not once through his long, almost professorial, portion explaining the two concepts to which he has dedicated his leadership.

At one point during this part of the speech, Mr. Ceausescu pushed aside the Rumanian text he was following and looked at his wristwatch.

Gorbachev Cuts Off Applause

While the Rumanian leader, in his speech, appeared to be encouraging outbursts of applause and frequently prolonged them with waves of his hand over his head, Mr. Gorbachev often showed impatience with interruptions, gesturing as if to cut them off.

During his host's speech, as well, the Soviet leader was often the first to stop applauding, cutting short the long waves of ovations that are standard at Mr. Ceausescu's speeches.

The differences were not only those of style between Mr. Gorbachev, who is 56 and the youngest Communist leader, and Mr. Ceausescu, who is 69. Mr. Gorbachev also raised two issues capable of being interpreted as indirect references to Rumanian conditions.

The Soviet leader cited Lenin's writings on the treatment of nationalities. Such issues need to be treated with "delicacy and carefulness," Mr. Gorbachev recalled, referring to Lenin. "I think Lenin's words on this matter are applicable to this day," he said.

Dispute Over Transylvania

Rumania, whose territory includes the Transylvania and Banat homeland of a Hungarian minority estimated to total up to two million, is involved in an open quarrel with Hungary about treatment and rights accorded the minority.

The Soviet Union, as leader of the Warsaw Pact, is concerned about the outbreak of a rare open dispute between two members. While asserting that the Soviet Union has no intention of acting as mediator, a Soviet diplomat said that Moscow had asked both sides to strive for a settlement without open polemics.

Another reference by the Soviet leader, which analysts said was not necessarily intended to criticize Mr. Ceausescu, was a condemnation of Communist Party officials guilty of nepotism.

Mr. Gorbachev has made this point in other speeches, and the Russian word for nepotism—"kumovstvo"—is also open to a wider interpretation of favoritism going beyond the family circle.

But the official English translation provided by Rumania was "nepotism," and the word has a special meaning in a country whose leader's wife is a First Deputy Prime Minister and member of the party's ruling body, whose son is the leader of the Communist Youth League and whose brother heads the armed forces political department.

* * *

June 28, 1987

BELGRADE BATTLES KOSOVO SERBS

Special to The New York Times

BELGRADE, Yugoslavia, June 27—The police clashed here early today with about 1,000 Serbs and Montenegrins protesting what they called terrorism against them by ethnic Albanians in Kosovo Province.

The clash occurred shortly after a meeting of the country's Central Committee during which there were 16 hours of debate on ways to ease tension between Kosovo's 1.7 million ethnic Albanians and 200,000 Serbs and Montenegrins.

Witnesses said squads of policemen seized demonstrators and forced them into buses to be driven back to their homes in Kosovo. Some protesters were detained for several hours.

The Central Committee meeting was the first in six years dedicated solely to the Kosovo problem.

Tensions have been high in the province in southwestern Yugoslavia since the Albanians rioted there in 1981 to back demands for higher status as a republic.

Since then, more than 22,000 Serbs and Montenegrins have fled Kosovo.

The Government asked people from Kosovo not to come to Belgrade during the Central Committee meeting, but hundreds came here overnight.

Published excerpts from the debate showed continued splits in the party ranks, and no decisive action was considered likely.

The police also prevented large groups of Belgrade residents from joining the protesters by cordoning off the entire center of the city.

Serbs have said the ethnic Albanians in Kosovo have committed atrocities against them, including murder, rape, desecration of graves and churches and blinding of cattle.

* * *

July 13, 1987

EVEN IN YUGOSLAVIA, A RICH-POOR SPLIT

By HENRY KAMM
Special to The New York Times

LJUBLJANA, Yugoslavia—Slovenes are political realists, so no one here in their capital raises the subject of separating from Yugoslavia except to reject it.

"One has to practice mimicry, be diplomatic," said Matjaz Kmecl, the Communist Party's cultural chief and member of its collective presidency in this small Slavic republic. "It doesn't work otherwise. If you resist by force, you perish. This relationship continues with Yugoslavia."

But the political and economic crisis that has long confronted Yugoslavia has sharpened Slovenia's awareness that its two million people have the highest level of economic development among the republics and provinces that make up this federal country of 23 million.

Agence France-Presse

A street in downtown Ljubljana, Yugoslavia, the capital of Slovenia.

The New York Times/July 13, 1987

Slovenia helps to subsidize Yugoslavia's southern republics.

A Major Debate

No Yugoslav city debates more intensely how to deal with differing levels of development in a federal structure, and no city asks more pointedly whether northern Yugoslavia is paying too dearly for the south.

"Slovenia's share of the population is 8 percent; its share of the gross national product is 18 percent," said the republic's Premier, Dusan Sinigoj.

"And our share in exports to the convertible-currency area is 25 percent," he added, citing what may be Slovenia's proudest statistic. With Yugoslavia's foreign debts at nearly $20 billion, dollar exports are the principal criterion of economic performance for the six republics and two autonomous provinces.

The southern republics, Bosnia and Herzegovina, Macedonia and Montenegro, as well as the province of Kosovo, are subsidized by the more prosperous areas through a federal fund and direct contributions.

'Not a Productive Discussion'

Mr. Kmecl estimated the cost at 20 to 30 percent of the national product of Slovenia, the northernmost republic, but others said this figure seemed high. No reliable statistics are available.

"It is not a productive discussion whether it is a sacrifice for us or useful to us to live within Yugoslavia," said Viktor Zakelj, principal economic adviser to the collective presidency of Slovenia. "Looking at numbers does not contribute to the cohesion of our country."

Although the drain on Slovenia prompts a good deal of discussion here, questions are not raised about the principle of responsibility for advancing the underdeveloped regions.

"The question is not, 'solidarity, yes or no?' but how," said Bozo Kovac, who is editor of Delo, the main Slovenian daily newspaper, and chairman of the federal Assembly's internal affairs committee.

In Slovenia, it is generally assumed that much of the republic's assistance to the south has been badly misused. So the question being asked is how to restructure Yugoslavia politically and economically to assure the continuing development of all its parts.

Different Answers

To some Slovenian officials, the answer lies in freeing the Yugoslav market from Government interference and applying the laws of supply and demand. Others suggest reorganizing the relationships among the republics and with the federal Government.

All recognize that these ideas raise issues that involve central power in a one-party state—issues that no Communist country has yet faced so openly.

"We in Slovenia see a solution for emerging from the crisis in a more open market and economy," Mr. Zakelj said. "In Kosovo, because of their much lower level, they find it easier to be content with distribution more programmed by the state.

'Fewer Bad Investments'

"We here believe firmly that to reach our objectives we have to work out a different form of socialism, effective from the economic point of view, respecting the market but socially just."

Discussing the contention that northern money has been misused in the south, Mr. Kovac noted that Slovenia's factories are more efficient than those elsewhere in the country. "Capacity in Slovenia is better utilized and managed than in the south," the editor said. "There have been fewer bad investments."

Because each republic and province firmly insists on its autonomy within Yugoslavia, those receiving aid have been free to invest it as they wish.

"Fantastic sums go to the south, and they don't know how to use them economically," said Milos Kobe, a board member of Iskra, Slovenia's leading industrial concern and an exporter of electronic and electrical products.

Premier Sinigoj and other officials said that under new rules the donors have acquired more control, particularly when Slovenian enterprises were allowed to invest directly in southern plants and share in their management. But such innovations are in the experimental stage.

Stanislav Valant, executive vice president of Ljubljanska Banka, Slovenia's leading bank, showed impatience with Government plans to deal with Yugoslavia's crisis. "We need more initiative and less interference," he said. "We need deregulation, not additional regulation."

'Standing Still Could Be Fatal'

Some officials and critics believe that such arguments are delaying necessary decisions. They believe that in a period of rapid technological change the Slovenian economy falls behind its competitors every day that it turns over money to ineffective economies instead of using it to keep up with the state of the art.

"Standing still could be fatal," said Premier Sinigoj.

Mr. Kmecl, who spoke gloomily of a brain drain and intellectual disaffection, said: "We cannot invest in renewal because our capital is going for the development of the underdeveloped. A small country like this cannot afford this. After 40 years of this policy, they are still not developed, and we can't maintain the pace. We are immobilized." He added: "A technologically highly developed society like Slovenia needs always more for its own science and culture, while the underdeveloped need more for social protection than they produce. This is a turning point in every way."

* * *

September 10, 1987

FINANCIAL SCANDAL SHAKES YUGOSLAV LEADERS

By HENRY KAMM
Special to The New York Times

BELGRADE, Yugoslavia, Sept. 9—A financial scandal involving one of Yugoslavia's largest companies has embarrassed the country's political leadership and the man scheduled to become the country's next President.

The state-run company, a major food producer, had issued promissory notes estimated at $350 million, but possibly worth as much as $500 million, to at least 57 banks, and per-

haps as many as 63, it was disclosed late last month. The company, Agrokomerc, is unable to meet its obligations, as are several of its creditor banks. The scandal was disclosed at a time when Yugoslavia, whose foreign debt is at more than $17 billion, is preparing to discuss with its creditor banks and the International Monetary Fund a further rescheduling of its obligations.

Revelations of the scope of internal indebtedness are expected to intensify demands by foreign creditors that Yugoslavia put itself under a standby agreement with the monetary fund, giving the I.M.F. the right to insist on rigid fiscal and economic austerity.

In a nation where perhaps half the industrial and commercial enterprises habitually lose money and are kept going only by infusions of state funds, companies have traditionally bailed one another out with loans that are not backed by cash.

One effort to deal with the losses is a stricter bankruptcy law. Under the law, which took effect this year, companies habitually in debt could be forced into bankruptcy. But if strictly applied, the law could eliminate 7,000 companies and 1.5 million jobs. As a result, Yugoslav political analysts and economists do not expect it to be widely enforced. Unemployment is about 1 million in a work force of 6.8 million.

The Agrokomerc scandal has been depicted as evidence that the Government of Prime Minister Branko Mikulic is unable to deal with Yugoslavia's deepening economic problems.

The Yugoslav press has reported that the State Auditing Office discovered that promissory notes worth $8.8 billion were created between enterprises or between banks and enterprises last year alone, and that this partly explains why the monetary supply expanded by 109 percent in 1986. Inflation at the end of August was 116.6 percent compared to August 1986.

When Mr. Mikulic took office last year, he had a reputation of authoritarianism. But he has failed to instill the discipline that Yugoslav and creditor bankers and economists see as the only way out of the economic crisis.

In this decentralized nation of six federal republics and two autonomous provinces, each jealous of the other's prerogatives and those of the Federal Government, Mr. Mikulic is also hurt by the fact that Agrokomerc is from his republic of Bosnia-Herzegovina.

Company Executive Arrested

The company's chief executive, Fikret Abdic, is a member of the Central Committee of the republic's Communist Party and a member of the Federal Parliament. On Tuesday, Mr. Abdic's arrest on the charge of counter-revolution was announced. Moves have also been initiated to purge the party of officials connected with the scandal.

The State Auditing Office has demanded the arrest of 92 officials of Agrokomerc and creditor banks. Six senior company officials had previously been charged with malfeasance.

Mr. Abdic has embarrassed the national political leadership by stating that his principal political supporter was Hamdija Pozderac, the Bosnian member of the collegial federal Presidency. Under a system of rotating leadership, Mr. Pozderac is to be the country's nominal President next May.

Mr. Pozderac has denied a personal connection with Mr. Abdic, but the link between political leadership in the republic and its top enterprises will clearly be an embarrassing issue in next year's Presidential succession.

Until the disclosures, Agrokomerc was considered a successful company, employing 13,500 people and exporting to 22 countries. Suspicions have been voiced in the press that its downfall was not its commercial operations in food production and processing but extraneous ventures it undertook under political pressures, such as creating enterprises with little chance of commercial success.

* * *

September 18, 1987

'HEY BABU RIBA,' BELGRADE IN '53

LIVES OF THE PARTY—HEY BABU RIBA, directed by Jovan Acin; screenplay (in Serbo-Croatian with English subtitles) by Mr. Acin, from the memories of Petar Jankovic, George Zecevic and Mr. Acin; photography by Tomislav Pinter; edited by Snezana Ivanovic; music by Zoran Simjanovic; produced by Dragoljub Popovic and Nikola Popovic; production companies, Avala Film and Inex Film. At Embassy 72d Street 2, at Broadway. Running time: 109 minutes. This film is rated R.

Gala Videnovic (Esther); Relja Bacic (Glen); Nebojsa Bakocevic (Glen); Marko Todorovic (Sacha); Dragan Bjelogrlic (Sacha); Srdjan Todorovic (Kica); Milos Zutic (Kica); Djordje Nenadovic (Pop); Goran Radakovic (Pop); Milan Strljic (Rile); Dragomir Bojanic-Gidra (Rile).

"Hey Babu Riba" was shown as part of this year's New Directors/New Films Series. Here are excerpts from Walter Goodman's review, which appeared in The New York Times March 15. The film opens today at the Embassy 72d Street 2, at Broadway.

Set in Belgrade in 1953, when Yugoslavia was in the throes of breaking away from the Soviet camp, "Hey Babu Riba" focuses on a once-privileged set that has found itself in difficulties under the Tito regime. Esther's father is a former Royalist officer who has fled to Italy; her mother is languishing for want of streptomycin. The father of one of her friends is in jail; another, a doctor, has been put out of business by socialized medicine. All are selling off cherished possessions to eke out an existence, and their "surplus living space" is occupied by Communist Party favorites.

What makes the movie much more interesting than a Serbian variation of "Stand By Me" is its political perspective. The director, Jovan Acin, was born in Belgrade in 1941, and his screenplay, drawn in part from his own memories, is

about a generation entranced by American popular culture, from Glenn Miller to Levis, and by a Western spirit of freedom as well. When Esther's boyfriends defeat some party types in a rowing competition, it's a victory for their class.

The young protagonists—whom we meet again after life has taken its toll—are amiable if a bit colorless. More flavorsome performances come from characters churned up by the postwar changes: a woman known as "the vulture," who goes about trading nylons and powdered milk for the pianos and music boxes of the once-rich, and as a sideline initiating their offspring into sex and cigarettes; a conscientious official who tries earnestly to persuade Esther to get her father to collaborate with the regime, and, especially, a rapacious apparatchik named Rile, a handsome blackguard who falls for Esther and is unscrupulous in his pursuit. One of the movie's good jokes is that Rile, ever on the make, had his wrists tattooed with pictures of Stalin and Lenin just before the break with Moscow; now he wears wristbands and is taking a crash course in English instead of Russian.

Incidentally, if you've been dying to hear "Comin' Round the Mountain" sung in Serbo-Croatian, here's your chance.

* * *

November 1, 1987

IN YUGOSLAVIA, RISING ETHNIC STRIFE BRINGS FEARS OF WORSE CIVIL CONFLICT

By DAVID BINDER
Special to The New York Times

BELGRADE, Yugoslavia—Portions of southern Yugoslavia have reached such a state of ethnic friction that Yugoslavs have begun to talk of the horrifying possibility of "civil war" in a land that lost one-tenth of its population, or 1.7 million people, in World War II.

The current hostilities pit separatist-minded ethnic Albanians against the various Slavic populations of Yugoslavia and occur at all levels of society, from the highest officials to the humblest peasants.

A young Army conscript of ethnic Albanian origin shot up his barracks, killing four sleeping Slavic bunkmates and wounding six others.

The army says it has uncovered hundreds of subversive ethnic Albanian cells in its ranks. Some arsenals have been raided.

Vicious Insults

Ethnic Albanians in the Government have manipulated public funds and regulations to take over land belonging to Serbs. And politicians have exchanged vicious insults.

Slavic Orthodox churches have been attacked, and flags have been torn down. Wells have been poisoned and crops burned. Slavic boys have been knifed, and some young ethnic Albanians have been told by their elders to rape Serbian girls.

Ethnic Albanians comprise the fastest growing nationality in Yugoslavia and are expected soon to become its third largest, after the Serbs and Croats.

The New York Times/David Binder

A street in Pristina, in Kosovo, Yugoslavia, where ethnic Albanians form 85 percent of the population.

Radicals' Goals

The goal of the radical nationalists among them, one said in an interview, is an "ethnic Albania that includes western Macedonia, southern Montenegro, part of southern Serbia, Kosovo and Albania itself." That includes large chunks of the republics that make up the southern half of Yugoslavia.

Other ethnic Albanian separatists admit to a vision of a greater Albania governed from Pristina in southern Yugoslavia rather than Tirana, the capital of neighboring Albania.

There is no evidence that the hard-line Communist Government in Tirana is giving them material assistance.

The principal battleground is the region called Kosovo, a high plateau ringed by mountains that is somewhat smaller than New Jersey. Ethnic Albanians there make up 85 percent of the population of 1.7 million. The rest are Serbians and Montenegrins.

Worst Strife in Years

As Slavs flee the protracted violence, Kosovo is becoming what ethnic Albanian nationalists have been demanding for years, and especially strongly since the bloody rioting by ethnic Albanians in Pristina in 1981—an "ethnically pure" Albanian region, a "Republic of Kosovo" in all but name.

The violence, a journalist in Kosovo said, is escalating to "the worst in the last seven years."

Many Yugoslavs blame the troubles on the ethnic Albanians, but the matter is more complex in a country with as many nationalities and religions as Yugoslavia's and involves economic development, law, politics, families and flags. As recently as 20 years ago, the Slavic majority treated ethnic Albanians as inferiors to be employed as hewers of wood and carriers of heating coal. The ethnic Albanians, who now number 2 million, were officially deemed a minority, not a constituent nationality, as they are today.

Were the ethnic tensions restricted to Kosovo, Yugoslavia's problems with its Albanian nationals might be more manageable. But some Yugoslavs and some ethnic Albanians believe the struggle has spread far beyond Kosovo. Macedonia, a republic to the south with a population of 1.8 million, has a restive ethnic Albanian minority of 350,000.

"We've already lost western Macedonia to the Albanians," said a member of the Yugoslav party presidium, explaining that the ethnic minority had driven the Slavic Macedonians out of the region.

Attacks on Slavs

Last summer, the authorities in Kosovo said they documented 40 ethnic Albanian attacks on Slavs in two months. In the last two years, 320 ethnic Albanians have been sentenced for political crimes, nearly half of them characterized as severe.

In one incident, Fadil Hoxha, once the leading politician of ethnic Albanian origin in Yugoslavia, joked at an official dinner in Prizren last year that Serbian women should be used to satisfy potential ethnic Albanian rapists. After his quip was reported this October, Serbian women in Kosovo protested, and Mr. Hoxha was dismissed from the Communist Party.

As a precaution, the central authorities dispatched 380 riot police officers to the Kosovo region for the first time in four years.

Officials in Belgrade view the ethnic Albanian challenge as imperiling the foundations of the multinational experiment called federal Yugoslavia, which consists of six republics and two provinces.

'Lebanonizing' of Yugoslavia

High-ranking officials have spoken of the "Lebanonizing" of their country and have compared its troubles to the strife in Northern Ireland.

Borislav Jovic, a member of the Serbian party's presidency, spoke in an interview of the prospect of "two Albanias, one north and one south, like divided Germany or Korea," and of "practically the breakup of Yugoslavia." He added: "Time is working against us."

The federal Secretary for National Defense, Fleet Adm. Branko Mamula, told the army's party organization in September of efforts by ethnic Albanians to subvert the armed forces. "Between 1981 and 1987 a total of 216 illegal organizations with 1,435 members of Albanian nationality were discovered in the Yugoslav People's Army," he said. Admiral Mamula said ethnic Albanian subversives had been preparing for "killing officers and soldiers, poisoning food and water, sabotage, breaking into weapons arsenals and stealing arms and ammunition, desertion and causing flagrant nationalist incidents in army units."

Concerns Over Military

Coming three weeks after the ethnic Albanian draftee, Aziz Kelmendi, had slaughtered his Slavic comrades in the barracks at Paracin, the speech struck fear in thousands of families whose sons were about to start their mandatory year of military service.

Because the Albanians have had a relatively high birth rate, one-quarter of the army's 200,000 conscripts this year are ethnic Albanians. Admiral Mamula suggested that 3,792 were potential human timebombs.

He said the army had "not been provided with details relevant for assessing their behavior." But a number of Belgrade politicians said they doubted the Yugoslav armed forces would be used to intervene in Kosovo as they were to quell violent rioting in 1981 in Pristina. They reason that the army leadership is extremely reluctant to become involved in what is, in the first place, a political issue.

Ethnic Albanians already control almost every phase of life in the autonomous province of Kosovo, including the police, judiciary, civil service, schools and factories. Non-Albanian visitors almost immediately feel the independence—and suspicion—of the ethnic Albanian authorities.

Region's Slavs Lack Strength

While 200,000 Serbs and Montenegrins still live in the province, they are scattered and lack cohesion. In the last seven years, 20,000 of them have fled the province, often leaving behind farmsteads and houses, for the safety of the Slavic north.

Until September, the majority of the Serbian Communist Party leadership pursued a policy of seeking compromise with the Kosovo party hierarchy under its ethnic Albanian leader, Azem Vlasi.

But during a 30-hour session of the Serbian central committee in late September, the Serbian party secretary, Slobodan Milosevic, deposed Dragisa Pavlovic, as head of Belgrade's party organization, the country's largest. Mr. Milosevic accused Mr. Pavlovic of being an appeaser who was soft on Albanian radicals. Mr. Milosevic had courted the Serbian backlash vote with speeches in Kosovo itself calling for "the policy of the hard hand."

"We will go up against anti-Socialist forces, even if they call us Stalinists," Mr. Milosevic declared recently. That a Yugoslav politician would invite someone to call him a Stalinist even four decades after Tito's epochal break with Stalin, is a measure of the state into which Serbian politics have fallen. For the moment, Mr. Milosevic and his supporters appear to be staking their careers on a strategy of confrontation with the Kosovo ethnic Albanians.

Other Yugoslav politicians have expressed alarm. "There is no doubt Kosovo is a problem of the whole country, a powder keg on which we all sit," said Milan Kucan, head of the Slovenian Communist Party.

Remzi Koljgeci, of the Kosovo party leadership, said in an interview in Pristina that "relations are cold" between the ethnic Albanians and Serbs of the province, that there were too many "people without hope."

But many of those interviewed agreed it was also a rare opportunity for Yugoslavia to take radical political and economic steps, as Tito did when he broke with the Soviet bloc in 1948.

Efforts are under way to strengthen central authority through amendments to the constitution. The League of Communists is planning an extraordinary party congress before March to address the country's grave problems.

The hope is that something will be done then to exert the rule of law in Kosovo while drawing ethnic Albanians back into Yugoslavia's mainstream.

* * *

February 18, 1988

IT'S MOTHER NATURE, NOT CEAUSESCU, WHO RELENTS

By HENRY KAMM

Special to The New York Times

BUCHAREST, Rumania, Feb. 11—An exceptionally mild winter, days on end of spring sunshine instead of the usual leaden skies of February, have brought an air of well-being to Bucharest. It is an illusion.

"Things better?" a visitor asked a friend. "No," she said. "Did you expect them to be?" A dry laugh made clear that she did not.

The fine weather has meant no more than that the miseries of Europe's most deprived nation and the most repressed, according to the State Department's annual human rights report, have for the first time in years not been made worse by the extra hardships of Rumanian winter.

There is still almost no heating in Bucharest's apartments, but at least temperatures have been above freezing. Lighting remains too dim for comfortable reading. It is hard to find bulbs stronger than 30 watts in the stores, and officially a family is supposed to light only one room.

Ban on Private Cars Lifted

Only today, after more than a week of warm weather, the Government lifted its ban on the use of private cars. It was put into effect, as in every recent winter, with the first snowfall.

The pretext is that cars would snarl traffic; the reason is that the ban saves gasoline. Rumania exports millions of tons of petroleum products and uses the earnings in convertible currencies to meet President Nicolae Ceausescu's priority goal of ridding the country of foreign indebtedness.

The Government also exports vast quantities of Rumania's bounty of meat, dairy products, cereals and produce. A result has been a drastic reduction of the foreign debt from about $10 billion in the early 1980's to about $5 billion.

Another consequence is that a nation of 23 million people spends an inordinate amount of time in food lines and much of its inventiveness and energy in scheming how to buy food and other necessities under the counter or through backdoors.

"I go to the restaurant," a chauffeur said when asked how he got meat for his family. "I buy the meat at the restaurant, and my wife cooks it."

Some Stores Do Not Open

Much of the meat and other products allotted to restaurants is never served there. Their staffs sell the goods at the backdoor.

The food lines at the shops, all state-owned, have a conspiratorial air. Often the stores do not even open. The scarce goods are sold at the door, and when the supply is exhausted the door shuts and the disappointed shoppers look for another store at which to line up.

At one shop a saleswoman wordlessly handed a small parcel through the window of a door to each customer as he

Magnum/Martine Franck

A market in Bucharest. In a nation that exports agricultural products, Rumanians spend an inordinate amount of time in food lines and in scheming how to buy food under the counter.

reached the head of the line. "Cascaval," explained one man taking advantage of the rare occasion to wait behind about 50 others for a small piece of cheese.

At the office of Balkan, the Bulgarian airline, Rumanians do not line up. They crowd around an outside display case. Pencil and pad in hand, they wait until those within reading distance finish taking notes and cede their places.

Joys of Bulgarian Television

Rumanians are copying the program listing for the next two weeks of Bulgarian state television. With a good antenna they can receive Bulgarian broadcasts, although few speak the language. As a means of saving energy, Rumanian television is on the air only two hours a night, and a disproportionate amount of the time is devoted to Mr. Ceausescu.

Although Rumanians obviously prize it, many Bulgarians speak disparagingly of their television and say they much prefer to watch the Soviet station, which is beamed into their country. They prefer the new openness from Moscow, which has not yet reached Sofia and seems even farther away from Bucharest.

A pecking order of viewing across national borders has taken hold in Eastern Europe. In Hungary and Poland, many people scorn their national networks in favor of Western satellite broadcasts. Dish antenna kits are privately but openly sold in both countries. East Germans watch West Berlin stations, and many Czechoslovaks and Hungarians are fans of Austrian television.

A block from the airline office, clusters of Rumanians gaze throughout the day across a wide sidewalk at another set of display cases. They are attached to a fence surrounding the office of the United States Information Service and display pictures of American life that the information service puts up at its offices around the world.

But nowhere is the distance between the pictures and the viewers as great as here. To keep their citizens from getting too close to foreign embassies, the sidewalks in front of such buildings are forbidden zones, blocked off and guarded by armed police. Still, Rumanians peer intently across a 20-foot gap to see photos of President Reagan greeting visitors whom they do not know.

To make it easier, the embassy has the captions printed in king size characters.

'Bridge of Misery'

Rumanians are painfully conscious of a change in Balkan rankings exemplified by their predilection for Bulgarian television that has been brought about by their years of hardship. In the past, for reasons neither just nor explainable, Bulgaria had borne the mark of being deemed the most underdeveloped of the five Balkan nations. (A sixth, Albania, is so deeply isolated that no one includes it in the ranking.) Now, however, life is clearly more agreeable in Bulgaria than here.

Because of the many Rumanian shoppers who cross the Friendship Bridge, heavily barbed-wired and guarded on the Rumanian side, to buy Bulgarian groceries in Ruse, on the opposite bank of the Danube, Bulgarians mockingly call it the "bridge of misery."

Bulgaria has become a favorite destination for weekend excursions for the fortunate few who are allowed the rare privilege to leave their country even to visit another Communist nation.

A member of a recent group recalled that the shivering passengers rejoiced when the heat was turned on in the train on the Bulgarian side. "You see how far behind the Bulgarians are?" said one. "Twenty years ago, we had heated trains."

*   *   *

February 27, 1988

RUMANIA REJECTS U. S. TRADE BENEFITS OVER HUMAN RIGHTS DISPUTE

By CLYDE H. FARNSWORTH
Special to The New York Times

WASHINGTON, Feb. 26—Apparently rebuffing American demands for improvement in human rights policies, Rumania has told the United States it no longer wants the trade benefits that Washington links to such policies, the State Department announced today.

This means that tariffs on imports from Rumania beginning July 3 would rise about tenfold and that the number of imports would probably decline. In 1987 Rumania's exports to the United States were nearly $800 million, while its imports of American goods slightly exceeded $200 million.

The trade benefits make up what is known as most-favored-nation treatment, which the United States accords to most of its trading partners. Trade policy toward Eastern Europe and the Soviet Union has been linked to humanitarian concerns since the mid-1970's.

Dissatisfied With Policies

Deputy Secretary of State John C. Whitehead informed the Rumanian leader, Nicolae Ceausescu, at a meeting in Bucharest three weeks ago that the United States was dissatisfied with Rumanian human rights policies.

Mr. Whitehead later told reporters that Mr. Ceausescu replied in effect that the United States should mind its own business.

The State Department spokeswoman, Phyllis Oakley, said today that Rumania had just informed the United States through diplomatic channels that it had decided to "renounce" the trade benefits.

In addition to higher duties, which a Rumanian Embassy official said would cost the country up to $250 million in lost exports, Rumania would also lose eligibility for United States Government-supported export credits through the Commodity Credit Corporation and the Export-Import Bank.

Congress has been closely following the trade and human rights situation in Rumania. Both houses of Congress passed trade legislation stripping Rumania of the trade concessions for six months.

But House-Senate conferees, apparently anticipating today's announcement, dropped the six-month suspension from the bill Thursday.

Representative Chris Smith, Republican of New Jersey, said Rumania's decision was "clearly intended to pre-empt the annual Congressional scrutiny of Rumania's deplorable human rights record."

But Mrs. Oakley said that despite today's announcement, Rumania "stated to us that it will continue to allow emigration for family reunification purposes, without relation to economic ties with the United States."

*   *   *

May 29, 1988

HUNGARY ASSAILS RUMANIA ON VILLAGE RAZINGS

By HENRY KAMM
Special to The New York Times

BUDAPEST, May 28—Hungary has charged that a vast program in Rumania to consolidate villages is intended to erase the Hungarian heritage in areas of Transylvania that were severed from Hungary after World War I. The Hungarian Foreign Ministry, which has not made a formal statement on the matter to the Rumanian Government, has given foreign reporters translations of articles from Hungary's Government-controlled press. The articles protest the program. The articles charge that President Nicolae Ceausescu has decided to accelerate a program to reduce the number of villages in Rumania from 13,000 to 6,000 and to convert the land where the villages stood to agriculture. Rural populations are to be consolidated in small agricultural towns.

Western diplomats confirmed that Rumania has been consolidating villages on a small scale since the program was adopted in 1978. The fear now is that the project will be stepped up. Rumania acknowledges the program but denies that its intention is to decrease the rights of minorities

Diplomats assume that the program is a personal project of Mr. Ceausescu, similar to his destruction of much of central Bucharest, Rumania's capital, to replace traditional homes and historic churches with a grand avenue. With one of the lowest population densities in Europe—90 people for each 247 acres—Rumania is not thought to suffer from a shortage of tillable land.

Hungarian newspapers said Mr. Ceausescu has ordered all the agricultural towns to be under way by 1995 and to be completed by the year 2000.

The Western diplomats agreed with Hungarian charges that the mass relocation of villagers would dilute the cultural identity of the two major ethnic minorities in Rumania—Hungarians and Germans. Hungary says the number of ethnic Hungarians in Rumania exceeds 2 million, while Rumania puts the number at 1.7 million. There are 350,000 ethnic Ger-

The New York Times/May 29, 1988

Budapest wants to protect Transylvania's Hungarian heritage.

mans. Rumania has a population of 23 million. Hungary's population is 10.5 million.

Villages in Transylvania, in northwest Rumania, have historically been distinctly Rumanian, Hungarian or German in character, with only small representations of the other ethnic groups. Hungarians fear that the consolidation of population will further diminish the number of schools and classes using the Hungarian language.

Magyar Ifjusag, the newspaper of Hungary's Communist Party youth organization, has accused Rumania of threatening to erase the Hungarian heritage. It lamented the expected loss of "the native villages of grandparents, the monuments, the cemeteries where tombstones speak the ancestral language, the churches, where psalms are sung in the Hungarian language."

Hungary admits Rumanians seeking asylum, 80 to 90 percent of them ethnic Hungarians. A Hungarian official said 4,000 Rumanians were registered as "temporary settlers" this year.

The Hungarian official said ethnic Germans and Rumanians among the refugees are quietly sent to Austria, marking the first time a Warsaw Pact country has helped citizens of a member nation go to the West.

The Hungarian press has reported that since last month, Rumanian minority-language publications have been forbidden to use minority place names. Most Transylvanian villages have three names—Rumanian, Hungarian and German—and only the Rumanian names are now permitted.

*   *   *

July 2, 1988

RAZING RUMANIA

Even as Stalinism's disastrous legacies come under attack in Moscow, the old tyrannical style flourishes in Rumania. Nicolae Ceausescu's harsh 20-year rule has turned one of Europe's traditional breadbaskets into a land of legendary deprivation. He has razed acres of ancient houses and churches in Bucharest, its once-elegant capital, to make a parade ground. Now he pushes a program to destroy half the nation's villages and move their inhabitants into new "agro-industrial" centers.

Mr. Ceausescu is unmoved by the pleas of those whose carved fences, ancestral cemeteries and family homes will be plowed under. He touts the gain in food production promised by converting the land now occupied by 6,000 to 7,000 "non-viable" small villages to agriculture. Yet Rumania already has Europe's lowest population density; it suffers no shortage of tillable land.

Even so, Rumanians are hungry. They're also cold in winter, thanks to severe fuel rationing. They are grateful even for 30-watt light bulbs. And they are brutally repressed day to day. This state of affairs is the direct result of Mr. Ceausescu's corrupt, nepotistic, megalomaniac rule. First, his grandiose projects piled up unsupportable levels of foreign debt. Then he managed to halve the indebtedness by imposing unimaginably severe austerity. Now, he wants to tighten his iron control more by destroying the villages.

Mr. Ceausescu used to win plaudits in the West for his occasional departures from Moscow's foreign-policy dictates. No more. His brutalities have broken even the steely unanimity among East bloc nations, where he is now openly criticized.

Late last year, when he again tightened fuel rationing, thousands took to the streets in Brasov, Rumania's second-largest city. Even some among the Communist Party elite assayed tentative criticism. But the rioters were met with tanks, dogs and tear gas. Rumanians, beaten down by years of repression, have been mostly quiet since.

Quiet is just what others shouldn't be. Mr. Ceausescu has now headed off likely American trade sanctions—but only by ending Rumania's favored trade status himself. Other forms of leverage are needed too. Mr. Ceausescu's Stalin-style contempt for human rights, cultural legacies and foreign opinion have no place in today's Europe, East or West.

PART VIII

THE STRUGGLE FOR DEMOCRACY, 1989–2000

March 14, 1989

EX-AIDES CRITICIZE RUMANIA'S LEADER

By Reuters

VIENNA, March 13—Six former officials of the Rumanian Communist Party have sent a letter to President Nicolae Ceausescu attacking the Rumanian leader's hard-line policies, Western diplomats and Eastern bloc journalists in Bucharest said today.

The letter accused Mr. Ceausescu of violating human rights agreements signed by Rumania, of ignoring the constitutional rights of citizens and of mismanaging the economy and agriculture. The six signers are prominent Rumanians who have held senior Communist Party posts. The letter is seen as the biggest challenge to Mr. Ceausescu's 24-year rule since worker riots in Brasov, in central Rumania, in 1987.

In the letter, a copy of which was made available here by Rumanian emigre groups, the signers attacked Mr. Ceausescu for failing to observe the 1975 Helsinki Accords on human rights, which Rumania has signed.

Changes Rejected

It also accused the Rumanian leader, who has rejected changes pressed by the Soviet Union and other Communist nations, for ignoring the Constitution.

The letter was signed by these six officials: Silviu Brucan, 73 years old, a former Ambassador to the United States and delegate to the United Nations; Corneliu Manescu, 73, a former Foreign Minister and onetime chairman of the United Nations General Assembly; Gheorghe Apostol, 77, a former union leader and Politburo member; Alexandru Birladeanu, a former Politburo member and Deputy Prime Minister; Constantin Pirvulescu, 94, a co-founder of the Rumanian Communist Party, and Grigore Raceanu, who was described as a veteran party member.

Relocations Criticized

The letter singled out Mr. Ceausescu's program to slash the number of villages and to move peasants to new urban centers, saying this violated the constitutional right to property.

The letter took issue with an unpublished but widely feared law banning Rumanians from talking to foreigners.

The signers appealed to the Rumanian leader to scrap the rural reorganization program, to restore the constitutional guarantees of citizens and to end food exports. "Once this has been done, we are willing to take part in a constructive dialogue with the leadership,'' the signers concluded.

* * *

June 19, 1989

PAPANDREOU LOSES MAJORITY CONTROL IN GREEK ELECTION

By CLYDE HABERMAN
Special to The New York Times

ATHENS, Monday, June 19—Prime Minister Andreas Papandreou lost control of the Greek Parliament in national elections on Sunday, but his conservative challengers may not have won the majority needed to form a government.

If they did not, Greece will be headed for a period of intense political negotiations and may even have to go through another round of elections within a few months.

It was clear from returns early today that Greek voters had repudiated Mr. Papandreou, who has been plagued by scandals and who since 1981 has led his moderate Socialist Government in a forceful if erratic style.

Party-by-Party Statistics

The Pan-Hellenic Socialist Movement, trailed the conservative New Democracy Party headed by a longtime adversary of Mr. Papandreou, Constantine Mitsotakis.

With 53 percent of the popular vote counted, New Democracy had 45 percent, the Socialists 38.5 percent, a coalition of Communists and other far-left groups, 12.8 percent, and small parties, 3.5 percent.

"New Democracy has won—it's a clear victory," Mr. Mitsotakis told cheering supporters this morning. More than 60 percent of the Greek people condemned the corrupt and incompetent Government."

Makeup of Government Unclear

Still, he effectively acknowledged that the question of who will lead Greece was undecided. "I am waiting to see whether we will have a self-sufficient government," he said.

For his part, Mr. Papandreou conceded that he had lost the popular vote. "But New Democracy cannot form a government," he told reporters, "because there is a progressive majority in Parliament."

His statement suggested that he was prepared to try forging an alliance with the Communists to create the first coalition Greek government since a military junta gave way to civilian rule in 1974. In evaluating the returns, the percentages were critical. It was believed that Mr. Mitsotakis would need 46 percent or 47 percent of the vote to be able to capture 151 of Parliament's 300 seats. Projections on the Government-run television network showed him winning 147 seats, to 124 for the Socialists, and 29 for the left-wing coalition.

Reuters

Constantine Mitsotakis, head of the New Democracy Party, which yesterday led in Greek Parliamentary elections, after voting in Athens.

Payanotis Lambrias, a New Democracy spokesman, challenged these returns, saying that his party's calculations showed it had enough votes for a parliamentary majority. He said the party was counting on a strong showing in Athens and other large cities where the returns were coming in slowly.

Should the 70-year-old Mr. Mitsotakis fall short, he would have a difficult time finding coalition partners, and, in fact, he has said he does not want them.

Therefore, later this week, President Christos Sartzetakis may call on Mr. Papandreou, who is also 70, to try forming a new government. In short, despite the rejection at the polls, his political career may not be finished.

If he fails to persuade left-wing party leaders—and many of them have said they would never unite with Papandreou-led Socialists—Greece may be forced to go through elections again in late summer or early fall.

No Shortage of Contenders

The confusion of the situation was reflected in the paper ballots handed to voters as they went to polling places on a sun-splashed day. There were 25 parties in the race, many of them tiny groups led by former Papandreou associates who had defected from the Socialists in protest over scandals that have dogged him for nearly a year.

In addition to choosing a new national Parliament, Greek voters also selected 24 representatives to the European Parliament in Strasbourg, France.

Scandals in Mr. Papandreou's private life and his Government dominated the campaign to the exclusion of nearly all other issues.

His political troubles began last summer when he went to London for open-heart surgery, and at the same time disclosed his romance with Dimitra Liani, a 35-year-old former flight attendant.

It is common and even accepted for Greek men to have extra-marital relations. But many Greeks were upset by what they perceived as the Prime Minister's public flaunting of his affair and his rejection of his American-born wife, Margaret, 65. They were divorced last week.

In the no-holds-barred campaign, opposition newspapers published nude photos of Ms. Liani. In retaliation, a pro-Papandreou daily claimed to have tapes of telephone conversations between Mr. Mitsotakis and his mistress.

Payoffs Are Alleged

Far more devastating for the Prime Minister were charges that he and close associates received millions of dollars in payoffs in a bank-embezzlement scheme.

The scandal centered on the activities of George Koskotas, a financier and newspaper owner who is awaiting extradition hearings in Massachusetts and is accused of siphoning off $230 million from the Bank of Crete when he owned it. From jail, Mr. Koskotas charged that some of the money went to Mr. Papandreou and his friends, and so far a dozen officials have been arrested and forced out of the Government.

The Prime Minister protested his innocence, accusing American intelligence agents of concocting the scandal to destabilize Greek politics.

That Mr. Papandreou could run a race at all was widely seen as testament to his personal magnetism and, perhaps, to Mr. Mitsotakis's lack of it.

Mitsotakis Fought Nazis

The New Democracy leader is mild-mannered and reserved. He was born on Crete, where he joined the Greek Resistance against the occupying Germans in World War II. Twice, the Nazis sentenced him to death.

He was first elected to Parliament in 1946, at 28, and later served in various Government positions, including Finance Minister in the early 1960's.

After a military coup in 1967, Mr. Mitsotakis was arrested, but he was released and fled to exile in Paris. He returned when the military dictatorship fell in 1974, joined the New Democracy Party in 1978 and became its leader six years later. He and Mr. Papandreou do not try to conceal their dislike of each other, an antipathy that goes back to the mid-1960's when Mr. Mitsotakis led the party of George Papandreou, the Prime Minister's father.

Over the years, Andreas Papandreou developed a reputation as a keen but often erratic politician, keeping decisions to himself, often not making them until the last minute.

When he swept into office eight years ago, it was on a cry for "allaghi," or change. This time, he pleaded for continuity.

Presented as an Opposite

Mr. Mitsotakis presents himself as Mr. Papandreou's opposite in every way.

On substantive matters, he has promised to promote free enterprise, cut taxes and reduce the size of the Government so as to stimulate Greece's faltering economy. He also pledged to foster smoother relations with Washington, which has not hidden its disapproval of Mr. Papandreou.

Key issues between the two nations are continuing negotiations over leases for American bases in Greece and Washington's demand for the extradition of Mohammed Rashid, a Palestinian jailed here and wanted in connection with the bombing of a Pan American airliner seven years ago.

The Greek Supreme Court has ordered the extradition, but the new Government will have the final word.

* * *

July 2, 1989

GREEK COMMUNISTS JOIN WITH RIGHT TO FORM CABINET

By MARLISE SIMONS
Special to The New York Times

ATHENS, July 1—After more than half a century as bitter enemies, Greek Communists and conservatives joined forces today, forming a new Government for the single purpose of prosecuting officials accused of wrongdoing in the departing Socialist Government of Andreas Papandreou.

The decision brings a temporary end to the national crisis that has followed the June 18 elections, when no single party won the majority needed to form a government.

The coalition is expected to be short-lived. Conservative and Communist party officials said today that new elections would probably be held in three months.

Differences Are Buried

But for the moment, the officials said, they had buried their differences because a coalition was the only way to insure that a new government could start proceedings in an array of financial scandals. There are charges that officials have stolen millions of dollars of Government funds.

The accord has created a difficult situation for Mr. Papandreou, the departing Prime Minister and the politician who has dominated Greece for the last decade.

He immediately issued a statement saying the Greek people would not accept the new government. A radio station owned by Mr. Papandreou's Socialist Party called on citizens to "mobilize and take to the streets."

Capital Is Calm

But Greeks appeared relieved that the period of uncertainty had ended, and Athens remained calm today.

The Communists were outlawed and persecuted in Greece after they lost a bloody civil war to conservative forces 40 years ago. Now the party, led by Charilaos Florakis, has sud-denly gained a measure of power because for the first time since 1945 it holds the balance of the seats that the major parties need to form a government.

Mr. Papandreou, who is ailing, appears to face an unstoppable political and judicial process that could tear apart his powerful Socialist Party and perhaps lead to his own indictment.

Accountability Stressed

Constantine Mitsotakis, the leader of the conservative New Democracy Party, now the largest in the Government, has said that even if Mr. Papandreou proves not to be tainted personally in the corruption scandals, he will be held politically accountable.

From his sick bed this week, Mr. Papandreou has made repeated efforts to form his own government. But the Communist Party rebuffed him, calling his terms unacceptable.

Mr. Papandreou, 70 years old, remains hospitalized and has received treatment for pneumonia and heart and kidney failure. Officials of his party said the news that he had been outmaneuvered had infuriated him.

The new Cabinet, to be sworn in on Sunday, will be led by Prime Minister Tzannis Tzannetakis, a member of Parliament from the New Democracy Party. Mr. Tzannetakis, 62, is a former public works minister and former officer who was jailed and expelled from the navy during the military regime that ruled Greece from 1967 to 1974.

A member of the Communist Party today described him as a man who has "the honesty of an officer and the temperament of a gentleman."

As prime minister, he will be responsible for opening the parliamentary investigations into the scandals. His candidacy broke the deadlock of almost two weeks in which efforts to form a government were attended by high political drama and considerable constitutional confusion.

Mr. Mitsotakis, whose New Democracy Party won a plurality, first failed to form a government.

On the day after the June 18 election, Mr. Mitsotakis proposed that the Communists and other parties join him in a temporary government to punish guilty members of Mr. Papandreou's Government, but the Communists rejected the proposal.

Then Mr. Papandreou directed coalition talks from his hospital bed but failed to persuade the Communists to join him.

The Communist group, a coalition of a Moscow-oriented party and a moderate party of Euro-Communists, clearly wanted to savor their position and waited until Tuesday when they received a three-day mandate to form a government.

Demands From Communists

Mr. Florakis, the Communist leader, once a resistance fighter and rebel leader who spent 18 years in jail, demanded that Mr. Papandreou and Mr. Mitsotakis step aside and that a multi-party government be formed. After much wheeling and dealing, both men reluctantly accepted the demand, but Mr. Papandreou's party was finally excluded when he said the only acceptable coalition would be one of Socialists and Communists.

The new Parliament will hold its first session on Monday, and one of its priorities, politicians said, will be to lift the immunity from Cabinet and Parliament members of the Papandreou Government.

Mr. Papandreou has announced that he will leave the hospital briefly and go to Parliament to be sworn in as a deputy. If his health permits, he will be the opposition leader.

But whatever his political skills, Mr. Papandreou may find it difficult to influence proceedings against him or his political associates. With only 125 seats, he will be outnumbered by his opponents in the new governing coalition, who jointly hold 173 seats in the 300-member Parliament.

The scope of the coming parliamentary investigations is still unclear. In his electoral campaign, Mr. Mitsotakis spoke of more than 40 political and financial scandals and schemes affecting the Papandreou Government in its eight years in office. Even if true, it is not likely that the Parliament and later the judiciary can tackle such a vast array.

Mirage Deal Is Questioned

The issues that the conservatives and the Communists have focused on include these:

- Charges that officials of the Papandreou Government were paid illegal multi-million dollar commissions when they ordered 40 French Mirage jet fighters. The first of the fighters was delivered this year. Full details of the contract were never fully disclosed.
- Charges that the Government in recent years defrauded the European Community of agricultural subsidies by falsely labeling sales of corn and wheat. Who benefited from these subsidies is not known. Proceedings against Greece have been initiated in the European Court of Justice.
- The best-known scandal is the Koskotas affair, named after its central figure, George Koskotas, a 34-year-old financier and newspaper owner who is now in jail in Massachusetts.

Mr. Koskotas is accused of embezzling close to $230 million from the Bank of Crete when he was its owner. In published interviews he has said his financial dealings were part of a large scheme that permitted Mr. Papandreou and other officials to skim off interest payments on Government funds deposited at his bank.

Mr. Papandreou has denied any wrongdoing in all these cases and has said rivals have created the scandals to destabilize his Government.

8 Cabinet Members Are Out

So far, however, eight Cabinet members of the Papandreou Government have either resigned or have been dismissed in the Koskotas affair. Several high-ranking civil servants accused of financial wrongdoing in this and other cases may not leave the country.

The parliamentary investigations in the Koskotas affair, which began several months ago, were interrupted in May when the Cabinet suddenly adjourned a week early, before a report on the case was due.

Whatever the outcome of the investigations, the short-term government followed by new elections will mean that other major issues are not likely to be dealt with until well into the fall.

For the United States, this will mean postponement of delicate negotiations on the four American military bases here. The lease ran out in December and any renewal must be made within 17 months of its expiration date.

The United States has also requested the extradition of Mohammed Rashid, a Palestinian imprisoned here and wanted in connection with the 1982 bombing of an American jetliner in Hawaii.

* * *

August 6, 1989

YUGOSLAVS ASTIR OVER SERBIAN'S RISE

By HENRY KAMM
Special to The New York Times

BELGRADE, Yugoslavia—The hottest political topic in Yugoslavia is Slobodan Milosevic—what he has done and, even more, what he might do next.

The 47-year-old President of Serbia, the country's largest republic, has aroused such hopes and fears that Yugoslavs say that no leader here since Tito, who ruled autocratically from World War II until his death in 1980, has made himself such a dominant personality.

The political career of the former banker and industrial executive began only five years ago. But since then he has made himself the undisputed leader of Serbia and has done so with such determination, which his many opponents describe as ruthlessness, that many say they believe—or fear—that the Serbian chief will not stop short of seeking to rise to the top of the nation, a federation of six republics.

Because the six republic leaders now take turns being president in the collective national leadership, Mr. Milosevic would have to have the Constitution changed to have himself installed for a longer term as president of the nation. Some of Mr. Milosevic's influential associates say they believe that he may seek such changes.

'Delicate Question' of Ambition

Many Yugoslavs and diplomats say they believe that the Serbian leader has national ambitions. Members of his entourage reject one widespread opinion, that he considers himself "a new Tito," but agree that he might seek national power.

A political scientist who holds a position in the Milosevic camp and requested anonymity said: "His ambition is a delicate question. It is too early to talk about his departure from Serbia before Yugoslav conditions have been created for him to move on. It is pointless to hold a federal position when such jobs hold no power. I doubt he would leave until the constitutional system changes and collective leadership is abolished."

The hopes that Mr. Milosevic will continue to rise are concentrated among the Serbs, the largest nationality in this multinational country, where population groups coexist uneasily. But because Serbs number about 9 million in a nation of 23.3 million, double the size of the next-largest group, the emergence of an exceptionally strong and popular Serbian leader has spread fear among the other nationalities in the other republics, Croatia, Slovenia, Bosnia and Herzegovina, Montenegro and Macedonia, and two autonomous provinces, Vojvodina and Kosovo.

Since Yugoslavia was formed in 1918, keeping Serbia from exerting its numerical and historic power has been widely considered the key to preserving national unity. Yet an appeal to Serbian nationalism has been the fuel powering Mr. Milosevic's rise.

Support From Anti-Communists

To Serbs, "Slobo," as most call him, has righted the wrongs inflicted on their nation since Yugoslavia was created in the wake of World War I. Most other Yugoslavs believe that Mr. Milosevic (pronounced mee-LOH-sheh-vitch) has aroused nationalism to its highest pitch, thereby threatening the delicate ethnic balance that keeps the country's peace.

"Serbia was politically and economically dominated in Yugoslavia," said Prof. Kosta Mihailovic, an economist and member of the Serbian Academy of Science. "An anti-Serbian coalition existed for a long time. We occupied a vassal position in Yugoslavia. This was totally changed by the appearance of Slobodan Milosevic."

The enthusiastic support for a Communist leader by men like Professor Mihailovic—and even by anti-Communist dissidents—is a phenomenon as new as Mr. Milosevic's rise and a major reason for concern among non-Serbs. Since Communism came to power in the person of Marshal Tito, Serbian intellectuals have been reluctant to support the party, because of curbs on intellectual freedoms and a belief that the President kept Serbia from exercising its rightful weight.

"Revanchist ambitions against Serbia characterized the post-war period," Professor Mihailovic said. "The others wanted the rate of growth of Serbia's economy to be the lowest. Serbian wartime leaders were chased from power. The Serbian intelligentsia was under terrible pressure. I was eliminated from public life for 20 years. The dignity of the Serbian people was infringed."

Issue of Kosovo

Mr. Milosevic has restored what Serbs consider their dignity. Other Yugoslavs and foreign diplomats, depending on their point of view, say he has merely roused nationalism or even chauvinism in his people.

"Milosevic has full support in Serbia, from the peasants to the Academy of Science," said Budimir Kostic, president of the Serbian Investment Bank. "He'd get 90 percent of the vote in any election." Mr. Kostic spoke as a longtime friend

The New York Times/Aug 6, 1989

Nationalism in Serbia worries the other Yugoslav republics.

of his former fellow banker, but his assessment of Mr. Milosevic's support is that of most Yugoslavs and diplomats.

Mr. Milosevic reached a new high point this year over the issue of Kosovo, an autonomous province of Serbia where ethnic Albanians are the majority and ethnic strife is endemic. He laid the base of his popularity in Kosovo two years ago, when the police used force to hold back a crowd of Serbians protesting against Albanians. He made the police halt, saying: "No one has the right to beat you. No one will ever beat you again."

Large pro-Milosevic and anti-Albanian rallies have been held in Serbia and elsewhere in support of stronger Serbian rule over its two autonomous provinces. Finally, this year, federal consent was obtained for an amendment to Serbia's Constitution to that effect; a result was an ethnic Albanian protest movement that was put down by military force and mass arrests.

Collective Leadership Opposed

A Communist Party Politburo member told an ambassador that the other republics agreed to the constitutional change in a hope that Mr. Milosevic would "stay in Serbia." They are no longer sure their hope will be fulfilled.

One of Tito's legacies is a Constitution written to prevent his successors from holding the exceptional powers he exercised. Yugoslavia and its constituent parts, as well as the ruling Communist Party, are run by collective, rotating leaderships.

"Milosevic is against collective leadership because it is an alibi for individual irresponsibility," his associate said. "He believes in personal responsibility, courage and competence. We don't have that yet in Yugoslavia."

Duran/Weco

Slobodan Milosevic, the President of Serbia, Yugoslavia's largest republic, with supporters in Kosovo last March. Mr. Milosevic, who has become Yugoslavia's most talked-about politician, may try to change the Constitution to allow himself to hold the office of President permanently, some associates say. The Presidency is now rotated among the leaders of the country's six republics.

The comment lends support to a belief that Mr. Milosevic will eventually demand the creation of a Federal President with strong executive powers and propose himself for the post.

Push for Economic Changes

The Serbian leader has made an unusually rapid rise. He was an active Communist at the University of Belgrade, where he graduated with a law degree in 1964. He worked in the party apparatus in economic posts until he became an executive at a state-owned gas company in 1968. Five years later, he became its chief. In 1978, he was named president of the Belgrade Bank. In that post, he visited the United States many times and speaks conversational English.

He entered the political scene in 1984 to head the Belgrade party organization. In 1986, as a protege of Ivan Stambolic, then Serbian leader, he rose to the top of the hierarchy by being elected President of the Serbian Communist Politburo. In May he became head of the republic's presidency, in effect chief of government. Along the way, in 1987, Mr. Milosevic led a Serbian party purge that removed his sponsor, Mr. Stambolic, from the leadership.

Mr. Milosevic has put himself in the forefront of the national campaign for economic restructuring. But few enforcing actions have followed.

Mr. Milosevic's supporters say committees that he formed for economic and political change have proposed constitutional changes to create a stronger Federal Government that will be able to make the needed difficult decisions. They contend that the other republics are not ready to join in.

Atmosphere of Suspicion

But Mr. Milosevic's opponents in other republics assert that Mr. Milosevic, an ebullient and sometimes pugnacious public speaker, is merely stating the obvious, and add that he has not contributed to the creation of national consensus needed for far-reaching constitutional changes.

In fact, they assert, his incitement of nationalism has created an atmosphere of suspicion that makes all Yugoslav agreements difficult.

Critics also noted that a major proposal for political liberalization published in late July makes clear that Mr. Milosevic does not support the creation of opposition parties.

In a return to a state of mind that prevailed under Marshal Tito and seemed to have disappeared with his death, Yugoslavs critical of Mr. Milosevic are again asking journalists not to quote them by name. Unconfirmed reports circulate accusing Mr. Milosevic of vindictiveness against critics.

One of the purported victims is the American Ambassador, Warren Zimmerman. He and Deputy Secretary of State Lawrence S. Eagleburger have apparently angered the Serbian leader with public criticism of the treatment of ethnic Albanians. As a result, Mr. Zimmerman, who has been here since March, has failed to obtain an appointment with Mr. Milosevic.

Another reported target is the Yugoslav Ambassador to the United States, Zivorad Kovacevic. Mr. Kovacevic has been recalled after only two years' service despite Yugoslav and American recognition of exceptional performance because, according to informed Yugoslavs and diplomats, Serbia objected that he failed to prevent Congress from passing two resolutions against human-rights violations against Kosovo Albanians.

For better or worse, diplomats agree, Mr. Milosevic has made himself Yugoslavia's principal political figure. "It is very clear," said Dusan Mitevic, head of Belgrade television and radio, a Milosevic loyalist. "You can't make Yugoslavia today without Slobodan Milosevic."

*   *   *

December 14, 1989

COMMUNISTS IN BULGARIA EXPEL ZHIVKOV

By CLYDE HABERMAN
Special to The New York Times

SOFIA, Bulgaria, Dec. 13—Todor I. Zhivkov, who had been Eastern Europe's longest-ruling leader until a month ago, was expelled today from the Bulgarian Communist Party, a humiliation that may increase his chances of facing formal corruption charges.

"I don't imagine anyone would want to be in his shoes now," a senior party official said.

Mr. Zhivkov's continued fall from grace came on a fast-paced day in which the party's Central Committee supported a call by its new leader, Petar T. Mladenov, to give up its guaranteed monopoly on political power.

It asked Parliament, which meets on Thursday, to repeal two paragraphs from Article 1 of the Bulgarian Constitution, which declares the Communists to be the country's "leading force."

"Our glorious party does not need that article any more," Mr. Mladenov said to tens of thousands of party loyalists summoned to an outdoor rally tonight in central Sofia to support the latest changes and to declare that Communism was not finished in Bulgaria.

Self-Critical Meeting

"It is only socialism that can grant social and economic development in our society," Mr. Mladenov told the cheering crowd, which was filled largely with older people. But from now on, he said, the party must make its way not through constitutional fiat but rather by proving itself against a competitive opposition in free elections.

Besides proposing the constitutional change, the Central Committee ended a highly self-critical three-day meeting by recommending parliamentary elections next spring, discussing in general terms ways to revive a failing economy and outlining possible changes in "all basic areas of social life."

Reuters

Petar T. Mladenov, the new Bulgarian leader, as he addressed a Communist rally in Sofia.

Much of the debate seemed intended to keep Communist leaders from falling too far behind the strong popular demands for rapid democratic change that have risen dramatically since the Politburo coup that toppled Mr. Zhivkov on Nov. 10.

But as much as charting the future, the party seems intent also on punishing Mr. Zhivkov and blaming him for just about every sin that has brought Bulgaria, in Mr. Mladenov's words this week, to "a near-heart attack condition."

'Gross Violations of Laws'

Mr. Zhivkov's expulsion from the party was the result of "gross violations of laws and gross mistakes in politics that brought the country to a serious crisis," said Andrei Lukanov, a Politburo member who heads a party investigation into the Zhivkov family's finances and reported penchant for lavish spending.

Mr. Lukanov, in effect the No. 2 party figure now after Mr. Mladenov, made his remarks at a news conference that he held with another Politburo member, Alexander Lilov. The mere scheduling of such a gathering, in which they answered free-wheeling questions from Bulgarian and foreign reporters, was of itself a remarkable event in this country where, Mr. Lilov acknowledged, fear had been rampant.

Since taking control of the party, Mr. Mladenov has purged the Politburo and the Central Committee of many Zhivkov loyalists. During this week's meeting, several committee members, including Foreign Minister Boyko Dimitrov, called for a broader house-cleaning, but it appeared that surviving members of the old guard managed to hang on, at least for now.

The only personnel change announced today was the expulsion of Mr. Zhivkov and two close allies—his son, Vladimir, who is reported to have accumulated enormous gambling debts, and Milko Balev, a widely disliked power broker in Mr. Zhivkov's 35-year rule.

Accusations of Abuse of Power

But Mr. Lukanov insisted that by getting rid of the disgraced former leader, "we are not only saying goodbye to a person, we are saying goodbye to a policy."

Over the last few weeks, there has been a steady drip of allegations in the controlled press about Mr. Zhivkov's high living and abuses of power. Reports say that he acquired as many as 30 houses and hunting lodges, that he was paid hundreds of thousands of dollars in royalties for books written by others, that state funds were improperly used to pay for a grandson's schooling in Switzerland.

Citing the Switzerland case, Mr. Lukanov said: "When that is done by a head of state it can no longer be considered a mild frailty. It is a grave malpractice."

The disclosures of longstanding financial abuses have been a particular sore point for Bulgarians, whose standard of living, Mr. Lukanov said tonight, has been declining. Their average monthly income is about $100 a month, using a semi-official rate. At commonly used black market rates, the monthly income, as measured in dollars, drops to as low as $25.

Feelings Are Hostile

"Since Nov. 10," Mr. Lukanov said, "popular feelings toward Mr. Zhivkov have been not only hostile, but very acutely so—so hostile that I don't imagine anyone would want to be in his shoes now."

The two Politburo members declined to discuss the likelihood that the 78-year-old Mr. Zhivkov would be brought to trial. They also insisted that the former leader, who reportedly is staying inside one of his houses outside Sofia, was not under house arrest.

But the probability that his troubles would deepen was strongly suggested in a Central Committee proposal that Parliament begin a parallel inquiry into Mr. Zhivkov's finances, one that members of the Bulgarian public would be allowed to join.

The investigation was characterized as a necessary part of the restructuring the Communists now say they seek. According to Mr. Lukanov, the party wants to sharply reduced "nonpriority" Government spending, emphasize consumer goods more than military production and perhaps move toward private land ownership.

In another area of major concern, Mr. Lilov said the party would set up a committee to re-examine Mr. Zhivkov's policy of forced assimilation of Bulgaria's large ethnic Turkish minority. The five-year-old program, especially a requirement that the Turks take Slavic names, led last summer to the exodus of 310,000 of these people to Turkey.

Mr. Lilov offered no specific suggestions, but he said that "we are willing to find a new solution to this problem."

* * *

December 14, 1989

IS RUMANIA NEXT TO GO?

By KATHERINE VERDERY

BALTIMORE—Astonishing changes have swept every Eastern European country except Rumania, which might have been expected to change as drastically as its neighbors but has not. Why?

The answer is complex, but here are some of its elements: police repression, disorganized opposition, a unified party leadership.

The Government's level of surveillance and repression is higher than any other in the bloc. It has isolated or expelled would-be dissidents, contained opposition movements and crushed riots and strikes. Government force is combined with extensive collaboration (incentives include otherwise unobtainable goods, apartments, jobs, etc.), which increases the effectiveness of the secret police.

Second, and partly in consequence, the population has little experience in organizing opposition. Leaders of movements comparable to Czechoslovakia's Charter 77 died mysteriously or were "exported" to the West. Thus, Rumanians accumulated less of the organizational experience that Hungarians, Czechs and Poles have acquired over the past three decades. The West contributed to this by failing to support opposition to a regime viewed as independent from Moscow, even as the West encouraged dissidents in other Eastern bloc countries.

Third, the Czech, Polish, East German, Hungarian (and, to a lesser extent, the Bulgarian) Communist Party leaderships all were divided between various kinds of hardliners and reformists. In Rumania, reformist voices have been systematically eliminated from the leadership, which remains unified behind President Nicolae Ceausescu's family rule.

The lack of a split in the party leadership deprives opponents of leverage. (Support within the party was crucial to Solidarity's brief success in 1980.) Nor has there been any faction in the inner circle likely to take advantage of public disturbances to make a grab for power, or waiting in the wings to assume power when public opposition forces the hardliners out.

Reformist factions in the other countries owe much to Soviet support, enhanced by the presence of Soviet troops, upon which reformists might count. In Rumania, which has had no Soviet troops since 1958, the absence of this resource further impeded internal splits from developing.

Thus, it is almost impossible for Rumanians to mount demonstrations similar to those in Prague and East Germany.

Moreover, if one were to occur, there is not much likelihood of its serving as the basis for a transfer of power to a reformist leadership. It might be objected that, until two months ago, East Germany seemed just as unsusceptible to change as Rumania. But on each of the three points, repression, lack of opposition and the unity of leadership, Rumania is more extreme than East Germany.

What are the prospects for change? Changes elsewhere have put tremendous pressure on the regime, and it is clear that the Soviets will not oppose a transfer of power. Thus, there is an outside chance that "opportunistic fissures" might develop at the top, leading to Mr. Ceausescu's ouster by some of his erstwhile allies. This could be either in reaction to a spontaneous demonstration or independent of one.

Recent events suggest another possible route to the same outcome. In a major speech, Mr. Ceausescu blamed some of his chief ministers for sabotaging the planned distribution of food and fuel, extreme shortages of which have made the lives of Rumanians a nightmare for most of the past five years. He promised to prosecute these ministers, hoping, it seems, to redirect to them the public hatred focused on his leadership.

If, indeed, he launches a purge among his closest advisers, whose fate he deserves to share, this might provoke them to unite and drive him out. The new leadership, while less harsh than Mr. Ceausescu's, is unlikely to be truly reformist.

At least as likely as a change at the top is a spontaneous demonstration that almost assuredly would be crushed by security forces. Should this occur, a world reaction of outrage and condemnation could help end a dictatorship that has been an embarrassment to Europe and a torment to its own people.

Katherine Verdery is professor of anthropology at The Johns Hopkins University.

* * *

December 18, 1989

RUMANIAN POLICE, TRYING TO OUST DISSIDENT CLERIC, BATTLE THOUSANDS

By The Associated Press

VIENNA, Dec. 17—Rumanian security forces, using tanks and water cannon, battled thousands of anti-Government demonstrators after the police tried to deport a dissident clergyman, the Hungarian press agency and people familiar with the unrest said today, It was believed to be one of the largest outbreaks of anti-Government protest in at least two years in Rumania, where the hard-line Communist leadership of President Nicolae Ceausescu has crushed dissent and rejected the efforts for reform under way in much of Eastern Europe.

Hungary's state press agency, quoting a television reporter in the southern city of Szeged, said an eviction order against the Rev. Laszlo Toekes of the Reformed Church in Timisoara,

250 miles northwest of Bucharest, the Rumanian capital, was to be carried out this afternoon.

A Human Chain

The press agency said Mr. Toekes and his family had been guarded for several days by hundreds of ethnic Hungarian and other Rumanian citizens who formed a human chain to protect him. The minister has championed the rights of people of Hungarian stock in Rumania.

"They tried to prevent the eviction of their clergyman, when hell broke loose and the human chain changed into a demonstration of thousands against Ceausescu and his regime," the Hungarian press agency said, citing the accounts of witnesses.

"Riot police tried to suppress the demonstration, and a bloody brawl started," the Hungarian report went on. "It took almost two hours for the policemen to gain the upper hand."

It did not say what day the violence broke out, but other people familiar with the unrest reported protests both Saturday and today.

Deportation Intended

They said the authorities had intended to deport the minister on Saturday. His fate was not known, the Hungarian agency said.

Quoting the television reporter in Szeged, the Hungarian agency said: "Witnesses saw bloodied young people in the streets of Timisoara, and Ceausescu pictures floating on the Bega Canal. They said many of the demonstrators were arrested."

Quoting travelers returning from Rumania, the Hungarian agency said the police used water cannon against the demonstrators. A Czechoslovak citizen was quoted as saying he had seen tanks and blockaded streets.

A Report From Budapest

Earlier, a worker at Hungarian television in Budapest said that at least 10,000 Rumanians had demonstrated today against Mr. Ceausescu's authoritarian rule in Timisoara, which is about 30 miles from the Hungarian border.

Yugoslav travelers returning from Timisoara said in Belgrade that tens of thousands of people were milling about the streets this morning. The Yugoslavs said that "the entire city seemed on the streets."

The Hungarian television worker said the angry crowd broke display windows of bookstores and threw out books by President Ceausescu.

The police reportedly attacked the protesters and managed to control the crowd by late afternoon.

Many Reported in Streets

Late today, a caller told the Danubiusz radio station in Budapest that tens of thousands were still in the streets of Timisoara. He said he received his information by telephone.

The West German newspaper Die Welt said hundreds of supporters had prevented the cleric's deportation on Saturday. According to the report, in its Monday issue, a crowd of 500 people had ringed the church where he sought refuge after having been stabbed by masked, unknown assailants on Nov. 2.

The faithful, initially only ethnic Hungarians, took turns because of sub-zero temperatures, the West German paper reported. Later, ethnic Rumanians and members of the Rumanian Orthodox Church joined the crowd, it said.

The Rumanian state press agency did not report on the weekend demonstrations.

Mr. Ceausescu, who was elected Rumanian Communist Party chief on March 22, 1965, is the longest-serving Soviet bloc leader. His problems in governing have included an autocratic style and severe ethnic strife involving the Hungarian minority, many of whom have complained of systematic discrimination against them.

*   *   *

December 23, 1989

CEAUSESCU FLEES A REVOLT IN RUMANIA BUT DIVIDED SECURITY FORCES FIGHT ON

By DAVID BINDER
Special to The New York Times
WASHINGTON, Saturday, Dec. 23—After ruling Rumania as a dictator for a quarter of a century, President Nicolae Ceausescu was forced to flee Bucharest Friday when angry crowds of anti-Government demonstrators, backed by army units, took over large sections of the capital.

Reports spoke of fierce fighting in the capital between the army and the pro-Ceausescu security police, but by early today the army appeared to be gaining the upper hand.

Bucharest radio said the head of the security police changed sides and ordered his forces to support the army and the Rumanian people, Reuters reported Friday evening. The broadcast also said the Interior Minister and a Deputy Prime Minister had been arrested by anti-Ceausescu forces.

"The forces of democracy are in the ascendant," a State Department official who is following the situation said Friday evening.

4,500 Bodies in Open Graves

Loyalist forces also were reported Friday evening to be attacking Timisoara, the western city where the uprising began last Saturday. But the army said that it had repulsed that attack.

Early today, Maj. Gen. Stefan Gusa, the Army Chief of Staff, said regular army units opposing Mr. Ceausescu had taken control of almost the entire country from security police forces, Reuters reported.

Open graves were discovered in Timisoara Friday with what were believed to be as many as 4,500 bodies, many of them women and children, who were believed killed by security forces over the weekend.

Once Mr. Ceausescu and his wife, Elena, fled, the changes that took place in Rumania were more sudden and dramatic than any in Eastern Europe.

Prisoners Reported Freed

Early today, the Bucharest Radio reported that all Rumanian political prisoners had been freed.

The television and press, which yesterday had been the most rigidly controlled in Eastern Europe, declared their freedom. Viewers around the world saw live images of demonstrations and heard calls for freedom and change that had been inconceivable before. But shortly after midnight in Bucharest, the television station went off the air while heavy fighting was going on in the vicinity.

The anti-Ceausescu forces—a combination of army generals, veteran Communist politicians who had been placed under detention and student leaders—moved swiftly on Friday to form a provisional government under Corneliu Manescu, a former Foreign Minister who was put under house arrest in March for signing a letter urging Mr. Ceausescu to resign.

But with the Government in disarray and the opposition still organizing, reports were often sketchy and sometimes wildly contradictory. For example, there were initial reports Friday that Mr. Ceausescu and his wife, whom he had made his second in command, had fled Bucharest seeking to fly to a country like China or Iran, but that they had been captured in a car near a military airport. But later, the Rumanian radio said those reports were wrong, and that Mr. Ceausescu and his wife had apparently escaped capture.

Late Friday evening, the Soviet press agency reported that the Ceausescus were believed to have left the country.

But their son Nicu, who had been in charge of security forces in central Rumania, was captured and brought to a television studio and shown to the public.

Friday night, the old royal palace in Bucharest, which has served as the presidential residence, was on fire, and there were explosions in the Communist Party Central Committee headquarters. Before it went off the air, the Bucharest television station reported a gunbattle under way inside its building.

Flee by Helicopter

Mr. and Mrs. Ceausescu fled by helicopter, which lifted them off the roof of the Central Committee building and apparently flew them initially to the town of Tirgoviste, 45 miles northwest of the capital.

According to Rumanian and Yugoslav press reports, the trail of the escaping couple grew cold after Tirgoviste, as they raced away, changing cars at times.

The demonstrations in Timisoara started when the authorities moved to deport an ethnic Hungarian priest, the Rev. Laszlo Tokes, and crowds of his supporters came to surround his house and prevent his being taken into custody. Between 2,000 and 4,000 people were believed killed that day, including a number of children.

Then bloodshed began on Thursday in the capital of two million people as security troops opened fire on demonstrators in University Square, and again Friday on the vast square named for Gheorghe Gheorghiu-Dej, Mr. Ceausescu's predecessor.

Rumanians cheering soldiers who joined forces with them yesterday in Bucharest against the rule of President Nicolae Ceausescu.

Reports of Killings

Witnesses said several hundred residents of Bucharest had been killed by automatic weapons in that square. Friday evening, Bucharest television showed huge crowds in the square, against the backdrop of the burning royal palace, Mr. Ceausescu's official residence.

There was a large explosion in the Central Committee building and witnesses also reported that the National Archives, a few blocks to the west, had been set ablaze. There was a suspicion that that had been done by security troops to destroy damaging evidence about the Government.

Mr. Manescu, who is 73 years old, and Silviu Brucan, a former Ambassador to the United States, joined others to form a Committee of National Salvation Friday to organize free elections, according to a live broadcast of the television station, which was renamed Free Rumania Television.

Appeal From 4 Communists

They and four other veteran Rumanian Communists had been arrested last March when they issued a joint appeal to Mr. Ceausescu to end his tyrannical rule. They were relegated to dirt-floor dwellings on the edge of the sprawling capital and were forbidden contact with anyone but their police guards. An unidentified student leader appearing with Mr. Manescu and Mr. Brucan in an impromptu broadcast said young intellectuals had endorsed the men as brave patriots.

Other television broadcasts showed not only the dramatic scenes of a crowd of 120,000 celebrating their victory in Timisoara, but also the burning royal palace that had housed Rumania's kings until 1946.

Another broadcast showed Nicu Ceausescu, the favorite son of the presidential pair and lately considered the crown prince, being led into a television studio with his face severely bruised. The son, who is 39 years old, had been the party chief in Sibiu, in Transylvania, and was captured and disarmed after he tried to take command of a security police unit and to take hostages, the radio reported.

Nicu Ceausescu has been widely detested in Rumania since he ran over and killed a teen-age girl about 15 years ago on Aviator Square while driving fast under the influence of alcohol in his sports car in broad daylight. Well-documented stories of his debauchery have circulated for years in Rumania

Other Family Members

But there was no word of the fate of the other 40 members of the extended Ceausescu family, many of whom, like Lieut Gen. Ilie Ceausescu of the Army and Lieut. Gen. Nicolae Andruta Ceausescu of the Interior Ministry, the president's brothers, acquired prominent posts in recent years.

The key to the revolution Friday appears to have been the defection of key army commanders to the side of the growing mass of civilian protesters.

One of Mr. Ceausescu's last official acts Friday morning was to declare a state of martial law. Evidently the Defense Minister, Col. Gen. Vasile Milea, refused to carry out the Ceausescu order.

Bucharest Radio, still in the hands of Ceausescu loyalists, reported that General Milea, whom it described as "a traitor," had committed suicide. Later, however, the radio station on Nuferilor Street, a mile north of the Central Committee building, reported that General Milea had been shot, apparently by security forces loyal to the President.

Battle at TV Station

The radio station had been invaded and taken over by students. Army tanks came to defend it against attacks by security troops during the afternoon. Similarly, the headquarters of Rumanian television next to Lake Floreasca had been taken over by rebels and then besieged for a time by security troops, who later fell back.

Leading the army commanders who rose up against Mr. Ceausescu after the death of General Milea was General Gusa, the chief of the general staff.

About 6 P.M. Friday, Bucharest time, the radio station broadcast the following "particularly important" communique:

"Upon the order of General Gusa, anti-terrorist army troops have to come urgently to Boteanu Street 3 at the basement exit, the cafeteria, whose entrance is from the Plenarelor Street. The second entrance is opposite a garage. Signed by General Gusa." The site on Boteanu Street is adjacent to the Central Committee building and opposite the palace.

General Addresses Rally

Shortly before, General Gusa, addressing a rally while standing next to Ion Iliescu, a former Central Committee member who had been denounced by Mr. Ceausescu as a rival in 1971, said over the radio:

"Brothers, the army throughout the country is at the side of the people. It is the people's army. All army units, all garrisons, and all our country's cities are quiet. Please, do understand that we have to put order into things in Bucharest as well. Therefore, you have to help the military to be able to go where they have missions to fulfill. The army will always be with us and with you. We swear, we swear, we swear."

The task facing the army in cleaning out the pockets of security forces appeared to be formidable. According to radio reports, security forces tried to occupy both Otopeni International Airport six miles north of the center of Bucharest and the nearby Baneasa airport, which handles domestic flights.

"The Otopeni attack was repulsed first," said Romilo Limonedis of Radio Free Europe's Rumanian service. Both assaults occurred about 6 P.M. Friday, Bucharest time.

Recruited From Peasantry

The security troops are mostly recruited from the Rumanian peasantry and were handpicked for their loyalty to Mr. Ceausescu, and are paid twice the wages of university professors, with starting pay of about $420 a month.

Asked to explain the forces that came together to bring about his downfall, one of the United States Government's leading analysts of Rumanian affairs said today:

"I think it was a people in despair of their physical survival under Ceausescu, facing at last the choice to die fast or die slowly."

The analyst, who asked not to be identified, said a combination of desires for "religious rights and wanting to live like human beings finally reached a stage where helplessness was replaced by rage."

* * *

December 24, 1989

RUMANIAN INSURGENTS CAPTURE CEAUSESCU; HIS POLICE BATTLE WITH ARMY FOR SURVIVAL

By DAVID BINDER
Special to The New York Times

WASHINGTON, Dec. 23—Nicolae Ceausescu, the deposed Communist President of Rumania, was reported captured today as the army continued to do battle with the dictator's powerful security police in Bucharest and in at least half a dozen other Rumanian cities.

Truckloads of empty coffins were delivered to hospitals, and bodies were reported lying in the streets of various parts of the capital. But much of the fighting was in the center of the city, most notably near the television station where the news of the capture of Mr. Ceausescu and his wife was broadcast. The secret police launched rocket and grenade attacks at the broadcast center in an effort to seize the building and cut off the information that was sustaining the insurgents fighting with forces loyal to Mr. Ceausescu.

Pluralist System Promised

Despite those attempts, the Rumanian broadcast service was able to carry communiques from a hurriedly constituted Council of National Salvation giving credit to the army and to young people for leading the revolt. The messages were read by Ion Iliescu, who has been mentioned as a potential national leader.

He pledged to abandon the monopolistic pre-eminence of the Communist Party and adopt a pluralist system. In his appearance Mr. Iliescu referred to Mr. Ceausescu as a "poison hyena."

A few hours later, at around 5 P.M. Bucharest time, the radio and television reported that the 71-year-old Mr. Ceausescu had been arrested along with his wife, Elena, who had been his chief deputy. The announcement ended rumors that the couple managed to escape abroad on Friday.

Sites Change Hands

But confusion remained over which communications and transportation hubs in the country were in the control of insurgent forces that joined civilians in the national uprising, and

Rumanians taking refuge beside tanks that engaged security forces still loyal to Nicolae Ceausescu, the deposed Communist President, yesterday in Bucharest.

which were in the hands of secret police units still loyal to Mr. Ceausescu or fearful of reprisals from citizens if they were disarmed. Apparently some sites changed hands several times.

Artillery and mortar shelling and machine gun fire was heard in Bucharest all day, as well as in Timisoara and Sibiu, the radio and press agency reported.

At one point, officers in the Soviet Embassy in Bucharest said they had come under fire several times.

In Moscow, President Mikhail S. Gorbachev, said that he plans to confer with Warsaw Pact members because "the next day or two there could be some help needed, or medicine, because of this trouble." As the fighting continued in Bucharest, Xinhua, the Chinese press agency, reported that its office in the capital and the Chinese Embassy, "six kilometers away from the city's center," had been struck by bullets. A French television station reported that Jean-Louis Calderon, a 31-year-old reporter, was crushed to death by an army tank outside the Communist Party Central Committee building on Gheorghe Gheorghiu-Dej Square.

Americans Gather at Embassy

An American Embassy spokeswoman said that all Americans in Bucharest, including about 50 private citizens, had assembled at the Embassy on Dionisie Lupu Street and that all were safe. She also said that the Bucharest airports remained closed because of the fighting.

Otopeni, the international airport, and Baneasa, used for domestic flights, were both assaulted by forces of the security police, Securitate, in the night, but the army said both attacks were repulsed. The army also said it turned back an attack by Securitate paratroopers at Timisoara's airport Friday night.

Armed clashes with security forces were also reported today in the Danube port of Galati, Brasov, Arad, Cluj and Svintu Gheorghe. In Sibiu, according to a Rumanian radio report, Securitate forces in the Continental Hotel were besieged by students from the Sibiu Military Academy.

Hospitals Filled With Wounded

The security police also attacked gas pipelines, the Bucharest blood bank and, again and again, the 13-story main television building just below Lake Floreasca on the northern edge of the capital. Today, it was struck by rocket-propelled grenades for a time.

Bucharest's hospitals filled with wounded and dead, with the Emergency Hospital alone receiving 54 bodies today.

But in the broad boulevards, jubilant citizens waved the Rumanian flag, from which the Communist symbols, including a red star, pine trees, an oil rig and ears of wheat, had been ripped.

Tonight, the 1-day-old National Salvation Committee under Mr. Iliescu, a former Central Committee member, announced the formation of a provisional committee to run the country and prepare for free elections next spring. The committee announced that its Defense Minister would be Gen. Nicolae Militaru, an Army officer who was demoted by President Ceausescu.

Fighting Not Affected by Capture

The news of the capture of the Ceausescus, which was broadcast by Bucharest radio and television stations just before 5 P.M. Rumanian time, apparently had no immediate impact on Securitate units still fighting with army forces this evening.

Also under arrest are the Interior Minister, Tudor Postelnicu, 57, and the Deputy Prime Minister, Ion Dinca, who holds the rank of lieutenant general.

But today, Col. Gen. Iulian Vlad, the 58-year-old chairman of the Department of State Security, went on the state radio to declare that he was siding with the insurgents. He ordered the security troops to side with the people and the Army "against the Ceausescu clan." It was not immediately clear how widely his order was being obeyed, or, indeed, if it was being obeyed at all.

The relationship between the security police and the army is complex, according to a United States Government official who is a specialist on the Rumanian armed forces. The Securitate troops number 30,000, while the army has about 176,000, the official said. But the security police, though lacking the heaviest weapons, are said to be much better trained and equipped and more highly paid than the army. They also enjoyed privileges denied most Rumanians, receiving generous allotments of food, fuel and electricity that are strictly rationed.

As Many As 12,000 Dead

Rumanian and Yugoslav press agencies spoke of thousands of dead, including as many as 12,000 citizens killed in the city of Timisoara alone. It was there, some 280 miles west of Bucharest that the first anti-Ceausescu demonstrations began on Dec. 15. In addition, reports said hundreds of citizens have been killed in Bucharest since mass demonstrations against the regime began there on Thursday, when President Ceausescu was booed and shouted into a stunned silence for three minutes as he tried to deliver a speech a day after his return from a three-day state visit to Iran. Security police opened fire on the jeering crowd.

Despite the carnage, the crowds returned on Friday, gathering in huge demonstrations throughout the city, including one in front of the former royal palace where Mr. Ceausescu lived with his 70-year-old wife, who served as his deputy. By Friday afternoon the couple fled the capital by helicopter.

The Ceausescus landed in Tirgoviste, a medieval town 45 miles northwest of Bucharest that he designated as the nation's second capital in 1986. They raced off in an automobile and were later seen switching to a second car. Then they vanished until this afternoon.

But the Ceausescus' eldest son, Nicu, a 39-year-old who was the party leader in Sibiu, in central Transylvania, was captured Friday evening after he tried to take command of the Securitate forces in his region. He was shown on Rumanian television with a bruise on the left side of his face.

Today, the army announced that it had also placed under arrest Mr. Ceausescu's brother Lieut. Gen. Ilie Ceausescu, who headed the Communist Party's political directorate of the army. There was no word about the fate of the 35 or so other members of the extended Ceausescu family, many of whom held high Government positions.

The initial report on the apprehension of the Ceausescus carried by Agerpres, the Rumanian press agency, said they had been "captured and arrested in Tirgoviste." Subsequent reports indicated they might have taken refuge at a nearby military airport.

Personal Stake for Securitate

The official who is expert on Rumanian defense force noted that the Securitate troops have had a personal stake in remaining loyal to Mr. Ceausescu because of the privileges they have received. He added that the wrath directed at the Securitate left some of its men and women with the sense that they were fighting for their own lives as well as those of the Ceausescus.

The army, on the other hand, scrimping with a sharply reduced defense budget, has had to curtail military exercises in recent years and now rates as the most poorly trained in the Warsaw Pact.

The official cautioned, however, against a "black and white" depiction placing all of the army on one side of the fighting and all of the security troops on the other. "There may have been some crossovers," the official said.

But there is a strong suspicion among United States Government analysts that some of Mr. Ceausescu's loyal aides, or perhaps Mr. Ceausescu himself, may have spent last night and early this morning sending out orders to security forces for specific attacks in Timisoara, Sibiu and Bucharest itself.

"It looks too well coordinated," said one official, noting that the Securitate assaults on the Bucharest airports and the Timisoara airport late last night were almost simultaneous, as were attacks on the Bucharest radio and television stations, which are about one and one-half miles apart.

If indeed as one report suggested, the Ceausescus spent the night at the military airport at Titu, 18 miles south of Tirgoviste, that would have provided the deposed leader the communication equipment he needed to send out orders to his security troops.

*   *   *

December 26, 1989

ARMY EXECUTES CEAUSESCU AND WIFE FOR 'GENOCIDE' ROLE, BUCHAREST SAYS

By JOHN KIFNER

Special to The New York Times

BUCHAREST, Rumania, Tuesday, Dec. 26—Nicolae Ceausescu, absolute ruler of Rumania for 24 years, and his wife were executed on Monday by the army that he once commanded, the Free Rumanian Television of the new provisional government said.

A first brief announcement said an "extraordinary military court" had tried Mr. Ceausescu and his wife, Elena, who was widely viewed as the country's second most powerful figure until widespread demonstrations forced the pair to flee the capital on Friday morning. They were reportedly captured on Saturday in Tirgoviste.

At 1:30 this morning, a few hours after the report of the executions, the television showed its first footage of the Ceausescus in captivity.

Evidence of Capture

Some of the footage appeared to be from Monday's trial. The words "condemned to death" were barely audible on the fuzzy sound track. At one point, Mr. Ceausescu slammed his fur cap on the table. At times he seemed contemptuous. His wife appeared frightened.

The film, which opened with a doctor taking Mr. Ceausescu's blood pressure, was the first solid evidence that he had indeed been captured. The sound track also referred to the billion dollars he was said to have secreted abroad.

"The sentence was death and the sentence was executed," said the television announcement. It was proclaimed in the name of a largely faceless revolutionary government, the Council of National Salvation, which took power after the Ceausescus fled.

Few Details on Execution

It has not been made clear exactly when, where, how or on whose authority the Ceausescus were put to death, and their bodies had not been shown.

The charges against the Ceausescus, according to the television announcement, included the "genocide" of 60,000 people, many of whom died in the last week of fighting; undermining state power; destroying the country's economic and spiritual values, and trying to escape the country to claim $1 billion reportedly hidden abroad.

The Rumanian television said this morning that fighting near its studios in the capital was preventing staff members from getting footage of the execution on the air, Reuters reported.

The television studio has been the focus of heavy fighting between the Rumanian Army, which has sided with the popular uprising, and the security police, which is loyal to the Ceausescu regime. It is not known whether the security forces will fight on after the death of their leaders, but the

CNN

In a picture taken from Rumanian television, President Nicolae Ceausescu and his wife, Elena, are shown in a courtroom during a military trial before their reported execution. No pictures of the execution were shown.

insurgents clearly hope to demoralize them by showing proof of the executions.

The announcement of the execution came as Rumanians celebrated a bittersweet Christmas, treasuring their newfound and tentative liberties but mourning the many hundreds and perhaps thousands slain in the uprising.

The capital was calmer on Monday, with Rumanians strolling the boulevards and only an occasional burst of gunfire. The army appeared to be consolidating control over the remaining bands of now-renegade secret policemen, the backbone of the old order.

A Christmas tree stood on the balcony of the Communist Party headquarters this afternoon. It was placed in the spot where only last Thursday Mr. Ceausescu was hooted into shocked silence, jeered by a crowd that had been summoned to hear him condemn protests in a western city, Timisoara.

Sightseers wandered where fighting took place over the weekend between diehard security forces, who had sustained the reign of the Ceausescus, and a spontaneous coalition that united army units and irate civilians. Among those who turned out were several hundred people who gathered in front of party headquarters early this morning chanting, "We want Ceausescu hanged here at the palace!"

Shrines for Slain Students

New newspapers have been printed in the last few days with names like Freedom, Liberty and Free Rumania. One paper that appeared as Spark when it was put under sanctions by Mr. Ceausescu renamed itself Truth. On Monday, when truckers drove by tossing out copies of the new papers, crowds rushed into the streets to grab them. "We had cold, hunger and terror," was the way one of the papers, Free Youth, described the past regime.

At a Christmas Mass at the Rumanian Orthodox Cathedral, the center of the major religion, Patriarch Teoctist Arapafu hailed "these brave young people, these young boys and girls who have died for freedom."

"They will live in our hearts forever," he said. At the same time, the Patriarch, who had cooperated with Mr. Ceausescu's Government, acknowledged that despite what he called shocking times, "I did not have the courage these children have shown."

Although orthodox, the Rumanian Church observes the same calendar of holy days as does Catholicism, the next-largest denomination in the country. But under the old regime, observances of Christmas were celebrated in private or in secrecy.

Downfall of 'Leader for Life'

The reported execution of Mr. Ceausescu and his wife, along with the capture of his brother, son and daughter, ended nearly a quarter-century of absolute power. Mr. Ceausescu was routinely idolized as the "leader for life," with accounts of his daily routine dominating the local newspapers and the two hours each day that Rumanian television was on the air.

His harsh rule, enforced by a hated secret police and a system in which one in four Rumanians was said to be an informer, included drastic measures to pay off the foreign debt. Those included cutting off heat and electricity during the fierce Central European winter and exporting harvests of food while keeping citizens on meager rations.

But as in other Communist countries, a privileged inner circle of the party elite enjoyed amenities like ski and hunting resorts and special food shops.

The television made much of the luxurious circumstances in which Zoia Ceausescu, the ousted leader's daughter, lived, noting that $100,000 had been found in her home after she was captured over the weekend.

As in several other parts of the Soviet bloc, rigid and seemingly entrenched one-man and one-party rule has collapsed in the face of popular protest. Here the process was tougher and more violent both during the years of oppressive rule and in the days that have seen it toppled.

Accounts of extraordinary brutality that have been widely circulated included massacres by the secret police and confirmed reports of people buried in mass graves in Timisoara after they were shot for protesting 10 days ago. Still, no thorough accounting of the death toll has been made.

Thousands have died in the last two weeks, said Victor Ciobanu, the Health Minister in the old regime, as he appeared on television tonight. Mr. Ciobanu has given his support to the new but so far formless revolutionary leadership. But he rejected as grossly exaggerated the reports broadcast on Sunday by the Hungarian radio that as many as 60,000 had been killed. That figure would amount to more than twice the 30,000 who were thought to have died in the Hungarian uprising of 1956, crushed by Soviet force.

The membership of the new government has not been made public for what its spokesman says are security reasons. But it is known to include a number of members of recent governments, some of whom had fallen out with Mr. Ceausescu.

Those include Corneliu Manescu, a former Foreign Minister; Ion Iliescu, a onetime member of the Politburo who had quarreled with the former President; and two top military figures: the chief of the general staff, Gen. Stefan Gusa, and the Deputy Foreign Minister, Ion Stanculescu.

All along the main boulevard, named for Ana Ipatescu, a Communist heroine, thousands of people strolled today, pausing to look at handbills hailing the revolution that were posted in store windows. They barely flinched as bursts of gunfire sounded a few blocks away, although at one point a group took refuge in doorways when the gunfire sounded too close.

The demonstrators chanted "Arafat and Qaddafi, you have taken our bread!" reflecting a widespread resentment of Arabs, who had formerly received privileged treatment here.

There are constant rumors on the street that the security police is made up of Arabs and Iranians. A Rumanian television cameraman, racing from the television headquarters late Monday afternoon, said, "We are fighting four armies here: Palestinians, Syrians, Libyans and Iranians."

* * *

December 27, 1989

FOR AN UNREPENTENT CEAUSESCU, SUMMARY JUSTICE

By Reuters

BUCHAREST, Rumania, Dec. 26—Nicolae Ceausescu and his wife, Elena, went to their deaths by firing squad defiantly spurning the right of their military accusers to judge them.

"I do not recognize this court," the deposed Rumanian leader repeatedly told the military prosecutor in a videotape broadcast by Rumanian television tonight. "I will be judged only by the people."

Mr. Ceausescu, seized on Friday after the revolution that overthrew him, was executed with Mrs. Ceausescu after a swift trial on Monday found them guilty of genocide and other crimes against the state.

The television did not show the couple's faces when their death sentence was pronounced, but Mr. Ceausescu was heard clearly to say: "It doesn't matter. It has no importance."

'Read the Constitution'

The hourlong videotape of the final hours of the couple who ruled Rumania with an iron hand for 24 years showed Mr. Ceausescu, 71 years old, arguing angrily at the army tribunal and declaring in a loud voice: "I do not recognize this court. Read the Constitution."

"We've read the Constitution," an off-screen voice answered. "We know it better than you."

"I will not answer a single question," Mr. Ceausescu said. It ended with a final scene of Mr. Ceausescu lying on his back alongside his wife in front of a concrete wall, his eyes open and blood oozing from his head.

The television never showed his accusers but broadcast their voices.

At one stage, challenged on what he had done for society, the deposed President said, "I built hospitals."

Questioned about food shortages, he curtly retorted, "The people have 200 kilos of corn."

Mr. Ceausescu and his wife, who was also his second-in-command, were shown sitting at a table in a sparsely furnished room. Both were dressed neatly, he in a black coat and she in a fur-collared topcoat.

They sat grim-faced, listening attentively to the accusers. From time to time Mr. Ceausescu put his hand on Mrs. Ceausescu's to reassure her.

'I Will Answer Nothing'

"I will answer nothing," Mr. Ceausescu said. "I will sign nothing. I will not recognize this court."

The interrogator asked, "Who ordered the shooting of the people?"

"I will not answer a single question," Mr. Ceausescu replied. "Do not interpret my silence as answers."

"I will only answer to the working class," said Mr. Ceausescu, who often stared at the ceiling during the proceeding. "I will tell the people. I will answer to the working class."

"The people should fight to destroy this band, which together with foreign powers wants to destroy the country and has carried out a coup!" he screamed, pointing frantically with his finger.

He often wagged his finger in a lecturing gesture and sometimes waved his hand. Mrs. Ceausescu occasionally smiled and mumbled.

The interrogator asked: "What possessed you to reduce the people to the state they are in? Not even the peasants had enough wheat and had to come to Bucharest to buy bread. Why did the people have to starve?"

Mr. Ceausescu replied: "This is a lie. Think carefully. It is a lie and proves the lack of patriotism currently in the country."

The interrogator said: "You destroyed the Rumanian people and their economy. Such things are unheard of in the civilized world."

'Everything It Needed'

Mr. Ceausescu said: "We do not intend to argue with you. The population had everything it needed."

"I will answer only to the people's Parliament in connection with treason and the coup and how things happened in Rumanian history, and you will all answer to the people," Mr. Ceausescu said.

Mrs. Ceausescu stared absently with apparent lack of interest. She seemed exhausted and was slumped against the wall in her chair most of the time. But sometimes her eyes darted back and forth.

"How can you let them speak to you like that?" she asked her husband at one point.

The off-screen voice said, "Let Elena Ceausescu tell us about the costs of publishing her books abroad."

She replied angrily, "I gave my entire life for my people," and made chopping motions with her hand. "Our people."

'We Condemn You to Death'

The off-screen voice said: "On the basis of the actions of the members of the Ceausescu family, we condemn the two of you to death. We confiscate all your property."

There followed a freeze-frame on the tape, and the accused pair's reactions were not visible.

"Please enter into the minutes that all the conditions exist to bring a verdict of guilty," the voice said.

The off-screen voice, in a tone that was angry and decisive, then listed the articles under which the two were found guilty.

"Your crimes were such that you merit the biggest penalty," the voice said.

Mr. Ceausescu tried to comfort his wife by touching her hand. She looked down and licked her lips.

"It is sad that you do not wish to confess the crimes you have committed against the Rumanian people," the voice said. "You have not only deprived the people of bread and heating, but you imprisoned the Rumanian spirit, which could not express itself in any way. You took oxygen from the wounded."

"Your terrorists supplied themselves in the underground and opposed the people," the voice said. "You have drained us. You call on the people. How can you face this very people?" Mrs. Ceausescu laughed. "This laugh says all that needs to be said about you," the voice said. "On the basis of your behavior, you belong in a madhouse. The two of you, if you beg my pardon, should listen to what I am saying."

"You have nothing to say about the revolution? The blood spilled in Timisoara?" the voice continued, referring to the reported massacre of thousands of anti-Government demonstrators that ignited the current unrest 10 days ago.

'You Are Putschists'

Mr. Ceausescu stood up. "I can only be accused by the people's Parliament," he said. "You are putschists, the destroyers of Rumania's independence." He sat down again. "I was respected when I went to the factories—"

But the voice interrupted him before he could finish.

When ordered to stand, the Ceausescus refused.

"It is unanimously decided that Ceausescu Nicolae and Ceausescu Elena be given the maximum sentence for genocide against the Rumanian people and the destruction of the Rumanian land," the voice said.

Mr. Ceausescu declared, "I refuse to recognize this court." The footage stopped. Then scenes of Mr. Ceausescu's blood-stained corpse, previously shown on television, were screened again.

* * *

December 28, 1989

RUMANIANS MOVING TO ABOLISH WORST OF REPRESSIVE ERA

By CELESTINE BOHLEN
Special to The New York Times

BUCHAREST, Rumania, Dec. 27—Seeking to dismantle the legacy of Nicolae Ceausescu, the executed dictator, Rumania today lifted some of the controls that have made this country one of the most repressive in Europe.

The new provisional Government abolished a requirement that all typewriters be registered with the state, and legalized abortion, an offense for which violators were jailed. And under a decree published today, Rumanian citizens are freed of the obligation to address each other as "comrade."

But even as calm descended on the capital after five nights of gunfire, the Government invoked "revolutionary" conditions as it instituted special military tribunals to track down, try and punish armed Ceausescu supporters.

Caution Returns at Night

Although Bucharest was quiet tonight, pedestrians picked their way home cautiously, accustomed to the frequent and random sniper shots of recent days.

But during the day, crowds strolled leisurely past the hull of the burned-out national library on Palace Square, and past the offices of the Communist Party's Central Committee, scene of fierce fighting over the weekend, to look at the tanks parked there.

In the subways, self-appointed youths checking people's documents and searching for weapons have set up shop for the long haul, even as the threat from the renegade security forces of Mr. Ceausescu seemed to lessen. Today, for the first time, there were no spontaneous demonstrations in the center of the city of the kind that have filled the streets here since the ouster of Mr. Ceausescu last Friday.

Scenes of Trial and Death

The Government-controlled television tonight again showed tapes of the former ruler's trial on Christmas Day, during which he angrily dismissed the charges against him and vowed to take his case to the "working class."

Today, for the first time, a full view of the body of Elena Ceausescu, the President's wife, was shown on television. Both she and her husband were laid out on army cots, their bloody coats loosely draped around them.

Workers at Free Rumanian Television said today that the tape of the Ceausescu trial, first shown in still pictures on Monday night, had to be edited to delete the faces of the judges because of their fears of retaliation by Ceausescu loyalists. A Government spokesman today refused to disclose where the executions had taken place.

A witness to the executions, who asked not to be identified, said in an interview that soldiers in the firing squad "could not restrain their hate" and "fired immediately, with abandon."

There have been widely varying estimates of the number of people killed in the years that Mr. Ceausescu was in power, with the tribunal that condemned him to death hearing a figure of 60,000. However, specifics and dates of the killings remain elusive. There seems general agreement that thousands have died, many of them since the revolution began in the western city of Timisoara almost two weeks ago.

These days, some Rumanians are troubled by the heavily propagandistic character of the television and the newspapers under the control of the Council of National Salvation, the formal name for the revolutionary leadership. They are carrying Government decrees and exhortatory articles with little commentary, investigative reports or analysis, leading some to question whether the new council is abusing its control over the media.

Also, they note, some essential rights—like freedom to travel outside the country—have not yet been clarified. Debates on these and other issues among the 37 members of the ruling council are not publicized, and some groups, particularly students, are demanding more openness at the top.

With the Communist Party in tatters after the collapse of the Ceausescu leadership in this month's uprising, the role to be played by former Communists in the new Government has become an important issue.

Students and dissident intellectuals have expressed dissatisfaction at the appointment of several onetime Communist officials, including the President, Ion Iliescu, a former Cabinet minister and party secretary, to top jobs in the Government. Mr. Iliescu spoke by telephone today with the Soviet President, Mikhail S. Gorbachev, and thanked him for backing the revolution, the press agency Tass reported from Moscow.

Mr. Iliescu and Mr. Gorbachev reportedly are friends from their college days in Moscow.

And the new Vice President, Dumitru Mazilu, told reporters that people with a record of collaboration with the Ceausescu regime would have no role in the new Government.

New Plans, New People

"Such people who are not clean, we will not work with them," said Mr. Mazilu, a former diplomat who was placed under house arrest after he criticized Rumania's human rights record. "We have a plan for a new Government, with new people."

However, the problem is a delicate one in a country where four million people are past or present members of the Communist Party. Rumanians and Western diplomats agree that the new Government will have to draw on the pool of former Communist bureaucrats to keep things running.

And today, at a news conference, a spokesman for the Foreign Ministry ruled out any kind of a witch hunt in the bureaucracy. "We believe we will have to proceed very carefully," said Corneliu Bogdan, a new Cabinet minister. "There are some people who expressed their views and suffered, and some complied. We have to remember that not everyone can be a hero."

"The first question will be competence," said Mr. Bogdan, a former Ambassador to the United States, who in recent years had been regarded as a dissident. He added that it is inaccurate to describe new political parties springing up as anti-Government. "There can be no opposition party because there is no party in government," Mr. Bogdan said.

No Confusion at the Top

The council, he said, is made up of a "remarkable consensus, one of the great unique features of the Rumanian revolution." He denied that there was any confusion in the new Government, which will serve until elections in April.

"We have a program, but we need tranquillity," he said.

From its makeshift headquarters at the Foreign Ministry, the Government has been issuing a stream of decrees this week. The army has been put in charge of the Securitate, the security force many of whose members remained loyal to Mr. Ceausescu. Harsh residence laws that restricted mobility have been dropped, and the Government has promised to pay back to its citizens money taken out of their paychecks for "economic development" in recent years.

Since 1966, Rumania has practically banned abortions, first for women with less than four children and later for those with less than five. The law, drawn to promote population growth in this country of 23 million, was hated by most women here, some of whom resorted to dangerous self-induced abortions. Because the law also penalized doctors who treated women who had performed abortions on themselves, hospitals often turned away patients or treated them under a different guise.

"It was the most horrible law," a young Rumanian woman said. "Even pregnant women did not want to be checked, which meant a lot of people who needed care were frightened to get it." Abortion is a primary means of birth control throughout Eastern Europe.

Also halted was a hated modernization program that had razed villages and destroyed old buildings in Rumania. In its place, a program has been created to preserve national monuments, and a call has been issued for historians to write "the true history of the country." Another measure adopted today resurrected the Rumanian Society of Philosophy, an 80-year-old institution that had been dissolved under Communist rule.

Feeding Rumanians First

But for the population, the most visible changes have come from swift measures taken to ease the harshness of life under Mr. Ceausescu. Food saved for export will be used at home.

And today in Bucharest, crates with Cyrillic lettering filled with chickens headed for the Soviet Union showed up at local stores, along with oranges and lemons.

Rationing was immediately lifted after Mr. Ceausescu's ouster last Friday, and Rumanians did not wait for instructions to turn up the heat in their apartments, celebrating the end of a painful austerity program.

Today, the Government announced "emergency measures to strike at the lingering threat from members of the Securitate, who until Tuesday were waging urban guerrilla warfare against the army.

*   *   *

December 31, 1989

IN A DICTATOR'S PALACE, LAVISH ECHOES OF POWER

By ALAN COWELL
Special to The New York Times

BUCHAREST, Rumania, Dec. 30—For the last five years, 8,000 workers and 7,000 soldiers toiled each day to build the House of the Republic, a great and solid palace measuring 300 feet from ground to flagpole that was to have been a memorial to a man and his wife—Nicolae and Elena Ceausescu.

Today, a week after the couple's execution, the forbidding three-tiered building, still uncompleted, stands pale and solid in the snowstorms that have blanketed Bucharest for the last two days, dominating the Boulevard of Socialist Victory that runs two-thirds of a mile before it, lined by 1,500 empty apartments once destined to house the party faithful.

But its huge bulk holds none of the glory supposed to be encased in its salons and galleries of marble lighted by crystal chandeliers, one of which is said to weigh as much as five tons.

Rather, it and other official buildings here reflect the twin poles of the dictator's 24 years in power—the will to cow and subdue a people through raw power and its daunting symbols and the constant nagging fear of revolt that prompted Mr. Ceausescu to couple the grandeur above ground with labyrinthine tunnels, escape routes and bunkers below it.

A Bleak Memorial

It stands thus as a monument of a kind different from the one its myriad architects planned—a bleak memorial to hubris brought low.

"There are tunnels, tunnels and bunkers below us," said Col. Constantin Luta, a three-star officer who was Mr. Ceausescu's master builder for the House of the Republic, but who like the rest of the army now supports the new provisional Government. Reporters could not enter the tunnels, he said, because they may have been booby-trapped by "terrorists," the name commonly used for the pro-Ceausescu security forces that opposed last week's rebellion.

Elsewhere, however, reporters have gained access to some of these complexes, notably those that lie beneath what used to be the Central Committee headquarters of the Rumanian Communist Party, where soldiers said today they feared that somewhere far below them scores if not hundreds of "terrorists" may still be holed up.

"No one is sure where the tunnels lead or how they are laid out," said a soldier on guard outside the Communist Party headquarters today. "It is not safe to go there."

Rumanian troops marching in the snow past the unfinished House of the Republic, Nicolae Ceausescu's palace, under construction for five years.

3 Levels of Tunnels

The soldier said that below the Communist Party building was three levels of tunnels, stocked with food and guns and fresh water and leading to a bunker supposedly capable of withstanding nuclear attack. Reporters have visited only the upper layers, where one refrigerator, the soldier said, is filled with beef and ham and where soldiers keep a nervous guard.

The soldiers say many weapons have been found there, including sniper rifles with night scopes.

Yet for those who live here, the fascination is as much with what is above the ground as with what is below it.

"Generally, the Government buildings were not open for the people," said Nicolae Padararu, an official guide who acted as a translator for Colonel Luta at the House of the Republic today. The old royal palace elsewhere in Bucharest that was the presidential residence was set ablaze in the wave of outrage that prompted the Ceausescus to flee the capital on Dec. 22.

Discovering a Gilded Life

Over the last week, as the secrecy has been stripped from a dictatorship that ruled in the name of socialism, Rumanians have discovered many things about how their leaders lived a gilded and whimsical life while they strained under hardships.

At the Ceausescus' villa outside Bucharest, for instance, reporters have been shown the twin apartments where the couple, both of lowly origins, maintained separate suites of rooms, adorned by expensive works of art.

Mrs. Ceausescu, according to visitors in the villa, had accumulated a wardrobe of shoes that rivaled in style and number those of Imelda Marcos in the Philippines. Some, the visitors said, had diamond-encrusted heels designed and bought in Paris.

At the House of the Republic, the Staircase of Honor, the wide marble steps leading from the chandeliered entrance hall to the rest of the complex, stands unfinished. The reason for this, Colonel Luta said, is that Mr. Ceausescu could not quite decide how he wanted it so it has been rebuilt seven or eight times.

Extensive Lighting

More telling at the House of the Republic is the lighting.

Colonel Luta did not permit reporters to visit the plenary hall, where the five-ton chandelier is found. "How big is it?"

reporters asked another army officer. He grimaced, struggled for words, then shrugged and said: "Big." Then how much power did it consume? Colonel Luta said he could not guess, but volunteered that the lighting in Ceausescu's offices at the House of the Republic devoured 85,000 watts.

Under the austerity that prevailed here for the majority of the people, electric power was scarce and rationed. Whole villages would be cut off if they consumed more than their quota. Power was regularly severed in midwinter, leaving homes dark and freezing, so as to save money to repay a huge foreign debt. Apartments were limited to one 60-watt bulb a room, so that Mr. Ceausescu's offices consumed the same power, roughly, as 350 four-room apartments.

The House of the Republic has "thousands" of rooms, Colonel Luta said. Its floor space is over 400,000 square feet and 13 stories. It was to house the State Council and other institutions of power as well as the Ceausescus in their still-unfinished apartment.

50,000 People Displaced

The Rumania Hall—the central area for receptions—is almost as big as a football field, 240 feet long and 90 feet wide, with tower ceilings covered in gold leaf on pink gypsum. The marble columns are hand-carved. Up to 50,000 people lost their homes, so that the site for it could be cleared when building started in 1984. Its outer dimensions are roughly 840 feet long, 720 feet wide and 330 feet to the top of the soaring stone needle that acts as a flagpole. It is about two-thirds finished and the cost has run into "tens of billions of lei," the local currency traded in the banks at nine to the dollar. Whole industries were set up to feed the palace's demands for marble and timber. Construction accidents claimed 20 lives.

Yet by Colonel Luta's account, the Ceausescus oversaw its building with the same solicitousness as a couple keeping watch on a more modest renovation.

"Ceausescu came every week, sometimes three times a week," Colonel Luta said. Sometimes, he and Elena, who was regarded as the second most powerful person in the land, could not quite agree on the features and fittings.

"First he wanted some of the floors to be all marble. Then when his wife came she said she wanted wood. So all the marble was torn up and destroyed," Colonel Luta said, adding that "as a rule she agreed with his decisions." "When there was an argument, they delayed and would come back with a common solution worked out in the family itself."

*   *   *

January 3, 1990

RIGHTS OF THE TURKS PROTESTED

By Reuters

KURDZHALI, Bulgaria, Jan. 2—Angry Bulgarians chanting anti-Turkish songs dating back to Ottoman rule demonstrated in this southern town today against a decision to grant religious rights to local Bulgarian Turks.

Policemen with riot sticks kept about 1,000 Bulgarians and Bulgarian Turks apart at the protest outside Communist Party headquarters. Shouts of "Bulgaria! Bulgaria!" and "No to Turkish slavery!" were answered with: "Give us our names back! We want our rights!"

The Bulgarians are angry at a decision by the country's new Communist leaders to grant religious rights to Bulgarian Turks and to allow them to use Muslim names.

About 10,000 Bulgarians staged a similar protest Monday in Kurdzhali, 160 miles south of the capital, Sofia, and about 600 Bulgarians in 120 cars were en route to Sofia, where they planned to protest at the National Assembly building.

Program of Equal Rights

Local Communist authorities in Kurdzhali, a predominantly Turkish town of 50,000 people, decided Saturday to defy the Central Committee's decision to overturn the policy of forced assimilation of Bulgarian Turks.

The Bulgarians, who said they were not consulted about the decision, demanded a national referendum to decide the fate of the country's 1.5 million Bulgarian Turks, many of whom live in this mountain region near Turkey.

In Istanbul, the Bulgarian Consul, Nicolay Buvcukov, said today his Government planned to free Bulgarian Turks jailed for opposition to a now discredited assimilation campaign.

"The new leadership of the Bulgarian Communist Party is now openly and sincerely telling the truth," Mr. Buvcukov told a news conference in Istanbul. "It will strive for equal rights for every citizen without considering religion or race."

He said the amnesty bill would be submitted to Parliament Jan. 19 and would probably take effect by the end of the month. He could not say how many prisoners would be affected.

*   *   *

January 3, 1990

BUCHAREST SAYS ENTIRE POLITBURO RULED BY CEAUSESCU IS IN CUSTODY

By CELESTINE BOHLEN
Special to The New York Times

BUCHAREST, Jan. 2—All members of the Rumanian Politburo commanded by Nicolae Ceausescu, the executed dictator, are in detention, a spokesman for the current Government declared today.

Constantin Girbea, a Foreign Ministry official, said that more than three dozen members of the ruling body of the Rumanian Communist Party were taken into custody in the wake of the flight and execution of Mr. Ceausescu and his wife, Elena.

Mr. Girbea added that 20 other close associates of Mr. Ceausescu were also in prison. He did not disclose what charges had been filed in all these cases, but he declared that all "evildoers from the old regime will be brought to justice."

Press Agency Reorganized

The spokesman also reported that the official Rumanian press agency, Agerpress, had been disbanded for having lost credibility in the Ceausescu years. A new agency formed to take its place, to be called Rompress, would no longer be under state control.

These announcements came as people at the very center of the revolution were debating whether their efforts were fully spontaneous or whether the spark of protest had been fanned by a small conspiratorial group that first coalesced as long as six months ago.

An amateur video, taken just as power was changing hands in Rumania on Dec. 22, shows Gen. Nicolae Militaru—who was later made Minister of Defense—saying that the ruling Council of National Salvation had been in existence for six months.

This comment and other details of contacts among core members of the council in the days before the fall of Mr. Ceausescu suggest that plans for a new government were further along than spokesmen have been willing to admit.

The issue of how the council was formed is a delicate one here as small parties emerge in opposition to the ruling group, and as many Rumanians complain that the council is not practicing the pluralist policies it says it has adopted.

Government spokesmen asserted today that General Militaru's comment could not be heard on the film, which was shown Monday night during a joint French-Rumanian broadcast with a French voice-over. During the broadcast, Prime Minister Petre Roman also denied that the Council of National Salvation predated the revolution.

"Absolutely not," he said in French, showing anger at the French commentator. "We had no contact. It was spontaneous. The front was created on the spot."

But today, Rumanians listening to the conversations on the videotape, filmed four hours after Mr. Ceausescu and his wife fled Bucharest, confirmed that General Militaru did make the comment during a debate on what to call the new provisional government.

President Ion Iliescu and Prime Minister Roman were present, along with General Militaru, at the filmed meeting, described as the first gathering of the council. Also shown were Dumitru Mazilu, the new Vice President, and Silviu Brucan, an influential member of the council's Executive Bureau.

According to the tape, someone proposed calling the new Government the Democratic Front, a name that was dismissed as too vague. General Militaru then proposed the name Council of National Salvation, since it "has been functioning for six months."

'At the Head of a Wave'

Since they first announced their existence on national television on Dec. 22, members of the council have said they first came together during the early, chaotic hours of the revolution, after demonstrators stormed the giant headquarters of the Rumanian Communist Party on Palace Square.

"We found ourselves at the head of a wave," Mr. Roman said on television Monday night. "There was nothing organized ahead of time."

Western diplomats said today that a letter from an anonymous organization calling itself the National Salvation Front had been received by Radio Free Europe several months ago on the eve of the 14th congress of the Rumanian Communist Party.

But, they said, many such open letters, without signatures, are sent to foreign embassies or news organizations. "There have been a number of different groups writing letters but they are very ephemeral," said one diplomat.

In an interview this week, Mr. Brucan said that Mr. Iliescu and Mr. Roman, who have a long friendship, had been in touch between Dec. 17, the day Government troops fired on civilians in the western Rumanian city of Timisoara, and Dec. 21, when the violence spread to Bucharest.

'We Could Count on Militaru'

He also said that he and other dissidents were aware of the sympathies of General Militaru, a retired army general who had served as commander of the Bucharest garrison. The army in Rumania had long been considered a weak link in the chain that Mr. Ceausescu had forged to keep Rumania under his control.

"We knew from the very beginning—that is for many years—that we could count on Militaru," Mr. Brucan said. "We knew he is a man of courage, an adversary of Ceausescu."

Although General Militaru was retired, Mr. Brucan said he had kept up contacts with his old colleagues.

"Militaru had his men he knew he could trust. There were very many generals who were against Ceausescu, but few who were ready to act against him," Mr. Brucan said. "It was very risky."

The decision of the army on Dec. 22 to support the revolution was critical to its success. In the new Government, the army plays the most prominent role, with four officers—including General Militaru—holding ministerial posts.

Mr. Brucan said the conversations last month between Mr. Iliescu and Mr. Roman were not intended to create a shadow government, but to discuss who still serving at high levels of the Ceausescu regime might be receptive to clandestine contacts.

"They were talking in general about who among those in power they should contact, who among the generals," he said.

Council Has Expanded

Neither Mr. Brucan nor Mr. Mazilu were part of the conversations, because both were under house arrest before Dec. 22.

The first public announcement of the council's makeup listed 39 members, including dissidents, former Communist Party members, intellectuals and artists. It has since expanded to 150 members, but key decisions are made by an 11-member bureau, which according to one member now meets every other day.

The videotape, which showed the first meeting of the new Government, also revealed its careful relations with the

Soviet Union, a neighboring country which had bad relations with Rumania during the Ceausescu era. On the tape, President Iliescu is heard saying on the afternoon of Dec. 22 that he had been in touch with the Soviet Embassy.

"I have been in contact with the Embassy of the U.S.S.R. and have kept them abreast of the situation we are in, so that they can tell Moscow who we are and what we want," he is heard as saying.

*   *   *

January 13, 1990

RUMANIAN LEADERS OUTLAW OUSTED COMMUNIST PARTY

By DAVID BINDER
Special to The New York Times

BUCHAREST, Jan. 12—Bowing to demands of thousands of irate demonstrators, leaders of Rumania's governing Council of National Salvation agreed tonight to outlaw the Communist Party and to hold a national referendum on restoring the death penalty.

An estimated 5,000 people joined the rally, the first public demonstration against the new leadership that took power last month in the revolution against the Communist Government of President Nicolae Ceausescu.

Rumania is the only country in the Eastern Bloc to have outlawed the Communist Party, the only party it had before the revolution in December. But the country's new political picture is by far the most chaotic, with a hastily organized Government that has not been elected and almost no organized opposition.

Appearing increasingly shaky in their three weeks of rule, the Council's chairman, Ion Iliescu, and Prime Minister Petre Roman also agreed to appoint a commission to receive complaints from the public.

Council Seems to Lose Ground

The Council of National Salvation appeared to have lost ground in a number of Rumanian cities. There were reports tonight that local governments affiliated with the Council had been ousted in Timisoara, Brasov, Iasi and other major cities. In at least one of those cities, Iasi, the army was reported to have taken control.

The demonstration in Bucharest began at noon as a commemorative ceremony in Palace Square to mourn the thousands of Rumanians killed in the uprising against Mr. Ceausescu.

The crowd grew, and soon there were cries for the ouster of Silviu Brucan, a veteran Communist who was held under house arrest by the dictatorship until Mr. Ceausescu's fall. Mr. Brucan, a senior member of the Council of National Salvation, said on Thursday in an interview that he remained a convinced Communist.

"Out with Communists!" the crowd chanted as it moved to Victory Square. The shift in mood seemed spontaneous;

there were no placards or banners to suggest that the anti-Government outburst had been planned.

When Mr. Iliescu, Mr. Roman and others tried to address the demonstrators this evening, they were often shouted down.

There were chants demanding that Mr. Iliescu, who is also considered to have been an anti-Ceausescu dissident, step down, and Mr. Roman with him.

'Death to Loyalists!'

By 8 P.M. the demonstrators turned their fury on Ceausescu loyalists. "Death to Ceausescu's people!" they cried. "Death to loyalists!" Then there were shouts demanding restoration of the death penalty, which the Council abolished after ordering the execution of Mr. Ceausescu and his wife, Elena, after a secret military trial.

"Death! Death! Death!" shouted the crowd.

"All right, we will hold a referendum on the death penalty," Mr. Iliescu said.

"Try all his chief aides!" the crowd shouted. "We're not leaving!"

The crowd then demanded that the Communist Party be outlawed. The party collapsed with the ouster and subsequent execution of Mr. Ceausescu, but the protesters evidently feared that it could be reorganized.

"The Rumanian Communist Party is outlawed, considering that it is against the national spirit and our ancestors' law," Mr. Iliescu said in remarks broadcast live on state radio and television.

That seemed to satisfy most of the demonstrators, who chanted, "Victory! Victory!" and began trickling home. But a core of protesters were still gathered in Victory Square after midnight, chanting anti-Communist slogans.

*   *   *

January 16, 1990

BULGARIAN PARTY LOSES DOMINANCE

By CELESTINE BOHLEN
Special to The New York Times

SOFIA, Bulgaria, Jan. 15—This country today became the last of the Soviet Union's East European allies to strip the Communist Party of its dominant role, following the others in a halting transition to multiparty democracy.

The Bulgarian Parliament, following a pattern that has become almost routine among former Soviet clients, deleted from its Constitution the once-standard phrase that has guaranteed the Communist Party a monopoly of power for more than 40 years.

On most questions today, Parliament voted unanimously for change, just as it once voted unanimously to uphold the old rigid system under Todor Zhivkov, deposed as Bulgarian Communist Party leader in November after 35 years in power.

But in the lobby and in the hallways, a new informality was evident as legislators mingled easily with reporters, and doorkeepers cleared the way for strangers without challenging their right to be there.

The one-day session of Parliament came as the Communist Party this week enters negotiations with opposition groups in another ritual common in the countries now forswearing authoritarianism—round-table talks about the composition of a transition government.

The Parliament session also concluded five days of talks on the conflicts between Bulgarians and ethnic Turks, with the formal adoption of a 11-point declaration pledging equal rights for the Muslim minority.

In a move intended to strengthen Bulgaria's transition to democracy, Parliament gave new life to opposition parties that had been crushed during the early years of Communist rule and rehabilitated opposition figures who had been jailed, exiled or killed for their political views.

But it stopped short of demands, pressed at a rally on Sunday in Sofia and again by some lawmakers today, to amend the opening phrase of Article I of the nation's Constitution and delete references to Bulgaria as a "socialist state headed by the working class."

"There is no socialist or bourgeois democracy," a legislator said, arguing for new terminology. "There is either democracy or there isn't."

Decision Put Off

A debate on that phrasing was postponed until the end of February, when Parliament will be asked to consider about 25 constitutional amendments, striking out inconsistencies and contradictions created by the abrupt shift of political power since the ouster of Mr. Zhivkov on Nov. 10.

The vote in Parliament today to abolish the Communist Party's dominant position changes little in a concrete way, some prominent opposition members said. "All these paragraphs are not important," said Petar Beron, a spokesman for the opposition group Eco-Glasnost.

One opposition demand was met when the Government announced that Communist Party control of the Interior Ministry, which oversees the police, will be eliminated.

Andrei Lukanov, head of the Communists' parliamentary group and the second-ranking figure after the new Bulgarian leader, Petar Mladenov, said in an interview on Sunday that he does not expect any change in Bulgaria's constitutional status as a "socialist state."

He said the phrasing about the working class' leading role would certainly be eliminated, but he doubted that Bulgarians wanted to abandon their economic system.

"The question is one that only the people can decide," he said, "and our opinion is that the majority of the Bulgarian people will vote for socialism."

In other East European countries, the old Communist Parties are in retreat, running for cover behind a facade of free-market reforms. In contrast, Mr. Lukanov appeared confident that in Bulgaria, a socialist system would remain a strong lure for voters.

Value of System Upheld

"We think people will soberly assess the situation," he said, "and they will properly criticize us for following Stalin and for our own peculiar deformities. But in spite of this, we think socialism gave something to Bulgaria."

Parliament also repealed a 1946 law that banned the old Agrarian Party, a leading political force in Bulgaria before World War II. The party was later revived, but as a servant of the Communists. Today's vote restored the party's political rights.

In the gallery today sat a victim of the postwar repression, Ruen Krumov, the 76-year-old former editor of the Social Democratic Party newspaper, The Free People. In 1945 and 1946, Mr. Krumov watched as about 30 members of his party leadership were arrested and jailed, some for 10 years. He spent five years in a concentration camp, later learning that Sveti Ivanov, his colleague on the newspaper, and then 36, had died in prison.

"I am very happy," said Mr. Krumov, after Parliament voted to undo the deeds done 40 years ago. "They asked us what we wanted, we told them and they did it. It is enough."

Mr. Lukanov said the commission could examine more cases of victims of political repression, but he said "rehabilitations would be made on a case-by-case, name-by-name basis."

On Tuesday, Communist Party leaders are to begin the first round of talks with leaders of several loose-knit opposition groups, grouped under the Union of Democratic Forces. The two sides, each represented by 33 people, will negotiate over how Bulgaria is governed in the months before elections, now scheduled in the spring.

*　　*　　*

January 30, 1990

ZHIVKOV IS PLACED IN BULGARIAN JAIL

By The Associated Press

SOFIA, Bulgaria, Jan. 29—Todor Zhivkov, the deposed Bulgarian leader, has been moved from house arrest to a prison for people accused of murder and other major crimes, the chief prosecutor's office said today.

The prosecutor's statement also announced indictments against Mr. Zhivkov's son-in-law, Ivan Slavkov, and an investigation into Milko Balev, a former Zhivkov aide.

The statement, carried by the official press agency, said Mr. Zhivkov, ousted as Communist Party chief on Nov. 10 after more than 35 years in power, was being questioned. The Bulgarian radio said Mr. Zhivkov was undergoing medical tests because of concern about his age and health.

The 78-year-old former leader already has been charged with misappropriating state property, inciting ethnic hostility and abuse of power.

Detained on Jan. 19

Misuse of state property, the most serious charge, carries a maximum penalty of 30 years. The ethnic-incitement charge arose from discriminatory policies against the ethnic Turkish minority in Bulgaria. The authorities detained Mr. Zhivkov on Jan. 19 and placed him in investigative custody. Earlier reports said he was kept in a villa adapted for the purpose.

Mr. Zhivkov's arrest was ordered last week, but today's statement from the prosecutor did not say when Mr. Zhivkov was moved to the Prison of the Criminal Investigation Department, which houses people suspected of serious crimes, or charged with them.

Mr. Slavkov and Mr. Balev were among several relatives or close associates of the former leader also accused of crimes. Mr. Slavkov, president of the Bulgarian Olympic Committee and a member of the International Olympic Committee, was charged with illegal possession of a large quantity of firearms, with receiving questionable payments and with malfeasance in office, the statement said.

Mr. Balev, a former Politburo member, faces charges of malfeasance in office and misappropriation of public property, the statement said. It did not say whether the two were in custody.

Negotiations began today between the Communist Party and the opposition. A Communist Party congress opens on Tuesday, and a showdown is expected between conservatives and advocates of change.

Foreign Debt of $11 Billion

The foreign debt, now about $11 billion, and growing economic problems were the main items of discussion by party delegates and the Union of Democratic Forces, a loose alliance of 12 independent groups and parties.

A spokesman for the opposition union, Georgi Spassov, said on Sunday that the opposition would not join any coalition government before elections, scheduled for May, because it does not want to be a scapegoat for economic failures or have reforms blocked by the Communist-controlled Parliament.

*   *   *

February 8, 1990

ROMANIA'S AIDS BABIES: A LEGACY OF NEGLECT

By CELESTINE BOHLEN
Special to The New York Times

BUCHAREST, Romania, Feb. 5—The babies, about 60 of them, are on the third floor of the drab gray hospital, the only AIDS clinic in Romania. In some rooms, there are two babies to a crib. In one small cubicle, four infants, close to death, lie in a row under a single blanket.

Amid the wailing and quiet moans of the children, nurses scurry about with vials, syringes and wet cloths. But it seems they cannot keep up. Many of the babies lie in wet clothes. The ones with shrunken, wrinkled faces die without anyone noticing.

Of all the grim legacies of the Nicolae Ceausescu era, this may be the most chilling. According to statistics gathered by

Romanian virologists and confirmed by French doctors, Romania is threatened with an unusual pediatric epidemic of AIDS, concentrated in crowded orphanages and clinics, spread by an old-fashioned practice of giving blood transfusions to newborn infants.

Figures on AIDS Cases

Doctors here say that of 2,000 children tested so far in targeted clinics and orphanages, 250 have AIDS, and another 200 have tested positive for the HIV virus, which causes AIDS. [The World Health Organization said an emergency team had been sent to Romania, where W.H.O. doctors said 700 children had been found to be infected with the AIDS virus.]

While this is not a thorough epidemiological survey, and does not reflect the incidence of AIDS among all Romanian children, it points to a critical situation whose proportions are still unknown.

'A Case of Extreme Urgency'

"I have never seen this anywhere," said Jacques LeBas, an AIDS specialist who is president of Doctors of the World, a Paris-based medical assistance program. "This is a case of extreme urgency."

The plight of babies with AIDS is not unique to Romania. But here, the authorities' willful neglect of the disease allowed it to spread quickly, compounding problems already created by poverty, poor equipment, bad medical practices, large numbers of abandoned children and other social distress common to the Ceausescu era.

On the third floor at the AIDS clinic, the Victor Babes Hospital, the nurses know that they are dealing with hopeless cases. Two nurses, Paula Efta and Miora Cojan, said they have seen 20 or 25 babies die in the last months, and that 2 or 3 children would die that night. "It is a work of big love," Mrs. Cojan said. "These children have no parents, so they attach themselves to us like real mothers."

An Old, Dangerous Practice

Almost two-thirds of the AIDS babies were brought to the hospital from orphanages. These homes, overcrowded, ill-equipped and underheated, are another Ceausescu legacy, the product of draconian policies against birth control that resulted in thousands of unwanted children.

An old practice of injecting blood transfusions into the umbilical cord, to stimulate the growth of small infants is now seen as one reason for the rapid spread of AIDS among babies. Since the practice requires only a small dose of blood, one pint of AIDS-contaminated blood could be used many times over.

The practice of injecting blood from adults into infants and small children fell out of use long ago in the United States, and is very rare today if it is practiced anywhere outside Romania, specialists in the history of medicine said. The last known use of a similar practice in the United States was in the 1930's, when parents' blood was injected into children

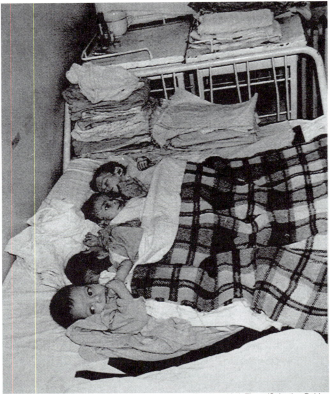

The New York Times/Celestine Bohlen

Four AIDS-stricken babies sharing a blanket at the Victor Babes Hospital, the only AIDS clinic in Romania. Doctors say that of 2,000 children tested so far in targeted clinics and orphanages, 250 have the disease AIDS, and another 200 have tested positive for the HIV virus.

to immunize them against measles. The practice not only did not work but caused severe health problems and was stopped by the 1940's.

Contaminated needles or syringes are another frequent cause of AIDS, as they were in Elista, a Soviet city in the northern Caucasus where an AIDS epidemic broke out among hospitalized babies last year. Many less developed countries do not have disposable syringes, and sterilization may be slipshod.

While children in the West or in third world countries suffer from AIDS, typically they inherit the disease from their mothers, who contracted it either by sex or by dirty needles.

The story of AIDS in Romania has unfolded a bit at a time. Until Dec. 22, when Mr. Ceausescu was overthrown in a revolution, there was no official acknowledgment that AIDS existed in Romania, which meant that any data about the spread of the disease was a state secret. Blood donors, already barely controlled against hepatitis B, an acknowledged health problem in Romania, were not screened for AIDS.

Still, a few adult cases were reported, about a dozen in all. The first documented case in the country was a 40-year-old barman who was hospitalized at the Babes hospital in 1985.

Hard evidence about AIDS among Romanian children was first reported last June, when Dr. Ion Patiescu, laboratory chief at The Institute of Virology, and his assistant, Dr. Stefan Constantinescu, were doing random testing for viruses among children hospitalized at Bucharest's Fundeni Hospital, a cancer treatment center.

An Alarming Discovery

To their surprise, their first patient, a 12-year-old girl, turned out to have AIDS. As they kept testing, the results became more startling. Of 150 children, 31 tested positive for the HIV virus. But what was most alarming was the age of those infected: 29 of the 31 were under 3 years old.

"We were surprised because we had taken the young ones as a control group, not expecting to find anything," Dr. Constantinescu said. The other shock was that the majority had clinical AIDS, meaning they had not been infected recently. "And yet," he said, "they were being treated for pneumonia, diarrhea and infections."

In the political climate of the Ceausescu era, the doctors' findings were trouble. The Ministry of Health instructed them not to test anymore, and moved the children from Fundeni Hospital to the Babes clinic. But, according to the two doctors, most of the children were eventually sent home, since there were no centers to treat them.

Using testing kits sent by the World Health Organization, the two doctors pressed on with their research, convinced that the problem was not limited to the Fundeni Hospital. "We had tested the parents and they were negative," Dr. Constantinescu said, "and yet we were already seeing antibodies in the children."

Since Fundeni Hospital serves the cities of Giurgiu, on the Danube River opposite Bulgaria, and Constanza, a port city on the Black Sea, the doctors went to both places. In each city, pediatricians told them that for the past year and a half, they had been noticing children with persistent infections who were not responding to treatment. Yet, said Dr. Constantinescu, a diagnosis of AIDS had never occurred to them. "If you are told there is no such virus in Romania, why study it?" he asked.

Eventually, the Health Ministry responded with some testing of its own and, Dr. Constantinescu said, it found 40 children in each city with AIDS.

By chance, the results from one set of tests done at the Novodari orphanage near Constanza came back to the Virology Institute, and not to the Babes Hospital, which is next door. Alarmed, Dr. Patiascu and Dr. Constantinescu rushed to the ministry. "Of 138 samples of blood, 92 were positive," Dr. Constantinescu said. "At that moment, the authorities said, 'stop, you are playing around.' "

Even more damaging than the Novodari results was the news from Arad, a city on Hungarian border. Two patients there were found to have the AIDS virus. That was enough to accuse Dr. Patiascu and his assistant of provoking anti-Romanian sentiment in Hungary.

Testing Is Halted

At that point, the doctors stopped their testing, and never sent their earlier findings to the World Health Organization. Last fall, a Romanian pediatricians' conference on AIDS in children was canceled and its program was withdrawn from the printers.

Since the revolution, the climate has changed. Testing has begun again, but equipment and a comprehensive program are still lacking. More than 2,000 samples of blood are awaiting testing at the Virology Institute, yet the two doctors only have 500 testing kits. The World Health Organization is sending experts to help examine test results.

But on the third floor of the Babes Hospital the children, all under 3 years old, lie or sit in their cots, with bewildered looks on their faces as doctors, nurses and reporters troop by. The weakest, thin as sticks, lie silent under the blankets. The sturdier ones stand at the edge of their cribs, craving attention.

Mother Describes Ordeal

On the first floor, three mothers share a small, narrow room with their babies. One baby had already been shown to have AIDS. His mother, Adriana Alexandru, 24, sat holding him silently on a cot at the back of the room. Impassively, she described how she and Gabriel, 6 months old, had been living in the hospital for the past two weeks, sent there from Giurgiu after she had become alarmed at his rapid weight loss. She said she had no idea how he caught the disease, except that he had been hospitalized often after his birth.

Dr. Gheorghe Jipa, director of the Babes Hospital, said older children who have been found to have AIDS are sent home after treatment, and readmitted only when they become critical. Hospital records show that 94 patients had been admitted for treatment since Jan. 1.

Last week, the new Health Minister, who is the fourth since the revolution, went on national television and gave a rough outline of the situation. But the doctors are still waiting for more facts. "We can only get out of this impasse with the truth," Dr. Jipa said.

*   *   *

February 15, 1990

ALBANIAN-SERB TENSION TOUCHES ALL IN KOSOVO

By JOHN KIFNER
Special to The New York Times

PRISTINA, Yugoslavia, Feb. 12—The Albanians gather in a haze of cigarette smoke in the university coffee shop, complaining about the ruling Serbs. A few blocks away, in a little restaurant named for the tomb of an epic Slavic poet of resistance to the Ottomans, Serbs grumble about the majority Albanians.

Here in Kosovo Province, where the ornate Serbian Orthodox village churches and monasteries give way to the homes of Albanians with their distinctively Middle Eastern surrounding walls and the white minarets of mosques, ethnic tension is never far away. It is a constant reality whose impact far overrides the fading of Communist ideology.

Late last month, protests against what Albanians perceive as Serbian domination broke out once again, with the federal and local police firing tear-gas bullets into crowds of demonstrators. Albanians say they have documented 32 deaths by police gunfire. The outburst was caused, Albanians here said, by reports that an Albanian in the neighboring Macedonian republic was killed by a falling rock when the traditional wall around his house was bulldozed as a zoning violation.

"During the last year, there were many problems, more and more repression of the Albanian people," Isuf Berisha, an Albanian who is president of the Society of Philosophers and Sociologists of Kosovo, said in a booth in the crowded coffee shop. "The only question was when, and it was now," he said referring to what he described as the inevitability of the Albanian response.

90 Percent Are Albanians

Of the two million people in the impoverished province— the average per capita income is $800—about 90 percent are Albanians. This demographic imbalance has resulted from the high birth rates among the Albanians, among the highest in Europe, and the long emigration of Serbs from the area.

But despite the overwhelming numbers of Albanians, what is officially called the "autonomous province of Kosovo" is more and more effectively under the control of Serbia, the largest and most assertive of the six republics that make up this hodgepodge country, which encompasses five major nationalities, many smaller ethnic groups, three dominant religions and two alphabets.

Indeed, after Albanian protests, much of the autonomy was formally taken away last March, and Kosovo's government, police, courts and Communist Party structure were placed under the control of Serbia.

Serbia is run by Slobodan Milosevic (pronounced mee-LOH-suh-vitch), a gray-haired populist politician who has become a hero for the Serbs and for Communist regulars by making the Kosovo issue his stock in trade and raising it with clear undertones of Serbian nationalism and resentment of Albanians.

For many Serbs, the Albanians are seen as a people who are proliferating and encroaching on hallowed Serbian ground, for this is the site of the Battle of Kosovo in 1389, which sealed the Turkish conquest of Serbia. The defeat of Prince Lazar and his Christian allies at the hands of the Muslim legions of Sultan Murad I—both leaders were killed—is savored by Serbs the way Texans remember the Alamo. The battle, one of the largest of medieval times, makes Kosovo an emotional heartland of the Serbs. The site itself, outside of town, is commemorated by a tower, hard by a soft-coal power-generating plant spewing vast clouds of pollution.

Icons of Serbian Nationalism

The little restaurant in the Serbian quarter of this glum city is decorated with icons of nationalism: a large photograph of Mr. Milosevic, who is known to all as "Slobo," a portrait of Prince Bishop Petar Petrovic-Njegos, the bard whose epic poem, "The Mountain Wreath," hails Slavic uprisings against the Turks in the 17th and 18th centuries, and a picture of his grave in a chapel atop Mount Lovcen. There is a poster commemorating last year's 600th anniversary celebration of the battle, which shows Prince Lazar in medieval fashion, holding his severed head in his hand, and a popular romantic depiction of a woman giving a sip of wine from a jug to a dying Serb lying atop the Turk he had killed.

"Sure, you don't see any of them here," the proprietor said, referring to Albanians, as he plopped down a platter of grilled meat, "or any of ours over there."

The radio playing in the restaurant said, "The situation in the province has calmed down enough for us to enjoy an afternoon of music," and it proceeded with the Serbian equivalent of country and western songs of lost love and hard drink.

Indeed, the only reminders of last month's violence are a few bored-looking policemen staked out reading newspapers in cars at the edge of the city, and gray-haired local policemen draped in helmets and bulletproof aprons in the center of town. By the side of the road the other day, a handful of Albanian women raised their hands in V signs as cars went by carrying Albanian men wearing traditional cone-shaped hats.

400,000 Sign Albanian Petition

But no one here thinks the trouble is over, least of all the Albanians, who have abandoned demonstrations and gained about 400,000 signatures on a petition for change and alternative political structures.

"The situation does not allow us to be happy," said Mr. Berisha, a 34-year-old unemployed philosopher. "The problem is the Serbs are being manipulated as a means of taking and perpetuating power."

"The biggest problem is that the Serbs want to make this just a Serbian land, like before, when there was a monarchy," put in Meriman Kamberi, a young woman at the table. "They consider us like a foreign power here and say we are the enemy."

"It's a national frustration," Veton Surroi, an Albanian intellectual who is the local president of the Union for a Democratic Initiative, said in a separate interview. "It is an Albanian rebellion against Serbian leadership. The majority of the population is against the party dictatorship."

* * *

March 24, 1990

TITO'S IMAGE, A FEW RELUCTANT STEPS BEHIND STALIN'S, IS SLOWLY CARTED AWAY

By DAVID BINDER
Special to The New York
BELGRADE, Yugoslavia, March 23—Hardly a day has gone by in recent months without some act to cut the heroic image of Tito down to size, revealing the late President as exceptionally greedy, mendacious and vainglorious.

There are eight cities named after Tito in Yugoslavia, one in each of the six republics and two autonomous provinces. In every one, citizens' initiatives have sprung up seeking the removal of the designation.

In the Serbian city of Titovo Uzice, more than 1,000 people have signed a petition demanding that the city's name revert to just plain Uzice. There is some poignancy to this. In 1941, Tito's Communist Partisans briefly liberated Uzice from German occupiers and declared it the capital of the Uzice Republic.

The process of what is known here as de-Titoization encompasses not only the cult he fostered in his lifetime but the historical record, which he plainly falsified, and the immense properties that he accumulated.

De-Stalinization Compared

De-Titoization in a country where Tito was treated like a god for 35 years, and where he acted like a king, is comparable to the process of de-Stalinization in the Soviet Union, but it started much later. Tito died in 1980.

The cult of Tito was one of the few unifying factors that bound this country of rancorous and mutually suspicious republics, and the demythologizing of the man has accompanied and accelerated renewed regional conflicts.

There are practical matters involved in the debate, like what to do with his Blue Train, a $40 million combination of 20 luxuriously appointed cars and 2 locomotives that he used to travel around the country. It cost $145,300 to keep up last year, and the Government wants to sell it, but there are no buyers. Similar disposal problems have arisen over his Danube River yacht.

In addition, the Government is wrestling with the disposal of many of Tito's houses, which cost $726,500 a year to keep up. Other villas and palaces used by Tito around the country have become the property of the governments of the republics in which they are situated.

Art Works Were Seized

Questions have also been raised about art and antiquities seized during Tito's rule and given to him. Among the treasures are Dutch Masters, including a Rembrandt and a Memling confiscated from a Zagreb physician after the war.

The paintings are at Tito's coastal residence on the Adriatic island of Brioni.

Also on the island is a section of a remarkable Roman mosaic discovered near the Serbian city of Zajecar some years ago. The Mayor of Zajecar presented the mosaic section to Tito under duress, he now says. Zajecar is demanding the return of the gift.

One group of revelations has convincingly portrayed Tito as much more of a devoted follower of Stalin before and during World War II than he ever acknowledged. Stalin expelled Yugoslavia from the Cominform in 1948 in a split that set the Balkan land on a path of independent Communist rule, making it the first country to leave the Soviet bloc.

Was Admired in West

Tito's break with Stalin was widely viewed with admiration in some circles in the West, where the Yugoslav leader was held up as an example of independent leadership. That image was further enhanced when, along with Nehru of India, Nasser of Egypt and Sukarno of Indonesia, he helped establish the movement of nonaligned nations. Documents long kept secret by Tito have now come to light showing that acting as Stalin's agent, together with a small circle of Yugoslav Communists, he purged 800 members of the party in 1939, including founding members.

All of those expelled in 1939 were in exile in Moscow. Some had already been killed in the great purges by Stalin that swept away millions of Soviet Communists and thousands of foreign Communists. Those Yugoslavs on the Tito purge list who survived in Moscow were later killed as a result of their expulsions from the Yugoslav party.

The documents dealing with this were found by Pero Simic, who disclosed them in a book published at the end of 1989, "Tito: When, How, Why."

"It was the basis for Stalinizing the party," Mr. Simic said of the 1939 purge. "Tito said later it was to make the Yugoslav party independent, but the documents show it was to make it Stalinist."

Falsification Documented

Mr. Simic has also caught Tito in a major falsification of his career in the party. Tito asserted that he became Secretary General in the summer of 1937. The documents Mr. Simic unearthed show that Tito did not acquire that post until the autumn of 1940, although he clearly played the leading role in the party for at least a year before that.

Tito also falsely maintained that he had taken part in the Bolshevik Revolution in 1917. "He lied," the author said in an interview.

In a second book based on other secret party documents, Mr. Simic and a co-author, Jovan Kesar, disclosed that Tito arranged to have Aleksandar Rankovic, his longtime associate, framed at a Central Committee meeting in 1966 and forced to resign from the party.

The principal allegation against Mr. Rankovic, previously the Interior Minister but then Vice President of Yugoslavia, was that the secret police installed electronic devices in Tito's home, including his bedroom. "They eavesdropped on me," Tito said at the time.

A General Is Implicated

In fact, the devices were installed just before the so-called Brioni meeting of the Central Committee by two military intelligence officers under the authority of Ivan Krajacic, a Croatian general who was close to Tito.

"Rankovic was completely innocent," Mr. Simic said. "He was always loyal to Tito. But he never admitted responsibility for the bugging." Nor was a court case ever pressed against Mr. Rankovic, who died in disgrace in 1983 at age 74.

The Kesar-Simic book, published this year, is entitled "Pardon Without Mercy." It has served partly to rehabilitate the man once considered a possible successor to Tito.

Another victim of Tito's whims, Milovan Djilas, who spent 9 ½ years in prison for criticizing the Yugoslav leader, has also returned to public favor. His long-banned books are being published here, and he was interviewed on national television recently. "I have been half-rehabilitated," said Mr. Djilas, who will turn 79 in the spring.

Still emerging in the process of de-Titoization is the extent of torture and killings that took place in the early postwar years in Yugoslavia's prison camps on the islands of Goli Otok, which held male prisoners, and Sveti Grgur, for women.

Gestapo-Like Torture Charged

About 7,000 men were sent to Goli Otok. According to witness accounts being published in the Yugoslav press, torture practices there were equal to those of the Gestapo. New prisoners were compelled by the secret police to run a gauntlet of older prisoners who were forced to beat them with clubs and spit on them as an initiation rite.

It is unclear where the de-Titoization process will end. His picture still hangs in all government offices, and there are hundreds of streets still named after him, including Belgrade's Marshal Tito Boulevard.

Some Yugoslavs have been relishing scandalous details of Tito's personal life, including the assertions in the magazine Intervju that he was married more than the three times officially acknowledged, and was the father of more than the two sons he acknowledged. The women in question include a high-born Viennese, a Kirghiz tribal chief's daughter and a Turkish silk dealer.

One Yugoslav who is not amused is Tito's widow, Jovanka Broz. She wrote a letter published on Monday in the Belgrade daily Politika complaining that the press was intruding on her private life with sensational reports about her late husband and herself.

* * *

March 27, 1990

BULGARIAN INQUIRY REVEALS 50'S CONCENTRATION CAMPS

By DAVID BINDER
Special to The New York

SOFIA, Bulgaria, March 26—A special commission of the Bulgarian Government has uncovered a series of concentration camps where some prisoners were tortured and killed in the 1950's and early 1960's under the rule of Todor Zhivkov, the Communist leader ousted last November.

The existence of the camps was made public in an article on Friday in Demokratsiya, the newspaper of the opposition coalition called the United Democratic Forces, and more reports with new details and allegations have appeared since in other newspapers and on Bulgarian television.

Iordan Ormankov, a lawyer who is the spokesman of the Ministry of Interior, said today in an interview that Mr. Zhivkov himself might be implicated by the investigation of "the serious crimes" committed in the camps.

"In an authoritarian regime such as existed before Nov. 10 it was not possible for such things to be neglected by the ruler," Mr. Ormankov said. "Todor Zhivkov at least knew or gave the orders. The problem is that from this period there were few material traces. It was done on the telephone."

Zhivkov Is Confined

Mr. Zhivkov is now confined in a military hospital on the southwestern edge of Sofia, while the state prosecutor continues an investigation of other possible crimes committed during his 35-year rule.

The concentration camps under investigation were at Kotsian, Bogdanov Dol, Belene Island in the Danube and at Lovech. The disclosures most shocking to ordinary Bulgarians concern Lovech, situated in the northern center of the country. Some Bulgarian press reports are calling it "a death camp."

Mr. Ormankov said a preliminary examination of Interior Ministry archives and interviews with former inmates indicate that between 700 and 1,000 people were interned at Lovech starting in 1959 and that about 100 died there or were killed. The inmates included common criminals, people who refused to work and possibly some members of the Communist Party.

As to who was directly responsible, Mr. Ormankov said: "Documents show that the activities of these units, or 'objects' as they were called, were under the control of the Deputy Minister of Interior, Col. Gen. Mircho Spasov. He issued the directives, mostly verbally, although there are several documents bearing his signature."

General 'Alive and Well'

General Spasov, who retired several years ago, occupies a large brick villa surrounded by a steel fence in Dragalevtsi, a village on the north slope of Mount Vitosh overlooking the capital. "He is alive and well," the spokesman said, "but if I were in his shoes, I would use my gun on myself. That is strictly a personal opinion."

Lovech was apparently opened in 1959 and, according to Mr. Ormankov, closed by a decision of the ruling party Politburo on April 5, 1962. The spokesman said the remaining prisoners were freed and several camp officials dismissed or otherwise disciplined. "None was convicted," he added. A nearby parallel camp for women, mostly prostitutes, was also closed down.

Would other former Interior Ministry officials besides General Spasov face trial? Mr. Ormankov said: "I don't exclude it. Very probably some will face trial for serious crimes. We want to make a clean break with the past and to be governed by the rule of law."

Many Employees Dismissed

To this end, he pointed out, the former State Security secret police has been dissolved and the Ministry of Interior completely reorganized. "A major part of the employees have been dismissed," he said.

Among the incidents described by surviving camp inmates are a visit to Lovech by General Spasov, who was quoted as ordering a major, "Beatings for everyone and work, work, work." Some prisoners were clubbed to death, the former inmates said.

Another inmate who was doing forced labor at the camp charged that he heard Mr. Zhivkov say of the prisoners during a visit, "These are weeds that should be cut at the roots without mercy."

A former inmate, Dimiter Mitov, said that at Lovech some prisoners, including three former army colonels and a physician, had been compelled by guards to drag chunks of ice from the River Osam in winter and that those who collapsed were left to freeze or drown.

Last weekend, about 5,000 Bulgarians demonstrated at Lovech carrying signs saying, "Death to the Killers."

* * *

April 7, 1990

ALBANIANS' NEW WAY: FEUDS WITHOUT BLOOD

By CHUCK SUDETIC
Special to The New York Times

PRISTINA, Yugoslavia, March 31—Libibe Dragacina extended his hand to Beslim Betushi, and when the handshake was concluded, a group of witnesses broke into happy applause.

The ritual superseded an older custom in this region of Albanian clans, one that called for a Dragacina kinsman to kill a male Betushi to avenge a killing of the past.

The age-old practice of blood vengeance continues among the ethnic Albanians of Yugoslavia's Kosovo province, but a campaign is under way to end the carnage of feuds and vendettas.

Motivated in part by what they say is the need for Albanian unity in the face of Serbian designs on this overwhelmingly Albanian region, ethnic Albanian intellectuals and students have gone out among the region's rural families to persuade them to abandon the tradition of revenge.

Resolution of 150 Conflicts

The group says that it has reconciled about 150 family and clan conflicts since Feb. 1, and that it is confident that it can settle many of the 450 to 550 remaining cases.

"In this situation, which has been difficult for Albanians, we wanted to have at least a reduction in this evil," said Anton Cetta, a retired cultural anthropologist from Pristina University here in Kosovo's capital. Mr. Cetta, who initiated the reconciliation effort, added, "In difficult times, it is a natural law that a man wants to be more secure."

"It is not easy for the families who are required to draw blood to forgive," he said, adding that for centuries families who did not carry out vengeance were considered cowards.

The law of blood vengeance requires the family of a victim of a slaying or accident either to kill an adult male from the family of the person who caused the death or to force that family to make a stiff payment for the loss. The elders pick a male family member to exact the vengeance, which can be carried out in any way.

Fear of Vengeful Attacks

"Even from behind," said Ismail Haradinai, whose family is negotiating a reconciliation with a neighbor over the fatal shooting of his brother during a dispute. "It is best to kill the murderer himself, but if you can't, then you kill a brother, father, uncle or anyone you can get."

Blood vengeance has accounted for as many as 100 deaths a year in recent years in Kosovo, said Muhamet Pirraku, a researcher at Pristina's Institute for Albanian Studies who has studied the tradition. In contrast, in the last 15 months, 51 Albanians and 1 Serb are officially reported to have died in protests against Serbia's cancellation of the regional autonomy that Kosovo, with its 90 percent ethnic Albanian majority, had previously enjoyed from the Serbian republic.

Fear of vengeful attacks has many times forced Albanian men to flee abroad or to remain inside their walled family compounds for decades, he said. In some cases, only women venture out of the compound.

Traditionally, Mr. Cetta said, elders from the two hostile families formally settle the conflict once the vengeance has been exacted. But he noted that there have been instances when blood vengeance set off a chain of killings that did not end before claiming 25 to 30 lives.

From Tradition to 'Cult'

The practice, which extends to neighboring Montenegro, has survived despite its being forbidden by the regions' two religions, Islam and Christianity. Government campaigns have also failed to end the practice.

Judges usually give 10- to 20-year sentences to men convicted of blood-vengeance killings, Mr. Cetta said, adding that such sentences have not deterred the killers. "They think they have to do it," he said. "It is a tradition that has grown into a cult."

Mr. Cetta said his group was trying to change behavior by appealing to patriotic instincts in a time of turmoil, when many Albanians are resisting what they contend is growing pressure from the central government in Belgrade.

The government of the Serbian republic, which administers Kosovo, is preparing an ambitious program to settle Serbs in the once-autonomous province, an effort that Albanians consider colonization.

Serbian-Albanian Tensions

"Ours is a voluntary effort to destroy blood vengeance as an evil entirely," he said. "We don't want to carry this stigma any longer."

The current ethnic tensions in Kosovo are the latest in a centuries-long struggle between the Serbs and Albanians for the region. The Albanians assert that they are Kosovo's original inhabitants and they trace their tenure as dating long before the 15th century, when many converted to Islam after the conquest of the area by the Ottoman Turks.

For their part, Serbs lay claim to Kosovo based on the fact that it was the core of medieval Serbia before it was conquered by the Ottoman Empire. They argue that the Albanians originally moved into Kosovo only after the Ottomans arrived.

At blood-vengeance reconciliation ceremonies last Saturday, speakers won applause and victory signs for their calls for progress and solidarity.

"When women took off the veil it was difficult, but now they sit among us," Mr. Cetta said to the families of one village. "Now it is difficult to make the gift of blood, but later it will be normal. We must swear that we will not kill each other anymore."

"We hope to enter the European Community, and we should go in without these old burdens from the ancient past," he said. "There are many things we have to become more civilized about. We will be more civilized when a grandmother says to her grandson, 'Bring me the newspaper.' We will be civilized when grandmothers know how to read and care about what is happening in the world."

* * *

April 12, 1990

NEW LEADER OF THE GREEKS: CONSTANTINE MITSOTAKIS

By PAUL ANASTASI

ATHENS, April 11—His political career may be said to have its origins in the mid-19th century, when his grandfather founded the Komma Xipoliton, the Party of the Bare-Footed Ones, liberals who opposed the right-wing establishment then in power.

Today, Constantine Mitsotakis, 71 years old, was sworn in as Greece's Prime Minister, paradoxically representing the victory of the center-right forces after nearly a decade of Socialist rule.

His career exemplifies the struggle of a man who has shifted from the center to the right, overcoming decades of controversy and feuding within his own party and contesting three elections in the last 10 months.

Mr. Mitsotakis, who was born on the island of Crete on Oct. 18, 1918, was sworn in with a 39-member team of ministers.

A conservative government became possible when a former rival, the leader of a small center-right party, provided the one seat Mr. Mitsotakis needed for the required parliamentary majority, or 151 of the 300 seats.

Washington Visit Expected

Mr. Mitsotakis's New Democracy party won the elections Sunday with 46.9 percent of the vote and 150 seats in its third attempt to clinch a majority after failing by only a few seats in elections in June and November. Although New Democracy defeated the Socialist Party, which had been in power since 1981 under Andreas Papandreou, in those elections, its failure to win a clear majority necessitated a series of coalition governments.

Mr. Mitsotakis said today that a primary task would be to improve Greece's international image. Under Mr. Papandreou, he said, "Greece had strained relations with the West and looked like a center for international terrorism and political and economic instability."

Mr. Mitsotakis is expected to visit Washington soon at the invitation of the Bush Administration, something denied Mr. Papandreou throughout his rule as Prime Minister.

To his supporters, Mr. Mitsotakis is known as the Tall One, a reference to the fact that at 6 feet 3 inches he towers above the average Greek. To his opponents, he epitomizes Byzantine politics, a shrewd and cunning dealer who has shifted political alliances on many occasions in his rise to power.

A Break With Party

Mr. Mitsotakis was first elected to Parliament in 1946 at the age of 27 and was appointed to his first Cabinet post, Under Secretary of Finance, in 1951. Before 1967, when the military seized power in a coup, he held a number of Government posts in the liberal Center Union Party of Mr. Papandreou's father, George.

But in the mid-1960's, during one of Greece's most bitter political periods, he broke from that party to support the center-right Government, laying the foundation for his bitter rivalry with Andreas Papandreou.

The center-left labeled him the "arch-apostate," accusing him of selling out his principles for personal benefit and easing the imposition of the military dictatorship. Mr. Mitsotakis denies the charges, saying he has always advocated moderation and political stability.

He formed his own New Liberation Party in 1974 when the military junta collapsed and four years later merged it with the more conservative New Democracy party. He held several government posts, including Foreign Minister and Minister of Economic Coordination. After a long struggle within the party, Mr. Mitsotakis was elected leader in September 1984.

Arrested by the Nazis

When the Nazis invaded Greece in 1941, Mr. Mitsotakis fought as a commissioned officer and then headed a resistance group on Crete. He was arrested twice and sentenced to death each time, but escaped execution, first through an amnesty and then in an Allied-backed exchange of prisoners. He represented the Allies when the Germans surrendered on the island at the end of the war.

Mr. Mitsotakis was also jailed in 1967 when the junta seized power. After his release, he escaped abroad. The Government retaliated by arresting his entire family, including his 5-month-old son. From abroad, Mr. Mitsotakis appealed for the release of "the youngest political prisoner in the world." He was jailed on his return to Greece in 1973,

and was freed only on the restoration of democracy the next year.

Mr. Mitsotakis and his wife, Marika, have three daughters and a son and nine grandchildren. A son-in-law, Pavlos Bacoyannis, who was New Democracy's chief parliamentary spokesman, was killed by left-wing terrorists last year.

Mr. Mitsotakis is Prime Minister today largely because of his skill at behind-the-scenes maneuvering, especially reconciliation, which makes up for his lackluster image as an orator. In June he prevented a Socialist comeback by forming a government with the Communists. In November, he gave his support to an all-party Government.

On Monday, he obtained a vital single seat from Constantine Stephanopoulos, who had abandoned New Democracy in 1985 after an unsuccessful struggle for the leadership with Mr. Mitsotakis.

"I feel an enormous burden as Prime Minister," Mr. Mitsotakis said today. "Our economy is in ruins and our international image is badly shaken. But I am honored by the fact that my government will be leading Greece into the united Europe of 1992, in the midst of a rapidly changing world. With God's help, we hope to succeed."

*   *   *

April 26, 1990

VICTORY SEEN FOR NATIONALISTS IN YUGOSLAV REPUBLIC

Special to The New York Times

ZAGREB, Yugoslavia, April 25—A conservative nationalist party appears to have swept to victory in the opening round of the first free multiparty elections to be held in the Yugoslav republic of Croatia in more than 50 years.

The nationalist party, the Croatian Democratic Association, has so far won 16 of the 80 seats in the main chamber of Croatia's Parliament, according to the latest official results. The party is led by Franjo Tudjman, a onetime Communist partisan who became an anti-Communist dissident. The Communist Party, which has controlled Croatia's government since 1945, has taken only two seats.

Runoff elections scheduled for May 6 and 7 will determine who will occupy the remaining seats.

But even where the Croatian Democratic Association's candidates have failed to win the clear majority needed to bypass the second tier of voting, they have generally led the field and are expected to win in most of the runoff races.

Calls for a Confederation

Mr. Tudjman, a historian, said the first task of the government he expects to form will be to draft a new Croatian constitution. After that, he said, the republican government will approach the other Yugoslav republics to work out Croatia's future relationship with them.

Mr. Tudjman has publicly called for a confederal Yugoslavia, but many people suspect that he wants Croatia's eventual severance from Yugoslavia. Moves in that direction would almost certainly set off a conflict with Serbia over lands claimed by both republics.

Mr. Tudjman emphatically denied that his party favors initiating a realignment of Yugoslavia's internal borders to bring parts of the republic of Bosnia and Herzegovina into Croatia unless Yugoslavia at some time breaks up.

In that case, he said, his party would seek a referendum on the question in Bosnia and Herzegovina.

Slovenian Talks on Federation

The scale of the victory by Mr. Tudjman's party came as a surprise to many in Yugoslavia and has particularly stunned Communists and Serbs living in Croatia and throughout the country.

The Serbian-populated regions of Croatia, which account for about 11.5 percent of the republic's population, are reported to have voted overwhelmingly in favor of the Communists and the Serbian Democratic Party.

As he studied election results, Mr. Tudjman said his government would take steps to reduce what he asserted was a preponderance of Serbs in Croatia's government, police and news organizations.

In Slovenia, the president of the Christian Democrats, Lojze Peterle, discussed ideas for distancing Slovenia from the Yugoslav federation that stopped short of outright secession.

Mr. Peterle is regarded as likely to become that republic's new prime minister once the coalition of parties known as Demos receives the mandate to form a government when the new Parliament convenes in about two weeks.

* * *

May 17, 1990

ROMANIA, PREPARING TO VOTE, WEARS A LOOK OF MENACE, SQUALOR AND FEAR

By CELESTINE BOHLEN
Special to The New York Times

BUCHAREST, Romania—Five months after the only violent revolution in Eastern Europe, Romania heads into its first free elections on May 20 with only a tenuous hold on its newly won freedoms, facing a future that looks almost menacing.

The streets of Bucharest are still dark at night, even though restrictions on electricity use, one of the most hated measures imposed by Nicolae Ceausescu, were lifted days after the dictator was overthrown in December after 24 years of oppressive rule.

Romanians will tell you there is more light now than before, but it is just enough to cast shadows on the main boulevards and radiate a pale glow from the giant apartment blocks on the city's edge. On many side streets, pedestrians still pick their way blindly at night past potholes, stray dogs and the occasional armed soldier out on patrol.

No matter how one arrives in Romania, the country looks as if it is falling apart. Bucharest's airport would be a dis-

grace anywhere. Water drips from the ceiling, floor tiles are cracked, plants are dead or dying in their pots and the first word of greeting for a visitor, passing an armed sentry at a makeshift checkpoint, is a whispered, "Cigarettes."

The darkness in the capital heightens the uneasy feeling many people have about Romania as the elections approach. About 80 parties are competing for seats in Parliament, and three candidates—two emigres and a former high-ranking Communist official—are vying for the presidency, a post likely to have considerable power.

To Many, the Front Is Not Salvation

Violence has already erupted between opposing groups— some of it, many people believe, orchestrated by the ruling National Salvation Front, which took command of the country during the revolution and has since acquired a reputation among many Romanians as protector of the old order, even of former members of the dreaded Securitate secret police.

The Liberal Party presidential candidate, Radu Campeanu, was attacked in a provincial town last week. The Peasants Party candidate, Ion Ratiu, has reported similar assaults. And a round-the-clock anti-front, anti-Communist protest in one of Bucharest's main squares since April 22 has kept up pressure on Ion Iliescu, the leader of the National Salvation Front and the country's interim President. Despite this, the front retains support in regions outside the capital, and Mr. Iliescu is considered the favorite in the presidential race.

From its earliest moments, the ruling front has been caught in contradictions of its own making. In the days after Mr. Ceausescu fled Bucharest, it appointed itself guardian of the revolution; for the last few months, it has been repeatedly accused of selling out the revolution in order to hold onto power.

The credibility of the front, still the dominant partner in the provisional government, is the central issue in the election campaign. Opinions on both sides of the debate are held with a vehemence that brooks no compromise; for many, it is a simple article of faith that the front and its top leaders are bent on destroying Romania's infant democracy, and turning the clock back toward a kind of Gorbachevian Communism.

Slow to Dismantle The Old Apparatus

Sitting in a darkened corner of a small mansion on Calle Victorei, which now houses the Independent Group for Social Dialogue, Gabriel Andreescu, a former dissident, explained his bleak view of recent developments in Romania.

"I see the situation going from bad to worse," he said. "If the front wins, it will be a long time before the Romanian people regain a civil society. If they win fairly, it will be painful enough. If they cheat, it means they will have to go from abuse to abuse."

Others say this deep pessimism flies in the face of the hands-off policy toward public protests, and the open criticism of the front that appears daily in the glut of newspapers and journals being sold in Bucharest; the criticism even makes its way onto state-controlled television.

"We have never in our history had such freedom of the press," said Marin Sorescu, a poet and essayist. "What is good is the lucidity of the intellectuals, who are now free to criticize. But an excess of lucidity can also be negative."

"The front is criticized from all sides, for being too authoritarian, for being too weak," he said. "But their main problem is their slowness in changing the old apparatus. They say they cannot do more because this is only a provisional government. But it has created a nervousness, and a lack of confidence that is not healthy."

Vistas of Neglect In City and Country

The poverty of the country is apparent everywhere. To drive across the border from Hungary is to be sent lurching backward in time. Horse- or ox-drawn carts are frequently seen, bearing loads of hay, or entire gypsy families; potholes the size and even the depth of watermelons appear in the middle of the road.

The farmland, although often beautiful, is usually scraggly; in the foothills of the Carpathian Mountains, shepherds stretch out to sleep on the side of the road, a few feet from passing cars. In industrial areas, factories lie exposed and neglected, with machinery rusting in open yards and huge pipes running overground, sometimes over the road itself.

On the road from Hungary, children rush toward the road at the sight of a foreign car, jumping, shouting and yelling out for candy or gum. The practice apparently began with the arrival of international aid trucks soon after the revolution, but has since turned into a game. In Oradea, a city right across the border, children besiege cars at traffic lights. The only lingering connection to the first euphoria of the revolution is the V sign they flash as traffic moves on.

In Bucharest, half of the city looks like an abandoned construction site. Huge cranes still tower over half-finished apartment buildings, just as they did four months ago. Those buildings, part of Mr. Ceausescu's hated reconstruction project, have been halted for political reasons as the Government tries to figure out what to do with them. But other buildings in the countryside, also half-finished but already collapsing, stand as a testament to the appalling waste and shoddiness of long decades under Communist rule.

Poor Health Care: No Moral Urgency?

The worst damage done by Mr. Ceausescu and his predecessors is not visible to the traveler passing through Romania: the crowded and unsanitary orphanages, home to about 14,000 abandoned children; hospitals where patients sleep two to a bed; mental asylums where in winter patients go through the snow to the toilet; clinics where harried nurses try to keep up with the ceaseless demands of babies with AIDS, a disease that under Mr. Ceausescu was decreed to be nonexistent.

The result has been the systematic erosion of human values, damage that has lingered after the revolution. Romanian and foreign doctors lament the lack of moral urgency on the part of some officials, even in the medical profession itself.

Even since the discovery of AIDS among children, officials have been slow to contain the spread of the disease.

"I don't know who is responsible for new children being infected now," said Dr. Stefan Constantinescu, at the AIDS laboratory at the Institute of Virology in Bucharest. "It is not Ceausescu anymore."

"We have to start from zero," said Mr. Sorescu. "We have to make an inventory of what we have, and what we don't, and simply state the facts. We have to face the crisis sincerely and admit that at this point, Romania is poorer than countries in Africa."

The Prospects For a Coalition

With three strong personalities in the race, the presidential contest has captured the public's attention and its emotions. Mr. Iliescu is the favorite, and draws huge crowds outside Bucharest, where people welcome him with signs calling on him to "be like a parent." Of the other two, Mr. Campeanu, who has served as interim Vice President, has the most credibility, although he and Mr. Ratiu, who lived abroad for the last 17 and 50 years respectively, are handicapped by the time they spent out of Romania.

In outlying regions, the ruling front has established itself as the party not only of Mr. Iliescu and the revolution, but also of local notables.

Despite those and other advantages, including prime-time coverage on television, the front might not win a majority of seats in Parliament, which would force it into a coalition with one of its two major opponents. Such a coalition, some Romanians say, would provide the balance needed to keep the front from sliding into old authoritarian habits.

A balanced Parliament might also help Romania avoid another dangerous option—a takeover by the armed forces, which played a critical role in the revolution and must view the current disarray in society and the economy with alarm.

Hunting Cohorts Of the Old Order

The main objection to the front is that it is filled with former Communists who have not abandoned either the party's ideology or its old methods. But as the other parties are finding, it is not easy in post-Ceausescu Romania to bar all former Communists from political life. There were 3.8 million Communist Party members in Romania, out of a total population of 23 million—the highest proportion of party membership of any country in Eastern Europe.

"We know that a large majority were in the party against their will," said Valentin Gabrielescu, spokesman for the Peasants Party. "We do not congratulate them for their weakness, but we will let them in our party. It would be stupid not to. But the ones we will never tolerate are the Securitate, the ministers and the members of the Communist aristocracy—the grand chefs."

Since the execution of Nicolae and Elena Ceausescu on Christmas Day, the search has been on to find those who were more than passive participants in the Ceausescus' grotesque cult of personality.

And yet, even as Romanians continue to uncover new horrors committed by the old regime, they are having great difficulty in figuring out who to blame, and how best to mete out justice.

The Securitate: Where Did It Go?

The slow pace of justice has frustrated many people, particularly the young, and added more weight to the suspicion that the front is not committed to sweeping out survivors of the old regime.

Even Silviu Brucan, a leading figure in the front, has not been able to track down his old tormentors. Mr. Brucan, both a veteran Communist and a dissident who spent much of the end of the Ceausescu period under house arrest, recently retrieved his dossier from the Securitate files—three volumes, thick as phone books, blackened and charred around the edges where someone apparently tried unsuccessfully to destroy them by fire.

The files, which Mr. Brucan now keeps in his desk, are a testament to the Securitate's thorough and obsessive regard for its enemies. There are verbatim transcripts of breakfast conversations recorded between Mr. Brucan and his wife in the village outside Bucharest where they lived under house arrest, and meticulous records of his morning trips to the neighborhood store to buy bread and milk.

From the file, Mr. Brucan learned for the first time the names of those who interrogated him when he was arrested in 1988 after he and five others published a letter critical of Mr. Ceausescu. After the revolution, all three men have disappeared without a trace. But, said Mr. Brucan, "I am still looking."

* * *

May 21, 1990

FRONT IN ROMANIA SEEMS VICTORIOUS IN FREE ELECTIONS

By DAVID BINDER
Special to The New York Times

BUCHAREST, Romania, May 20—The National Salvation Front, the group dominated by former Communists that has run Romania since the violent revolution last December, appeared to be headed toward a convincing victory today in the country's first free national elections in more than 50 years.

According to projections based on polls outside 252 voting sites across the country, Ion Iliescu, the head of the Front and the interim head of state, won 83 percent of the vote for a new President. The Front also won 66 percent in elections for the National Assembly and the Senate, according to the polls conducted by Infas, a West German political-opinion research organization. Most opposition parties had disappointing showings, far below their expectations.

No votes have been counted and scores of thousands of voters were still lined up outside polling stations in Bucharest at midnight, when the polls officially closed. Casting ballots was a tedious procedure in Romania's first free elections since 1937, with each voter expected to read through and stamp choices on a total of 37 pages of candidates.

Official Results Tuesday

The earliest official results are expected to be issued by the national election board on Tuesday.

Still, the polls projected a strong showing for the Front, which would snap a string of election victories by conservative political parties elsewhere in Eastern Europe, where Communist governments have been ousted in the last 12 months, in Poland, Hungary and East Germany.

Led by Mr. Iliescu, a 60-year-old former Communist Party secretary, the Front took power last Dec. 22 after President Nicolae Ceausescu fled from his office in the face of a popular uprising, ending a tyrannical reign of 24 years; Mr. Ceausescu and his wife, Elena, were executed on Christmas Day. The Front has enjoyed the powers of incumbency ever since, even though it has faced fierce criticism and rejection by many Romanians for being made up mostly of former Communist Party members who had served the Ceausescu Government.

Others Lack Resources

Opposition parties formed since the December revolution include revivals of the prewar National Peasants Party and National Liberal Party. But they lacked the resources and time to organize a truly effective alternative to the Front.

The Peasants Party's presidential candidate, Ion Ratiu, received only 6 percent of the vote, according to the Infas projections, and the party got only 4 percent in the National Assembly and 3.5 percent in the Senate races.

The Liberal presidential candidate, Radu Campeanu, like Mr. Ratiu long an exile until returning to Romania early this year, received 11 percent.

In the National Assembly races, the Liberals received 10 percent and for the Senate, 9.5 percent, according to the polling.

Those showings, if confirmed in the final count, appear to render moot the question of whether the Liberals could offer themselves as coalition partners of the Front or accept a coalition offer from Mr. Iliescu.

Militants in Opposition

At the same time, such a gigantic endorsement may cause Mr. Iliescu further problems with more militant members of the opposition, many of whom were still out in the streets of the capital tonight shouting anti-Communist slogans against him and the Front.

His taking 83 percent of the vote might lend greater credence to charges of fraud; Mr. Ceausescu used to declare himself victor with 98 percent of the vote in his unopposed election races.

One of the election's surprises, judging by the Infas sampling of 16,000 voters, was the strong showing of a new envi-

Romanians waiting to vote outside Bucharest. The National Salvation Front, composed largely of former Communists, appeared far ahead.

ronmental party, which gained 5 percent in both parliamentary races.

Apparently the exit polls were unable to take account of the thousands of independent candidates running by themselves or as candidates of one of the 80 other small parties registered in the elections. Their standings will become apparent only later.

Still, the elections would appear to be a personal victory for Mr. Iliescu, who has vowed that he has shed his Leninist past and wants to lead Romania on a path of social democracy. He himself had been relegated to minor posts in the 1970's after being deemed insufficiently loyal by Ceausescu.

An Offering of Stability

In interviews at polling stations, Romanians in and around Bucharest said they liked Mr. Iliescu and felt the Front would offer more stability in a country that is still fraught with chaos.

There were signs here and there that former members of the defunct Communist Party might attempt to manipulate the results in their districts in favor of the National Salvation Front.

As the evening wore on, reports coming in from some of the 500 foreign observers spread out through the country indicated a number of acts of intimidation and outright infractions of missing ballots, missing rubber stamps for voting, and ballot-box stuffing.

In Election District 122 in the center of the capital, for example, the independent chairman of the election board,

Florin Gloteanu, was suddenly replaced by a man identified with the Front named Mircea Carlin.

Protests From Engineer

When Mr. Carlin showed up with some toughs at his side, a district representative of the National Liberal Party demanded to know what was going on and who the extras were.

"I can bring my dog if I want to," Mr. Carlin told Bogdan Grigoroiu, the Liberal Party official.

A hot argument ensued. When Mr. Grigoroiu called the Mayor's Office to inquire what had happened to Mr. Gloteanu, the previous chairman, he was told, "Maybe he died."

Mr. Grigoroiu, a bearded young electrical engineer, protested the substitution and he also protested the arrival of an excessive and uncounted number of ballots and, stranger still, of the rubber stamps to be used by voters at the polling place. The rubber stamps were not supposed to arrive until 5 A.M. Sunday morning.

'Watching Like a Hawk'

Mr. Grigoroiu said he had made certain that the large ballot box with two slots for District 122 was empty when voting started at 6 A.M. in the schoolhouse on Mihai Eminescu Street.

He also pointed out that both Mr. Carlin and Mr. Gloteanu were present this afternoon, saying of the latter, "You see, he is not dead."

The dead of Romania may yet play a problematic role in the election, since, according to experts, roughly a million citizens have died since the last national census in 1977, while their names have remained on the voting lists.

Huge Turnout in Village

A few miles north of Bucharest in Tunari, a village of 4,000 inhabitants, 2,800 of them of voting age, there was a huge turnout as there seemed to be all over the country.

Inside the polling station, infractions of the election law passed in March by the provisional parliament could be observed, such as polling officials paging through the lengthy ballots for Parliament before they were cast by voters and voters going behind the yellow curtains of the balloting booths in pairs.

Outside the village clinic, the spirit was festive, with voters, a third of them of gypsy nationality, in Sunday best.

"It is not so important who wins," said Anton Chirita, a gypsy who is a radio parts maker. "The main thing is that we have democracy and freedom."

"Those who don't vote are their own enemies," said another Tunari voter.

Between Tunari and Balotesti, the next village, four miles north, a whole community of 3,000 houses was torn down several years ago as part of the Ceausescu "systemization" plan of eliminating thousands of Romanian villages and concentrating their inhabitants in large apartment buildings.

"It is an awful life in the flats," said a Tunari voter, "no running water and the toilets are outside!"

"We are happy that our own houses were not destroyed," said a Balotesti voter. "They were scheduled to go last March if Ceausescu had lived. We barely escaped." In fact those facing demolition had been told to level their own houses or face fines of 7,000 lei.

In the capital itself, Mr. Iliescu cast his ballot at 6:14 A.M. early enough, he said, to avoid television cameras and a crush of news photographers. A crowd of 1,000 cheered Radu Campeanu, the Liberal candidate, when he went to vote later in the morning in the capital.

*　　*　　*

June 10, 1990

ROUND ONE: ELECTIONS IN BULGARIA

THE VOTING

Two rounds of secret-ballot voting will be held to fill the 400 seats in Bulgaria's unicameral Grand National Assembly. In its next session, the Assembly will function both as a constituent assembly and a legislature.

The first round of voting is today and the second is June 17. It is the first free, multi-party election in Bulgaria since the Communists took power after World War II.

Voters will elect deputies by a simple majority, one each in 200 electoral districts; the other 200 deputies will be elected by a proportional representation scheme in 28 multi-member districts. There are about 3,100 candidates.

About 6.7 million of Bulgaria's nine million people are registered to vote. A heavy turnout is expected.

THE PARTIES AND MOVEMENTS
Bulgarian Socialist Party
Formerly the Bulgarian Communist Party

It has monopolized Bulgarian political life since World War II. Its main strength lies in its financial resources and still entrenched party apparatus, in the government bureaucracy, economic enterprises and military. Its platform endorses the multi-party political system and a gradual introduction of a market-based economic system.

The party's leader, Aleksandar Lilov, and Bulgaria's President, Petar Mladenov, and Prime Minister, Andrey Lukanov, won considerable popular support after unseating the Communist dictator, Todor Zhivkov, last November. The Socialist Party's support has waned as the opposition has solidified and struggled to focus public attention on the party's 45 years of totalitarian rule rather than the reforms it has introduced in the last six months.

Union of Democratic Forces

A coalition of 16 political parties and organizations, the Union of Democratic Forces is Bulgaria's largest opposition political group. Member organizations include Ecoglasnost, an environmental organization; the Club for Glasnost and Democracy, an intellectuals' organization that has given the coalition several of its top leaders; Podkrepa, an independent trade union; the Bulgarian Agrarian National Union-Nikola Petkov, a party offshoot that is named for an agrarian leader executed in 1947 and that is opposed to the Communist takeover of Bulgaria after World War II; and the Bulgarian Social Democratic Party.

Opposition to the Socialist Party bonds the coalition's disparate member organizations together. Under the chairmanship of Zhelyu Zhelev, a dissident philosopher, it has won considerable support in the capital, Sofia, and has recently gained momentum in the countryside with its anti-Communist message and called for "shock therapy" to solve Bulgaria's economic and social woes.

Bulgarian Agrarian National Union

Once a satellite party to the Bulgarian Communist Party, the "official" Bulgarian Agrarian National Union left the government last November and purged its former leaders. Its chairman, Viktor Vulkov, has proclaimed the party a part of the opposition and hopes to make it the country's third political force. It is a centrist party whose main goal is land redistribution.

The Movement for Rights and Freedom

The movement is largely a Muslim party that in recent weeks has emerged as the main representative of Bulgaria's two million ethnic Turks, Bulgarian Muslims and Gypsies.

The party's leader, Ahmed Dogan, who spent over three years in prison for leading demonstrations against enforced cultural assimilation of Bulgaria's ethnic Turks in 1984-85, hopes the party will win 30 to 40 assembly seats and plans to work to secure minority and religious rights.

Other Parties

There are 32 other, smaller parties, ranging from extreme right-wing nationalists to a party that wants a return of the king from exile.

* * *

June 12, 1990

BULGARIAN VOTING STUNS OPPOSITION

By CELESTINE BOHLEN
Special to The New York Times

SOFIA, Bulgaria, June 11—Stunned by the Bulgarian Socialist Party's decisive victory in Sunday's parliamentary elections, leaders of the main opposition group told a rally today that they would keep up their fight against the former Communists, refusing all offers to form a coalition government.

"We will enter the National Assembly as an opposition that will confront the Communist Party with its crimes, and insist that it take responsibility for everything it has done under its rule," vowed Zhelyu Zhelev, head of the Union of Democratic Forces, before a crowd of about 50,000 people who gathered to protest the election results.

Official results on the elections to the 400-seat Grand National Assembly were not complete today. But preliminary results show the Socialists ahead with about 48 percent and the Union of Democratic Forces with 34 percent.

Many Bulgarians are still absorbing the news that after 45 years of Communist rule, almost one in two voters gave the Communists' successor, the Socialist Party, a mandate to lead the country again.

Although Bulgarian Communists have shed their old name and eased their grip on economic and political life, their victory still set a precedent—it was the first time that a ruling Marxist party has competed in multiparty national elections and won since the collapse of Communist rule began in Eastern Europe last year.

Socialist Leader Urges Calm

In a television appearance tonight, Andrei Lukanov, the Socialist Prime Minister and an architect of the party's changes, appealed for calm. He called the election "the first step toward the creation of a democratic society."

At a news conference, representatives from several international observer teams declared that the elections had been free and fair, although a separate, unofficial group of monitors, led by Americans, maintained that "fear is still a factor."

The opposition accused the Socialist Party of resorting to fraud and intimidation to win the elections, but its leadership stopped short of calls to invalidate the vote. A second round of voting will be held on June 17 in districts where no candidate won more than 50 percent.

Tens of thousands of disappointed opposition supporters paraded peacefully for several hours through the capital tonight, without any interference from the police, who in some cases moved to the sidewalk to let the chanting, flag-waving protesters pass by.

A breakdown by Bulgaria's 28 electoral districts, based on a tally drawn from 1,300 selected precincts, showed the Socialists winning in all but three districts.

Ethnic Turks Give a Pledge

Sofia, the capital, was captured by the Union of Democratic Forces, while the Turkish Rights Movement won in Razgrad and Kirdzhali, two regions where ethnic Turks make up a majority. The Turks' leader, Ahmed Dogan, pledged cooperation with the Union of Democratic Forces in the second round.

Projections for the 200 Assembly seats apportioned by proportional representation show the Socialists with 100 seats, compared the Union's 67 and the Turkish Rights Movement's 17. The Bulgarian Agrarian Party has so far captured only 16.

Results from the 200 single-member districts were still not available.

The Assembly, which will sit for 18 months, has the responsibility of rewriting the Bulgarian Constitution. But the new Government first must tackle the worsening economic situation, in particular a $10.3 billion debt and a severe cutback in factory orders from the Soviet Union.

To deal with these problems, the Socialist Party has said it will seek a broad-based coalition. But the rejection by the Union of Democratic Forces, a group made up of 16 parties and movements, means the Socialists' narrow majority will be put under considerable pressure.

The victory by the former Communists in Bulgaria, the last country in Eastern Europe to hold free elections, was in part a reflection of people's reluctance to embrace change, some people here said.

Living Standards Improved

Members of the Socialist Party said the vote was also an indication of the people's loyalty to a Government that since World War II has increased the standard of living and kept the peace, although with an iron hand.

But many people who were out demonstrating in the streets of Sofia said the vote showed the continued hold that local Communist authorities still have on the population, particularly in the countryside.

"People think the Communists are omniscient," said Filip Dmitrov, deputy chairman of the Bulgarian Green Party. "That is how they are intimidated."

At back-to-back news conferences, two groups of observers differed over the fairness of the Bulgarian elections.

Although repeatedly given second-hand accounts of intimidation, Geoffrey Tordoff, a member of the House of Lords and head of the British team, said he could find no corroboration of a single instance of political pressure.

Associated Press

Leaders of the opposition to the Bulgarian Socialist Party said they would continue to fight against the former Communists despite their victory in Sunday's elections. Tens of thousands of opposition supporters paraded through Sofia yesterday, demonstrating in front of the National Assembly.

But a team of 60 observers from 23 countries led by the National Democratic and Republican Institutes in Washington, D.C., reported finding evidence of the legacy of dictatorship—"psychological and sociological" pressures "not visible to the naked eye."

"One could smell it," said Tibor Vidos, director of the Alliance of Free Democrats, a major Hungarian party, who came here as an observer. "People coming from Eastern Europe have a nose, and we can identify how people behave."

The official United States delegation did not issue a statement in Sofia. A spokesman said it will be delivered first to the White House.

Reports of intimidation by local Communist authorities, who continue to have considerable control over jobs, housing and other necessities, had surfaced before the elections in interviews to opposition figures, journalists and human rights monitors.

Today, speaking to the protesters, Mr. Zhelev said such behavior should have been expected. "It would have been strange and naive to expect any other way of proceeding on the part of a party that came to power by fraud and violence and kept power for 45 years by fraud and violence," he said.

*   *   *

June 14, 1990

ROMANIAN TROOPS FIRE ON PROTEST; 4 DIE, 93 ARE HURT

By The Associated Press

BUCHAREST, Romania, June 13—Soldiers shot demonstrators outside the Romanian Interior Ministry tonight after protesters raided state television offices and burned down the police headquarters, witnesses said.

The state radio reported that 4 people were killed and 93 were hospitalized, 4 of them in a "grave state." Two of those killed were shot to death, the broadcast said, quoting the Health Ministry.

The Soviet press agency Tass, in a dispatch from Bucharest, said "many cars" near the Interior Ministry and the police

Romanian troops reportedly fired on demonstrators who rampaged through Bucharest yesterday. Police officers and soldiers clashed with protesters after a 53-day anti-Communist demonstration was broken up.

headquarters had been overturned and set ablaze, and two buildings nearby were also on fire.

Worst Violence Since December

The violence was the worst in Eastern Europe since December, when a popular revolt in this country led to the ouster of the dictator Nicolae Ceausescu. Mr. Ceausescu was executed with his wife, Elena, on Dec. 25.

The Romanian Interior Ministry occupies the building that was formerly the headquarters of Mr. Ceausescu's secret police, the Securitate.

President-elect Ion Iliescu today accused extremist elements of organizing what he termed an "Iron Guard rebellion" against the Government, a reference to a pre-World War II party that supported the Nazis.

Long Occupation Ended

The violence was touched off by a police raid before dawn that ended a 53-day anti-Communist protest in University Square in downtown Bucharest. The police clubbed and dragged away the protesters.

These demonstrators had been demanding that former high-ranking Communists like Mr. Iliescu be banned from holding public office for 10 years and that independent television stations be established. [In Washington, the State Department said

it deplored the use "of excessive force by the authorities in clearing the square." A State Department statement said: "We are concerned that this action by the Romanian authorities may set off a cycle of violence. President Iliescu and his Government must now exercise restraint."] A witness to the violence said she helped carry 12 bodies from the Interior Ministry area. Another witness reported seeing at least two bodies. These reports could not be independently confirmed.

Demonstrators halted broadcasts for about 45 minutes at the television station, the scene of heavy fighting and urgent on-air appeals for an end to Communist rule in December.

The Romanian press agency reported that people were "seriously wounded" near the Interior Ministry, the police headquarters and the television station.

Government Musters Backers

Thousands of Government supporters gathered at Government headquarters at Victory Square late this afternoon in response to Mr. Iliescu's appeal for "responsible people" to protect public buildings. The press agency said 5,000 miners and thousands of other Government supporters were bound for Bucharest from outlying areas.

An opposition leader, Senator Radu Campeanu, chief of the Liberal Party, said the influx of Government backers into the capital would only aggravate the situation.

The violence came weeks after Romania's first free elections in more than four decades on May 20. The elections were marred by allegations of campaign and electoral irregularities.

The demonstrators have said that Communists still dominate the National Salvation Front, in power since December and the overwhelming winners of last month's elections.

The protesters fought the police in the afternoon in University Square, then fanned out to the police headquarters, the Interior Ministry, the television station and Victory Square.

Coup Attempt Is Charged

"We are now facing an organized, planned attempt to overthrow through force and violence the leadership elected in a free and democratic way," Mr. Iliescu said in a statement tonight. Mr. Iliescu, the first former Communist to win a free presidential election in Eastern Europe, pleaded for support for the army and security forces "to liquidate this Iron Guard rebellion and reinstate calm."

A Government statement said demonstrators stole weapons, ammunition and police uniforms from the Interior Ministry. It said a filling station near the ministry was attacked and gasoline stolen to make firebombs.

A protester, Rebecca Doina Cercel, said she and others helped carry 12 bodies to ambulances outside the ministry. She said the bodies were taken to the morgue.

Mrs. Cercel's 4-year-old son was killed in the uprising last December. She had been in University Square since the protest began in April.

Mrs. Cercel, 25 years old, said the police clubbed her. She had bruises on her face and abdomen.

Photographer's Account

A freelance photographer, Jeremy Sutton-Hibbert, of Scotland, said he saw soldiers shooting from inside the ministry and the body of a man shot in the head.

Gabriel Paslaru, a reporter for The Associated Press, said demonstrators who tried to break through the main gate of the ministry building were met with rifle fire or single shots.

"I saw one man with an injured hand who fainted before he was rushed into a car and another man who was hit in the neck," Mr. Paslaru said. "His face was a red mask of blood—it is hard to believe he could survive."

Earlier in the day, the police had said that about 260 people had been detained.

At the height of the protest, the state-run television station was raided by protesters who occupied one of the main studios. An announcer said they might not be able to transmit any longer.

Minutes later, the picture was cut and then the sound but the station went back on the air 45 minutes later.

"A bunch of people who were drunk got into the TV, and it is a grave situation which we hope will never again occur," said the station's director, Razvan Teodorescu.

Before taking over the station, demonstrators carrying gasoline cans and clubs broke into police headquarters in central Bucharest, then set fire to nearby cars and trucks and a wing of the building.

About 1,500 people gathered outside and booed when helicopters approached. Some protesters marched toward Victory Square, headquarters of the National Salvation Front.

Tent Camp Destroyed

The violence began before dawn, when the police sealed off the central square with trucks and buses, then moved in on the sleeping demonstrators with clubs.

The police ripped down the tent camp the protesters had built, where some had been on hunger strikes.

By midafternoon, the steel-helmeted policemen were battling about 1,000 protesters who overturned a police van and freed two prisoners, then set the van ablaze, witnesses said.

Fleeing demonstrators smashed glass doors to get inside the nearby Inter-Continental Hotel but were dragged away by the police. The protesters hurled rocks at the policemen, who threw the stones back.

*　*　*

June 15, 1990

ROMANIAN MINERS INVADE BUCHAREST

By CELESTINE BOHLEN
Special to The New York Times

BUCHAREST, Romania, June 14—Responding to an emergency appeal by President Ion Iliescu, thousands of miners from northern Romania descended on the capital city today with wooden clubs and rubber truncheons and sought crude revenge for anti-Government rioting Wednesday.

In grimy work clothes and helmets, their faces blackened by soot, the miners took control of Bucharest's main boulevard and central square, menacing and beating passers-by whom they apparently suspected of having tried to bring down the Iliescu Government.

Associated Press

Miners from northern Romania attacking an anti-Government demonstrator with clubs yesterday in University Square in Bucharest. The miners were responding to an appeal to help President Ion Iliescu.

Their suspicions appeared to be indiscriminate; motorists in their cars, well-dressed professors, students, photographers, reporters, mothers with children and girls walking their dogs were chased off the street, sometimes hit across the shoulders with rubber hoses.

By evening, the miners had emptied University Square, which was the setting of a marathon anti-Government demonstration that was broken up in a police raid before dawn Wednesday.

Summoned by Mr. Iliescu to save the Government from a "fascist rebellion," the miners joined other workers loyal to the governing National Salvation Front early this morning and ransacked the headquarters of the two main opposition parties, setting fires, breaking windows and carting off or destroying equipment and documents.

The miners' arrival in the city came the day after soldiers opened fire on anti-Government demonstrators outside the Interior Ministry, killing at least four and wounding scores in the worst violence in Eastern Europe since December, when Nicolae Ceausescu was overthrown in a popular revolt.

Opposition Papers Seized

In the violence today, pro-Government workers laid siege to the apartments of prominent Government opponents and halted the publication of Romania Libera, the main opposition newspaper.

By the afternoon, the miners were still in control of the headquarters of one opposition party, the Peasants Party, lounging in the courtyard and on the balconies amid broken typewriters and piles of trash. At the Liberal Party headquarters, militiamen guarded the doors, while party members stayed away.

"We took a common decision to stay home and stay in touch by telephone," said Sorin Botez, a spokesman for the Liberal Party. Other critics of the Government also stayed off the streets today.

The rampage by the miners and other workers, tolerated by the few policemen visible today in Bucharest, came just as Romania's new Government, headed by Mr. Iliescu and the front, is about to take office. Although bitterly opposed by students, liberal intellectuals and the so-called historical parties, the front won the May 20 election by a landslide, buoyed by Mr. Iliescu's personal popular appeal.

Attacks by Miners Assailed

The extent of the Government's role in bringing the miners to the city, beyond Mr. Iliescu's appeal, was not known. A Government spokesman, Ion Pascu, said the police and the army had not responded to save the Government in what he called a coup attempt by opposition forces. The spokesmen said that in the absence of an adequate police force, the Government would continue to rely on the miners, who he said might stay in the capital for another two or three days. The miners are thought to number about 7,000.

Although the miners said that they came to Bucharest spontaneously after Mr. Iliescu's summons, the Government

has clearly taken responsibility for them. This afternoon buses arrived at University Square to take the miners to an exhibition hall where they watched the World Cup soccer match before being bused back to the square and then to some location in the city where they were spending the night.

Mr. Botez criticized the attacks against the Government on Wednesday, but said they did not justify Mr. Iliescu's call to the miners. "It is not a good beginning for a new Government to start with acts of terrorism," he said. "It is a unique case in European history, a world premiere, for a president to incite one part of the population against the other."

Dumitru Mazilu, who resigned from the leadership of the front last winter in a dispute over the Government's response to a demonstration against the front, said today that his apartment was surrounded for about five hours by a group of belligerent miners, armed with sticks, who threatened to kill him.

In a pre-dawn raid Wednesday, the police cracked down on the protest that had occupied University Square for seven weeks.

Witnesses to the raid Wednesday said a number of protesters were beaten as they were dragged off by the police and 253 were arrested—although all were released a few hours later.

Later in the day anti-Government protesters armed with gasoline bombs and guns seized in a raid on Central Police Headquarters, laid siege to the Interior Ministry, the state TV station and the Government's central offices at Victory Square. Five people were killed and 277 were wounded, the Health Ministry said.

Because of the crisis, sessions of the assembly and senate scheduled for today were postponed until Monday. A joint session after that is formally to appoint Mr. Iliescu head of state.

A miners' spokesman said in a statement carried by the Rompres press agency that they would stay in Bucharest as long as necessary. "We shall stay here until we are sure that order is reinstated and people go back to work," the statement said. "Nobody called us to Bucharest so we won't accept anyone telling us to go back home."

Mr. Pascu said the Government would continue to rely on the miners while examining the creation of a new police force, a kind of national guard, that would supplement the function of the municipal police.

'Vigilante Violence' Assailed

WASHINGTON, June 14 (Reuters)—The United States accused Romania today of using vigilante violence against anti-Government demonstrators and said it would defer a decision on normalizing trade ties.

"The United States condemns in the strongest possible terms the rioting of the past two days, and the Government-inspired vigilante violence that departs from the commonly accepted norms of democracy and the rule of law," said the White House spokesman, Marlin Fitzwater. "We are concerned that the deplorable events of the past two days are being used to justify the suppression of legitimate dissent in Romania."

The State Department spokeswoman, Margaret D. Tutwiler, replied affirmatively when asked if it was fair to assume that Washington would defer a decision on granting most-favored-nation-status to Romania until it is satisfied with the human-rights situation there.

The British Government accused the Iliescu Government of using the tactics of the Ceausescu regime. In London, a Foreign Office official, William Waldegrave, said: "What is depressing is both the rhetoric—talking about all their opponents being fascists and gypsies, just like Ceausescu—and the way in which they called out the 'rent-a-mob' of coal miners who were bused in, armed with pickax handles and knives, and loosed off into the streets."

* * *

June 30, 1990

ALL WE CROATIONS WANT IS DEMOCRACY

By FRANJO TUDJMAN

ZAGREB, Yugoslavia—Last month the Croatian people, sick and tired of Communist oppression, joined the peoples of Eastern Europe in looking away from Communism and toward a democratic future. We have set the goal of a Croatian society that, like the United States, is based on political and economic freedom, respect for human rights, the protection of individual liberties, an independent judiciary and a government that is truly "of the people, by the people, and for the people."

There are those, however, even in America, who fear any measure of Croatian democracy. This surge of national identity and authority will, some say, lead to the breakup of Yugoslavia, to civil war, or both.

These fears are misplaced. Freedom and self-determination do not threaten stability; repression and tyranny do. To reject Croatia's transition to a democracy on the pretext of preserving regional stability only delays the inevitable—and heightens the risk of regional chaos and violence at some date in the future.

The democratization of Croatia will lead neither to the breakup of Yugoslavia nor to civil war. These threats represent a last desperate ploy by the central Communist government in Belgrade to win Western neutrality on the issue of Croatian democratization.

Belgrade has learned and implemented the lesson of Lithuania: rather than condemning democratization, the Communists argue that the price of democratization is higher than the West should be willing to pay. This crude bit of disinformation threatens to undermine Western support for the emergence of democracy, based on free and fair elections, in a Communist country.

In fact, if Belgrade does not cause a civil war by military intervention, there will be no civil war. Croatia is wealthier and more productive than all but one of the other Yugoslav republics. That republic, Slovenia, has held elections recently that also resulted in a mandate for greater autonomy.

It is up to Belgrade whether Yugoslavia will continue to profit from a confederation including Croatia, or whether Yugoslavia will forgo a relationship that remains crucial for the economic stability of the other republics.

It is we, the Croatian people, who have risked our lives to put forward a democratic party and to vote our conscience. And it is we who continue to risk our lives in defiance of totalitarian Communism. If Belgrade chooses to attack us for choosing freedom, we remain prepared to defend our liberty with our blood. It is the height of arrogance for the U.S. to dismiss Croatian democracy on the ground that regional stability is at stake, when we Croatians are willing to put our lives at stake for our freedom and dignity.

The end of Communist rule in Croatia will not result in a domestic bloodbath, as the Belgrade propaganda asserts; there will be no purges against Serbians or retribution against Communist officials and their families.

And I know well the temptation of retribution. Three years ago, when I was 65 years old and after the Communists had sent me to prison twice, I learned the names of the Communist soldiers who shot and killed my father and stepmother in cold blood. These men live today in the Republic of Croatia. For more than four decades, I believed the lie that my parents had been killed by Nazi collaborators. Similar ghastly stories are common in Croatia.

The Croatian Democratic Union and I were elected to end such tyranny. And, despite 45 years of brutal Communist rule, and despite the association of many people with these oppressors, I vow to allow no reprisals in a newly democratic Croatia. I will work to build a society which is a vibrant marketplace of ideas and initiative, where disagreement and debate are signs of strength.

The Communist soldiers who murdered my parents will be judged by God alone. I no longer yearn for revenge; the murderous, inhumane system that killed my parents and tens of thousands like them has been judged for its crimes—in free and fair elections—by the Croatian people. That system has been decapitated.

Franco Tudjman is President of the Republic of Croatia. His conservative, nationalist party recently won a majority in the Croatian parliament.

* * *

July 6, 1990

SERBIA SUSPENDS GOVERNMENT OF ALBANIAN REGION

By CHUCK SUDETIC
Special to The New York Times

BELGRADE, Yugoslavia, July 5—The Parliament of the Yugoslav republic of Serbia today suspended the Assembly and the Executive Council of the Kosovo region, which has a

90 percent ethnic Albanian population and has been the scene of ethnic disorders.

The Parliament also dismissed the editors of Kosovo's main Albanian-language newspapers and the managers of its radio and television stations.

The action extinguishes what remained of the Kosovo region's autonomy and it is certain to exacerbate already bitter relations between the region's ethnic Albanian majority and Serbian minority.

"The Albanian people are nervous but remaining calm," said Ibrahim Rugova, a leader of the ethnic Albanian opposition. "It is very dangerous now," he said by telephone from Kosovo.

Policemen seized the radio and television stations in Pristina, the regional capital, at 3 A.M., Belgrade television reported.

Stations Go Off the Air

Mr. Rugova said Albanian-language radio and television broadcasts have gone off the air, and that the police were guarding the newspaper building and the radio and broadcast stations.

"The police even took over the headquarters of the Kosovo Writers Association at 4 o'clock this afternoon," Mr. Rugova said, referring to a building that the Albanian opposition used for meetings and news conferences. "There is no more Albanian authority in Kosovo now."

"Everything the Serbs say about democracy is now obviously exposed as demagoguery," he said. "They take care of themselves and repress us."

Mr. Rugova added that the ethnic Albanian opposition would continue even if outlawed.

The Serbia Parliament's action followed a vote last Monday by ethnic Albanian members of the Kosovo Legislature to declare the region a constituent territorial unit within the Yugoslav federation, with all the rights and powers of the country's six republics, said Aleksandar Prlja, the Serbian Secretary for Foreign Relations.

Albanian Vote Worried Serbs

The ethnic Albanians' vote brought condemnation throughout Serbia. It was seen as evidence that the ethnic Albanians would eventually want to sever Kosovo, a center of ancient Serbia, from Yugoslavia and merge it with neighboring Albania.

Yugoslavia's republics have a vaguely defined right to secede from the federation, and newly elected non-Communist governments in the republics of Slovenia and Croatia are threatening to exercise that right.

Kosovo, which had de facto republican status under Yugoslavia's 1974 Constitution, lost most of its autonomy in March 1989 when the Serbian Government pushed through constitutional amendments. More than 50 ethnic Albanians have died in the last 18 months in clashes with the police.

"It is unthinkable that Kosovo's Assembly could declare a state within the Yugoslav federation," Mr. Prlja said. "There is no room for a second Albanian state either in Serbia or in Yugoslavia. The sooner the Albanians shed their illusions that there could be the possibility of having a second state in Serbia, the better it will be for everybody."

Serbs Assume All Powers

Serbia's Parliament and Executive Council have assumed all legislative and administrative powers in Kosovo. The Serbian police took control of law enforcement there three months ago.

Ethnic Albanian members of the Kosovo Assembly are reportedly traveling to Belgrade to consult with Yugoslav federal authorities.

Kosovo's legislature will not be reconvened until after the Serbian Parliament adopts a new republican constitution and free multiparty elections are held, Mr. Prlja said.

Under the Constitution, the Kosovo Assembly appoints the region's Executive Committee and the managers of press and broadcasting organizations. Mr. Prlja said that last year's amendments gave the Serbian Parliament the right to carry out the suspensions.

The move by Kosovo to declare equal status within Yugoslavia came in the wake of a hastily called referendum throughout Serbia last weekend, in which 90 percent of the voters opted to delay free, multiparty elections in the republic until after the Communist-controlled Parliament adopts a new constitution.

The ethnic Albanians boycotted and obstructed the referendum.

Six-Day Notice of Referendum

Faced with angry anti-Communist demonstrations in the streets of Belgrade twice in the last few months, calling for free multiparty elections, Serbia's hard-line leader, Slobodan Milosevic, announced the referendum only six days before it was held.

He originally characterized the referendum as a chance for Serbia's voters to indicate clearly whether they wanted free, multiparty elections before a new constitution.

It is expected that the referendum would result in a limited role for the Communists in setting up a constitutional framework, as had been the case elsewhere in Eastern Europe, or to have the elections come after leaving the constitutional work to the present party dominated legislature.

However, as drafted, the proposition linked endorsement of the present Parliament to the acceptance of a broad statement of national and territorial unity.

"There is no question that a new constitution is necessary but what is in question is who should draft and adopt it," said Kosta Cavoski, president of the opposition Democratic Party Executive Committee, who said he expected free elections to be delayed for a year or more.

"Must we allow the existing illegitimate, one-party, Communist Parliament to draft the constitution or do we want a legitimately elected constituent assembly?"

* * *

July 7, 1990

BULGARIA'S LEADER QUITS POST OVER CRACKDOWN ON PROTEST

By Reuters

SOFIA, Bulgaria, July 6—President Petar Mladenov quit today over accusations that he ordered tanks to disperse an anti-Government protest in December, and his resignation set off rejoicing by thousands of Bulgarians.

"Never again a Communist President in Bulgaria!" a member of the Union of Democratic Forces told about 5,000 people gathered outside Mr. Mladenov's office after he quit.

"Never!" they shouted back. "Never!" Many chanted "Victory!" and danced and hugged each other. Some carried banners that called Mr. Mladenov a liar. Others pulled model tanks up and down the pavement, mocking Mr. Mladenov.

But Prime Minister Andrei Lukanov asked Bulgarians in a statement on television not to strike or demonstrate for one week, so that the new Parliament could open in an atmosphere of calm.

Threat of a General Strike

Mr. Mladenov submitted his resignation to Bulgaria's newly elected Parliament "in order not to be a reason to increase political tension," Bulgarian television reported.

Political opposition parties, hundreds of street protesters and even Mr. Mladenov's party newspaper had joined in calls for his resignation, prompted by a videotape showing him ordering tanks to move against protesters on Dec. 14.

Student leaders had issued a declaration demanding that Mr. Mladenov quit by 8 P.M. and had threatened to call a general strike beginning on Monday if he did not resign.

Mr. Mladenov, 53 years old, was initially regarded as a reformer after ousting the veteran Communist Party leader Todor Zhivkov in a party purge in November.

Tape of Chief Ordering Tanks

He became President in April and led the country to its first free elections in four decades last month.

The new 400-seat Grand National Assembly convenes on Tuesday and is expected to discuss Mr. Mladenov's resignation. It is dominated by Mr. Mladenov's party, the Bulgarian Socialist Party, formerly the Communists, which won a landslide election victory.

The Union of Democratic Forces, which released the videotape showing Mr. Mladenov calling for tanks to quell the December protests, had demanded that he quit before Tuesday.

Even the newspaper of the former Communist Party, which Mr. Mladenov led for three months after ousting Mr. Zhivkov, joined calls for his resignation.

Experts Report on Tape

"Politics is a man's game," the newspaper Douma said in a front-page editorial. "Someone who is not good enough has to leave the stage."

In an earlier report, Douma said a panel of experts had studied the tape and it clearly showed Mr. Mladenov saying, "The tanks had better move in."

Mr. Mladenov initially insisted the tape had been doctored. But in a television statement earlier this week, he did not deny making the remark.

"Society is disappointed with weakness of the President who couldn't find strength to admit what he said on Dec. 14," the Douma editorial said. "After that he made one blunder after another."

* * *

July 10, 1990

BULGARIA'S RENAMED COMMUNISTS IN DISARRAY AFTER ELECTION

By CLYDE HABERMAN
Special to The New York Times

SOFIA, Bulgaria, July 9—Despite their solid victory in elections to Parliament last month, Bulgaria's renamed Communists are acting like a party in disarray.

Now known as Socialists, the Bulgarian Communists were the only ones in Eastern Europe to emerge from elections more or less intact after the upheavals that have swept away one totalitarian system after another.

But political commentators and foreign diplomats described the party as a ship without a captain, lacking clear direction or initiative.

In the three weeks since the election, they say, the Socialists have done little more than react fitfully to public demands for swifter democratic change and cleaner breaks with the Stalinist past.

In the process, there are increasing signs of splits between conservatives and reformers allied with Prime Minister Andrei Lukanov, who said changes must come faster to rescue Bulgaria from a worsening economy.

The Socialists' troubles were underscored and intensified by the resignation Friday night of President Petar Mladenov, who engineered a palace coup last November that toppled the country's hard-line leader of 35 years, Todor Zhivkov.

Mr. Mladenov gave way to student strikes and other protests as he lost all credibility because of a comment last December that tanks should to be called in to crush anti-Communist demonstrators.

Now, an unexpected priority for the new Grand National Assembly, which convenes on Tuesday, is to find a successor to fill the largely figurehead presidency. The Socialists lack the two-thirds majority to do it by themselves. Speculation ran high today that they might support a non-Socialist candidate.

Opposition Is Wary

Thus far, the main opposition group, a collection of former dissidents known as the Union of Democratic Forces, has resisted attempts to lure it into a coalition. The Socialists continue to try, however.

Mr. Lukanov says a broad consensus is essential to deal with pressing national problems. But the tasks ahead are so daunting that some political specialists are convinced that the Socialists want to be able to share the blame should things go wrong.

"I think they're scared to death of holding power by themselves," a Western diplomat said.

If the ruling party had hoped that the Mladenov resignation would end the protests that have filled Sofia streets for weeks, they were disappointed. The protesters, almost giddy over a victory that would have been unthinkable a few months ago, started to raise new demands.

The agenda includes calls for the resignation of Mr. Lukanov and other officials and members of Parliament regarded as tainted by their Communist Party past. In addition, protesters insist that a date be fixed for a public trial of the 79-year-old Mr. Zhivkov, who is reportedly in a prison hospital while the commission investigates corruption and abuse of power charges.

Today, the Government sought to meet this demand by announcing that the inquiry would end on July 18 and that an indictment would be drawn up over the next month.

*   *   *

July 11, 1990

BULGARIA CONVENES A POST-COMMUNIST PARLIAMENT

By CLYDE HABERMAN
Special to The New York Times

VELIKO TARNOVO, Bulgaria, July 10—Bulgaria reached down to its roots today to convene its first Parliament elected in genuine elections after more than 40 years of Communist rule.

Symbolism and substance dovetailed when the 400 members of the new Parliament, the Grand National Assembly, traveled to this gingerbread town in the Balkan Mountains to invoke the spirit of the country's first modern Parliament, convened here in 1879.

That gathering followed centuries of Turkish domination, spoken of with bitterness even today.

Veliko Tarnovo, 150 miles east of Sofia, the capital, signifies freedom for Bulgarians. And so to many, it seemed a good place to begin the process of undoing the political and economic ravages of Communist domination.

Dissidents Turned Legislators

Meeting in a pastel-blue building that is now a museum, members of Parliament sat on long benches and listened to party leaders pledge themselves to democracy and national reconciliation. They were an assortment of Government officials, farmers, writers, laborers and intellectuals. Perhaps the most remarkable aspect of their largely ceremonial first session was that they were there at all.

Many of them, especially in the main opposition group, the Union of Democratic Forces, were dissidents against the

Government of Todor I. Zhivkov, the Stalinist leader toppled in November after 35 years in power. Only a short while ago, they were still meeting one another furtively and measuring their words carefully when talking to foreigners.

But all that is in the past, insisted Alexander Lilov, chairman of the Bulgarian Socialist Party, as the Communists now call themselves. The Socialists, presenting themselves as born-again democrats, won a surprisingly strong victory in parliamentary elections last month, winning 211 seats to the union's 144. The remaining 45 seats went to small parties.

"We won't betray our campaign platform," Mr. Lilov told members of Parliament. "And we will work with all of you for democracy and prosperity in Bulgaria."

Calls for Purge of Communists

His main opponent, Zhelyu Zhelev, leader of the union, responded with reserve. But he also indirectly reminded the Socialists that power had passed from a single party to Parliament. "This National Assembly will lead Bulgaria on the road to democracy and to Europe," he said.

But moderate words could not conceal the serious political tensions confronting Bulgaria, problems put off today as Parliament adjourned until next week to buy time for consensus building.

The country remains without a President after the sudden resignation under fire last week of Petar T. Mladenov, a Communist Party veteran who had led the anti-Zhivkov rebellion. The Socialists, despite their victory, have also been unable to put together a new government reflecting the election results.

Moreover, student protesters, who have set much of the political agenda in recent weeks, insist that more Communist's must resign, including the reform-minded Prime Minister, Andrei Lukanov.

'A 2d Cyprus' Is Resisted

One fundamental division was graphically displayed in Veliko Tarnovo today, that between Bulgarians and the large ethnic Turkish minority.

Several hundred militant nationalists filled the streets, threatening to blockade the old Parliament building to keep out 23 members elected from a party of ethnic Turks, the Movement for Rights and Freedom. The nationalists did not succeed, and were kept far from the building by militia squads.

But they were allowed to rally, and they used the occasion to denounce the 1 million ethnic Turks, according to estimates, that are in their midst—11 percent of the population—as a disloyal fifth column intent on reconquering Bulgaria. "We don't want a second Cyprus," a protester said, referring to the 1974 Turkish invasion there.

Under Mr. Zhivkov, ethnic Turks suffered a campaign of forced assimilation that required them to take Slavic names and give up some Islamic rituals. That policy was reversed by the new national leadership soon after it took over. But the action set off protests by ardent nationalists exercising their new right to take to the streets.

The volatility of the issue was reflected inside the Parliament building today. Three political leaders addressed the session, but they did not include Ahmed Dogan, head of the Turkish party, even though his group is No. 3 in terms of seats in Parliament. His turn was delayed until next week, and went instead to the head of the smaller Agrarian Union.

"They didn't want to scare the public by having Dogan speak," said Rumen Danov, an opposition lawmaker.

*   *   *

July 20, 1990

EMBALMED BODY OF BULGARIAN COMMUNIST IS TAKEN FROM MAUSOLEUM AND CREMATED

By CHUCK SUDETIC
Special to The New York Times

SOFIA, Bulgaria, July 19—The embalmed body of the man regarded as the founder of Communist Bulgaria, Georgi Dimitrov, was removed from a mausoleum in Sofia's main square on Wednesday and cremated, news reports in Sofia said today.

The glass-encased body, which had been on public display in the temple-like white stone mausoleum since soon after Mr. Dimitrov's death in 1949, was removed before dawn on Wednesday by government workers and cremated in Sofia's central crematorium soon afterward, the reports said. Only close friends and relatives were said to have witnessed the cremation.

Mr. Dimitrov's ashes will reportedly be buried alongside the grave of his mother.

The removal of Mr. Dimitrov's body, which has been hotly debated here since the downfall of Bulgaria's last Communist dictator, Todor Zhivkov, in November, was carried out secretly and under the noses of anti-Communist protesters camped out in tents on the sidewalk.

Honor Guard Relaxes

Under mounting pressure from the protesters, who have made an issue of the homage paid to Mr. Dimitrov, Bulgaria's Prime Minister, Andrei Lukanov, announced last week that the body would be removed. But he did not specify when it would be done.

Outside the mausoleum, an honor guard dressed in smart white uniforms rotated shifts normally on the hour on Wednesday, but the once-stone-stiff guards were visibly relaxed while on duty and often bent over and glanced around at the gathered protesters. The honor guard was absent this morning.

Tonight, only a few military policemen watched over the mausoleum, chasing away photographers and curiosity seekers who strayed onto the reviewing stand built into its facade, which was once used by Bulgaria's Communist leaders to view May Day parades and other celebrations.

The protesters had lined a metal railing in front of the mausoleum with posters depicting sphinxes and slogans saying, "Bulgaria is no ancient Egypt," "We don't need any Pharaohs" and "It stinks!"

'Son of the Working Class'

Across the street, in front of the headquarters of the Bulgarian Socialist Party, this country's former Communist Party, some party members were visibly upset.

"I'm hurt terribly," said Lilian Kraieva, a working mother of four. "Georgi Dimitrov was a son of the Bulgarian working class. He was a son of the working class of the whole world."

"It was an uncivilized act," she said about the body's removal. "They should have asked the Bulgarian people what they thought before they did anything."

Veterans of Bulgaria's wartime anti-Fascist resistance had called last week for a referendum on the question.

Some members of the Young Socialist League, who have pitched a pro-Socialist Party tent near what has become a tent city of anti-Communist protesters, applauded the removal of Mr. Dimitrov's body.

"For us there is no single opinion," said Yuri Borisov, the league's president. "But personally, I think it was necessary because the conflict with the opposition is very sharp now and there were facts that compromised Georgi Dimitov's work."

An Enigmatic Figure

While reviled as a Stalinist by some, Mr. Dimitrov remains an enigmatic and colorful figure in the history of world Communism and is renowned as one of this century's staunchest fighters of Fascism. He helped found Bulgaria's Communist Party in 1919, won acquittal on charges brought by Germany's Nazi Government of plotting the fire that destroyed that country's Parliament building in 1933, and served in Moscow as secretary of the Communist International from 1935 to 1943.

After coordinating anti-Fascist activities in Bulgaria from abroad in World War II, Mr. Dimitrov returned to his homeland to become its dictator in 1946.

No official decision has been made on what will become of Mr. Dimitrov's mausoleum. Many Bulgarians have called for it to be dismantled.

"I think they should make it a monument to all our national heroes," said a member of the Young Socialists' League.

*   *   *

August 2, 1990

BULGARIAN OPPOSITION LEADER
TO BECOME PRESIDENT

By CHUCK SUDETIC
Special to The New York Times

SOFIA, Bulgaria, Aug. 1—After a bewildering series of turnabouts, Bulgaria's Parliament today elected the leader of the main opposition political coalition to the national presidency.

Zhelyu Zhelev, the 59-year-old head of the Union of Democratic Forces, a coalition of 15 opposition parties, was chosen Bulgaria's first non-Communist President in four decades.

Mr. Zhelev ran unopposed, but collected only 284 of the 389 votes cast; he needed a two-thirds majority of the members present to win the election. The Bulgarian Socialist Party, formerly the Communist Party, remained the majority party.

Applause, and a Show of Hands

"I thank you for the trust you have put in me," Mr. Zhelev told the Parliament after the vote. "My only guiding principle will be the interests of Bulgaria, to turn it into a modern, democratic, prosperous nation."

After taking the oath of office to resounding applause, Mr. Zhelev nominated Atanas Semerdjiev, the Socialist former Interior Minister, to become Bulgaria's vice president.

Shouting down a proposal to put off voting on the vice presidency until Thursday, the legislators then elected Mr. Semerdjiev by an overwhelming majority in a show of hands.

Mr. Semerdjiev resigned as Bulgaria's Interior Minister in a fit of anger last Friday night after a row over the plans, now postponed, for an appearance before the Parliament of Bulgaria's deposed Communist dictator, Todor Zhivkov.

Despite Mr. Zhelev's election, leaders of the Bulgarian opposition vowed again today not to enter into a coalition government with the majority Bulgarian Socialist Party.

Mr. Zhelev is expected to ask Andrei Lukanov to stay on as Bulgaria's Prime Minister.

Coalition Is Ruled Out

"Our support for a strong and competent government does not mean that we are about to enter a coalition," said the Union's spokesman, Stoyan Ganev.

Others said, however, that while leaders of the Union of Democratic Forces might not enter into a new government some of its supporters might be willing to take posts in what Mr. Zhelev has termed a "Government of experts."

Despite their assertions that they are avoiding entry into a coalition to guarantee Bulgaria a real political opposition for the first time in the post-war era, the Union's leaders have also said that they are loathe to enter the Government because they want to avoid shouldering political responsibilities for the tough, unpopular decisions Bulgaria's Government will have to take to deal with economic ills.

Associated Press

Zhelyu Zhelev at Parliament in Sofia yesterday after he was elected President of Bulgaria.

Mr. Zhelev will have the power to call Parliamentary elections, which will give him the ability to schedule elections at a time most advantageous to the opposition.

Bulgaria's presidency was vacated almost four weeks ago by Petar Mladenov after the Union produced evidence that he supported the use of force to put down anti-Government demonstrators last December.

* * *

August 27, 1990

BULGARIAN SOCIALIST OFFICES ARE
STORMED BY PROTESTERS

By CHUCK SUDETIC
Special to The New York Times

SOFIA, Bulgaria, Aug. 26—Several hundred rioters tonight stormed the headquarters of Bulgaria's Socialist Party, the country's former Communist Party, to protest the continued presence of Communist symbols in public places throughout the country.

The rioters set fires that destroyed most of the first floors of the main party headquarters and an adjacent party office building. While about 15,000 sympathizers gathered at the main square, the rioters also broke into the back entrance of the party headquarters and ransacked parts of the building that were not in flames.

By late tonight, the police had moved in to disperse the crowds and the fire brigades were putting out the blaze.

The Associated Press reported that several people were injured by falling debris.

The A.P. said the police had sealed off roads into the capital and announced a national alert.

'Mafia! Mafia! Mafia!'

Earlier, the police stood by as the crowd rampaged through the building and ripped up yellow bricks from Sofia's main

Reuters

Anti-Communist demonstrators in Sofia burning ransacked contents of the offices of the governing Socialist Party, which has been accused of keeping hard-line Communists in top positions.

square to throw through the building's windows. The rioters also scattered the contents of the building onto the front and back steps and built bonfires. Fire brigades twice attempted to extinguish the fire, but rioters both times prevented them from turning on their hoses.

The violence stemmed from political tensions that have been steadily growing between the governing Socialist Party, which this summer won the first free elections in Bulgaria in more than two decades, and the minority opposition, which has accused the Socialists of keeping hard-line Communists in important positions.

Tonight, as the protesters unleashed their anger, Bulgaria's Socialist Vice President, Atanas Semerdzhiev, implored the rioters to stop. But members of the crowd shouted him down with cries of "Mafia! Mafia! Mafia!"

Mr. Semerdzhiev, who resigned as Interior Minister several weeks ago, told the rioters, "I promise you, if there is someone here who can go there and remove the star, I will go there with him."

The red star above the Socialist Party headquarters has for weeks been the source of anger among the anti-Communist demonstrators, who want it removed.

Opposition Backs Protesters

The crowd attacked and began beating Filip Bokov, a member of the Socialist Party's supreme party council, before the police moved in to rescue him. Bulgaria's President, Zhelyu Zhelev, the former leader of the opposition coalition, Union of Democratic Forces, was reportedly away at the coastal city of Varna and was said to be rushing back to the capital.

In a radio broadcast, Mr. Zhelev said: "This is pushing the country toward chaos and violence, toward military dictatorship, toward civil war. This is a crude violation of public order which cannot in any way be justified."

No leaders of the opposition made any move to stop the rampage. In fact, opposition members expressed solidarity with the protesters.

"This is the Bastille," said Bogdan Atanasov, a Social Democrat member of Parliament. "I wish to see those people go. I don't want to wait the next 15 years."

A police officer said, "We can't do anything," while looking into the flames leaping from the party office building. "We have no law for such cases," he continued. "And the firemen could do nothing because the people will not let them."

Several rioters appeared to be overcome by smoke and sought help in a tent near the site where other protesters had doused themselves with gasoline and threatened to ignite themselves unless the red star above the party headquarters is taken down.

The violence today was by far the worst in Bulgaria since the toppling of Todor Zhivkov in November.

*   *   *

September 19, 1990

BIRTHPLACE OF GAMES SHOCKED AND ANGERED

By PAUL ANASTASI
Special to The New York Times

ATHENS, Sept. 18—Greeks reacted with shock and anger today to the vote by the International Olympic Committee to award the 1996 Golden Olympics to Atlanta.

Melina Mercouri, the actress and former Minister of Culture and one of the members of the Greek delegation at the I.O.C. meeting in Tokyo, charged that American business interests had won over Greece's historic right to hold the Games. "Coca-Cola won over the Parthenon temple," she said.

Greece was the home of the ancient Olympic Games and Athens was the site of the first modern Games in 1896. Its bid for the 1996 Games was based on the idea that the 100th anniversary should be held at the original birthplace.

Papandreou Expresses Regret

"I express my deep regret that the international community did not respect history and the spirit of the Olympic Games and, yet again, committed an injustice against Greece," said Andreas Papandreou, a former Prime Minister and the head of the Socialist Party.

The Government, in a lengthy statement by Deputy Prime Minister Athanasios Kanellopoulos, said that the decision would damage the Olympic spirit. He said the only hope of restoring their original principles was for the Games henceforth to be held permanently in Greece as in ancient times, in accordance with a proposal first made by Athens a decade ago.

"Greece, the country which gave birth to the Olympic spirit and fostered peaceful competition, knows both how to win and to lose," Kanellopoulos said. "Our conscience is clear."

'Rage and Disgust'

"The decision provokes rage and disgust," said Sotiris Papapolitis, a Conservative Party parliamentary deputy and candidate for mayor of the Greek capital's port city of Piraeus.

Speaking on the state-run television network, he described the vote by the I.O.C. as "unacceptable theft" and added that "it does not in the least correspond to the ancient spirit of the Olympic Games."

The Greek shock over the decision was also seen in the reactions of thousands of bystanders who had gathered in the streets to watch giant television screens put up by the Government to watch the I.O.C. announcement live from Tokyo.

In Athens. platforms had been erected for local dance groups, highways were decorated with flags, and cannon salvos were to be fired from atop the city's central Lycabettus Hill.

Byron Polydoras, a Government spokesman speaking at a news briefing shortly before the international committee's decision, said that Greece would never attempt to hold the Games again if it was denied the right this time.

* * *

September 28, 1990

DO 4 BEHOLD THE VIRGIN? BISHOP IS NOT A BELIEVER

By CHUCK SUDETIC
Special to The New York Times

MEDJUGORJE, Yugoslavia, Sept. 23—The Vatican has warned that church-sponsored pilgrimages to this mountain village are banned, but that has not stopped Roman Catholic pilgrims from crowding into Medjugorje, where the Virgin Mary is said to have been appearing daily to four young people for the last decade.

Promoted by countless books, brochures and videotapes, Medjugorje (pronounced MEHD-joo-gore-yeh) has become Yugoslavia's hottest tourist attraction, a hard-currency wellspring whose yearly cash flow even church and Government officials are loath to gauge.

Since 1985, the number of communion wafers distributed annually at St. James Church here has more than doubled to over a million, parish records show.

But in a recently published letter, Joseph Cardinal Ratzinger, head of the Vatican's office on doctrine, warned that the church forbids official pilgrimages to Medjugorje.

This ban has been interpreted to mean that Catholic parishes may not organize tours and that priests, nuns and lay church workers may not officially lead pilgrimages here until the Vatican makes a pronouncement on the apparition's authenticity. Such a pronouncement may be years off.

Private Tours Organized

The Cardinal's warning has not dampened the fervor with which St. James's Franciscan priests promote Medjugorje and the messages of peace that the Virgin is said to be delivering. Catholics circumvent the ban by organizing private tours accompanied by clergymen cast as "spiritual advisers."

The Franciscans' ardor has rankled the local bishop, who says the apparitions are a Franciscan-perpetrated hoax.

"Propaganda in favor of Medjugorje is being rushed in order to place the church and the world before a 'fait accompli,' " Bishop Pavao Zanic said in a statement detailing his personal objections to the reported appearances. "No one even mentions that which throws doubt on the 'apparitions.' "

Once a poor peasant village, Medjugorje has taken on the trappings of a bustling beach town, complete with kitsch mongers and bed-and-breakfast places. The streets are jammed with tour buses, campers, cars and pilgrims.

'The Greatest Propaganda'

"The majority of the pious public has naively fallen victim to the great propaganda, the talk of the apparitions and the feelings," the Bishop said in his statement. "These people themselves have become the greatest propaganda for the event. They do not even stop to think that the truth has been hidden by deliberate falsehood. They do not know that not one miraculous healing has occurred that could have been verified by competent experts."

"These are all outright lies," said the Rev. Ljudevit Rupcic, a Franciscan priest, pointing at Bishop Zanic's written statement. "None of the Bishop's arguments hold any water when people compare them with the books and studies that have been written about Medjugorje," said Father Rupcic, whose latest book on Medjugorje, his fourth, rebuts the Bishop's charges.

The dispute between the Franciscans and Bishop Zanic over Medjugorje is just the latest skirmish in a church turf war touched off a century ago when Austria occupied Bosnia and Herzegovina and took steps to establish a Catholic diocese in the region, said the Rev. Vjekoslav Milovan, secretary of the Yugoslav Bishops' Conference.

The Franciscans have been working with the region's Catholics since the Middle Ages, he said. They forged strong bonds with the villagers and resented Vienna's push for the establishment of diocesan parishes and the appointment of non-Fanciscan bishops, he said.

Ivan Dragicevic, one of the four who report seeing the Virgin, said that the Virgin appears to him in three dimensions standing on a cloud and that on occasion he has even touched her.

On a recent evening, Mr. Dragicevic and Marija Pavlovic, another of the four, knelt in a cramped room in the church bell tower and began saying the Lord's Prayer aloud and in unison to prepare for the vision.

Twice during the prayer they slipped into several minutes of silence and stared up toward a wall where they said the Virgin appeared. Occasionally, Mr. Dragicevic nodded his head and muttered a few sounds. After both periods of silence they resumed their prayer at the same point.

"The whole thing is an ecstasy," the 25-year-old Mr. Dragicevic said, adding that his conversations with the Virgin have lasted 5 to 30 minutes.

Many Lives Are Changed

Authentic or not, there is little doubt that the Medjugorje apparitions have changed many lives.

"My friends thought I was becoming crazy and fanatic, but my heart just pulled, pulled, pulled," said Milona von Habsburg, a 32-year-old Archduchess in Austria's former ruling family who abandoned a job in a fashionable Geneva auction house to do volunteer work in Medjugorje.

The Rev. Theodore Cassidy from St. Joseph's Parish in Sykesville, Md., who has made several trips to Medjugorje, said: "There is so much happening here, so many stories, so many events, that it's hard to put it all together. Most priests have doubts about this when they first come. But I believe it."

"There is an awful lot of good that comes from it," he said. "You can see it in improvements in family life and people giving up drugs. No one has to believe this, but I would encourage people of all faiths to come here, and they should be ready to change."

*   *   *

October 2, 1990

CROATIA'S SERBS DECLARE THEIR AUTONOMY

By CHUCK SUDETIC
Special to The New York Times

BELGRADE, Yugoslavia, Oct. 1—In an atmosphere of rising ethnic tension, Serbs in the Yugoslav republic of Croatia today declared the republic's predominantly Serbian-populated counties to be autonomous. The declaration, based on the results of a vaguely worded referendum on Serbian autonomy conducted throughout Yugoslavia over the last two months, was signed by Milan Babic, a local politician who heads the Serbian National Council, a Yugoslav press agency report said.

More than 99 percent of the approximately 750,000 participants in the referendum voted for autonomy, the report said. Serbs officially account for 11.5 percent of Croatia's 4.7 million people, but any Serb born or living in Croatia was allowed to vote.

The autonomy declaration comes after a weekend of unrest in Croatia's Serbian-populated counties that has set off

a storm of criticism across Serbia. Extreme nationalist opposition political figures in Serbia threatened today to form paramilitary units "to defend" the Serbs in Croatia if the Yugoslav Government does not do so.

The unrest began after special Croatian police units began confiscating arms and ammunition from police stations in Serbian-dominated areas and from weapons depots belonging to units of Yugoslavia's territorial defense organization, a kind of national guard.

On Friday night, a group of Serbs broke into an arsenal in a police station in the town of Glina and made off with weapons.

Croatian riot policemen using tear gas clashed with the crowds in several predominantly Serbian-populated towns on Saturday. A police officer and a civilian suffered gunshot wounds.

Late Sunday night, an anonymous group based in Knin, an almost completely Serbian-populated Croatian town, blocked area roads and rail lines in reaction to the police detention of Serbs for illegal weapons possession and disorderly conduct, a press agency report said. In a statement released today, the group gave the Croatian authorities an ultimatum to release the detainees, the report said. Barricades still blocked several main roads tonight, radio reports said.

Croatia's government has repeatedly said that the Serbs' referendum is illegal and asserted that the actions of the republic's Serbian minority are an effort to undermine Croatia's democratic order and deflect attention from Serbian police repression against ethnic Albanians in that republic's Kosovo region.

*   *   *

October 30, 1990

ROMANIANS BRACE FOR FIRST HARD LESSONS IN MARKET ECONOMY

By CELESTINE BOHLEN
Special to The New York Times

BUCHAREST, Romania, Oct. 29—Ten months after the revolution that freed them from Eastern Europe's harshest Communist Government, Romanians are bracing for their first lesson in free market economics this week.

The Government has planned drastic increases in prices on consumer goods on Thursday, and has also announced that people are going to have to get back to work, including working two Saturdays a month.

Working Saturdays had been one of the most hated burdens imposed by the Government of Nicolae Ceausescu, and it was one of the first to be lifted when the dictator was forced from power and executed in December. But in the months that followed, as the country's political turmoil continued, the Government discovered that people had stopped working not only on Saturdays but during most of the rest of the week as well, leading to a 28 percent drop in production for the first nine months of the year and a 46 percent drop in exports.

Slacking off has become so much a national pastime as to become a national joke. With Saturdays now "free," people work half days on Fridays, often less. Asked what a missing colleague was doing, one Romanian, looking at the empty desk, replied bitterly, "Eating democracy."

Time to End Long Weekend

Prime Minister Petre Roman, who is trying to push a series of radical economic measures through Parliament, is banking on the hope that Romanians themselves know that it is time to end the long weekend.

"I know they know that we are not working as much as we should," he said in an interview with two American journalists. "They are aware that with such a performance, we will not solve our problems."

"We are at the moment of truth," he said. "There is no other alternative."

The announcement of the two Saturday workdays, which will increase the average work week from 40 to 44 hours, comes just as people are getting ready for the shock of price reform. That begins Thursday when the Romanian currency, the leu, is devalued from 21 to 35 to the dollar.

The decision to let prices rise to market levels on all but certain basic goods—including heat, electricity, housing and food—is expected to unleash a steep inflationary spiral, with prices on some items jumping 100 to 125 percent.

Lowest Salaries to Rise

To soften the effect on poorer Romanians, the Government is proposing to raise salaries and pensions at the lower end of the scale. The cost of the compensation package will be 25 billion lei in 1991, Mr. Roman said. The costs of food and other subsidies are still being negotiated, he said.

Although the price increases were announced by Mr. Roman on Oct. 18, they have prompted little panic buying because, as Romanians point out, state-run stores were already virtually empty. Items from shoes to shampoo can now be found only on the black market, or in the private shops that opened after the Government, in its first and meager attempt at privatization, allowed entrepreneurs to set up small businesses last spring.

An estimated 50,000 small businesses now operate in Romania, but as in the Soviet Union, these early swallows of capitalism have only soured people's view of the coming economic order. Shoes that cost 300 to 400 lei in state stores—when there are any shoes—cost 1,500 lei when sold by private vendors.

Mr. Roman agreed that the results of the small-enterprise law had been disappointing since only a handful were involved in manufacturing or production. He described the majority as "hit and run" merchants, interested in the quick profits made possible by the widespread shortages.

Encouraged by Farm Reform

On the other hand, he said he was encouraged by results from Romania's first attempts at agricultural reform, which redistributed almost a third of the country's arable land to private farmers, who on their leased plots have managed to increase the supply of meat and fresh produce sold at the unregulated farmers' markets.

According to Mr. Roman and Romanian economists, the principal reason for the shortages in the state shops has been the dramatic rise in incomes. To keep on top of the wave of protests and strikes that have swept the country since December, managers have let wages rise 26 percent even as productivity plummeted.

Other costs have also soared. As the country has been released from the semi-darkness decreed by Mr. Ceausescu, electricity consumption has gone up 23 percent even as Romania, like the rest of Eastern Europe, faces an energy crisis caused by the drop in Soviet imports and the rise in world oil prices.

Mr. Roman's economic package, now making its way through Parliament, calls for a series of radical changes in banking, agriculture, labor policies and other areas. In televised interviews and speeches, he has described his approach as a more wide-ranging version of the "shock therapy" now being applied in Poland. Unemployment is expected to rise—perhaps to as many as one million people—as Romania's bloated and outdated industries struggle to survive.

Old Guard Said to Resist

Mr. Roman has made himself the plan's principal salesman but he said it has the full support of President Ion Iliescu, who has been less visible in recent weeks. Mr. Roman identified the opponents of change as holdovers from the old guard, still entrenched in the government bureaucracy and exemplified by the 18 deputy ministers who were dismissed last week as examples of "resistance."

Mr. Roman said foreign companies have expressed interest in investment projects totaling $2 billion. But he acknowledged that Romania's image was badly hurt in June when bands of miners, wielding axes and bats, descended on the capital to defend the Government after a day of violent opposition protests.

* * *

November 11, 1990

WITH YUGOSLAVIA IN TURMOIL, MACEDONIA HOLDS FIRST FREE ELECTION

By CHUCK SUDETIC
Special to The New York Times

OHRID, Yugoslavia, Nov. 10—In an election laced with anxiety over this country's possible breakup, voters in Yugoslavia's southern republic of Macedonia will go to the polls on Sunday in the first free multiparty parliamentary elections in the republic's 45-year history.

The voting in Macedonia will be the first in a series of elections in the next seven weeks that should leave all of Yugoslavia's six quarrelsome republics with democratically chosen governments and set the stage for their leaders to begin working out a new agreement on future relations.

This spring, nationalist coalitions unseated the ruling Communists in Slovenia and Croatia and began pressing to scrap the present Yugoslav federation and create a loose confederation of independent states.

The Slovene and Croatian Governments have threatened to secede if a confederation proves impossible, but the ruling Communists in Serbia, the largest of the six republics, are staunchly opposed to a confederation.

Four-Way Political Race

The election campaign in Macedonia, Yugoslavia's least-developed republic, is shaping up to be a four-way race involving the reconstituted Communist Party; the Reform Party of Yugoslavia's Prime Minister, Ante Markovic; a coalition of anti-Communist Macedonian nationalist parties, and an ethnic Albanian party.

No single party is expected to win a majority of the Parliament's 120 seats, but sketchy polling results indicate that the pro-Yugoslav Communist and Reform parties are poised to win about half the votes.

Perhaps nowhere in Yugoslavia is popular support for the Communists and the continued existence of the Yugoslav state, federal or confederal, stronger than in Macedonia. The republic owes its existence to Yugoslavia's wartime Communist Partisans, and photos of Marshal Tito, the country's longtime Communist dictator, are still seen in shops and restaurants.

"Here, there isn't the kind of anti-Communism that there is in Slovenia and Croatia," said Petar Gosev, the Communist Party's leader.

Surge in Popularity

Mr. Markovic's Reform Party, a likely coalition partner for the Communists, appears to have surged in popularity since it began an energetic campaign in Macedonia several weeks ago.

Mr. Markovic won great popular support nationwide by engineering an economic program that succeeded in harnessing runaway inflation.

Macedonia constitutes the Reform Party's first test at the polls, and here at least the party seems to be drawing significant support from intellectuals, business executives and others fed up with nationalist rhetoric and economic mismanagement.

"People look at Mr. Markovic's pragmatic approach and see in it a guarantee that Yugoslavia will survive," said Mirce Tomovski, a magazine editor.

Leaders of Macedonia's nationalist parties, who support a confederal Yugoslavia, claim that a Reform Party victory would usher in a new period of "foreign domination" of Macedonia.

'Colony of the Northern Republics'

"Macedonia has been a colony of the northern republics, and we can't allow this anymore," said Tome Kostadinovski, a spokesman for the All-Macedonian Movement for Action.

Macedonians argue that in 1913 Serbia, Bulgaria and Greece divided up their land and that large, unrecognized ethnic Macedonian populations live in the countries that border the republic.

Both the All-Macedonian Movement and the more radical Internal Macedonian Revolutionary Organization support unification with Macedonians living in Greece and Bulgaria.

The Communists and the Macedonian nationalist parties find common ground in their alarm at the growth of Macedonia's Albanian population.

Officially, ethnic Albanians constitute about 20 percent of Macedonia's 1.9 million people. But Macedonian and ethnic Albanian party leaders claim that the Albanian population is significantly higher and that the success of the Albanian party may be the election's biggest surprise.

*   *   *

November 15, 1990

THE HURDLES ARE MANY, BUT THE REWARD IS A CHILD

By CELESTINE BOHLEN
Special to The New York Times

BUCHAREST, Romania—Moved by pictures she had seen of the desperate conditions in Romanian orphanages, Linda Tresgaskis came here from Austin, Tex., for the first time last July to find a year-old child to take home with her.

She recently came through a crash course in the ordeals of Romanian adoption with flying colors—and a 2-week-old son named Charles Michael.

Her friend from Rochester, N.Y., who had come hoping to adopt two or three babies under one year old, is leaving with a 7-year-old daughter, a 2 ½-year-old son, an infant and prospects for adopting a fourth baby, not yet born.

"It is funny how it works out," said the new mother, who spoke on condition of anonymity. "You cannot predict which ones you will fall in love with."

In the last few months, the adoption of Romanian children by people from the West has been steadily increasing, after a halt last summer as the Bucharest Government established new regulations. Veterans of the process say the new rules, instituting formal court proceedings in the place of President Ion Iliescu's personal signature, are still ragged, and the experience exhausting.

Hardships Worth Enduring

But those who come are prepared to put up with anything so long as they can leave with a healthy child, a prize that is increasingly hard for adoptive parents to find in North America and Western Europe, particularly for single mothers like Ms. Tresgaskis.

The plight of Romania's abandoned children—offspring of a Communist system that first forbade abortions for most women and then made it economically impossible for them to care for large families—has opened up new reserves in the worldwide search for children in need of homes.

Under pressure from relief organizations, the Romanian Government is now trying to coordinate aid for the 130,000 children left stranded in 379 institutions, of whom almost half are considered mentally or physically handicapped.

A recent report produced some chilling findings: of the 32 hostels for handicapped children, not one is considered fit for use, and yet the children remain. Calculating the shortages of food, clothes, materials and medicines, the Government estimated it needs $27 million in immediate aid, $100 million for the long term.

Foreign adoptions, properly controlled, are one way to rescue some of the children, although proportionately the numbers are small. No national figure is available, but the flow seems to be steady.

Last summer, 67 families from Canada came here as a group, and left with 130 children. One estimate put the number of adoptions by Americans by September at 160.

Fewer Newborns Available

Since January, when the draconian anti-abortion law was lifted, the number of births in Romania has fallen and the number of abortions has soared. As a result fewer newborns are available for adoption, and some organizations are turning their attention to needier children.

As they tour the orphanages and asylums, the new parents are walked past cribs of children—often wet, unwashed and with running noses—and asked which one they want. Older children besiege foreign visitors, calling the women "mama" and asking to be taken away on a plane.

"It feels like shopping for shoes," Ms. Tresgaskis said. "It can be an awful experience, saying no, not this one, not that one. Never in your wildest dreams did you ever think you would be in a situation like that."

At the Hotel President here, a former guest house of the Romanian Communist Party that has become a popular campground for adoptive parents, the war stories told around dinner tables are all about the bureaucratic bungling, petty corruption and 19th-century working conditions that plague the collection of the necessary adoption papers.

The court procedure can take as little as 15 minutes, or as long as five hours. In one rural town, the proceedings ended up including five judges and a full jury, drawn from citizens called in off the street to pass judgment on why one American family that already had four children wanted to adopt two more.

In this baffling maze, the prospective parents have nowhere to turn but to each other. They complain that the United States and other embassies provide conflicting, sometimes inaccurate information and that in many cases their Romanian lawyers know little more than they do.

Those who come to adopt come prepared to stay for weeks, sometimes months. Not knowing how old their child will be, they arrive with clothes and diapers for all ages, and then swap among themselves. Other essentials include dollars and cigarettes, the most acceptable form of currency in Romania's current economic crisis.

"When I came I was handing out candy bars and packs of cigarettes," said one frustrated American. "Now I am up to $20 bills, and by tomorrow it may be 50's."

Costs Relatively Low

Still, the costs are relatively low. Ms. Tregaskis figured that she spent $5,000 for everything, including one round-trip ticket, hotel room, taxis, taxes and various fees. Lawyers' fees, which include a mandatory $606 state tax, can range from $1,000 to $2,500, but after bitter experience many new parents advise doing without lawyers altogether.

To save money, people can also live in private apartments, where they can stay for $20 or less a night. But often they find the hardships of Romanian life more than they bargained for—sometimes no refrigerator and elevator and now, in parts of Bucharest, water only at certain times of the day.

The misery of ordinary life in Romania, little improved since the revolution last December, when Nicolae Ceausescu was overthrown and executed, hits the adoptive parents hard.

"I have traveled a lot, I have been in the interior of Mexico, I have seen poor people in our own country," Ms. Tresgaskis said. "But in Europe, you don't expect the ignorance, the lack of basics, this kind of poverty. When you see the homes, you can understand why the mothers had to give the children up."

Getting the legal consent from the biological parents is emotionally draining, although in some cases the parents may not have seen their institutionalized children in years. Some people report cases where the Romanian families have pressed for money or some kind of material help.

But most mothers who give their newborn infants directly to foreigners do so hoping that their child will have a better life. "The only way she could handle it was to block out all emotions," Ms. Tresgaskis said of the 23-year-old woman who gave birth to Charles Michael.

Ms. Tresgaskis, a 40-year-old nursing home administrator, said she wants her son to know where he came from. "I want him to know his heritage," she said. "I want him to know that his country is in the middle of a crisis and that his mother did what she did out of love."

* * *

November 28, 1990

YUGOSLAVIA SEEN BREAKING UP SOON

By DAVID BINDER
Special to The New York Times

WASHINGTON, Nov. 27—United States intelligence is predicting that federated Yugoslavia will break apart, most probably in the next 18 months, and that civil war in that multinational Balkan country is highly likely.

The predictions, included in a long National Intelligence Estimate produced under the auspices of the Central Intelligence Agency, are unusually firm and sharp for such a document, a senior Government official said.

The intelligence estimate runs counter to views of Yugoslavia's future in the State Department, although some specialists in that department also subscribe to the premise.

The intelligence prediction received backing in Yugoslavia on Nov. 15 when Prime Minister Ante Markovic declared: "The acts of the highest state organs of Slovenia, Serbia and, partly, Croatia inevitably lead to a straining of political relations in Yugoslavia and directly threaten the country's survival."

Nationalism Is Growing

The Prime Minister continued, "The situation is characterized by growing nationalism and separatism and an alarming worsening of ethnic relations, all of which is expressed in violence, a drastic threat to public order, peace and citizens' safety."

According to United States officials who have read the intelligence document, its two basic findings are that "the Yugoslav experiment has failed, that the country will break up" and that "this is likely to be accompanied by ethnic violence and unrest which could lead to civil war."

"It did not predict absolutely that there would be a civil war, but said it was highly likely," one official noted. He said he was "startled by its stark terms."

Yugoslavia, a federation of six republics formed under Tito's victorious Communist partisan army at the end of World War II, has been plagued by increasing internal tensions since the death of Tito in 1980. The stresses in the country of 23 million have been worsened by political rivalry between Serbia, the largest of the six republics, and Croatia and Slovenia, the most prosperous; and by Serbia's repression of its Albanian minority of nearly two million in the region called Kosovo.

Democratic Elections Held

In the spring, Slovenia and Croatia held democratic elections that ended Communist Party rule, while Serbia—also facing elections—retains a Communist government under its president, Slobodan Milosevic.

The authors of the intelligence estimate, and virtually every other American official concerned, blame Mr. Milosevic as the principal instigator of Yugoslavia's troubles, both for initiating the latest repression of the Kosovo Albanians and for stirring Serbian nationalist passions.

After an auspicious start with an economic reform program last winter, Prime Minister Markovic has seen his federal authority wither in the face of mounting disputes among the various republics. Slovenia and Croatia have threatened to secede from the federation and Mr. Milosevic has lately pursued a go-it-alone policy for Serbia.

The United States intelligence estimate on Yugoslavia's future is set in this context.

Army Termed Fraying

"I think you can almost write the death certificate now," a Government official who specializes in Yugoslav affairs said recently. He pointed to moves by Belgrade authorities to impose customs duties on goods entering Serbia from other Yugoslav republics and to withhold Serbia's payments to the Federal Government. He also said the Yugoslav People's Army "is beginning to fray."

"I could see a formal breakup by mid-1991," this official said.

Another American Government specialist took a more cautious view of Yugoslavia's future, saying, "I am not willing to write them totally off" at this moment.

The C.I.A.'s pessimism is shared by some State Department officials, including Deputy Secretary Lawrence S. Eagleburger, who served two tours in Yugoslavia, most recently as ambassador, and who is widely respected in the country as a friend.

It is also shared to a degree by American scholars specializing for many years in Yugoslav politics and history—among them Steven L. Burg of Brandeis University, Charles Jelavich of the University of Indiana and Denison I. Rusinow of the University of Pittsburgh.

Late last month, the House and Senate passed an amendment to the Foreign Operations Appropriation law that bars any United States loans or credits for Yugoslavia unless the assistance is directed to a republic "which has held free and fair elections and which is not engaged in systematic abuse of human rights."

The legislation was fueled mainly by members of Congress who desire to penalize Serbia for its repression of the Kosovo Albanians.

* * *

December 11, 1990

RULING PARTY WINS SERBIAN ELECTIONS

By CELESTINE BOHLEN
Special to The New York Times

BELGRADE, Yugoslavia, Dec. 10—The struggle over the future of Yugoslavia took an ominous turn today when Serbia's ruling party, whose hard-line policies have helped push the country toward a breakup, emerged victorious in free elections.

The still incomplete tally from Sunday's elections showed the Serbian president, Slobodan Milosevic, received about 60 percent of the vote and the Socialist—formerly Communist—Party he heads poised to capture a solid bloc of seats in the republic's Parliament. The Yugoslav press agency said the Socialists won 80 out of 140 seats already counted for the 250-seat Parliament.

Mr. Milosevic's victory in free elections—the first in Serbia since 1938—sent a defiant signal to Yugoslavia's other five republics, particularly Slovenia, where the Government has called for a referendum on independence on Dec. 23. Slovenia and Croatia have been pressing for more autonomy within a looser, confederated Yugoslavia, in part to distance themselves from Serbia and its attempts to impose its conservative policies nationwide.

Stunning Size of Victory

"I think Slovenians who are preparing themselves for the plebiscite now have one more reason to say they are in favor of independence," Stane Stanic, the spokesman for the Slovenian Government, said today.

The apparent size and sweep of Mr. Milosevic's victory stunned the Serbian opposition, which had portrayed him as the unrepentant heir to Serbia's Communist past. In his campaign, Mr. Milosevic, who rose to power three years ago, offered himself as the candidate of stability and the protector of Serbia's national interests.

Mr. Milosevic's main rival, Vuk Draskovic, the leader of the nationalist but anti-Communist Serbian Renewal Movement, conceded defeat today, but in a bitter speech he portrayed the race as a contest between good and evil.

"On Dec. 9, Serbia voted to decide between Bolshevism and democracy, the past and the future, darkness and light, ruin and salvation, disgrace and honor," Mr. Draskovic said. "Official results show that the citizens voted for bondage, Bolshevism, the past, darkness and disgrace."

A Warning of Civil War

Though his policies are perhaps more nationalistic than his opponent's, Mr. Draskovic seemed toward the end of the campaign to be more open to negotiations with Croatia and Slovenia for a new union that would keep Yugoslavia together. Mr. Milosevic, by contrast, pushed for a strengthening of the existing federation, which the others fear would become a mechanism for domination by Serbia, the most populous republic. Mr. Milosevic has spoken of the threat of civil war if other republics seek independence.

The victory of Serbia's ruling party echoed election results earlier this year in Romania and Bulgaria, where reconstituted Communist parties were also the winners.

The ruling Communists won in Montenegro, a southern republic that also held elections on Sunday. In contrast, former Communists lost to nationalist parties in elections held in Yugoslavia's other four republics this year.

A second round of voting may be held in Serbia on Dec. 23 for those parliamentary seats in which no candidate won a majority of the vote in Sunday's balloting. The main opposition parties have vowed to join forces for the Dec. 23 election in hopes of stopping the former Communists from winning control of the Parliament.

Fear of Economic Change

In Serbia, much of Mr. Milosevic's support came from those who fear they might lose in the republic's halting change to a market-based economy.

"I think he never lost the mass of people who live behind the times," said Zoran Djindjic, a member of the opposition Democratic Party. "They haven't heard the Berlin wall has fallen."

By endorsing Mr. Milosevic and the former Communists, Serbian voters signaled their support for an economic program that has combined regional protectionism with resistance to free-market policies in local industry.

In recent months, Mr. Milosevic's Government has taken economic steps against other Yugoslav republics, including raising tariffs and other trade barriers to slow the import of Slovenian and Croatian goods. Mr. Milosevic has also appealed to Serbia's industrial workers with promises to protect them from unemployment, which is rising elsewhere in Eastern Europe.

Albanians Boycotted Vote

The victory was also an endorsement of Mr. Milosevic's policies within Serbia, particularly toward the province of Kosovo with its majority Albanian population. Over the last year, the Serbian Government has stripped Kosovo of its political autonomy, laid off Albanian workers and closed institutions, including hospitals. On Sunday, ethnic Albanians boycotted the elections.

What happens next in Kosovo is one of the pressing questions facing Yugoslavia, and the results of Sunday's elections offer no clue of a resolution to the standoff. Some political analysts say that by strengthening Mr. Milosevic's hand, voters may have served to provoke Albanian resistance.

"The Government with its election victory has only solved the problem of its own legitimacy," said Leon Kojen of the opposition Democratic Forum. "It has not solved the problem of Kosovo, Yugoslavia's future, the problem of Serbs outside Serbia, the economy and the problem of international isolation."

*   *   *

December 13, 1990

FORMATION OF AN OPPOSITION PARTY ANNOUNCED AT A RALLY IN ALBANIA

By DAVID BINDER
Special to The New York Times

WASHINGTON, Dec. 12—Amid scenes of jubilation, the formation of the first opposition party in Communist-ruled Albania was announced today at a huge rally in Tirana, the capital.

Called the Democratic Party, the new group has already applied at the Ministry of Justice to establish its legal status, one of its founding members, Gramoz Pashko, who is a prominent university economics professor, said in a telephone interview from Tirana. That ministry was recreated last summer after having been abolished 23 years earlier.

On Tuesday, after three days of anti-Government demonstrations by university students, the Communist Party central committee endorsed in an emergency session "the creation of independent political organizations."

No Multiparty Tradition

Albania has been ruled uncontested by the Communist Party since 1946, and until Tuesday the party leadership had consistently declared that it would never permit opposition parties.

The small Balkan country of 3.3 million has no traditions of political parties or parliamentary government. During World War II opposing groups of nationalists, royalists and fascists tried to gain political footing, but were swept aside by the Communists.

Six weeks ago, Mr. Pashko, who is 35 years old, began describing himself to foreign visitors as "a dissident." He was at the time still a member of the Communist Party, as was his friend, Ismail Kadare, a prominent writer, who defected to France in October.

Joining the economist in announcing the founding of the Democratic Party at today's rally in the university's "Student City" were Azem Hajdari, 28, a philosophy student who played a leading role in organizing the student revolt, and Dr. Sali Berisha, 45, a Tirana cardiologist.

'Democracy! Democracy!'

Mr. Pashko said about 80,000 people attended the rally— "workers, of course students, artists, lawyers, all kinds of people." Others at the scene estimated higher numbers. Tirana has a population of 300,000. The crowd chanted "Democracy! Democracy!" The economist said that although some students had been injured in clashes with special police forces on Sunday and Monday there had been no fatalities.

As yet the Democratic Party founders have chosen no leaders, Mr. Pashko said, and they have only begun to sketch out a party platform, which he said would include advocating a multiparty system, protection of human rights, a free market economy and good neighborly relations.

In a departure, however, Azem Hajdari, the student leader, said the Democratic Party would "work for the peaceful democratic union between Albania and Kosovo," the neighboring Yugoslav province of Serbia whose inhabitants are 90 percent ethnic Albanians. This call from Tirana could lead to friction with the Belgrade authorities.

Both Mr. Hajdfari and Mr. Pashko paid respects to Ramiz Alia, the Communist President and party chief, for introducing a reform program that paves the way for multiparty system. National elections are set for Feb. 10.

*   *   *

December 20, 1990

ALBANIA RECOGNIZES FIRST OPPOSITION PARTY

By The Associated Press

VIENNA, Dec. 19—The Albanian authorities formally recognized the country's first opposition party today, paving the way for multiparty elections after decades of one-party Communist rule.

But the Government continued its clampdown on suspects accused of taking part in rioting last week. The official Albania press reported that courts had sentenced 18 people to prison terms of up to 12 years. More than 150 people were on trial for anti-Government acts after the violence last week in four provincial centers, the Albanian state radio reported.

Justice Minister Enver Halili issued a signed and stamped document recognizing the new Democratic Party of Albania exactly one week after its founding, said a party spokesman, Genc Pollo.

The approval came a day after the new party applied for registration and the parliamentary presidium passed a decree formalizing a Communist Party decision of last week to legalize independent political parties.

The decision appeared to reflect growing pressure on the authorities to speed up democratic reforms. After the democratic revolutions that swept the former Soviet bloc last year, Albania is the last country in Europe still under Stalinist rule.

*   *   *

December 22, 1990

ALBANIA REMOVES STATUES OF STALIN

By Reuters

TIRANA, Albania, Dec. 21—Albania, convulsed by political upheaval, has torn down Eastern Europe's last towering statues of Stalin.

The isolated, hard-line nation, now embarked on cautious political change, also sent the widow of the late Albanian Stalinist leader, Enver Hoxha, into retirement.

Albania's Government, a target of anti-Communist riots last week, chose Stalin's 111th birthday today to exorcise the political ghost.

The latest developments follow a frenzied 10 days of political change in which Mr. Hoxha's successor, President Ramiz Alia, permitted independent political parties for the first time. A leader of the newly founded Democratic Party, Gramoz Pashko, said his group had been given permission to hold a rally on Saturday. It would be the first opposition rally to be held legally.

Lenin's Statue Remains

These events were a spectacular break with more than four decades of one-party Communist rule installed by Mr. Hoxha, who died five years ago. His widow, Nexhmije, stepped down as leader of the People's Democratic Front, which controls Communist mass organizations.

A crane moved into Tirana's Stalin Boulevard at midnight on Thursday and loaded the dark bronze statue onto a truck, its head hanging over the back. It left behind a statue of Lenin, the founder of the Soviet state.

Only a handful of passers-by and a few policemen were there for the symbolic act that seemed to seal the end of Stalinism in Europe.

At daylight, behind a red curtain, workers chipped away with powerful drills to remove the statue's remaining marble and concrete platform, drawing crowds of curious young onlookers.

The Tirana radio said Stalin's name and symbols associated with him were to be removed from streets, institutions and the city named for him.

Multiparty Elections Due

The Albanian Communist Party is preparing to begin its campaign next week for the first multiparty elections in 45 years, due to be held in February.

Churches, sealed under a rigorous policy of state atheism for more than 20 years, have begun reopening as Christmas approaches.

The first Masses were celebrated over the last few days in several Greek Orthodox churches in Greek minority communities in the south, people there said.

But there was no sign that any mosques had started to reopen for the country's Muslims, who once accounted for 70 percent of Albanians.

* * *

December 24, 1990

SLOVENES VOTE DECISIVELY FOR INDEPENDENCE FROM YUGOSLAVIA

By BRENDA FOWLER
Special to The New York Times

LJUBLJANA, Yugoslavia, Dec. 23—In another strike at the already shaky unity of Yugoslavia, Slovenes voted overwhelmingly today in favor of independence from this ethnically diverse country of 23 million, preliminary and unofficial results showed.

With 75 percent of the vote counted, 94.5 percent voted for independence and 4.5 percent voted against. Approval by 51 percent was needed for the plebiscite to pass. Voter turnout was estimated at 90 percent, and 1 percent of the ballots were invalidated.

But the vote for independence in this northern republic of two million will not mean an immediate break with Yugoslavia's other five republics and its two autonomous provinces.

"We're fully aware that we still need the federal Government," said France Bucar, president of the Slovenian republic's Parliament. "But at the same time, we can't allow it the latitude to overlook our decision or to continue to function in the same constitutional framework."

A Six-Month Plan

The plebiscite endorses a six-month plan by the Slovenian republic to take gradual control of military, foreign and monetary policies, which are now largely in the hands of the federal Government in Belgrade, the Yugoslav capital.

But officials here said that if Slovenia fails to reach agreement with the other republics and the provinces on a system of confederation similar to that of the European Community, secession will not be out of the question.

"This country is disintegrating," Dimitrij Rupel, Slovenia's Secretary of Foreign Affairs, declared at a news conference.

"There is great instability, especially from the point of view of the legal system, so we are forced to search for a new form of coexistence."

The process toward autonomy was set in motion in July, when the republic's newly elected democratic government declared its sovereignty.

Moves toward secession by Slovenia and the neighboring republic of Croatia have been criticized by the federal Government, which is dominated by Serbs, the biggest ethnic nationality in Yugoslavia. Some of the more than 50,000 ethnic Serbs living in Slovenia also oppose such a plan.

"They want to have a confederation that is not a confederation at all," said Dusa Damjanovic, president of the Serbian Democratic Party, which was formed just over a week ago.

She said that many Serbs in the republic did not vote today because they wanted neither to oppose Slovenes nor to cast ballots for independence.

Fearing that the vote would only increase the deep divisions in Yugoslavia, some Slovenian parties initially urged that negotiations on the future of Yugoslavia be held first with the other republics and the two provinces.

But resistance to the vote gradually came to be viewed as unpatriotic, and nearly all parties threw their support behind it, said Mile Setinc, vice president of the Liberal Democratic Party. His party, the second-biggest in the Slovenian assembly, had originally opposed holding the plebiscite now.

Alerting Slovenes Abroad

"The first thing I am going to do is an interview with the Radio Cleveland to inform Slovenes abroad of our decision," the Prime Minister of the republic, Lojze Peterle, said after the voting.

Mr. Setinc and other politicians here say they doubt that secession would be embraced by other republics.

The mix of nationalities is greater in other republics, they said, and the borders between them are less clear-cut than that between Slovenia and Croatia.

"There are lot of Croats in Bosnia-Herzegovina, and there are lots of Serbs in Croatia, so every involvement with those groups risks real civil war," Mr. Setinc said.

But Croatia's new Constitution, approved by its Parliament on Saturday, includes provisions that provide for secession.

* * *

February 22, 1991

NEW PROTESTS IN ALBANIA; CRISIS MOUNTS

By DAVID BINDER
Special to The New York Times

WASHINGTON, Feb. 21—With thousands of Albanians demonstrating in the streets of the capital for an end to Communist rule and with the country's economy in a shambles, President Ramiz Alia began today to try to form a crisis government.

The 65-year-old leader, who is also First Secretary of the Communist Party, has assumed personal control of the entire governmental apparatus. Mr. Alia declared Wednesday night on television that he would meet the demands of protesters by replacing the 23-member Government of Prime Minister Adil Carcani, 18 of whom hold the rank of Cabinet ministers.

The Communists, who came to power in 1944 on the strength of the Albanian Partisans' struggle to drive out the Axis occupiers, have ruled Albania uncontested since.

Since mid-December, when mass protests swept Tirana and every other major city in the country of 3.5 million, Albania has been in the throes of what amounts to a popular uprising.

Protests Against Hoxha Symbols

In Tirana this morning, the wrath of demonstrators again focused on the monuments and symbols associated with Enver Hoxha, the onetime partisan leader who ruled the country as a pro-Stalinist dictator until his death in 1985 after designating Mr. Alia as his successor.

Protesters moved on the Enver Hoxha Museum, apparently bent on ransacking the building, which is shaped like an eagle, on Boulevard of Heroes, the capital's main street. They turned back when warning shots were fired in the air by members of an armored unit posted at the entrance.

Tanks and armored cars also barred access to an adjacent bloc of villas occupied by members of the Communist Party elite, including Hoxha's widow, Nexhmije.

After turning back to the city center at Skanderbeg Square, named for the 15th-century leader who is Albania's national hero, the protesters dismantled most of a huge sign of red painted metal letters atop the Palace of Culture praising the Communist Party, leaving only the letters for "Albania." Then a crowd of several hundred demonstrators made a pyre of Hoxha's books and pictures at the base of the 40-foot statue of Hoxha that was demolished yesterday.

Troops Ordered Not to Fire

Although earlier demonstrations led to violent clashes with army units and police, causing injuries to dozens of Albanian law enforcement officers and protesters, it appears that no one has been killed in the popular uprising.

In a telephone interview today, a Tirana opposition leader attributed the lack of bloodshed to President Alia, saying that he had personally ordered police and troops not to open fire on protesters.

So far, President Alia has given in step by step to virtually every one of the demands raised by protesters. Having begun what he called a "democratization process" last May, he has retained a measure of personal popularity and, until now, the mass protests have not called for his removal.

It was not immediately clear whether Mr. Alia's emergency government would include members of newly formed Albanian opposition parties. A leading opposition figure, Gramoz Pashko, said today that his Democratic Party would refuse any offer to take part in a coalition with Communists.

Associated Press

Anti-Communist protests continued in Albania as efforts began to form a crisis government. On Wednesday, demonstrators in Tirana pulled down a statue of Enver Hoxha, the Stalinist dictator who died in 1985.

Elections Set for March 31

Along with three other new opposition parties, Mr. Pashko's two-month-old party is campaigning against the Communists in elections scheduled for March 31. The elections had originally been set for Feb. 3, but were postponed by President Alia at the request of the opposition.

A Tirana resident said President Alia conferred today with Ibrahim Rugova, leader of the Kosovo Democratic Alliance, the largest political organization of the Albanian minority in neighboring Yugoslavia.

This move added another dimension to the popular unrest sweeping Albania, since it is almost certain to have repercussions among the Serbian leadership in Belgrade, which in recent years has maintained a policy of repressing the 1.7 million ethnic Albanians in the Kosovo region of Serbia.

*   *   *

February 27, 1991

CORRUPTION TRIAL OPENS FOR ZHIVKOV

By CHUCK SUDETIC
Special to The New York Times

SOFIA, Bulgaria, Feb. 26—With defiance and self-possession, the former Communist dictator of Bulgaria, Todor Zhivkov, was in Sofia's Supreme Court today to answer corruption charges in the illegal distribution of apartments, cash and other privileges to his relatives and political minions.

Though perceived generally here as necessary to purge the evils of the totalitarian government that Mr. Zhivkov led for 35 years until his overthrow in November 1989, the trial seems to leave Bulgarians of all political persuasions dissatisfied.

In a three-hour display of savvy and stamina, gingered with wit, Mr. Zhivkov, age 79 years old, insisted that all the charges against him are groundless. They carry a maximum of 20 years.

"I plead not guilty," Mr. Zhivkov stated in a robust voice. "Behind this arrest and behind this trial there are political forces and political figures that will be unmasked by the people sooner or later."

Rights Charges Raised

Many Bulgarian political figures, especially leaders of this country's ethnic-Turkish minority, want the former dictator tried on charges relating to human-rights abuses, including the incitement of ethnic hatred during the sometimes-vicious official campaign in the mid-1980's to force the ethnic-Turks to adopt Bulgarian names.

"The trial is being held now to satisfy the human need for justice," said Ira Antonova, an opposition member of Parliament. "This proceeding is enough only for those who do not think, those for whom money is the only thing. But it is very unsatisfying for the thinking man."

"It is the remnants of the old nomenklatura putting him on trial," she said, referring to the former Communist elite and echoing a charge Mr. Zhivkov himself made today.

"First you should try the entire Communist Party," Mr. Zhivkov stressed, arguing that all party decisions were taken collectively and not by him alone. "Then you should try the Constitution, which placed the Communist Party above the state."

"Everything that has been done in this country has been sanctioned by the collective spirit," he said.

'Living in Another Time'

Much of today's testimony centered on a secret 1962 decision by the Communist Party Politburo ordering the highest government body, the Council of Ministers, to transfer state funds through the secret police to privileged party members, ostensibly for special food allowances.

"We were living in another time," Mr. Zhivkov told the court. "We were living in a time when we were creating a big illusion that did not coincide with real life. The Council of Ministers was obliged to follow any decision taken by the plenum of the Politburo."

The former dictator scoffed at the charges that he had illegally distributed apartments to family members, to children of his most loyal political supporters and to house servants who had worked for the secret police.

"It's normal everywhere," he said, referring to housing perks for high government officials. "When Mrs. Thatcher lost her job, she gave up her state villa, got into her own car and went home."

"I suggested that some flats be given to the needy," he said. "I remember the case of one woman with 10 children who came to me and said, 'Todor Zhivkov, I'm going to kill them if you do not give me an apartment.'"

Blames His Ministers

At times during today's session, Mr. Zhivkov seemed to exert his personal will over the judge and prosecutor. Waving his arms, turning to the public and joking, he even brought

Associated Press

Todor Zhivkov, former Communist leader of Bulgaria, at court yesterday in Sofia.

the prosecutor down from his rostrum by maintaining that deafness kept him from hearing the questions.

"Let's have a closed meeting and I'll tell you lots of things," Mr. Zhivkov said, offering to reveal information about the secret police.

The former head of state charged that his ministers were responsible for the wrongs he has been accused of committing.

"It was not my style to interfere in what the ministers were doing; I had other channels," he shouted at one point just before the presiding judge called a recess. "You won't find Todor Zhivkov's name where the things were done."

"These things were not within the scope of my duties," he cried. "You have made a mistake, Mr. Prosecutor. You might have been misled."

*   *   *

March 13, 1991

U.S. AND ALBANIA TO RESTORE FULL LINKS

By DAVID BINDER
Special to The New York Times

WASHINGTON, March 12—The United States will resume full diplomatic relations with Albania on Friday, ending 52 years of nonrecognition, American and Albanian officials announced today.

Administration officials said Foreign Minister Muhamet I. Kapllani was flying to Washington to take part in the formal act of diplomatic recognition with Assistant Secretary of State Raymond G. H. Seitz.

Months will pass before a United States ambassador to Tirana is named and still more time before an American embassy begins functioning in the Albanian capital, an Administration official said.

But the Bush Administration has concluded that it is desirable to act now because "we want to get engaged in the democratic process in Albania," the official said and because the Communist Government of President Ramiz Alia "is at least attempting reform."

'Greater Engagement' Urged

On March 31, Albania is to hold its first multiparty elections since the Communists seized power in late 1944.

The Administration official said the State Department would send a small group of American diplomats to Tirana to become acquainted with the situation before the elections. Since early December, Albania, a country of 3.5 million, has been swept by waves of unrest marked by popular demonstrations against the Communist system.

Richard A. Boucher, a State Department spokesman, said the turmoil called for "greater engagement, not less" by the United States. He also cited humanitarian concerns. There is currently a food shortage in Albania.

The United States and Albania had close ties before World War II. Americans of Albanian origin returned to the Balkans in 1912 to help establish the first Albanian Government. President Wilson was credited with having been the most powerful defender of Albania's territorial integrity in international councils immediately after World War I, when Italy, Yugoslavia and Greece vied to seize chunks of the country. There was also an American teachers college in Albania.

U.S. Reviled as Evil

Diplomatic ties between Washington and Tirana were severed in June 1939 after Italy's invasion of Albania. An informal American observer mission was sent to Tirana in 1945 to explore resumption of relations. The Communist Government refused to honor prewar treaties and harassed the members of the mission so much that they were withdrawn in November 1946.

The Albanian Government resumed diplomatic relations with the Soviet Union last year, after a break of 29 years. Albania and China have also agreed to increase trade and economic cooperation as part of Albania's effort to improve its international ties, and Albania has obtained observer status at the Helsinki talks in Europe, which emphasize human rights.

Until a little more than a year ago, the Communist Government regularly reviled the United States as an evil superpower bent on subjugating small countries like Albania.

In fact, in the early 1950's, the United States was actively engaged in a plot to overthrow the Albanian Communists with paramilitary forces.

Talks on renewing ties were begun last summer and were virtually concluded in September. But senior State Department officials objected to moving ahead on the ground that human-rights abuses were continuing in Albania, causing the project to be delayed.

Political Prisoners Pardoned

VIENNA, March 12 (Reuters)—The Albanian Government said today that it had pardoned all the country's remaining political prisoners.

"Following this pardon, there are no more political prisoners in re-education centers and prisons in Albania," the said Albanian radio, monitored by the BBC.

The report did not say how many people were affected by the pardon. The International Helsinki Federation, a human rights monitoring group, estimated that there were 200 political prisoners in Albania's jails.

* * *

May 29, 1991

BULGARIA RELEASING DATA ON SHOOTING OF POPE

By JOHN TAGLIABUE
Special to The New York Times

SOFIA, Bulgaria, May 28—Bulgaria is releasing more than 127 volumes of documents to investigators from several countries, including the United States, in an effort to discover the truth about allegations of Bulgarian involvement in a 1981 attempt to assassinate Pope John Paul II.

The documents, from the archives of the Bulgarian secret police, document an official investigation mounted in the early 1980's at the request of Bulgaria's Communist Government. It came to the conclusion that Bulgaria played no part in the assassination attempt, which was carried out by a Turk, Mehmet Ali Agca.

Mr. Agca was convicted of trying to kill the Pope and is serving a life sentence in a Rome jail. Mr. Agca said that he had been recruited by Bulgarians acting at the behest of the K.G.B., the Soviet secret service. But seven other defendants in the supposed Bulgarian plot, including three Bulgarians, were released by a Rome court in 1986 after it concluded that there was insufficient evidence to convict them.

Italian prosecutors contended that Soviet leaders wanted the Polish-born Pope dead because he supported the independent Solidarity labor movement in his native country.

But Soviet and Bulgarian Communist officials always denied having any role in the May 13, 1981, attack on the Pope, which left him seriously wounded. Moscow and Sofia said Mr. Agca, whose testimony was marked by frequent contradictions and retractions, was coached by Western intelligence services to damage the Soviet bloc countries.

The decision to turn over the documents stems from Bulgaria's non-Communist President, Zhelyu Zhelev, who has pledged to uncover the details of crimes committed within Bulgaria and abroad by the country's former Communist Government.

Bulgaria's Communist leaders commissioned their own internal investigation, which absolved the nation's secret services of involvement. The records of that investigation form the documentation handed over to an American historian, Allen Weinstein, who is to head a commission of international historians that will examine the papers.

Asked whether these documents were not possibly the record of a whitewash, Mr. Weinstein said in a news conference on Monday that he had obtained "iron-clad assurances" that any further documents necessary in the course of the investigation would be made available.

"What I have been offered is the starting point, not the closure," Mr. Weinstein said.

Stefan Tafrov, the chief foreign policy adviser of the Bulgarian President, said that the commission headed by Mr. Weinstein would have access to any materials it deemed necessary and would be able to freely question Bulgarian witnesses.

Addressing the news conference. Mr. Tafrov said that President Zhelev, who spent 17 years under house arrest under the Communist Government of Todor I. Zhivkov, believed that "the truth should be uncovered without any bias, and that Bulgaria is the most interested party in discovering the truth."

Italian officials, who were forced to shelve the case after the 1986 verdict, have announced their intention to reopen the inquiry, and Mr. Weinstein traveled to Rome today to seek their cooperation.

*   *   *

June 26, 1991

2 YUGOSLAV STATES VOTE INDEPENDENCE TO PRESS DEMANDS

By CHUCK SUDETIC
Special to The New York Times

LJUBLJANA, Yugoslavia, Wednesday, June 26—The Parliaments of the Yugoslav republics of Slovenia and Croatia overwhelmingly passed declarations of independence Tuesday that could lead to full secession if their demands for a new, more loosely bound Yugoslavia are not met by Belgrade.

After an emergency late-night meeting, Yugoslavia's federal Government responded early this morning by calling the republics's actions illegal and ordering national army and police units to seize control posts along Slovenia's borders.

It remains uncertain when the military and police forces would attempt to take control of Slovenia's border crossings, which now include posts along the republic's border with Croatia. A Slovene government official reached by telephone this morning said that the federal troops had not yet taken such action.

The New York Times

Parliaments in Solvenia and Croatia passed secession measures.

It is clear, however, that the battle of wills between federal authorities and the leaders of the two renegade republics has entered a new phase that raises the possibility of bloodshed.

Army Intervention Sought

Leaders in both republics have said that federal authorities, including the national army, would be required to ask for permission to move across the republics' territories.

"We still favor negotiations," President Milan Kucan of Slovenia said Tuesday. "But in order that real negotiations take place, we have opted for independence."

Even though the Slovene and Croatian leaders clearly prefer to remain in a decentralized Yugoslav federation, the political atmosphere is charged because of the possibility of bloodshed and instability through miscalculation.

Citing such concerns, the European Community and the United States have both said they will not recognize the independence of Yugoslavia's two most pro-Western and wealthiest republics. Many Western leaders have recalled that World War I had its roots in the fiery nationalism of this region.

In response to the action by the two republics, the federal Parliament in Belgrade asked the national army Tuesday evening to intervene immediately to prevent the country's dismemberment. The national Parliament, however, has no power to order the army into action.

Prime Minister Ante Markovic has repeatedly warned that he would resort to all legal means to prevent the republics from becoming truly sovereign states, as the declarations say they now are.

Both Slovenia and Croatia have warned for a year that they would secede from Yugoslavia if the country was not recast as a loose confederation. But even now leaders of both republics are insisting that despite the independence declarations they are still eager to discuss creation of a new Yugoslav union with the other four republics.

Both independence declarations spoke of "disassociation" from Yugoslavia. A draft of the Croatian version, obtained by The Associated Press, proclaimed a "sovereign and independent state" and declared: "By this act the Republic of Croatia initiates the process of disassociation from the other republics."

Slovenian and Croatian leaders maintain that the national army, whose Serbian-dominated officer corps commands a multi-ethnic force, would disintegrate if it were ordered to put down the movements toward independence.

'A Few Armored Cars'

"Any military action would amount to occupation," said Janez Jansa, Slovenia's defense minister. "It would take more than a few armored cars."

Yugoslavia's currency, the dinar, will remain the sole legal tender in Slovenia and Croatia for the time being, although the parliaments of both republics have adopted laws providing for the creation of their own currencies and national banks.

The Yugoslav Army will also maintain bases in Slovenia and Croatia for the present, But both republics have already organized their own armed forces and plan to negotiate the army's withdrawal in discussions that they are already likening to the German-Soviet talks on the Red Army's withdrawal from what was East Germany.

Warnings From the West

Republican leaders say Ljubljana will recall Slovenian representatives from the federal Parliament and bureaucracy and replace them with officials designated to negotiate and oversee a gradual breaking of ties with the Belgrade Government.

In the last week, the European Community and the United States have warned Slovenia and Croatia that they would not extend diplomatic recognition to the republics as independent states nor would they offer any economic aid.

"This was to be expected," said President Kucan at a news conference here Tuesday morning. "Under international law, the legal entity is still, for the time being, the Socialist Federated Republic of Yugoslavia."

Croatia's president, Franjo Tudjman, in a speech to his republic's parliament Tuesday night, said: "We understand completely the worries of individual states and the entire European Community about the Yugoslav crisis. But we must take our own interests into consideration first."

Mr. Tudjman also said that Croatia would redouble its efforts to gain international legitimacy by sending representatives to foreign capitals and appealing to international organizations.

In contrast with the demands of Slovenia and Croatia's for a loose confederation, Serbia, the largest and most populous

Steps to Independence: Two Yugoslav Republics

Croatia and Slovenia have approved declarations of independence in their campaign for a looser Yugoslav federation.

	Slovenia	Croatia
GEOGRAPHY	The northernmost of Yugoslavia's six states, covering 12,584 square miles and accounting for nearly 8 percent of the federation's territory.	Yugoslavia's second-largest republic, covering 35,132 square miles from the Adriatic coast to the agricultural heartland of Slavonia.
PEOPLE	Population: 2 million, about 9 percent of Yugoslavia's inhabitants. There are small Italian and Hungarian minorities.	Population: 4.8 million (including 500,000 ethnic Serbs), or about 20 percent of the federation's 23.5 million people.
HISTORY	Slovenia was ruled by a succession of German princes until the Middle Ages, when it was incorporated into the Austrian Empire. In 1918, Slovenia joined the new kingdom of Serbs, Croats and Slovenes that later evolved into Yugoslavia. It first gained limited autonomy in the 1930's. After Yugoslavia was reconstituted as a Communist federation in 1945, all states were granted considerable self-government.	The Croats created a small kingdom in the 10th century that united with Hungary in 1102. The Turks occupied much of it before being ejected by the Austrians in the 18th century. With the fall of the Austro-Hungarian Empire, Croatia joined Serbia in forming Yugoslavia. Croatian secessionists set up a Nazi puppet state that murdered hundreds of thousands of Serbs and Jews during World War II.
ECONOMY	Traditionally one of the poorest parts of the Austro-Hungarian Empire, Slovenia developed rapidly after it joined Yugoslavia and became its economically most prosperous region after World War II. Its industries, including the Elan ski factory, were badly hit by free-market reforms and unemployment has risen.	The Adriatic coast accounts for about 80 percent of Yugoslavia's $3 billion annual earnings from tourism. Leading industries are shipbuilding, petrochemicals, food processing and agriculture. Tourism has been halved by a rebellion of ethnic Serbs near the main resorts. About a quarter of the work force is unemployed.
GOVERNMENT	Ruled by Demos, a coalition of six center-right parties that defeated the reformed Communist Party last year. Milan Kucan, a former Communist, was elected president.	Governed by the Croatian Democratic Union, a nationalist party. The party's leader, Franjo Tudjman, a former Communist general, was named president by the legislature. Serbs have declared independence for Krajina in western Croatia.
CURRENCY	Yugoslav dinar. A parallel currency is planned.	Yugoslav dinar. A new currency is planned.
ARMY	Yugoslav national army is present. A Slovenian territorial defense has 70,000 members, not all mobilized.	Yugoslav national army is present; a republican army is in training. It consists of a 10,000-member National Guard and 10,000 to 20,000 police.
FOREIGN AFFAIRS	Representative offices in several European capitals and in Washington.	Representatives in European capitals and the United States, Canada and Australia.
PASSPORTS	Yugoslav passports, Slovenian in preparation.	Yugoslav passports, Croatian in preparation.

The New York Times

Yugoslav republic, has called for strengthening the Yugoslav federation. Serbia's Government of renamed and reconstituted Communists is often blamed for undermining Yugoslavia's market-based economic reform program. Serbia's government has said that a confederation is acceptable only if all of Yugoslavia'sSerbs are brought within the borders of a single state. Croatia, which has a large Serbian minority, strongly opposes this.

Leaders here in Slovenia admit that they were driven to take their step to independence in part by a desire to escape the costs of conflicts between Serbs and ethnic Albanians in southern Yugoslavia as well as those involving Serbs and Croats, which have claimed several dozen lives in the last five months.

"Slovenian leaders hope that independence will lead to an improvement in the republic's political-risk assessment and pave the way for new private investment," said Joze Mencinger, a top economist and former Slovenian vice president, adding that the republican government is not counting on economic aid from foreign governments.

Subjects of Austria for about 800 years, the Slovenes chose to join Yugoslavia after the collapse of the Austro-

Hungarian Empire in the waning days of World War I. This alpine republic, which has few minorities and is predominantly Roman Catholic, will find little internal resistance to moving away from the Yugoslav federation, which has been eroding since the 1980 death of Tito, the country's postwar Communist dictator.

'Soft Border Crossings'

Slovene workers are already erecting what republican officials are calling "soft border crossings" at eight points between Slovenia and Croatia. Officials said the border guards would make only cursory identification checks.

Croatia, which was connected with Hungary from the beginning of the 12th century until its leaders chose to join newly formed Yugoslavia after World War I, has already met stiff opposition to its independence move from a large portion of its Serbian minority. The Serbs in Croatia have a vivid memory of mass killings by Nazi-backed Croatian nationalists during World War II and strongly oppose coming under the complete control of the Zagreb government.

Voters in Slovenia and Croatia have passed popular referendums calling for the republics to become sovereign states.

* * *

June 28, 1991

YUGOSLAV ARMY USES FORCE IN BREAKAWAY REPUBLIC; SLOVENIA REPORTS 100 WOUNDED OR KILLED

By JOHN TAGLIABUE
Special to The New York Times

BELGRADE, Yugoslavia, Friday, June 28—Yugoslav Army units used force today to take control of several border posts from the Slovenian authorities and deployed tanks and troops around Slovenian airports to keep the republic from putting its independence proclamation into effect.

On Thursday, two days after the republics of Slovenia and Croatia proclaimed their independence, the first skirmishes were reported between national Yugoslav troops and militias loyal to Slovenia. The Slovenian Defense Minister, Janez Jansa, reported fighting in at least 20 places and estimated that more than 100 people had been killed or wounded.

"To put it briefly, Slovenia is at war," said Mr. Jansa, who was dressed in combat fatigues.

The clashes fed tensions here and in the breakaway republics by forcing the question of whether the crisis in Yugoslavia could be solved peacefully. Diplomatic efforts seemed to be going nowhere.

Helicopters Downed

There were conflicting reports on casualties and the extent of the fighting. Seeking to calm Yugoslav citizens, the federal authorities in Belgrade emphasized that only a few thousand troops were involved and that they were under orders to avoid clashes.

But the Slovenian Defense Minister said Thursday night on television in Ljubljana, the republic's capital, that in addition to the 100 casualties reported in the fighting, six federal army helicopters had been shot down. And this morning, a Slovene government spokesman in Ljubljana said a member of a Slovene police patrol passing a national army barracks in Maribor was shot and killed by a soldier in the barracks.

Convoys of federal tanks were reported near Ljubljana, with some involved in a tense standoff with Slovenian forces at the city's airport.

Yugoslav television showed army tanks plowing their way toward Gorica, on the Italian border as glum Slovenes stood silently by. The tanks shoved aside buses and bulldozers that Slovenes had parked in the streets in a vain effort to halt the federal troops.

Slovenian officials said this morning that 15 army tanks had been disabled by anti-tank missiles and that federal soldiers were using helicopters to ferry troops to the less accessible border points.

On Thursday, republic officials reported shooting at a checkpoint on the Slovenian border with Austria, where Yugoslav army troops used grenades to dislodge regional defense forces.

In an emotional statement, the Slovenian President, Milan Kucan, called the federal army action an "aggression against the sovereignty of the country" and an "attempt at permanent occupation" of Slovenia. He called on Slovenes to defend their fatherland and urged young people serving in the federal army to desert.

In Belgrade, the Government described the crisis in equally dramatic terms, declaring in a statement that the situation was "highly critical" and that failure to defuse it would "unavoidably lead to bloodshed with unforeseeable consequences for all the people of Yugoslavia."

Unrest Brewing for Months

Political and ethnic unrest has been brewing for months in the two breakaway republics. Both Slovenia and Croatia have warned that they would secede if Yugoslavia was not remolded as a looser federation. Despite the independence declarations, leaders of Slovenia and Croatia, both relatively wealthy and pro-Western republics, have said they are still willing to negotiate a new Yugoslav union.

But they have met resistance from Serbia, the largest and most populous republic, and the one that controls the national military.

Serbia, which is governed by renamed and reconstituted Communists, is frequently blamed for undermining Yugoslavia's attempts at market-based economic reforms. Serbia wants to strengthen the splintering federation and said it would accept the loose confederation advocated by Slovenia and Croatia only if all the country's Serbs were brought within the borders of a single state. Croatia, which has a large Serbian minority, opposes that idea. And that minority, which accounts for about 500,000 of Croatia's 4.8 million people, is rebelling against attempts by the republic to break away.

A major catalyst to Croatia's independence movement was Serbia's refusal last month to accept the appointment of a Croatian, Stipe Mesic, as chairman of the collective Presidency because of his separatist leanings.

2 Republics Largely Cut Off

Efforts to reopen lines of communication with the two dissident republics were bearing little fruit today. After a session of the Yugoslav Cabinet, the federal Prime Minister, Ante Markovic, offered to meet his Slovenian counterpart, Lojze Peterle. He proposed that declarations of independence by the Slovenian and Croatian parliaments on Tuesday be frozen for a three-month period, giving regional representatives and federal officials time to negotiate. But the Slovenian leadership rejected the proposal, calling on Belgrade to remove its soldiers and then talk.

Concern among Yugoslavia's neighbors appeared to be mounting.

Austria said it would invoke new rules of the Conference on Security and Cooperation in Europe that empower member nations to demand information about unusual troop movements.

Several tourism companies were reportedly preparing to evacuate at least 15,000 British tourists from Yugoslavia, whose beaches along the Adriatic attract large numbers of foreigners each summer.

There was concern that the conflict between the Yugoslav Government and the two republics would widen further when Croatia warned that it would order its lightly armed forces to attack federal army units in the region if they did not return to their barracks.

On Thursday, Yugoslav television showed army tanks positioned between the Croatian police and armed Serbs in lanes of the Croatian village of Glina, where roughly two-thirds of the population is Serb. The tanks were deployed after an officer and two civilians were killed.

After a meeting in Zagreb, the republic's capital, on Thursday, Croatian leaders said that federal troop movements in the republic might be a harbinger of military action similar to the crackdown in Slovenia. The reports could not be independently confirmed.

Reports of casualties varied widely. Slovenian officials said that a Yugoslav Army officer was killed in fighting near Ormoz, toward the Austrian border. But the federal Deputy Defense Minister, Vice Adm. Stane Brovet, denied there had been any deaths. He said three army officers, two of them helicopter crewmen, were wounded when their aircraft came under small-weapons fire.

Belgrade television said that three soldiers died when a helicopter crashed in downtown Ljubljana.

The Government appeared to be seeking first to bridge the gap with Slovenia, since that republic went further on Tuesday by declaring itself a sovereign and independent republic.

In a gesture toward Croatia, the Yugoslav Cabinet said that the country's collective presidency should convene as soon as

Reuters

A Yugoslav Army tank pushing aside a truck that formed part of a barricade on a road leading to the airport in the Slovenian capital of Ljubljana. About 100 casualties were reported in the clashes, but estimates varied.

possible and suggested that it would no longer block the appointment of Mr. Mesic as chairman.

But this evening, Belgrade television said that the Serbian leadership continued to reject Mr. Mesic.

At a news conference Thursday, Admiral Brovet said the army hoped to secure the borders by the evening, and Belgrade television, which usually presents the central Government's views, said that the goal had been achieved. But a Slovene spokesman in Ljubljana said this morning that the Yugoslav national army controls 7 border crossings to Italy and 5 to Austria, while the republic forces hold the remaining 15. The spokesman said the national army attacked a border crossing at Holmec at about 5:30 A.M. and the small mortar fire caused an undetermined number of injuries.

* * *

July 6, 1991

QUIET WAR SPILLS BLOOD INSIDE CROATIAN BORDERS

By STEPHEN ENGELBERG
Special to The New York Times

GLINA, Yugoslavia, July 5—The shops are locked, the streets deserted. At the hospital, nearly all the doctors and nurses have fled. The police station, the bus station and even the museum commemorating a World War II massacre are pocked with bullet holes, the aftermath of a shootout last week that left two local policemen and two civilians dead.

While international attention has focused on the fighting in Slovenia, towns like this one in Croatia are the front lines for a less-publicized but increasingly lethal battle between the Croats and the Serbian minority within the republic's borders.

It is this conflict, diplomats say, that poses the greatest long-term risk of violence in Yugoslavia. Militants among the 600,000 Serbs living in Croatia—they make up about 12 percent of the population—have waged a guerrilla war for the past year.

Now, with order breaking down across Yugoslavia, they have sharply stepped up their challenge to Croatia, attacking police in dozens of cities.

Police Officers Killed

Croatian officials say 25 policemen have been killed in fighting since the republic approved a declaration of independence last week. In Glina, 16 policemen who surrendered to rebel Serbs last week are being held hostage. There were reports today that at least one policeman was shot in the nearby town of Sisak.

On Thursday, in some of the sharpest clashes between Serbs and Croats since the end of World War II, firefights raged between the two groups in eastern Croatia.

Senior Croatian officials say the ethnic fighting has brought the republic to the verge of chaos, with heavily armed civilians attacking each other and the police overwhelmed by the scale of the violence.

The officials said the fighting raises the possibility of warfare between Croatia and Serbia. Croatian officials say the rebels are armed by the government of the politically dominant Serbian republic; Serbs deny that, but some Serbian extremists have acknowledged assisting their countrymen in Croatia.

In Glina, in the heart of Croatia, the peace is being kept by Yugoslav Army tanks and soldiers deployed after the battle last week between the Croatian police and local Serbs.

Glina, which is about 70 percent Serb, brings together the mixture of history and ethnic hatred that makes Yugoslavia such a volatile country.

Serbs came to Croatia more than 400 years ago, when Serbia was under Turkish rule and Croatia was part of the Austro-Hungarian Empire.

After the creation of Yugoslavia in 1918, this Serbian enclave co-existed uneasily with the nearby Croats.

Massacre, Not Sanctuary

In August 1941, the pro-Fascist puppet state installed by the Germans in Croatia massacred 1,200 Serbs in Glina. The Serbs were brought to this town from a neighboring village and told they could convert from their Orthodox faith to the Croats' religion, Roman Catholicism. But when they arrived at the church, the doors were locked and the Government's security forces slit their throats.

After the war, Serbs stayed on, partly out of their deep commitment to remaining near the graves of ancestors. Where the church had stood, the Communist Government erected a museum and monument.

The fears of the Serbs grew exponentially when a nationalist party won last year's presidential elections and restored some of the same emblems used during the war by the independent Croatian state.

Serbs in Glina say that if Croatia secedes from Yugoslavia, they will secede from Croatia and join Serbia.

Police Surrender

The town exploded with violence last week on Wednesday, when Croatia passed a resolution moving the republic closer to independence.

There were conflicting versions of how the shooting started. But it seems clear that a Croatian police patrol came under fire and retreated to a bar owned by a Croat. A full-scale attack on the police station led eventually to the police surrender and the arrival of the army and Croatian paramilitary police.

Milan Korac, the Deputy Mayor of this town and a Serb, said he hoped the Yugoslav Army would stay. "We are afraid of what would happen if the army goes out," said Mr. Korac, who himself wears a pistol. "We are afraid of the Croatian police."

For Gavran Blazen, a 26-year-old bartender, the rising ethnic tensions are a quandary. His mother is a Serb, his father a Croat, and he grew up in a mostly Serbian village. Still, he feels the pressure to choose sides in a country that has increasingly little room for the uncommitted.

"I'm Yugoslav," Mr. Blazen said. "I can't find my nation."

While he believes that the Serbs in Croatia should be allowed to go their own way, perhaps by joining with the Serbian republic, he has little sympathy for their methods. "This must stop," Mr. Blazen said, standing beneath the bullet-pocked windows of Glina's bus station. "We can finish this only with conversation. With guns, you settle nothing."

*   *   *

July 19, 1991

YUGOSLAV FEDERAL ARMY TO PULL OUT OF SLOVENIA

By CHUCK SUDETIC
Special to The New York Times

BELGRADE, Yugoslavia, July 18—Yugoslavia's federal presidency decided tonight to order the withdrawal of all Yugoslav National Army units from the breakaway republic of Slovenia, an official statement said.

The order was the clearest sign yet that Yugoslav Federal officials have given up hopes of preventing Slovenia from seceding from this crumbling federation of six republics.

"The pullout is supposed to begin immediately and, according to a plan, be completed in three months," Serbia's representative to the presidency, Borisav Jovic, said in a television news broadcast after the meeting late tonight. "The Yugoslav National Army does not have to be stationed in those parts of the country where it is considered an occupying army."

Tonight's announcement is certain to set off a popular sigh of relief in Slovenia, Yugoslavia's most developed republic, which declared itself independent on June 25 and thwarted an army attempt to take over its international borders the next week.

'Significant Step'

"We consider that with this we have made a significant step toward a resolution of the Yugoslav crisis and enabled further discussion of Yugoslavia's future in a peaceful manner and without conflicts between the Yugoslav National Army and the Slovenian military," Mr. Jovic said.

A new series of meetings of the eight-member Federal Collective Presidency and the Presidents of Yugoslavia's quarrelsome republics is set to begin on Monday in the Macedonian resort town of Ohrid.

"The meeting will consider the future of Yugoslavia, the question of resolving the Yugoslav crisis and all other key questions concerned with finding a way out of this situation," Mr. Jovic said. "We agreed that this work will continue without recess until we find a way out."

The discussion at today's presidency session centered around a proposal by the Slovenian Parliament for an army withdrawal from the republic, an official close to the presidency said before the breakup of the meeting, which he characterized as stressful.

Croatia Opposes Withdrawal

The four Serbian-controlled members of the federal presidency supported the army's withdrawal. Croatia's representative, Stipe Mesic, cast the only no vote.

While Slovenian authorities have been pushing for a complete army pullout, officials in Croatia, which declared its independence from Yugoslavia on the same day as Slovenia, have expressed fears all week that an army exit from Slovenia would allow for a redeployment of military units to counties in Croatia where Serb rebels have been carrying out an armed uprising since last August.

On Saturday the federal presidency ordered the disarming of all armed forces in Yugoslavia except for the National Army and regular police units by midnight tonight.

At least eight people have died in violence in Croatia's Serb-populated counties since last Sunday.

The Federal Defense Ministry in a report to the Federal Government today, charged Slovenia and Croatia with failing to carry out elements of a European Community-mediated peace accord reached on July 7, including failure to return Slovenia's border crossings to Federal Government control and demobilization of troops.

Fierce clashes between Serbs, who account for about 11.5 percent of Croatia's 4.5 million people, and Croatia's militia have increased dramatically since Croatia and Slovenia declared their independence.

Serbs suffered atrocities at the hands of Croat nationalists during World War II. The resulting fear of a resurgence of Croatian nationalism has been whipped up by Serbia's press.

Croatia Opposes New Borders

Croatian officials say the trouble in the Serb-populated counties is the work of a few Belgrade-backed and army-backed militants who launch hit-and-run attacks on Croatian police patrols in villages and induce Serbs to take up arms in "self-defense," against Croatian police efforts to maintain order. The Serb attacks and Croatian efforts to ferret out "Serb terrorists" have galvanized the fears of many Serbs in Croatia.

Both Slovenia and Croatia threatened for more than a year to secede from Yugoslavia if the country could not be transformed into a loose confederation of independent states. Slobodan Milosevic, Serbia's President, has repeatedly stated that his republic would agree to Yugoslavia's breakup, so long as all of the country's Serbs are brought within the borders of a single state.

Croatia's leaders vehemently oppose any changes in the country's present internal borders because Croatia would stand to lose sizable amounts of territory.

National Army personnel in movable equipment will be redeployed from Slovenia to Serbia and Bosnia-Herzegovina, the statement said.

* * *

July 31, 1991

A DAY OF TERROR AND DEATH ON A SERB-CROAT DIVIDE

By STEPHEN ENGELBERG
Special to the New York Times

SISAK, Yugoslavia, July 30—Terror still creased the faces of the Croatian villagers of Struga today as they described how their Serb neighbors rounded up dozens of their kinsmen four days ago and used them as human shields for a methodical march of death and destruction.

"It was a human wall," said Melita Blazevic, a 20-year-old Croat who described how she was pulled from her house by Serbian schoolmates, beaten and forced to join a procession of townspeople prodded forward by knives and gun butts.

The Serbs, she and other witnesses said, steadily fired a heavy machine gun mounted atop a truck as they moved behind the civilians toward the Croatian police, who were trying to maintain authority in a region of Croatia where Serbs outnumber Croats. The police defenders were reportedly paralyzed by the sight of their families held hostage and did not return fire.

"We were all together, walking in front," Miss Blazevic recalled, "and they were walking behind us, house by house, shooting at the houses."

Miss Blazevic's account was confirmed by two other villagers and in two separate reports by Yugoslav journalists who witnessed the events Friday in Struga, a rural community about 60 miles south of Zagreb, the Croatian capital. She and other witnesses said the Serbian advance was finally halted when a Croatian policemen jumped atop the truck and detonated grenades he was carrying in what was apparently a suicide mission.

The increasing violence in Croatia is starting to look, feel and smell like an old-fashioned Balkan war. There are no smart bombs or laser-guided weapons to keep the conflict impersonal or the adversaries at a distance from each other.

Instead, the struggle between the republic of Croatia and the Serbian guerrillas is being waged village by village with classic infantry weapons—automatic rifles and mortars.

Croatia's state-run television and security officials have been portraying the battle for Struga as an atrocity. The television reported that nine policemen had been killed in the fighting there, and it broadcast footage Sunday night that showed some of the bullet-riddled bodies with their throats slit.

It was unclear how many civilians died in the fighting. Witnesses spoke of at least two, including Manda Begic, 70, who lay wounded and screaming for help on the main street for more than an hour before she died.

Some historians estimate that more than a million people died in Yugoslavia during World War II, about half in clashes with the Axis forces, while the rest were machine-gunned, knifed or set afire by their fellow Yugoslavs. Many thousands of Serbs, Jews and gypsies died in concentration camps set up by the Nazi-installed Government of Croatia. Croats were also killed in large numbers by Serbian guerrilla forces.

Tito Suppressed Rivalries

Tito and his Communist successors managed to suppress this legacy of violence for 45 years. But the victory of nationalist parties in last year's Serbian and Croatian elections appear to have returned this country to the most bitter era of its modern history.

The skirmish in Struga was part of a broad offensive on Friday and Saturday that saw Serbian rebels push the Croats from a number of villages south of Zagreb. Struga, home to about 200 people, is on the edge of a predominantly Serbian area that has declared its independence from Croatia and calls itself Krajina.

Witnesses from Struga say last week's attack began in the morning with an onslaught of mortar rounds. Then the Serbs began moving through the neighboring hamlet of Zamlaca, collecting hostages.

Miss Blazevic, who has a black eye and shattered teeth, said she was hiding in her home at the outskirts of Struga when the Serbs kicked down the door. Outside, she saw the flatbed truck with the machine gun bolted to its floor. Her 24-year-old brother, Zdravko, had left the house to join in the firefight.

Assailants Were Schoolmates

"Almost all of them of them were schoolmates, the people with whom I used to meet for drinks," she said of the Serbs. "I told them, 'You are garbage.'"

"They asked me, 'Where is your brother?' I said, 'I don't know.' And they started to beat me."

"One started to beat me with his pistol on my face," she continued. "When he broke three teeth—he was standing on my left side—I directly blew my teeth out. He said, 'Why are you spitting at me?'"

The villagers seemed bewildered by the speed with which hatred has overwhelmed all other feelings between local Serbs and Croats. Several said Predrag Orlovic, a Serb who has openly boasted of cutting Croatian policemen's throats,

only last year shared a combine with his Croatian neighbors to bring in the harvest.

257 Mortar Rounds in Hour

Maria Kizevic, who gave her age as "over 60," said she knew nearly all of the assailants from her years of work at the local school. Mrs. Kizevic said she was terrified by the initial artillery barrage, and gave up counting the sounds of exploding mortar rounds after reaching 257 in one hour.

She and a 56-year-old man who declined to be identified said they had witnessed the deaths of three policemen, who were stripped to their underwear and then slashed on the legs with knives. The three were said to have been led to a cornfield and told run for their lives. As they struggled to escape, they were said to have been hit with a burst of machine-gun fire.

The witnesses complained that the Yugoslav Army was late in arriving, but all agreed that the military subsequently played a constructive role in protecting the Croats.

On Monday, the army stood guard as the villagers of Struga formed a convoy of tractors and set out for Sisak, a Croatian city about 25 miles north. The refugees, with a few scattered belongings in carts, traveled a circuitous route to avoid the Serbian towns. They arrived in Sisak today, greeted by small crowds of tearful local residents.

* * *

August 12, 1991

ITALY'S HANDLING OF ALBANIANS IS DRAWING CRITICISM

By ALAN COWELL
Special to the New York Times

ROME, Aug. 11—As fighting and tension intensified between Albanian refugees and Italian security forces in the southern port of Bari, criticism mounted in Italy today over the authorities' handling of the Albanians, whose visions of a new life in Italy have collided abruptly with official determination to send them back home.

Pope John Paul II today commented on the Albanians' reception in this country by saying, "No one can remain indifferent before the dramatic scenes of men, women and entire families." Analysts took the remark as implicit criticism of the oft-repeated and hard-line official position aimed at discouraging more Albanians from seeking refuge here.

The Pope's remark and much criticism from the press and elsewhere were inspired by the squalid conditions in which the thousands of Albanians have been held since their arrival last week. They are crowded into a soccer stadium and along the dockside in Bari, subsisting on bread and water and living without bedding, sanitation or shelter from the searing August heat.

Echoing criticism from several Italian newspapers, the Rome daily La Repubblica castigated what it called "behavior that shows lack of foresight, preparation and improvisation."

But Deputy Prime Minister Claudio Martelli defended Government policy, saying, "We absolutely will not tolerate a new clandestine immigration from Albania after that of recent months."

Albania is Europe's poorest country, seized by economic crisis as it slowly and uncertainly emerges from decades of Stalinism that sealed it off from the outside world. About 24,000 Albanians fled to Italy in March, and some received shelter. This time, however, the authorities have apparently decided to demonstrate that Italy is not prepared to act as a haven for new arrivals.

The crisis began Thursday when 10,000 Albanians aboard a commandeered freighter forced their way into Bari harbor. Many of them literally jumped ship and swam ashore, but the police rounded them up.

Since then, there have been several clashes between refugees and the police as waves of Albanians have tried to break out of the stadium.

Early today, reporters in Bari said, the clashes reached new intensity when Albanians at the port barricaded themselves on a pier and stoned police officers distributing food in what seemed a protest over the meager rations and poor conditions. The police fired tear gas, which promptly wafted back on a morning breeze into police lines, and a fire-fighting vessel doused the Albanians with its hoses.

The Italian authorities have accused the Albanian Government of allowing the refugees to head for Italy so as to blackmail Italy into granting Albania more financial aid. The Government said today that Foreign Minister Gianni De Michelis would fly to Albania on Monday to discuss the issue with the authorities there. Some fugitives in Bari have said they encountered no official resistance when they commandeered the freighter after rumors spread that they would be able to leave.

The authorities said that as of this afternoon about 4,000 of the Albanians had been sent back by plane or boat.

Italy, having decided to send the refugees home, seems to be finding it difficult to do so quickly. A requisitioned ferry that left for Albania two days ago was reportedly denied permission to dock at the Albanian port of Durres to discharge its returnees.

* * *

September 28, 1991

IN SHRINE TO VIRGIN, THREAT OF WAR DARKENS STREETS

By CHUCK SUDETIC
Special to The New York Times

MEDJUGORJE, Yugoslavia, Sept. 23—Scared off by the war in Croatia, all but a few perseverant Roman Catholic pilgrims have disappeared from this mountain town, where four youths have reported seeing apparitions of the Virgin Mary each evening for the last decade.

The millions of Catholics drawn here from all over the world by devotion to the Virgin, curiosity and reports of miraculous healings transformed this once down-at-the-heels hamlet into a tourist haven. But this afternoon it resembled a wind-blown off-season beach town.

On Sunday, only local worshipers and a handful of American and Salvadoran pilgrims attended the evening Mass and rosary at Medjugorje's St. James Church, where the nightly communal prayer for peace has for years drawn overflow crowds.

Now, policemen with automatic weapons man checkpoints along the almost deserted roads leading to Medjugorje, which is in the republic of Bosnia and Herzegovina. Ranks of powder-blue Madonnas cast blank stares at the town's empty streets from display windows in darkened souvenir shops.

Neon Signs Turned Off

"We were ordered last week to switch off all neon signs," said Mladen Bavcevic, who manages a hotel opened only 16 days ago that now boasts one of the town's two restaurants still serving meals.

"I have to admit that we haven't a single guest tonight," he said. "We're more like night watchmen than hoteliers these days."

An army reserve contingent, made up mostly of rugged men marshaled from the outback of the neighboring republic of Montenegro, have dug in a little more than a half-hour's drive from Medjugorje across the Neretva River valley. Reserve officers say the units are engaged in a routine exercise, but their gun emplacements all point toward positions held by the Bosnian republic police.

Sporadic gunfire has erupted from the army's encampments day and night, and drunken reservists toting automatic weapons have invaded cafes in nearby villages. Bands of reservists have also broken into private homes and shops, taking canned food and searching for weapons, republic police officials said.

"These men aren't soldiers, they're scum, a drunken mob," said a police commander in the nearby town of Capljina.

Memories of Atrocities

Several thousand Croats and Muslim Slavs have fled the area where the troops are bivouacked, while Serbs, fearing retaliatory violence if clashes erupt, have fled to towns behind federal army lines. This region's Muslim Slavs, Croats and especially Serbs have vivid memories of atrocities committed against them by one another during World War II, including a mass killing of Serbs by Croatian fascists committed near Medjugorje itself.

"There is a very flimsy peace now," said the Rev. Ivan Landeka, an assistant at St. James. "We told people that columns of army reservists have come from Montenegro and Serbia and that there is a possibility of clashes nearby."

"People here are just not used to having an army around," Father Landeka said.

"Jet fighters overflew Medjugorje several times each day last week," he said. "Last Tuesday, we had 10,000 people at

Mass on the mountain above Medjugorje. We could hear bombs exploding in the town of Ploce, about 20 miles away. We didn't know what was happening."

A Few Americans Remain

The few American pilgrims left in Medjugorje speak of anxiety, but many of them say they intend to remain here to pray and meditate.

"I'm going to try to stay through Oct. 7," said Linda Enfield, who operates a landscape business with her husband in Boca Raton, Fla. "I'm just supposed to be here. I don't know why, but I am."

John Mattras, a tax lawyer from Hoboken, N.J., planned since January to spend today, his 26th birthday, in Medjugorje. He and his travel companion, Paul Kelly, a 29-year-old one-time actor who plans to take up a religious vocation in the South Bronx after his return home, avoided watching television footage of the war in Croatia to keep from becoming discouraged.

Prudent to Leave

"It kept getting more depressing every day," Mr. Mattras said, referring to the news during the few weeks before their departure. "We almost had to wrestle with our travel agent to book our trip because he insisted it was too dangerous to go."

"We prayed a lot," he said.

Mr. Kelly said: "We were planning to stay for two weeks. But the American priest told us at Mass last night in the strongest terms that it would be prudent for us to make plans to leave."

"They tell us that everything around here is going to close up and that the English-speaking priests are going to leave if things get bad," he said.

Ed Ennis, a 68-year-old retired fishery-department worker from Ocean Park, Wash., making his fourth pilgrimage to Medjugorje, insisted that he was not worried at all.

"I have too much faith in the Blessed Lady," he said.

"This is a place of total peace," he said. "But this is the first time I've been here and been angry."

"I am very angry to see it so empty because of the fear people have for their mortal hides," he said. "The rosary is the strongest weapon that exists."

Thank You for a Cure

Mr. Ennis's daughter-in-law, Virginia Ennis, a 51-year-old bus driver, said nothing could have kept her from Medjugorje this year.

"I suffered from bone cancer," Mrs. Ennis said. "I came here last year and was healed during a Mass. I knew I was cured. I felt different."

"The doctors had said that I would be in a wheelchair within six months," she said. "After the Mass I walked up the mountain."

"The doctors couldn't explain my recovery," she said, "but they told me to keep doing what I was doing."

"No war could scare me away," she said. "Wouldn't you come back to say thank you?"

* * *

October 15, 1991

BULGARIAN OPPOSITION CLAIMS VICTORY IN A CLOSE VOTE

By The Associated Press

SOFIA, Bulgaria, Oct. 14—Thousands of Bulgarians took to the streets tonight to celebrate an opposition group's claim of victory in parliamentary elections that could oust the Government of former Communists.

Projections based on partial returns gave the Union of Democratic Forces a narrow lead, but the former Communists, now called Socialists, said it was too early to concede defeat. Final returns from Sunday's voting are not due until late in the week.

The projections also indicated that the first non-Communist government since World War II might have to rely on the Turkish ethnic minority's party for survival, an unsettling prospect for many Bulgarians because of the country's ethnic tensions.

Opposition Backers Rally

About 50,000 opposition supporters rallied in downtown Sofia to cheer the Union of Democratic Forces.

"You are free!" shouted Filip Dmitrov, the leader of the opposition coalition and its candidate for Prime Minister. "The age of Communism in Bulgaria is over!"

As Mr. Dmitrov spoke, the demonstrators, many in tears, waved the blue flags of his anti-Communist coalition. They shouted: "Victory! Victory!" and "Communists are rubbish!"

President Zhelyu Zhelev, a former chairman of the United Democratic Forces, called the election "a new step toward democracy." Mr. Zhelev was chosen by a Socialist-controlled Parliament in a move to mollify the opposition after elections in June 1990, and his power has increased in recent months.

Despite the jubilation, the Socialists, who won last year's elections after the ouster of the hard-line Communist leader Todor Zhivkov, seem likely to hold more than a third of the 240 parliamentary seats, enabling them to block key legislation.

The Union of Democratic Forces wants quick privatization of state-owned businesses, while the Socialists favor a slower transition to a market economy.

4 Percent Margin Projected

According to a projection by the local affiliate of Gallup International, the Union for Democratic Forces won 36 percent of the vote, compared with 32 percent for the Socialists.

The Socialist leader, Alexander Lilov, refused to concede defeat, telling his supporters that the counting was not over. "Cheer up, dear comrades," he urged.

The Turkish minority's Movement for Rights and Freedoms was projected to win 7 percent of the vote. It is the only other party forecast to exceed the 4 percent minimum required to gain parliamentary seats.

Nearly a quarter of the estimated five million votes went to 58 other small anti-Socialist parties, which failed to pass the threshold. Some foreign observers who monitored the election predicted that the high proportion of votes going to parties without seats could cause political instability.

Gordon Heald, director of the Gallup affiliate, said the vote projection was based on returns from 250 representative polling centers out of 11,000 nationwide. He said it had a margin of error of one or two percentage points.

That appears to give the balance of power in Parliament to the Turkish minority, which accounts for about 11 percent of Bulgaria's nine million people.

Before the ouster of Mr. Zhivkov in November 1989, the ethnic Turks suffered widespread discrimination, which they say continues.

Mr. Lilov ruled out a coalition between the Socialists and the Turkish party. Leaders of the Union of Democratic Forces took no public stand on the possibility of a coalition.

*   *   *

October 17, 1991

BULGARIA VOTE GIVES KEY ROLE TO ETHNIC TURKS

By CELESTINE BOHLEN
Special to The New York Times

SOFIA, Bulgaria, Oct. 16—Its rights restored after years of forced assimilation under Communist rule, Bulgaria's ethnic Turkish minority has emerged from national elections last Sunday with a critical role to play in the formation of the next Government, thrusting the volatile issue of ethnic relations to the forefront of Bulgarian politics.

The Movement for Rights and Freedom, representing the country's one million Muslim Turks, won about 7 percent of the vote. As a result. it is seen as the most likely coalition partner for the Union of Democratic Forces, the opposition group that on Sunday pulled ahead of the Bulgarian Socialist Party—as former Communists here now call themselves—to take its place as the country's major political force.

But even as its members were celebrating the Communists' final fall from power, the Union of Democratic Forces, which split three ways on the eve of the elections, fell short of the majority it needs in Bulgaria's new, 240-seat Parliament. The latest unofficial results, with 90 percent of the vote counted, showed the Union's lead had dwindled to 34.4 percent, compared with the Socialists' 33.8 percent.

Since no other party has won the 4 percent minimum required to gain parliamentary seats, the Union of Democratic Forces, a loose alliance of center-right parties, may have little choice but to form a coalition with the Turks. It is a political equation that makes many in this Balkan country of nine million people worry about an ethnic Bulgarian backlash.

'Not a Popular Idea'

"It is not a popular idea for many Bulgarians to be dependent on the Movement for Rights and Freedom," said Andrei Lukanov, the former Communist who served as Prime Minister in the transitional Socialist Government. "It may be prejudice, but there it is."

Raising the specter of a Government "held hostage" to an ethnic minority, Mr. Lukanov signaled a nationalist theme that could spell trouble for the new Government as it tries to guide Bulgaria through a period of painful economic change.

Tensions between Orthodox Christian Bulgarians and Muslim Turks date from the Turkish Ottoman Empire's 500-year occupation of Bulgaria, which ended in 1878. But they became more acute in the 1980's, when the Communist leader, Todor Zhivkov, began a campaign of cultural assimilation that forced ethnic Turks to adopt Slavic names, closed their mosques and prayer houses and suppressed any attempts at protest. One result was the mass exodus of more than 300,000 ethnic Turks to neighboring Turkey in 1989, a spectacle that deeply hurt Bulgaria's image abroad.

The legacy of Mr. Zhivkov's policies—now the basis of criminal charges against the 78-year-old deposed leader—has continued to poison Bulgarian politics even after his ouster in November 1989 and the demise of the single-party state. When the Socialist Government, then led by Mr. Lukanov, moved in January 1990 to restore the Turks' long-denied rights, ethnic Bulgarians in regions with mixed populations rose up in protest, fanning fears of a rise of a militant pan-Islamic movement in Bulgaria.

Prominent Role Expected

In the previous Bulgarian elections, held in June 1990, the Turkish Movement, led by Ahmed Dogan, a former political prisoner, also came in third, but its victory then gave it fewer than 6 percent of the parliamentary seats. Its members' voices were barely heard in the battles that raged between the Socialists and the opposition Union of Democratic Forces.

This week, with predictions that the Movement could have as many as 27 seats in Parliament, Mr. Dogan continued to keep a low profile, shunning both the foreign and Bulgarian press. But in an interview today, Yunal Lyufti, a spokesman for the Movement, made it clear that this time Bulgaria's ethnic Turks would expect a prominent role in return for their support of the next Government.

Mr. Lyufti said his party expected "a few ministerial posts," including a spot as Deputy Prime Minister and involvement in Bulgaria's foreign policy "as a balancing factor."

He played down alarmists' predictions about the Turks' participation in Government as the work of a "handful of nationalist leaders."

"I think both Bulgarians and Turks are mature enough to understand the real activities of the Movement," he said. "We have to overcome the psychological burden carried since the Ottoman occupation, and then people will regard the Movement as an ordinary political party."

But at a news conference today, Alexander Yordanov, a leading member of the Union of Democratic Forces, hinted that his party was not yet ready to grant the Turkish Movement a prominent role in Government. "Not every party that passed the 4 percent threshold is entitled to ask for a ministerial post," he said.

Mr. Yordanov said the first task of the new Government would be to introduce new laws on the privatization of state property, to make changes in laws on land ownership and foreign investment, and to start confiscation of property illegitimately held by the former Communists.

But as the election campaign receded, so did the vehemence of the anti-Communist language of the Union of Democratic Forces, echoed in the last days by President Zhelyu Zhelev, who openly discarded his neutral role.

And as passions rise over the issue of Turkish participation, many here predict it will be days, maybe even weeks, before a new Government emerges.

"Bulgarians in the mixed regions will make trouble and the Socialists will exploit this issue," said Krassimir Kanev, an adviser on minority affairs for President Zhelez. "This will be a very unstable situation."

*   *   *

November 9, 1991

EUROPEAN NATIONS DECLARE SANCTIONS AGAINST BELGRADE

By ALAN RIDING
Special to The New York Times

ROME, Nov. 8—Frustrated at its continuing failure to halt Serbian-led attacks on Croatia, the 12-nation European Community placed broad economic sanctions on Yugoslavia today and urged the United Nations Security Council to order an oil embargo in the hope of cutting off fuel for the conflict.

Conferring on the fringes of a two-day NATO summit meeting, community foreign ministers also said that a peace conference being mediated by Lord Carrington of Britain had been put in jeopardy by "fighting and indiscriminate bloodshed" taking place in violation of repeated cease-fires.

The punitive measures announced today referred broadly to Yugoslavia, but European officials said they were aimed at Serbia and Yugoslavia's Serbian-led army. The community said it would compensate republics that continue to cooperate with peace efforts and are hurt by the sanctions.

Most Drastic Moves Yet

Western Europe's moves today were the most drastic since the community intervened in the Yugoslav conflict soon after Slovenia and Croatia declared their independence on June 25. Until now, the community has focused on trying to end the fighting and promote peace talks. So far, 12 cease-fire agreements have collapsed.

Noting that the oil embargo could help end the fighting, European officials said the community had decided to seek action through the United Nations because Serbia's main suppliers are the Soviet Union and Libya, countries that would not be affected by any embargo dictated by the community.

Britain, France and Belgium—community nations that are on the Security Council—are to sponsor an embargo resolution at the United Nations in the coming days. Foreign Minister Hans-Dietrich Genscher of Germany said, "I know from the Soviet Union that they want to support all measures the community proposes." China was also expected to approve the embargo.

Bush Promises Statement

Shortly before leaving here, President Bush hinted that the United States may follow the European lead. "We'll have more to say on that in the not-too-distant future," Mr. Bush said. Asked about the proposed oil embargo, he added, "We'll have a U.S. position on that very soon."

Foreign Secretary Douglas Hurd of Britain said he did not think force would be necessary to carry out an embargo. "It would have the force of international law, and it will be the countries through which the oil passes who will have to bear the brunt of enforcing it," he said.

Economic experts have questioned whether the sanctions can help end the fighting since Yugoslav leaders have done nothing to shield the economy from war damage. Some experts also fear that the Serbian President, Slobodan Milosevic, might use the measures to rally public opinion behind him.

While dismissing any suggestion of a European peace-keeping force in Yugoslavia, Mr. Hurd said the community would use every peaceful means to persuade Yugoslavs "to pull themselves out of this downward dive into disaster."

In a separate statement, the NATO leaders condemned the use of force to achieve political goals, noting that attacks by Yugoslavia's Serbian-led federal army on Dubrovnik and other Croatian cities were "out of all proportion to any provocation, cease-fire violation or requirement to protect Serbian communities or army garrisons."

They also recalled that Croatia had not fulfilled its pledge to end its blockade of federal army barracks and stressed that recognition of republics seeking independence could only come in an overall settlement that included guarantees for rights of minorities.

Eager on Recognition

Officials said Germany was still eager to recognize the independence of Slovenia and Croatia, the two republics whose moves for independence led to the fighting, but had agreed not to act alone. "Undue recognition may trigger off processes far worse than the situation now," the Dutch Foreign Minister, Hans van den Broek, said.

The community left open the door by urging the two republics to prepare legal provisions protecting human rights and minority rights. "The train towards recognition has already started to roll," Mr. Genscher said.

Announcing sanctions approved last Monday after Serbia rejected a community peace plan, the European foreign ministers said a 1980 trade and cooperation agreement with Yugoslavia would be immediately suspended. Yugoslavia currently does 60 percent of its trade with community countries.

The community also placed new limits on imports of Yugoslav textiles, stripped Yugoslavia of trade benefits under the so-called General System of Preferences and suspended Yugoslavia from participation in an economic recovery program for Eastern Europe that is backed by 24 Western countries.

The community foreign ministers are expected to meet soon to determine what compensatory measures will be adopted to help cushion republics other than Serbia from the impact of the sanctions.

The community is also expected to compensate Greece, which borders on Yugoslavia. With 40 percent of Greece's trade passing through Yugoslavia, Athens estimates losses up to $10 million per day and has asked the community for $500 million in emergency aid.

The foreign ministers decided against recommending a suspension of the Yugoslav peace conference, but they also recognized there was little room for optimism. Lord Carrington said he was willing to continue negotiations if all six Yugoslav republics participate. "But the difficulties some are posing make it very difficult to reach a political conclusion," he said.

* * *

November 16, 1991

DUBROVNIK DIARY:
SHELLING, SNIPER FIRE, CHAOS AND
FOR A FEW, ESCAPE BY SEA

By DAVID BINDER

The writer of this article was evacuated on Thursday after spending a week in Dubrovnik, Yugoslavia, whose Croatian defenders are besieged by Yugoslav federal forces. Here is a diary of the final five days of the visit.

Nov. 10

The Hotel Belvedere caught fire about 10:15 A.M. under heavy shelling from two Yugoslav Navy patrol boats and from mortars on Mount Zarkovica, just above. It belches dark-gray smoke and flames.

Snipers are firing past the Hotel Argentina from Zarkovica, where the army is entrenched, and from the ridges below Mount Srd, where the Croatian defenders have a stronghold in a Napoleonic fort.

The Dubrovnik Crisis Committee evacuated the 70 Croatian refugees who had been given shelter in the Belvedere to the Argentina, 800 yards up the coast. All of them are from nearby towns that were largely destroyed by the advancing army. For the Belvedere refugees, it was the second move in a couple of weeks and most probably not their last. They have only the clothes on their backs.

Also at the Argentina is the European Community, a 13-member team of military officers from seven countries sent by Brussels to monitor the fighting between the Serbs and the Croats. They wear white pants and shirts. Local residents call them the ice-cream men.

The monitors aren't cowards. But when mortar and cannon shells explode and sniper bullets whiz nearby, they duck, scramble and sprawl on the floor just like those without combat experience.

Like many others here, the ice-cream men are trying to get out. They show up at the harbor in their white van with a police escort, and stand in the bright sunshine below the St. Ivan Fortress, watching the shells detonate. The stench of untreated sewage is strong. The army cut off Dubrovnik's water and electricity weeks ago.

The monitors decide the firing is too intense to risk sailing across the bay to Cavtat, about half an hour away on the army side, so the group heads back to the Argentina. The shelling and sniper fire is intensifying. The explosions are nerve-wracking, so loud they stop conversation.

Eight people were wounded today on the Croatian side as far as we can tell.

"I have stones," says Nives Cicin-Sain. "I think I could throw them on their heads. I was kind of a pacifist. Never hated anybody. But now?"

Nives is a sculptor, 30 years old, from Split. She volunteered to work here helping refugees—there are more than 10,000 in shelters around the city.

She says the first person killed in the siege of Dubrovnik by the Serbian-led federal army was a Serb, a 50-year-old poet named Milan Miesic. A shell hit his house near the Argentina on Oct. 5. The siege is 40 days old.

Nov. 11

The shelling and sniper fire is getting worse. The monitors aren't even going to try to get out.

Except for the explosions, the Old Town is eerily quiet: Only the hourly tolling of the bell in a 15th-century tower at the top of the Stradun boulevard, the swish of waves, and the hum of a generator used to light the wretched shelters in the catacombs of the forts. A few citizens trot along the edges of the Stradun, fearful of incoming fire. Now and then, a stray cat zips by in search of food. Birds fly up in flocks whenever there is an explosion.

It is the second day of really heavy bombardment. The federal gunners hit the 17th-century Jesuit monastery, a Baroque masterpiece, the 16th-century Sorkocevic Palace, which served in the summer as a stage for Shakespeare performances, the St. Ivan and Lovrijenac Forts and other monuments inside or near the ancient city walls.

They also pound the Hotel Excelsior, right next to the Argentina, and some boats in the new harbor at Gruz.

Officials announce that 58 people have been killed in the last four weeks on the Croatian side, including five today. The number of wounded has reached 300. The weather remains sunny and warm.

"I love this city," said Ranko Bautovic, a Red Cross worker who is 35. "I was a tourist guide for 17 years. But now I have lost this love. I care only about the people."

Nives and her fellow volunteer Vesna Cucic are asked whether it is really worth defending Dubrovnik.

"They have to fight from somewhere," says Nives of the Croatian forces.

"They're going to destroy it anyway," says Vesna, a 31-year-old librarian. "It's the people who count."

Nov. 12

The federal forces' bombardment is heavier still: Cannon, mortars, rockets, wire-guided missiles. It started just before dawn. Terrific explosions.

Half the journalists and photographers are in the Argentina, the rest inside the town walls. Nobody is safe in either place. A Briton took a piece of shrapnel near his spine, but he's still running around.

At 9:30 A.M. two British photographers are blown against a wall right outside the Argentina by a mortar shell, scaring the daylights out of them. But they are not wounded.

Standing on the seaside terrace, the European monitors watch the navy and the army slam old Dubrovnik—first the St. Ivan and Minceta towers, then boats in the old harbor, then the top floors of the Town Hall and the city cafe.

Rockets swish by in multiples. Then the army tries out its wire-guided missiles. We see their tail flares streak toward the port, followed by huge bangs.

At 11:00 the bell of the clock tower tolls the hour. At noon it is silent. Somewhere in between, a missile hit it.

We can see that it struck the "green men," the two bronze figures carrying hammers to strike the bell that Dubrovnik bought from Venice in the 15th century. The Dubrovnik people call them Maro and Baro. In the old harbor, pleasure boats are on fire, the flames jumping from craft to craft until all are ablaze.

At 12:45 P.M., a wire-guided missile hits the Argosy, the boat chartered to the European Community, as the European monitors watch in dismay. They had promised me a lift. We watch the boat burn, wondering if we are really trapped.

Nov. 13

More shelling and shooting. The Argentina has run out of beer and fresh water. They serve disgusting coffee made with sea water.

Croatian Radio reports 23 were killed and 11 wounded in Dubrovnik yesterday. It's still sunny. This place is beautiful even in these hours of torture.

All at once a tiny bit of hope. The European monitors have finally got a relief ship, the Slavija, moving from down the coast at Zelenika, where the Feds are in control.

The firing is dying down. Only an occasional volley from automatic rifles and machine guns.

At 2 P.M., the vessel appears on the horizon to the west. The Europeans have arranged to take 1,600 refugees with them—women, children, old men.

I pack, pay and say goodbyes to brave Nives, Vesna, Ranko and Inspector Lukic and head for the harbor.

The Slavija has sailed in under the watchful eyes of the federal forces and anchored in the Gruz harbor next to a burning dockyard. Trucks emerge from its cavernous maw with fresh supplies of desperately needed food, mineral water, propane gas, medicine.

Good supper in the Slavija's restaurant. Great shower in cabin No. 232. A little sleep. Bad dreams.

Nov. 14

Up at 7 with loud shouts from the dock.

The first of thousands of Dubrovnik people are crowding aboard. Maj. Per Hvalkof of the Danish special forces is grim.

"There are people on shore who should be on the ship," he tells an official by telephone in Zelenika, the Slavija's next port of call. "There are people on the ship who should be on the shore."

Pregnant women, babies, 80-year-olds with canes, Croatian guards carrying rifles. Later we hear there are 2,200 on board. About 56,000 are estimated to be left behind.

One of the passengers is Toni Dratovic, a 47-year-old who studied business administration in Wisconsin, came back to Dubrovnik and owned 16 apartment houses and boats here. He was wounded in the back by shrapnel.

"I lost everything here," he said.

The Slavija motors rev up and we pull away from the wharf in the rain, a sitting duck for any Yugoslav gun crew that decides we should not be leaving. But we are allowed to pass safely through the lines. Seasickness sets in as the calm waters of the harbor give way to the Adriatic chop, but for the refugees, their nausea is a sign of deliverance.

*   *   *

November 21, 1991

CROATION CITYSCAPE: STRAY DOGS, ROWS OF WOUNDED, PILES OF DEAD

By CHUCK SUDETIC
Special to The New York Times

VUKOVAR, Yugoslavia, Nov. 20—After 86 days of shelling, aerial bombardment and house-to-house combat, Vukovar is a wasteland of gutted homes and churches, burning storefronts and bloated, bullet-riddled bodies littering the streets.

Today, a day after the last Croatian snipers abandoned the city to the victorious Yugoslav Army, civilian survivors of the siege continued to emerge from the basement shelters where they have survived three months with little water, food and medicine, and without electricity and heat, to seek the relative comfort of refugee camps. This afternoon, about 450 wounded men, women and children, including a dozen newborn babies, were evacuated from the basement corridors and fallout shelters of the town's hospital.

Only about 2,500 of Vukovar's 50,000 residents stayed throughout the battle, and no estimate of the death toll was available here today. Estimates of the overall toll in five months of fighting in Yugoslavia range from 3,000 to 7,500.

Only soldiers of the Serbian-dominated army, stray dogs and a few journalists walked the smoky, rubble-choked streets and the ruins of the apartment buildings, stores and hotel in Vukovar's center. Not one of the buildings seen in a daylong visit to this town could be described as habitable.

In one park, shellfire has sheared thick trees in half like so many blades of grass cut by a mower. Across the street, the dome of an Orthodox Christian church had fallen onto the altar.

Automatic weapons fire erupted every few minutes as the prowling Serbian soldiers, some of them drunk, took aim at land mines, pigeons and windows that had survived the fighting.

In two courtyards across the street from the hospital, about 50 bodies were lined up in rows and tagged with numbers. Some were covered with blankets. Soldiers searched through the city's basements for more dead, and for evidence to back up the army's assertions that fleeing Croatian extremists killed scores of Serbian civilians in and around Vukovar.

Photos of the Dead

Belgrade television tonight broadcast grisly photos reportedly depicting the bodies of men and women strewn about the streets and yards of Borovo Naselje, a settlement for shoe-factory workers next to Vukovar, who were allegedly butchered by Croatian soldiers with knives and axes.

The pictures shed no light on whether the victims were Serbs or Croats, or on who killed them. But the reports of atrocities appear to have led to reprisal killings of Croats by Serbs.

This morning, two Western journalists said they saw army reservists shoot two Croatian men in civilian clothes on Vukovar's main street on Tuesday afternoon. They reported seeing other freshly killed bodies nearby, apparently the victims of similar summary executions.

"They dragged some of the bodies into a nearby department store," said one of the journalists, who insisted on not being identified. "They were trying to hide some of them."

Today the bodies of seven Croat men lay in a vacant lot next to the department store. All were pocked with bullet holes. A white bath towel tied to a broomstick lay about 20 feet away.

'They Have All Been Killed'

A soldier said Serbian troops had shot about 80 men they suspected of committing atrocities against Serbian civilians.

"Our guys shot them immediately, on the spot," said the 28-year-old volunteer, who comes from the Serbian town of Arandjelovac.

Some of the Croatian militiamen changed into civilian clothes and hid among the wounded and civilians at the town's hospital, the soldier said. His account was confirmed by hospital personnel.

"Local people identified them," he said. "They have all been killed."

Fred R. Conrad/The New York Times

Some of about 50 corpses that lay yesterday across from the hospital in Vukovar, Yugoslavia.

"I saw it," he said. "It was about noon. Every one of them admitted that he had killed people. They used hostages as a human shield."

In the late afternoon twilight, a pair of Serbian soldiers wandered among the streets with plastic store bags and a camera.

Serbs' Overland Route

"I'm taking pictures of the dead for a remembrance," said one. "They are all Ustashe."

The Ustashe were Croatian fascists who carried out atrocities against Serbs during World War II. The Serbian-controlled Government in Belgrade asserts that it is fighting to prevent similar depredations in Serb-populated regions of Croatia, which declared independence from the Yugoslav federation in June.

By seizing Vukovar, the Serbs have also secured an overland route from Serbia to a group of Serb-controlled villages in the area of Croatia north of the town. They have also removed the Croats' last foothold on the Danube River.

The Serbs have already captured about a third of the breakaway republic's territory, including many regions with overwhelmingly Croat populations.

Yugoslav Army troops in Vukovar said today they are sure the army's commanders will now train their sights on the nearby Croatian towns of Vinkovci and Osijek.

"In the end, after all this," said a teen-age Serb in Vukovar's territorial defense corps, "there will be an agreement."

In the bomb-proof bunker under the parking lot of the hospital, hundreds of wounded men and women were stacked on three-level bunk beds, the mattresses only two feet wide, awaiting evacuation later in the day.

"I don't know whether it's night or day," said Jozo Oklopcic, a 56-year-old bricklayer, who was wounded in the stomach by an exploding shell two weeks ago. "I only want to know if my family is alive."

Outside, a group of young Croatian and Serbian mothers waited for buses that would evacuate them to Zagreb and Belgrade respectively.

"I gave birth 20 days ago," said 21-year-old Sonja Djudjar, who said she dodged shellfire to travel from her basement to the hospital when she was ready to give birth. "I don't know where my husband is."

"Thirteen babies were born in the hospital during the siege," said Sister Damira, a Roman Catholic nun, who held an infant who has not seen its mother in months because she could not make it through the blockade that has sealed off Vukovar since mid-September. "We have no idea why the army shot at the hospital. Nobody has explained that to us."

*   *   *

November 24, 1991

FOR BLACK SEA, SLOW CHOKING BY POLLUTANTS

By MARLISE SIMONS
Special to The New York Times

VARNA, Bulgaria—For centuries, the Black Sea produced dolphin skins and caviar and fish so plentiful that no one thought such bounty could ever end. But now this ancient highway between Europe and Asia is suffering extensive changes, the proportions of which are only just becoming fully known.

All along its 2,500-mile coastline, fishing boats sit in port, idled by the collapse of sturgeon, mackerel, anchovy and other commercial fisheries.

Bathing beaches near Constanta in Romania and Odessa in the Ukraine have been closed for the last two summers because of chemical pollution and the smelly froth of algae blooms. Now scientists warn that this inland sea is rapidly losing its oxygen and its ability to purge itself.

Specialists Meet

The Black Sea and its unusual biological traits, which are still little understood, have long fascinated scientists. This year, the end of Communism permitted specialists from the whole region to meet and debate the Black Sea's problems freely for the first time at a conference in this Bulgarian city.

But political turmoil in the Soviet Union is holding up a new international agreement to stop the marine pollution already banned off other coasts, and ships from many nations still clean out their oil tanks, flush their ballast and dump loads of dangerous sludge and toxic waste into the Black Sea.

Biologists also worry about the growing tide of human, farm and industrial discharge pouring in from the four Black Sea countries—Bulgaria, Romania, the Soviet Union and Turkey. Newly published surveys show that every town, industry and mine along its shores uses this land-trapped water as dump and sewer.

More than 60 rivers and streams deliver waste from a catchment area of 160 million people. The four largest are the Danube, the Don, the Dnieper and the Dniester, and they arrive here after sweeping through a region now recognized as one of the most polluted in the world.

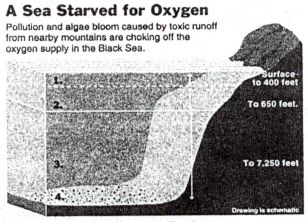

A Sea Starved for Oxygen

Pollution and algae bloom caused by toxic runoff from nearby mountains are choking off the oxygen supply in the Black Sea.

Surface to 400 feet
To 650 feet.
To 7,250 feet

Drawing is schematic

1. **Oxygenated Water** Where most life exists.
2. **Boundary Zone** Combination of oxygenated and stagnant water.
3. **Deep Water** Devoid of oxygen and most life. Contains hydrogen sulfide.
4. **Sediment** Contaminants sink, concentrating at the bottom.

Source: Ken O. Buesseler, Woods Hole Oceanographic Institution

Scientists say that every year these rivers carry many tons of toxic materials—oil, lead, phosphorous, nitrates, chromium, cadmium and others.

Fallout From Chernobyl

In spring, when the melting snow washes the land, the river waters from the north, especially the Dnieper, carry radioactive fallout from the 1986 nuclear accident at Chernobyl.

"I know of no other inland sea under such pressure," said Stanislav Konovalov, director of the Soviet Institute for Biology of the Southern Seas at Sebastopol. "This is much more degraded than the Baltic."

Biologists like Mr. Konovalov who have spent much of their lives exploring the Black Sea say they are shocked and surprised by the collapse of its fisheries and other extraordinary changes in its ecosystems.

At Vinizi, a small community of summer houses and fishermen on the Bulgarian coast, Atanas Stefanov remembers the time that he and his father hunted dolphins and seals to sell the fat and the skins.

"Our biggest year, we shot 1,024 dolphins," said Mr. Stefanov, who has been going to sea for 55 of his 68 years. "That was 1947. Everybody did it. Of course it's forbidden now."

Only Little Fish Now

For much of their lives, these fishermen have caught three-foot-long, caviar-laden sturgeon and loads of fat horse mackerel. "Today we get these little things," Mr. Stefanov lamented, showing a pot full of small scad.

Aboard the Bulgarian research vessel Akademik, Hinko Klisarov said that the crew still spots dolphins, but that the other mammals, the seals, have disappeared altogether. And like creatures in a science-fiction tale, some jellyfish are getting bigger and bigger. "They are now appearing at 30 pounds or more," he said.

Yuvenaly Zaitsev, a Soviet biologist based in Sevastopol, argues that the sturgeon were finished by overfishing. The total catch, he said, dropped from more than a thousand tons per year in 1950 to less than 10 tons two years ago. Worse than that, he said, of the 26 commercial fish species abundant in 1970, he said, today only five are left in commercial quantities.

Mr. Zaitsev says a proliferation of jellyfish has caused part of the problem because they eat the eggs and the larvae of other fish. A new arrival is a plague of ribbed jellyfish, a recent intruder that is found on the Atlantic coast of North America and probably arrived here in bilge water.

Anchovy Fleets Paralyzed

Whatever the cause of the changes, they are far-reaching. Some two million people live directly or indirectly off fisheries. On Turkey's 700-mile Black Sea coast, fishermen have been hit hardest, and anchovy fleets are paralyzed at Trebizond, Sinop, Samsun and other ports. The Ankara Government says that between 1987 and 1989, the Turkish Black Sea catch dropped almost 95 percent, from 340,000 tons to less than 15,000 tons, and it has declared a moratorium on anchovy fishing.

"Nobody really knows why all this is happening," said Umit Unluata, an oceanographer at the Turkish Institute of Marine Sciences. "It may be a combination of overfishing, pollution, climate change and shifts in the food chain."

Geologists say the greatest change in these waters happened some 8,000 years ago, when the Black Sea was still a fresh-water lake but the sea level rose and the Mediterranean spilled through the Bosporus.

As salt water rushed in, geologists believe, it killed the life adapted to fresh water, and this produced the mass of hydrogen sulfide, which remains trapped in the deep waters beneath the thin surface lid of oxygen.

Nine-Tenths Lifeless

Only the top 100 yards or so is oxygen-bearing water, and more than nine-tenths has such high levels of hydrogen sulfide that it is lifeless.

"It's really a geological freak," said David Aubrey, a senior scientist at the Woods Hole Oceanographic Institution in Massachusetts, which organized the first large international Black Sea conference in October in Varna. "If you put a piece of metal in deep enough, it will come out black. If you turned the Black Sea over, it would smell of rotten eggs."

"In this fragile setting," Dr. Aubrey added, "man has now created an environmental catastrophe."

The mass of hydrogen sulfide and methane is sealed off by the lid of oxygenated water. Scientists say that if the sea "turned over" because of an earthquake or a chemical upheaval—something that they call unlikely but possible—the escaping gasses could kill people on the shore.

Sea Receives Less Water

Modern change began 30 years ago with the frantic industrialization along the rivers in Eastern Europe that brought

The New York Times

toxic chemicals, detergents and fertilizers. Soviet dams and irrigation projects have diverted so much river water that by Soviet estimates, the Black Sea is today receiving almost one-fifth less fresh water and becoming more salty.

Some scientists believe that the poisonous hydrogen sulfide is welling up, reducing the oxygen layer and thus causing fish kills. But others blame the detergents and fertilizers.

In the estuary of the Danube, a 70-mile-wide wetland of channels, lakes and swamps, the algae blooms have grown wildly in the 1980's.

"By the end of the summer, much of the delta is covered in spume," said Mircea Staras, a Romanian biologist. Mr. Staras lives in Tulcia, close to the mouth of the Danube. "When the algae die, everything else is killed," said Mr. Staras, "even the underwater plants. This was an important spawning ground for sturgeon, for carp, for pike. We lost all the big fish."

'An Unexpected Bonus'

Radioactive fallout from Chernobyl is being monitored by scientists. They say the signals given off by particles like cesium 137 and strontium are traceable and therefore allow monitors to see how pollutants behave, how long they stay on the surface, how fast organisms take them up and how the Black Sea mixes and circulates.

"It's an unexpected bonus," said Gennadi Polykarpov, a Soviet monitor. "The fallout is a problem in the Dnieper water because it is used for irrigation, but it is not a health hazard in the Black Sea."

As awareness of the degradation grows, hopes of reversing it are running up against the reality that the Black Sea countries do not have the means or the political will to change their practices in the short run.

"Even if we stopped all the pollution as if by magic," Mr. Zaitsev said, "it would be impossible to go back to the 1950's. Nature has its own laws."

Cleaning up many areas would cost a fortune. The large and handsome bay at Burgas, Bulgaria, was a popular beach resort until two decades ago, when chemical plants were built on its shores. Today the bay is off-limits to bathers, and water and air here look equally greasy and opaque with contaminants.

Farther south, near Chernomoritz, researchers have found hot spots of uranium radiation along the inlets and beaches that they believe was spilled by a nearby mine. Local guest-house owners, though, have repeatedly taken down signs warning people to keep away due to radioactivity. They say the signs ruined their business.

But the scientists at the Black Sea conference agreed that even if a cleanup would be too costly or too difficult in the short run, a huge effort should be made to stop the sea from getting worse. A convention to diminish pollution of the Danube, which is fed with sewage and waste from eight nations, was agreed upon in August. But most of the eight nations have not yet signed it.

A convention to protect the Black Sea has been in the works for two years. While the Soviet military had first held it up, a new complication now is that the Ukraine, Russia and Georgia, caught up in their own domestic political turmoil, will probably have to debate and sign the agreement separately.

"The two conventions are absolutely essential for any future action," Dr. Aubrey said. "They will help change legislation in the different countries, and they can trigger foreign aid."

"A new legal framework will be a quantum leap," said Lawrence Mee, of the United Nations Environmental Program. "It made a tremendous difference in cutting back pollution in the Baltic Sea. It showed us that the law can work."

*   *   *

December 10, 1991

20,000 ALBANIANS RALLY IN CAPITAL

By Reuters

TIRANA, Albania, Dec. 9—About 20,000 Albanians rallied in Tirana today to celebrate the first anniversary of pro-democracy protests that ended more than four decades of Stalinism in Europe's poorest country.

But the mood was dampened by a lack of heating in many cities as a cold wave swept the country, increasing the misery of a weary population already suffering from chronic food shortages and a paralyzed Government.

People who ran out of wood for their apartment stoves turned to electric heaters, overloading the creaking power grid and blacking out many parts of Tirana and towns throughout the country.

"We demand food and heating," Gezim Kalaja, a trade union leader, told the crowd. "But this can only be achieved by clearing Communists out of the administration and bureaucracy. Those who had political power now have economic power. We have no more confidence in the Government or President."

Armed police with orders to shoot if necessary accompanied soldiers distributing bread and guarded stores after Albanians, fearing famine, raided food warehouses over the

weekend. Two people were killed in Lac, northeast of Tirana, in the disturbances.

People lined up for hours in Tirana for bread today, but no incidents were reported.

There was no word of progress in President Ramiz Alia's efforts to forge a compromise between the country's main parties to insure stable government through the winter.

Prime Minister Ylli Bufi resigned under fire last week and now heads a caretaker team.

"Our hopes for freedom, democracy and better living have been sabotaged by the servants of the dictatorship and Communism," Mr. Kavaja said.

The crowd marched to the headquarters of the Democratic Party, the biggest opposition party, where the party leader, Sali Berisha, pledged to continue to press for early elections.

Mr. Berisha also defended his party's decision last week to quit the coalition Government, a move that plunged the country into political crisis.

"If necessary we are ready to overthrow 100 governments," he told the demonstrators.

The Democrats withdrew their seven ministers from the 25-member cabinet after the Government, dominated by former Communists, refused to schedule early elections.

*   *   *

December 24, 1991

SLOVENIA AND CROATIA GET BONN'S NOD

By STEPHEN KINZER
Special to The New York Times

BONN, Dec. 23—Germany flexed its new diplomatic muscle today by recognizing the independence of two breakaway Yugoslav republics, Slovenia and Croatia.

German consulates in the two republics will be upgraded to embassies on Jan. 15, the Foreign Ministry said in a statement.

"In the view of the German Government, the republics of Slovenia and Croatia fulfill the conditions set by the European Community," the statement said.

At a fractious European Community meeting last week, Germany announced to its partners that it was planning to recognize Slovenia and Croatia, even if it had to do so alone. To preserve a semblance of unity, the 12 member countries approved a resolution authorizing recognition of new nations that meet certain conditions, including stable borders, respect for democracy, and protection of minority rights.

Thousands Killed in Fighting

Several European leaders, as well as President Bush and Secretary General Javier Perez de Cuellar of the United Nations, had urged Germany not to proceed with plans to recognize the two republics immediately. They suggested instead that recognition be withheld until it could be granted as part of an overall peace settlement.

Both supporters and opponents of recognition say their position will help end the fighting, which has claimed thousands of lives since Slovenia and Croatia declared independence this summer. Troops of the Serbian-dominated regular army and militias have taken over a third of Croatia's territory in their attempt to block Croatian secession.

Under the European Community resolution, today was the first day on which a member country could declare that Croatia or Slovenia had met the conditions for recognition. The community set Jan. 15 as the first day for formal recognition, and whether Germany has adhered to that deadline or acted too quickly was described in Bonn as a matter of interpretation.

After the community's decision was announced last week, Chancellor Helmut Kohl hailed it as "a great victory for German foreign policy." He dismissed charges by Yugoslav leaders that Germany was building a sphere of influence that would form the basis of a "Fourth Reich."

"We Germans are concerned about the fate of these people and about their future in democracy—nothing else," Mr. Kohl said.

Germany has pledged not to send military aid to Croatia, but is ready to begin a quick civilian aid program that will include reconstruction of war-damaged cities.

Chancellor Kohl hopes the recognition will signal to Yugoslavia's Serbian leaders that their country is doomed to break apart, and perhaps persuade them to accept a peace settlement. He argues that unified Germany, a central European nation that is geographically close to the conflict zone and that has itself benefited from the protection of foreign democracies, is in a special position to understand the yearnings of isolated republics.

A Gamble by Kohl

Chancellor Kohl's policy is a gamble that diplomatic isolation will force Serbian leaders to accept defeat. If it does not, Germany will be in no position to back up its recognition with force. The Constitution forbids sending German troops abroad, and all political parties oppose the shipment of weapons to crisis regions.

The Munich newspaper Süddeutsche Zeitung, one of whose correspondents was killed this year while covering the Yugoslav conflict, today criticized the Government's action as "an empty gesture" that was "a foreign policy reaction to domestic political pressure."

There are about 700,000 Yugoslav workers in Germany, most of them Croats. Many have deep roots in Germany, and an estimated 200,000 are voting citizens. They have been highly active in demanding that the Bonn Government recognize Croatia.

Germany's haste to recognize Croatia has disturbed some Europeans, for various reasons. Among them is the memory of World War II, when Germany supported a pro-Nazi government in Croatia.

Bosnia Appeals to U.N.

SARAJEVO, Yugoslavia, Dec. 23 (Special to The New York Times)—The President of Bosnia and Herzegovina for-mally appealed to the United Nations Security Council today to deploy peacekeeping forces in this Yugoslav republic as soon as possible to reduce the risk of a serious outbreak of ethnic violence.

"This would secure the peace," said President Alija Izetbegovic, adding that he hoped peacekeeping troops would be stationed throughout the republic but especially along its borders with Croatia and Serbia.

"It would be desirable that they come before Jan. 14," he said.

* * *

January 12, 1992

BULGARIANS VOTING FOR PRESIDENT FOR FIRST TIME

Special to The New York Times

SOFIA, Bulgaria, Jan. 11—Bulgarians will vote Sunday to elect a president directly for the first time in the country's history.

It is the third election since June 1990, the date of Bulgaria's first free parliamentary elections in 40 years.

Sunday's election is a veiled contest between the Union of Democratic Forces and the Socialist Party, the successor to the Communist Party, which ruled Bulgaria between the end of World War II and November 1989.

For some, the vote is also a referendum on the progress of reforms that brought huge price rises last February, followed by a 3.5 percent monthly inflation rate and a current unemployment rate of 10 percent.

Three days ago, tens of thousands of workers and pensioners demonstrated for higher minimum wages and pensions. The Socialists have sought support from the 2.3 million pensioners and the new unemployed, the biggest losers in the economic hard times.

Sofia's stores offer a variety of imported citrus fruits, liquors and other goods, yet many remain almost empty of customers as cash-poor Bulgarians live off reserves of canned goods put by last summer.

Next to the economy, the other major campaign issue is nationalism, directed against the country's Turkish minority and by extension to Turkey.

The president, who has a five-year term, will be Bulgaria's head of state and commander in chief. The office's only significant political prerogative is the right to send legislation back to Parliament for reconsideration.

Yet Bulgarians take the election seriously. "The presidential institution at this stage of our development is exceptionally important," said Alexander Yordanov, the Democrats' parliamentary leader. "If there's a parliamentary crisis, it's important that the presidency be in the hands of a democrat so Bulgaria won't return to a totalitarian system."

The incumbent President, Zhelyu Zhelev, and his vice presidential running mate, Blaga Dimitrova, supported by the Democratic coalition, are facing 21 rival pairs.

The two main contenders are the Democrats and the Socialists. The Socialists did not nominate a presidential candidate from among their ranks but instead are supporting a nominally independent candidate, Velko Valkanov, and his running mate, Roumen Vodenicharov.

While the Socialist Party captured over half the parliamentary seats in elections in June 1990, it won only one-third of them last October. The Democrats won the October election, taking 34.4 percent of the vote.

Democratic sympathizers accused the Valkanov-Vodenicharov team of appealing to nationalism.

But Elena Poptodorova, a Socialist member of Parliament, counters: "They have alerted the public to the danger of a new type of segregation. It's true that both reacted strongly against the registration of parties on the basis of nationality and religion, because such parties lead to the division of the country."

She was referring to the predominantly Turkish Movement for Rights and Freedoms, which won 24 of Parliament's 240 seats in October.

Many have criticized President Zhelev for defending the nearly one million-member Turkish minority in its quest for win political rights. But the popular Mr. Zhelev, a Communist-era dissident who was appointed President in August 1990, is expected to win.

*   *   *

January 13, 1992

INCUMBENT LEADS BULGARIA'S PRESIDENTIAL VOTE

Special to The New York Times

SOFIA, Bulgaria, Jan. 12—President Zhelyu Zhelev appeared to be leading in Bulgaria's first direct presidential vote today but short of a majority, projections based on partial returns indicated.

The projections estimated that Mr. Zhelev received about 45 percent of the vote, followed by Velko Valkanov, a nominally independent candidate backed by the former Communists, with about 31 percent, said the Bulgarian Association for Fair Elections and Civil Rights. The group is a nongovernmental organization that conducts separate tabulations of vote results.

Official results are not expected until Monday evening, but the partial returns suggested that the candidates would face a tight runoff for the presidency next Sunday. A majority was required to win on the first ballot.

The Government election commission said about 75 percent of eligible voters had cast ballots in the election, which pitted Mr. Zhelev, the nominee of the Union of Democratic Forces, which holds the majority of parliamentary seats, against 21 other candidates.

An independent businessman, Georgi Ganchev Petrushev, was running third with about 16 percent, the projections indicated.

The victor in the presidential election gets a five-year term as head of state and Commander in Chief of the armed forces. The president will also have the power to send legislation back to the Parliament for reconsideration.

Mr. Zhelev, a 56-year-old philosopher who was a dissident under Communist rule, has served as President since August 1990, when he was appointed to the post by the Bulgarian Parliament.

Despite the big field of candidates, the vote today was considered a contest between the Union of Democratic Forces and the successors to the old Communist Party, the Socialists, who have been vying for leadership since a hardline Communist Government was ousted in November 1989. Many Bulgarians considered the election a report card on economic reforms, which have brought hardships like huge price increases and job losses. In endorsing Mr. Valkanov, a 54-year-old lawyer not officially a Socialist candidate, the Socialists sought support from pensioners and people left jobless as a result of free-market changes.

"The Government is feeling a lot of pressure from every direction," said Prime Minister Filip Dimitrov, chairman of the Union of Democratic Forces, which assumed leadership of the Government after narrowly defeating the Socialists in parliamentary elections last October. "Without enough money to answer all these demands, the Government has no choice at all but to withstand the pressure."

*   *   *

March 2, 1992

TURNOUT IN BOSNIA SIGNALS INDEPENDENCE

By CHUCK SUDETIC
Special to The New York Times

SARAJEVO, Yugoslavia, March 1—A large turnout of voters appeared today to have guaranteed a victory for independence in a referendum in the ethnically mixed central Yugoslav republic of Bosnia and Herzegovina.

A vote in favor of independence would further the disintegration of Yugoslavia that began last summer with the secession of the republics of Slovenia and Croatia, touching off the first major war on the European continent since World War II. A cease-fire took effect in early January.

Slovenia and Croatia have already won international recognition, and Macedonia hopes to follow them soon.

Leaders of Bosnia-Herzegovina's Croats and Muslim Slavs, who together account for 60 percent of its four million people, expect the European Community to grant the republic diplomatic recognition soon after the official results of the referendum are announced on Tuesday.

"We expect an automatic recognition because the referendum was the only condition set by the European Community," said the republic's Foreign Minister, Haris Silajdzic, a Muslim. "This is a condition we accepted gladly because we are sure of the results."

The New York Times

Voters turned out in large numbers to cast ballots for an independent Bosnia and Herzegovina.

Vote in Montenegro

In another referendum today in the neighboring republic of Montenegro, which is almost entirely Serb-populated, voters are expected to give overwhelming support to the republic's union with Serbia in a truncated Yugoslav state.

Despite new reports of scattered violence, well over 50 percent of the electorate voted in Bosnia and Herzegovina's referendum.

Diplomatic recognition of Bosnia and Herzegovina would be a severe blow to the republic's Serbs, who account for 32 percent of the population and oppose independence because they do not want to be cut off from Serbia.

The Serbs, most of whom boycotted this weekend's vote, have formed a "Serb Republic of Bosnia-Herzegovina" and have threatened to secede if the existing republic is recognized as independent. Serbs control about 60 percent of Bosnia-Herzegovina's territory and warn that they are ready to defend it with arms.

Armed gangs of masked Serbs and Croats blocked roads in several areas of the republic today, two days after a shooting incident at a Serb-manned barricade that killed a Muslim and two Serbs. This afternoon in central Sarajevo, unidentified gunmen attacked a wedding party, wounding a Serbian Orthodox priest and killing a Serb carrying a Serbian flag.

Attack on Barracks Reported

The pro-Serb Yugoslav Army reported that unidentified assailants had attacked a barracks near the town of Bihac overnight.

The republic's President, Alija Izetvegovic, a Muslim and the only President of a Yugoslav republic who was never a Communist, plays down the danger of major violence here.

"There may be a few isolated incidents," he said, "but a general armed conflict will not erupt."

Leaders of Bosnia and Herzegovina's main ethnic groups have failed to make substantive progress in three rounds of European Community-sponsored talks aimed at breaking the republic's logjam of snarled national ambitions. All parties, however, call for the talks to go on.

*   *   *

March 3, 1992

REBEL SERBS DISRUPT TRAVEL INTO YUGOSLAV REPUBLIC

By CHUCK SUDETIC
Special to The New York Times

SARAJEVO, Yugoslavia, March 2—Gangs of masked and armed Serbs, angered by the results of a weekend referendum on independence for the republic of Bosnia and Herzegovina, set up barricades today and blocked all transportation routes leading to this mountain capital.

But by late tonight, television reports said the Serbian guerrillas had agreed to lift the seige and that some of the barriers were being dismantled. At the same time, bursts of gunfire continued to echo off the mountains that surround this city, where four people had been reported killed and at least seven wounded in clashes near the barricades.

The blockade prevented trains from entering, and only a few ambulances and police cars were allowed to pass the barricades for most of the day. The action also choked roads in other parts of Bosnia and Herzegovina, including the main highway to Croatia. Muslim Slavs and Croats had also erected barricades near some of their enclaves in the republic.

Sending a Message

The well-coordinated effort was clearly intended as a signal by the Serbs, who make up almost a third of the republic's population, that they were not only dissatisfied with the vote for secession but that they were also ready to stall or derail efforts to carry it out.

The message was intended for the Muslim Slavs and Croats, the two ethnic groups that account for 60 percent of the republic's four million people. They favor independence and are eager to have the European Community recognize Bosnia and Herzegovina as an independent country.

Well over 60 percent of the republic's 3.1 million eligible voters cast ballots in favor of independence, according to unofficial results based on a tally of 78 percent of the votes. The republic's Serbs boycotted the referendum.

With the departure of Slovenia and Croatia from Yugoslavia, Muslim Slavs and Croats in Bosnia and Herzegovina fear the prospect of being left behind in what is certain to be a Serb-dominated rump Yugoslav state.

On the other hand, Bosnia and Herzegovina's Serbs reject the notion of being cut off from Serbia by an international frontier and argue that the other two nations are forcing independence on them by using the "tyranny of the majority."

Serbian leaders in Bosnia and Herzegovina have proclaimed their own Serbian polity, which they define as covering about 60 percent of the present republic's territory. They have warned for months that they would take up arms to keep the republic inside the frontiers of what is left of Yugoslavia.

An explosion of serious intercommunal strife is the worst nightmare of everyone living in this highly charged territory, which has a grim history of internecine violence, including atrocities committed here during the civil war that gripped Yugoslavia from 1941 to 1945.

"If the Gordian knot in Bosnia-Herzegovina is not untied to the satisfaction of all three nations, then we will have here, I assure you, Belfast or Beirut," said Rajko Dukic, a member of the Serbian Democratic Party's so-called crisis committee, which organized the barricade action. "There is little room to iron out a compromise."

The party has demanded that Bosnia and Herzegovina's government halt all further steps toward independence.

But Bosnia and Herzegovina's foreign minister, Haris Silajdzic, a Muslim, said there was no chance that the Government would change its mind on independence.

"Immediate recognition of Bosnia-Herzegovina would be the best contribution the European Community could make towards peace and order in this part of the world," Mr. Silajdzic said.

Like the Serbian rebels in neighboring Croatia, Serbs in Bosnia and Herzegovina have been armed by Serbia and the Yugoslav National Army. But the army disavowed the blockade. In a local radio broadcast, the commander of the army's Sarajevo garrison called the action "sheer banditry."

"The army is not involved in these activities as far as we know," said the republic's Muslim deputy prime minister, Rusmir Mahmutcehajic. "The army has offered us its complete cooperation in finding a solution to this situation. We have decided to refrain from any use of force."

Most of the Yugoslav Army's forces, including an estimated 100,000 troops, are concentrated in Bosnia and Herzegovina. The republic is also the site of most of the army's weapons factories.

* * *

March 23, 1992

EX-COMMUNISTS LOSE IN ALBANIA VOTE

By HENRY KAMM
Special to The New York Times

TIRANA, Albania, Monday, March 23—The opposition Democratic Party declared a landslide victory over the former Communists today after voters turned out in heavy numbers on Sunday to elect a new Parliament.

"We have won 65 to 70 percent of all the votes, and the Socialists a maximum of 25 percent," the leader of the centrist Democrats, Dr. Sali Berisha, said in an interview at the party's headquarters, which was surrounded by an ever-growing crowd of cheering supporters. "It is the end of the Communist night in Albania."

The leader of the Socialists, former Prime Minister Fatos Nano, conceded defeat early today in an interview at his party headquarters, a gloomy place deserted by all but a handful of supporters. "We wish the winners good luck," he added. His party had not yet released any concession statement to the public.

The Socialists, who renamed themselves last June after governing for decades as the Communist Party of Labor, appear to have suffered from the sharp economic decline over the last year in this long-isolated country, the poorest in Europe.

The Socialists have also renounced their former ideology, which for decades was dogmatic and hostile to outside influence by Communist and capitalist nations alike. They won a parliamentary majority in the first multi-party elections a year ago. But chronic shortages of food, medicine, fuel and electricity have bred deep resentment.

Dr. Berisha, a 47-year-old cardiologist, said he based his announcement on telephone reports from Democrats on election boards throughout this Balkan land of 3.3 million people. The Central Election Commission said it hoped to make an announcement later today.

Dr. Berisha said his party's triumph resulted largely from a dramatic reversal of the vote in the countryside, where two-thirds of all Albanians live. In the elections last year, the Democrats won in all the towns but were badly beaten in rural regions.

If Dr. Berisha's vote estimates are confirmed, they would bear out reports that Albania's peasant farmers have shifted allegiance because of disappointment with the results of the return of farmlands to private ownership under the renamed Communists. Many had hoped the move would raise living standards.

Turnout in the voting on Sunday was described as heavy. More than 500 candidates ran in direct district elections for 100 parliamentary seats, and 40 to 50 more seats will be filled by proportional representation from national party lists. Run-off elections will be held next Sunday between the top two contenders in districts where no candidate won a majority.

People in villages visited last week were nearly unanimous in expressing support for Dr. Berisha and disaffection from the Socialists.

In the village of Griqan, chosen arbitrarily because of its remoteness, most of the people interviewed on Sunday said or hinted that they had voted for the opposition after supporting the Communists a year ago.

Griqan lies in the mountains south of this capital. The only signs of modern development are electrical power lines and the asphalt paving that covers the first half of the feeder road into Griqan.

The village of 400 inhabitants has no plumbing and no indoor toilets. Since the breakup of the collective farm into which it had been converted by the Communists, it has no tractors or tools and almost no seed wheat, corn, fertilizer or insecticide.

Shortly after 11 A.M. Sunday, 150 of Griqan's 198 eligible voters had cast their ballots in the largest room of the largest house, which had been converted into the polling station. Voters stepped behind a red curtain strung across a corner of the bare room while the five members of the town's election committee, representing four parties and an independent, stood about.

The committee members greeted a foreign visitor—the first ever, they said—with enthusiasm and proclaimed their faith in the victory of democracy. In Griqan, that translated into support for the small Republican Party, whose candidate there was supported by the Democrats. Dr. Berisha is their man, they said.

'Time to Think Through'

Sheepishly, they said the trend in voting undoubtedly differed from the result last year, when 170 of 184 votes were for the Communists. "It was just the beginning," a committee member said. "People hadn't had time to think things through."

Another man said: "Our land has been heavy on our hands since we got it last year. We have only our hands to work it. Only 10 to 15 percent is planted."

Ferit Balla, the 36-year-old Democratic committee member, said villagers were voting for the opposition "because they think that's the way to Europe." Now that Albania's Communist-imposed isolation from the world has been broken, he said, the people want to live on "the European standard."

"We no longer want to have to put on these old shoes," said a young man, as the conversation turned into a village forum. The men wore threadbare clothes and shoes beyond repair.

Mr. Balla said the Albanian radio, television and press reports had indicated that opposition leaders, particularly Dr. Berisha, had established ties with Western countries, particularly the United States. "We hope that after the elections they will provide more assistance." he said.

*   *   *

March 27, 1992

ALBANIA'S CLERICS LEAD A REBIRTH

By HENRY KAMM
Special to The New York Times

TIRANA, Albania—"Even a dog would not have slept where we had to," said Haxhi Hafiz Sabri Koci, the religious leader of Albania's Muslims, the largest of this country's three major religions. Mr. Koci, whose title is Mufti, showed his hands—toilworn, the joints of some fingers swollen out of shape from his years in prison.

"Twenty-one years at hard labor," he said, nodding toward them. "In the copper mines. I was a welder, a plumber. I did every kind of work, just like the other prisoners. They were mainly political."

At the age of 71, Mr. Koci and other clergymen—Muslim, Roman Catholic and Eastern Orthodox—have stepped out of the shadows of nearly a half-century of persecution and are leading a rebirth of religion. Of the population of three million, estimates are that more than 65 percent are nominally Muslim, 20 percent Orthodox and 13 percent Catholic.

Icons Ripped Out

The Albanian Orthodox Annunciation Church in the center of this capital is beginning to resemble what it was until the old Government ripped out the iconostasis, the wall of icons that is a feature of Orthodox churches, painted over the frescoes and destroyed most paintings while sending the oldest to a museum. Workers are busy reconverting the church, which has served as a gymnasium.

A wizened man entered and crossed himself. He made his way through the masons at work to the rear of the iconostasis, then knelt, kissed some sacred pages and muttered a prayer.

He was the Rev. Theodor Plushko, 74 years old, returning to a consecrated church for the first time since the Government closed his village church in the north in 1967 and gave the roof tiles and other removable materials to a collective farm. Father Plushko was sent to work in its orchards. Asked if his church would be repaired, he answered, "With God's help."

Albania staged a witchhunt for people in all religions, like other nations where Communist Governments took power in Eastern Europe in 1944–45. Then, in 1967, Albania's dictator, Enver Hoxha, declared this country officially atheist and wrote the ban on all religious observance into the Constitution.

Then, without public announcement, the wreckers went to work throughout the country to raze and gut what leaders of all faiths now estimate to have been 95 percent of the mosques and churches.

The few that were spared were either marked by plaques identifying them, without mentioning their purpose, as "cultural monuments," like this capital's 18th-century Ethem Bej Mosque, or desecrated for state use, like the Roman Catholic Cathedral of Shkodra, once the seat of an archbishop, which became a sports arena.

Religious leaders of different faiths now speak hopefully of rebuilding plans, but in this impoverished country's state of economic collapse and total dependence on foreign aid even for its minimal food needs, construction is not at the top of the agenda.

Bardhyl Fico, a Muslim cartoonist who heads the new State Secretariat for Religion, said of Mr. Hoxha's campaign to destroy religious buildings: "He also destroyed the human soul. This will take generations to restore."

Ignorant of Religion

Bishop Ivan Dias, a Vatican diplomat here, said, "More than the churches, we need to build up the human person." Monsignor Dias, an Indian prelate, is Papal Nuncio, or ambassador, to Albania, and he was also named by Pope John Paul II to be bishop in charge of all Roman Catholics, in the virtual absence of Albanian priests still able to serve.

Of 300 priests in this country when the Communists came to power, only 30 survive, said Monsignor Dias.

Mr. Fico said: "The Catholics suffered the most. They were the most loyal to their faith, the most intransigent. It is to their honor that they were the most persecuted."

Because of the terror engendered by a vast network of informers, people here say, parents did not dare pass on their faith.

"We were afraid to tell our children that secretly we continued to pray," said Peter Rama, 77 years old, an elder of Annunciation Church. "We feared they might talk about it outside."

As a result, the many who now flock to mosques and churches are for the most part ignorant of the religion they are learning to profess.

"The mosques are full of young people who know nothing about Islam," said Sali Tivari, Secretary General of the Muslim Community.

All faiths have started seminaries and schools, and several Islamic countries have sent young men here to teach Albanian youths. Christian teachers report that their task is made exceptionally difficult by what Monsignor Dias says the Pope called "Communism at its worst" when he sent him here.

"They reduced them to subhuman condition," the Bishop said. "I find the material sometimes is very raw."

*   *   *

April 4, 1992

COMMUNIST QUITS AS ALBANIA CHIEF

By The Associated Press

TIRANA, Albania, April 3—Ramiz Alia, the former Communist leader, resigned as President today, less than two weeks after Albanians elected a non-Communist Parliament.

Mr. Alia's resignation removes the most visible remnant of hard-line Communist rule in this impoverished Balkan country and opens the way for the Democratic Party to consolidate its election victory. The Democrats pledged after the elections to oust Mr. Alia rather than submit their Cabinet nominees to him for approval.

Mr. Alia, 66 years old, was the ideological chief and the chosen successor of Enver Hoxha, the Stalinist dictator who ruled Albania for four decades until his death in 1985.

President Alia announced his resignation on the eve of the first session of the new Parliament, in which the Democrats hold 92 of 140 seats. The Socialist Party, a regrouping of former Communists, won only 38 seats in the March 22 voting among Albania's 3.2 million people.

In a statement that was read on state radio, Mr. Alia said he had governed for the sake "of people's unity, political progress of the country and the consolidation of democracy.

"For the same reason I now am resigning as President, hoping that the new Parliament will trust the life of the country to a new personality who is able to move Albania in the direction the majority wants," he said.

Successor to Be Chosen

It was not immediately clear whom the Democrats would choose to replace Mr. Alia. The leader of the Democratic Party, Sali Berisha, refused to say whether he would seek the post.

The new government will face the task of rebuilding a shattered economy and restoring stability after months of food riots and rampant crime. The country has been surviving largely on relief shipments from abroad.

The Democrats argued during the election campaign that their anti-Communist credentials would attract foreign aid and investment.

After the collapse of Communist governments across Eastern Europe and mass protests by Albanians in December 1990, Mr. Alia eased the Communist Party's absolute grip on power and allowed some political opposition.

In Albania's first multiparty elections a year ago, the Socialists won a majority of seats in the Parliament. But the Socialists were unable to turn the economy around and demands grew for new elections.

*   *   *

April 7, 1992

EUROPE NODS TO BOSNIA, NOT MACEDONIA

By ALAN RIDING
Special to The New York Times

PARIS, April 6—The 12-nation European Community decided to recognize the independence of Bosnia and Herzegovina today, arguing that the move could help end the latest outbreak of ethnic violence in the former Yugoslav republic.

But it once again bent to pressure from Greece by delaying a response to the Macedonian republic's request for recognition. Greece, which is a community member, has accused the republic of trying to usurp the name of its northern province of Macedonia and of harboring territorial ambitions over the region.

Community governments have already established diplomatic relations with breakaway Slovenia and Croatia, while Montenegro has decided to remain part of Yugoslavia along with Serbia.

The Bush Administration is going to recognize the independence of Bosnia and Herzegovina, Croatia and Slovenia on Tuesday with an announcement by the White House and a policy statement by the State Department. Officials expect the statement will shed some light on what the United States intends to do about Macedonia and the remaining members of the old Yugoslav federation, Serbia and Montenegro.

Community foreign ministers meeting in Luxembourg also agreed to end economic sanctions against Serbia so long as it continues to cooperate with European-sponsored peace talks, restores air links with the other republics and recognizes the legal authority of United Nations peacekeeping forces.

Sanction Is Lifted

On a separate issue, the community today lifted its last remaining economic sanction against South Africa—a 1985 embargo on the sale of crude oil and other oil products—in recognition of its moves to dismantle apartheid. The decision was warmly welcomed by South African officials.

Today's meeting, though, was dominated by the Yugoslav question, with foreign ministers eager to demonstrate that the community can still play a mediating role in the crisis even though its failure to end the fighting in Croatia last year forced it to turn to the United Nations for help.

When the community recognized Slovenia and Croatia in January, it spelled out its terms for recognizing other new states. European officials said Bosnia and Herzegovina and Macedonia had since fulfilled these conditions, which included popular endorsement of independence through referendums.

After the ethnic violence of recent days in Bosnia and Herzegovina, Portugal's Foreign Minister, Joao de Deus Pinheiro, the current community chairman, said the new republic would be recognized on Tuesday because there was "no reason" for a further delay.

Violence Called Worrisome

"We are worried about the violence," Mr. Deus de Pinheiro went on, referring to opposition by the Serbian minority in Bosnia and Herzegovina to the republic's independence. "We hope the violence will not continue, we hope that it is just an outburst that will fade away."

The republic is made up of 1.9 million Muslim Slavs, 1.4 million Eastern Orthodox Serbs and 750,000 Roman Catholic Croats.

Italy's Foreign Minister, Gianni de Michelis, said that making "no decision today would have worsened" the situation.

A British official in Luxembourg quoted by The Associated Press also asserted that a delay would bring more trouble. "The whole business would simply be repeated next time," he said.

On the question of Macedonia, Mr. Deus de Pinheiro said the community was negotiating with both Greece and Macedonia to find "an acceptable solution" that would permit recognition of the republic. He said he was optimistic about a breakthrough before community foreign ministers meet again next month.

In a statement today, Macedonia's President, Kiro Gligorov, reiterated that the republic did not claim any Greek territory and warned that postponement of recognition of its independence could lead to "very severe consequences," including the risk of "a wider Balkan conflict."

*   *   *

April 10, 1992

ALBANIANS ELECT NON-COMMUNIST PRESIDENT

By Reuters

TIRANA, Albania, April 9—Sali Berisha, a 47-year-old heart surgeon who leads the Democratic Party, was elected by lawmakers today as Albania's first non-Communist President since World War II.

Dr. Berisha said his first task would be to introduce legislation to attract investment to Albania, the poorest country in Europe. He also pledged to live like an ordinary Albanian.

"The President of one of the world's poorest countries should live like the rest of its citizens," he said after he was elected to the post by a wide majority of the new Parliament. He was the only candidate.

Mr. Berisha, whose party won a landslide victory over the former Communists in elections last month, was elected 96 to 35 by the 140-member Parliament. Fatos Nano, leader of the Socialist Party, as the renamed Communists are known, was among eight deputies absent from the session today.

Dr. Berisha's Communist predecessor, Ramiz Alia, resigned as President last week rather than face dismissal by the Parliament, in which the Democrats and their allies hold a two-thirds majority. Mr. Alia came to power in 1985 after the death of the Stalinist dictator Enver Hoxha, who ruled Albania for four decades.

*   *   *

April 15, 1992

BREAKING CEASE-FIRE, SERBS LAUNCH ATTACKS INTO BOSNIA

By CHUCK SUDETIC
Special to The New York Times

SARAJEVO, Bosnia and Herzegovina, April 14—Serbian and Yugoslav Army forces shattered a European Community-brokered cease-fire in this newly independent republic today, overrunning regions populated by Muslim Slavs.

The major penetration by Serb forces from Serbia into Bosnia and Herzegovina is the first large-scale incursion by Yugoslav Army units based outside Bosnia. The move is the latest phase in a military campaign to cut away huge swaths of Bosnia and Herzegovina for an emerging Serb state as Yugoslavia disintegrates.

The United Nations special envoy on Yugoslavia, former Secretary of State Cyrus R. Vance, is scheduled to arrive in Belgrade on Wednesday in an attempt to quell the violence in Bosnia and Herzegovina.

Protest by U.S. Envoy

The Serb offensive today came four days after the United States Ambassador to Yugoslavia, Warren Zimmermann, delivered a strong protest to Serbia's President, Slobodan

Milosevic, against his republic's use of paramilitary organizations to destabilize Bosnia and Herzegovina.

The United States Government, in a statement on Monday, said it holds the civilian and military authorities in Belgrade accountable for the "aggression" against Bosnia and Herzegovina.

Fierce clashes were reported today in the towns of Foca and Mostar, and gun battles and artillery fire again rocked the capital, Sarajevo.

Heavy fighting in Bosnia and Herzegovina broke out two weeks ago before the recognition of this republic as an independent state by the United States and the European Community. The fighting has left hundreds of people dead or wounded, but reliable casualty figures are not available.

Visit by U.N. Official

"There are bodies lying in courtyards that no one has the nerve to go out and pick up yet," said Fabrizio Hochschield, spokesman for the United Nations High Commission on Refugees, who visited the besieged town of Foca on Monday.

The hard-line nationalists leading Bosnia and Herzegovina's 1.4 million Serbs vehemently oppose independence and threatened for months to unleash a war to partition the republic.

The republic's 1.9 million Muslim Slavs and most of its 750,000 Croats favored independence because they oppose being left behind in a Serb-dominated state whose record on respect for minority rights has been condemned as Europe's worst by Western diplomats and human rights groups.

The major Yugoslav Army move into Bosnia and Herzegovina today shattered a cease-fire arranged on Sunday night. A column of about 100 trucks carrying regular army troops and reservists, artillery pieces and supplies rolled into the mainly Muslim Slav town of Visegrad on the Drina River, an army statement said. Visegrad is the fifth major Muslim Slav town captured by the Serbs in the last two weeks.

Serb army units also moved today on the town of Gorazde, the population of which is about 70 percent Muslim Slav, a Serbian news agency said.

Belgrade Television, a voice of Serbia's Government, asserted tonight that the army units had been "invited" in to Visegrad by its Muslim Slavs and Serbs.

"The Serb and Muslim populations along the Drina River Valley have seen that their only salvation lies in the arrival of Yugoslav Army troops," the army said in a statement tonight.

But Western diplomats called the army's move aggression.

Western diplomats asserted that the Serbs have mounted an orchestrated campaign to drive the Muslim Slav populations out of certain areas. "There is a lot of ethnic cleansing going on," a Western diplomat said. "The Serbs are trying to consolidate ground on the western side of the Drina."

The Yugoslav Army has for months armed the Serbs in Bosnia and Herzegovina and emptied civil-defense arsenals in Muslim Slav and Croat regions of the republic. Now Sarajevo's defense forces are without the weaponry to stave off the Serb offensive.

Bosnia and Herzegovina's leaders said today that at present they can only rely on international pressure on the Serbian Government and Yugoslav Army to stop the Serbs' dismemberment of the republic.

"These people are not going to stop at threats," Haris Silajdzic, Bosnia and Herzegovina's Foreign Minister, said by telephone from Washington. "This is first and foremost a land grab and only secondly an attempt to bolster the Communist regime in Belgrade with yet another nationalist cause."

U.S. Help Is Sought

WASHINGTON, April 14 (AP)—Mr. Silajdzic asked for American help today to spare his country from more "mass massacres," which he said are being committed by irregular forces sent from Serbia.

With Secretary of State James A. Baker 3d standing at his side, Mr. Silajdzic blamed Serbian authorities for a "great human tragedy" he said was taking place in his homeland and recommended they be prosecuted for war crimes.

Mr. Baker called the situation "extraordinarily tragic" and said the United States had sent another strongly worded protest note to the Serbian leadership. He said American officials would be in touch with European Community representatives to see what could be done.

Later, the State Department issued a statement in which it condemned "the use of force, intimidation and provocation to nationalist violence by militant nationalist Serbian, and to a lesser extent, Croatian leaders in Bosnia."

"Their strategy and tactics are clearly aimed at promoting the forceful disintegration of Bosnia and Herzegovina," it said.

The statement also condemned the "clear pattern of support" for the destabilization of Bosnia, primarily on the part of the Yugoslav military and the Serbian President, Slobodan Milosevic.

At a news conference after he met with Mr. Baker, Mr. Silajdzic said that as he spoke, hundreds of bodies of children, women and men were lying in the streets across his country.

"We are confronted with—I don't know if we can call them people—irregular forces very well-equipped and ready to kill civilians," Mr. Silajdzic said.

He called for reorganization of the United Nations peacekeeping force in neighboring Croatia so some could operate in Bosnia.

* * *

April 17, 1992

FOR THE NAME OF MACEDONIA, A BURST OF GREEK PRIDE

By MARLISE SIMONS
Special to The New York Times

ATHENS, April 12—Greece seems hypnotized once again by its past, not in study of its glorious achievements, but in an extraordinary burst of nationalism set off by the disintegration of Yugoslavia to the north.

The object of this passion is the name Macedonia. Marching in the streets, putting stickers on cars and shop windows and waving flags, Greeks are heatedly proclaiming that the name Macedonia is exclusively Greek, that it has been theirs for 3,000 years and must remain so.

The threat, as they see it, is that a small territory long part of Yugoslavia now wants recognition as the independent republic of Macedonia. Greeks say a combination of ethnic Albanians and Slavs are thus trying to usurp the name of a Greek region that was made famous by Macedonians like Aristotle and his pupil Alexander the Great.

And as important here, the name evokes the painful history of northern Greece, a land that has been constantly fought over, the last time barely 40 years ago. The Greeks say they have no designs on the territory to the north, but they fear that Yugoslav Macedonia has designs on Greece.

'A True Balkan Puzzle'

The issue has come to a boil here in recent weeks because of growing signs that both the European Community and the United States are eager to find a way of recognizing the new state, whose capital is Skopje, to help stabilize the volatile situation in the republic.

"This is a true Balkan puzzle," a Western diplomat said. "Skopje says this part of Yugoslavia will destabilize if it's not recognized quickly. Athens says that recognizing a new Macedonia will destabilize all of the southern Balkans."

Bowing to intense Greek pressure, the community and Washington have postponed a decision until May, but they have urged Athens to find a compromise with the Skopje Government, though talks in January broke down. They have also proposed other names for the new republic, like New Macedonia and Slavo-Macedonia.

But no name that includes the word "Macedonia" is acceptable to Greece, the Government and most of the opposition have solemnly reiterated in recent days. And if Western European governments decide to ignore Greece's protestations, many Greeks say Athens should close the country's northern border in retaliation and paralyze an important international transit route.

An imprecise geographical region that was home to Greek-speaking tribes more than 3,000 years ago, Macedonia has not been a stable nation-state with fixed borders since the time of Alexander in the fourth century B.C. Slavic tribes settled in the region around the seventh century A.D.

In modern times, it has been a particularly troublesome political faultline and the scene of much bloodshed. The formerly Yugoslav republic of Macedonia covers nearly 26,000 square kilometers and has 1.9 million people. The dominant language is a dialect of Bulgarian. The Macedonia region of Greece has about the same number of people in a 34,600-square-kilometer area.

At the beginning of this century, Macedonian rebels in Greece and Bulgaria were fighting not only against the Turks but also against each other in the final days of the Ottoman Empire. Subsequently, two Balkan wars were fought over the

The New York Times

Greeks fear that the Yugoslav republic of Macedonia has designs on their Macedonian region.

territory until it was finally carved up in 1913. Bulgaria got 10 percent, Serbia got 38 percent and just over half went to Greece.

But frustrated Macedonians in Bulgaria, who wanted union with the Macedonians of Serbia and Greece, formed a guerrilla movement, and between the World Wars they terrorized the region with assassinations and cross-border raids. In World War II, Bulgaria, which was pro-Hitler, saw its chance to take Greek Macedonia and moved in, but it was forced to withdraw toward the end of the war.

Worse fighting came during the Greek civil war, from 1946 to 1949, in which an estimated 100,000 Greeks died. Greek Communists had their bases in this region and got supplies from Yugoslavia in exchange for promises to deliver Macedonia to Communism. At the peak of the civil war, both Tito and Stalin wanted Salonika, the exit to the Aegean Sea.

Washington became alarmed when Tito created a Yugoslav Macedonia, seeing it as a springboard into Greece and an embryo for a Greater Communist Macedonia. Secretary of State Edward R. Stettinius Jr., in a 1944 memorandum, condemned any reference to a Macedonian "fatherland" or "national conscience," calling it a potential "offensive action against Greece."

The right-wing Athens newspaper Estia reprinted the memorandum last week, saying Washington should read up on its recent diplomatic history. The text says, "The solid policy of the U.S. Government is to oppose strongly any resurgence of the Macedonian question as far as Greece is concerned."

Today, Greece seems consumed by anger and insecurity over the issue. "We are so furious because the Yugoslav Communists falsified and stole our history by saying that Macedonia is basically Slavic," said Eugenia Koukoura, a historian, who insisted on taking a visitor to see a 2,500-year-old Macedonian tombstone that bears Greek inscriptions. She is eager to point out that Tito, when he carved a new Macedonia out of the Serbian region called Vardar in 1944, had his followers rewrite history to create a local Macedonian identity.

In recent weeks, Greek officials have been busily reasserting their claims over the name, although they make no claims on the Yugoslav territory. They have rebaptized several warships and northern airports. Salonika's airport is now called Macedonia and Kavalla's was renamed Alexander the Great. Fresh archeological finds have been unveiled to link the area's history to Greece. This month, two museums in Athens put on Macedonia exhibits.

Many citizens have joined what seems to be a wholesale reaffirmation of identity. The Macedonian star, the emblem of the ancient empire, appears in stickers on shop windows and streetlamps. Men wear the star in their lapels, and women have them on brooches and earrings. A few weeks ago, the Government issued new 100-drachma coins that carry the Macedonian star and the image of Alexander.

"Greeks often are not good patriots; they emigrate; they send their money abroad," said Andreas Ekonomides, a lawyer. "But they are very sensitive about their heritage and their history."

Thus, what to outsiders might appear to be merely a dispute over semantics has taken on the dimensions of a battle for Greek cultural heritage against the heirs to a Yugoslav Communist Government that long harbored territorial ambitions over Macedonia.

Government officials here said that ever since Tito created a Yugoslav Macedonia, radical groups in the territory had spoken openly of the need to "liberate" the rest of their region to form a "Greater Macedonia." The officials say such talk goes on with ominous insistence. The Skopje Government says that it has no territorial designs but that it does not want to change the republic's name.

The six-month-old dispute has had the unusual effect of uniting this often quarrelsome and divided nation in an intense wave of nationalism. But this has also enormously complicated the Greek Government's efforts to find a solution. "We have reached a nationalistic delirium," a senior official said.

Some Fault Government

Foreign diplomats in Athens said the Government itself had helped stir up the highly charged mood, and that it now had little room for maneuver. Apparently seeking to widen his freedom of movement, Prime Minister Constantine Mitsotakis dismissed his hard-line Foreign Minister, Antonios Samaras, on Monday. Mr. Samaras had insisted on closing the border.

When asked what they fear from their small and impoverished neighbor, Greeks recall that competing claims over "Macedonia"—both name and land—have often led to war.

In Athens and Salonika, the northern capital, Greeks say they believe that the Skopje Government is not looking to start offensive actions now. But they fear that militant groups might start trouble in the future under a Macedonian banner. Therefore, they say, the territory must be prevented from calling itself Macedonia. Radicals reportedly include former Greek Communists who fled to Skopje and never got over their defeat in the civil war.

* * *

April 28, 1992

CONFIRMING SPLIT, LAST 2 REPUBLICS PROCLAIM A SMALL NEW YUGOSLAVIA

By JOHN F. BURNS
Special to The New York Times

BELGRADE, Yugoslavia, April 27—Serbia and Montenegro today proclaimed the establishment of a new, truncated Yugoslav nation shorn of the four republics that have seceded over the last 10 months. The move amounted to a confirmation of the breakup of the old Communist Yugoslavia and an implicit acceptance of the independence of Bosnia and Herzegovina within its existing borders.

The decision to proclaim a new Yugoslavia was rushed through in a subdued, almost regretful, ceremony of less than 10 minutes, reflecting the discomfort of people acting to accommodate demands from Europe and the United States.

In finally acknowledging the demise of the Yugoslavia that had existed since 1946 and proclaiming a nation with less than half its area and with a population of 10.5 million compared with 23.5 million, the leaders of Serbia, dominant partners in the new nation, were effectively seeking to evade or forestall growing pressures for Serbia's international isolation.

In the Constitution for the new Yugoslavia proclaimed today, its leaders declared the borders to be those of Serbia and Montenegro as they existed in the Communist Yugoslavia established by Tito after World War II. In an accompanying declaration, the leaders said the new nation, to be called the Federal Republic of Yugoslavia like its Communist predecessor, "has no territorial claims" on neighboring republics.

Diplomats said this amounted to a renunciation of the claim made in the past by Slobodan Milosevic, the Serbian President, and by other Serbian nationalists that all Serbs in the old Yugoslavia had the right to be included in a single state that others called "a Greater Serbia."

The significance of this appeared to extend not only to Bosnia and Herzegovina, whose 1.7 million Serbs are the largest Serbian group outside Serbia, but also to the three other republics that have seceded: Croatia, Slovenia and Macedonia. Serbia fought a war on behalf of Croatia's 580,000 Serbs last year similar to the one in Bosnia and Herzegovina.

The New York Times

Newborn Yugoslavia is considerably smaller than the federation created after World War II. The Republics were carved from the kingdom that emerged after World War I and later took the official name Yugoslavia.

The pressures on Belgrade to give such assurances, led by the United States and the European Community, intensified last week after Serbia gave its backing to a military offensive in Bosnia and Herzegovina.

Offensive Kills 200

The offensive, in which a dozen or so towns were captured, killed at least 200 people and forced tens of thousands of Muslim Slavs and Croats to leave their homes. It also raised fears that Serbia would eventually annex the captured territories or seek to partition Bosnia and Herzegovina by recognizing a separate Serbian republic there.

The decisions announced here today created new optimism among the Muslim Slavs and Croats in Bosnia and Herzegovina, who approved the republic's independence in a vote eight weeks ago. The vote was boycotted by the republic's Serbs, who account for about 30 percent of the population.

The proclamation of the new Yugoslav nation and its renunciation of territorial claims served as a signal for the new Government in Bosnia and Herzegovina to renew pressures for removing 10,000 Yugoslav Army troops who have been garrisoned there.

Tonight, a statement from the Bosnia and Herzegovina presidency, issued on behalf of the Muslim Slav and Croatian leaders, formally demanded the withdrawal of the army from the republic, and said that those Yugoslav troops who wished to remain should join the republic's newly established territorial defense force.

Another Cease-Fire Broken

But the statement had hardly been read over the radio in Sarajevo, the capital, before Serbian forces in the suburb of Ilidza responded with a barrage of recoilless cannon and machine-gun fire that appeared to be the most serious breach yet of the cease-fire that was agreed between the rival forces last week.

At the weekend, as part of its moves to ease Western pressures for its diplomatic isolation, Serbia dispatched the acting Yugoslav Defense Minister, Gen. Blagoje Adzic, to open negotiations on the army's presence in Bosnia and Herzegovina with Alija Izetbegovic, a Muslim Slav who is the republic's President. But in a seeming effort to allay the concerns of the republic's Serbs, the army commander in Bosnia and Herzegovina, Col. Gen. Milutin Kukunjac, a Serb, told reporters in Sarajevo today that while the army might pull out of "certain areas," it would remain in Bosnia as "the army of the people who accept us." This appeared to imply that the army would remain in areas of Serbian population.

The declaration accompanying the new Constitution included other gestures toward Western governments, among them a pledge that the new nation would abide by the principle of "not using force to settle open questions."

The declaration also said that Yugoslavia, in its new form, would be a democracy based on respect for human rights and on the principles of a "market economy." Further, it pledged to negotiate with the four breakaway republics on all "open questions," including the division of the old Yugoslavia's assets, through the European Community's Conference on Yugoslavia.

Many Serbs who attended today's ceremony at the copper-domed parliament building were subdued, and their spirits seemed unimproved by efforts to foster a spirit of celebration. Few joined in when a choir of women in white robes sang "Hey Slavs!" the anthem of the old Yugoslavia and of the new one, and only a small crowd gathered outside to watch the raising of the new flag, the same tricolor of red, white and blue that was flown by Communist Yugoslavia, minus the red star at the center.

Some of those present saw the new nation as a poor relation to the two previous ones: the Kingdom of Serbs, Croats and Slovenes, which lasted from 1918 until the Nazi invasion in 1941, and Tito's republic, which covered 98,765 square miles, more than double the 39,380 square miles of the new state.

"I was born in one Yugoslavia, grew up in another, and now I'm a citizen of a third, and it is the smallest of the three," a woman said at the ceremony.

*   *   *

May 29, 1992

SERBIAN CHURCH ASSAILS BELGRADE

By CHUCK SUDETIC

BELGRADE, Yugoslavia, May 28—The Serbian Orthodox Church called on President Slobodan Milosevic today to step aside and supported calls by opposition leaders for a boycott of elections for the Parliament of the new rump Yugoslav state this weekend.

It was the church's sharpest criticism of any Belgrade Government since before the Communist era.

In its statement, the church called for "the creation of a government of national unity and salvation that will enjoy the confidence of all the people."

"We remind all those in power, especially in Serbia, that no one's armchair is more important than the destiny and freedom of the entire people and that no one has a monopoly over the people and the future of our children," the statement says.

A Western diplomat said: "This is a direct assault on Milosevic. The church is rejecting Milosevic's claim to speak for the Serbs. This is certainly the furthest they have ever gone."

Opposition Boycotts Vote

The church's statement backed a call by opposition leaders for voters in the Serbian-Montenegrin state not to take part in the elections.

"The Serbian Church ultimately takes exception to and distances herself from this and such authorities and their standard-bearers, from the Constitution which was adopted without the people's consent, as well as from the planned elections," it says.

"The ruling parties in Serbia and Montenegro, inheriting the structures and organs as well as the means and principles of the postwar Communist system, even today do not make possible equal rights for a democratic dialogue in society," the bishops' statement says. "The authorities promise to correct historical injustices and attacks upon the church and the consciences of men, but in practice do not fulfill a single essential promise."

The Orthodox Church, which preserved the Serbs' national identity during centuries of foreign domination, is the most influential nongovernmental institution in Serbia. Indeed, the principal defining characteristic of traditional Serbian culture is Christian Orthodoxy.

But the church's power waned significantly in the postwar era because the Communists confiscated church lands, banned parochial schools and discriminated against church-goers in the allocation of jobs, and no precise figure for church membership exists. The Western diplomat said it remained to be seen whether the statement would significantly increase support for the election boycott among the 6.5 million Serbs in the rump Yugoslavia.

"Serbia is not Poland," the diplomat said, alluding to the political strength of the Roman Catholic Church there.

Serbian opposition leaders called for the election boycott because the Communist Government in Belgrade monopolizes the nation's television. A long report by Belgrade television tonight on the church's statement did not mention the bishops' criticism of the Government.

The bishops also lashed out at the European Community, saying it was singling out the Serbian people, rather than the Governments of Serbia or Croatia, for responsibility for the wars in Croatia and Bosnia and Herzegovina.

The European Community and the United Nations are preparing to impose economic sanctions on Serbia, assigning Belgrade the lion's share of responsibility for the fighting in Bosnia and Herzegovina, which has left more than 2,300 people dead and displaced more than 750,000. "The European Community," the eight-page bishops' memorandum says, "apparently identifies the Serbian people with the regime which ruled over them and in large part still rules today."

"It would be dishonorable and short-sighted to ascribe to any people, especially the Serbian people, the evils committed in our days on the part of Broz's generals on both sides of the front," the statement says, referring to Tito, the longtime leader of postwar Yugoslavia, by his real name, Josip Broz. "It was not necessary for them to turn their incompetence in negotiations and inability to reach agreement into a war between peoples who were finally being liberated from Communist slavery and degradation."

Appeal by Milosevic

Tonight, President Milosevic appealed to Serbs to rally behind the month-old Yugoslav state despite mounting international pressure and the impending imposition of sanctions.

"These pressures are primarily designed to destabilize Yugoslavia," Mr. Milosevic said in a 45-minute televised interview.

"Is this new world order one in which some nations rule and others are ruled?" he asked. "We shall have no foreign overlords."

"Some powers are doubtless dictating solutions and their relationship toward us," the Serbian President said. "This cannot last for long."

Taken together, Mr. Milosevic's appeal to patriotism and the Orthodox Church's criticism of his Government highlighted a yawning rift between pro- and anti-Government forces in Serbian society, a rift that many people here say portends civil war in Serbia itself.

10 Killed in Bosnia

At least 10 people died in violence in Bosnia and Herzegovina overnight and today. The Sarajevo radio reported tonight that Serbian forces were firing rockets at the city from positions on the mountainsides above it.

The bishops repeated their support for unification of all Serbs in a single state and blamed Yugoslavia's Communists for dividing the Serbian population with republican borders that the European Community, the United States and the United Nations have in recent months recognized as international frontiers between Slovenia, Croatia, Bosnia and Herzegovina, and the new rump Yugoslavia consisting of Serbia and Montenegro. A sixth republic of the old Yugoslav federation, Macedonia, has declared independence but has not received international recognition.

While favoring the unification of the Serbian nation in a single state, the church distanced itself from the use of violence to attain that national goal.

"Our church favors the unity of the Serbian people and Serbian lands but also supports a just solution of the national rights and existential problems of all people with whom the Serbs live," the statement said.

* * *

May 30, 1992

SERBIAN GUNNERS POUND SARAJEVO

By CHUCK SUDETIC
Special to The New York Times

BELGRADE, Yugoslavia, May 29—Defying international threats of sanctions against Belgrade, Serbian forces in Bosnia and Herzegovina pounded Sarajevo with artillery and rocket fire early today in the heaviest bombardment the capital of the war-torn republic has faced, and kept up the shelling throughout the day, officials and witnesses there said.

At least six people were reported killed in Sarajevo and scores more wounded in the latest barrages, officials in the city said. Serbian gunners also shelled the ancient Croatian port of Dubrovnik for the first time since December, damaging the stone tower that guards the old city's harbor.

The president of the self-styled Serbian Republic of Bosnia and Herzegovina, Radovan Karadzic, said economic sanctions now being drawn up by the United Nations, United States and European Community against the rump federal Government of Yugoslavia in Belgrade would not stop the fighting in Bosnia and Herzegovina.

"No threat of sanctions will make the Serbs accept domination," Mr. Karadzic said, denying that the Belgrade Government was involved in the Bosnian Serbs' battle against the Croatian and Muslim Slav forces in Bosnia and Herzegovina.

Western diplomats link Serbia's Communist leader, Slobodan Milosevic, and elements of the Serb-led federal Yugoslav Army with Mr. Karadzic's party, the Serbian Democratic Party. The Serbian forces in Bosnia have overrun more than 60 percent of the republic and carried out what they call "ethnic cleansing" operations, expelling thousands of Muslim Slavs.

The fighting in Bosnia and Herzegovina has left an estimated 2,300 people dead and 7,700 wounded, and driven more than 700,000 from their homes.

The Serbs' main attack on Sarajevo began before midnight local time Thursday and lasted about four hours, witnesses said. Intermittent shelling of the city continued all day today.

The bombardment damaged two mosques and tore through dozens of houses, stores and office buildings, including the presidency building. Fires ignited by the shells damaged several office towers, a tobacco factory and the arena where figure skaters competed in the 1984 Winter Olympics.

At least 10 shells hit the main radio and television broadcast center, which the Serbs have been trying to disable throughout their two-month campaign to carve up Bosnia and Herzegovina and partition Sarajevo itself.

"I cannot believe that Stalingrad was any worse than this," said Sulejman Sulic, a member of Bosnia and Herzegovina's Parliament, referring to the World War II battle between Soviet and German forces that raged for nearly five months, cost both sides hundreds of thousands of casualties and razed the city. "The center of the city is like a ghost town, with stone fragments, shards of roof tiles and broken glass all over."

Western diplomats and local officials link the bombardment with the continuing blockade of the Marshal Tito Barracks in central Sarajevo by pro-Government forces, which consist mostly of Muslim Slavs and Croats but also many loyalist Serbs.

Sarajevo residents received a warning to return to shelters at about 3:30 P.M. The warning came after the commander of the army of the Bosnian Serbs, Gen. Ratko Mladic, told the Sarajevo Government that his forces would level the capital if pro-Government militiamen did not allow federal Yugoslav Army troops to leave a barracks in Sarajevo with their weapons.

General Mladic insists that the Yugoslav Army officers, soldiers and civilians inside the barracks be allowed to leave with their heavy weaponry, a Western diplomat said. But officials in Bosnia and Herzegovina asserted that the general was dragging out the barracks evacuation in order to give his forces time to secure a corridor from Serbian positions to the barracks, a move that would virtually enable the Serbs to cut Sarajevo in half.

Most of Bosnia and Herzegovina's 1.4 million Eastern Orthodox Serbs oppose the republic's independence and support the formation of the republic of Bosnian Serbs, which would be linked to the new rump Yugoslavia.

Bosnia and Herzegovina's 1.9 million Muslim Slavs and most of its 750,000 Croats favor independence.

The army of the Bosnian Serbs consists of ill-disciplined local militias, volunteers from Serbia itself, and about 80,000 Bosnian Serbs who were members of the Yugoslav Army until it withdrew from the republic this month.

* * *

May 31, 1992

U.N. VOTES 13-0 FOR EMBARGO ON TRADE WITH YUGOSLAVIA; AIR TRAVEL AND OIL CURBED

By PAUL LEWIS
Special to The New York Times

UNITED NATIONS, May 30—Rejecting last-minute Serbian appeals for a delay, the Security Council voted overwhelmingly today to follow the Bush Administration's lead and impose tough economic sanctions on the Yugoslav Government in an effort to force Belgrade try to bring peace to Bosnia and Herzegovina.

In addition to calling for the establishment of a "security zone" around the Sarajevo airport to allow emergency supplies to be flown into the Bosnian capital, today's resolution committed the Council to "consider immediately, whenever necessary, further steps to achieve a peaceful solution in conformity with relevant resolutions of the Council."

U.S. to Seize Yugoslav Assets

Although the resolution, which passed with 13 votes in favor and two abstentions, made no specific reference to using force, some Council members are informally discussing the possibility of a naval blockade of the Adriatic ports and closing Bosnian air space to Serbian planes that are supporting forces fighting there. In Sarajevo today, Bosnian Serbs and Muslim Slavs battled at an army barracks, but the Serbs were later reported to have ordered their troops to halt artillery fire..

Tonight, President Bush ordered the Treasury Department to seize all Yugoslav Government assets in the United States by Monday. The White House said they amounted to about $200 million.

"The grave events in Serbia and Montenegro constitute an unusual and extraordinary threat to the national security, foreign policy and economy of the United States," Mr. Bush said in a statement.

Loopholes Are Seen

Together with the comprehensive ban on all commercial and financial links imposed on Iraq before the Persian Gulf war, today's decision by the Security Council represents the second time that it has taken punitive action against an aggressor nation since the end of the cold war.

In Belgrade, the capital of Serbia, economists and Western diplomats agreed that the sanctions would impose hardships on the republic but that contingency plans and loopholes were likely to enable the Serbian economy to function for a long time.

Today's embargo, which closely resembles the sanctions against Iraq, requires all the countries of the world to cease trading in any commodity, including oil, with the Yugoslav federation formed by Serbia and Montenegro and to freeze all its foreign assets.

All air traffic links to and from the country must also be suspended and no one may repair, service, operate, insure or provide spare parts for aircraft registered in Serbia or Montenegro.

In addition, the resolution bans Serbia and Montenegro from participating in any international sporting events. It requires all countries to suspend cultural, scientific and technical contacts with Belgrade and to reduce the size of its foreign diplomatic missions.

Russia dropped its earlier reservations about the embargo and voted in favor of the sanctions. In a strong statement issued in Moscow today, Russia said Belgrade had "brought upon itself the United Nations sanctions by failing to heed the demands of the international community."

China, traditionally reluctant about Security Council interference in any country's internal affairs, abstained, but did not threaten to block sanctions with its veto as a permanent Council member. Zimbabwe, one of the Council's six third-world members, also abstained. But the other five, India, Cape Verde, Venezuela, Ecuador, and Morocco, one of the embargo's sponsors, supported the move, as did Austria and Japan. Other members voting for sanctions were the other sponsors of the resolution: the United States, Britain, France, Belgium and Hungary.

As the Council voted, Serbia began an eleventh hour bid to avert sanctions. In letters to President Bush and President Boris N. Yeltsin of Russia, President Slobodan Milosevic of Serbia asked the United States and Russia to place "all the forces involved" in the fighting in Bosnia and Herzegovina under their joint command.

Serbs Appeal for Conference

Earlier today the Serbian leadership cabled Secretary General Boutros Boutros-Ghali to ask him to propose an international conference on the Balkans crisis instead of sanctions.

"It's bobbing and weaving," said a Western diplomat in Belgrade. "The time for proposals like this has long passed. The Serbian side has to act quickly and unilaterally to stop the brutal destruction of Sarajevo and the aggression against Bosnia and Herzegovina. Words are not enough."

The new sanctions package came some 10 days after Secretary of State James A. Baker 3d lost patience with the European Community's efforts to negotiate a peace settlement in the former Yugoslav federation. He bluntly accused Serbia of stirring up a civil war in Bosnia and Herzegovina and said the Security Council should impose sanctions on Yugoslavia. At the time he pointedly refused to rule out international military intervention to end the fighting and allow relief supplies to reach suffering people.

After the United States sat on the sidelines for months, the Secretary of State's intervention, made at a conference in Lisbon, represented a reassertion of American leadership in the Balkans crisis and finally forced the hesitant Europeans to approve a separate, less onerous sanctions package against Belgrade earlier this week.

Explaining his decision on Yugoslav assets, Mr. Bush said, "The measures I have taken today express our outrage at the actions of the Serbian and Montegrin governments and will prevent those governments from drawing on monies and properties within U.S. control."

Weapons Deliveries Banned

The Security Council has already banned all deliveries of weapons and other military material to any of the constituent republics of the former Yugoslav federation.

The aim of these sanctions, the resolution says, is to force the Serbian authorities in Belgrade to cooperate with the demands the Security Council laid out earlier this month in Resolution 752, which called for an immediate cease-fire and an end to ethnic oppression in Bosnia and Herzegovina.

This means Belgrade must cease all interference in Bosnia and Herzegovina and use its influence to promote a general cease-fire, oversee the disbanding and disarming of elements of the Yugoslav National Army and irregular forces and end efforts to create an purely Serbian enclave by driving out other ethnic groups.

Belgrade Condemned

In the Security Council discussion, speaker after speaker condemned the authorities in Belgrade for deliberately encouraging ethnic conflict in Bosnia and Herzegovina.

"There is no doubt the principal responsibility lies with the civil and military authorities in Belgrade," said Sir David Hannay, the British representative. "Multiple rocket launchers are not found in Serbian peasants' barns. Somebody puts them there."

But while today's resolution is directed principally at Serbia, it also expresses concern at cease-fire violations and acts of racial discrimination in Croatia and calls on all parts of the former Yugoslav federation to cooperate with the European Community's peace conference for the region.

France Opposes Ban on Sports

The vote was also delayed by a last-minute attempt by France to delete the ban on sports at the personal request of President Francois Mitterrand. But France eventually dropped its demand in return for language clarifying that the Serbs are not solely responsible for the crisis in the Balkans, diplomats said.

At least 2,200 people are known to have died in Bosnia and Herzegovina since Croats and Muslim Slavs, who together make up more than 60 percent of its 4.3 million people, voted in February to secede from the Yugoslav federation.

Bosnia's Serbs opposed independence and have fought with help from Belgrade and the Yugoslav Army to carve out an enclave for itself by driving away other ethnic groups.

The United Nations has already dispatched a large peace-keeping force to monitor the fragile truce that ended ethnic fighting in Croatia and Slovenia that broke out after they declared independence. But the organization was forced to withdraw its token presence from Sarajevo earlier this month as a result of the intense fighting there.

In addition, the United Nations and other relief agencies have been hindered and harassed in their efforts to help the more than 500,000 people driven from their homes by the fighting.

And the Secretary General has said that many of the warring factions there are actively trying to deny food and medicine to some civilians to force them to move elsewhere.

Sales of medicine and food were exempted from today's trade embargo, but the Security Council committee established to monitor compliance must be notified of such shipments.

*   *   *

June 1, 1992

TENS OF THOUSANDS CALL FOR REMOVAL OF SERBIA'S LEADER

By CHUCK SUDETIC
Special to The New York Times

BELGRADE, Yugoslavia, May 31—Tens of thousands of demonstrators crowded downtown streets today calling for the resignation of Serbia's President as the first effects of United Nations sanctions were being felt.

The President, Slobodan Milosevic, criticized the sanctions imposed on Saturday, saying Serbia was not responsible for the fighting in Bosnia and Herzegovina, which continued today.

"This is the price we have to pay for supporting Serbs outside Serbia," Mr. Milosevic said early this morning after he cast his vote in elections for the Yugoslav Parliament. "As far as the accusations that we have committed aggression against Bosnia and Herzegovina are concerned, surely every citizen of Serbia knows that they are ridiculous. We have not committed any aggression against Bosnia."

Election Boycotted

Mr. Milosevic appeared tired as he voted today. All major opposition parties were boycotting the elections in Serbia and Montenegro, the only remaining Yugoslav republics, and the Serbian Orthodox Church denounced the vote.

Polls opened just hours after the United Nations Security Council imposed the economic sanctions.

[Bush Administration officials Sunday expressed deep reluctance to use military force to enforce the sanctions, saying Washington's immediate goal was to force the Serbian-backed military to lift its two-month blockade of Sarajevo. Administration officials said they wanted to assess the effects of the embargo before taking any further steps to punish Yugoslavia.]

The first outward signs of the embargo were lines forming at gasoline stations in the Belgrade area and the disruption of air links.

Flights Are Canceled

This morning, hundreds of stranded travelers milled around Belgrade Airport watching the word "Canceled" click up next to one departing flight after another on the large black timetable. Within hours, only flights for Paris, Copenhagen, Moscow and London were left and it was unclear whether they would actually depart.

Yugoslavia also has been disqualified from the European soccer championship in Sweden as a result of the United Nations embargo.

The peaceful demonstrators, many dressed in black, took over downtown Belgrade streets for about three hours this afternoon, unfurling a mile-long black banner along the city's main shopping thoroughfare before protesting outside the television station, the hub of the Serbian Government's propaganda network.

Demonstrators jeered and shouted "Slobo Must Go!" outside the republic's Presidency Building, referring to President Milosevic.

The demonstration was the largest anti-Government gathering in Serbia since violent protests in March 1991 brought Yugoslav Army tanks to Belgrade streets.

Bombing of Belgrade

"I am against the war and the regime that has sucked our sons into war," said a Yugoslav Airline flight attendant, laid off last week after 30 years on the job because of the cancellation of the airlines' landing rights by the United States and Canada.

"I want to show the world that all Serbs are not the same," she said. "We all expect to be bombed, and we remember when the Americans bombed Belgrade in 1944."

Slobodanka Karic, a 50-year-old health worker, said, "It's only a matter of time before the armed conflict comes to Belgrade. The international community should stop all the armed attacks by all sides, and then the Communists must be removed."

The demonstrators scoffed at today's elections, calling them a "farce."

Reports on Turnout

Election officials reported only a 38 percent turnout at Serbian polling stations at 2 P.M., and by evening were asserting that 60 percent of the electorate had voted. In Montenegro, turnout reports ranged from 6 to 60 percent. About 7.3 million people are eligible to vote. Final results are not expected until Wednesday.

Western diplomats said a weak turnout would not necessarily be interpreted as a vote of no confidence in Mr. Milosevic, who rose to power through the Communist Party's apparatus and has deflected criticism and held power by appealing to Serbian nationalism and controlling the republic's large enterprises and most influential media.

Serbia's main opposition parties, the Serbian Renewal Movement, Democratic Party and Serbian Liberal Party called for the boycott because they said the Government pushed through the country's new Constitution without adequate discussion, allowed only a short period for campaigning and refused to end its virtual monopoly on the country's main television channel.

'Duty to Liberate Serbia'

The leader of the Serbian Renewal Movement, Vuk Draskovic, said: "The Serbs' enemies are not in London, New York, Paris or Moscow. They are right here in Belgrade. It's our duty to liberate Serbia."

"The Serbian people are not guilty," Mr. Draskovic said. "Sanctions are needed against the regime, not the people."

The Serbian Orthodox Church denounced the Serbian and Yugoslav Governments last week, disassociated itself from the new Constitution and the elections and called for the formation of a government of national salvation.

Only the renamed Communist Party of Serbia and Montenegro, two ultra-nationalist parties, and several dozen tiny political groups ran candidates.

Successor to Old Yugoslavia

The elections were scheduled after the new Yugoslavia was formed on April 27 in an attempt to claim the status of the successor to the Yugoslav Federation as well as its assets.

Government leaders say the elections are important because they will allow the Yugoslav Government to begin functioning normally again after huge gaps were torn in the Legislature and administration by the secession of Croatia, Slovenia, Bosnia and Herzegovina and Macedonia.

Officials of the United Nations peacekeeping forces in Sarajevo today won agreements from Serbian leaders in Bosnia and Herzegovina's government for a new cease-fire scheduled to begin on Monday at 6 P.M. local time, an official in Sarajevo said. The cease-fire agreement provides for the evacuation of a besieged Yugoslav Army barracks in the city center.

Bosnian Serb forces this morning continued their bombardments of Sarajevo, while Yugoslav Army and Bosnian Serb forces also shelled the historic port city of Dubrovnik, lobbing about 17 shells into the walled Old Town.

More than 2,300 people have been killed and 7,700 wounded since the Serbs began their military campaign to seize most of Bosnia and Herzegovina. The fighting has driven well over 700,000 people from their homes.

* * *

June 1, 1992

IN SARAJEVO, ANGER AND GRIEF AMID RUINS

By JOHN F. BURNS
Special to The New York Times

SARAJEVO, Bosnia and Herzegovina, May 31—When the Serbian Orthodox priests lifted the top off Predrag Merjanovic's coffin for his family's last farewells today, his grandmother leaned over, moved the black scarf from his face and kissed him.

"Your brothers who survive you will avenge you!" she said, her anguished voice riding above the wailing of the dead man's mother and sister.

Around them, in the caramel colored church in the hills above the besieged city, Serbian men in camouflage fatigues with pistols, knives and grenades strapped to their belts wept for their comrade, a 27-year-old Serbian policeman. He died on Friday when a sniper in Sarajevo shot him in the back as he pulled his pajamas from a clothesline.

After their farewells, the mourners stepped out into the drizzle and vowed to keep fighting until Sarajevo was "liberated" from the Croats and Muslim Slavs who control much of the city.

"If this land is not going to be Serbian, it will be nobody's," said a 30-year-old Serbian policeman, also named Predrag, who gave only his first name.

A day after the United Nations Security Council imposed sweeping sanctions on Serbia and identified it as the principle aggressor in Bosnias and Herzegovina's civil war, the mood among the ethnic Serbian forces encircling Sarajevo, the Bosnian capital, was defiant, and at time apocalyptic.

In their vows to keep fighting, to avenge lost comrades and to capture Sarajevo—or at least to carve out Serbian enclaves that can be governed as part of an autonomous Serbian republic—the fighters offer little hope that they will yield at any time soon to international pressure.

On the Serbian front lines, along the slopes of the 6,500-foot mountains that cradle Sarajevo, the mood was one of a people who consider themselves maligned, above all by the United States, which led the drive for sanctions.

Sometimes in anger, sometimes in what seemed like despair, officers and men alike assailed American reporters entering Sarajevo for which they said were misleading Western news accounts that had helped push the United Nations into the embargo on trade, oil, civil aviation and sports.

At the funeral, at paramilitary checkpoints along the rutted mountain roads that are the Serb's supply lines, and at military barracks on Sarajevo's outskirts where Serbian commanders direct their operations, the Serbs insisted that atrocities attributed to their forces—including a mortar attack on a bread line in the center of Sarajevo in which at least 20 people died—were "provocations" by Muslim Slav units seeking to push the world into punitive actions against Serbia.

Fear of Extinction

The Serbs also represented themselves as men fighting to save their historic foothold in Sarajevo against the Muslim-dominated Government of Bosnia and Herzegovina, which they said was committed to a program of Islamic fundamentalism, and ultimately to the extinction of the Serbian Orthodox Church and other aspects of Serbian culture that have been rooted here since Sarajevo in its present form was founded 535 years ago.

Finally, the Serbs said, they were fighting to save their families and fellow military men who have been trapped in Sarajevo by the fighting.

As mortar and machine-gun fire broke the stillness outside his office, Col. Tomislav Sipcic of the newly formed army of the so-called Serbian Republic of Bosnia and Herzegovina, was preoccupied with the plight of Serbs trapped in Sarajevo. At intervals during the evening, the granite faced officer at the Lukavica barracks in Sarajevo's outskirts picked up a telephone on his candle-lit desk to speak with a Croatian commander of the opposing Muslim-Slav and Croatian forces in Sarajevo.

Until 12 years ago, Colonel Sipcic, who is 50 years old, was an officer in the Yugoslav Army. It has transferred at least 55,000 troops to the new army after the Serbian Government, under pressure to respect Bosnia and Herzegovina's independent status, ordered Yugoslav forces to withdraw. Now, in addition to maintaining a blockade on Sarajevo, the Colonel's tasks include bargaining with the Croatian commander, Col. Stjepan Siber, over 734 Serbs who are trapped in the Marshal Tito barracks in the heart of Sarajevo.

For more than two months, the Serbs, who include 486 women and children and 248 officers and teen-age military cadets, have been besieged in the barracks by Croatian and Muslim Slav forces inside the huge military encampment, covering the equivalent of 10 city blocks, the Serbs are trapped without electrical power or fresh food, and their fate has become intertwined with that of Sarajevo itself. In effect they have become hostages to the heavy bombardment of the city by Serbian artillery, mortar and rocket batteries in the surrounding hills.

Tonight, in one of the curious human twist to the Sarajevo battle, Colonel Sipcic agreed to allow a Muslim Slav chess team safe passage in their way to the World Chess Olympiad in the Philippines, if Colonel Siber, a former army colleague, held to an agreement to allow the evacuation of the Marshal Tito barracks on Monday.

Similar agreements have been made and broken at the last moment, raising fears of a massacre if the walls of the barracks should be breached.

But if ties forged in the old Yugoslavia still count for something among military officers, much else about Sarajevo attests to the rupturing of human bonds and the resurgence of the ethnic and religious hatreds of the past.

Many of the Serbian fighters described their Muslim foes as lazy, and as under the spell of Alija Izetbegovic, the President of Bosnia and Herzegovina, a man they described as a Muslim extremist.

"What they didn't succeed in achieving 500 years ago they want now," said Grujo Sudzum, a 36-year-old Serbian mechanic serving as a military volunteer, referring to the Turkish drive into Europe in the 15th century.

As dusk settled over the low hills separating the Lucavica barracas, Mr. Sudzum was surrounded by a group of Serbian volunteers. Asked if they would agree to United Nations demands that they stop fighting if it meant the end of their bid for a Serbian republic within Bosnia, they replied in a chorus; "Never!"

One man exclaimed: "I lost my house!" Another man said he had lost contact with his wife and three children in Pofalici, a district where, the fighters said, Muslim Slav militiamen had killed at least 70 civilians 15 days ago, burning some alive in their homes.

In the village of Pale, 10 miles from Sarajevo, the funeral of Mr. Marjanovic left no doubt about the bitterness stirred by the fighting. After Serbian priests in black and golden vestments had performed a liturgy over the coffin, and mourners with lighted candles had filed under the oil-painted icons to kiss the dead policeman, Nedeljko Rasevic, a 41-year-old hotel manager now serving as a military volunteer, blamed President Bush for what be said was the United Nations' victimization of the Serbs.

"If Mr. Bush was here he wouldn't do such things to our people," Mr. Rasevic said. "He should come here to see the truth. He should come here and learn about eight people that the Muslims took to a school basement in Sarajevo and burned alive. We are burying our people all the time."

*   *   *

June 4, 1992

SERBS SAY MUSLIM SLAV AND CROATION GUNMEN KILLED CIVILIANS IN 6 VILLAGES

By JOHN F. BURNS
Special to The New York Times

SARAJEVO, Bosnia and Herzegovina, June 3—In accounts that appeared to confirm that atrocities against civilians are being committed by all sides in the ethnic war here, Serbs from a mountainous area outside Sarajevo said today that Muslim Slavs and Croatian gunmen swept through at least six villages in the region last week, executing Serbian men after they had been forced to kneel and recite the Muslim incantation "God Is Great."

The Serbs also said the attackers looted and burned their homes, then rounded up large numbers of survivors and forced them to spend three to five days in darkened, damp railroad tunnels with virtually no food or water.

It was not clear from the accounts what had become of the captives after they were removed from the mile-long Ivan-Sedio tunnel near the village of Bradina, 25 miles southwest of Sarajevo, but several of the Serbs said that they had heard that the detainees had been placed in internment camps in Muslim controlled villages in the area.

Charges of Atrocities

Much of what the Serbs said could not be verified, although the United Nations military group in Saravejo said the allegation about people being held in the railroad tunnel had been confirmed when the Muslim-led Government in Sarajevo, responding to inquiries by the United Nations, had given assurances that the Serbs had been removed from the tunnel.

It remained unclear, from the Serbian accounts and from what the United Nations officers were told, what the Muslim Slav and Croatian captors had intended to do with the detainees in the tunnel before the United Nations intervened. The detainees were said to have included women and children and many elderly people.

It was not clear whether the use of the tunnel would have led to a massacre without United Nations help, as the Serbs who relayed accounts of it said they had feared, or whether some of those held in the tunnel died, as the Serbs also maintained. The accounts of merciless killing and mistreatment of Serbs by Muslim Slav and Croatian militants by witnesses and others were strikingly similar to accounts of Serbian atrocities against Muslim Slavs and Croats that had been given elsewhere in this former Yugoslav republic.

Last week, accounts of Serbian atrocities played a major role in prompting the United Nations Security Council to punish Serbia with the most sweeping economic and other sanctions it has ever imposed, including a trade embargo, a ban on oil, and an end to all sports and cultural links.

The accounts given today by Serbs from the region around Bradina, a village 25 miles southwest of Sarajevo, appeared to confirm that some Muslim Slav and Croat groups, who have made a loose alliance with the fight against the Serbian forces, have been using similar tactics to clear Serbian civilians from other contested areas in the republic.

The assertion by Zeljko Gligorevic, a 28-year-old clerical worker from Bradina, that Muslim Slav gunmen had executed some men in the village after forcing them to say Muslim prayers also seemed to lend support to Serbian assertions that some Muslim Slavs, who are the largest ethnic group in the republic, want to turn Bosnia and Herzegovina into an Islamic state.

Mr. Gligorevic reached the Sarajevo suburb of Ilidza on Tuesday after what he said had been a 50-mile trek across the mountains of Bradina, during which, he said, he was shot twice in the thigh by men he said were Muslim Slav fighters with automatic rifles.

Western reporters who spoke with him at a Serbian home in Ilidza were taken to see him after they had learned of the Bradina incident and of the herding of Serb survivors into the tunnel, from other Serbs. These included Col. Tomislav Sipcic, who commands Serbian forces in the region that includes Bradina, and a Serbian reporter raised in Bradina who said that he had been given details of the tunnel incident by a Croatian acquaintance in the region whom he had reached by telephone.

In the Serbian colonel's account, about 3,000 people were held in the tunnel, from Bradina and at least five other villages with Serbian populations in the area, including Brdjani, Donje, Selo, Konjic, Pazaric and Tarch. The Serbian reporter said the number he had been given was 2,000 to 4,000.

Exaggerated Reports

In many other reports of atrocities in the two-month-old war in Bosnia, the number of those alleged to have been killed, wounded or otherwise mistreated have sometimes proven exaggerated. However, the involvement of several villages suggested that the number of people taken to the tunnel could have easily run into the hundreds.

The fact that villagers were held in the railway tunnel was confirmed when Serbian requests for intervention that were put to the United Nations military group stationed in Sarajevo were relayed to the Bosnian Government.

Col. Kari Hoglund, deputy commander of the 120-man United Nations force that is attempting to negotiate a cease-fire in the war and to arrange safe passage for relief convoys, said that the charges that thousands of people were being held in the tunnel were relayed late last week to senior officials of the Government, which is shared between Muslim Slavs and Croats.

Colonel Hoglund, a Finnish officer, said that the Sarajevo Government had not responded for "two or three days." When it did, he said, it indirectly confirmed that the charge was true. "We were just told that they were now out of the tunnel," Colonel Hoglund said, referring to the Serbian villagers. He said that the United Nations had been unable to verify anything else, including the whereabouts of the captives after they were moved.

Mr. Gligorevic, the survivor who was interviewed, was red-eyed and sunburned and broke down frequently during his account. He said that he had survived for three days, with about 20 other Bradina villagers in a hole they had dug in a hillside outside the village and covered with branches and ferns.

He said that they had occasionally climbed a tree to watch what was happening in the village and had seen attackers looting and burning about 150 houses, all of them owned by Serbs. He said he had learned from others of an incident in which a village elder, Pero Mrkajic, a restaurant owner who was 65 years old, had been doused with gasoline and burned to death.

Description of Killings

Mr. Gligorevic said that he had learned of the reported massacre, in which several Bradina men were made to kneel and say Muslim prayers before being shot, during one of the trips he made into the village at times when the attackers withdrew. He said that a relative, sheltering in the burned-out shell of her home, had told him that she had seen the executions.

Like other Serbs who relayed accounts of the attacks, Mr. Gligorevic said that he had lost contact with most members of his family, including his father, mother and 23-year-old pregnant sister, and feared that if they had survived they were now in what he called "concentration camps."

This is a term used by several of the Serbs to describe the internment camps that they said had been set up by the Muslim Slav and Croat forces in a former military barracks at Konjic, a town about 12 miles south of Bradina, and at another in Butorvic Polje, about 10 miles farther south.

'A Piece of Land'

As was the case with Muslim Slavs who survived similar atrocities by Serbian gunmen in areas of eastern Bosnia adjacent to Serbia, Mr. Gligorevic's account was given with a striking lack of bitterness against Muslim Slavs, with whom he had said he had played as a child, shared classrooms, and accompanied the local football games.

But he said that his experience had persuaded him that Serbian leaders who are leading the fight for exclusively Serbian enclaves were right. "What I want is a piece of land that is Serbian, where I can go free, no matter how small, no matter whether I ever see my own village again," he said.

*   *   *

June 8, 1992

A PEOPLE UNDER ARTILLERY FIRE MANAGE TO RETAIN HUMANITY

By JOHN F. BURNS
Special to The New York Times

SARAJEVO, Bosnia and Herzegovina, June 7—As the 155-millimeter howitzer shells whistled down on this crumbling city today, exploding thunderously into buildings all around, a disheveled, stubble-bearded man in formal evening attire unfolded a plastic chair in the middle of Vase Miskina Street. He lifted his cello from its case and began playing Albinoni's Adagio.

There were only two people to hear him, and both fled, dodging from doorway to doorway, before the performance ended.

Each day at 4 P.M., the cellist, Vedran Smailovic, walks to the same spot on the pedestrian mall for a concert in honor of Sarajevo's dead.

The spot he has chosen is outside the bakery where several high-explosive rounds struck a bread line 12 days ago, killing 22 people and wounding more than 100. If he holds to his plan, there will be 22 performances before his gesture has run its course.

Two months into a civil war that turns more murderous by the day, Sarajevo, the capital of Bosnia and Herzegovina, is a skeleton of the thriving, accomplished city it was. It is a wasteland of blasted mosques, churches and museums; of fire-gutted office towers, hotels and sports stadiums, and of hospitals, music schools and libraries punctured by rockets, mortars and artillery shells.

Parks have been pressed into service as emergency cemeteries, and the pathetic lines of graves march ever farther up the hillsides toward the gun emplacements.

What is happening here, in a European city that escaped two World Wars with only minor damage, is hard to grasp for many of those enduring it.

It is a disaster of such magnitude, and of such seeming disconnectedness from any achievable military or political goals, that those who take shelter for days in basement bunkers, emerging briefly into daylight for fresh supplies of bread and water, exhaust themselves trying to make sense of it.

Many, like Mr. Smailovic, who played the cello for the Sarajevo Opera, reach for an anchor amid the chaos by doing something, however small, that carries them back to the stable, reasoned life they led before.

Mr. Smailovic, 36 years old, spoke over the blasts of the shells that have poured down on the city unremittingly for the last 48 hours. The barrages by the Serbian forces seem to be a paroxysm of fury at their failure to capture the city after weeks of dumping thousands of tons of high explosives from the hillsides.

He could have been speaking for all the survivors trapped here, in defiance of the Serbian nationalists' insistence that only the ethnic partitioning of the city, and of the republic, can bring them security.

"My mother is a Muslim and my father is a Muslim," Mr. Smailovic said, "but I don't care. I am a Sarajevan, I am a cosmopolitan, I am a pacifist." Then he added: "I am nothing special, I am a musician, I am part of the town. Like everyone else, I do what I can."

In Sarajevo, as in many cities, towns and villages across this former Yugoslav republic, Serbs, Muslims and Croats, the third major ethnic group in the population of 4.4 million, have lived for centuries side by side, so much so that their cultures, families and life styles have grown into each other—creating a society of striking depth and variety.

Symbol of Civility Now Symbol of Pain

They have done so in a landscape that is one of the most beautiful in Europe, a place of Alpine mountains and blue-green rivers, of terra cotta-roofed houses that cling to precipitous hillsides, of white stone mosques with green copper domes and pencil-slim minarets.

Sarajevo, in a narrow valley bordered on all sides by mountains, has long been the symbol of this richly textured life, enchanting generations of travelers since the present city was established by a Turkish sultan in 1462.

Now it is a symbol of another kind—of a place where Muslims, Serbs, Croats, and other religious and ethnic minorities, including Albanians and a tiny population of Jews, suffer together. They endure the gunfire of Serbian nationalists who believe that the independent nation of Bosnia and Herzegovina proclaimed on March 2, and led by Muslims and Croats, will dominate and eventually persecute Serbs.

From this conviction—met with increasing ferocity in many parts of the republic by Muslims and Croats, some of whom have adopted tactics as brutal as those of the Serbs—has grown the war that is draining the life from Sarajevo.

The conflict here had small beginnings early in April, when decisions by the European Community and the United States to recognize the new nation led to barricades being thrown up around the city by rival ethnic militias.

Early in May, it got out of control after Alija Izetbegovic, the Muslim who is President of the new republic, was kidnapped by the Serbian forces, and Muslim and Croatian troops retaliated by ambushing a convoy of the Serbian-led Yugoslav Army as it evacuated an army headquarters in the city.

The President, who was released in exchange for guarantees of safe passage for the convoy, was out on Marshal Tito Street in the center of Sarajevo this afternoon. He walked gin-

gerly around piles of broken glass and rubble from the shattered facades of apartment buildings built during the time before World War I when Sarajevo was an outpost of the Austro-Hungarian Empire.

The 67-year-old leader, a lawyer and economist who spent nearly 10 years in prison under Yugoslavia's Communist rulers for his writings on Muslim beliefs, sought to reassure scattered groups of people he met along the way. But he made no effort to hide his own anxiety after weeks of heavy shelling.

"Are you scared?" he asked a group of militiamen standing guard with Kalashnikov automatic rifles under an archway leading into the Solomon Palace, a six-story apartment building that was once home to some of the city's leading Jews, many of whom died in the Nazi terror.

"A little," one militiaman replied, shifting nervously in a denim jacket embroidered with the fleur-de-lis badge that is the emblem of the new republic.

"I am afraid too," replied Mr. Izetbegovic, who has spent long periods in a basement bunker in a nearby Government building. "But we must hold out."

For many here, that has become a prospect of appalling bleakness. Although the United Nations on Friday reached the outline of an agreement to take control of Butmir Airport, on the city's outskirts, from the Serbian forces and to open a corridor into town, there is little confidence here that the Serbs will carry it out.

By lifting the siege, the Serbs would effectively acknowledge that they have lost the city, many in Saravejo believe. Already, all but a few of Sarajevo's suburbs are controlled by Bosnian territorial forces made up of Muslims, Serbs and Croats.

But if relief supplies do not arrive soon, desperation may turn to catastrophe. Only a handful of Government services still operate, and those in skeletal state. No one seems to know how many people remain, but it appears to be at least half the city's prewar population of 560,000—possibly many more.

Food and Hope Are Running Low

The Serbian nationalist forces allow no food to pass through their roadblocks on the periphery of town, and supplies that have been sneaked past their gun positions on the hills have been minimal. Most families have only loaves of bread baked by the single bakery that continues to function, using reserve supplies of flour from silos that are in a part of town under Mr. Izetbegovic's control.

To this, some families have added a thin gruel made of water and nettles taken from the lower slopes of the surrounding hills. With inventive cooking, and private supplies of flour, Sarajevans produce the likes of French bread and a sugared Turkish cake called kevlici.

But no one outside the Government knows how long the flour supplies might hold out, and fear of starvation is widespread. When two Western reporters entered the city on Friday, one of the first people they encountered was a professor

Agence France-Presse

A man reflecting at a grave yesterday in a newly reopened cemetery in Sarajevo, the capital of Bosnia and Herzegovina. Many ethnic groups use the Serbian cemetery because it is considered the safest in the city.

of biophysics from the medical faculty of Sarajevo University, Dr. Hamid Pasic.

"I am hungry!" he said. "I am 76 years old, I am a professor, and I am hungry!"

Those who venture out for food do so at great risk. Although some of the gunnery appears to be aimed at military targets, most of the rounds land in densely populated parts of the city. The sections of town taking the worst punishment include the central district and Bascarsija, an old quarter of mosques, narrow alleyways and wooden-front workshops and boutiques.

The toll has risen rapidly, particularly this weekend, when the Serbian gunners began their most merciless barrage. Every minute or two, with only a few pauses, shells slammed into apartment buildings and the remnants of commercial districts, each volley hitting with a blast that could be heard miles away.

At night, the skyline was a facsimile of Baghdad during the gulf war—with gunners' flares lighting the high-rises of the city center in silhouette, and tracer fire skipping across the sky.

From a vantage point in the old town, fires blazed at every point of the compass, some of them huge conflagrations that burned for hours.

Wisdom and Tears of a Barkeeper

The number of dead and wounded was another unknown, but gravediggers were hard pressed to keep up with the new bodies arriving by the hour.

At Kovlaci Park above Bascarsija, 185 new graves, each with a coffin-shaped wooden marker bearing the Muslim emblems of a star and a crescent moon, lay row upon row on the hillside. The graves were piles of freshly turned earth beneath clusters of wild roses, carnations and violets.

Shells hitting the hillside drove a steam-shovel operator who was digging the graves into the cover of a ridge abutment. While he took shelter there, two middle-aged women carrying plastic bags of bread were hit by a new blast. Both were killed.

For Kemal Aljevic, the 45-year-old owner of a bar in Bascarsija called Alf, after the American television puppet character, the sight of the Kovlaci graves was too much. With tears streaming down his cheeks, Mr. Aljevic said that the Serbian gunners appeared to be repeating the destruction of Vukovar, the Croatian town of 45,000 that was reduced to rubble by artillery fire last year.

"This will be three times worse than Vukovar," he said.

As in Vukovar, the Serbs seem to use the heaviest weapons of the Yugoslav Army, which formally withdrew from

Bosnia and Herzegovina three weeks ago and turned at least 55,000 men over to a new force of Bosnia's ethnic Serbs.

One of two Sarajevo newspapers still being produced, Oslobodenje, quoted Yugoslav Army officers who had defected to the Bosnians as saying that weapons being used in the barrage included 155-millimeter howitzers, 120-millimeter mortars, 104-millimeter tank cannon and 132-millimeter multiple-rocket launchers. The paper said a total of 4,000 tons of high explosives had been fired into the city.

Some of the artillery shells are coming from a former Yugoslav Army barracks at Hampjesic, 20 miles east of Sarajevo, the officers reportedly added.

Houses of Worship Become Targets

The destruction has reached every quarter of Sarajevo, and almost every landmark. Fifty of the city's 80 mosques have been damaged or destroyed, including the oldest in the Balkans, Tabacki Mesdid, which dates to 1450. The Morica Han, a 15th-century Turkish inn stop for caravans, and the Islamic Theological Faculty, also from the 15th century, were damaged.

The main synagogue and the Roman Catholic cathedral have been hit, though only lightly damaged. The main broadcasting center and its transmitter have been repeatedly shelled; repairs at feverish speed have kept the radio and television stations on the air.

The Serbian nationalists seem to have taken little care to avoid buildings of historic importance to the ethnic Serbs who live here, 38 percent of the city's population before the fighting.

One building was extensively damaged by a shell that pierced its glass dome. It was the National Library, formerly the city hall, where in 1914, Archduke Franz Ferdinand of Austria-Hungary attended a reception minutes before he and his wife, Sophie, were assassinated by a 19-year-old Serbian nationalist, Gavrilo Princip. Half a mile away, at the site of the assassination, the museum dedicated to Mr. Princip has now been destroyed.

The main Serbian Orthodox church in the city center has also been extensively damaged.

Sites linked to the 1984 Olympics have come under fire, too. Both cupolas have been destroyed atop the former United States Consulate building, a neo-classical structure on a rise above the city center, which served as the Olympic museum. Its roof was penetrated by a shell, and all its windows were shattered.

The hospitals are packed with the wounded, many with amputated limbs from shrapnel blasts. Doctors report an unusually high incidence of heart attacks and of psychological distress.

With gasoline unavailable, many of the doctors walk miles to work through streets where every intersection offers clear sightlines to snipers in the hills. Along the way, hundreds of cars, buses and trams lie destroyed, many of them burned-out hulks.

A lung specialist who walks back from the Vrazova Health Center every day spends her nights in a shopping-center storage room in the city's old quarter with her husband, a cardiologist.

With them, on mattresses on the floor, are a taxi driver, dentist, fireman, electrical engineer, waiter and computer scientist, together with their families—a cross-section of Sarajevo life, pressed together as they rarely were before the fighting. Amid occasional tears, there are moments of joy over chess games, crossword puzzles and surprise meetings with old friends from other parts of town.

"You're alive!" a professor exclaimed to another who appeared in a shopping arcade on Saturday night, hugging him tightly for a full minute as both wept.

On a radio broadcast that was frequently drowned out by exploding shells, an announcer urged people to turn up the volume on the station's Bosnian patriotic songs and Beatles music. "We cannot kill these maniacs with guns," he said, "so let's kill them with love and music."

Escape Mechanisms: Music and Disbelief

In an apartment nearby, with only a candle burning to deny the gunners a target, the 16-year-old daughter of a Muslim electrical engineer and his architect wife, Meliha Dzirlo, lingered at a piano into the small hours playing Beethoven's "Pathetique" Sonata and a polonaise by Chopin.

Everywhere, when they were not arranging forays for food or water or exchanging names of those killed or wounded, people appealed for help from the outside world. After listening to a shortwave-radio account of the United Nations plans for relief convoys, Asim Hadzic, a 30-year-old Muslim who is a food-company salesman, shook his head.

"It would be a good start but it isn't enough," he said. "We want military intervention."

The doctor who walks every day to the Vrazova Clinic, a Muslim who, fearing for her house, asked not to be identified, took a wider view.

"I can't believe this is all real," she said, gesturing toward a pile of rubble from an apartment building. "Here we are on the eve of the 21st century—in Europe, in a beautiful city and a country that offered people every possibility of a good life. How can such a thing happen? And how can a so-called civilized world allow it to continue?"

* * *

July 20, 1992

IN SARAJEVO, A HAM OPERATOR CAPTURES THE HORRORS OF WAR

By JOHN F. BURNS
Special to The New York Times

SARAJEVO, Bosnia and Herzegovina, July 19—Like ham radio operators the world over, Ramiz Bisic used to muse about the day when he and his shortwave set would become the pivotal point in a great human drama. Now his musing has turned to reality, but instead of a dream come true he is living a nightmare.

For 15 hours each day Mr. Bisic hunches over his American-made equipment, reaching out to besieged towns across the mountainous republic that have no other way of communicating. What he and a handful of other radio operators here learn, and pass on to other Bosnians and the outside world, is a piecemeal account of the misery the war has brought to tens of thousands of people in towns that have been surrounded by Serbian troops for as long as three and a half months.

On Saturday night, as he has every night since early April, Mr. Bisic, a 39-year-old land surveyor, was spinning up and down through the frequencies. He was trying to maintain a link to Gorazde, the only predominantly Muslim town in eastern Bosnia that has not yet been captured by the Serbian nationalist forces. If Gorazde falls, as the Bosnian Governement in Sarajevo has predicted it will, many fear there will be little left to distract the Serbian forces from their unrelenting battle for Sarajevo, the capital.

As dusk fell on the hills overlooking the school where he is based in Sarajevo, Mr. Bisic was discussing a cease-fire agreement signed on Friday in London. The accord was signed by the Bosnian government, whose forces hold Sarajevo, Gorazde, and a diminishing number of other towns, and by representatives of the Serbian and Croatian nationalists, who have used their superior military power to carve out their own autonomous states on Bosnian territory.

Most of the military gains have come at the cost of the 1.9 million Muslims who are the largest group in the territory. If honored, the cease-fire would have meant an end to the Serbian attacks on Gorazde at 6 P.M. today, the time set by the London pact for the guns across Bosnia and Herzegovina to fall silent.

If observed in full, the accord would also mean that the people of Gorazde—50,000 to 100,000, according to differing estimates by the Sarajevo Government and by Gorazde's defenders—would be free to leave to seek the food and medical care the Serbian blockade has denied them.

At midnight, six hours after the truce deadline, the defender of Gorazde reported by radio that the city was still being pounded by intense Serbian artillery and mortar fire and that the night sky was lit by fires resulting from the new attack. It was a situation that had been predicted by the defenders during the radio link on Saturday night.

"The whole world must know by now that the Chetniks are liars," said the commander of Gorazde's army, who identified himself only as "Chief."

"They have constantly lied in the past, and anyone who believes they are going to stop their killing now should know that they are still lying," he added.

A Word Adopted With Pride

By Chetniks, the Gorazde commander meant the irregular Serbian forces who have played a major role in the Bosnian fighting and who have claimed the name of the Serbian guerrillas who fought the Nazis in Bosnia during World War II.

The name is used with pride by the Serbian fighters, but as an epithet by those fighting for the Bosnian government. The

Gorazde commander's use of it turned what had been a connection with Sarajevo into a debate with a Serbian military radio operator who had been listening in.

"We'll cut your head off, Turcin," a scratchy voice said, using the Serbo-Croatian word for Turk, which is often used by Serbian nationalists to refer to Bosnian Muslims. This was followed by the sound of music identified by Mr. Bisic as a recording of an old Serbian nationalist song about ancient battles between Serbian armies and the Ottoman Turks.

When the song finished, the intruding voice resumed, "This is a Chetnik in the hills outside Gorazde," the voice said.

Mr. Bisic, who is accustomed to Serbian operators interrupting and drowning out his calls, spun the tuning dial, jumping to an alternate radio frequency prearranged with the Gorazde defenders. But discussion of the situation in the besieged town had hardly begun when the "Chetnik" butted in again, more politely this time but insistent on having his version of the Gorazde battle heard by the reporter at Mr. Bisic's side.

"This reporter gentleman should come to Serbian territory and hear the truth," the man said, this time in English.

Almost immediately, other operators joined the discussion—from Belgrade, the Serbian capital, and from Zagreb, capital of Croatia, as well as from other parts of Bosnia. For an hour, the radio turned into a Balkan seminar, linking fighters and civilians on opposite sides of the bloodshed, each delving into his own version of history.

Mr. Bisic, looking exasperated, stuck with the frequency. "I've heard this all before," he said.

The tale told by the Gorazde commander, typical of those that Mr. Bisic records each night, was grim. The man calling himself "Chief" said that parts of the town center were burning form Serbian incendiary shells, adding to the damage from a week of shelling by Serbian armored units.

The steady barrage has destroyed several factories, the town's main hospital, two emergency clinics, several schools, the main sports hall, the post office, both of the town's drug stores and the bus station.

By the commander's account, Gorazde's last stocks of flour were exhausted last week, ending the baking of bread that has been the town's staple during the siege. He said doctor's were still operating on the wounded with anesthetics and that about 25,000 people in the town, refugees from Serbian attacks elsewhere in eastern Bosnia, were living on the open air.

'We Are Living in Hell'

With gasoline supplies also exhausted, vehicle traffic had been halted, and people were moving about only when mist from the Drina River made the streets invisible to Serbian gunners in the hills.

"We find it hard to believe that we are living in Europe at the end of the 20th century," the Commander said. "We are living a hell here, experiencing horrors that would be hard for anybody that is not here to comprehend."

This was followed by a request in English from another man that a message be relayed to President Bush.

"The people of Gorazde would like to say hello to President Bush," the man said. "Mr. Bush is a great man, he's a great opponent of world terrorism, but please tell him that we need American military intervention, to stop this spilling of innocent blood."

When the fighting in Bosnia and Herzegovina began, the Serbian attackers moved quickly with fighter-bombers and artillery to sever all communication links between Government-held outposts, blasting microwave relays towers and other crucial telephone, television and radio links. The forces struggling to resist the offensives were often totally cut off, while the Serbian troops retained their own communication networks, mainly those of the Serbian-dominated Yugoslav Army.

Mr. Bisic, a leading member of the ham radio club in Sarajevo before the war, stepped into the gap. Recruiting fellow club members, he organized an informal network that began by taking messages from people in besieged towns and villages and relaying them to radio operators elsewhere.

Messages Are Broadcast

Each message is recorded on a thick pad. Messages for Sarajevo, where the radio and television station still operate, are passed on to be broadcast. Responses are relayed by telephone to the radio operators, who pass them on.

The list of messages makes for poignant reading, since many of the earlier ones came from families in Muslim towns in eastern Bosnia like Zvornik, Bratunac, Visegrad and Foca that have since been captured by the Serbian forces, usually with many Muslim dead. Most of the messages were hopeful, in situations that promised little.

One, from Visegrad in early April to relatives in Sarajevo, said simply, "Tell Alija, Hamed and others that we are all safe and sound."

The Bosnian Government army, rapidly organizing itself from the scattered militias that existed when the war began, turned to Mr. Bisic and his fellow operators for help in maintaining its own links across the republic. This added role has turned the elementary school where Mr. Bisic operates from a cramped basement room into a target for the Serbian forces. The building, on one of the highest points in Sarajevo, has been hit several times with artillery shells.

On one occasion, when Mr. Bisic was talking to the Government forces in Mostar, 80 miles south of Sarajevo, a Serbian military operator interrupted to warn that he would be shelled if he continued.

School Is Attacked

When he switched frequencies and continued to take the Mostar report, the school, closed to students for the duration of the fighting, was immediately attacked, and a shell destroyed the antenna that Mr. Bisic had used to relay news of the Bosnian fighting to operators as far away as American Samoa, Hong Kong and Sydney, Australia.

As Mr. Bisic spoke, shells could be heard striking parts of the old Muslim quarter below the school, the explosions reverberating around the hills.

Asked if he was afraid, Mr. Bisic—call sign YU4AAQ—replied: "Anybody in this world who is not afraid is not thinking clearly. The situation arose when we had an opportunity to use the skills we had built up over many years, and it was clear what we should do.

"If we are helping a little bit to lessen the suffering, the effort has been worthwhile."

*   *   *

August 1, 1992

EUROPE'S CAUTION ON BOSNIA PROVOKES GROWING CRITICISM

By Craig R. Whitney
Special to The New York Times

LONDON, July 31—Western European governments are facing increasing public criticism of their muted response to Serbian aggression in the Balkans and the millions of refugees made homeless by the Serbs' policy of "ethnic cleansing." But officials in key European capitals are showing little inclination to take a more active role.

Most European governments have so far confined themselves to symbolic gestures, such as naval monitoring—but not enforcement—of the United Nations economic sanctions against Serbia. But recent news reports that Serbian nationalists have been driving Croat and Muslim men, women and children from their homelands in sealed freight cars and cattle trucks to modern day concentration camps have stirred public outrage.

Prime Minister John Major has called a broad peace conference of foreign ministers and international organizations to discuss the crisis in the Balkans on Aug. 26-28, but some British politicians now are beginning to say that this is not enough.

Ex-Official Criticizes Major

Following a string of vivid press reports about atrocities, a former British Foreign Secretary, Lord Owen, said on Thursday that he had written to Prime Minister John Major demanding immediate military action to stop them.

"When faced with concentration camps and sealed trains, we have done nothing," Lord Owen said in an interview. "We made that mistake with the Jews in the Second World War."

He added that if the Western allies and the United Nations could mobilize to force President Saddam Hussein to stop attacks on the Kurds in Iraq after the war in the Persian Gulf, they should be able to force Serbs to stop attacks against their neighbors in the Balkans as well.

"It is perfectly within the power of NATO" to enforce an immediate cease-fire, he wrote to Mr. Major. "Satellite and air reconnaissance could pinpoint any unauthorized military activity and retaliatory air strikes could be mounted from

NATO airfields that ring Yugoslavia or by planes flying from aircraft carriers. This could be implemented within hours, not even days, once the requisite authority had been got from the U.N. Security Council."

Officials at 10 Downing Street said that Mr. Major had received the letter and would reply in due course, but that Britain's skeptical view of outside military intervention in the Balkans remained unchanged.

President François Mitterrand of France flew into Sarajevo under fire earlier this month, and has assigned French troops to the airlift of food and medicine into the city, but only after making clear that France, too, had no intention of asking the troops to try to enforce peace. Two influential national newspapers, Liberation and Le Monde, wrung their hands this week about the collective European failure to stop the fighting, but stopped short of proposing to send soldiers in to do anything about it.

German officials have been sounding increasingly urgent alarms about the inadequacy of existing measures.

"I grant that we have so far been unsuccessful in stopping this terrible murdering and killing," Foreign Minister Klaus Kinkel said in an interview with the Süddeutsche Zeitung on Wednesday. "I have always said that in the end military intervention should not and cannot be excluded."

Parallels to Nazi Crimes

Some European politicians have drawn parallels between the Serbian actions and what the Nazis did to the Jews and the Slavs in World War II, when Western democracies also stood by until it was too late for millions of Nazi victims.

"Ethnic cleansing" of Muslim and Croatian areas in Bosnia and Herzegovina and elsewhere by Serbian militias has been going on for months, and two and a half million refugees are now homeless in the Balkans, the largest number since World War II.

The Prime Minister of the truncated Yugsolav state, the Yugoslav-born American businessman Milan Panic, has acknowledged that these actions invite comparisons to the Nazi barbarity, and he said here on Thursday that he would go to Sarajevo, the Bosnian capital, to try to stop the fighting.

Paddy Ashdown, the leader of the opposition Liberal Democrats in Britain, said today that he was also going to Croatia and Bosnia "to draw attention to the failure of Britain's Government and governments throughout Europe to rise to this appalling human tragedy." Mr. Ashdown called on the British Government to help create militarily protected safe zones for the refugees in the Balkans, like the ones the allies created for the Kurds in Iraq after the war in the Persian Gulf.

Germany, with a large population of Croatian immigrant laborers, has already accepted more than 200,000 refugees from the fighting, Mr. Kinkel said, but German requests to their European Community partners this week to accept country-by-country quotas fell on deaf ears.

In Austria, where more than 50,000 refugees have already arrived, Chancellor Franz Vranitzky said that the country would be tougher about admitting many more, because Austrians were worried about being overwhelmed by indigent and desperate foreigners. "Now it's time for somebody else to take a turn, not us," Mr. Vranitzky said.

Under another former British Foreign Secretary, Lord Carrington, the European Community has been trying for the past year to mediate negotiations to stop the fighting. But it has become increasingly clear that Lord Carrington's efforts have had little effect on the Serbian nationalists who all European leaders agree are behind the worst violence. On Wednesday, his latest peace effort on Bosnia and Herzegovina ended without progress.

Meanwhile, the fighting continues. The United Nations has neither enough troops nor a mandate to expose them to the kind of hostile environment that would be necessary to impose a ceasefire.

A Mandate to Observe

Adm. Jeremy M. Boorda, an American who commands the NATO task force now in the Adriatic, told reporters here a few days ago that it has a United Nations mandate to observe whether any shipping tries to violate the economic sanctions that were imposed on Serbia earlier this summer, but not to fire a shot if any violations are observed. The Western European Union force operating in close cooperation with NATO operates under the same rules of engagement.

Despite the pressure to change, European governments have yet shown little sign of moving toward military intervention.

"Those who allow Serbia to wage its war are responsible for the streams of refugees," the Frankfurter Allgemeine newspaper wrote last week. "The West is thinking about this, but rethinking by governments has yet to be done."

* * *

August 4, 1992

BOSNIANS PROVIDE ACCOUNTS OF ABUSE IN SERBIAN CAMPS

By STEPHEN ENGELBERG
Special to The New York Times

KARLOVAC, Croatia, Aug. 3—They differ in the details, but the outlines of their stories coincide with chilling clarity. These are Croatian and Muslim refugees who have fled the fighting in Bosnia and Herzegovina, and they speak of having been herded by the tens of thousands into camps were they witnessed beatings and shootings of prisoners by masked Serbian guards.

None of the factories, schools and stores reportedly being used as human holding pens are on the lists of prison camps that Serbian authorities in Bosnia and Herzegovina permit the International Red Cross to visit.

Charges about concentration camps have been raised by all sides in the conflict, often as part of propaganda offensives, and no independent observer or journalist has visited any of the three sites described by these refugees, in Trnopolje, Prijedor and Prnjavor.

Disease a Threat, Too

But the refugees all spoke of heavily guarded places where inmates lived in unspeakably filthy conditions and disease was as much a threat as execution. The refugees sheltering beneath trees in the heat of the makeshift camp 40 miles south of Zagreb did not appear to be recounting rehearsed stories or rumors. Four women and one man all agreed to be quoted by name as they described the three sites, all in northern Bosnia, where they said they themselves were held captive or which they visited.

Three talked of a prison in a primary school in Trnopolje, a village near the Bosnian town of Kozarac.

"They were beating people, killing them," said Rebija Alic, a 32-year-old woman who said she was held there with her 4-year-old son for 17 days. "I saw it."

She said that men and women slept on the tile floors of the classrooms. The guards wore masks, she said, and inmates were allowed only a few drops of dirty water a day from the pump out front.

Mrs. Alic said that food was limited to a piece of bread every two days, although some other witnesses said some local villagers were permitted to bring in additional provisions to friends or relatives.

'Looked Hungry, Thirsty'

Hava Grabic, 39, said she went to a ceramics factory in the nearby city of Prijedor in search of her missing husband. She said she walked the chain-link fence surrounding the building and saw hundreds, perhaps thousands, of men on the other side.

"They were like those hungry people in Africa who crave bread," she said. "They had long hair, beards. They wore rags. They looked hungry, thirsty."

She said she did not see her husband.

Josip Stec, a 56-year-old retired clerk who walks laboriously with the aid of a cane, said he spent 61 days in prison after Serbs moved into his hometown, Kukavica, near Derventa. He acknowledged that his first captors, Serbian military policemen, had treated him "correctly."

But he showed scars on his arms from beatings in a second location, a furniture store in the town of Prnjavor, which he said held 68 men and 15 women. During his time there, Mr. Stec said, he saw a man kicked, pinched and beaten with a pole until he died.

All five people come from the area near Kozarac, a heavily Muslim town that was the target of a Serbian "ethnic cleansing" operation in late May and early June. They said that they saw civilians executed on the spot by men with automatic rifles and that some buildings in the town had been leveled.

Afterward, they said, the survivors were driven to camps in the area between Prijedor and the Serbian stronghold of Banja Luka. Bosnian Government officials have charged that the Serbs held as many as 33,000 people in 13 locations in this area, although some have since been released.

One Woman's Account

Nerima Besic, 25, tells her story in a calm voice, but her hands tremble as she threads a piece of paper over and over between her fingers.

She said two masked Serbs came to the house in Kozarac where she and her mother-in-law were taking shelter with other women and children during shelling.

"They took my sister up to the attic of the house, intending to rape her," she said. "By coincidence they didn't. They brought her back down having done nothing."

"Then they took me," she continued. "They took my child out of my arms and took me away to the ground floor. They took my mother-in-law out and pointed a gun at her, while I was taken to another room where he pointed a gun at me and started taking my clothes off. I begged him and tried to pull away. I hit him. Then he pointed the gun directly at me and I had to do everything he asked for.

"The man who raped me was masked," she said. "But I knew him."

A Beating by 15 Reported

Mrs. Besic said she believed her life was saved when a Serbian policeman, a neighbor, saw from the outside that her mother-in-law was being held at gunpoint and went into the house cursing the two men as "chetniks." The word was used in World War II for anti-fascist Serbian fighters.

Later, she and her mother-in-law were taken to Trnopolje where they were held for a few days and then released. During that time, she said, she saw one person killed in a beating by about 15 Serbs.

Mrs. Besic had an indirect account about a prison camp in Omarska, generally described by Bosnians as among the worst of these places. She said her 15-year-old cousin had been among a small group of very old and very young people released from Omarska.

She quoted her cousin as having said that water was taken into the camp in tanks tainted with oil. She said her cousin, who spent two months in Omarska, had spoken of 5 to 10 people dying every day.

"I'm not sure, I haven't been there," she said simply.

Mrs. Besic said her cousin, "Used to be a tall, strong boy," adding, "Now he's thin and pale, and his head is shaved."

Red Cross Cites Violations

By CHUCK SUDETIC
Special to The New York Times

BELGRADE, Yugoslavia, Aug. 3—After visiting 10 prisons and internment camps throughout Bosnia and Herzegovina, the International Committee of the Red Cross today accused all sides in the four-month conflict of blatantly violating the human rights of civilians.

"Violations of humanitarian law and of basic human rights perpetrated by all parties to the conflict have reached such a point that they have become common practice," said the Red Cross statement, issued today at the headquarters of the organization in Geneva.

The violations have continued despite public and confidential appeals to officials at all levels by Red Cross officials since the fighting began last year, the statement said.

Since July 9, Red Cross teams have visited about 4,000 people held in 10 sites operated by Serbian and Croatian combatants as well as by the Bosnian Government, said Judith Nushagen, a Red Cross spokeswoman in Belgrade.

A Complaint by Belgrade

Officials in Belgrade said the Red Cross had visited only a small number of the civilian internees they believe are being held against their will across Bosnia and Herzegovina, and they complained that the organization's teams were not being given access to all such sites. They said the organization would demand the release of all civilians.

The Red Cross president, Cornelio Sommaruga, said at a United Nations conference in Geneva last week that all of the ethnic groups fighting in Bosnia and Herzegovina had been "cleansing" entire regions of members of opposing ethnic groups.

"Whole populations are being terrorized, minorities intimidated and harassed, civilians interned on a massive scale, hostages taken and torture," Mr. Sommaruga said. "Deportation and summary executions are rife."

The United Nations, the United States and most other Western countries have accused the Serbians of undertaking an operation to expel Muslims and Croats from the so-called Serbian republic they are carving from Bosnia and Herzegovina's territory.

The war in the former Yugoslavia has displaced nearly 2.5 million people and left untold thousands dead.

*   *   *

October 4, 1992

MACEDONIA, IN FIGHT OVER A NAME, IS REELING FROM TRADE EMBARGOES

By DAVID BINDER
Special to The New York Times

WASHINGTON, Oct. 2—Macedonia, the odd republic out in the Yugoslav conflict, is groaning under the weight of trade embargoes imposed by Greece in the south and Serbia in the north, officials here and in the Macedonian capital say.

The embargoes have blocked critically needed imports, especially of oil, two Macedonian officials told members of the Senate Foreign Relations Committee late last month.

Michalis Papaconstantinou, the Greek Foreign Minister, acknowledged this week that Greece had cut off oil supplies to Macedonia. But he said at a news conference here on Thursday that his country was prepared to renew the shipments under a European Community arrangement. "We don't want to do any harm to them," he said.

Issue of Recognition

Three former republics of the old Yugoslav federation—Slovenia, Croatia, and Bosnia and Herzegovina—now enjoy international recognition as sovereign states. And the republics of Serbia and Montenegro, reconstituted as a truncated Yugoslavia, retain widespread diplomatic ties despite the expulsion of Yugoslavia from the United Nations General Assembly and the imposition of heavy sanctions on it.

But Macedonia is recognized by only a handful of countries. The rest are holding off because of objections by Greece. For nearly 12 months, the Athens Government has demanded that Macedonia change its name, asserting that the use of the word "Macedonia" should be the exclusive right of Greeks.

The resumption of oil supplies from Greece has been held up by a Greek demand that the authorities in Skopje sign end-user certificates with a name other than "Macedonia." The Macedonian Government has so far refused.

Economy Falters Week by Week

The Republic of Macedonia is a multi-ethnic country whose majority is Slavic, as is its official language.

Robert Frowick, a retired American ambassador posted to the Macedonian capital of Skopje on an international peace mission, said by telephone that he had noticed a deterioration of the economy in just two weeks.

"It is worse now," he said. "They are in an energy crisis. Precious few tractors are pulling wagons filled with people because there is no fuel for buses."

Mr. Frowick is leading a mission created by the 51-member Conference on Security and Cooperation in Europe in an attempt to prevent the Balkan war from spilling over into Macedonia.

The visiting Macedonian officials, Jane Miljovski, the Minister of Privatization, and Ljube Trpeski, the Minister for Economic Relations, said Greece added to Macedonia's problems last month by imposing a total embargo.

The two officials said that ambulances in their republic lacked fuel to carry sick people and babies, and that there was not enough diesel oil for tractors to haul in the harvest.

'A Very Hungry Winter'

Serbia, which opposes Macedonia's declaration of independence, has barred shipments of vitally needed food to the republic, the officials said.

"We are expecting a very hungry winter," Mr. Miljovski said.

He and Mr. Trpeski attended the annual International Monetary Fund meeting here late last month in an effort to get some financial relief for their country, but to no avail.

"We need the I.M.F. endorsement to help attract business to Macedonia," Mr. Miljovski said. "The Greek blockade, especially, is killing us."

The two Macedonians also called on Senator Claiborne Pell, the chairman of the Committee on Foreign Relations, but they immediately faced a seemingly impossible demand.

"Just drop the name 'Macedonia' and everything will be all right," the Rhode Island Democrat said by way of greeting.

*   *   *

October 13, 1992

STOP SERBIA. BOMB SERBIA

By DON M. SNIDER

WASHINGTON—Western intervention in the former Yugoslavia has been impeded by a lack of agreement on long-term goals and by the urgency of attending to humanitarian help. In Sunday's debate, President Bush repeated that he was opposed to committing U.S. forces to the region.

But the ends that Mr. Bush and other Western leaders should seek are now clear, if they were not earlier. With Serbia prepared to move on two new fronts—against the Hungarian minority in the Vojvodina region of northern Serbia and the Albanian majority in the Kosovo region—the West cannot just provide another hapless negotiator with no power to back up its words.

To keep the conflict from spreading, a coalition of democratic powers under the United Nations should use a military force against Serbia, including a strategic air campaign, along with economic and political pressures. Fortunately, U.S. technological strength makes this undertaking possible, in concert with our allies.

Make no mistake: this would be a campaign to isolate Serbian leaders from the civilized world and inflict maximum destruction on their military. The aim is not simply to punish, but to demonstrate to Serbian leaders that only through accommodation can they avoid such continuing pain in the future. Exploiting this ability to hurt creates bargaining power for ultimate diplomatic resolution.

The campaign would have three components. First, the coalition should tighten the U.N. economic and arms embargo to quarantine Serbia. All commerce must stop, including telecommunications and transportation links to other countries. The coalition would need a naval contingent for the Danube as well as ground forces on major transportation arteries. The militaries of our European allies have the means to do this.

Second, since Western powers are wisely unwilling to join an unconventional ground war, the coalition should arm— and perhaps train—the Bosnian forces willing to fight and sacrifice for their freedom. Right now, the Yugoslav Army backing the Serbs in Bosnia has an uncontested military advantage. Banning Serbian military flights in the region would negate Belgrade's overwhelming air-power advantage within Bosnia. At the same time, U.N. forces should greatly increase humanitarian aid.

The third component is a strategic air campaign by the coalition against Serbian military targets, wherever they are located. These would include airfields, military installations, arms depots, power plants and communications lines. As they did against Iraq, American and coalition air forces, with Stealth aircraft and cruise missiles, can quickly neutralize Serbian air defenses. The allied air forces could then strike with relative impunity from bases close by in NATO countries, as well as from offshore carriers and other vessels.

Such a military plan certainly carries risks. The Serbians may respond by stepping up their brutal "ethnic cleansing" in the near term. There may be more casualties among civilians and U.N. forces in Bosnia. The air campaign would put American fliers in danger. But there will be no risk of escalation, since coalition forces will use maximum force from the start. Perhaps the greatest risk of this campaign is that it sets up a potentially protracted contest of political will between the coalition and the renegade nation. The West must be prepared to inflict punishment longer than Serbian leaders can tolerate.

Yet these risks are less of a threat to U.S. interests than doing nothing and allowing Serbia, and every other renegade nation, to flout norms of international and human relations.

The objectives are clear as are the measures of success. And most important, this plan emphasizes the strengths of the U.S. and coalition military forces. We need to respond to the crisis now and fight on our terms, not theirs.

Don M. Snider, deputy director of political military studies at the Center for Strategic and International Studies, served on the staff of the National Security Council in the Reagan and Bush Administration.

*   *   *

October 22, 1992

SERBS AND CROATS NOW JOIN IN DEVOURING BOSNIA'S LAND

By JOHN F. BURNS
Special to The New York Times

SARAJEVO, Bosnia and Herzegovina, Oct. 21—After months of merciless artillery bombardment, this mostly mountainous republic has been reduced to a handful of desperate cities and towns controlled by the Government, with its people increasingly accepting that their struggle for survival is lost.

Outside Sarajevo, Serbian forces have seized at least two-thirds of the country. Croatian troops control most of the rest.

But what deepens the pessimism is the realization that the Croatian forces have turned their backs on their onetime Bosnian allies and are now joining with the Serbs to carve up Bosnian territory for themselves.

Bosnia Being Partitioned

Indeed these two sides are now mopping up and consolidating their gains in areas that nationalist leaders in their respective homelands have coveted for a century.

Since April, the Serbian nationalists have unleashed murderous fusillades on Sarajevo that have made casualties of at least 10 percent of the 400,000 residents. The Serbian strategy has been to force the city to yield without a battle because of the pressure of hunger, shelling and winter cold.

The Serbian forces have long enjoyed the logistical support of what remains of Yugoslavia, which is dominated by the republic of Serbia. But of equal significance, the Croatian Defense Council, which has been leading the Croatian drive, has received weapons, troops and leadership from Croatia's army, based in Zagreb.

"The Croats have proclaimed a Croatian state within the state of Bosnia and Herzegovina," said Emir Fazilbegovic, a member of the Muslim Council in Mostar, 85 miles southwest of the capital. "Muslims now see no difference between the policies of the Serbian and Croatian leaderships."

A significant sign of cooperation between Serbs and Croats in carving up Bosnia occurred earlier this month when Franjo Tudjman, the Croatian president, ordered Croatian forces under the control of the Bosnian wing of Croatia's governing party to pull out of Bosanski Brod, a refinery town along the Sava River border between Croatia and Bosnia.

The pullout left Serbian forces with only two remaining hurdles to completing a corridor between Belgrade in the east and Serbian-controlled areas of Croatia in the west.

Gains for Croatia

And while international attention has been centered on the Serbian offensives, Croatian forces have seized control of a broad chunk of Bosnia west and south of Sarajevo. From the Croatian headquarters in Mostar, forces of the Croatian Defense Council, nominally allied to the Bosnian army but in practice following Mr. Tudjman's orders, have cemented control of western Herzegovina, where more than 90 percent of the population are Croats.

From there, they have pushed north and east, capturing towns and villages where Croats and Muslims are about equally numerous.

In areas of eastern Herzegovina, where Serbs are more numerous, more signs of a Serbian and Croatian accord to partition Bosnia are showing up.

According to Bosnian officials, Croatia has agreed not to challenge Serbian control of the region around Trebinje, in a southern triangle of Bosnia adjacent to Montenegro, Serbia's ally in the truncated federation of what was once Yugoslavia.

Croatian Dissident Assassinated

In August, these accounts say, Croatia arranged for Croatian Defense Council troops to ambush and assassinate Blaz Kraljevic, commander of a fiercely anti-Serbian Croatian military faction known as the Croatian Armed Forces, when Mr. Kraljevic's units challenged Serbian units around Trebinje.

For months, Mr. Tudjman, the Croatian leader, encouraged the Bosnian Government to hope that Croatia would join the battle against Serbian forces, particularly around Sarajevo.

But pledges given to the President of Bosnia and Herzegovina, Alija Izetbegovic, in visits to Zagreb were not fulfilled, and Mr. Tudjman has recently dropped the pretense of being Mr. Izetbegovic's ally.

Shift in Alliances

Instead the Croatian leader has been speaking as if his alliance is with Slobodan Milosevic, the Serbian leader, and

The New York Times

In Bosnia and Herzegovina, Serbs and Croats are consolidating gains in areas long coveted.

Government-controlled newspapers in Zagreb have been attacking the Izetbegovic Government as "a hotbed of Islamic fundamentalists."

In Sarajevo, and in the handful of other towns under Government control, the collusion between Serbia and Croatia in partitioning Bosnia has fostered an increasing militancy among hard-line Muslims, particularly in the private militia groups that form a large part of Bosnian fighting strength.

Threat of Assassination

Privately, some of these Muslim militia commanders have threatened to assassinate Mr. Izetbegovic or any other Bosnian official who accepts a peace settlement at the Geneva talks that stops short of rolling back the gains that Serbian and Croatian forces have made.

"If Izetbegovic or anybody else thinks that we have fought as long as we have to capitulate now, they will not live five minutes," one militia commander said. He was speaking at a frontline Bosnian position in Stup, a western suburb of Sarajevo where Croatian troops pulled back in September and allowed Serbian units to tighten the Sarajevo siege.

The Bosnian Government's hopes for survival had once rested on Western military intervention, the possibility of an effective military alliance with Croatian forces, or perhaps a coup in Belgrade that might have toppled Mr. Milosevic's nationalist government.

A Tour of the Front

Mr. Izetbegovic has turned recently to a clandestine tour of the few patches of territory his Government still controls, usually to proclaim that the battle for a sovereign, unified Bosnia will continue.

And although those in power here accept that Serbia and Croatia have effectively annexed most of the country, and that the Muslim-led Bosnian militia can only hope to hang on to the little it still holds, they still say they are a long way from giving up.

"We know only too well that fighting on involves enormous hardships and dangers, but the alternative would be still worse," said Kemal Muftic, a senior adviser in Mr. Izetbegovic's office. "What faces us is genocide, the extinction of the Muslim people of Bosnia, and the end of 500 years of history. So we must either confront our enemies now, with all that entails, or accept still greater suffering and death."

Appeal for Outside Aid

For months, senior officials here have been speaking in apocalyptic terms, partly out of a desire to prick the conscience of the United States and its European allies, which have said that they have no intention of committing troops here in support of the Bosnian Government.

But by almost every measure—casualty counts, refugees, cities and towns emptied of their populations or substantially destroyed, reports from the battlefronts of new setbacks and defeats—the situation facing the government and those who depend on it could scarcely be worse.

All figures here tend to be sketchy, since the Government has no telephone connections outside Sarajevo, and the reports it does receive, by messengers traveling through the mountains and by shortwave radio links, are taken mostly from those areas it still controls. These are augmented by sketchy accounts from tens of thousands of Muslim refugees who survived Serbian "ethnic cleansing" offensives only to end up living with a few miserable bundles of belongings in tent camps and school gymnasiums.

From these sources, the Health Ministry in Sarajevo has estimated that 127,000 people are dead or missing, of whom 16,000 have been confirmed as having been killed. Hospitals and clinics are said to have treated 129,000 people who have been wounded. In Sarajevo alone, more than 3,700 people have been killed, 30,000 wounded, and 7,150 have been listed as missing.

As for property damage, the Health Ministry has said that 80 percent of all the hospitals and clinics in the country have been heavily damaged or destroyed, at a replacement cost of at least $2 billion.

Recently, the worst news has come from the battlefront. In hospital wards in Sarajevo, men, women and children with debilitating wounds lie listening to radios that blare scratchy accounts recorded from short-wave radio links with

towns like Gradacac and Jajce and Bihac, Government-held outposts that have been hanging on in the face of relentless Serbian offensives.

For weeks, there have been nothing but reverses, each one tightening the pocket around the Government forces and the mostly Muslim populations of the besieged towns.

Dream Stillborn

Just 200 days ago, on April 6, Bosnia and Herzegovina emerged from 1,000 years of tumultuous history to a status many Bosnians had dreamed of since childhood—that of an independent state, recognized by the major powers of Europe, with many of its mixed population of Muslims, Serbs and Croats eager to put years of Communist stagnation as a republic of Yugoslavia behind them.

Now, the dream has been shattered by a war of a scale and malevolence not seen in Europe since 1945.

According to documents possessed by the Bosnian Government, Mr. Milosevic and Radovan Karadzic, the 47-year-old psychiatrist who leads the Serbian nationalists in Bosnia, secretly agreed to annex what they referred to in their own internal messages as a "frame" around the small heartland of Bosnia.

The mood of desperation in Bosnia was captured two weeks ago when the Government commander in Tuzla, center of Bosnia's chemical industry, threatened to create an ecological disaster by dynamiting railroad cars and trucks full of chloride and chlorine.

Threat to Poison River

In Jajce, a besieged town 60 miles northwest of Sarajevo, another commander threatened to pour cyanide into the Vrbas River, sending it downstream to the junction with the Sava.

The Tuzla commander, Zeljko Knez, said that use of the chemicals was all that was left to the Tuzla defenders after Croatian forces had intercepted and confiscated arms supplies.

"We have been reduced to the point where we can no longer mount an adequate defense," he said.

In his tour of Government-held areas, Mr. Izetbegovic is said to have worked to undermine Mr. Tudjman's control of Croatian Defense Council forces by appealing to units with large numbers of Muslim fighters to support the Government in defiance of Mr. Tudjman's orders. In Mostar, the commander of the Croatian units, Jasmin Jaganac, is a Muslim, and in some areas Muslims are said to comprise nearly half of the Croatian forces' fighting strength.

Croatia Controls Supplies

But the Croatian units' arms supplies and finance come through Croatia, and so far there has been no sign of Croatian units, some of them only 20 miles from Sarajevo, helping to break the Serbian siege.

Nor has there been any let-up in a practice sanctioned by Mr. Tudjman, of imposing a "war tax" of 30 percent on all supplies and arms funneled through Croatian-held areas to Sarajevo. Often, the supplies, costing millions of dollars in cash to black marketeers, have been seized before reaching the city.

Before the latest round of the Geneva talks on the future of the Balkans, which began on Monday, Mr. Tudjman said that he expected an agreement establishing a formal cease-fire between Croatian and Serbian forces in Bosnia. In other interviews, he has suggested that the "Muslims," meaning the Bosnian Government, may have to accept that they have been reduced to a rump of central Bosnia, where they can establish what the Croatian leader has called "a small Muslim and Islamic state," separate from other Bosnian territories that could be annexed to Croatia and Serbia.

* * *

October 25, 1992

A BOSNIAN MOVIE MAKER LAMENTS THE DEATH OF THE YUGOSLAV NATION

By DAVID BINDER

He is a displaced person: a Bosnian who cannot return to Bosnia, a Slav of Muslim origin who never practiced Islam, a Yugoslav patriot whose Yugoslav culture has been demolished.

Emir Kusturica, the director from Sarajevo whose films have won major international awards, is living the title of his last movie, "Time of the Gypsies." As he alternates residences between a room in Morningside Heights in Manhattan and an apartment in Paris, he wonders whether anything remains of his family memorabilia in his place of birth, the shattered capital of Bosnia and Herzegovina.

Talk pours out of him like the water of the swift-flowing rivers of his homeland; he spoke recently for a stretch of three hours in an Upper West Side cafe near Columbia University, where, with breaks for filming, he teaches film studies.

"I never wanted an independent Bosnia," he said of his homeland, the breakaway Yugoslav republic now engulfed by war. "I wanted Yugoslavia. That is my country."

He said that for several years after Tito died in 1980, "Yugoslavia was a kind of superpower. Great movies. Beautiful novels. Great rock-and-roll. We became a superpower in basketball.

"The problem is that people needed to identify more strongly with it after Tito and his awful, tricky way of leading the country," Mr. Kusturica said. "Instead, religion got in the way through nationalism—the same as 500 years ago—as the main generator of emotions. At a certain moment, Yugoslavia stopped being rational, and then you end up going to war."

At the beginning of October, Mr. Kusturica, 37 years old, returned briefly to a fragment of the former Yugoslavia, the Montenegrin coastal town of Herceg Novi. He went there to bury his father, who had died of a heart attack at age 70 in an apartment the son had leased after getting him out of the war zone.

"This war killed him, too," he said. "My father got hit by invisible lightning. I compare the death of my father and the death of the country."

While on the Adriatic coast, the director encountered Bosnian Serbs on furlough from the front lines of fighting in the republic. One of them related an experience that to Mr. Kusturica epitomized the absurdity of the Balkan war.

"I spoke to a Serbian warrior who told me of coming home to his apartment in Bosnia and finding it looted—by Serbs—but not just stealing his belongings and money," Mr. Kusturica said. "They actually scraped the wallpaper off his walls." He said the pillagers apparently presumed that the dwelling belonged not to a Serb but to a Muslim.

'Plunder on All Sides'

"Scratching off wallpaper, that is the symbol of this war," Mr. Kusturica said. "The essence of this war is plunder on all sides. In May, Muslim militiamen looted my father's apartment in Sarajevo. They even took my film prizes."

Mr. Kusturica said his personal heritage reflects the essential Bosnian experience of domination by the Ottoman Turks from the 15th century until early this century.

"I am a living illustration of Bosnian mixing and converting," he said. "My grandparents lived in eastern Herzegovina. Very poor. The Turks came and brought Islam. There were three brothers in the family. One was Orthodox Christian. The other two took Islam to survive."

Bosnians, in Mr. Kusturica's view, are not very religious, and though he read the Bible and the Koran "for personal education," he described himself as having "a nice pagan, tolerant point of view." This, he said, corresponds to the "certain paganism which appears in paintings, in movies, in books" that is characteristic of Bosnian culture, although Bosnia was also a nexus of Catholic, Orthodox and Islamic faiths and a center of Jewish culture as well.

Mr. Kusturica's films have almost by definition been transcultural—the oddball Sarajevo love story, "Do You Remember Dolly Bell?" which won the Gold Lion award at the 1981 Venice Film Festival; the growing-up-in-Sarajevo story, "When Father Was Away on Business," which won the Golden Palm in Cannes in 1985, and "Time of the Gypsies," about a Gypsy boy lured abroad from Yugoslavia by an unscrupulous con man, which helped him win Italy's prestigious Rossellini award for directing in 1989. His Sarajevo films got him into a lot of trouble with Bosnian Muslims "because I showed that Muslims could be silly, too."

He has just completed his first English-speaking film, a view of American society called "Arizona Dream," which is scheduled for release early next year, and he soon will start work on a version of "Crime and Punishment" set in Brighton Beach.

A conversation with Emir Kusturica (his name is pronounced EH-meer KOO-stoor-eet-sah) comes back again and again to Ivo Andric, the Bosnian writer who won the Nobel Prize for Literature in 1961 for his epic "Bridge on the Drina." The late author's 100th birthday on Oct. 10 went unmarked in the lands of the former Yugoslavia.

Since Mr. Andric's death in 1975, Mr. Kusturica has wanted to make a film based on the novel, which chronicles

Bosnian history using the Turkish bridge of stone at Visegrad and the role it plays in the lives of people living along the river. "I should make this film," he said. "But they would kill me."

A Literary Hero

"It is like the Bible," he said. "Andric was a Serb, with a Croat name, Ivo. He was one of the very few people who understood Bosnian Muslims. He tells what it means when people's minds are poisoned. But I know people in Sarajevo who think Andric was a criminal." One of those, he said, is Alija Izetbegovic, the President of Bosnia and Herzegovina, who is a Muslim fundamentalist.

He said that when a Muslim blew up the Andric statue at the Visegrad bridge, the Izetbegovic Government hailed the bomber as a hero. "You can't lead the country thinking Andric was an awful writer and a bad person," he said.

At 6 feet 3 inches and 185 pounds, Mr. Kusturica has the look of an athlete. He was once offered a contract by a soccer team, he said. "I was a big fighter when I was younger," he recalled. "In bars I was ready to explode and fight.

"The last fight I had was in Sarajevo," he said. "May 1990, a literary club was to be opened, with a chair dedicated to Andric. I was invited to speak. I was going to read an Andric story on hatred in Bosnia. Before I came to it, a drunk poet, not a good poet, started screaming, 'You traitors, Serbs, go to Belgrade! This is not Belgrade!' A second, a third time. He was destroying the evening. I just lost it. I pulled him out. I hit him. I came back breathing hard while I was reciting Andric, that Andric warning against hatred. Next day those small Titoists who became democrats all of a sudden started attacking me as a Serb.

"That was the time I said, 'So long.'"

Was the creation of Yugoslavia—mixing nations, religions and languages under one Government—a mistake? "I don't think so. No Yugoslavia means no Andric."

Could he return to Sarajevo?

"I don't think so. They told me they're going to kill me if I came."

* * *

October 30, 1992

IN A 'CLEANSED' BOSNIAN TOWN, CROATS, NOT SERBS, AIM GUNS

By JOHN F. BURNS
Special to The New York Times

PROZOR, Bosnia and Herzegovina, Oct. 29—In the year of "ethnic cleansing," there is little in this mountain town that is not chillingly familiar.

Stores and restaurants still burn on the main street, three days after notices were posted on lampposts and shattered storefronts ordering the pillaging halted. Along forest roads leading from the town, terrified Muslim refugees hasten away with pitiful bundles of belongings.

Heavily built men in camouflage gear lounge amid the ruins, engaging in sporadic looting and insisting that nothing terrible has happened.

Serbs Are Spectators

The scene has been played out scores of times since Serbian nationalist troops began offensives across Bosnia and Herzegovina in April, emptying towns and villages of Muslims so that the land could be claimed for a Serbian ministate free of other ethnic groups.

But here, Serbian soldiers have been spectators, watching from gun batteries in the hills while another unsparing army, of Croatian nationalists, has inflicted its wrath on Muslim townspeople.

"Kill, kill," a young Muslim man with brimming tears whispered in English to a reporter who drove into Prozor past roadblocks of suspicious Croatian troops to find what has become a ghost town. "They kill all—man, woman, child, no difference. It is great tragedy."

Of at least 5,000 Muslims who lived here quietly until last week, the only ones remaining were on a hill a few hundred yards from the main street, apparently under arrest by Croatian forces.

How many Muslims died here is impossible to tell. But the extensive damage to the town, and accounts given to reporters by refugees in the hills who spoke of Croatian fighters storming through the streets, shouting through megaphones, "Come on boys, let's get the filthy Muslims!" suggested that the estimate given by the town's Croatian Mayor, Mijo Jozic, of 6 Muslims dead and 68 wounded was probably low. The Muslim-led Government in Sarajevo, 40 miles to the east, has estimated at least 300 Muslim casualties here.

Before the war that has broken Bosnia and Herzegovina into a jagged patchwork of territories ruled by ethnic warlords, Prozor was a quiet mountain town where the main activity was a bicycle factory that shipped its products to Austria and Germany.

But since Friday, the factory has been a Croatian military headquarters, and Prozor has become synonymous, among Bosnian Muslims, with the collapse of an alliance between Muslims and Croats that the Muslims had counted on in their increasingly desperate war with the Serbs.

No More Pretense

Starting 10 days ago, and spreading quickly through the towns and villages that cluster along the Bosna and Vrbas rivers north and west of Sarajevo, Croatian troops have forsaken the pretense of a pact with the Muslims to preserve Bosnia and Herzegovina as a sovereign state.

Instead, the Croats have followed the Serbian lead, fighting street battles with the Muslim-led forces of the Sarajevo Government in what appears to be a bid to consolidate the frontiers of a Croatian ministate.

Localized fighting has erupted at half a dozen towns along the river valleys, some of it, as in the town of Vitez, involving such matters as which side will control the local gas station. But a drive along 200 miles of mountain highways and dirt tracks in the region reveals a pattern of an impatient and often ruthless bid to impose exclusive Croatian control over an area where Croats and Muslims have lived side by side for centuries.

The fighting has mostly subsided, with sullen standoffs in towns like Vitez, Travnik and Novi Travnik. But urgent appeals by the Muslim-led Bosnian Government, fighting to hold onto a handful of towns from its seat in Sarajevo, appear unlikely to persuade the Bosnian Croats and the man who ultimately controls their fighting units, President Franjo Tudjman of Croatia, to revive the alliance.

An Ideal Appears Dead

What has happened here—and especially the Croatian onslaught in Prozor, where the Croatian fighters appear to have been merciless in their attacks on Muslims—has sounded across Bosnia like a death knell. In the spring and summer, when Serbian fighters were seizing two-thirds of this former Yugoslav republic, the ideal proclaimed in Sarajevo—that Muslims, Serbs and Croats could somehow come together again in a single state—had seemed more and more unrealizable. Now it looks all but dead.

With their tightening control up and down the valleys around Prozor, the Croatian forces have virtually completed their takeover of western Herzegovina, where 90 percent of the residents are Croats. With this and a few other parcels of land around predominantly Croatian population centers in northern Bosnia, they have assembled the territory they need for their ministate, which they have named Herzeg-Bosna.

Croatian and Serbian forces are fighting now in only a few places, where their ministates overlap, and even these battles are rapidly diminishing.

At dusk today, the Sarajevo Government announced that Serbian forces had captured the mixed Croatian and Muslim town of Jajce, 50 miles northwest of Sarajevo, which a joint Croatian and Muslim force had defended since the war began. Jajce, with 10,000 residents, was one of only half a dozen towns of any size still under the Sarajevo Government's control.

Holding onto the town, when the only path through the Serbian siege lines was a mountain track that was used only at night by vehicles with extinguished lights, had become increasingly difficult. But reports from the area said the Serbs did not break through until this morning, after the town's fate was sealed by mistrust between the Croatian and Muslim defenders.

Feud Leads to Downfall

Ivica Saric, a Croatian spokesman, told reporters that survivors of the Croatian units that were overrun in Jajce reached Travnik today after hiking through the mountains and reported that the Croatian and Bosnian Government units had begun feuding in Jajce after fighting between the two groups erupted elsewhere.

"They said the reason Jajce fell was the distrust between Croatian and Muslim soldiers," Mr. Saric said.

Although powerful officials in the Sarajevo Government have advocated fighting a two-front war with the Serbian and Croatian forces, President Alija Izetbegovic argued successfully in emergency meetings last weekend that the Muslims had no choice but to try to renew the alliance with the Croats.

Part of Mr. Izetbegovic's reasoning was that Mr. Tudjman, the Croatian leader, is not likely to make the partitioning of this republic into Serbian and Croatian ministates official for fear that Croatia could be subjected to United Nations trade sanctions, as the truncated Serbian-dominated Yugoslavia was in May after the offensives in Bosnia began.

Also, the Croatian forces include thousands of Muslim fighters. Many of these, as well as at least some Croats, are opposed to the partitioning of Bosnia.

At the Croatian headquarters in Prozor, where scores of fighters were relaxing after seizing the town, some said they still considered the Serbs the enemy and the Muslims as potential allies.

"Don't forget, most Croats here voted for an independent Bosnia back in February," said a 38-year-old commander, who gave his name only as Zeljko. "If the politicians can work out the details, that would still be the first choice."

But talks between Muslim, Serbian and Croatian leaders in Geneva have deadlocked, with the Serbs and Croats holding out for powerful ethnically based governments in areas under their control, and the Muslims, the largest ethnic group, opposing any breakup along ethnic lines.

Meanwhile, Herzeg-Bosna, the Croatian ministate, as well as the ministate proclaimed by the Bosnian Serb leaders in April, are operating like provinces of Croatia and Serbia. The Croatian dinar is the currency in Herzeg-Bosna, and Croatian flags, with their red and white checkerboard badge, fly in every village and town.

And after the bloodshed in Prozor, it would seem that re-establishing a normal life between Croats and Muslims could take years. From accounts given by Muslims, it seemed clear that Croatian units showed little restraint once they gained the upper hand.

An indication of the Croats' attitude could be found in the fact that some Croatian fighters encountered along the main street wore armbands with skull-and-crossbones motifs and the letter U for Ustashe, the World War II Nazi collaborators who ruled Croatia and Bosnia with great brutality. One teenage fighter posed for photographs in front of burning Muslim stores in a wartime German officer's cap bearing an Iron Cross.

While the handful of Muslims encountered in the town appeared too frightened to talk, except in quick bursts when the Croatian fighters were out of earshot, those who reached predominantly Muslim villages in the surrounding hills offered grim accounts of Croatian units firing at random on houses and stores, then sending tractors through the town to collect bodies.

Many of the Muslims said they had lost touch with family members, and were trekking from village to village looking for survivors.

*   *   *

April 25, 1993

SERBS AGAIN REJECT VANCE-OWEN PEACE PROPOSALS

By JOHN DARNTON
Special to The New York Times

BELGRADE, Yugoslavia, April 24—Courting the risk of allied air strikes and virtually assuring that new international sanctions will descend on Yugoslavia on Monday, the leader of the Bosnian Serbs said today that a proposal to link Serbian enclaves in Bosnia with a demilitarized corridor was not acceptable.

After meeting for three hours with Lord Owen, who is trying to mediate an end to the Bosnian war, the Serbian leader, Radovan Karadzic, said the latest version of the peace plan "is absolutely anti-Serb" and "didn't meet a single Serbian need."

Western diplomats said more talks could be held on Sunday, when Lord Owen is to return from an overnight trip to Zagreb, Croatia.

He is also supposed to meet again with Slobodan Milosevic, the President of Serbia, who is widely assumed to call the shots for the Serbs in Bosnia. The ability of the Serbs in Bosnia to continue their battle for territory depends on the Serbian-dominated Yugoslav federation of Serbia and Montenegro.

Among the Dandelions

With the United Nations deadline for acceptance of the plan creeping closer, diplomats could not rule out an 11th-hour move by the Bosnian Serbs to wrest some final concessions that would lead them to a grudging acceptance of the peace plan.

But most thought that was unlikely, given the vehemence of Dr. Karadzic's rejection, and they viewed his stand as a critical step toward deeper international involvement.

The meeting today took place in a villa on the outskirts of Belgrade, a pale yellow stucco house with drawn shades and an overgrown lawn resplendent with yellow dandelions. As the talks wore on, more and more maps—ever larger—were sent for and delivered.

But when Lord Owen left, he pushed through a mob of reporters, his face drawn. Asked if any progress had been made, he responded with a curt no.

Plugging Loopholes

The rejection means that sanctions mandating the seizure of all Yugoslavia's assets abroad and prohibiting the transshipment of goods across Yugoslavia will automatically come into effect on Monday. These steps are expected to plug major loopholes in a trade embargo imposed a year ago that is already choking the Yugoslav economy.

The New York Times

At the same time, the intransigence of the Serbs will test the patience of the Clinton Administration, which is under growing pressure to take military action to end "ethnic cleansing" and to support the Muslim-led Bosnian Government.

President Clinton said on Friday that he was giving serious consideration to air strikes against Serbian positions, adding that he expected that European allies would join Washington in such an action.

The foreign ministers of the European Community met in Denmark today to weigh military action. For Britain and France, which both have troops with the United Nations peacekeeping forces in Bosnia, a decision to bomb Serbs could expose their soldiers to retaliation.

Any decision on military strikes could also be complicated by the long siege of Srebrenica. Under a cease-fire agreement, Muslim defenders surrendered some weapons to United Nations troops there, or slipped through the encircling Serbian lines. Now all that is protecting a desperate and hungry civilian population of some 30,000 Muslims from attack by Serbian artillery is a lightly armed 145-member United Nations force from Canada.

The Offer of a Corridor

The five-day mission to the region by Lord Owen, the European Community mediator, had the air of a last-ditch attempt to win approval of the peace plan that he devised with Cyrus R. Vance, who was the United Nations mediator. The plan would carve Bosnia into 10 semiautonomous provinces virtually parceled out among Muslims, Croats and Serbs.

The Croats and Muslims have signed the agreement. In an effort to overcome the objections of the Serbs, Lord Owen has proposed a 6-mile-wide, 50-mile-long corridor patrolled by United Nations forces that would link the Serbian area around Banja Luka in northwestern Bosnia with the Serbian province in the east, which borders the republic of Serbia in Yugoslavia.

The corridor, while not under Serbian sovereignty, would at least provide a transit link, as the Berlin corridor linked the city to West Germany during the cold war, Lord Owen said.

Dr. Karadzic rejected both the corridor and the historical analogy.

"The German corridor went through Germany," he said, "but that is not the case here," meaning that the Bosnian corridor would traverse territory held by Croats. Without a more solid corridor under their own jurisdiction, the Serbs living in the northwestern Bosnia would flee in terror, he suggested.

'We Should Be Separated'

"We asked Lord Owen, where are we going to put 500,000 Serbs who would run away?" Dr. Karadzic told reporters. He said that he took the threat of Western air strikes very seriously, but that he had no alternative to rejecting the proposal.

Insisting that Serbs, Croats and Muslims had been fighting for centuries, he castigated the West for pressing a plan that would force them to live in the same country. "Why are you pushing us together, like a dog and a cat in the same box?" he asked. "We can't live together. We should be separated to be good neighbors."

This statement pointed toward the resolution preferred by the Bosnian Serbs. They want to sit down with the Croats and perhaps the Muslims and simply cut the country into three parts.

The Serbs, who control about 70 percent of Bosnia, would be in a dominant bargaining position. They would most likely try to arrange a trade with the Croats that would give the Serbs their corridor in exchange for a more consolidated Croatian area around Mostar and other towns in the southwest.

'Greater Serbia'

The Serbs have other objections to the Vance-Owen map. They feel it deprives them of major industrial areas and power stations. They also want more territory around Trebinje in the south and in the northwest.

The self-styled parliament of the Bosnian Serbs is meeting today and Sunday in Bijeljina, in northeastern Bosnia, to reconsider the Vance-Owen plan, which Dr. Karadzic said he would present without recommending acceptance or rejection. The parliament, which is even more militant than he is, already turned it down on April 2.

The parliament voted to establish an assembly between Serbs in Croatia and Serbs in western Bosnia, a step that Croats and Muslims are bound to regard as a provocative move toward creation of a "greater Serbia."

*   *   *

April 25, 1993

DOES THE WORLD STILL RECOGNIZE A HOLOCAUST?

By JOHN DARNTON

BELGRADE, Yugoslavia—Lady Thatcher, in her scorching indictment of Western inaction over Bosnia and Herzegovina two weeks ago, said: "I never thought I'd see another holocaust in my life." And then to her fellow Tory, Prime Minister John Major, she gave the unkindest cut of all. During the Battle of Britain the country was overwhelmed and inadequately prepared, she said, but at least it had "a Prime Minister with a lion heart." The implication was unmistakable: Mr. Major is no Churchill—he is Neville Chamberlain.

Not for half a century has the world witnessed events in Europe that have stirred such an agonizing echo of past horrors. The television footage of houses reduced to rubble, the bombed-out churches and mosques, the lined-up bodies and mass graves—they all evoke the flickering black-and-white newsreels of World War II. The words "genocide," "massacre," "holocaust," "civilian bombing" and "ethnic cleansing" haunt everyday speech and stir up guilt-ridden memories like smoke rising from a crematorium.

For European leaders and now, especially, the Clinton Administration, the ever-worsening events in what once was Yugoslavia throw up difficult questions: When does dithering negotiation turn into appeasement? Is it finally time for intervention?

Last week the questions were thrown into the sharpest relief by a letter from 12 State Department officials to Secretary of State Warren Christopher, telling him that the course of diplomacy followed so far had failed and urging him to advocate the use of military force to save the Muslims of eastern Bosnia. The stakes were larger than Bosnia alone, the letter said, because failure to take military action there, it said, "would teach would-be conquerors and ethnic bigots throughout the world that their crimes will go unpunished."

Throughout the conflict, the most compelling argument for not getting involved in the defense of Bosnia against Serbian nationalists has been that outside meddling might only raise the general level of suffering and death. But just in the last two weeks, Western sufferance for the Serbian nationalists has been strained more than ever as they relentlessly hammered Srebrenica to the point of submission. And there now seems less reason than ever to hope that the way to contain the evil let loose in the Balkans is to let the conflict just play itself out. Last week, even as Serbian ethnic cleansing went unpunished in the east, Croats and Muslims who had been nominal allies fell upon each other in spasms of their own ethnic cleansing, rending villages where Croats and Muslims had long lived side by side.

By coincidence last week, Poland commemorated the 50th anniversary of the Warsaw ghetto uprising—the insurrection against the Nazis by several hundred Jewish fighters that is the 20th century's most powerful example of heroic resistance against insurmountable odds. But it also carries a message of universal reproach, for during the uprising, which led to the razing of the ghetto and was a critical chapter in the extermination of Poland's Jews, the world stood by and did nothing. A parallel to ships filled with Jewish refugees searching for a harbor can be found today, when refugees from the fighting in Bosnia and Croatia are kept out of most European countries and form huge crowds outside embassies in Belgrade in hopeless quests for visas.

The point was made Thursday at the opening of the Holocaust Memorial Museum in Washington, when Elie Wiesel, the Nobel Prize-winning author and survivor of the Holocaust, stopped talking about events of 50 years ago during his speech and said to President Clinton: "And Mr. President, I cannot not tell you something. I have been in the former Yugoslavia last fall. I cannot sleep since what I have seen. As a Jew I am saying that. We must do something to stop the bloodshed in that country." An ironic footnote to the opening of the museum came when Mr. Wiesel and Simon Wiesenthal, the Nazi hunter, objected to an invitation to Franjo Tudjman, Croatia's President, pointing out that a 1988 book he wrote claimed that only 900,000 Jews, not six million, died in the Holocaust.

Grand Disillusionment

Behind the guilt lies grand disillusionment, for the generations that grew up in the shadow of the Second World War came to terms with the concentration camps through an unspoken assumption that never again would evil of that magnitude be tolerated. Not war itself, which was perhaps unavoidable, but war waged ruthlessly against everyday civilians who are selected for slaughter solely on the basis of ethnicity or religion—that would be ruled out of bounds for all time.

With the collapse of Communism, one hope was that the demise of superpower rivalry might allow foreign affairs to be conducted around a fulcrum of morality, with more focus on economic development, the conservation of resources and the discouragement of anti-democratic petty tyrants.

It has not worked out quite that way. In the matter of long-suppressed ethnic identities, it appears in retrospect, Communism acted as something of a hermetic seal. Once the seal was broken, acts of hatred and ethnic crimes from 40 years ago, when exploited by unscrupulous leaders, lose the distance of history and are experienced as if they happened yesterday.

Under Marshal Tito, the expression of ethnic sentiment in Yugoslavia was a crime. Memories of the ugly deeds of the Nazi state of Croatia, where thousands and thousands of Serbs perished in concentration camps, were suppressed. Mass graves were covered over by concrete. The recent opening of those graves by Serbs who carefully reburied the heaps of bone was not only an act of reverence for the dead. It also was a fanning of the flames of insecurity for Serbs who lived outside Serbia, in the Krajina area of Croatia.

Western diplomats based here agree that Serbs have every reason to recall their barbarous treatment at the hands of the Croatian Ustashe. They note that in the current conflict there is an ample record of atrocities on all sides—Serbian, Muslim and Croatian. But they will also acknowledge that the prime mover of Yugoslavia's descent into chaos has been the engine of Serbian nationalism as driven by President Slobodan Milosevic. Its mission is to draw together the Serbs in other former republics of the now-defunct federation—the "precani," meaning literally "the ones across the river."

Warnings

The first alarm bells should have gone off six years ago when Mr. Milosevic took his now famous trip to Kosovo, the southern region that nurtured Serbian nationalism but where Albanians now constitute 90 percent of the population. Appearing before a crowd of thousands of Serbs, who were pushed back by police truncheons, he declared, "No one has the right to beat you!" The frenzied response taught him the power of the force at his disposal.

Several former ambassadors from European countries privately expressed frustration to Western journalists during the ensuing years. They said their cables to their home offices warning about the genie that Mr. Milosevic had freed from the bottle were being ignored. In 1991, the secession of Croatia and Slovenia precipitated the Serbian-Croatian war that turned, a year ago, into civil war in Bosnia. The Bosnian Serbs, supported by Serbia, now control about 70 percent of the territory.

The time for effective intervention, many people now argue, was in May or June of last year, when the Serbian siege of mostly Muslim Sarajevo was getting under way. It might have given pause to the Serbs before they felt the power of their own dominant position, before ethnic cleansing had advanced so drastically and while there still was a semblance of civil society in Sarajevo and cities like Mostar. Now, Mr. Milosevic is at the peak of his strength despite a trade embargo against Serbia that is almost a year old, a year of war in Bosnia and an on-again, off-again war with Croatia.

These days, with reports of atrocities continuing and nightly footage on international television of wounded and orphaned children, the pressure for some form of action to stop the slaughter is building. Once again, diplomats are contemplating the lesson of Chamberlain's umbrella: Move in quickly and stamp out the infection, because otherwise the pathology will spread exponentially.

Two Faces of the Facts of War

For weeks now, the fate of Bosnia has seemed intertwined with the fate of one eastern town, Srebrenica. Perhaps 50,000 Muslims, including refugees and defenders, remain surrounded there by Serbs who had besieged and all but captured the town before a cease-fire was worked out by the United Nations. The truce put the town under U.N. protection to allow the disarming of the Muslims and some evacuations. At the climactic moment last weekend, when Srebrenica appeared on the brink of surrender following ferocious Serbian shelling, the newspaper readers of Sarajevo, the Bosnian capital, and Belgrade, Serbia's capital, were offered radically different versions of the events. In these excerpts, Tanjug refers to the Yugoslav news agency; Republika Srpska is the name Serb nationalists give to their self-proclaimed government in Bosnia; Karadzic is Radovan Karadzic, leader of the Bosnian Serbs; Milosevic is President Slobodan Milosevic of Serbia, and Mladic is Gen. Ratko Mladic, commander of the Bosnian Serb forces, sometimes called *Chetniks.*

In Sarajevo

Tomorrow, a Canadian battalion serving with the United Nations Protection Force should enter Srebrenica as a result of negotiations between Lieut. Gen. Lars-Eric Wahlgren, commander of the U.N. force, and the war criminal Karadzic. A Golgotha continues for the citizens of Srebrenica . . . Zlatko Lagumdzija, the Deputy Prime Minister of Bosnia and Herzegovina, has told the world that Mladic's army, that is Milosevic's army, has to be stopped, that the only thing that the aggressor army understands is force, and that the only way it can be stopped is by confronting it with a greater force. . . . The aggressor forces continued their offensive at Srebrenica throughout the day yesterday with undiminished intensity, and the people of the town continued to give a heroic account of themselves in resisting the attempt by the more numerous and better-armed attackers to penetrate the town's outskirts. Besides their push across the front lines, the Chetniks continued to use their heavy artillery to shell the center of Srebrenica, massacring civilians. During the morning hours alone, the Chetnik artillery killed six people and injured 15, including several children. In Tuzla . . . local and foreign reporters were presented with a transcript of an intercepted radio-telephone conversation between war criminal Mladic and the Chetnik commanders in the area . . . in which he ordered them to press their attacks so as to enter Srebrenica before he began his negotiations on a cease-fire.

Oslobodjenje
April 17, 1993

In Belgrade

In spite of the fact that the Muslim armed forces are facing a total military defeat, they again launched attacks this morning from various directions from the territory of Srebrenica. According to Tanjug reporting from this region, the Muslim units are using all their artillery and firing equipment. The Serbian sources say that Serbian defenders had tens of dead and wounded following attacks by Muslim forces which lasted for days. The army of the Republika Srpska was forced to respond strongly in a counterattack and it has reached strategically important peaks around Srebrenica. The Serbian lines are only about one kilometer by air from Srebrenica. Using the fact that the Serbian side is not undertaking any action against Srebrenica itself, the Muslim extremists continued to attack. During the morning the most severe attacks of the Muslims were launched on Ratkovic, Zeleni Jadar, Podravanje and Milici. According to Tanjug, the Serbian sources are reporting that Muslim soldiers have started sur-rendering arms yesterday. There were such individual cases in the region of Skelani, Bratunac, Derventa and Podravanje. The Muslim extremists are in a hopeless situation from the military point of view. They are still reluctant to surrender because they were the ones to destroy 56 Serbian villages near Srebrenica, Bratunac and Skelani and on several occasions have killed in a most brutal way more than 1,300 Serbs, mostly women, children and aged people.

Politika
April 17, 1993

*   *   *

June 10, 1993

'HALLELUJAH' IS HEARD IN THE ARCH-ATHEIST'S TEMPLE

By HENRY KAMM
Special to The New York Times

TIRANA, Albania—If Enver Hoxha, Albania's dictator for more than 40 years, is turning in his monumental grave on a hillside above this capital, it would not be surprising.

On the steps of the spectacular marble-and-glass structure resembling a winged pyramid that was built to honor the man who made Albania the only country that outlawed religion, men and women who said they came from the Foursquare Gospel Church of Los Angeles were laying hands on shattered limbs, blind eyes and aching bodies the other day, and with many a "Praise the Lord!" and "Hallelujah!" prayed for healing.

True, the police barred their way into the building on the ground that the crowd seeking to enter was too big for the former Hoxha Museum, now the Hall of International Culture. And the police finally made the members of various groups of reborn Christians from the United States, Canada, Romania and the Netherlands, who held several days of meetings devoted to healing through faith, disperse from the steps.

But their outdoor rallies met no obstacles, and the many disabled people who gathered at the former shrine of atheism proved by their presence the effectiveness of religious propaganda in post-Communist Albania and the completeness of the break with the past, in which Albania ranked with North Korea as the most dogmatic and reclusive of Communist nations. The gatherings also bore witness to the inadequacy of medical services in this deprived country.

Albania's last census, before the Italian invasion of 1939, showed the population to have been 70 percent Muslim and virtually all the rest Orthodox or Roman Catholic. Religious practice in this land of 3.2 million people is reviving today; most Albanians questioned say they consider themselves nonpracticing Muslims.

Many here still call the Boulevard of the Martyrs of the Nation, on which the former museum stands, Stalin Boulevard because of the larger-than-life statue of the dictator that adorned it. Today, a privately owned coffee bar has been erected in front of it, hiding its empty pedestal. Across the street, where Lenin's likeness once towered, the pedestal has been decorated with a tribute from a spray can to Pink Floyd.

The boulevard runs through the center of this city of 200,000 from the vast square on which stands the Tirana Hotel, a grim example of the massive, featureless Communist architecture of the 1960's, to the university, a specimen of the Fascist style that dominated in the 1930's, even before Italy occupied Albania.

In the Communist era, the broad avenue about half a mile long was the image of Hoxha's Albania. There were the statues and soulless buildings housing the all-powerful party leadership, the Government, the Presidency and the feared Ministries of Internal Security and Defense.

There were neither houses in which people lived nor shops. There was no private trade—just as there were no lawyers, because Albania's Communist society was deemed so perfectly just that they were not needed.

Police officers and soldiers bearing automatic rifles at the ready kept pedestrians at respectful distances from the houses of power. The rare cars in a country that had no privately owned vehicles conveyed the leaders between villas and offices.

The buildings still stand, and armed soldiers still guard the ministries. But they no longer inspire awe.

In midafternoon on these warm days, pedestrians take over the boulevard. Young and old, whispering lovers and boisterous teen-agers, humanize the charmless thoroughfare by being themselves despite a setting that was meant to intimidate.

The end-of-day promenade had not stopped in the Communist years, but the flow of strollers was kept at a distance from the halls of the mighty by the guards, and this cast a pall over gaiety. Albanians say the scene was monotonous because of the virtual uniformity of dress in a country that offered modest, dark or white clothing in a few standard models.

Nowadays, strollers treasure eccentricity in dress and carry the messages of the T-shirt culture.

Albanians marvel at what seem to them multitudes of private cars, mainly old vehicles that failed safety checks in other countries. But cars are still few enough for the curbs on both sides to be lined with people sitting to chat.

Along the sidewalks, private dealers lay out small quantities of illegally imported candy bars, cookies, soft drinks and beer and sacks of dried pumpkin seed. The poverty of this largely unemployed city can be measured by perhaps 20 sellers waiting until late in the evening with a stock whose total value, for the length of the boulevard, would fall short of three digits in dollars.

Comza Gjeci sells rarer goods. On sheets of newspapers, he displays books—novels of Albanian and foreign writers deemed publishable by the former authorities and, even rarer, books from earlier days in foreign languages that Albanians kept, often hidden because the old leaders considered them "bourgeois."

The 63-year-old retired teacher and his wife, whose joint monthly pensions total less than $30, share their two-room apartment, plus a small room rented nearby, with their three grown children and their families, 10 people in all. None have regular jobs. Mr. Gjeci does not want to sell his own books yet, he said, so he buys books others are forced to part with in this time of need.

"When I take their books, it seems to me I take their hearts," he said.

* * *

August 3, 1993

ALBANIA CRUMBLES INTO A 'LEAST DEVELOPED' NATION

By HENRY KAMM
Special to The New York Times

TIRANA, Albania—Albania has no economy to speak of, an unemployment rate of about 40 percent of the remaining work force after about one-tenth of the population has fled abroad to find work, few public services and pervasive poverty of a degree not seen in Europe since World War II.

The railroad no longer functions, and buses are rare. There never was an airline. Hospitals lack virtually everything, and schools have no textbooks since 27 million of the heavily ideological books of the past were scrapped. The United Nations has classified Albania as a "least-developed nation," the only one ever in Europe.

Foreign officials here believe that this classification would have been appropriate even before the authoritarian Communist Government collapsed in stages in 1991–92. But under its founder, Enver Hoxha, who ruled from 1944 until he died in 1985, and his successor, Ramiz Alia, Albania was extremely secretive toward outsiders and allowed virtually no access to important information.

Alireza Mahallati of the United Nations Children's Fund said 970 out of 8,000 schools had been destroyed as Albanians turned on many buildings that they connected with Communism or their collectivized society.

'Schools Without Texts'

"Children go to schools without windows, texts and hardly any heating," he said. Parents lack money to clothe or equip their children, so absenteeism is high.

The average wage is less than $30 a month, and salaries even for top jobs are little higher. Lieut. Gen. Ilia Vasho, chief of the army general staff, said he earned $45 a month and consoled himself in the knowledge that President Sali Berisha earned only $120.

"Albania is far more stable than it has any right to be," said an ambassador of a major power, summarizing the state of this Balkan country of 3.2 million people, which last year elected its first non-Communist Government.

Until the elections of March 1992, which were won in a landslide by the Democratic Party of Dr. Berisha, a cardiologist, Albania was in chaos. The Communist Party, now called Socialist, was nominally in power, but the totalitarian system by which it ruled since 1944 had fallen apart with the collapse of Communism in Eastern Europe.

Factories Abandoned

The collective farms were disbanded, their properties dismantled or destroyed, and production virtually halted. Workers abandoned the primitive factories and mines.

Crime was rampant. Throughout the night, gunfire was heard in Tirana, the capital, and few dared leave their houses after dark. Electric power, heat and water became rare. Albania, in effect, became a ward of Western Europe.

Because the police did not interfere, most of the tens of thousands of trees that for centuries lined the roads have been cut for firewood, leaving endless rows of stumps.

They, together with the hundreds of thousands of concrete pillboxes that Mr. Hoxha had built all over the landscape in paranoiac fear of invasion, are cited by Albanians as symbols of the folly that ruled their nation.

Dependent on the West

Albania today remains dependent on the West, mainly Europe. Officials of international organizations believe that it receives more foreign aid per citizen than any other country. Its only export is its unemployed; more than 300,000 Albanians work abroad, most in Greece.

In nine days of travel across Albania, hardly a factory chimney was seen smoking. Many plants have been dismantled by their workers, partly in a widespread phenomenon of fury against institutions of their former oppressors, partly to use tools for private pursuits or beams or window frames in their own homes.

The chromium and copper mines that were Communist Albania's main producers of foreign exchange are paralyzed. "The mechanism that made them work was slave labor; now it's gone," said Kutlay Rebiri, chief of the World Bank mission here.

Major foreign investment is needed to make the mines competitive, but the Balkan instability provoked by the breakup of Yugoslavia has discouraged any investment.

Migrants' Money Is Vital

The money the migrant workers send back, estimated at $400 million a year, and the resumption of some subsistence agriculture are virtually Albania's only contribution to its economic survival.

With land privatized, agriculture has resumed. But instead of the large collectives, which produced enough to maintain a low but adequate nutritional level, the land has been split up into inefficiently small units averaging 3.5 acres. Farm productivity is one-tenth of that in the European Community.

"The whole village, all the men, are looking for work abroad," said Bashkim Xaka, a 30-year-old farmer in Noi, a village about 30 miles north of here. "We don't have enough land to farm." Under the market economy introduced by Dr. Berisha, there is no substitute for the state, which in the past provided seed and other necessities and the use of mechanical equipment. The fields are green, but nothing but hand tools are in use.

$1.2 Billion in Aid

Since mid-1991, according to European Community statistics, the prosperous nations of the G-24 group have given $1.2 billion in aid. The community provides 30,000 to 40,000 tons of wheat a month for bread, the staple food.

International officials believe that when owners get formal title to land, many will sell to permit the restoration of more productive agriculture. "Then the former owners will move to the cities and increase unemployment there," an official said. Land privatization has largely taken place, but distribution of title deeds is far from complete.

Mr. Eribi said Government revenues covered only 20 percent of the national budget of $300 million. He said 50 to 60 percent is financed by foreign aid and the rest through the printing press. He explained the stability of the national currency, the lek, at about 105 to $1 by the effect of the workers' remittances.

Foreign and international officials say that despite the great inflow of aid funds and "soft" loans, the Government has proved incapable of spending or accepting much of what it receives. They attribute this to Albania's inexperience, the shortage of competent officials and a tendency to pass decisions up to a higher level rather than take responsibility for making them.

Of $40 million granted by the International Monetary Fund to finance vital imports since July 1992, no more than $12 million has been spent, Mr. Ebiri said.

A German Government aid official visiting the northern town of Kukes, center of an exceptionally deprived region, said he had come to deliver two projects as outright gifts, each worth more than $3 million—a water-supply system and a hospital. But he said officials had refused to sign the contracts, demanding changes that the German believes mask their unwillingness to put their names to any decision.

Trading in Greek Goods

A few Albanians are profiting from trades based largely on the accessibility of Greek goods and free-market currency exchanges. The area in front of the National Bank is the open, if not fully legal, meeting place for money dealers and customers. For most Albanians, freedom has meant, at best, maintaining the low standard of life of the Communist decades.

But after the first destructive fury against state property, followed by the enthusiasm that brought Dr. Berisha to power, the docility of the past has for the moment redescended.

Dr. Berisha is still viewed favorably by many Albanians and foreign officials. But disenchantment with the economy and a split from his Democratic Party by leading intellectuals, who accuse the President of disregarding their rights, signal the erosion of power of a Government whose means to meet the expectations Dr. Berisha raised in his campaign are severely restricted. For the moment, hopes still prevail over disappointment.

A Gallup poll in the formerly Communist countries done for the European Community and published in February showed Albanians leading all in optimism. Seventy-seven percent said they believed that their country was moving in the right direction; 72 percent expressed confidence in the market economy; 71 percent said they believed that the economic situation would improve over the next 12 months.

Diplomats and international officials said they envied this optimism and wished they could share it.

* * *

October 10, 1993

OLD RIVALS BATTLE IN GREEK ELECTION

By ALAN COWELL
Special to The New York Times

ATHENS, Oct. 9—The banners are furled. The campaigning is done. The bullhorns have blessedly fallen silent.

All that remains for Greek voters to do in elections on Sunday is to deliver what the pollsters insist will be one of Europe's most remarkable political resurrections: the revival and reinstatement of Andreas Papandreou.

Remember him?

Mr. Papandreou was the Greek Socialist leader of the 1980's who tweaked the United States' tail over the American military presence here, consorted with the likes of the Libyan leader, Muammar el-Qaddafi, and infuriated his European Community partners with his profligate spending of their money.

Once Seemed Doomed

The problem child of the NATO alliance, Mr. Papandreou seemed doomed by disgrace, ill health and a disastrous record when, in April 1990, Greece's eight million voters last dusted off the ballot boxes in the cradle of democracy to elect Constantine Mitsotakis, a conservative, as Prime Minister.

At that time, Mr. Papandreou was conducting an openly adulterous relationship with Dimitra Liana, a flight attendant half his age who is now his wife, faced grave corruption charges, seemed debilitated by open-heart surgery in 1988 and, after nine years in office, had left Greeks saddled with the European Community's biggest debts.

Some were tempted to write him off altogether. But now, on the eve of the election, his party, the Pan-Hellenic Socialist Movement, is running a clear six percentage points ahead of Mr Mitsotakis's New Democracy in public opinion surveys.

If that margin is maintained in the voting booths, it will be enough to give Mr. Papandreou a whopping majority in the 300-seat Parliament under election legislation introduced by Mr. Mitsotakis to favor the front-runner.

While there may still be some slippage, many Greeks seem to be taking Mr. Papandreou's victory as virtually assured, and not necessarily because they like him.

Voting Against, Not For

"In Greece, people vote to oust someone, not to install someone," said Photis Photopoulos, a central Athens travel agent of conservative inclination.

The prime reason voters have turned against Mr. Mitsotakis, many Greeks say, is the economic austerity program through which he sought to pay off the debts and untangle the economic mess inherited from Mr. Papandreou. The program has hurt Greeks in their businesses and their pocketbooks.

"The market is dead," said Nicolas Continis, a businessman. "Gas has gone up. Rents have doubled. New Democracy blew it. The people who are voting for Papandreou are all hoping that he'll spread some money around again."

In some ways, it has been a campaign of titanic proportions. Spectators have been offered the vision of two 74-year-old men slugging out the last battle of a personal feud that has overshadowed Greek politics since Mr. Mitsotakis broke with Mr. Papandreou's father, Prime Minister George Papandreou, in 1965 in what the Papandreou camp still terms "the betrayal."

For Mr. Mitsotakis, the campaign is supposedly his last shot at power: if he loses, he has said, he will quit, an assertion that not everybody believes.

For Mr. Papandreou, the vote provides probably a last chance to vindicate himself after all the tribulations: corruption charges that he narrowly avoided when a panel of judges voted 7 to 6 to acquit him in January 1992; accusations of quixotic mismanagement of the Greek economy, the European Community's poorest, and the sense that age and ill health had consigned him to history's has-beens.

By many accounts, the campaign has been a grubby one. Mr. Mitsotakis's television advertising, orchestrated by American advisers including James Carville of President Clinton's campaign, has gone so far as to suggest that in voting for Mr. Papandreou, Greeks would be voting for a dying man.

A Conspiracy Theory

Naturally, the campaign would not be complete without a nefarious conspiracy, this time centering on the billion-dollar business of Greece's vast, inefficient but potentially lucrative state telephone corporation.

Mr. Mitsotakis offered a 35 per cent stake and management rights to six foreign bidders to pursue his drive for privatization and economic renewal, offending Greek tycoons with their own interest in the telephone corporation.

So, as the unsubstantiated theory goes in Mr. Mitsotakis's campaigning, and in the coffee shops of Kolonaki Square where loose talk is as much the point as the beverage, the businessmen decided to bring him down, using their control of influential newspapers and radio stations to discredit him, and fanning the flames of revolt in New Democracy.

All good conspiracy theories need a clinching argument. In this case, Mr. Papandreou has already provided it: he has said that if he is elected, he will not sell the telephone corporation to the foreigners. Greek interests, thus, would be protected, and, for some, the conspiracy theory proved beyond all doubt.

"It is difficult to rule," Mr. Mitsotakis said, "when you're being stabbed in the back with a stiletto, or a pack of stilettos."

*   *   *

October 12, 1993

GREEK VICTOR NOW FACING TOUGH TASK

By ALAN COWELL

ATHENS, Oct. 11—With Andreas Papandreou back in power in Greece, borne by a remarkable political resurrection, the question is whether the Socialist leader, onetime firebrand and perennial master of surprise, will go back to his old quixotic ways.

Mr. Papandreou's Pan-Hellenic Socialist Movement has emerged with a solid majority of 170 seats in the 300-member Parliament after Sunday's national election.

His victory over Prime Minister Constantine Mitsotakis has thrust Mr. Papandreou, a Harvard-educated economist and onetime United States citizen, into a changed world where his cold war stock-in-trade no longer has currency. And despite the result of the election, the campaign left more questions than answers.

First of all, there is the issue of his health, which has not been good since open-heart surgery in 1988.

European Community Post

"If the question is whether he can run a hands-on, day-to-day Government, the answer is probably not," said a diplomat. The 74-year-old Greek leader's frailty is doubly important because in January, Greece assumes the rotating, six-month presidency of the European Community, which entails a potentially grueling travel schedule that Mr. Papandreou may be loath to undertake.

Similarly, his health may well constrain him from a more flamboyant foreign policy, as he concentrates on the more pressing problem of economic policy at home that forms the biggest question mark.

As he acknowledged victory last night, Mr. Papandreou spoke of "difficult problems" inherited from Mr. Mitsotakis and promised "economic policies that will bring stability, development and social security."

Inherited Austerity Plan

What Mr. Papandreou has inherited from Mr. Mitsotakis, though, is not so much a problem as an unpalatable solution to Greece's chronic economic woes: an austerity program that was intended to curb inflation, cut huge state deficits and begin selling off chunks of Greece's vast state sector to private business—in essence, a reversal of everything Mr. Papandreou stood for in the 1980's.

His last spell as Prime Minister, from 1981 to 1989, ended in scandal, corruption charges and accusations of mismanagement that left him isolated and discredited among the swing voters who decide Greek elections. His successful quest for vindication will have a price, however.

As his supporters careened through Athens into the small hours today with car horns blaring and banners flapping from motorcycles and car windows, the message they were sending Mr. Papandreou was one of anticipation: now that Mr. Mitsotakis is gone, they were saying, let's get back to the good old days when the money ran freely from the state coffers.

Pressure From Public Workers

"He has an obligation to his voters who want him to reverse privatization and the hold-down on public spending," said Sotirios Papasotiriou, an economist. "He has to give something." Specifically, Mr. Papandreou is under pressure to increase wages for the 670,000 Government employees who, along with their families, make up a large chunk of his constituency.

At the same time, though, Mr. Papandreou needs economic growth and European support. Greece is the poorest nation in the community, and its signature on the Maastricht Treaty on European integration obliges it to keep pace with its partners.

"Greece is so dependent on the European Community, that I don't think Papandreou will be able to do anything like he did in the past," said Mr. Papasotiriou.

The conservative New Democracy party of Mr. Mitsotakis, with its 111 seats, was humbled by defections and the huge personal unpopularity that accrued to its leader after three years of biting economic austerity.

As he conceded defeat last night, Mr. Mitsotakis, also 74, said he would begin the process of holding elections for a new party leader, possibly a younger man like Miltiades Evert, former Mayor of Athens, to stanch the hemorrhage of voters towards Antonis Samaras, a 42-year-old maverick who broke with Mr. Mitsotakis and set up his own party, Political Spring.

With barely a majority at Mr. Mitsotakis's command, the revolt stripped New Democracy of its parliamentary edge, forced elections seven months ahead of schedule and split the one-time monolith of the Greek right.

By today, Mr. Samaras's party had won 4.6 per cent of the vote and 10 parliamentary seats, all of them taken from New Democracy.

*   *   *

May 20, 1994

COCA-COLA REACHES INTO
IMPOVERISHED ALBANIA

By JOHN TAGLIABUE
Special to The New York Times

TIRANA, Albania, May 19—Dirt-poor Albania has hardly an economy to speak of, but as of today it has Coke.

The average wage is less than $30 a month. Its main export is its unemployed, with an estimated 300,000 Albanians working abroad, mostly in Greece and Italy, and sending money home.

But today, in a lush field outside the capital, President Sali Berisha joined Coca-Cola executives from the United States and Italy to cut a red and white ribbon that opened a $10 million Coca-Cola bottling plant, the first major foreign investment in the country and another step in Coca-Cola's march into formerly Communist, now liberated, Eastern Europe.

"It might not be what they need the most," said Hans Christian Jacobsen, a food industry expert with the European Bank for Reconstruction and Development, who attended the opening today, "but it has symbolic value to create awareness that Albania is still here."

Coca-Cola's Shrinking Globe

Albania becomes the 197th country where Coca-Cola is made, leaving only a handful of blank spots on the Coca-Cola globe, most notably Libya, Iraq, Cuba and North Korea, where the soft drink remains banned.

But for some of Albania's struggling 3.3 million people, the reinforced-concrete factory gleaming under sunny skies resembled a Martian spacecraft landed amid the country's pervasive poverty and shimmered like light at the end of the tunnel.

"This is a country where only three years ago foreign investment was forbidden by law, and foreign investors were considered agents of treason," Dr. Berisha, a cardiologist, said before the ribbon ceremony.

"It's a real symbol of the deep changes that have taken place in Albania in the last two years."

Dr. Berisha later pressed a button, and bottling machines shook and hissed while young Albanians clad in red T-shirts emblazoned with the Coca-Cola logo scurried about loading bottles or shouted orders at each other.

The factory is a joint venture involving the development bank, Coca-Cola, an Albanian company called Invest P.F. that is affiliated with the Ministry for Foodstuffs and Italy's Busi Group, the largest franchised bottler of Coca-Cola in Italy. The factory will have the capacity to turn out 24,000 bottles of Coke an hour and will provide jobs directly for about 100 Albanians and indirectly for another 400 to 500, like truck drivers or distributors.

"It's a completely different experience, in every sense," said Lalo Idlir, a 33-year-old mechanical engineer who joined Coca-Cola three months ago. "The organization, the discipline, the manner of working, the technology—it's a totally new experience."

Mr. Idlir guessed that Albanians, who traditionally drink beer or wine with their meals and consume enormous quantities of clear white raki, a potent grape brandy, would snap up Coke.

Fatbardh Ganai, a 40-year-old engineer who worked for 12 years at the Government's Institute for Food Research before joining the factory, said the jobs there were prized. "We get about twice what you'd make outside," he said, casting nervous glances at the rattling line of six-ounce refillable bottles.

At current wage levels outside the Coca-Cola plant, an Albanian would have to work about an hour and a half to buy a bottle, which costs 25 lek, or about 25 cents.

Mr. Ganai tasted cheap imitations of Coca-Cola brought in from Greece about three years ago, "but there's no comparison with the real thing," he said.

A Media Event

Coca-Cola celebrated the plant opening with a media event, chartering an Alitalia jetliner to haul 38 reporters and eight television crews into Tirana's scruffy airport.

Coca-Cola officials stressed their commitment to rebuilding Albania, which United Nations officials have classified a "least developed nation," the only one in Europe.

E. Neville Isdell, senior vice president of the Coca-Cola Export Corporation, said Coke was "doing more than opening a bottle plant."

"This is the crucial first step in building a strong, thriving, world-class business system," he said.

The Stalinist totalitarian regime that ruled Albania since 1944 fell apart several years ago with the collapse of Communism in Eastern Europe. Albania was in chaos until the elections of March 1992, which the Democratic Party of Dr. Berisha won in a landslide.

His Government has been committed to shock therapy, and today Dr. Berisha boasted of its achievements to reporters. Inflation, he said, fell to 30 percent last year from 400 percent two years ago, and is projected to drop below 20 percent this year.

Albanians bought 50,000 new cars last year, he said, and installed 30,000 satellite dishes, a revolution in a country whose old Communist leadership allowed Albanians virtually no access to outside information.

In downtown Tirana, traffic is bustling and boutiques and snack bars are sprouting. Everywhere, big gray satellite dishes have been affixed to crumbling apartment blocks.

Foreign officials like Mr. Jacobsen agreed that projects like the Coca-Cola plant served a useful function, galvanizing local efforts to transform the economy.

According to the Government, foreign investors have committed $290 million to Albania, more than 50 percent of it from Italy, and the figure is expected to double this year. But little of the investment money has flowed in yet.

Muhtar A. Kent, the 41-year-old president of Coca-Cola East Central Europe, said the company expected a positive cash flow in Albania "very soon," perhaps within 18 months. The capital, he said, would be plowed back into more trucks, equipment and retailing capability.

Mr. Isdell said Coca-Cola's success in Eastern Europe was based on pent-up desire for the symbols of the West.

"We're all about refreshing people around the world," he said. "That's what we do."

*　*　*

December 19, 1994

BULGARIA'S COMMUNISTS CLAIM PARLIAMENT ELECTION VICTORY

By JANE PERLEZ
Special to The New York Times

SOFIA, Bulgaria, Dec. 18—The former Communist Party took an early lead in parliamentary elections here today and its leader claimed victory.

The party leader, Zhan Videnov, a 35-year-old former Communist official who is likely to be the next Prime Minister, said his party would reverse the country's deep economic decline.

With less than 5 percent of the vote counted, the Bulgarian Socialist Party, as the former Communists call themselves, had 43 percent. Its main opposition, the anti-Communist Union of Democratic Forces, had 25.6 percent. Of 49 parties vying for the 240 seats in Parliament, four other small parties appeared likely to win representation.

"This is a victory for the country," Mr. Videnov said tonight. "We can solve the problems." He has described the party's approach as the way forward, rather than a return to the past.

In many ways, Mr. Videnov, who has marshaled his power in the last two years, is a direct political descendant of Todor Zhivkov, who ruled Bulgaria as a Communist leader for 33 years until 1989.

Mr. Videnov, who had a reputation as a young hard-line apparatchik, became leader of the Socialist Party after Mr. Zhivkov's lieutenant, Aleksandur Lilov, was pushed out in 1992.

The Socialist Party, the main supporter of the "non-party" government of technocrats that was in power from December 1992 to September this year, is less inclined toward a market economy than the ex-Communists who have won elections in Hungary and Poland. Popular support for radical changes to the economy is far weaker in Bulgaria than in Hungary or Poland.

The core of the Socialist Party support comes from the three million retirees who make up a disproportionately large share of Bulgaria's 8.7 million population. The party, which was well disciplined for election day, also appealed to young people, many of whom are unemployed.

Opinion surveys have shown widespread disgruntlement with the economy, which is one of the least privatized in Eastern Europe. But the surveys show that more than 70 percent of the people blamed the anti-Communist Union of Democratic Forces for the problems, rather than the former Communists who have wielded more power in Parliament.

Western economists here say the former Communists will begin to prop up the ailing heavy industries that for the last five years have had rapidly declining output but have not laid off workers or begun restructuring. The party is also unlikely to give peasants their own land.

The party favors closer ties to Russia, a country for whom there is some reverence here rather than the fear that is prevalent elsewhere in Eastern Europe. There will be efforts to recapture at least some of the huge past trade with Russia; more than 70 percent of Bulgaria's exports went to Russia before 1989.

* * *

April 5, 1995

VANGA

FOR A REVERED MYSTIC, A SHRINE NOW OF HER OWN

By STEPHEN KINZER

RUPITE, Bulgaria—This remote hamlet has become a shrine for the sick and troubled from throughout the Balkans and beyond. Every day they come by the hundreds, hoping for a word from an extraordinary woman who they believe is blessed with great mystic power.

The visionary, known only as Vanga, is widely believed to be able to see and feel things that are beyond the senses of ordinary people. There are countless stories of her ability to explain the past, predict the future and prescribe cures for physical and spiritual pain.

Vanga, who is in her 80's and has not used a family name for decades, was blinded in a windstorm that swept through southwestern Bulgaria when she was a young girl. Soon afterward, Bulgarians say, she began to show remarkable psychic gifts. Her fame grew steadily, and today there is hardly a Bulgarian who does not know of her.

In her youth, Vanga was often consulted by members of Bulgaria's royal family, which was deposed in the 1940's. In the Communist era, although few reports about her were allowed to appear in the press, senior members of the ruling elite traveled regularly to seek her counsel.

Journalists in Sofia, the Bulgarian capital, say Leonid I. Brezhnev, the Soviet leader until his death in 1982, consulted Vanga at least once. More recently, they say, leaders of several former Soviet republics have taken time out from state visits to make the three-hour trip here from Sofia.

At first sight, this dusty outpost near the Greek border seems unremarkable. There are only about a dozen modest houses, and in the one where Vanga lives chickens feed in a petunia garden as laundry flaps from clotheslines.

But there is one striking edifice here: an extremely unorthodox Orthodox church. It was designed by one of Bulgaria's most daring architects, Bogdan Tomalevski, and looks nothing like an Orthodox church is supposed to look. There are no domes, and inside there is no gold, no altar, no alcove for praying. The only decorations on the pale walls are boldly stylized portraits of saints by Svetlin Roussev, a Bulgarian painter known for his experimental art.

The church was paid for with contributions that pilgrims left here in tribute to Vanga, and built according to her specifications. Although it has been open only since October, the murals inside have already had to be retouched because they have been kissed so many thousands of times.

Orthodox bishops at first refused to consecrate the church because it does not conform to normal standards, but they later relented, apparently unwilling to make an enemy of Vanga. Politicians, writers, actors and diplomats, including Bulgaria's Foreign Minister and the Russian Ambassador, were among the thousands who turned up for the consecration service.

One recent day, several busloads of pilgrims arrived here. A few were admitted to the small adobe house where Vanga lives, but most had to be content with a glimpse of her as she briefly stepped outside. She walked haltingly, long gray hair flowing over her shoulders. The crowd fell silent, but she made no gesture to acknowledge its presence.

Many of those who came seemed burdened with sadness. Several told stories of disappeared loved ones or families afflicted with illness.

"I came here once before, many years ago, and everything she predicted for me came to pass," one woman said. "She told me that my mother's sickness could not be cured, and she was right. She said that my nephew had been murdered, and we found the body exactly where she told us to look. I absolutely believe everything she says. I adore her. She is a saint."

Each time Vanga predicts an event correctly, as she did before an earthquake that shook northern Bulgaria in 1985, her legend grows. Inaccurate predictions, like her vision that the World Cup soccer final last year would be played between "two teams beginning with B," are quickly forgotten. One finalist was Brazil, but Bulgaria was eliminated by Italy in the semifinals.

Vanga, who rarely gives interviews, has said the area around Rupite attracts unexplained cosmic forces. Boiling water bubbles from the earth outside her house, and many believe it has curative power.

Although Vanga's visitors come from as far away as Japan and South America, some of her neighbors are skeptical.

"Local people don't believe in her," said a peasant woman walking through the streets of Petric, a nearby town. "She just looks at you, asks you what's wrong and then repeats phrases she has memorized. A lot of what she does is for money. And the way she talks is vulgar. She uses words that no woman should use, especially not a godly person."

Such doubting, however, evidently has no effect on Vanga's legion of admirers.

"Vanga is religious in the most noble and elevated sense of the word," a Bulgarian journalist wrote recently in the magazine Literary Forum. "Her unique capacity to resurrect past events and to look into the future is one of the greatest secrets of our time."

*   *   *

April 28, 1995

BULGARIA NOT SURE WHETHER IT SHOULD TURN EAST OR WEST

By STEPHEN KINZER

SOFIA, Bulgaria—Any night of the week, one of the hottest spots here is Eddy's Tex-Mex Diner, where young Bulgarians guzzle Jack Daniels, eat chili burgers and Cajun shrimp, and listen to local bands belt out songs about tequila sunrises and flat-back Fords. A large American flag dominates the decor.

Several blocks away stands Sofia's most imposing Orthodox church, the splendid golden-domed Alexander Nevsky Cathedral. It is named for one of Russia's most heroic saints, and a plaque inside explains that it was built to express gratitude for Russia's role in freeing Bulgaria from Ottoman rule in the 1870's. Nearby, a heroic equestrian statue of Czar Alexander II conveys the same message.

Bulgaria is torn between West and East. Pro-Russian sentiment is strong, and the new Government, which is run by former Communists, is anxious to avoid offending Moscow. Yet some Bulgarians fear that strengthening ties to Russia may lead to anti-Western sentiment and perhaps to curbs on the personal freedoms this country has just begun to enjoy.

"There's a certain amount of wrestling for Bulgaria's political soul going on," said an American who frequents Eddy's Diner. "They feel somewhat pushed aside and isolated. They just don't know where to go. That accounts for some of the desire to look east again."

One Bulgarian who is seeking to deal with these questions is Vladimir Andreev, a film maker. He is working on "The Way to Europe," a film that will explore Bulgaria's identity crisis through the stories of men and women who ride the bus line that connects Sofia to Berlin.

"Identity is the real question facing Bulgaria right now," Mr. Andreev said. "We are looking for a big brother. For 50 years it was easy, because the Soviet Union was our big brother. Now there is no more Soviet Union, and many people want nothing to do with Russia. So they are looking to Western Europe and the United States."

"It's a question of where we are. Geographically we're in Europe, but there is quite a strong tendency, as in Russia, to believe that we're something special, with our own history and problems, and that the principles of Europe can't be exactly implanted here. There is a great debate going on about whether we should face Russia or face Europe."

President Zhelyu Zhelev is pro-Western and supports efforts to bring Bulgaria toward membership in the European Union and NATO.

After a period of rule by the pro-Western United Democratic Front, Bulgarian voters last December returned the former Communists, who now call themselves the Bulgarian Socialist Party, to power. Since then, Foreign Ministry officials have stopped saying they seek membership in NATO.

Instead they say only that they want to become "associated" or "work closely" with the alliance.

"Bulgaria will not do anything with regard to NATO which it is not totally confident that the Russians approve of and want to happen," a foreign diplomat here said.

Deputy Foreign Minister Vasily Baitchev said in an interview, "Although we do not consider Russia's position to be decisive, we do believe that Russia's legitimate rights cannot be ignored."

Determined to push their country westward, several prominent Bulgarians have formed the most active lobby of its type in Eastern Europe, the Atlantic Club of Bulgaria, intended to shape public opinion in favor of NATO. Indeed, public opinion surveys suggest that as recently as three years ago most people here opposed the idea of Bulgarian membership, but that most now favor it.

*   *   *

June 15, 1995

A RAGTAG BOSNIAN ARMY BECOMES A CREDIBLE FORCE

By ROGER COHEN

SARAJEVO, Bosnia and Herzegovina, June 14—The Serbs still shell this city, as they have for more than three years. But there is a difference today. The outgoing mortar fire from Bosnian Army positions is often as intense as the Serbian bombardment.

The 82-millimeter mortars, brought through the dank tunnel that is this city's single connection with the outside world, are only the most visible sign of the emergence of a credible Bosnian Army from the ragtag collection of thugs, kids and patriots armed with hunting rifles who faced the Bosnian Serbs in 1992.

This force of about 130,000 soldiers has more than held its own against the Serbs over the past year. It has taken strategic high ground, most recently Treskavica Mountain south of Sarajevo, and resisted against all odds in the isolated western enclave of Bihac. But a major victory of a kind that could change the course of the war has eluded it.

The absence of such a victory may help explain the current massing of Bosnian troops around Visoko, northwest of Sarajevo, in possible preparation for an attempt to break the city's siege.

"We are tired of dying for hillsides and mountains," said a Bosnian soldier who asked not to be identified. "We want to fight now for something decisive."

There are two potentially decisive battles in the Bosnian war, Western analysts say.

The first is to lift the siege of Sarajevo: victory would lift the morale of Bosnians to an almost incalculable degree and link the capital with the Government-held heartland around Zenica. At a single stroke, the state called Bosnia would pass from a tenuous idea to something with a semblance of physical coherence.

The second is for the narrow corridor near Brcko linking Serbian-held parts of Croatia and western Bosnia with eastern Bosnia and Serbia itself. A Bosnian victory closing the corridor would probably doom all Serb-held territories to the west.

But the area around the corridor is tank country, which suits the Bosnian Serbs, and it is close enough to Serbia to make it almost inevitable that the powerful Serbian-dominated Yugoslav Army would be drawn into any major battle.

The strength of the Serbs around Sarajevo is also formidable. They are believed to have 500 to 800 heavy weapons within range of the city. Civilians are vulnerable to Serbian tank, mortar and artillery fire at any time and the Serbs have repeatedly shown their readiness to use terror as a weapon of war. All the high ground is in Serbian hands.

But scrambling to circumvent an arms embargo whose initial effect was to perpetuate their vulnerability, the Muslim-led Bosnian forces now have some means of hitting back.

Paul Beaver, a London-based military analyst, said they had succeeded in acquiring large number of mortars, some long-range anti-tank weapons and a few tanks. Smaller weapons are increasingly produced domestically in places like Novi Travnik and Bihac.

"The Bosnians have very rapidly become a proper army," he said. "They can probably mount one small battle group of about 30 tanks and 50 guns. They also have some increasingly good special units capable of breaking through enemy lines."

Western analysts say most of the Bosnians' weapons have come from Turkey, Malaysia and Iran, three countries with which the Sarajevo Government has established close commercial and diplomatic relations.

"Our relations with Iran are quite firm," said Kemal Muftic, the chief aide to Alija Izetbegovic, the Bosnian President. "If you find yourself in as hard a situation as we are in, you accept the help you can get."

The conduit for most of the weapons has been Croatia, a nominal ally of the Bosnian Government whose own intense armaments program has been tolerated by the United States despite the embargo on all the states that emerged from the former Yugoslavia.

But Croatia, still wary of the Bosnian Government after the Muslim-Croat war of 1993, has been reluctant to allow the Bosnian Army to obtain the tanks and heavy guns it most needs to push through entrenched Serbian artillery positions like those around Sarajevo.

"The biggest problem for the Bosnian Army is still artillery," said an American official.

There is no question that the Bosnian Army outnumbers the Serbs, probably by about 45,000 men, and its motivation is widely viewed as superior. The Serbs are stretched thin and their unity of purpose has been sapped by political divisions.

But does it make sense to use the Bosnian manpower and motivation to attack into Serbian strength? Some Western analysts believe the Bosnian Army would suffer a devastating defeat around Sarajevo and should continue to concentrate on smaller targets.

One alternative objective would be to take Serbian territory in the Ozren Mountains, allowing the big Government-held towns of Tuzla and Zenica to be linked more directly. An attempt to achieve this failed last year.

Such an incremental approach would probably bring some successes and the long-term military trend is certainly in Bosnia's favor. But incremental successes are not going to change the fact that the 300,000 people of Sarajevo are close to the breaking point.

More than 38 months after the city was encircled, it is today without water, electricity, gas, or a usable road out of town. Food is scarce and former bank managers and executives now spend their time tending vegetable gardens. The Bosnian Government is aware of the extent of civilian exhaustion.

After being devastated and waiting for somebody to help them, Bosnia's Muslims, helped by Croats and Serbs loyal to the Government, now know that only they can rescue their capital. They have no further illusions about the intentions of Western governments.

In this context, the civilian impatience and military restiveness in and around Sarajevo is such that a bold gamble cannot be excluded, one that most United Nations military observers here give a 50-50 chance of success.

* * *

August 5, 1995

IN BROAD ATTACK, CROATIA IS TRYING TO DISLODGE SERBS

By RAYMOND BONNER

ZAGREB, Croatia, Aug. 4—The Croatian Government launched a long-threatened offensive at dawn today, sending tanks, troops and jets into action to retake a swath of territory that has been under the control of rebel Serbs since 1991.

More than 1,500 shells landed in Knin, the headquarters of the breakaway Serbian region, United Nations officials said. Other towns along the 90-mile-long Serb-held territory, known as Krajina, were also reportedly shelled or bombed.

A resumption of fighting between Croatia and the Krajina Serbs has long been feared for its potential to draw in the powerful forces of the Serb-dominated Yugoslav Government. But the Serbian leader in Belgrade, Slobodan Milosevic, said today that "escalation of the conflict must be prevented."

The number of civilian dead was not known—the Croats did not allow journalists into Krajina—but the United Nations commander in Knin, Col. Andrew Leslie, told The Associated Press there had been a "serious loss of human life."

The United Nations also reported that one peacekeeper was killed and two others were wounded in the attack, and that 98 more were captured by the advancing Croats. The United Nations has some 10,000 troops in the region, many along a 1992 cease-fire line.

The United Nations has threatened NATO air strikes to protect its troops in Krajina but no such raids were mounted today.

Indeed, the only NATO action was against a Serbian target. The United States Navy said two radar-jamming planes attacked a surface-to-air missile site near Knin after the missile battery's radar locked on to the planes in preparation for firing.

The planes, EA-6B's flying from the aircraft carrier Roosevelt in the Adriatic, were responding to a request for help from United Nations peacekeeping forces in the area, a Navy spokesman said in Washington. It was not immediately known what damage the site suffered; the planes returned safely to the carrier.

After the Croatian President, Franjo Tudjman, rejected a peace plan presented late Thursday by the United States Ambassador, Washington urged him to respect civilians and the peacekeepers. "On both counts, they're batting .000," an American official said late this afternoon.

Europe's chief peace negotiator for the Balkans, Carl Bildt, condemned the Croatian offensive, comparing President Tudjman to the Krajina Serb leader, Milan Martic, who has been indicted by an international tribunal on charges of crimes against humanity.

Noting that Mr. Martic had been indicted for a rocket attack on the civilians of Zagreb, Mr. Bildt said, "It is difficult to see any difference between these actions and the shelling of Knin, which President Tudjman must now be held responsible for."

On Thursday the United States Ambassador, Peter W. Galbraith had presented to President Tudjman an agreement extracted from a rebel Serb leader. Mr. Galbraith said the concessions substantially met Croatia's demands on the rebels.

The Krajina region is valuable to Croatia because all the roads and rail lines connecting Zagreb with the southern coastal region pass through it. The Serbs also control an oil pipeline from the Adriatic.

Mr. Galbraith has played an active role in seeking a negotiated settlement, but his efforts may have been undermined by Washington's lukewarm warnings against a Croatian offensive. Or it may be, as one diplomat here suggested, that Mr. Galbraith was so committed to the talks he had led for more than a year that he failed to see that they were doomed, given the intransigence of the two parties.

In any event, within hours of receiving the plan, the Croatian Government went to war.

There are several reasons why the Croats chose war rather than further talks to get Krajina back, diplomats and United Nations officials said. For one thing, the Croatians do not trust the Serbian leaders, and saw the proposal, which included talks on re-establishing Croatian sovereignty in Krajina, as a stalling tactic.

The Croatian Army, which has more than 100,000 men in uniform and modern weapons acquired in spite of the arms embargo, is far superior to the rebel Serbs, thought to be 50,000 strong. Politically, the Serbs do not have many friends in the world, and Washington and Bonn had essentially given Croatia a green light.

In short, the Croats saw a window of opportunity, but it was a window that Mr. Galbraith's proposal and other negotiating efforts were beginning to close, for it would be hard to justify war if the peace talks were making progress.

Under the Ambassador's plan, the Krajina Serbs had agreed to reopen the oil pipeline and were prepared to negotiate the reopening of the road from the Croatian port at Split to Zagreb. Thus today's action will bolster those who believe, as do some diplomats here, that what really lies behind the offensive is the determination of the Croats simply to expel the 150,000 Serbs in Krajina.

It was difficult to determine how successful the Croatian forces were today because their claims about towns and territory captured did not match what the United Nations said.

The United Nations reported Croatian assaults near Petrinja and Gospic, as well as Knin. But a spokeswoman, Maj. Rita LePage, said the Croats had met "stiff resistance."

In the early hours of the attack, a Danish peacekeeper was killed in a "deliberate" tank attack on his position, said the senior United Nations military commander, Lieut. Gen. Bernard Janvier. In a Croatian artillery attack on another position, two Polish peacekeepers were reported wounded, one critically. This afternoon, two Croatian jets strafed a Czech post with 30-millimeter cannon fire, Major LePage said.

Altogether, United Nations officials said, 16 posts were attacked by Croats and 98 peacekeepers were captured by Croatian forces.

There were no reports of Serbian attacks on United Nations peacekeepers, Major LePage said.

Beginning early this morning and continuing for most of the day, Government television suspended programming and ran patriotic songs and romantic images of soldiers defending the fatherland.

The war was less evident on the streets.

At the Croatian side of the front line, the town of Karlovac was eerily silent this afternoon after having been shelled briefly by the Serbs earlier in the day. The few brave souls who ventured out to what appeared to be the only food shop open went about their business quickly.

"We always thought there would be a diplomatic way to solve it," said Mile Jurjevic, who needed to buy some rations because he had to take his wife to the hospital, in a city several hours away.

Artillery fire thundered in the distance but it was outgoing fire, by Croatian forces.

Zagreb is only 25 miles north of Karlovac, but the atmosphere here was far different. There were people on the streets, lingering in cafes, eating ice cream cones. Workmen were carrying out routine street repairs. A huge air-raid shelter built into the side of a hill in World War II had no worried occupants at midday.

Around 6:30 P.M., an air-raid siren began to wail, and there was a report that a rocket had landed in a Zagreb suburb. Even after dark, however, there was still life on the streets.

*　*　*

August 8, 1995

TIDE OF FLEEING SERBS PUT AT 120,000

By JANE PERLEZ

BELGRADE, Yugoslavia, Aug. 7—The estimate of the number of Serbs fleeing Croatia after Government troops retook rebel-held land rose to 120,000 today, and relief officials said they faced the biggest refugee crisis of the Balkan war.

The president of the International Committee of the Red Cross, Cornelio Sommaruga, said here tonight that he was concerned about reports of attacks from areas held by Croatian troops on the refugees. Some of the refugees have traveled as far as Serbia, while others are in Serbian-held parts of Bosnia and others are trying to leave the area of Croatia taken by the Government.

There were reports of shelling, apparently from new Croatian positions in that region, which the Serbs called Krajina, toward three villages around Bosanski Petrovac, in western Bosnia, where refugees had gathered, a Red Cross spokesman said.

Refugees moving on the road toward Bijeljina, near the border with Serbia, were also shelled from Krajina, according to reports received by the Red Cross, the spokesman said.

The number of casualties was not known in either case. But the Red Cross sent emergency medical supplies to the local hospital at Petrovac, said the spokesman, Josue Ancelmo.

Mr. Sommaruga, who came to Belgrade today because of the crisis, said he would meet with President Slobodan Milosevic of Serbia and President Franjo Tudjman of Croatia and would call on them to "meet their responsibility to safeguard and respect civilians."

"We have a large humanitarian crisis here not only because of the number of displaced, but also because of the military attacks being done on the displaced," he said.

A large number of the refugees were armed, he said, complicating the situation and adding to the potential of new violence. Many Serb soldiers from the Krajina were among those who fled with their families in cars and tractors.

While earlier estimates of the number of refugees had ranged from 60,000 to 100,000, the Red Cross said today that it believed there were as many as 120,000.

The exodus of Serbian refugees from the Krajina was different from any other in the Yugoslav war, aid officials said.

While Bosnia has hundreds of thousands of refugees, and some of them have had to flee more than once as territory changed hands, they have been displaced over several years and in smaller groups.

Despite the many instances in which Bosnian Serbs troops have pushed Muslims out of their towns and out of United Nations protected enclaves, there has been no instance in which so many people have been displaced at one time.

Last month, when the United Nations-protected enclaves of Srebrenica and Zepa fell to the Bosnian Serbs, the Red

Cross said, 29,000 people were forced to flee. Most of them had already been expelled from their homes before coming to the enclaves.

Many of the Serbs who escaped from Krajina in advance of the Croatian forces had lived in that area for many years and had not previously been displaced by the war. Aid officials describes the new refugees as extremely tense, in large part because the unexpected speed of the Croatian offensive and victory was a shock and because they did not receive the military help to defend the Krajina that they expected from Serbia.

Serbia and Montenegro are the remaining entities in the current Yugoslavia, and it was the Yugoslav Army that secured the Krajina for the Croatian Serbs in the 1991 war.

Most of the refugees were on the move today in long columns of slow-moving tractors, carts, buses, trucks and—for the lucky ones—cars, on a 140-mile arc across northern Bosnia. But there were large clusters of refugees on a 70-mile stretch around Bosanski Petrovac, Prijedor and Banja Luka, in Western Bosnia, the Red Cross said.

Most of the refugees said they wanted to go to Serbia, and the Red Cross said today that the Serbian authorities were allowing the refugees to cross the border. Increasing numbers were reaching the capital here, and a group of refugees were camped outside the headquarters of the Yugoslav Red Cross waiting for help.

On the road just north of Loznica, in Serbia, cars packed with families from Knin, the capital of Krajina, were heading for Belgrade. By nightfall, the Red Cross said, an estimated 15,000 refugees had crossed the main border point at Sremska Raca into Serbia.

But the crossing there is over a narrow bridge and it was taking many, many hours for the refugees to be processed by the border guards, relief officials said.

*   *   *

August 10, 1995

SPY PHOTOS INDICATE MASS GRAVE AT SERB-HELD TOWN, U.S. SAYS

By ERIC SCHMITT

WASHINGTON, Aug. 9—The United States said today that it had spy photographs that it planned to make public of what appears to be a mass grave outside the Bosnian town of Srebrenica, where thousands of Muslim men and boys have been missing since they were rounded up after Bosnian Serbs seized the area last month.

The photographs, from spy satellites and U-2 planes, coupled with interviews with Muslim refugees who fled after Srebrenica's capture, provide the most compelling circumstantial evidence that Serbian troops executed at least several hundred military-age men and boys as part of an ethnic-cleansing campaign, Administration officials said.

"We've got some evidence from sensitive sources that tend to corroborate accounts of atrocities against the Bos-

nian men and boys who were prevented from leaving Srebrenica," David T. Johnson, a State Department spokesman, said today.

The chief United States delegate to the United Nations, Madeleine K. Albright, plans to present the evidence to the Security Council on Thursday. News organizations have reported refugees' grisly accounts of murders, rapes and other atrocities from Srebrenica. What are new are the reconnaissance photographs and a tip from a witness who knew of the mass graves, Administration officials said.

According to one American official who has seen the photographs, one shows hundreds and perhaps thousands of Muslim men and boys in a field near a soccer stadium about 5 miles north of Srebrenica. Another photo taken several days later shows a large area of freshly dug earth, consistent with the appearance of known mass graves, near the stadium, which is empty.

The International Red Cross has said at least 6,000 people are unaccounted for since the fall of Srebrenica. One senior American official said the graves in the aerial photographs could hold "many hundreds" of bodies. It is unclear how many of the other missing people are in hiding, dead or in refugee camps.

The timing of the Administration's disclosure of the photos, which Mr. Clinton discussed with his national security advisers on Monday, coincided with a new American plan to broker peace in the Balkans. Anthony Lake, the President's national security adviser, arrived in London today to begin talks with European allies.

One senior Administration official acknowledged that the photos "put some pressure on the Serbs and shows people we are watching them."

"People have to know what's going on," the official added. "We don't want people to think we're sitting on evidence."

The Administration said Assistant Secretary of State John Shattuck had gathered evidence of Serb atrocities during a visit to central and northeastern Bosnia last week.

Michael D. McCurry, the White House press secretary, said Mr. Shattuck "was presented with evidence of egregious human rights violations committed by Bosnian Serb forces in the aftermath of their attack on Srebrenica and Zepa."

"The Assistant Secretary heard eyewitness accounts of mass executions, beatings, rape and other flagrant violations of human rights and international humanitarian law," Mr. McCurry said, adding that the evidence would be turned over to the war crimes tribunal in The Hague.

The Central Intelligence Agency's Deputy Director for Intelligence, John Gannon, told a Senate hearing today that American intelligence had found a clear pattern of "ethnic cleansing" by the Bosnian Serbs since 1992.

He said that a C.I.A. analysis showed that more than 3,000 settlements, mainly in Serb-controlled areas of Bosnia, have been burned or destroyed and that up to 90 percent of non-Serbs will have no homes to return to.

As Administration officials in Washington discussed the reconnaissance photos, Mr. Lake and senior Defense and State Department officials prepared for talks with European allies on a new peace proposal for the Balkans.

American officials disclosed new details of the plan, which one top aide described as "a series of sticks and carrots" for the Bosnian Serbs and the Bosnian Muslims.

While Washington still favors a plan that gives the Muslim-controlled Bosnian Government 51 percent of the territory, the new proposal would give the Serbs the last remaining eastern Government enclave, Gorazde, in exchange for more valuable territory around Sarajevo.

To entice the warring parties to settle, the plan would lift economic sanctions against the Bosnian Serbs and promise a "mini-Marshall plan" of post-war economic aid to the Bosnian Muslims, an American official said. The United States and other Western nations would also help the Government build a military strong enough to defend its new borders.

If the deal falls through and the allies blame the Serbs, the plan calls for lifting the arms embargo against the Bosnian Government and launching air strikes against Serbian targets. If the Muslims are blamed for any failure, the United Nations peacekeeping forces would withdraw and leave the Muslims to their own devices.

If the new American peace effort succeeds, several thousand United States troops would be committed to a heavily armed NATO force to guarantee the plan, Administration officials said.

This planning has been in place for nearly two years, but until recently has not been much of an issue. But Croatia's successful military offensive against the Serbs and a split within the leadership of the Bosnian Serbs has presented an opportunity for a diplomatic settlement and forced the Pentagon to refine details on how to enforce it.

There are still several hurdles to clear before peace breaks out in the Balkans. Some Administration officials voiced skepticism that any deal was imminent. The European allies have to agree on the details. More important, the Serbs and Muslims must concur, which is far from certain.

"It has to be pursued in number of capitals," a senior Administration official said.

But if a durable peace is negotiated and Congress agrees to send troops, American forces would join a large NATO force to monitor Bosnian borders. Until the recent Croatian military offensive, NATO planners had estimated it would take as many as 35,000 NATO troops—half of them American—to enforce a Bosnia peace plan.

Pentagon officials said today that the loss of two eastern enclaves to the Serbs and the Croatian advances would mean there would be less territory to monitor and fewer troops, but they declined to say how many might now be required.

"Under the old plan, NATO would have done disarming and collecting heavy weapons," said a senior Pentagon planner. "This new initiative has much more limited tasks, like separating factions and providing some sort of protective envelope for the Bosnian Muslims."

The Pentagon official said the Administration "hasn't crystallized around any numbers, but it will be a smaller force with fewer missions."

"It all depends on how they the draw the map, where they put forces and what tasks would be assigned to them," the official added.

American officials say any NATO military involvement in Bosnia would most likely be measured in months, not years. "We are looking more to a Haiti model," a senior Administration official said.

*   *   *

August 29, 1995

HORROR AGAIN FILLS SARAJEVO'S MARKET

By The Associated Press

SARAJEVO, Bosnia and Herzegovina, Aug. 28—The air in Sarajevo, the besieged Bosnian capital, was thick with the screams of the wounded and dying and the wails of relatives and friends today after two shells hit the central market.

Gatherings had been prohibited at the marketplace in an attempt to prevent a repetition of the attack in February 1994 in which 68 people were killed and more than 200 wounded. A police officer said he had tried to disperse the teeming crowd minutes before the shell hit.

But today was the first sunny day after several rainy ones, and streets have been relatively busy in the past few weeks because the shelling had subsided as diplomats pressed for a new peace initiative in the Balkans.

Immediately after the market was hit today, women were seen crawling along the road, vomiting blood as they gasped for air.

Shopping bags lay dumped in the blood outside the main entrance of the once-elegant building that serves as the city's largest indoor market.

A man's body was hurled by the blast's force on to a railing that separated the sidewalk from the road. It hung there jackknifed.

Journalists joined taxi drivers and market vendors in heaping bodies into the back of vehicles to rush them to the hospital.

Some cars, bodies hanging out of them, sped off to hospitals, horns blaring.

Many of the dead were children, women or old people, some with legs and arms blown off.

One elderly man lay with his head bleeding, his motorcycle still between his legs.

The Bosnian Serb radio said that retaliatory mortar fire from Government positions hit the Serb-held Sarajevo suburb of Ilidza, hitting a wedding procession and wounding about 50 people, several seriously. There was no way to immediately verify the reports.

Hours after the attack on the market today, the city's streets were deserted. Somber classical music was played on radio and TV, interspersed with horrifying reports of the massacre, reminiscent of the attack in 1994.

At the city's main Kosevo hospital, normally hardened nurses wept and waved their arms in despair as they struggled to cope with more than 100 casualties. The shelling killed at least 37 people and wounded 80.

Like others whose wounds were not life-threatening, 50-year-old Nihada Hadziahmic, was forced to wait outside for her turn to be treated. Blood seeped through the cloth hastily wrapped around her wounded legs.

Doctors and nurses, their white robes splattered red, rushed casualties into operating rooms.

The hospital director, Dr. Fahrudin Konjhodzic, said that he thought Kosevo coped with the crush of casualties better than almost any other hospital in the world. The hospital has been dealing with the victims of shelling throughout the three years that the city has been under siege.

"Serbs did a great job again," shouted a doctor at the hospital as he rushed by. "And the world is just kidding around."

"Do they care for us?" he asked. Not waiting for a reply, he yelled, "Of course not!"

*   *   *

September 4, 1995

NATO DEMANDS SERBS WITHDRAW GUNS NEAR SARAJEVO

By ROGER COHEN

BELGRADE, Yugoslavia, Sept. 3—NATO issued an ultimatum to the Bosnian Serbs today to remove their heavy artillery from the Sarajevo area, and United Nations forces adopted a new policy by opening a road out of the Bosnian capital without asking for the Serbs' consent.

The opening of the road was largely symbolic in that it consists of a track across the airport and Sarajevans must still use the treacherous Mount Igman road to go anywhere beyond the city area. But the fact that the United Nations acted unilaterally was highly significant in that its policy has been to do nothing without the approval of the Serbs.

"The old United Nations policy was impartiality to the point of appeasement," one United Nations official said. "That has now changed." It has taken three and half years for this critical shift to occur.

A senior NATO official said that the Serbs had been told to start removing their guns to a distance of at least 20 kilometers (12.5 miles) from Sarajevo by 11 P.M. local time (5 P.M. Eastern time) Monday, or face a resumption of the 50-hour blitz on Serbian targets that ended early Friday.

But the official added that the Serbs would in fact almost certainly be given until 11 P.M. local time on Tuesday to comply with the three-point ultimatum from NATO. The NATO demands are that the withdrawal of guns must begin; that all attacks on Gorazde, Tuzla, Bihac and Sarajevo must cease; and that Sarajevo airport, closed by Bosnian Serb threats since April, must be reopened.

"The United Nations wanted a 72-hour pause that would end Tuesday, while NATO favored 48 hours," the official said. "So we came up with the formula of a review on Monday and a final cut-off on Tuesday."

Lieut. Col. Chris Vernon, a spokesman for United Nations forces in Sarajevo, said that Monday night would be "a key point when we assess how far we are getting." Asked if this amounted to a deadline, he replied, "I wouldn't go quite that far, let's just see what the situation is then."

When the bombing began last Wednesday, NATO said that it would not stop until the Sarajevo area was secure.

Colonel Vernon said there was no suggestion today that the Serbs had begun to remove their guns. Gen. Ratko Mladic, the commander of the Bosnian Serbs, has insisted that any withdrawal of the roughly 300 artillery pieces that have long terrorized Sarajevo must be accompanied by a cease-fire in Bosnia and a commitment from the Bosnian Government not to seize any military advantage from his army's actions.

The stand-off comes 18 months after NATO first issued an ultimatum for the removal of the guns. But at that time the real readiness of Western governments to use force was scant and an untenable compromise emerged that later opened the way for renewed Serbian shelling.

Only a mortar attack last week on the Sarajevo market that killed 38 people stirred a new resolve to ease the Serbian noose around the city.

That resolve was evident today in the United Nations' decision to open the road across the airport without asking the Serbs' permission. In the past, United Nations commanders have insisted that they could do nothing without the assent of both parties to the Bosnian war because to do so would be to take sides and risk being drawn into the conflict.

That was the firm position of Gen. Michael Rose, the British commander of United Nations forces in Sarajevo, who left the city early this year. He talked repeatedly of the "Mogadishu line" that could not be crossed—a reference to the way United Nations peacekeepers were dragged into the conflict in Somalia.

In fact, the United Nations mandate is not neutral and is clear in calling for the defense of the sovereignty and territorial integrity of Bosnia and Herzegovina, and in permitting the use of force to allow the delivery of food and other aid to cities including Sarajevo.

General Rose's successor, Lieut. Gen. Rupert Smith, has persistently attempted to adhere to this mandate and, with the arrival in recent months of the rapid-reaction force, he has secured the soldiers and firepower to do so. The nature of the United Nations mission has thus changed.

The road across the airport was opened early this year. But tensions mounted after some Serbian children were shot dead in the Serb-held section of town called Grbavica, and the road closed.

On the diplomatic front, Assistant Secretary of State Richard C. Holbrooke returned today to Belgrade after briefing the NATO allies in Brussels on Saturday. It appeared certain that he would press President Slobodan Milosevic of Serbia to persuade the Bosnian Serbs to comply with the NATO ultimatum to avoid a confrontation.

Up to now, the Bosnian Serbs, who have been persuaded by President Milosevic that peace is now in their best interest, have shown virtually complete restraint in the face of the NATO bombing.

In a gruesome piece of theater, they did instruct their television station to show images last Wednesday falsely suggesting that three Spanish diplomats had been killed by the NATO bombing, but there has been almost no retaliatory shelling.

The diplomats, accompanied by an Irishman and a Dutchman who were traveling with them, were in fact alive and in Bosnian Serb custody. They were released today and came to Serbia.

Mr. Holbrooke, who has been engaged in shuttle diplomacy during the last week, has secured agreement on a meeting in Geneva next Friday of the Foreign Ministers from Bosnia, Croatia and Serb-dominated Yugoslavia.

But the Clinton Administration is under some pressure from the Muslim-led Bosnian Government to resume the NATO bombing immediately. Muhamed Sacirbey, the Bosnian Foreign Minister, has suggested that he will not attend the talks unless the NATO campaign continues.

The breakthrough on direct talks in Geneva—it will be the first such meeting in two years—followed a power struggle between President Milosevic and the Bosnian Serbs in which Mr. Milosevic finally secured the authority to negotiate on behalf of his brothers west of the Drina River.

But if the Bosnian Serbs refuse to comply with the NATO ultimatum, it will suggest that President Milosevic's authority has its limits and that his ability to persuade the Bosnian Serbs to give up land in the interests of an agreement may not be absolute.

After 40 months of war, the Serbs, who accounted for close to a third of Bosnia's pre-war population, control about 70 percent of the territory.

Under the current proposal for an accord, they would have to give up about a third of the land they hold.

In an interview today with ABC News, Mr. Holbrooke said land would be the most difficult issue in peace talks. An international proposal offers 51 percent of Bosnia to a Muslim-Croat federation and 49 percent to the Serbs. But, he said, "each side's 51-49 looks more like 60-40 in their favor. The principle of 51-49 must be and will be maintained."

* * *

September 14, 1995

GREECE TO LIFT EMBARGO AGAINST MACEDONIA IF IT SCRAPS ITS FLAG

By CHRISTOPHER S. WREN

UNITED NATIONS, Sept. 13—Greece agreed today to take steps to lift its 19-month trade embargo against the former Yugoslav republic of Macedonia, in return for concessions from Macedonia that include scrapping the country's existing national flag.

The two neighbors have yet to settle a more intractable dispute over the name of Macedonia, which Greece contends belongs properly to its northern province. But the interim agreement, which came together after 28 months of shuttle mediation by Cyrus R. Vance, a former United States Secretary of State, defuses the longstanding threat of violence in a region already ravaged by ethnic warfare.

The accord was signed at the United Nations this afternoon by the Greek Foreign Minister, Karolos Papoulias, and his Macedonian counterpart, Stevo Crvenkovski, after some last-minute bargaining over the details.

It commits Macedonia to cease using "in any fashion" a 16-pointed star displayed on the red background of its national flag. Greece contends that the distinctive symbol, called the Sun or Star of Vergina, is intrinsic to its own cultural heritage.

Macedonia further pledged that nothing in its Constitution, which promises to protect all Macedonians, will be interpreted as constituting a claim to territory beyond its borders. Greece and Bulgaria both have ethnic Macedonian minorities.

Greece and Macedonia also agreed to establish diplomatic relations "at an early date," beginning with the prompt opening of liaison office in Athens and Skopje, and confirmed their common border as "enduring and inviolable." Greece had refused to recognize Macedonia, which declared independence after Yugoslavia disintegrated in 1991.

Mr. Vance said the steps needed to implement the accord fully would take place over the next few weeks. The agreement takes effect 30 days from today.

This would include lifting Greek trade sanctions, which have badly damaged Macedonia's landlocked economy. The agreement does not mention the sanctions but commits both nations to "refrain from imposing any impediment to the movement of people or goods between their territories." Mr. Vance had assured reporters last week that the sanctions would be lifted once the agreement was signed.

Two days of tough negotiations here preceded today's signing, with relations at first so frosty that the two Foreign Ministers stayed in different hotels here while Mr. Vance shuttled between them to resolve the final differences.

The Foreign Ministers finally met this afternoon under the auspices of Secretary General Boutros Boutros-Ghali to sign the agreement. But Mr. Papoulias and Mr. Crvenkovski did not speak to each other in front of reporters or take any questions.

Mr. Vance declined to specify the final sticking points, saying only that "there were a lot of technical things" to resolve in so wide-ranging an agreement. There were reports that the United States engaged in arm-twisting to get Greece to settle its dispute with Macedonia.

The negotiations over Macedonia's name are expected to resume in late October or early November. But Mr. Vance said, "The fact that they have a difference over the name is not going to affect progress" on what has already been achieved.

Mr. Vance said the agreement today "has possibilities of having a positive effect" on the ethnic fighting elsewhere in the former Yugoslavia. About 550 American soldiers are deployed in Macedonia as part of a larger United Nations force trying to prevent hostilities from spilling over from Bosnia.

* * *

September 16, 1995

SERBS, COMPLYING WITH DEAL FORGED BY U.S., BEGIN MOVES TO LIFT SIEGE OF SARAJEVO

By ELAINE SCIOLINO

WASHINGTON, Sept. 15—The Serbs of Bosnia today took the first steps to lift the siege of Sarajevo, reopening the roads and the airport and giving relief convoys free passage. They also withdrew a few tanks, howitzers and heavy artillery pieces from the hills surrounding the Bosnian capital.

President Clinton led a chorus of NATO allies and—after a week of intensifying criticism—the Russians in welcoming the brokered agreement, which calls for the Serbs to withdraw their heavy weaponry in exchange for a halt in the NATO bombing campaign.

But while relishing a rare moment of success in Bosnian diplomacy, the President warned of further military action if the Serbs renege.

"Let me emphasize: if the Bosnian Serbs do not comply with their commitments, the air strikes will resume," he told reporters.

Today's self-congratulation was punctured by protests from President Alija Izetbegovic of Bosnia that the deal, blessed on Thursday by the United States representative, Richard C. Holbrooke, allowed the Serbs to keep hundreds of their weapons within range of Sarajevo.

In the accord, brokered by Mr. Holbrooke, the Serbs agreed to withdraw artillery greater than 100 millimeters, mortars larger than 82 millimeters and all tanks, which American intelligence experts estimated totaled 350 to 400 weapons. The shell that killed 39 people in a Sarajevo market on Aug. 28 and precipitated the NATO bombing came from a 120-millimeter gun, according to a United Nations investigation.

But the agreement allows the Serbs around Sarajevo to retain several hundred smaller mortars, artillery guns and antiaircraft weapons that give them the ability to launch attacks with ease against the airport and other targets.

To make up for the gaps in the agreement, Lieut. Gen. Rupert Smith, the United Nations commander in Bosnia, sent a letter to the Bosnian Serb commander, Gen. Ratko Mladic, asking that Serb forces withdraw all mortars and artillery of 76 millimeters and larger and all antiaircraft weapons of 20 millimeters and larger.

"We admit there is a problem with the weapons that the Serbs have left out, and the United Nations is trying to resolve it," a senior Administration official said.

President Izetbegovic, whose troops are on the offensive in other parts of Bosnia, is also reluctant to agree to a formal end of hostilities around Sarajevo, and the United States at this point is uncomfortable about pressing him.

"It would put the victim on a par with the aggressor," said one senior Administration official involved in Bosnia policy. "They didn't lay siege to Sarajevo; the Serbs did."

The offensive by the Bosnian Army, in concert with Croatian allies, has uprooted a tide of angry Serbian refugees, causing potentially explosive turmoil in central Bosnia.

For their part, the Serbs are still fighting, and today fired two surface-to-air missiles at NATO warplanes outside Gorazde in eastern Bosnia, a United Nations spokesman said. The plane was not hit and NATO, apparently concerned about the fragile peace plan, did not retaliate.

Even as Sarajevo seemed to return to normal, Bosnian Government troops and their Croatian allies continued their offensive today in central and northwest Bosnia. And Serbs made clear that despite their commitment to withdraw their heavy weapons from a 12.5-mile zone around Sarajevo, they reserved the right to retaliate for Bosnian attacks.

"Should the Muslims attack Serb Sarajevo, our army will have to activate its heavy weapons, which will not be far away," Momcilo Krajisnik, the top aide to Radovan Karadzic, the Bosnian Serb leader, told the Bosnian Serb press agency.

Still, the Administration, the United Nations and the NATO allies share a wary optimism that this time, the Serbs may be serious about ending the three-and-a-half-year bombardment that has terrorized the 300,000 residents of Sarajevo.

In Banja Luka, in northern Bosnia, Dr. Karadzic, who signed Thursday's agreement, said his military would withdraw its heavy weapons "because if we have a cessation of hostilities agreement, it means there is not going to be war in Sarajevo any longer."

NATO's top commander in Europe, Gen. George Joulwan, said he was encouraged by the movements, but added that more weapons had to be withdrawn before NATO could extend its 72-hour pause in air strikes. "We have to see compliance," General Joulwan said. "We are very heartened that there is some movement of heavy weapons, but it is too early."

The suspension in bombing expires at 4 P.M. Eastern time on Sunday, but can be renewed for 72 hours if NATO decides the Serbs are moving to comply with the agreement.

The current strategy of the Clinton Administration is twofold: to take the Bosnian Serbs at their word, at least until they break it; and to nudge the Bosnian Government, which is recapturing territory, into peace. To that end, the Administration hopes to seize on what it calls the Serbs' desire to translate Thursday's concessions into a formal cessation of hostilities around Sarajevo and eventually a country-wide ceasefire.

In a sign that Washington is convinced tension in Bosnia is easing, Washington is withdrawing its request to send F-117 stealth fighters to Aviano Air Base in Italy for use in combat missions over Bosnia.

In Geneva today, Mr. Holbrooke, who will continue his shuttle diplomacy over the weekend, and mediators from Russia, Britain, France and Germany agreed to press for a peace settlement in the next few weeks.

But senior Administration officials acknowledge that the Muslim-dominated Bosnian Government, which has made dramatic battlefield gains against the Serbs during the air strikes, is resistant to the idea of a cease-fire.

"Given the state of play on the battlefield, the Bosnian Government is not immediately drawn to the idea of a country-wide cessation of hostilities," Alexander Vershbow, the senior official on Bosnia at the White House, said.

In a test today of the Serbian pledge to ease its siege, a French military plane carrying Defense Minister Charles Millon and relief supplies landed at Sarajevo and two United Nations relief convoys reached the city. Eleven relief flights are scheduled to land in Sarajevo on Saturday.

* * *

September 16, 1995

EUPHORIA IN STREETS
AS SUPPLY LINES OPEN

By KIT R. ROANE

SARAJEVO, Bosnia and Herzegovina, Sept. 15—This afternoon, Sabin Dzako heard a roar like thunder that shook the windows and brought tears to her eyes.

Outside, from the clear blue sky, the first of what she hopes will be a long line of cargo jets hit the tarmac of Sarajevo airport, bringing a long-awaited shipment of food and the first installment of psychological relief that citizens of the besieged city have known in months.

"We all hope that we will be able to sleep peacefully now and have water and power like we used to," the 52-year-old woman said. "I was so happy I cried when I saw the plane. It means the shooting has stopped and we are now free."

The opening of the airport was the fulfillment of the first part of a broad agreement with the Bosnian Serbs, who also opened the land routes into the city to relief convoys and, in the final hours of the day, began to remove their heavy weapons from the hills around the city.

In the neighborhoods around the airport—some of the worst-hit areas of the city—many citizens were euphoric.

Medzed Muzaferija, a local businessman, danced in the street as the second plane touched down. Then he spotted some of his company's trucks coming around the bend off the Mount Igman road, which has only recently opened to commercial traffic. Jumping in his Volkswagen Golf, Mr. Muzaferija popped a Roy Orbison tape into the tape-deck and cranked up the volume.

"I feel great," he shouted above the music. "This is the end of the war, definitely. It's over and there's no turning back."

Few people cared that the agreement signed by the Bosnian Serbs did not meet the original NATO ultimatum to pull all of their heavy weapons from the area, or that it was the Bosnian Serbs who would be listing just what they had and what they were willing to move. Dobrinja, a suburb of Sarajevo off a long corridor of sniper territory, has grown weary of war, and the NATO air strikes have proved to them that the world has finally become weary, too.

"Who cares about those Serbs' guns now, the U.S.A. has arrived and they are afraid to use them," added Mr. Muzaferija, pointing to the United Nations cargo plane about half-a-mile away. "This means the end of the Serbs."

Two aid convoys drove through Serb-held territory unimpeded today, carrying more than 350 tons of wheat flour and other food, while two planes reached the airport, one carrying aid, the other supplies for the United Nations forces.

Mans Nyberg, spokesman for the United Nations High Commissioner for Refugees, said that today was the first time convoys had passed Bosnian Serb checkpoints without being harassed. He added that eight planeloads of aid were slated to arrive on Saturday and that, if access continues, September would be the first month in five that Sarajevans received the 6,000 tons of food a month promised by the United Nations. He said he hoped the shipments would also allow aid organizations to begin filling their vacant warehouses for the bitter cold months to follow.

"This will amount to the end of the blockade," he said. "It is the end of this Serb weapon against the citizens of Sarajevo."

"And they stopped," he added, "for no other reason than the NATO bombing."

The NATO air strikes, which began on Aug. 30 in response to a Bosnian Serb mortar attack on a crowded market area in Sarajevo, opened the city to commerce several days ago. Food prices have plummeted, and shelling and sniping incidents have reached a year low.

In the markets, people recalled how at the height of the 41-month-old siege one egg cost $2. Now Sarajevans can purchase a box of 24 eggs for about $10. The cost of bananas and potatoes also reached record lows, and even alcohol is becoming affordable.

About the only hold-out has been the price of cigarettes, which some tobacco hawkers attributed to hoarding. That would break, they said, at the first sign of a Marlboro truck in town.

Despite the new optimism, Sarajevo still has its skeptics, who recall how Western guarantees to protect them from Serbian shelling were not acted upon in the past.

Throughout the city, memorials and shell holes mark the sites of personal loss and death and many people doubted that these tributes to Sarajevo's dead would be the last.

"I don't trust the Serbs and I don't care what they say," said Edina Hadzic, an 18-year-old student as she sat with her friends in one of the city's shaded squares. "I still feel under siege and getting cheaper food will change that. They are still on the hills and can create a massacre any time they want."

* * *

September 27, 1995

U.S. BACKS WAR-CRIMES LAWSUIT AGAINST BOSNIAN SERB LEADER

By NEIL A. LEWIS

WASHINGTON, Sept. 26—As the United States announced a preliminary agreement today to settle the war in the Balkans, the Clinton Administration has separately endorsed a lawsuit that would put the leader of the Bosnian Serbs on trial for war crimes—in New York.

In a brief filed with the Federal appeals court in New York last week, the Clinton Administration supported the right of two women to sue the leader, Radovan Karadzic, for suffering caused by what they claim is his participation in war crimes, torture and genocide.

The decision to support the women, whose names were withheld in court documents, came after an intense debate within the Administration over whether the spectacle of a trial and the Administration's support of it would make it more difficult to win Dr. Karadzic's support for a Balkan settlement.

A lower court had already ruled that the civil lawsuit could not be brought against Dr. Karadzic, but the United States Court of Appeals for the Second Circuit, which is now considering the case, has a history of favoring such lawsuits.

The two plaintiffs, identified only as Jane Doe 1 and Jane Doe 2, contend that Dr. Karadzic is responsible for what they suffered in the Balkans. The first plaintiff alleges that she was raped and mutilated by Bosnian Serb soldiers and the second woman alleges that she witnessed the rape and murder of her mother by Bosnian Serb forces.

Dr. Karadzic is represented by Ramsey F. Clark, a former United States Attorney General. Mr. Clark did not return telephone calls.

The Karadzic suit is the latest episode in a remarkable development in United States law in recent years—the use of American courts to enforce international human rights standards.

The Second Circuit has ruled that torturers and dictators may be sued in the Federal courts for acts that occurred abroad and that a judgment may be enforced if the subjects come to the United States or their assets here or abroad are located. That is the reasoning behind the multi-million dollar lawsuit against Ferdinand Marcos, the late Philippine dictator.

Dr. Karadzic was served with papers as he walked outside his hotel room when he came to the United Nations in February 1993.

Beth Stephens, an attorney for the Center for Constitutional Rights in New York who represents the two women, said she does not know whether Dr. Karadzic has any assets in the United States or elsewhere that could be seized to satisfy a judgment. "But our clients would be satisfied by a judgment that is just, even if they never receive any money," she said.

In supporting the women's right to sue, Drew S. Days, the Solicitor General, and Conrad K. Harper, a State Department legal adviser, said that while Dr. Karadzic is not an official of any recognized nation, he should be as liable for war crimes as were Nazi industrialists who were not government officials.

A State Department memorandum sent to Secretary of State Warren Christopher urging his approval of the brief argued that it would be an opportunity for the Clinton Administration to distinguish itself from its Republican predecessors in the field of human rights.

Dr. Karadzic, a psychiatrist, has also been indicted by a United Nations-sponsored war crimes tribunal sitting in The Hague for a variety of human rights abuses. As a result, he has avoided traveling outside the territory of the former Yugoslavia to avoid being taken into custody.

Administration officials have said the war crimes charges could become part of the peace negotiations. But Ms. Stephens, the lawyer for the two women, said governments and international authorities could not negotiate away the rights of the plaintiffs in the civil suit.

*   *   *

November 2, 1995

3 BALKAN PRESIDENTS MEET IN OHIO TO TRY TO END WAR

By ELAINE SCIOLINO

DAYTON, Ohio, Nov. 1—Barely suppressing their mutual distaste, three Balkan Presidents came together today at an American military base for ambitious peace talks aimed at ending four years of terror and bloodshed in Bosnia.

It was the first time the three men—Slobodan Milosevic of Serbia, Alija Izetbegovic of Bosnia and Franjo Tudjman of Croatia—have met face to face since they held a series of unsuccessful meetings in Yugoslavia in 1991 on the eve of the country's division and disintegration into war. Thus just bringing them into the same room represented a considerable achievement.

But the basic questions that they failed to settle four years ago and that have since provoked Europe's worst conflict since World War II remain unresolved: Can Bosnia survive, and what degree of self-government should be given to the Serbian minority living within its borders?

"We have an urgent and important purpose today," Secretary of State Warren Christopher said in opening the conference, which included representatives of France, Britain, Germany, Russia and the European Union. "We're here to give Bosnia and Herzegovina a chance to be a country at peace, not a killing field; a place where people can sleep in their homes, walk to work and worship in their churches, mosques and synagogues without fear of violence or death."

The United States, which hopes to keep the negotiations shrouded in secrecy and the three Presidents away from the television cameras, did not allow them to speak at the opening ceremony or answer a reporter's question about the prospects for peace.

And in a sign that the United States intends to control public disclosures about the talks, the State Department spokesman, Nicholas Burns, told reporters tonight that Mr. Milosevic and Mr. Tudjman agreed in a separate meeting today to a positive joint statement.

The statement, which Mr. Burns read aloud but did not release, declared their willingness to work toward full normalization of relations, including a mutual respect for human rights and the return of refugees, as well as the peaceful resolution of eastern Slavonia, a piece of Croatian territory that was seized by Serbs early in the war.

There was an air of awkwardness in the antiseptic, fluorescent-lit meeting room in the Hope Hotel Conference Center, named after Bob Hope, and the body language of the three Balkan leaders as well as the choreography of the Americans revealed much more than the official statements.

The main players—including the three Presidents, the Europeans, Mr. Christopher and Richard C. Holbrooke, the chief American negotiator—strode into the meeting room one by one. Each President was escorted into the room by the senior American diplomat serving in his country.

That allowed Mr. Christopher to avoid having to shake the hand of Mr. Milosevic, whom the Bush Administration said should be tried on war crimes charges.

But other handshakes were important to the American side today, and as soon as the group sat down around a small round table, Mr. Holbrooke gave Mr. Christopher a cue to rise, move toward the three Presidents, and nudge them into shaking hands with one another.

For the most part during the open-ended peace talks, the three Presidents will not meet face to face, but will relay their negotiating positions to each other via Mr. Holbrooke.

As the meeting opened on the 8,242-acre Wright-Patterson Air Force Base outside Dayton, about 100 demonstrators gathered outside the gates to protest Mr. Milosevic's presence and call for the independence of Kosovo, the province of Serbia populated mainly by ethnic Albanians.

"We will not negotiate with the war criminal," one sign said. "Milosevic's place is in The Hague, not Dayton," another said, referring to the center of the international war crimes tribunal.

Before the opening ceremony, Mr. Christopher conferred with the three Presidents in their personal quarters for about 45 minutes each.

He brought Mr. Izetbegovic, whose country the United States considers the "victim" in the war, a personal message from President Clinton to assure him of the American commitment to preserve the unity of the Bosnian state and strengthen its federation with Croatia, according to Mr. Burns.

As for Mr. Tudjman, Mr. Christopher "congratulated" him on the results of parliamentary elections on Sunday, which his party won by a large enough margin to keep a majority in Parliament.

But human rights organizations and independent American election monitors have criticized the election because the Serbs of the Krajina region were banned from voting, but ethnic Croats living in Bosnia were allowed to vote. Even some senior State Department officials said the United States should be protesting the results, not praising them.

As for Mr. Milosevic, Mr. Christopher expressed "grave concern" about reported massacres of Bosnians by the Bosnian Serbs, particularly paramilitary groups, in Srebrenica and Banja Luka. Mr. Milosevic, who has been authorized by the Bosnian Serb leaders to speak on their behalf during the peace talks, has always denied that he was involved in any massacres they have carried out or has any influence to stop them.

Asked for Mr. Milosevic's assessment of the meeting with Mr. Christopher, a Serbian delegate said, "The President was satisfied."

Mr. Christopher is said to distrust Mr. Milosevic and his intentions. The Secretary did, however, support an unsuccessful move in the Administration last week to have the United Nations Security Council suspend most economic sanctions against Serbia during the talks.

When Mr. Christopher was asked during one of three back-to-back television interviews today whether there was any doubt that Mr. Milosevic was involved in massacres last summer in Srebrenica, he sidestepped the issue, saying only that the United States was spending more than any other country to support the war crimes tribunal in The Hague and that the issue of a potential indictment of Mr. Milosevic "is not our judgment to make."

But Mr. Christopher also said NATO peacekeeping forces might not go into Bosnia if the two Bosnian Serb leaders indicted as war criminals were still in power.

"We can't really expect that forces of NATO would be there at the same time those individuals were in positions of power," he said of Radovan Karadzic, the Bosnian Serb leader, and Gen. Ratko Mladic, the military commander.

The American side imposed a news blackout on all the parties except Mr. Christopher and Mr. Burns.

Entering the conference hall, however, the Bosnian Foreign Minister, Muhamed Sacirbey, said, "If it fails, it won't fail because of us."

In an earlier interview, he laid out his country's position, including a demand that Mr. Milosevic deliver those indicted for war crimes to the tribunal.

"You cannot speak of peace in Dayton and continue to have ethnic cleansing in Banja Luka," he paraphrased his President as telling Mr. Christopher.

Mr. Holbrooke expects the peace talks to last about two weeks, although Carl Bildt, the former Swedish Prime Minister who represents the European Union, believes that agreement could be reached within a week.

*   *   *

November 22, 1995

ACCORD REACHED TO END THE WAR IN BOSNIA; CLINTON PLEDGES U.S. TROOPS TO KEEP PEACE

By ELAINE SCIOLINO

DAYTON, Ohio, Nov. 21—The presidents of three rival Balkan states agreed today to make peace in Bosnia, ending nearly four years of terror and ethnic bloodletting that have left a quarter of a million people dead in the worst war in Europe since World War II.

The leaders—Alija Izetbegovic of Bosnia, Franjo Tudjman of Croatia and Slobodan Milosevic of Serbia—initialed the peace agreement and 11 annexes in a hastily-arranged ceremony in the same conference room at Wright-Patterson Air Force Base where they opened their talks 21 days ago.

The agreement is to take effect when it is formally signed by the parties in Paris in mid-December.

Unlike previous peace accords that have collapsed, this one was reinforced by widespread fatigue of a war that has uprooted two million people from their homes and appalled the world with scenes of harrowing atrocities, and by the promise of enforcement by 60,000 NATO troops. President Clinton, hailing the agreement in a White House Rose Garden ceremony, reiterated his pledge that the NATO force would include 20,000 Americans.

"The agreement is a victory for all those who believe in a multi-ethnic democracy in Bosnia," said Secretary of State Warren Christopher, who spent several exhausting days brokering the final details of the accord. "It offers tangible hope that there will be no more days of dodging bullets, no more winters of freshly dug graves, no more years of isolation from the outside world."

But underneath the self-congratulation of today's ceremony was a grim awareness that the basic questions the parties failed to settle before the war remain: Can Bosnia, with its mutually suspicious populations of Muslims, Serbs and Croats, survive as a single state? What degree of self-government should be given to the Serb minority within its borders? And does Mr. Milosevic have the power to force the Serbs of Bosnia to do what he says?

Today the Bosnian Serb representatives who served in a delegation headed by Mr. Milosevic did not show up for the ceremony to initial the various annexes that affect the Serbian part of Bosnia.

The Bosnian Serbs were particularly upset by the military annexes in the agreement, which they charged essentially made NATO an occupying force, American and European negotiators said.

Under the agreement, NATO will have the right to remove or relocate specific forces and weapons from any location in the country whenever it determines that they constitute a threat to its troops.

The Bosnian Serbs were even more enraged by the map of the capital, Sarajevo, which turned Serb-held neighborhoods over to the Bosnian Government. One American negotiator said that when the Bosnian Serbs saw the map—which Mr. Milosevic refused to show them until today—they went "berserk."

"The agreement that has been reached does not meet even the minimum of our interests," said Momcilo Krajisnik, president of the self-styled Bosnian Serb parliament.

The Bosnian Serb Parliament scuttled a peace settlement in the spring of 1993, after the same three presidents signed the so-called Vance-Owen peace plan that divided Bosnia into 10 provinces along ethnic lines.

But in the antiseptic, fluorescent-lit conference room in the Hope Conference Center, the mood was palpably upbeat, as the Balkan presidents took turns at the podium to explain—in English—why making peace was important to them.

Reuters

From left to right, Serbia (Slobodan Milosevic, President), Bosnia-Herzegovina (Alija Izetbegovic, President), Croatia (Franjo Tudjman, President), United States (Warren Christopher, Secretary of State)

A CLOSER LOOK

The Dayton Accord: A Peace Agreement for the Balkans

The settlement is a compromise among conflicting aims. For the Muslim-dominated Government of Bosnia, it affirms the legal integrity of the country and restores the unity of the capital, Sarajevo. The Serbs get — if not the separate state they want — a semi-autonomous republic. The Croats secure their national borders and will be able to nurture ties to Croats in Bosnia.

An elaborate governmental structure is spelled out, involving a central elected presidency and parliament presiding over two entities — a Bosnian-Croat federation, and a Serb republic. Some issues, such as the fate of Bosnian Serb leaders who have been indicted as war criminals, are not fully addressed. The agreement does not take effect until it is formally signed, expected in Paris in early December.

The Final Disputes

Serbian Corridor

The Serbs wanted a wider corridor around the town of Brcko, linking the Serb-held areas of eastern Bosnia with the territory around Banja Luka. This will be decided by arbitration.

Sarajevo

The Serbs wanted some parts of the city to be part of the new Serb republic; the Bosnian Government wanted and won a unified, open city, the symbolic heart of the unified nation it seeks.

Path to Gorazde

The Bosnian Government regains control of a swath of land linking Sarajevo with the enclave of Gorazde, strengthening its presence in the east.

War criminals

People indicted by the international tribunal cannot hold elected office. The Governments pledge to cooperate with the tribunal, but are not explicitly required to arrest indicted people, who include top Bosnian Serb leaders.

BOSNIA AND HERZEGOVINA

- Serb republic
- Bihac
- Banja Luka
- Brcko
- Tuzla
- Srebrenica
- Zepa
- Bosnian-Croat federation
- Sarajevo
- Gorazde

Proposed new boundary between regions.

EXISTING AREAS OF CONTROL

Bosnian Government and Croatian

Serbian

The Next Steps

The United Nations will lift the arms embargo against all states of the former Yugoslavia. Trade sanctions against Serbia will be suspended, but limits remain on its participation in international organizations.

The peace agreement will be formally signed in Paris in December, after which a NATO-led force, including some 20,000 American troops, will enter Bosnia to police the settlement.

The Broad Outline

TERRITORY	CONSTITUTION	TROOPS	PEACEKEEPERS	REFUGEES
The Bosnian-Croat Federation will control roughly 51 percent of the land, the Serb republic 49 percent. Some areas of current control are to be given up by each side.	A constitution creates a central government with a group presidency, a two-house legislature, a court and a central bank. The two sub-entities, the Bosnian-Croat Federation and the Serb republic, will each have their own presidents and legislatures. Officials at all levels are to be chosen in internationally supervised elections. How much power the central government will have, in practice is a major question.	Parties must withdraw forces behind agreed cease-fire lines within 30 days. All heavy weapons and forces will withdraw to barracks areas within 120 days. Arms imports to all sides are temporarily halted and negotiations will begin on limits for heavy weapons and aircraft.	A peace-keeping force will be under NATO command, headed by an American general. The force will monitor the cease-fire and control the airspace. It will be "an active, robust force capable not only of implementing a peace agreement but also of defending itself vigorously."	Displaced people will have the legal right to reclaim their homes or receive compensation. A commission will investigate human rights violations.

For Mr. Milosevic, who longs to be embraced again by the West, the war in Bosnia was a merely "civil war" that "should be left to the past." What was important now, he said, was not only peace and understanding but also economic and cultural development. He portrayed himself as a conciliator, saying, "the solutions achieved here include painful concessions by all sides, however; without such concessions it would be impossible to succeed."

For Mr. Izetbegovic, who is determined to preserve Bosnia as a multiethnic democracy, the importance of the agreement is that it guarantees the sovereignty and territorial integrity of his country, he said, as well as the "development of an open society based on tolerance and freedom."

In announcing the agreement earlier in the day, President Clinton said, "The people of Bosnia finally have a chance to turn from the horrors of war to the promise of peace." He added, "Something stirred among the leaders themselves and they decided that they should not let this moment pass."

But it also means that he now will have to make good on his pledge both to the allies and to the Balkan nations to send American troops to Bosnia as part of the NATO-led force.

The agreement calls for the preservation of Bosnia as a single state. But it also divides Bosnia into two almost-equal parts, with one side controlled by a Muslim-Croat federation and the other by a Serb republic.

The plan also envisages a central government with an elected president and parliament, the return or compensation of refugees, the separation of Bosnian and Croatian troops on one side and Serbian troops on the other, and the reconstruction of the country. But it is not at all clear how a government made up of enemies who only recently have put down their arms will function.

The capital, Sarajevo, remains united—a key demand of the Bosnian Government—but some eastern suburbs, including the Bosnian Serbs' headquarters in Pale—are to remain under Serb control.

The agreement also leaves unresolved the fate of Radovan Karadzic and Gen. Ratko Mladic, the two Bosnian Serb leaders who have been indicted by an international war crimes tribunal.

Although the agreement prohibits any indicted war criminal from running for office, it does not meet the initial demand of the Bosnian Government that Mr. Milosevic turn the two men over to the United Nations-sponsored tribunal.

The agreement is to be followed by actions by the United Nations Security Council. One would suspend trade sanctions that have crippled the Serb economy in the last three-and-a-half years. Secondary sanctions, like a ban on Serbia's membership in the United Nations and access to World Bank loans, would remain until the Serbs showed compliance with the peace accord.

Another Security Council resolution would gradually lift the arms embargo on the six republics of the former Yugoslavia, beginning 90 days after the agreement is signed. The embargo is believed to have handicapped the Bosnian Government during the course of the war against the better-armed Serbs.

But while the embargo is to end, the rivals agreed today to temporarily forswear arms purchases.

Each side is to retain its own army. Throughout the talks the Serbs refused pleas by the negotiators to give up their heavy weapons, and the Bosnian Government was unable to get a side agreement with the United States pledging immediate American help in arming and training its army.

In a news conference after the ceremony, European negotiators, who will be responsible for organizing a plan to reconstruct Bosnia, stressed that success depends on how the agreement is put into effect.

"These agreements are not self-implementing," said Pauline Neville-Jones, the head of the British delegation. Even Richard C. Holbrooke, the chief American negotiator, warned that on every page of the agreement "lie challenges to both sides to set aside their differences," which he called "raw and open wounds." He added: "On paper we have peace. To make it work is our next and our greatest challenge."

Until this morning, there was no deal and the rollercoaster, marathon talks seemed doomed.

At first, the sticking point seemed to be the width of a 30-mile-long passage linking Serbia with the Serb-held territory in northwestern Bosnia, around Banja Luka. Last night the United States thought a deal was near, after the Serbs agreed to the Bosnian demand that the corridor be no wider than three miles.

At 10 P.M. Mr. Christopher went to the Bosnian delegation with a last, take-it-or-leave-it offer.

"If you can agree we have a final agreement and we can initial a peace," he told them. "If you don't, these proceedings are going to have to be suspended."

He said he needed their answer at 11:30 and went to bed. By that time, the Bosnians had no answer. Mr. Christopher called Mr. Clinton, told him he wanted to suspend the talks and went to bed.

About midnight the Bosnians issued a new demand—control over the town of Brcko in northern Bosnia, which is currently under Serbian control and is in the middle of the corridor linking the Serbs' Bosnian territories. By morning there was no accord. The defining moment came after all three presidents agreed that the issue of Brcko could be resolved by a still-undetermined method of arbitration over the next year.

The first tangible sign that the deal was complete was a gesture as the ceremony opened. On the first day, Mr. Christopher did not shake the hand of Mr. Milosevic, who is widely blamed for starting the war. Today he did—twice.

It was a personal achievement for both Mr. Christopher and Mr. Holbrooke, and the result of an extraordinarily complicated negotiating process in which the United States brought together the three Balkan presidents and their delegations and negotiators from Britain, France, Germany and Russia.

It also represented the evolution of Mr. Christopher's own thinking. Even before he was confirmed as Secretary of State, he was skeptical that diplomacy could bring peace to Bosnia. But he later came to the conclusion that the only way for the parties to make peace was if the United States seized control of the negotiations from the Europeans and pressured all the parties.

* * *

December 11, 1995

U.S. TROOPS IN BOSNIA FIND A 'SHELLSHOCKED' PEOPLE

By PHILIP SHENON

TUZLA, Bosnia and Herzegovina, Dec. 10—Just past midnight, Lieut. Col. Sidney Kooyman of the First Armored Division wandered into the bomb shelter that doubles as a television room for the handful of American soldiers who have already arrived in Bosnia.

He began to pull off his camouflage uniform, the fatigue evident in his face after another day of trying to make sense of a land that the United States will try to bring peace to.

"This place is shellshocked," he said of Bosnia. "The people are dazed, just dazed, and the trauma of what they have been through will take a while for them to understand what is happening now. They are welcoming us, but in the reserved manner of people who have been through a horrible time."

As they trickle in ahead of a large airlift of peacekeeping troops expected to begin arriving later this week, the first American soldiers to land in Bosnia had received a muted, even indifferent welcome from the people whose suffering they are supposed to end.

"It's hard to gauge their reactions," said Capt. Anthony Davit of the Air Force, who arrived in this bleak industrial city last week to oversee renovation work on Tuzla's airfield, where the Americans now live in a converted school house. Captain Davit, 28, from Lafayette, Ind., said he had met only a few Bosnians so far, "but they do tend to keep a lot to themselves."

For their part, Bosnians in the neighborhoods surrounding the airstrip say they are grateful for the American decision to risk sending troops here. But many also say that after more than three years of war, it is difficult to muster any sort of emotion, no matter how good the news.

"I think every Bosnian, everyone, will be happy to see the Americans," said Elvis Gargich, a 21-year-old Muslim. "My mother liked Elvis Presley—Elvis was a big star in Bosnia."

But Mr. Gargich, a day laborer at the Tuzla base, said the tentative response to the American deployment was understandable. "The war has killed our emotions," he explained. "So many killings, so much blood, and it is difficult for us to feel anything."

If there is a sense of happy expectation here, it is over the arrival of American consumer goods and the money that the American soldiers will bring and spend in this impoverished city, its borders ringed with squalid camps that house thousands of Muslim refugees from other parts of Bosnia.

Already one Tuzla bar has changed its name to the American Club, with a small Stars and Stripes on each table, while a restaurant has announced that it will soon begin pizza deliveries to the air base.

Mr. Gargich said that whatever the reputation of other Bosnians, Americans would find the people of Tuzla to be tolerant and desperate for peace. This mostly Muslim city has long had a reputation for progressive relations among ethnic and religious groups, and there is a large population here of Bosnian Serbs, with intermarriage common between Muslims and Serbs.

Tuzla, which bills itself in an investment-promotion brochure as the city "where reason prevails," is one of the few places in Bosnia that did not vote along ethnic lines in national elections after the collapse of Yugoslavia.

"I've lived here all my life, and I don't have anything against Serbs," Mr. Gargich said as he unloaded the bags of another group of arriving American soldiers. "When people say that Bosnia is like Vietnam, they do not know what they are talking about."

Dervis Sedic, 34, a Tuzla-born air traffic controller who will be helping to guide the Air Force planes into the city, said that although his mother was Muslim, he did not consider himself anything other than a Bosnian. "I do not describe myself by religion," he said.

Traditionally, he said, the people of Tuzla made their living as salt and coal miners, and that was the secret of their tolerance. Regardless of the ethnicity or religion, "miners know that they have to work together or die," he said.

"They have no choice in the mines. We must live and work together in Tuzla. That is our attitude today."

* * *

December 31, 1995

SPENT BOSNIA NOW TRIES TO MAKE ITS PEACE

By ROGER COHEN

SARAJEVO, Bosnia and Herzegovina—In the winter mists of this battered country, there is a silence deeper than the mere absence of gunfire. People seem muted, hushed, as war recedes and anguished retrospection meets fragile hope.

Peace has brought no joy. There is a flatness to everything. So much emotion had already been expended. "Laughter is strangely absent," said Zeljko Trograncic, a psychologist at Kosevo hospital in Sarajevo, the scene of repeated horror through 42 months of siege and war. "We spent everything."

In the absence of emotion, a sense of subsiding prevails, the subsiding of fear and fanatical folly. Rising in their place, it seems, there is a shadowy thing: Shrouded in fog, permeated by a damp cold, divided by mountains, marked by successive empires, this thing is called Bosnia.

But whose land is it?

The worst European conflict in 50 years was fought to settle this question. More than 200,000 people died. But the question is stubbornly unresolved. Indeed, the answer to the war's riddle that seems to hover today over the mist-clad valleys is that Bosnia belongs to itself. It is culturally and topographically different from its neighbors. All the bombardments, all the destruction, all the killing could not quite obliterate this fact.

For now, it is divided by war. The Serbs have half, the Croats about 20 percent, the Muslim-led Government the rest. Ottoman bridges and monasteries have been flattened, Catholic churches of Croats destroyed, Orthodox monasteries of Serbs razed. The people of Bosnia, particularly Muslims, have been herded from their homes and often massacred. All to prove that land belonged to one of Bosnia's ethnic groups and always had.

But that proof, it now appears, did not exist. The confluence of religions and cultures in this corner of Europe—a place the great Bosnian-born writer Ivo Andric called this "muffled land" of "silence and uncertainty"—was too intense. Indeed it was the very confluence, the very miscegenation, that defined the place.

The Serbs said the land was theirs because the Muslims of Bosnia were in reality Serbs who had made the mistake of converting to Islam under Ottoman Turkish rule. The Croats tried a similar argument to buttress annexation: The Muslims were really apostate Croats. As for the Muslims, with no other mother country, they said that they were Bosnians and that the Serbs and Croats who shared the land and made up half the prewar population should realize they were Bosnians too.

The arguments swirled, the artillery boomed. The world looked on, aghast at the horror, unsure how to end it.

Finally, it was American-led diplomacy backed by NATO force—the two things most conspicuously absent during most of the war—that stopped the killing. Bosnia, effectively, is under NATO rule today.

The Western alliance has thus followed in the footsteps of the Ottoman empire, the Austro-Hungarian empire, the Serbian monarchy, puppet-Nazi Croatian rulers and the Yugoslav Communists—the outside authorities that for centuries ruled Bosnia and bequeathed this land of mixed religions and peoples. The central question is: What will happen when NATO leaves?

The answer is still indistinct. The attempt to dissect Bosnia and so deny its existence goes on. "The minds are still at war," said Michael Steiner, a German envoy working on reconstruction.

The Serbs living in parts of Sarajevo that they are supposed to give up soon to the Muslim-led Government under the terms of the peace treaty have asked the United Nations for 20,000 coffins. They say they want to exhume their dead and take the remains with them when they leave.

Perhaps the approximately 60,000 Serbs in suburbs including Ilidza, Grbavica and Vogosca will go elsewhere. If so, another severe blow to the notion of a mixed Bosnia will be inflicted, for few areas of mixed population have survived wave upon wave of "ethnic cleansing."

But already, in Ilidza, some soldiers scoff at orders from the Bosnian Serb headquarters at Pale. Instructed to keep journalists out, they let them in. The barriers essential to sustain the myths of ancient hatred and the madness of war may thus be beginning to crack.

Loss Home, Husband, Then an Eye, Gone

Evlija Keric, a 30-year-old Muslim woman, caught one of the last spasms of the war. Now she lies prostrate at Kosevo Hospital, in tears and without an eye. After the Dayton peace agreement, after its signing in Paris, she thought it safe to return to Sarajevo to visit her sister. But on Dec. 21, a Serbian sniper opened fire on the tram she was riding, and the bullet took her left eye.

Mrs. Keric is from the Vogosca area, one of the Serb-held suburbs of Sarajevo that are supposed to be handed over to the Government. Early in the war, on June 15, 1992, as the Serbs "cleansed" areas under their control of Muslims, she escaped through the woods. Her husband, Ismet, stayed behind in their village of Tihovic.

On July 4, 1992, the Serbs entered the village. Mr. Keric and several of his cousins—including Ramiz Kozljak, Sead Kahriman, Sead Hera and Mahamud Kahriman—were rounded up. In all, about 30 Muslim men were taken away. None of them were ever seen again.

"I have tried the Red Cross, I have tried every means to try to find out what happened to my husband and the rest of the family," Mrs. Keric said. "But I never heard a thing."

Her story traces that of a conflict whose early months saw untold tens of thousands of Muslim civilians rounded up never to be seen again. Rather than war, in the classical sense of a conflict between armies, the first six months of this conflict amounted largely to organized Serbian terror.

Its full extent is still unclear, but this much is known. The elimination of Muslims was not systematic—2,000 German marks or so could often buy freedom from the Serbs—but it was devastating. It was not efficient genocide on the Nazis' industrial scale; it was a rampage aimed at removing all Muslims from much of Bosnia through execution or eviction.

Mrs. Keric lived as a refugee in Kakanj, only to return to her city and be wounded with one of the dying shots of the war. Her reasons for grievance—the loss of her home, the loss of her husband, and finally the loss of her eye—seem manifold, the stuff of future wars. Yet Mrs. Keric seems to have about her a peculiarly Bosnian patience and good will.

"I don't know who needed this war," she said. "We in Bosnia did not, but somebody must have. For myself, I just want peace now. I hope to see my husband again, recover my sight, to enjoy peace. But who knows? We live in hope."

But hope is tempered here with a strong dose of common sense. It has little to do with illusion. Bosnians have seen a lot—empires that pass, armies that get bogged down, political passions that die. From all this they have developed a stoical patience and a mocking sense of humor.

All the paraphernalia of division dreamed up by international diplomats—a new passport for the Muslim-Croat federation, a new flag for the federation, a new flag for the Serb republic, a new passport for the Bosnian state carrying the symbols of all the peoples—are thus greeted with a certain derision. All these things are "synthetic," people say with a dismissive wave.

Recovery Memory of Loss Begins to Loosen

Emina Dubravic, the director of the Sarajevo music school, was eight months pregnant when the war broke out. In March 1992, she and her husband were chased by the Serbs from their home in Ilidza. She gave birth to her son, Amir, on April 27, 1992, as the shells fell on Kosevo Hospital. Six months later her husband, Kenan, was killed.

Last year, Mrs. Dubravic, who is 30, could not talk about her husband without dissolving into tears. She could not bring herself to play her flute. She could not bring herself to tell Amir that his father was dead. When he asked, she would say, "Dad is sleeping." She could not see an end to the war.

Now, 18 months later, she seems to be changing. The past is beginning to loosen its hold on her. The future even beckons. She can speak calmly of her dead husband and equally calmly of the possibility of forming a new relationship. She is playing her flute every day; her music gives her pleasure. She has faced the truth with her son.

Scott Daniel Peterson/Gamma Liaison

As peace starts to take hold in Sarajevo, people can walk the streets and collect water without fear.

"This year," she said, "Amir started talking about his father so much. He said that he did not understand. He said everyone sleeps, but everyone also wakes up, so if dad is sleeping, why does he not wake up too?"

Amir watched television a lot. He saw the repeated images of wounded people bleeding. He asked what happens when all of the blood goes out of a person. He understood that when enough blood goes out, a person dies. He suggested to his mother that his father also lost all his blood like that.

"I could see that he was only 3, but he had understood," Mrs. Dubravic said. "I was forced to explain, and now I think it was better."

Amir became more quiet. He stopped asking about his father. But then another question occurred to him. He started asking his mother how it was possible that he had been born if he did not have a father.

"So I showed Amir a picture of him as a baby with Kenan, and he realized that his father was alive when he was born," Mrs. Dubravic said. "Then he asked me if I loved his father and if I had kissed him. I said yes I had. Now when he sees a couple kissing on the street, he says they will have a baby."

This summer, as Sarajevo was again subjected to some of the worst shelling of the war, Amir became very frightened. He was talking only about the shells and blood. He would wake up every night. He was scared of the dark. He only felt secure in the bathroom, where he and his mother would take refuge when the shelling was heaviest. At night, he insisted on sleeping on the floor of the bathroom.

Finally, Mrs. Dubravic decided that Amir should leave Sarajevo with her parents, who are also refugees from Ilidza. In August, they went to the central Bosnian town of Zenica. She has not seen her son for more than a month but does not want to bring him back to Sarajevo until the winter is over and it is clear whether the peace is secure.

So now, one late December day, Mrs. Dubravic returns to an empty apartment. She is lonely. It is cold. She wrestles still with the past. On Aug. 28, when a mortar fell on the Sarajevo market, killing more than 30 people and at last stirring NATO to decisive action, she was walking nearby. She was thrown off her feet. She saw bodies ripped in two. She saw a man on a bicycle keel over, dead.

"I am trying to forget those images," she said. But the tears and sobs that shake her show that she is still in their grip.

Everywhere, the palpable horror of the past contends with the insubstantial glimmer of a better future. If the past cannot be overcome, another war must surely come. If the future cannot be given form, it will be sucked into the vortex of Balkan bloodshed. Amir may then find himself, in his 20's, drawn like his father into a war he never sought.

Mrs. Dubravic is looking forward. She went up on Mount Igman with a pair of binoculars and saw her old house in Ilidza. It is standing. She has decided she wants to return. She also wants the Serbs who live in Ilidza to remain there.

"It was hard to see the house," she said. "I invested so much of myself and my hopes for the family in it. But even without Kenan, I want to go back because return, for me, will equal my new beginning and the recovery of my dignity. I know some of the Serbs there chased me out, but I also know that others helped to save me. I just do not have hate inside me. I cannot hate, and I cannot imagine life in a Sarajevo populated only by Muslims."

At the music school, all the religious holidays are celebrated: the Catholic Christmas, the Orthodox Christmas, the Muslim feast of Bairam. But the children voted overwhelmingly against having any religious education in the school. They want to study music, which knows no barriers.

As for Amir's education, Mrs. Dubravic said he would not be educated to hate. "All desire for revenge," she said, "leads only to another war."

Of course, for all Mrs. Dubravic's efforts, Amir may find a cause for hatred in his father's death. Perhaps the Serbs in Ilidza will leave, and Mrs. Dubravic's return there will be a bleak one. Perhaps the Serbs will stay and make her return impossibly difficult. Perhaps, when NATO goes, war will resume. Perhaps the lines now crisscrossing the mountains of Bosnia will solidify into permanent divisions, and the remaining open minds, like Mrs. Dubravic's, will close.

Despite everything, the music school director refuses to believe in the death of Bosnia. "We are all Bosnians," she said. "The Serbs here are Bosnians. When they leave Bosnia, they are miserable. The only difference is religion. Propaganda from the east in Serbia and propaganda from the west in Croatia made all this destruction. We Muslims were in the sandwich, and then we started with our own propaganda. But if propaganda could make all these divisions, it can also unmake them."

Reuniting Trying to Topple The Old Barriers

NATO insists that it will unmake the divisions by allowing freedom of movement. If it makes good on its word, if the barriers fall, Bosnia will surely prevail.

Before the war, Sarajevans used to drive to the beaches of the Adriatic in about four hours. They went through Ilidza and Hadzici, down the valleys to Konjic, on along the banks of the Neretva river to Mostar, and finally to the sea. It was a journey that captured all the astonishing beauty and variety of the Bosnian landscape. But the drive has long been impossible; the only way out of the besieged city was the mountain track over Mount Igman, treacherous and exposed to Serbian fire.

Now, on a December morning, there is a new NATO checkpoint at the entrance to Ilidza. The formalities are minimal. In Ilidza itself, in a single night of NATO presence, all the Serbs' military checkpoints that sealed off Sarajevo for 42 months have been removed. The drive through the suburb takes just 10 minutes.

In Hadzici, too, all the checkpoints have gone. The last NATO checkpoint, at the entrance to Government-held territory, is unmanned. The barbed wire coils and the barriers lie in the road: already they look like the relics of war. In the absence of any soldiers, a reporter removes them.

The road to the coast is open. It is littered with images of war: roofless houses, deserted settlements, churches battered to rubble, the slender minarets of mosques reduced to jagged stumps. In the brisk dawn, a Bosnian Army unit is out exercising. Their gear is new, their faces fresh. Perhaps, one day, they will want to fight again to avenge the loss of so much.

But there is something else in the air. The stirring of peace. The road is open. There are children on the way to school near Konjic, their bright sacks on their backs and their laughter rising. At Mostar, the old Ottoman bridge is being rebuilt and its soaring arch is beginning to take form.

The rivers rush on, as they always have, and the snow-capped mountains rise through the Bosnian mist above Jablanica. The guns are silent, and when, after just four hours, the sea beckons, its shimmering expanse is peaceful beyond words.

*   *   *

May 12, 1996

WAR CRIMES TRIAL SEEKS TO DEFINE THE BALKAN CONFLICT

By MARLISE SIMONS

THE HAGUE, Netherlands, May 10—Dusan Tadic, a Bosnian Serb and accused war criminal, sat through the first days of his trial this week looking pallid and shifting uneasily in his blue United Nations chair.

Much of the time, Mr. Tadic, a former cafe owner and policeman, simply stared across the courtroom, an ultramodern hall outfitted for this occasion with new computers and furnishings. He took notes as the prosecutor rose to list the charges of killing, rape and torture in the former Yugoslavia that brought Mr. Tadic to The Hague to face this United Nations war crimes tribunal.

But as the first international war crimes tribunal in half a century got under way, the focus quickly shifted from the stocky man in the dock to the nightmare of the war.

Since the trial opened, on Tuesday, the prosecution has insistently spoken of the enormous scale of the violence in the former Yugoslavia. It portrayed it as a result of a plan conceived in Belgrade that used the Yugoslav Army initially against Serbia's neighbors and subsequently to support local Serbian militias.

Court officials give several reasons for the prosecution's strategy. First, they say, the prosecutors are determined to show that what happened in Yugoslavia was not a local civil war, but an international conflict, with one state attacking others. This definition will be essential for the tribunal to try Mr. Tadic and other defendants on charges of "grave breaches" of the laws of war. If the conflict is defined as purely internal, a number of charges against Mr. Tadic and others will have to be dropped.

Similarly, the prosecution must demonstrate that the brutalities of "ethnic cleansing" committed against Muslims were part of a broad, state-organized policy. The existence of an official policy or system is needed in order to try Mr. Tadic and other defendants here for crimes against humanity.

For much of this week, therefore, Grant Niemann, an Australian and one of three senior prosecutors, presented a history lesson, for which he called on James Gow, a specialist in military history in the Balkans from the University of London.

As Mr. Gow outlined the start of the Yugoslav conflict, he used charts and video footage that appeared on computer monitors sunk into the table in front of each participant.

One segment, which Mr. Gow told the court was a key to the thinking of Serbia's President, Slobodan Milosevic, was recorded as the breakup of Yugoslavia loomed. It showed Mr. Milosevic proposing to rewrite the constitution and to include the right to secede "not just for republics but also for ethnic groups." Both the Croatian war of 1991 and the Bosnian war that began in April 1992 have centered on the Serbian minorities in Croatia and Bosnia that wanted to preserve ties to Belgrade.

Another video segment showed a Serbian nationalist leader accusing President Milosevic of arming and supporting Serbian paramilitary groups that fought in Croatia and Bosnia. In a third, a former Serbian paramilitary leader said his troops fought in Bosnia and Croatia with support from Belgrade. In the same section, taken from a BBC series, Mr. Milosevic dismissed this statement as ridiculous. He has consistently denied responsibility for any war crimes.

"This series of extracts, I think, shows how the paramilitary groups were operating and cooperating with official bodies of Serbia," Mr. Gow told the court.

The first courtroom clash occurred on Friday, when one of Mr. Tadic's lawyers challenged Mr. Gow's account of history, suggesting that he was biased against the Serbs.

It was clear, however, that the defense team, in addition to defending its client, is also trying to push the tribunal toward firmer definitions and rules. Michail Wladimiroff, the Dutch lawyer who heads the defense team, complained this week about the vagueness of the court's rules, definitions and standards of evidence. He said in an interview: "At issue here is the question: was this a civil war or an international conflict? What establishes an international nexus here? We don't know and the tribunal did not tell us."

Court officials seemed relieved this week at the arrival in The Hague of the first Bosnian Muslim in court custody. Zejnil Delalic is one of only three Muslims indicted by the tribunal for war crimes. He is accused of responsibility for murder, torture and rape committed by troops under his command against Serbian inmates of a prison camp in central Bosnia in 1992.

The court interrupted Mr. Tadic's trial for a pretrial hearing for Mr. Delalic, who pleaded not guilty. As of this week, the court has four accused war criminals in its custody. Another person indicted by the tribunal is awaiting transfer from a German jail and two others are held in Bosnia.

Officially, 57 people have been indicted by the court. But a court official said that seven others, some of "significant" rank, were recently indicted secretly.

* * *

May 28, 1996

PRO-WESTERN ALBANIAN CHIEF CLAIMS VICTORY IN CHAOTIC ELECTION

By JANE PERLEZ

TIRANA, Albania, May 27—In the most chaotic election in Eastern Europe since the fall of Communism, the Western-backed Albanian leader, Dr. Sali Berisha, claimed victory for his party of former Communists today despite concerns by international monitors about fraud and intimidation at the polls.

President Berisha, who had been rewarded by Washington with military and economic aid for his coolheadedness toward the explosive issue of the Albanian population in the Balkans, waged a strongman campaign.

He passed a law late last year that barred some prominent opponents from running because of their Communist past even though he was a senior Communist Party official himself. He criticized the opposition party as a "red front," and banned its final campaign rally here.

Toward the end of voting on Sunday, the main opposition party said it was withdrawing from the election before the counting started.

In pulling out of the election, the Socialist Party and its opposition allies said they would not recognize the new Parliament. The move appeared to leave Albania with a likelihood of one-party rule.

Election monitors from the European Union and the United States said they witnessed instances of police intimidation, open ballot boxes and voters' casting more than one ballot. In a district in the capital, the voting was held in the living room of the local leader of Dr. Berisha's Democratic Party.

One election monitor, Fabrizio Migliaccio of Italy, said he was stunned that in seven districts he visited in the seaside town of Durres, "basic violations" of the electoral process were made in front of him. They included more than one person being in the voting booth, unsecured ballot boxes and the stuffing of the boxes with ballots.

But Western officials, dependent in the last four years on Dr. Berisha to preach calm among the Albanians who make up 90 percent of the population of the Serbian province of Kosovo, appeared eager today to give the President the benefit of the doubt.

At a news conference today, Dr. Berisha thanked the West. "We won because we enjoyed the powerful support of our great friends in Europe and the United States," he said.

Western officials said it appeared from independent counting that Dr. Berisha's Democratic Party was a winner of the election anyway. It seemed, they said, that the Democratic Party polled more than 50 percent and the Socialist Party under 25 percent, with smaller parties failing to gain enough for the Socialists to form a coalition.

There was more support for the Democratic Party than expected and less for the Socialists than expected, Western officials said, but they said the voter fraud was not enough to have tipped the scales decisively.

*   *   *

May 30, 1996

DEMOCRACY DENIED IN ALBANIA

Albania, Europe's poorest country, suffered for decades under a fanatical strain of Communism. Now it seems to have graduated to a harsh form of post-Communist governance.

The Albanian economy, no longer sealed off from the world, has begun to revive and the old ideological tyranny has eased its grip. But last Sunday's deformed parliamentary elections make clear that democracy in Albania remains a distant dream. A new dictatorship may be in the making under the authoritarian rule of President Sali Berisha.

International election observers reported seeing stuffed ballot boxes, altered ballots and an intimidating presence of armed security forces and secret police at polling places. On Tuesday, riot police beat opposition demonstrators in the capital city of Tirana. The intimidation came despite the fact that Mr. Berisha's misnamed Democratic Party was considered a sure winner. Opposition parties withdrew from the election even before the votes were counted.

Yesterday two of the election-monitoring groups, including the nongovernmental International Republican Institute of the United States, condemned the numerous electoral violations. But the Clinton Administration has so far refrained from public criticism.

Mr. Berisha has won Western favor by preaching nonviolence to aggrieved ethnic Albanians living under Serbian rule, and by limiting illegal Albanian migration to Italy and Germany. But by ignoring his assaults on democracy, Washington risks signaling other countries in Eastern Europe that political repression is acceptable. Silence may also invite further abuses by Mr. Berisha that could produce political turbulence and increased migration from Albania. It would be wiser to speak the truth now.

*   *   *

May 31, 1996

FOR ALBANIANS, IN CARTS AND BMW'S, A HARD ROAD

By JANE PERLEZ

TIRANA, Albania, May 30—For Besa Mani, a 17-year-old high school student who watches American soaps, drinks Fanta soda and yearns to be a judge, her country is a confusing place.

For nearly three years, she has walked a few hundred dusty yards to school and retraced her steps back home. She is too scared to go anywhere else. Her father and mother venture as far as the garden gate and no farther.

The family is trapped indoors by a centuries-old custom of blood feud that dictates an eye for an eye. Besa's brother shot a man who tried to rape her mother, and ever since the Mani family has feared being killed by the dead man's relatives.

"We can't go out," said Besa, whose modern ambitions contrast with the ancient practices of her mountain region in northern Albania. "Who knows what would happen? The dead man was a bad man. He has a big family. They are everywhere. They have weapons." Albania, the poorest nation in Europe, sealed off for years by one of the world's most bizarre Communist governments, is struggling to come to terms with the contemporary world.

At the same time that Besa and her family stayed indoors, their neighbors went to the polls in the fourth election that Albania has held since the fall of the Communists in 1991.

But the experiment with democracy on Sunday went awry when the police under the control of President Sali Berisha intimidated voters and then beat opposition party supporters with truncheons in the capital's main square two days later.

Dr. Berisha, supported during his four-year rule by the United States, claimed victory for his post-Communist Democratic Party over a number of opposition groups. International election monitors said the vote was seriously flawed.

There are fears of a return of the deep vein of autocracy that has dominated Albania through the reigns of the Turks, of King Zog before World War II and finally of the hard-line Marxist Enver Hoxha, for whom even the Chinese Communists were too soft.

Switching from a collectivized society to a capitalist one is not proving easy.

When it comes to democratic elections, justice and freedom of the press, Albania has not fared well under President Berisha. But under the tutelage of the World Bank and the United States Treasury, a kind of capitalism—awash in corruption—has taken hold. The southern region of Albania has become one big bazaar.

There are probably more Mercedes—old, battered models that pound the rutted roads—per capita of population than many other places in the world. In a field outside the seaside town of Durres, hundreds of new and secondhand Mercedes, BMW's and fancy Volkswagens await buyers. The asking price for a new Mercedes stolen from Italy or Germany is $10,000 cash.

Private cars, which under the Hoxha Government were the perquisite of state officials only, now line up bumper to bumper at border posts, for day trips to trade and smuggle.

What is your profession? a border guard asked an Albanian awaiting to enter Montenegro. "Smuggler," the young man said from the window of his car, without the border guard flinching.

But around rural Koplik in the north, where Besa lives and which is the stamping ground of the clan of Ghegs who are thought to have come to the Balkans before the Greeks, the horse-and-cart is still supreme.

Profound mistrust abounds. About 10,000 men are believed to have gone into hiding in northern Albania since the collapse of the Communists. They are afraid, like Besa's father, Sali, that someone will hunt them down and seek revenge for an injustice—a killing, a land grab, a stolen donkey cart—deemed to have been committed yesterday or generations ago. Under the Communists, blood feuds were outlawed.

Even if they are dirt poor, Albanian farmers seem to be slightly better off. Land has been returned, although not always to the right owners.

Met Sula, a 66-year-old farmer in the village of Gose, 20 miles south of Tirana, has only a spade and his muscles as implements for his five acres of land where he is now fertilizing young watermelons with cow manure he shovels from the roadside.

"I have my own land now," Mr. Sula said. "It's not my family's old land and it is too far from my house. But it's better than under Hoxha." If he asked for his rightful land back, he would have his pension cut, he said.

The survival of the country, where the per capita income is $600 a year, now depends on three unusual sources of revenue, according to economists.

The first is foreign aid, which the Europeans have given generously as a way of keeping more Albanians from leaving and becoming illegal immigrants to Italy and Germany.

The second is earnings from the 400,000 Albanians who work abroad, mostly in Greece, and send remittances home. And third is contraband, including a high volume of hard drugs that transit through Albania to Western Europe.

In Shkoder, the northern city, new bungalows boasting smart roofs of red tiles imported from Macedonia—but no indoor plumbing—attest to the new wealth of the drug merchants.

Privatization of state property has started, although it is often accompanied by corruption that amounts to licensed stealing.

"The most common method of returning property owned before World War II is the following," a young businessman said. "The Government sets a price for the former owner which is prohibitive. The former owner can't afford it. So then the Government says they have offered it, been refused and they offer it instead to the state management at a much lower price."

Religion has been allowed a comeback. Declared an atheist state in the 1960's, Albania was traditionally about 70 percent Muslim, with the rest of the population Orthodox and Catholic.

Dr. Berisha, leaning to the West but looking for help where he can get it, allied Albania with the Islamic Conference. In the last several years, new mosques have been built at a rapid rate. In Shkoder, the biggest northern town, a domed mosque named Ebu-Bekr that is a gift from a Saudi family was opened last year.

So far, Albania's Islam is fairly secular. A fun-fair carousel does brisk business daily just outside Shkoder's mosque.

For Faik Spahia, a 38-year-old builder, the new mosque is a significant benefit. "I finished secondary school and I read lots of books," he said before attending prayer. "But I've

Agence France-Presse

Albania's experiment with democracy went awry this week. On Tuesday, two days after an election, the police under the control of President Sali Berisha forcibly broke up a demonstration in Tirana, the capital.

never found the truth except in the Koran, which I used to secretly read at home. To me, religious liberty is the most important thing."

*   *   *

June 23, 1996

ROAMING AN ANCIENT BULGARIAN CITY

By STEPHEN KINZER

For most Westerners and practically all Americans, Bulgaria remains a mystery. We associate it vaguely with yogurt, and perhaps with the haunting melodies of the women's choir known as Le Mystere de Voix Bulgares.

"The average European knows only that Bulgaria was Moscow's most loyal satellite, that its military industry was selling weapons all over the globe, and that it looked as if it had something to do with drug trafficking and with the attempt to assassinate the Pope," lamented the Bulgarian historian Bojidar Dimitrov in a recent essay.

For outsiders, one of the most thrilling aspects of the fall of Communism in Europe has been the chance to roam freely through lands that were once tightly controlled. Bulgaria is one of the last to be discovered, but it offers some of the richest rewards. Wedged between Romania and Turkey, with a long Black Sea coastline, Bulgaria has for centuries been a crossroads, and the variety of cultures it has absorbed makes it a fascinating tourist destination.

Like most visitors, I started my visit in Sofia, the capital, which lies near the western border with Yugoslavia. Sofia's monuments, among them the elegant golden-domed Alexander Nevski Cathedral and the St. George Chapel, which was built by the Romans in the fourth century and later turned into a Muslim and then a Christian sanctuary, whetted my appetite for the rest of the country. I chose Plovdiv, Bulgaria's second-largest city, as my destination for a weekend outing. Archeological finds date the first settlement in what is now Plovdiv to 500 B.C. Thracians arrived 2,200 years ago, and after Philip II of Macedonia conquered the region in A.D. 341, he took such a fancy to the town that he named it Philippopolis. Because it lay astride fault lines that divided great civilizations, it was often the target of conquerors. Between 1204 and 1364 alone, it changed hands 11 times.

Plovdiv lies just 100 miles east of Sofia, and the drive is along Bulgaria's only modern highway. At first the city looks undistinguished, a gray mass of smokestacks and prisonlike cement apartment blocks. But the "old town," which has been under government protection as a historic district since 1956, is among the most unusual in Europe. The various cultures that shaped Plovdiv—Thracian, Greek, Macedonian, Roman, Slavic, Gypsy, Armenian, Turkish and Bulgarian—have made the old town a delightful jumble of faces and architectural styles.

The streets of the old town are narrow and winding, and the whole district is small enough to explore on foot. Park your car as soon as you feel it bouncing on the ancient Roman cobblestones, then walk through the Hissar Kapija, one of the remaining town gates, which dates from the fifth or sixth century.

The Roman presence in Plovdiv is vivid in the form of ancient walls and fortifications, and especially in the spectacular amphitheater that is the city's greatest treasure. Built in the second century A.D., the amphitheater once held 3,000 people who gathered for theater performances and gladiator combats. It was smashed by Attila the Hun in the fifth century, but he left the semi-circular rows of benches and several sets of towering columns intact. Concerts are staged there in summer.

Walking past the amphitheater into the heart of the old town, you pass many striking examples of architecture from the 19th century, when a wave of anti-Ottoman patriotism was sweeping through Bulgaria. This period, which Bulgarians call the National Revival, saw a burst of creativity, including the development of a highly original style of building. The National Revival buildings in Plovdiv are quite different from one another, but several elements tie them together stylistically. They are built around living and dining areas on the second floor, and the ground floors, which were usually used for storage, have no windows.

One of these houses has a swirling, asymmetrical roof line, another is made of rough-hewn but handsome wood planks, and a third is built from a kind of adobe and distinguished by a series of white towers jutting through the roof. Together they form a most unusual ensemble.

Several of the most ornate National Revival buildings have been turned into museums. One of them, built in 1847, now houses the Ethnographic Museum, where lavish displays of locally produced jewelry, carpets, musical instruments, textiles, pottery and other crafts are on view. Just as interesting as the displays is the house itself. Each room is designed differently, according to its projected use. The painstakingly carved wooden floors, walls and ceilings are artworks in themselves.

Plovdiv's Archeological Museum, which is housed in a 19th-century Greek Revival building, is devoted principally to the Thracian culture—but was closed for renovations shortly after I left and no reopening date has been set. Among its most magnificent treasures are nine golden vessels ornamented with scenes from Greek mythology, and a collection of votive marble tablets and reliefs taken from burial sites.

Well worth a visit is the Museum of the National Revival Period, next to the Hissar Kapiya. Formerly a private home built in 1846–48 by the master architect known as Hadji Georgi, it tells the story of Bulgaria's rising against the Turks, focusing on the bloody April Uprising of 1876, in which Plovdiv played an important role. The building itself is a typically eccentric National Revival edifice with two facades, a rectangular one that juts out over the street and a bow-front next to it.

I was especially fascinated by my visit to a symmetrical, balconied National Revival building that houses works by the Plovdiv artist Zlatyu Boyadziev (or Zlatio Boyadjiev), who lived from 1903 to 1976. More than 70 of his paintings are on display, and the tour begins with a series of interesting but rather conventional ones, most of them flat, dark and traditional. Suddenly, however, the style changes dramatically. Boyadziev's later paintings are explosions of color, dazzling and highly evocative. The change came after Boyadziev suffered a stroke in 1951. "Doctors said the stroke affected his brain and gave him a new sense of color and a new way of seeing," a guide said.

Plovdiv is still an artistic center, and a young generation of talented painters is flourishing there. Many of the best display their work at the Red Pony Gallery, which is known to collectors throughout the Balkans. Others show at several of the old town's best restaurants. They include Philipopol, which foreign residents of Sofia often visit for weekend lunches; Janet, which has its own fashion house on the top floor, stocked with one-of-a-kind creations by local designers; and Ritora, which overlooks the amphitheater.

Not wanting to return to Sofia without seeing more of central Bulgaria, I traveled northeast from Plovdiv across mountain passes where great battles were once fought, and past a white spire marking the geographical center of the country.

I couldn't pass up a stop in Gabrovo, home of the House of Humor and Satire. Statues of Charlie Chaplin and Don Quixote stand guard outside, and inside is a display of drawings, paintings and sculptures from around the world. There is something here to amuse even the most somber of visitors; if you don't break out laughing at least a few times, you're probably dead. Can it be a coincidence that the artist Christo, famous for his surrounded islands, running fences and wrapped edifices, was born in Gabrovo?

A few miles past Gabrovo is Etar, a sprawling open-air museum where the crafts of the 17th and 18th centuries are practiced every day. There is a mill at which wheat is ground into flour which is then baked into bread; a coppersmith; a blacksmith; a studio for making musical instruments and one for making icons; and glass-blowers, weavers, furriers, woodcarvers, potters and even candy makers. About half the town is original and the rest was rebuilt in the 1960's in traditional style. It is worth a visit, especially if you are traveling with children, but I had the nagging feeling that life in a Bulgarian village a few hundred years ago might not have been quite as idyllic as the life portrayed here.

My tour ended in the town many Bulgarians consider their country's most beautiful, Veliko Tarnovo. Formerly the national capital, it is perched on a series of mountainsides facing the Yantra River about 30 miles northeast of Gabrovo. Unlike Plovdiv, which boasts only a concentrated historic center, Veliko Tarnovo is an entire island of beauty, with whitewashed houses and red-tiled roofs overlooking splendid National Revival buildings. Imposing fortresses, churches adorned with historic murals, and the palace from which Bulgaria's royal family ruled from the 12th to the 14th century are all open to the public.

Travel in Bulgaria, I found, is only modestly challenging. Most roads are easily passable though not up to western European standards. People seemed friendly and willing to help with directions even though few speak foreign languages. Gasoline is easily available, and every good-sized town has a selection of decent cafes and restaurants.

I never made it to the Black Sea, the country's most popular tourist destination. Nor did I visit any of the nine Bulgarian places that Unesco has designated "world heritage sites," among them the 1,000-year-old Rila Monastery, the intricately carved Thracian tomb at Sveshtari, or Pirin National Park near the Greek border. I must return before the word gets out.

Stephen Kinzer is the Berlin bureau chief of The New York Times

*   *   *

July 10, 1996

U.N. STARTS DIGGING UP MASS GRAVE IN BOSNIA

By CHRIS HEDGES

CERSKA, Bosnia and Herzegovina, July 9—United Nations war crimes investigators exhuming a mass grave in Bosnia unearthed nearly a dozen bodies today at a site believed to hold the remains of some of the thousands of Muslims slain last year by Bosnian Serbs after the fall of Srebrenica.

Working through an intermittent afternoon drizzle, the 20-member team dug up bodies with tattered clothes and bits of decaying flesh clinging to the bones. They used a seven-ton backhoe, picks, shovels, trowels and a small whisk broom to uncover the remains.

"We have found the edge of the grave by carefully removing the soil, rocks and debris on top of the bodies," said William F. Haglund, an American forensic anthropologist heading the team. "We're seeing some clothing and we are seeing some bodies now. I imagine there are going to be bodies that are maybe lying on top of each other. How many, and how spread out they are, we don't know yet."

The corpses all lay buried in a shallow grave along a 100-foot embankment near this village, 20 miles west of Srebrenica. Small red flags poked up out of the embankment along a dirt road where diggers had exposed bones, body parts or bits of evidence.

By the end of the day, human skulls, grayish thigh bones and soggy black boots were visible and marked off by yellow tape.

Investigators, who say the site is one of the smaller mass graves in this area, suspect that the Muslim victims were lined up by Bosnian Serb soldiers and gunned down along the steep embankment. The bodies, piled one on top of another, were covered with a thin layer of dirt. Many shell casings were found on the opposite side of the road.

The team, heavily guarded by American soldiers from the NATO peacekeeping force, began work on Sunday, checking for land mines, mapping, photographing and clearing the site. Late Monday and today, the specialists started to unearth bodies. They expect to exhume all of the bodies here within 10 days.

The forensic specialists, who will hand over the findings from the exhumations to the tribunal, will excavate seven or eight suspected mass grave sites in Bosnia and Croatia this summer. The work will take three months.

At least 4,000 Muslims killed after the fall of Srebrenica are believed to be buried in about a dozen mass graves dotted throughout the rolling hills surrounding the town.

The sites were located through interviews with survivors and from American spy satellite images. While the grave here in Cerska is suspected to hold a few dozen victims, others are said to hold hundreds, and in one case as many as 2,700 bodies, investigators said.

Witnesses have placed the Bosnian Serb military commander, Gen. Ratko Mladic, at sites around Srebrenica where mass killings are said to have taken place.

General Mladic and the Bosnian Serb political leader, Radovan Karadzic, have been charged with genocide by the international war crimes tribunal in connection with authorizing and overseeing the Srebrenica killings. The findings of the forensic specialists will be used in the trials of the two men if they are arrested.

"This is part of the process of collecting evidence and proving that crimes were committed," said Cees Hindriks, the Chief of Investigations for the tribunal, who visited the site today. "We will see if this evidence supports the statements of witnesses."

Team members said a refrigerated truck would arrive soon with special containers for the exhumed bodies. They will be moved in about two weeks to Tuzla, where specialists will try to identify each set of remains and determine the cause of death, a process that could take months.

Bodies that are identified will be returned to relatives, and the other remains will be turned over to the Bosnian Government, investigators said. The work, the specialists cautioned, will be slow and laborious.

"We will momentarily leave bodies where we find them," Mr. Haglund said. "We want to make sure we have each body carefully defined, so that when we go to pick them up we get all the finger bones, foot bones—everything that belonged to that body.

"Because the more complete the body is, the more complete the story that body or skeleton will tell, and the more complete the information we'll have for generating clues to identification."

*　*　*

November 3, 1996

ROMANIANS VOTE TODAY, BUT CHANGE ISN'T LIKELY

By JANE PERLEZ

BUCHAREST, Romania, Nov. 2—After seven years in power, Vaclav Havel of the Czech Republic and Ion Iliescu of Romania, have become the longest-serving leaders in Central Europe.

They couldn't be more different.

Mr. Havel is a dissident playwright turned President of 10 million people with a strongly Western orientation; Mr. Iliescu is a former high-ranking Communist and close aide to the late dictator Nicolae Ceausescu and has preserved many elements of the past.

Mr. Iliescu, 66, is up for re-election on Sunday and, according to the polls, he is likely to win a third term, although because of a crowded field he may face a runoff.

In parliamentary elections, which will also be held on Sunday, Mr. Iliescu's governing Party of Social Democracy, made up of former Communists, trails in the polls. Opinion polls indicate that a coalition of opposition parties, which bill themselves as proponents of market reforms, are likely to form the next government.

Why Mr. Iliescu has been able to hold on to power in the face of a precipitous drop in living standards is a puzzle. He has shown little of the flexibility of other former Communists, like Prime Minister Gyula Horn in Hungary, or President Aleksander Kwasniewski in Poland, both of whom came to power after Mr. Iliescu.

Romanians offer a variety of explanations that range from the weakness of a fractious opposition to what they call the inherent conservatism of many Romanians.

One analyst who offers a view from the inside, Silviu Brucan, a former Romanian Ambassador to Washington during the 1950's, said that Mr. Iliescu owes his tenure to Romanians' fear of change and the upheavals associated with capitalism. Many Romanians, inured by a tough past, were willing to suffer severe levels of poverty, he suggested.

"He has a chiefly conservative constituency," said Mr. Brucan, who has criticized Mr. Iliescu for his handling of the economy and for retaining elements of the secret police from the time of Mr. Ceausescu, who was overthrown and executed in 1989.

"There are four million members of the former Communist Party and their families who are afraid of retribution," he said. "There are workers in the big plants whose products have no markets who are afraid of unemployment. There are those who are renting apartments who are afraid the opposition will overturn the law on nationalization of property. And there are the people in the old state structures in the regions."

Here in the capital and in some bigger cities, though, Mr. Iliescu's popularity has plunged. At a campaign rally this week at a tractor plant in Brasov, north of Bucharest, Mr. Iliescu was confronted with angry protesters carrying placards reading "Enough of Your Humbug."

"We have disastrous living conditions," said a retired army colonel, Ion Popescu, 64, as he browsed among the second-hand books on outdoor tables near the University of Bucharest this week. "We can't afford anything but minimal survival."

As the piles of books in the nearby newspaper stand attested, Romanians can now read what they like—or, at least, what they can afford. But the Government controls the only nationwide television station, through which it broadcasts a dreary diet of circumscribed news and out-of-date entertainment.

Mr. Iliescu has done little to dismantle the centralized economy. At outmoded state-run steel, chemical and fertilizer plants, workers cling to jobs at 75 percent of full pay. The average pay in Romania is $100 a month, one-third of that in Poland. Despite recent wage increases, take-home pay in September was 71 percent of that of five years ago.

The health care system is regarded as the worst in Central Europe, with hospitals and the medical staff little changed since the Ceausescu era, when blood supplies were tainted and anesthesia often hard to come by. Recent opinion polls show that, after the high prices, inadequate health care is the biggest concern of Romanians.

One of the reasons for Mr. Iliescu's reluctance to change the old system seems to stem from his strict Communist background. He came from an impoverished family, but as a bright student was sent to the University of Moscow to specialize in hydroelectricity. He returned to Romania to take full-time positions in the Communist Party's hierarchy—first as head of the youth movement and then as head of propaganda in the Politburo.

The early 1970's, when Mr. Iliescu criticized Mr. Ceausescu's support of North Korea, he was sidelined from the inner-most party circles and sent to head up party secretariats in the cities of Jassy and Timisoara.

Despite Mr. Iliescu's career that was so close to Communist ideology, some say he is less a man of ideology than a political survivor.

*　*　*

November 18, 1996

NON-COMMUNIST IS ELECTED ROMANIA'S LEADER

By JANE PERLEZ

BUCHAREST, Romania, Nov. 17—After seven years of government rooted in the Communist past of the dictator Nicolae Ceausescu, Romanians made a clear break today and elected a mild-mannered geology professor and reformer, Emile Constantinescu, as President.

Ion Iliescu, Romania's leader since the overthrow of Mr. Ceausescu in 1989 and a former senior official in the Communist Party, conceded defeat soon after the polls closed this evening.

The victory of Mr. Constantinescu, combined with the victory two weeks ago of his opposition coalition, called the Democratic Convention, in parliamentary elections creates a totally new political alignment in Romania. Since the collapse of Communism in 1989, Romania had been the only country in Central and Eastern Europe to elect Governments of former Communists repeatedly and to shun opposition forces.

The dumping of Mr. Iliescu, 66, reflected deep disillusionment among all sectors of society with status-quo policies that brought about falling living standards and economic decline even as a coterie of former Communists around the President flourished. Many Romanians were bitter that they were faring so badly while other former Communist countries, like Hungary and Poland, were forging ahead—with average salaries three times as large and much lower inflation.

Addressing chanting crowds in University Square downtown tonight, a smiling and emotional Mr. Constantinescu appeared on the balcony of a university building and promised "the young, the mature and the elderly" that "there will be no more sacrificing of generations."

The crowd chanted "Down with the Communists!" and "We are home!" in the street where demonstrators were shot by Mr. Ceausescu's forces in December 1989. Today, the crowd roared approval when Mr. Constantinescu said, "I pay homage to those who died here in 1989 for freedom." Then, in a symbolic gesture that indicated a new era had opened in Romania, an Orthodox priest stepped onto the balcony, and in a deep voice that echoed through the night air, offered a prayer.

Conceding defeat, Mr. Iliescu said that he and his party, the Party of Social Democracy, would provide a critical but constructive opposition.

The victory and concession statements were made before any formal vote count but after national television, which is controlled by the Government, announced an exit poll that gave Mr. Constantinescu 53 percent of the vote and Mr. Iliescu 41 percent.

Today's election was a runoff, after Mr. Iliescu won 32 percent of the vote and Mr. Constantinescu 28 percent in the first round two weeks ago.

For educated, urban voters, the vote represented a critical juncture, a chance to catch up with the region and to step out of what many consider a demeaning status quo. "The future of Romania is at stake—it's as simple as that," Yolanda Stenaloiu, director of the Independent Journalism Center and a television interviewer, said before the outcome was announced. "If Iliescu is re-elected it will delay our future for another four years. If not, our future will start today."

In strident television ads redolent with the Marxist ideology in which he specialized as a Communist ruler, Mr. Iliescu contended that workers' factories and farmers' homes would be handed back to their pre-World War II owners if Mr. Constantinescu prevailed.

Since the end of the first round, the third major political party—the Union for Social Democracy, led by Petre Roman, a former Prime Minister and ally of Mr. Iliescu—has backed the challenger. Other parties, including nationalist groups, have also deserted Mr. Iliescu.

The campaigning between Mr. Iliescu, 66, and Mr. Constantinescu, 55, has been as much about the past as the future. In four television debates last week, Mr. Constantinescu said much had to be explained about what happened in 1989, when Mr. Ceausescu was deposed and executed by firing squad. Mr. Constantinescu said the Government must disclose the truth about the deaths of 1,500 people who demonstrated against the Communists then.

In order to attract voters, Mr. Constantinescu has made an array of promises in a "Contract with Romania" that will be almost impossible to keep—including lowering taxes and giving generous housing loans. He said in the debates that he would finance those programs by clamping down on the black market and catching tax evaders, including the many casinos in Bucharest, the capital.

But economists say that voters are not likely to experience rapid improvements in their well-being and that economic conditions are likely to get worse before they get better.

Even so, as younger voters went to the polls today, many of them said they were prepared for sacrifice in order to insure a sounder future.

Christiana David, a 22-year-old political science student, voted today in St. Sava High School, a few blocks from the central square in Bucharest where Mr. Ceausescu made his last public appearance in 1989 before being chased away by a crowd of tens of thousands of demonstrators.

"I voted for change," she said. "I want something new that would give people a chance to hope and to make Romania a different world for my child."

*   *   *

November 21, 1996

ROMANIA'S COMMUNIST LEGACY: 'ABORTION CULTURE'

By JANE PERLEZ

BUCHAREST, Romania, Nov. 19—Dorina Ciuplan, a 40-year-old mother of three teen-agers, recalled with a mixture of terror and emotion the nine self-induced abortions she endured during Communist rule under Nicolae Ceausescu.

"I sometimes think I'm lucky to be alive," said Mrs. Ciuplan, her eyes watering as she described forcing miscarriages at home and then going to a hospital, where doctors and nurses tormented her with abusive words and rough treatment as they finished terminating the pregnancies rather than let her die.

For more than two decades, contraception and abortions were strictly forbidden by Mr. Ceausescu in an attempt to build his country into a colossus through population growth. His government was overthrown in 1989, and one of its legacies was orphanages filled with unwanted and neglected children.

Another legacy of those horrific years, for Romania's women, is abortion. Some 10,000 women are believed to have died from complications of illegal abortions, and many more were permanently maimed.

Abortions were legalized as soon as Mr. Ceausescu was toppled, and contraception is theoretically available through the state health system.

But overwhelmingly, Romania remains what Western doctors call an "abortion culture," with an abortion rate that remains the highest in Europe. It also has by far the highest rate of pregnancy-related mortality, the strongest indication that Romania continues to lag far behind the rest of Europe and Russia in providing reproductive health services for women.

According to the United Nations Population Fund, Romania had 3.2 abortions for every live birth in 1990. By last year, the rate was 2.2 abortions per live birth. In 1995, the equivalent rate was 2.0 in Russia, 0.67 in the Czech Republic and Hungary and 0.2 in Germany.

The reasons why Romanian women turn to abortion center on the reluctance of the Government to promote family-planning despite healthy doses of Western aid to help the country establish such services, Western and Romanian doctors say. Iulian Mincu, who was Minister of Health until recently and who had been a personal physician to Mr. Ceausescu, publicly stated his opposition to family planning. After a public outcry over poor conditions in the health system, Dr. Mincu was dismissed this summer by Mr. Ceausescu's successor, Ion Iliescu, in an attempt to clean up the Government's image before parliamentary and presidential elections that Mr. Iliescu lost anyway.

The President-elect, Emil Constantinescu, made it clear during his campaign that he would make improved health services a priority, and family planning advocates said they were optimistic that the new Government would be more supportive of their efforts.

Without guidance from the Government, many Romanian doctors have been more enthusiastic about the more lucrative work of performing abortions than about recommending birth control, said Daniela Draghica, one of the administrators of 12 pilot family-planning clinics in Romania opened in 1995 and financed by the United States Agency for International Development.

The state pays for abortions, but as with almost all public health services women say they feel obliged to give the doc-

STATUS REPORT

Abortion Picture

ROMANIA

VIETNAM

BULGARIA

CHINA

HUNGARY

Abortion rate per 1,000 women, aged 15 to 44, for various countries, based on most recent data available.

U.S.

SWEDEN

CANADA

0   40   80   120   160   200

Source: The Alan Guttmacher Institute

The New York Times

tor a sizable extra payment, thus making abortions more financially rewarding.

A 28-year-old woman who would give only a first name, Adina, was at the gynecological clinic at Giulesti Hospital in Bucharest. She said she had had six abortions. An abortion costs 3,000 lei, a little less than $1, at public hospitals, where the vast majority of Romanians get their health care. But she said she had paid an additional $7 as a "gift" to the doctor.

On top of this, many doctors, repeating myths from the Ceausescu years, tell women exaggerated stories that oral contraceptives are deleterious to their health, Mrs. Draghica said.

"Women had these myths about contraception," Mrs. Draghica said. "The doctors had told them that pills were bad because they made women fat and gave them heart disease. It's a battle to get their confidence."

Some women are beginning to look for other alternatives. Maria Staicu, 41, who lives in the city of Sibiu and has two children, said the pain and debasement she endured in 1991 when she had a legal abortion left her determined not to go through it again.

"They did 20 women in a few minutes: 'Ready, go; ready, go,'" she said, describing the atmosphere in the state hospital. In the last five years of the Ceausescu regime, she had managed to buy Hungarian-made oral contraceptives on the black market, she said. After her abortion in 1991, she was fitted with an I.U.D.. "I would prefer anything else than an abortion," she said.

Romania remains the only country in Eastern Europe not to manufacture any kind of contraceptive. Thus supplies, including condoms, must be imported and are too expensive for many women, who say they have trouble even getting food on the table in the chaotic Romanian economy. Birth control pills imported from Hungary, the Netherlands or Germany cost as much for a month's supply—or in many cases up to two or three times as much—as an abortion, even though Western aid helps subsidize some of the cost.

The Western aid stems from publicity in 1990 about the plight of the unwanted Romanian children. Foreign assistance was sent to help care for the children, and for a longer-term solution, funds were offered to create family-planning services, including a $14 million World Bank loan and a $5 million grant from the United States Agency for International Development.

In the last year, a little progress has been made, but not enough given the resources that have been made available, those who work in the program say.

According to a report by Adriana Baban, a psychologist who counsels at one of the Romanian family-planning clinics funded by the A.I.D., and Dr. Henry P. David, director of the Transnational Family Research Institute, a nonprofit group in Washington, Romania had at least 445 deaths attributable to illegal abortion in 1989. By 1992, the number had been reduced to 120 and last year to 59.

But despite these reductions of deaths from self-induced abortions, the pregnancy-related mortality rate remains startlingly high. The World Health Organization reported that in 1990, for every 100,000 live births in Romania, 84 women died in childbirth. By contrast, the rate in Poland was 19. Last year, the number in Romania was 48. In the United States last year, the rate was 8, according to the Population Reference Bureau.

*   *   *

December 2, 1996

A NEW ROMANIA: NEITHER COMMUNIST NOR GODLESS

By JANE PERLEZ

ALBA-IULIA, Romania, Dec. 1—In a ceremony resplendent with the glittering robes and miters of Romanian Orthodox bishops in a site resonating with historic significance, Romania's new President today pledged a new start for his troubled country.

By supplementing his civil inauguration on Friday with a religious ritual in a cathedral adorned with golden icons, neo-Byzantine frescoes and royal portraits, Emil Constantinescu marked a milestone for the former Eastern bloc.

His defeat of Ion Iliescu in elections two weeks ago had already made history by sweeping away the last Government in the region that was an immediate descendant of the Communists and allowing what historians are calling Romania's first peaceful transfer of power.

Mr. Iliescu, a former senior Communist Party official, had been President of Romania since the violent overthrow of Nicolae Ceausescu seven years ago.

But today, by celebrating his ascendancy to the presidency with a religious service in the place where, 78 years earlier,

Romania was unified, Mr. Constantinescu, 57, signaled that the decades of official atheism under Communism were also being set aside.

No other post-Communist head of state, aside from Lech Walesa in Poland, has made such a personal point of sanctioning the resurgence of Christianity.

After listening as the head of the Romanian Orthodox Church, Patriarch Teoctist, spoke to him before the altar of Holy Trinity Cathedral, calling on him to preserve the country's spiritual and national dignity, Mr. Constantinescu moved outside to address about 20,000 people who braved a drizzle.

In personal tones avoided by his predecessors, the new President appealed for help in the difficult task of restoring Romania's shattered economy and defeated spirits.

"We have everything to do," Mr. Constantinescu said. "But to do it right, we must do it together. If it is going to be good, it will be good for us together. If it's going to be bad, it will be bad for all of us."

From the crowd, festooned with red-yellow-and-blue national flags, voices called out, "We love you."

Mr. Constantinescu acknowledged that the collapse of Communism in Romania had been accompanied by poverty and "cheated expectations." The future, he said, depends on "leaders who have to sacrifice and citizens who don't have to be sacrificed anymore."

Alba-Iulia, a small town 175 miles northwest of Bucharest, is revered in Romania as the place where, on Dec. 1, 1918, a unified Romania was proclaimed, comprising the provinces of Walachia, Moldavia and Transylvania. Fleetingly in 1600, the warrior Michael the Brave had succeeded in unifying the three regions by riding into Alba-Iulia on horseback and declaring the nation whole.

His efforts collapsed months later but fired the imagination of Romanian nationalists ever after. Walachia and Moldavia later won their freedom from the Turks and became the kingdom of Romania in 1881. And in return for entering World War I on the side of the Allies, Romania was awarded Transylvania, which had been part of Hungary.

Since the fall of Mr. Ceausescu in 1989, Dec. 1 has been celebrated in Romania as National Day. But even under Mr. Ceausescu, Romanian children were taught about Michael the Brave riding to the door of the Romanian Church of Unification here, where he was crowned King.

To commemorate the new unity of 1918, a new cathedral with fabulous friezes, a vast panel of icons of apostles and prophets above the altar and pink marble pillars was built in 1921.

King Ferdinand and his wife, Marie, were crowned here a year later. The monarchy was abolished in 1944, and murals of the King and Queen, dressed in fur-trimmed robes, were covered during the fiercely anti-monarchist period of Mr. Ceausescu. They were restored during a renovation of the cathedral two years ago.

Mr. Constantinescu has said that once the fanfare dies down, it will be difficult to fulfill the hopes his election has raised.

In his inauguration speech on Friday, at the enormous House of the People in Bucharest constructed by Mr. Ceausescu, he pledged to speed up privatization of state enterprises and to lower taxes. He has announced a short-term emergency plan to stabilize the overvalued currency, attract foreign investment and mend fences with the International Monetary Fund, which stopped disbursing loans last year.

Already, the former geology professor has displayed a low-key style that contrasts with the pomp of his predecessors. On Friday he threw open the doors of the presidential palace that he inherited from Mr. Iliescu, allowing reporters to roam rooms previously off-limits. He has refused what he calls the "army of bodyguards" and has his driver pick him up at his three-room apartment in downtown Bucharest.

"This is the first leader we have been able to trust," said an approving Nicu Stancu, 60, an artist, who cut short a trip abroad to attend today's ceremony.

*   *   *

January 13, 1997

WITH HARD TIMES, BULGARIAN PROTESTORS DEMAND ELECTIONS

By JANE PERLEZ

SOFIA, Bulgaria, Jan. 12—Tens of thousands of angry anti-Government demonstrators crammed in front of the flood-lit Orthodox cathedral tonight demanding early elections and an end to the worst economic crisis in Eastern Europe since the end of Communism.

The governing Socialist Party, an outgrowth of the former Communists, declined tonight to defuse the situation by accepting appeals by President Zhelyu Zhelev and the Speaker of Parliament to agree immediately to earlier elections.

The Socialists have been in power for the last two years as the country has slid into virtual bankruptcy. The former Prime Minister, Zhan Videnov, resigned in late December because of the economic crisis.

The chairman of the Socialist Party, Georgi Parvanov, said the first task in resolving the crisis was to "form a strong and powerful government that is not only for one day but for one and a half years ahead."

Inspired by the protests in neighboring Serbia, demonstrators backed by the Socialists' political opposition have taken to the streets in the last week to try to oust the Socialists by calling for new elections. And as in Serbia, the former Communists have not yielded, refusing on Friday night to vote on a motion in Parliament to call elections.

Mr. Parvanov said tonight that the "idea" of elections could be discussed, but he called on President Zhelev to ask the Socialists to form a new government in the next day or two.

The political turmoil in Bulgaria began before Christmas when, faced with national economic collapse, the Moscow-educated Mr. Videnov resigned at a heated Socialist Party congress. The Socialists, whose term does not expire until

December 1998, nominated Nikolai Dobrev, the Interior Minister, to replace him.

But President Zhelev, whose term expires this month, has refused to ask Mr. Dobrev to form a new government. Mr. Zhelev, a member of the opposition Union of Democratic Forces, supports the demonstrators—who, he said, had been reduced to a state of economic "humiliation" by the former Communists.

The political standoff has left Bulgaria without a Prime Minister and without a semblance of a stable government as average wages have plummeted in the last two months to $30 a month, lower than those in Albania, until now the poorest country in Europe.

Inflation for 1996 hit 310 percent, and the local currency, the lev, went from 70 to the dollar to 645 in 1996. Fifteen of the country's 42 banks are in receivership. Most of those that are still fully operating are described as minor banks with severe liquidity problems.

International financial institutions, in particular the International Monetary Fund, have said they will not help Bulgaria out of its financial predicament until a stable government emerges.

Members of the Union of Democratic Forces, which backs market reforms for the economy more strongly than the Socialists do, walked out of Parliament on Friday night after the Socialists refused to vote on the motion for new elections. The opposition has urged a nationwide strike and civil disobedience.

Tensions surged during a 10-hour siege of Parliament on Friday night and Saturday morning during which demonstrators surrounding the building and opposition members of Parliament who were trying to leave the building were beaten and hit with tear gas by the police.

The atmosphere remained volatile in the city today, with demonstrators newly angered after news spread from a private radio station, Radio Darik, that more than 200 people, including former Prime Minister Philip Dimitrov, had been wounded and had sought medical help after the melee outside Parliament.

Opposition members of Parliament said today that they would call for an investigation into why the Prime Minister-designate, Mr. Dobrev, called in squads of police officers to beat a path into the Parliament. They used clubs and fired blank cartridges to allow Socialist members to leave the building early on Saturday.

One member of Parliament described a bizarre scene in the chamber, where frightened members, cowed by the chants of demonstrators outside, were afraid that they would be barred from leaving. One member, George Granchev, the leader of a small-business party, was described as calling on his mobile telephone for a helicopter to land on the roof to ferry him off.

Unlike much of Eastern Europe—but like Romania—Bulgaria voted the former Communists into power in parliamentary elections in 1990, after the Communist dictator, Todor Zhivkov, was toppled in 1989.

The United Democratic Forces, with stronger anti-Communist roots, then won elections in 1991. But in a reaction against the rough transition to a market economy, which in Bulgaria was clouded with more corruption and crime than many other Eastern European countries, the former Communists won again in 1994.

Despite warnings from the World Bank and the International Monetary Fund that the economy was collapsing, the Videnov Government sat by as state industries were stripped of their assets by economic groups allied to the Socialist Party. As confidence in the Government sank, Bulgarians withdrew more than $700 million from banks during two months last summer.

Disillusionment with the Socialists became clear when the opposition candidate, Petar Roberto Stoyanov, easily won the presidential election last fall with 60 percent of the vote. He is to be sworn in Jan. 19, replacing Mr. Zhelev.

Faced with pressure from the I.M.F., which put its loan program to Bulgaria on hold last summer, the Socialist Party recently agreed to the recommendation that a currency board take over the functions of the national bank. Such a board would set a fixed rate of exchange for the currency and prevent the Government from printing money. But the I.M.F. is unwilling to set up the board, even with approval from the Socialists, until political stability returns.

The tolerance level of many of the demonstrators appeared to be dwindling fast today. Many said they had turned off heating in their apartments because they could not afford to pay the bills. More than 20 people, many of them elderly pensioners, died during a bout of subzero weather over the New Year. The quality of everyday items like sausages has deteriorated because the state meat factories fill them with soya instead of meat, a protester complained.

"Our situation is unbearable," said Zhana Boetri, a 38-year-old teacher who came to the protests with her husband, Valery, 43, an economist.

"We're supposed to be middle-class Bulgarians, but you can't call us that anymore," Mrs. Boetri said. "We had a car, but it was stolen last year. There is so much crime and no security.

"Our 13-year-old daughter was going to a special language school, but we had to pull her out. We could not afford the $250-a-year fees."

Mrs. Boetri's teaching salary has dropped in value to $20 a month and was paid a month late, she said. Mr. Boetri said his salary at a bank had dropped to $50 a month.

*   *   *

January 20, 1997

NEW PRESIDENT OF BULGARIA SEEKS REFORMS

By JANE PERLEZ

SOFIA, Bulgaria, Jan. 19—Faced with a political crisis that has brought huge crowds of protesters onto the streets, the new President of Bulgaria, Petar Stoyanov, was sworn in today.

He immediately called for new parliamentary elections, a major demand of the demonstrators, and said politicians who had "robbed the country" should be punished.

Speaking before Parliament, Mr. Stoyanov suggested that corrupt politicians had caused the country's economic collapse, which has left most Bulgarians living at subsistence level and put nearly half of the banks into receivership.

"The people on the streets have shown us what to do," he told Parliament, where the former Communists who are the target of the demonstrators sat stony-faced. "They are out there because they are desperately poor and because there have only been imitations of reform—and corruption."

Mr. Stoyanov, 44, a divorce lawyer and onetime star volleyball player, was elected by a wide margin in November in a protest vote against the governing Socialist Party, whose members made up the core of the former Communist Party.

As a previously little-known member of the opposition party, the United Democratic Forces, Mr. Stoyanov represents a new image for Bulgaria. But his inauguration highlighted the country's political standoff.

A demonstration that was to have coincided with his swearing-in was canceled in an effort to avoid a repetition of the police attacks on protesters during a siege of Parliament 10 days ago.

Instead, Mr. Stoyanov addressed a crowd of the protesters—and celebrators—who gathered outside Alexander Nevsky Cathedral this afternoon. In his speech, he repeated his call for an end to official corruption.

Reuters

Petar Stoyanov, who took office yesterday as president of Bulgaria, spoke to protesters in Sofia. He agreed to their demand for new parliamentary elections and blamed corrupt politicians for the country's economic crisis.

The political turmoil came to a boil on Jan. 10, when the Socialist Party members in Parliament—whose popular support, two public opinion surveys released last week indicate, has dropped to less than 10 percent—refused to vote on an opposition motion calling for new elections. The opposition then walked out of Parliament.

At the same time, the retiring President, Zhelyu M. Zhelev, also a member of the opposition party, refused to allow the Socialists to form a new government. Mr. Zhelev cited the discontent on the streets and the economic crisis.

The country had been without a government since just before Christmas, when the Socialist Prime Minister, Zhan V. Videnov, resigned. Mr. Videnov, a hard-line former Communist, was blamed by many Bulgarians for the economic disaster.

The Socialists nominated Nikolai Dobrev, the Interior Minister, to be Prime Minister, but Mr. Zhelev insisted that the Socialists reach an accommodation with the opposition on new elections and an economic program.

Mr. Stoyanov has been negotiating behind the scenes to find a solution. But his task has been difficult because the two parties, which totally mistrust each other, are themselves in turmoil with factions and internal fights.

Mr. Stoyanov said on Friday that his constitutional obligations might force him to let the Socialists form a new government, but today he seemed to have softened that approach.

What is at stake for Bulgaria is whether the country can begin to build economic stability.

The International Monetary Fund has stipulated that the only answer is the introduction of a currency board, but the fund has refused to help create one until a new government is in place. The board would set a fixed exchange rate for the currency and forbid the national bank to print any more money.

Such austere measures, which worked in Argentina, would in the short term bring even more misery for the population. Economists say, though, that in six months or so the economy would begin to normalize.

Western bankers have estimated that more than $7 billion of state money has been siphoned off since 1990, much of it thought to be in private bank accounts.

In a searing speech to the Socialist Party congress just before he was nominated as Prime Minister, Mr. Dobrev openly spoke of the corruption by his colleagues.

"Didn't we know that many state enterprises took credits without any intention of paying back their obligations?" he asked. "Was it not clear that the parvenu private bankers, living like oil sheiks, have neither the culture nor the ability to direct and manage these banks? Why didn't we dismiss the directors who emptied the state enterprises and filled their own bank accounts with the proceeds?"

Ivan Krustev, the director of an independent political think tank, the Center for Liberal Strategies, said Mr. Dobrev's analysis was in many ways the crux of the matter.

Mr. Krustev said one of the principal reasons that the Socialists were refusing to give up power was their financial interest. "There's a lot of money at stake," Mr. Krustev said. "Some people have two opportunities: to sit in Parliament or to sit in prison. Parliament may not be a nice place, but it's better for them than prison."

* * *

August 11, 1997

SUBWAY BURROWS PAST EGGSHELLS OF GRECIAN GLORY

By CELESTINE BOHLEN

ATHENS—Ever since Athens started building a subway system six years ago, archeologists have been holding their breath, fearing damage to the unknown treasures that lie beneath the city's surface.

As it turns out, buried treasures haven't been the chief problem. Working together with Attiko Metro, a company created by the Government, as it burrows beneath the city, Greek archeologists have unearthed a vast store of rich finds—Roman baths, a classical bronze head, ancient walls, undisturbed grave sites including one of a dog buried with his leather collar—much of which will be put on display inside the subway stations themselves.

Instead, what has raised alarms here and abroad is a plan by Attiko Metro that many feel could threaten one of the city's best-known and thoroughly excavated sites—the Kerameikos cemetery, where the dead were buried from the third millennium B.C. to Roman times.

Underlying the debate is the inexorable logic and pressure of the $3 billion, 11.4-mile subway itself, now well behind schedule. It is the largest construction project in Greece, almost entirely financed by loans and grants from European Union institutions, and a key element in the city's bid for the Olympic Games in 2004, as it was in its unsuccessful bid for the 1996 Games. Now, subway officials are saying that half of its 21 stations will be open by late 1999.

The new subway is considered critical for the future of Athens, where the population has doubled in the last 30 years to 3.5 million and the number of cars has skyrocketed. City planners see no other way to relieve the chronic traffic jams and, most important, the air pollution that they produce.

Pollution, which erodes marble's smooth surface and erases the features of statues, is also the biggest enemy of the monuments, a fact that makes archeologists and classical scholars supporters of the subway.

"Everyone knows Athens needs a metro," said Jutta Stroszeck, director of the German Archeological Institute in Athens, which has been responsible for excavations at the Kerameikos cemetery since 1913. Ms. Stroszeck noted that most of the most famous carved reliefs in the Kerameikos cemetery—including those in the Street of Tombs—have already been moved to museums, and substituted with plaster cast copies.

But the removal of some of the carved reliefs does not diminish the archeologists' concern for the integrity of the site itself—the tombs, the walls, the stones, everything that has made the cemetery an important clue in the discovery of Athens's past.

The original subway route beneath the cemetery would have run under the Sacred Gate and the walls of the ancient city, beneath the bed of the tiny Eridanos River. That plan raised such a storm of opposition that Attiko Metro last year agreed on a second route that cuts across only one corner of the ancient cemetery site.

But that corner happens to be directly beneath the Street of Tombs, an area lined by tomb-terraces topped with important pieces of classical funerary art.

No matter how much Metro planners insist that their new route will cause no damage to the monuments above ground, archeologists remain unconvinced, and opposed.

"The vibrations could crack and damage antiquities, damage that you cannot repair," Ms. Stroszeck said." You can not replace antiquities."

As part of its concession to archeologists, Attiko Metro agreed to start with a test tunnel, which will be about 3 yards wide and 15 yards deep, and will advance cautiously at the rate of about one yard a day, in order to be able to confront any problem.

But opponents of the plan are certain that the test tunnel will soon become the real thing.

"We don't want any tunnel built there at all," said Ms. Stroszeck. "but it is hard to have hope because the decision has already been made."

For their part, Metro officials say that in this case, as in others, they have bent over backwards to accommodate the concerns and wishes of the Central Archeological Council, a group of experts appointed by the Government, which has advised them at every step of the way. When the first Kerameikos route was proposed, the council approved it, noted Theodore G. Weigle Jr., an American consultant from the Bechtel Corporation, who is the Attiko Metro's chief executive.

"We have a clear history of giving the archeologists what they want," said Mr. Weigle. "At one time, the Kerameikos route was acceptable but views change, and the winds of public opinion blow in different directions. We don't believe a change in alignment was necessary, but we are willing to do it. There are some who argue that it never should have aligned in Kerameikos but then you would have to write off the station."

The Kerameikos subway station was among the first excavated by the subway consortium, and it is a good example of how the subway has been both good news and bad news for archeologists.

During excavations at the station site, thousands of new tombs were found, many with funeral objects and some dating to 429 B.C., the year Athens was hit by a plague that killed Pericles.

But the fact that work on the Kerameikos station has already begun has been one of the most powerful arguments for going ahead with a tunnel leading up to it, a tunnel that seems destined to lie beneath the Kerameikos cemetery.

Archeologists give the Metro team high marks for the excavations done along the route, particularly at its subway stations. "They have dug very slowly and very carefully at the stations," noted John Camp, director of the American excavations at the Agora. "I have followed several sites, and they have done it properly."

At the city's main Constitution Square, ruins of Roman baths dating to the third century A.D., stretching across about 170 yards, were discovered 10 inches under the congested Amalias Avenue. The bronze head from an almost-life statue from Greece's classical period was found beneath the National Gardens.

"There is always a struggle between antiquities and new ways, new streets," said Yannis Sakalarakis, a distinguished Greek archeologist." The need for a subway is great in Athens, yet it must be a balance between past and present. Often people who are working on the present are not able to foresee the future as well the people working on the past."

*   *   *

September 7, 1997

IS LIFE BETTER IN BULGARIA? IT'S A MATTER OF PERSPECTIVE

By BARBARA CROSSETTE

UNITED NATIONS, Sept. 5—The appearance this week of another index ranking countries by their social conditions—a study in which Bulgaria outranks the United States in quality of life—raises new questions about how and why these surveys are conducted.

In recent years, reports attempting to measure human progress and to evaluate the conditions that might serve as indicators of whether a nation will enjoy economic and social growth have been compiled by a number of international organizations. Among the most widely noted are surveys from Unicef, the World Bank and the United Nations Development Program, which publishes an annual Human Development Index.

The latest report is by a scholar of social work, Richard J. Estes, chairman of the program in social and economic development at the University of Pennsylvania's School of Social Work. Mr. Estes's study, using much of the same data available to United Nations agencies, nevertheless arrives at very different conclusions.

Denmark ranks highest among nations in the ability "to provide for the basic social and material needs of their citizens" in Mr. Estes's survey, compared with 18th in the United Nations Human Development Index. Mr. Estes ranks the United States 27th out of 160 countries, whereas the Human Development Index places it 4th out of 175.

According to Mr. Estes—who presented his findings this week at an international conference in Jakarta, Indonesia, and will publish them in a forthcoming book—Singapore and Cuba are almost equal in rank, at 51st and 54th place respectively.

By contrast, the United Nations index ranks Singapore in 26th place and Cuba in 86th. The United Nations says that Singapore enjoys nearly seven times the per capita gross domestic product of Cuba and slightly higher rates of life expectancy and school attendance. Unicef—the United Nations Children's Fund—reports in its 1997 Progress of Nations study that Singapore's child mortality and maternal death rates are lower than Cuba's. In Singapore, public housing is available to all.

"Both Singapore and Cuba suffer from their failures in the political sector," Mr. Estes said in an E-mail exchange from Jakarta, explaining that both countries rate highly unfavorably on his political index. Cuba's economy lags, he said, "largely because of the economic boycott/blockade of the country by the U.S. and its allies."

"In any case, Singapore is a country that has experienced miraculous economic changes, but where large segments of the population—mostly among the Malays—have minimal opportunity to benefit from the country's wealth," Mr. Estes said. Disparities in wealth, he said, "result in a lower overall score for Singapore than one might otherwise expect."

At the American Enterprise Institute in Washington, Nicholas Eberstadt, who studies demographic surveys, is critical of most attempts to measure social conditions and human progress.

"Human development indices are black boxes and the people who put them together can use any criteria they choose, and thus they can get almost any results they wish," Mr. Eberstadt said in an interview on Thursday.

"For example, there was a time when some specialists on workers' rights suggested using the number of strikes per year as an index of labor freedom," he said. "The lower the number of strikes, the more satisfied the workers. Of course, Communist Czechoslovakia turned out to be the country with almost complete labor freedom. The workers were so satisfied they never struck.

"The scope for error, both inadvertent and agenda driven, is vast in constructing human development indexes because at the bottom they pivot on arbitrary evaluations about which there is no universal consensus," he said.

Mr. Estes, who more than 20 years ago created what he calls the Weighted Index of Social Progress and has issued his ratings periodically, explained the criteria he uses to rank the United States below Bulgaria.

"The present social situation in Bulgaria is miserable," he said. "But in terms of responding to basic human needs, Bulgaria enjoys the legacy of social provision that characterized all of the states and partners of the former Soviet Union, i.e., high literacy, high access to at least basic health care, guaranteed housing, guaranteed income support during old age and other periods of income loss, and so on."

By contrast, Mr. Estes said, the United States loses points because it has 37 million people in poverty and many others on the edge of poverty and without adequate social benefits. He said that the United States trails other industrial nations in life expectancy, infant and child mortality, childhood immunizations and school attendance.

* * *

December 22, 1998

KOSOVO'S RIVAL FORCES ARE MOVING CLOSER TO A NEW WAR

By MIKE O'CONNOR

PERANE, Serbia, Dec. 21—Yugoslav forces and ethnic Albanian rebels seem to be goading each other into a major new round of fighting, with the people of Kosovo and Western countries able to do little more than watch.

Military and police units have been on the move in the last few days. Long convoys, including tanks and armored personnel carriers, are leaving bases where the Government had promised that their forces would remain and are putting men in new positions or taking territory from the rebels.

The rebels, who moved into many areas vacated by the Serbs in October, are stepping up the recruiting and training of fighters and are obtaining large amounts of military gear, according to diplomats. In the last week eight Serbs have been slain. Serbs are convinced that the rebels are responsible, and many are threatening to take their revenge against ethnic Albanian civilians.

The Supreme Commander of NATO, Gen. Wesley C. Clark, and senior American diplomats went to Belgrade today to tell top Yugoslav officials to rein in their forces.

But many Western diplomats in Yugoslavia say they doubt that they can stop renewed combat on a large scale, even though it had been believed that the harsh Balkan winter would prevent any new conflict. The chief Western diplomat in Kosovo, William Walker, an American, is more optimistic than others. Still, he said there was not much the West could do except try to persuade the rebels and the Government to act peacefully.

"I hope no one is overestimating the tools at our disposal," Mr. Walker said. "We don't have many."

In a month or so, as many as 2,000 international observers are scheduled to be on the ground in Kosovo, monitoring each side and trying to ease tensions. Now, however, there is a question whether war will erupt before most monitors are in place.

A senior Western diplomat, referring to the rebel-run Kosovo Liberation Army, said: "The Government's decided enough is enough; the K.L.A. is out of control. If the Government responds the way it seems to be getting ready to do, then the monitors will have to get out because there'll be war everywhere."

Today in this village, six tanks were involved in combat with rebel forces that recently moved into the area. The tanks left their base over the weekend for what the Government called a training exercise. New rebel trenches have been set up on the hills around the fighting.

The fighting here, along with the appearance today of heavily armed Serbian paramilitary policemen on the roads nearby, comes after a police official was shot to death as he walked to work this morning in a neighboring town.

None of this was supposed to happen after President Slobodan Milosevic, under threat of NATO air strikes, agreed to stop offensive operations and withdraw many of his forces from Kosovo in October. Diplomats, led by Americans, thought that if the Government halted their attacks, the rebels would honor a cease-fire, allowing negotiations.

But negotiations have made little progress. Most ethnic Albanians, who make up more than 90 percent of Kosovo's population, want independence. The Government is offering limited autonomy, and ethnic Albanian political leaders are deeply divided over what level of autonomy would be acceptable. Rebel leaders generally feel that they can win independence through war.

On Saturday, when the body of the Deputy Mayor of Kosovo Polje, a Serb, was found by the roadside shot to death, Miroslav Mijailovic, one of the 1,000 or so residents of the village of Velika Hoca, was welcoming guests to his home. The Serbian family was giving its annual homage to its patron, St. Nicholas.

Dishes of potatoes, sweet peppers, cabbage rolls, fish and cookies nearly overflowed the long table as people tried to find solace in talk of religion and tradition. But it did not work, because they said they could feel Kosovo sliding quickly into war.

"The people are not to blame for what is coming, not the Serb people or the Albanian," Mr. Mijailovic said. "Everyone wants what we had before, peace. But there are leaders on both sides who are setting a fire."

Historically, Serbs and ethnic Albanians have been very close in the area of western Kosovo near Velika Hoca. But now, the guests said, they are terrified by rebel fighters they see on the hills around the village.

The two peoples were so close that one guest, the Serbian Mayor of the city of Orahovac, three miles away, said one of his best friends was the man who is now the rebel commander for the area.

"When he started his chicken farm, he came to me for the money to buy the first load of chicken feed," said the Mayor, Andjelko Kolasinac.

"We are at the limits of our patience," Mr. Kolasinac said. "The West must put enough pressure on the K.L.A. that they stop what they are doing. Otherwise what I see coming will not be stopped."

When the Government has taken action against the rebels in the past, it has usually been so brutal that it has only increased the conviction among ethnic Albanians that they must create their own country.

A large military offensive over the summer forced as many as 300,000 ethnic Albanians to flee their homes. Government forces then looted and burned an estimated 20,000 houses. It was the prospect of mass starvation and deaths caused by exposure in the Balkan winter that prompted Western countries to intercede so that refugees could feel safe enough to move back to their villages.

But even now, in response to the rebel actions, Government forces often brutalize ethnic Albanians.

After the funerals last Wednesday of six young Serbs shot in a coffee shop in the city of Pec, the police went on a rampage for several days, arresting and severely beating dozens of ethnic Albanian men.

Many victims said they had not even been questioned about the killings, only beaten.

At the same time, Government forces retook a nearby village, causing hundreds of ethnic Albanian civilians to flee the area.

As his children packed clothes, blankets and bags of flour and a red kerosene lantern into a wagon behind the family tractor in the village, called Glodanje, Nysret Maloku echoed the appeal Serbs are making to Western countries. "You must stop these attacks on us," he said. "We want peace, but we want to survive."

And just as Serbs are insisting that Government forces be unleashed against the rebels, Mr. Maloku said he wanted the Kosovo Liberation Army to strike back at the Government.

"They have to protect us from the regime," he said. "Any army is supposed to protect its people."

*   *   *

February 15, 1999

ALBRIGHT BRINGS FOES FACE TO FACE AT KOSOVO TALKS

By JANE PERLEZ

RAMBOUILLET, France, Feb. 14—Alternately threatening and cajoling, Secretary of State Madeleine K. Albright brought the two warring sides in Kosovo together in talks here for the first time today but came away unconvinced that a settlement could be reached.

"I will not be able to say that the path to agreement is clear or that success is in sight," she said today, before she was expected to report back to President Clinton.

Empowered with Mr. Clinton's pledge of 4,000 American troops to police an eventual peace settlement in Kosovo, Ms. Albright journeyed to Paris and then to the 14th-century stone chateau here, 30 miles southwest of the French capital, to try to galvanize the Serbs and Albanians into reaching an accord this week.

Despite invocations of fond childhood memories as a diplomat's daughter in Belgrade, Ms. Albright encountered a recalcitrant Serbian delegation.

The Serbs' ultimate leader, President Slobodan Milosevic of Yugoslavia, has remained at home. His surrogate and close ally, President Milan Milutinovic of Serbia, flatly ruled out accepting NATO troops on his territory—considered a key part of any accord—and seemed impervious to Ms. Albright's renewed threats of air strikes by the alliance if the Serbs refuse an agreement.

The ethnic Albanians, who have been fighting for the independence of Kosovo, a province of southern Serbia, recognized the plan to offer them autonomy as a "fair deal," Ms. Albright said. But so far, only they seemed ready to sign a peace agreement at the end of the conference, she said.

The contact group of six nations—the United States, four Western European countries and Russia—whose foreign ministers met in Paris today to review the negotiations, set a deadline of noon next Saturday for ending the talks.

It was possible that Ms. Albright would return before the weekend deadline, officials said. She would come back for "closure or a showdown," one said. But it was also highly probable, he said, that the peace deal would have to be taken by the negotiators directly to Mr. Milosevic in Belgrade.

Ms. Albright used a variety of arguments, from the highly personal to the downright political, to tell Mr. Milutinovic why he should encourage his boss, Mr. Milosevic, to accept foreign troops. NATO envisages a force of some 28,000 troops to enforce an eventual peace accord.

An aide recounted that she told the Serbs today: "I know you all think that I'm anti-Serb, but my father said if he hadn't been a Czech first, he would want to be a Serb."

Ms. Albright spent part of her childhood in Belgrade, where her father was a senior Czechoslovak diplomat. But her exhortations, including remembering a Serbian lullaby, appear to have left her listeners unmoved.

Mr. Milutinovic, who dropped into the talks two days ago and is expected to report back to Mr. Milosevic on Monday, said the Serbs remained against the imposition of an outside force in Kosovo, the key element of the peace proposal.

"We are very much against it," Mr. Milutinovic said in a statement broadcast on Government-controlled Serbian television. "The differences boil down to what happens at the end. If an agreement is reached, who should implement it? We are of the opinion that we should implement it, that we have the strength do that."

He added that the Russians, traditional allies of the Serbs but part of the foreign team overseeing the talks, "are in full agreement with us" on the issue of foreign troops. The Russian Foreign Minister, Igor S. Ivanov, was expected at the Rambouillet talks on Monday.

Ms. Albright said she stressed to Mr. Milutinovic during their meeting at a Paris hotel that the foreign troops did not represent an invasion. "There's a big difference between if troops invade or are invited," she said at a news conference. "There are many places in the world where troops are invited to enforce the peace."

In contrast to the Serbs' position, Ms. Albright said, she was encouraged by the response from the ethnic Albanians. Besides meeting the 16-member delegation, she also spoke privately with one of the group, Hashim Thaci, a leading member of the rebel Kosovo Liberation Army, which has battled Serbian security forces for almost a year.

"They gave me every indication that they will be ready to sign on," she said, referring to a peace accord.

Diplomats here say little progress has been made so far in the talks, where the ethnic Albanians, representing 90 percent of Kosovo's estimated population of 2 million, and 13 Serbian delegates have been ensconced for the last week.

Progress is likely to remain difficult to assess, because the final decision rests with Mr. Milosevic in his palace in Belgrade.

The brunt of Ms. Albright's arguments with the Serbs centered on Mr. Milosevic's opposition to allowing foreign troops in Kosovo, a province of Serbia. Mr. Milosevic and his surrogates argue that foreign troops represent a breach of sovereignty.

In the draft plan that has been presented to both sides at the talks, Kosovo will become autonomous for three years, with its future after that undecided.

During the three years, a parliament, judicial system, police force and other institutions are to be developed. The aim is not only to give the ethnic Albanians control over their lives, but also to afford protection to the minority Serbs. While their security forces have ruled Kosovo harshly since Mr. Milosevic stripped away the province's autonomy in 1989, ordinary Serbs in the region say they fear the domination by the ethnic Albanians, who speak a different language, practice a different religion and live almost entirely separately. The Serbs are Eastern Orthodox, and the Albanians are mostly Muslim. The two peoples frequent different hospitals, schools, places of worship and entertainment.

Ms. Albright tried to impress on the Serbs, she said, that national sovereignty toward the end of the 20th century does not always mean what it meant 100 years ago. She cited as an example arms control agreements between great powers that decided to cede some of the armaments they could produce "for the greater good."

The Secretary also stressed that if Serbia did not accept an agreement for autonomy, Kosovo would descend into an even worse war that the Serbs could not win.

In the elegant rooms of the castle, Ms. Albright achieved some measure of success by bringing the leaders of the two delegations together.

They had not formally met with each other in their seven days of talking, eating and sleeping inside the chateau. The high point of the face-to-face encounter, according to an aide who was present, was the offer by the leader of the ethnic Albanian delegation, Mr. Thaci, who turned to the Serbs and said he wanted to find a way that they could live together. In reply, one of the Serbian leaders said they would like to be constructive, the aide recounted.

Because Mr. Thaci had been open-minded, Ms. Albright took him aside and encouraged him to think about the example of other militant groups that had offered to give up their weapons. As a model, she suggested Gerry Adams, leader of the political wing of the Irish Republican Army, who has forsworn arms for peaceful leadership, the official said.

Some diplomats have suggested that Mr. Milosevic is resisting foreign troops because it would be a "humiliation" for him to explain allowing outsiders on Serbian soil, particularly in the province that is at the heart of the Serbian national myth and was the site of Mr. Milosevic's first attempt to keep all Serbs in one state as the old Communist Yugoslavia disintegrated.

But others point out that Mr. Milosevic has the ability to explain anything he wants to his population, particularly through his control of key media.

On April 23 of last year, for instance, Mr. Milosevic organized a referendum in which a majority of Serbs agreed that there should be no foreign interference in the conflict in Kosovo. Less than three weeks later, the Clinton Administration envoy, Richard C. Holbrooke, the most prominent foreign mediator, met with Mr. Milosevic in Belgrade to try and get a peace effort started.

*   *   *

February 24, 1999

KOSOVO ALBANIANS, IN REVERSAL, SAY THEY WILL SIGN PEACE PACT

By JANE PERLEZ

RAMBOUILLET, France, Feb. 23—In a last-minute turnaround, the ethnic Albanian delegation at the Kosovo peace talks agreed in principle today to a settlement, turning what appeared to be an almost certain collapse for the Clinton Administration's effort into a limited success.

An hour after the 3 P.M. deadline for the end of the talks here, the ethnic Albanians presented Secretary of State Madeleine K. Albright and five other foreign ministers a declaration that promised they would sign the peace settlement after two weeks of consultation with the Albanian people in Kosovo.

The three-paragraph declaration was dragged out of the delegation after the chief American negotiator, Ambassador Christopher R. Hill, entreated the members to look into their hearts. Their statement saved the talks, where mediators have been trying for two and a half weeks to resolve the conflict with a proposal that calls for NATO peacekeepers. But Clinton Administration officials acknowledged that today's result was far from what they needed to press Slobodan Milosevic, the Yugoslav President, who remains opposed to NATO peacekeepers in Kosovo.

The United States' strategy was to get full agreement from the ethnic Albanians so negotiators would have more leverage to squeeze Mr. Milosevic, whose troops have viciously suppressed separatist rebels in Kosovo, a province of Serbia.

Without a final answer from the Albanians, it will be hard to carry out the threat of NATO bombing, a threat that is meant to force Mr. Milosevic's hand. Now the process essentially goes on hold for two weeks, and diplomats fear that Mr. Milosevic will try to exploit this delay by making inroads against the Kosovo Liberation Army, the separatist rebel group.

The conference organizers said they would reconvene almost three weeks from now, on March 15, in an unspecified place in France. By then the ethnic Albanians will have completed their consultations at home. The aim then will be to conclude a quick settlement that would give autonomy but not independence to Kosovo, guaranteed by a NATO peacekeeping force.

Ms. Albright, who appeared relieved that her investment of three days of coaxing and admonishing the Albanians had partly paid off, stressed that the Albanians "have a responsibility to make their 'yes' an unequivocal 'yes.' " She and the foreign ministers of Britain, Russia, Germany, France and Italy organized the conference here.

The 16-member Albanian delegation said it would take the proposed agreement back to Kosovo and explain its essential political and military elements to the 1.8 million ethnic Albanians. Both the delegation and the foreign negotiators said they believed that such discussions, in political circles and among citizens, would result in a final agreement.

They said it would be a popular document because it should give Kosovo's Albanians, who make up 90 percent of the province, considerable autonomy. It would also mean the removal of almost all the Serbian police and Yugoslav soldiers in Kosovo and would bring in 28,000 NATO-led soldiers, including 4,000 Americans, to keep the peace.

The Albanian delegation, which the Americans had expected to be the easier side to convince, balked at the agreement until the last moment, in large part because of objections by five members from the Kosovo Liberation Army, the rebel group that has been fighting the Serbs.

One guerrilla delegate, Hashim Thaci, was the last objector. But he was finally brought around when Mr. Hill and then another member of the Albanian delegation, Vetan Surroi, isolated him in discussions this afternoon. The stumbling block that Mr. Thaci had persistently raised—the guerrillas' insistence on a referendum at the end of a three-year interim period—was addressed with a face-saving reference to such a vote in today's declaration.

The statement says the delegation understood that at the end of the interim period, Kosovo "will hold a referendum to ascertain the will of the people." Exactly what this referendum would encompass was deliberately left unclear.

Negotiators said such a vote would not be legally binding, but the reference appeared to be enough to satisfy Mr. Thaci and others who see a referendum as a crucial first step toward independence. The agreement now offers Kosovo autonomy but keeps it a province of Serbia.

During the next two weeks, when the Albanians are back in Kosovo explaining the agreement, the threat of NATO air strikes against Mr. Milosevic will diminish.

But once a new round of talks opens on March 15, negotiators said, the threat of such attacks would renew the pressure on President Milosevic to agree to NATO-led ground troops as peacekeepers, which he has so far vigorously resisted.

The British Foreign Secretary, Robin Cook, said at the joint news conference of foreign ministers that the Secretary General of NATO, Javier Solana, was still empowered to order air attacks.

Ms. Albright said the Serbian delegation, led in the last days by Mr. Milosevic's close ally, Milan Milutinovic, the president of Serbia, had given a qualified "yes" to the political aspects of the agreement, including autonomy for Kosovo. But, she said, the Serbs remained "unengaged" on

Washington's insistence that the peacekeepers be led by NATO.

The Serbs said in a written declaration to the foreign ministers that they would "discuss" the possibility of an "international presence" in Kosovo. This proposal was an effort to accept something other than a NATO force, Ms. Albright said, and she found it unacceptable.

There remains the fear that President Milosevic will use his forces to harass the Kosovo Liberation Army, making the guerrillas perhaps less eager to settle than their representatives in Rambouillet.

NATO officials said there had been a substantial buildup of Serbian police forces and Yugoslav Army troops inside Kosovo and on the Kosovo border in the last several weeks. This could indicate that Mr. Milosevic is preparing for renewed fighting, they said.

In order to get the Albanians' conditional acceptance today, Ms. Albright offered incentives intended to show that Washington is a friend of Kosovo. For example, the United States will open a visa office in Pristina, the Kosovo capital, she promised, so Albanians would not have to travel to Belgrade, the capital of Serbia and Yugoslavia, to get consular services.

Officers in the Kosovo Liberation Army would also be sent to the United States for training in transforming themselves from a guerrilla group into a police force or a political entity, much like the African National Congress did in South Africa.

But in the end it appears to have been Mr. Hill's 11th-hour appeal, combined with the leadership of Mr. Surroi, that turned the tables.

Mr. Hill said he tried to prepare the Albanian delegation the night before for the consequences of rejecting an agreement to stop the war, which has squandered civilian lives in the last year and could only get worse. He said he asked the delegates to think about how they would think of themselves as individuals a week from now if they rejected the opportunity for peace.

This afternoon, as the ministers waited after lunch for the Albanians' final decision, Mr. Hill said, he went into the delegation room and sensed that a majority wanted to sign.

Then, he said, he pointed to a delegate and asked: "Do you want to sign?" The answer came back: po, the Albanian word for yes. Mr. Hill said he got a succession of po's until he got to Mr. Surroi, who stood up and started speaking.

"Vetan said, 'O.K, we can get this worked out,' " Mr. Hill said.

Mr. Surroi suggested a text of what became the declaration, in letter form, to the foreign ministers. Mr. Hill suggested that a translator sit at a computer in the room and type the words on the screen. There were no objections in the room, and with that, Mr. Hill said, the foreign ministers had what they needed.

Mr. Surroi, the publisher of the biggest newspaper in Kosovo, had worked feverishly during the two and a half weeks as a bridge in the delegation and had tried to bring the five guerrillas around.

He said late this afternoon: "This was done by consensus. We have everyone on board. What we have achieved here is Albanians working together. The biggest argument we saw was that this is an opportunity for peace."

*　　*　　*

March 1, 1999

THOUSANDS FLEE TO KOSOVO BORDER TO ESCAPE ARMY'S SURGE

By CARLOTTA GALL

GENERAL JANKOVIC, Serbia, Feb. 28—More than two thousand people fled villages during heavy fighting in southern Kosovo today and swamped a major border post in a desperate effort to cross to safety in neighboring Macedonia.

Yugoslav Army artillery and antiaircraft guns could be heard battering the mountainous region west of the border post of General Jankovic in the late afternoon. It was the most serious fighting in the Serbian province since the peace talks with ethnic Albanian separatists ended inconclusively last week. Serbia is one of two provinces in Yugoslavia.

Foreign observers trying to monitor a cease-fire in Kosovo for the Organization for Security and Cooperation in Europe have watched the army move large amounts of armor and troops into the border region in recent days. Now the soldiers seem to be putting it to use to clear and take control of a swath of territory along the border and overlooking the main road.

Refugees from several villages just west of the border post said that fighting had started early in the morning and that soldiers had stormed their villages in large numbers.

Imam Hasan Hasalari, the Muslim leader of the village of Rejance, said an army troop truck pulled up outside his home at 7:30 A.M.

"I was afraid to go out," he said. "Then just 500 yards away heavy shooting broke out and big explosions. Then I was afraid to stay in the house. I saw people running out the back and I climbed out of a window and ran."

Imam Hasalari ended up with 2,000 to 3,000 others clamoring to cross the border at General Jankovic, but they found their way blocked by Serbian police. Turned back because they had no papers or passports, the refugees stood in the street all day in rising panic as the police carried out house-to-house searches in the village. By early evening the refugees had been given shelter in houses there. In one house just off the main street, about 30 women and children filled a single room. Shemsije Sermjani, a nervous young woman with dark rings round her eyes, told of how they had fled their village, Palivodenica, at 10 in the morning. "We heard shooting and saw army patrols moving up into the hills above," she said.

"For two weeks, we had been watching the troop movements around. We were all ready to leave at any moment." She said her 80-year-old father and her brother had stayed in the village to watch their house and animals. "We don't know what will happen," she added. "It is very hard."

The New York Times

Refugees filled the Serbian border town of General Jankovic.

About 90 percent of Kosovo residents are ethnic Albanians, most of whom are Muslims.

Villagers said Serbian forces had begun their action by attacking the village of Pustenik, a known stronghold of ethnic Albanian guerrillas of the Kosovo Liberation Army, and then swept on through neighboring villages.

"They are ethnically cleaning villages in a five-kilometer area of the border," said one monitor there, who spoke on the condition of anonymity. He said that Serbian forces were trying to take territory before peace talks resume on March 15 and that the operation did not specifically seem to be against the rebels.

"They have moved to reinforce their position," he said. "It is all part of the politics."

* * *

March 18, 1999

SERBS' KILLING OF 40 ALBANIANS RULED A CRIME AGAINST HUMANITY

By CARLOTTA GALL

PRISTINA, Serbia, March 17—The 40 ethnic Albanians killed in the village of Racak in January were all unarmed civilians, and their slaying amounted to a crime against humanity, the head of a Finnish forensic team that examined the bodies said today.

The team leader, Dr. Helena Ranta, whose group performed autopsies on 40 of the 45 reported dead, announced the findings here in Kosovo's capital after handing her report to the Serbian authorities. She called for a criminal investigation of the killings and prosecution of the perpetrators.

The report sharply contradicts the official Serbian version of the incident, and coming as Belgrade has stepped up its military campaign in Kosovo and effectively stonewalled peace talks, the report turns the spotlight on Serbia's conduct in its southern province.

"This is a crime against humanity, yes," Dr. Ranta told a news conference.

She said the report would be submitted to the International War Crimes Tribunal in The Hague.

The Racak killings represented a turning point in the war. Upon hearing of the killings, William Walker, the American leading the observer mission sponsored by the Organization for Security and Cooperation in Europe, said the Serbian security forces had massacred the Albanians.

Mr. Walker was threatened with expulsion, and Serbia was threatened with NATO air strikes, setting off the chain of events leading to the first peace talks between the two sides.

Serbian authorities had said at the time that their forces had killed the people in a gun battle or in crossfire and that the dead were members of the separatist Kosovo Liberation Army, which is battling the government forces.

But the Finnish team concluded that "there were no indications of the people being other than unarmed civilians." Among those examined, there were several elderly men and one woman, Dr. Ranta said. Their clothes bore no insignia of a military unit, and there was no sign that badges or insignia had been removed, a summary of the report stated.

No ammunition was found on the victims, and a test for traces of gunpowder was negative. "It is most likely there was no fight," Dr. Ranta said.

The report also said that the clothes of the victims, marked as they were with bullet holes and congealed blood, could not have been changed or removed. This contradicts the official Serbian suggestion that the Albanians had removed the guerrillas' uniforms and dressed them as civilians to stage an apparent massacre.

Dr. Ranta emphasized that the 22 bodies found in a narrow gully above the village had not been moved, although most had been turned over when villagers first found them. "They were most likely shot where they were found," she said, further discounting Serbian accusations of a setup.

The dead were all killed by shooting and by more than one bullet, she said. One body bore wounds from 30 bullets, Dr. Ranta said.

Despite the exhaustive documentation, Dr. Ranta refused to draw conclusions as to the manner of death. She said it was not her role as a scientist to ascertain whether the killings were a massacre.

She said she had not visited the gully herself, which lies 25 miles southwest of Pristina, and so could not judge the distance from which the victims were killed.

* * *

March 20, 1999

CLINTON SAYS FORCE IS NEEDED TO HALT KOSOVO BLOODSHED

By JOHN M. BRODER

WASHINGTON, March 19—Preparing the American public for military action in the Balkans, President Clinton said today that the Serbs had crossed the threshold of acceptable behavior and that force was the answer to prevent further bloodshed in Kosovo.

"Make no mistake," Mr. Clinton said at an afternoon news conference at the White House, "if we and our allies do not have the will to act, there will be more massacres. In dealing with aggressors in the Balkans, hesitation is a license to kill. But action and resolve can stop armies and save lives." Excerpts, page A7.

Mr. Clinton spoke as ominous signs spread across Europe that NATO military strikes against Serbian targets could begin in days. Peace talks broke down in Paris as the Serbs refused to sign a peace accord accepted on Thursday by delegates of Kosovo's ethnic Albanian majority. Page A6.

Western Governments began removing cease-fire monitors and nonessential personnel from Yugoslavia.

The Pentagon announced that it was dispatching additional combat aircraft to the region in anticipation of a series of air strikes intended to reduce Serbia's ability to move against the separatist rebels.

Mr. Clinton spent most of his day making a case for United States participation in NATO-led military strikes in the Balkans, meeting a large contingent of members of Congress in the morning and speaking extensively on the subject with reporters this afternoon.

He also met senior foreign policy advisers to review plans for possible strikes, including timing, sequences and targets.

Congressional leaders emerged from the White House meeting skeptical about the reasons for United States involvement in hostilities in the former Yugoslavia.

Senator Trent Lott, the Republican majority leader, said the Senate would debate policy in Kosovo early next week.

"We believe that the President now recognizes the need to say to the American people," Mr. Lott said, "exactly what's at stake here, why would an action be taken, what would those actions be and what are the risks."

Senator Don Nickles of Oklahoma, the deputy Republican leader, said he had told Mr. Clinton that the United States should not initiate a bombing campaign unless President Slobodan Milosevic of Yugoslavia engaged in a systematic assault on the ethnic Albanians in Kosovo.

Mr. Clinton argued at his news conference that Mr. Milosevic had already carried out numerous massacres and other atrocities in Kosovo, as well as earlier in Bosnia.

"I think that the threshold has been crossed," Mr. Clinton said, citing the killing of more than 40 ethnic Albanian civilians in January in the village of Racak.

"With all the troops that have been massed, and what we know about their plans, and what they have publicly said about them, I would hate to think that we'd have to see a lot of other little children die before we could do what seems to be, to me, clearly the right thing to do to prevent it," the President said.

Later Mr. Clinton added, "I do not believe that we ought to have to have thousands more people slaughtered and buried in open soccer fields before we do something."

The conflict has created more than 400,000 refugees. An estimated 20,000 have been displaced just in the last week by military operations in and around Kosovo.

Mr. Clinton said the rationale to use force went beyond humanitarian concerns. He said a raging conflict in Kosovo could send tens of thousands of refugees across borders and, potentially, draw Albania, Macedonia, Greece and Turkey into the war.

"This is a conflict with no natural boundaries," he said. "It threatens our national interests. If we don't act, the war will spread. If it spreads, we will not be able to contain it without far greater risk and cost. I believe the real challenge of our foreign policy today is to deal with problems before they do permanent harm to our vital interests. That is what we must do in Kosovo."

Mr. Clinton faced pointed questioning on Kosovo both in his Congressional meeting and in the news conference.

He was asked why Mr. Milosevic should take American threats seriously, after Mr. Clinton and other Western leaders had backed down from earlier threats and allowed numerous negotiating deadlines to pass.

He was asked why NATO had delayed action, even though Mr. Milosevic has carried out a continuing campaign of repression against Albanians, Bosnian Muslims and other minorities in former Yugoslav provinces.

"I think he should take this seriously, because we were serious in Bosnia," Mr. Clinton said. "My intention would be to do whatever is possible, first of all, to weaken his ability to massacre them, to have another Bosnia."

He said the peace talks between the Serbs and the ethnic Albanians had been extended at the request of the two sides, not because of American irresolution. He noted that Russia had consistently opposed NATO military action against Moscow's allies in Serbia.

Mr. Clinton and European leaders have enlisted Russian support for peace efforts in Kosovo. But Moscow has steadfastly refused to endorse any threat of force against Belgrade. The issue is certain to arise when Prime Minister Yevgeny M. Primakov of Russia visits Washington beginning next Tuesday.

The House narrowly voted last week to endorse Mr. Clinton's plan to send American troops to Kosovo to enforce a peace accord if all parties reach one. The United States would supply 4,000 soldiers to a 28,000-member NATO peacekeeping force.

But Republicans have complained that the Administration is wading into a quagmire with no clear means of exit and without sufficient support.

"Americans are going to be killed," Senator Robert F. Bennett, Republican of Utah, said in a speech on the Senate floor today. "They are going to come home in body bags, and they will be killed in a war that Congress has not declared."

*   *   *

March 21, 1999

FEARS DEEPENS AS MONITORS QUIT KOSOVO

By CARLOTTA GALL

GORNJA KLINA, Serbia, March 20—Thousands of panicked refugees fled on foot, by tractor or by horse and cart today, carrying young children and clutching a few possessions, as Serbian forces pressed an offensive against the ethnic Albanian rebels in Kosovo.

These were people who had already abandoned their villages earlier this week for the comparative safety of Srbica, a town in the Drenica region, the heartland of the Kosovo Albanians' revolt against Serbian rule. Now, trudging through snow and bone-chilling cold, they were fleeing again, seeking safety deeper inside rebel-held territory.

The Serbian security forces—heavily armed police and Yugoslav Army units with tanks and other armor—appeared intent on smashing through the Drenica region northwest of Pristina, Kosovo's capital. That region was the birthplace of the armed revolt started by Kosovo's ethnic Albanians a year ago, and houses the headquarters of their Kosovo Liberation Army.

On the road to Srbica, burly policemen in dark blue camouflage uniforms, equipped with flak jackets and pistols in their belts, blocked access to most reporters. Journalists who did manage to enter the town described groups of gunmen, in white snow-camouflage and black masks, driving around the small community, and tanks and armored vehicles ranged in positions.

The policemen outside Srbica waved through a convoy of armored jeeps, police personnel carriers and a water truck, clad with crude metal sheets of armor, machine guns poking out of small slit windows. No other traffic was on the road.

In recent days, Srbica's population had swollen with some 5,000 refugees from outlying villages. Today, the town itself was under attack.

Shell fire resounded in the hills, and three houses in the town were in flames. A firefight was under way in the village of Poljance, just south of Srbica, which until Friday was under control of fighters of the separatist Kosovo Liberation Army.

Hours before, some 1,300 foreign monitors with the Organization for Security and Cooperation in Europe had evacuated to neighboring Macedonia. Their withdrawal followed the collapse of peace talks on Friday in Paris and increased NATO threats of punitive air strikes against Serbia for refusing to negotiate peace on foreign terms.

As monitors left in a coordinated motorcade of bright orange vehicles to the border, they watched large numbers of Yugoslav Army soldiers on the move. "They made signs, they blew kisses," said one monitor, speaking of the soldiers on condition of anonymity. "They are pleased to see us go." He had driven out from Pec, in western Kosovo, and passed a large column of armor headed the other way. There was also heavy military activity around the main army base outside Kosovo's capital, Pristina, he said.

"They are glad to see the back of us so they can finish the job," the monitor said. "They have a window of opportunity with the weather and they are going to put the squeeze on." Kosovo was coated in snow and low clouds, and the roads were thick with ice today—not good weather for NATO to bomb, he pointed out.

The monitors were given orders to withdraw on Friday as part of the West's preparations for a possible bombing of Serbia. Fears that the Serbian forces would block the monitors' departure proved unfounded today as they made their way on the hazardously icy roads toward the border crossing with Macedonia, where Serbian officials carefully invalidated the entry visas in the monitors' passports.

On Friday, President Clinton warned the Serbs that they had crossed the threshold of acceptable behavior. Nonessential foreign diplomats and their families began to leave Belgrade the capital of Yugoslavia, which consists of Serbia and Montenegro.

But neither warnings nor the weather deterred the Serbian police and Yugoslav Army today, as they pressed their offensive against the ethnic Albanian rebels. The Kosovo Liberation Army—financed by the Albanian diaspora and backed by the heavily ethnic Albanian population of this southern Serbian province—has grown in the past year from a ragtag force to a far more disciplined group increasingly equipped with sophisticated weapons as well as the standard Kalashnikov rifles.

But those weapons are still no match for the heavy armor of the Serbs. Today, tanks were ranged in firing position and mortars set up along the road looking south over the villages in the Cicavica mountain range.

The police manned a new position, and aimed their guns out from newly constructed sandbagged defenses. Columns of troop trucks and army artillery guns were drawn up in organized groups beside the road.

Farther north, the main road to Belgrade was cut by fighting. The police said the rebels had attacked a police station at Luzane Friday evening. That could not be independently confirmed but shooting and shelling continued much of today.

Starting in October, the foreign monitors had kept a check on army and police movements, trailing military convoys and watching their exercises and operations. While they were not able to force them to keep to barracks, the presence of the monitors appeared to have a restraining effect. They were particularly successful in negotiating local ceasefires.

As the foreigners left, many ethnic Albanians said they feared what the Serbs would do next. A woman who gave her name only as Sofia, a mother of three, was walking back to her house on the outskirts of Gornja Klina, to bring food to her husband and sons.

She had fled the village when shells landed in the area on Monday. She had heard that the monitors were leaving and said she now wanted to persuade her husband to abandon the house. "There is a lot of fear, everyone feels it," she said.

"When we fled the O.S.C.E. was there, they helped us. But now I do not know what will happen."

*   *   *

March 22, 1999

MILOSEVIC TO GET ONE 'LAST CHANCE' TO AVOID BOMBING

By JANE PERLEZ

WASHINGTON, March 21—The Clinton Administration today dispatched a special envoy, Richard C. Holbrooke, to meet with Slobodan Milosevic in what senior officials described as a "last chance" to persuade the Yugoslav leader to accept a peace agreement for Kosovo and avoid bombing by NATO.

Two days after President Clinton warned that the Serbs had gone beyond "the threshold" of violence in their southern province, Secretary of State Madeleine K. Albright said she was sending the envoy to present Mr. Milosevic with a "stark choice."

That choice, she said, was for him to agree to the settlement signed in Paris last week by the ethnic Albanians who make up most of Kosovo's population, or face NATO air strikes.

As Mr. Holbrooke prepared to leave tonight, Mr. Milosevic's forces appeared unintimidated, however. Taking advantage of the absence of more than 1,300 international monitors who withdrew from Kosovo on Saturday, they continued their rampage through Kosovo, burning ethnic Albanian villages in a region at the heart of the armed revolt.

At NATO headquarters in Brussels, where Mr. Holbrooke will stop Monday morning before flying on to Belgrade, American officials today presented NATO ambassadors with a stepped-up plan for bombing in Serbia, a move intended to strengthen Mr. Holbrooke's position with the Yugoslav leader.

The President's national security adviser, Samuel R. Berger, said today that another diplomatic push by Mr. Holbrooke was justified "one final time," even as the Administration came under new criticism that it was dithering over what to do about Mr. Milosevic.

"I think we owe it to the American people," Mr. Berger said on the CBS News program "Face the Nation." "We owe it to our military people, our allies, to make that final attempt, even as the preparations continue."

He stressed that plans for air strikes were simultaneously moving forward. "The preference is to find a peace agreement that will bring stability to Kosovo, peace to Kosovo, and rights to the Kosovar people," Mr. Berger said. "If we can achieve that with the imminent threat of force, that will be a good result."

Mr. Holbrooke, who negotiated a Kosovo cease-fire last October that Mr. Milosevic has flouted for two months, appeared to have a particularly difficult assignment this time.

Publicly, Clinton Administration officials said Mr. Holbrooke was being sent to deliver Mr. Milosevic the message of peace or war.

Mr. Milosevic has shown a pattern of backing down at the last minute. Should he show signs of doing so this time, Mr. Holbrooke will likely be left with the task of negotiating around the edges of the peace settlement that the ethnic Albanians signed at the Paris peace talks last week. Changes to the terms of the peace settlement could well drive the ethnic Albanians to renege on the agreement.

"If Mr. Milosevic is ready to agree to a NATO-led force which can include other nations, we're ready to discuss it without betraying the ethnic Albanians," a senior Administration official said. The official acknowledged there was "very little maneuvering room because of the 81-page document out of Paris."

By sending Mr. Holbrooke to what some officials are calling "last chance" talks, the Administration opened itself to accusations by even some supporters of being too accommodating toward Mr. Milosevic.

Former Senator Bob Dole, sent earlier this month by the Administration to break a logjam in the talks between the Serbs and ethnic Albanians, said he believed that Mr. Holbrooke's visit was unnecessary.

"I don't think we have to make any more overtures to Milosevic," Mr. Dole said on NBC News' "Meet the Press." "We've done enough of that."

Senator Joseph I. Lieberman, Democrat of Connecticut, who has been a proponent of the air strikes, suggested that the Administration was dithering. "Great alliances and great countries don't remain great if they issue threats and don't keep them," Mr. Lieberman said.

Others charged that the Holbrooke mission ran the risk of allowing Mr. Milosevic more time to conduct his new military offensive against the ethnic Albanian population and the guerrillas of the Kosovo Liberation Army.

"If you're going to send an emissary, every day you wait to do so you give Milosevic more time to attack," said James Hooper, the executive director of the Balkans Action Council, a nongovernmental group that has supported air strikes against the Yugoslav leader. "Why wait until Monday? And at least get it over quickly."

Members of the ethnic Albanian delegation, who signed the accords in Paris last Thursday, said they feared that Mr. Holbrooke, in an attempt to forge an agreement with Mr. Milosevic and avoid bombing, may undermine the terms of the accord.

They pointed out that Mr. Holbrooke went to Belgrade 10 days ago on a very limited mission—to deliver a message about the terms of the Kosovo settlement and to make clear that not signing would mean NATO air strikes—and failed to convince Mr. Milosevic to back down.

This time, they said, it appeared that Mr. Holbrooke would negotiate with Mr. Milosevic, even as Serbian forces were using tanks, heavy artillery and mortar in their new offensive in Kosovo, whose population is 90 percent ethnic Albanian.

The region was stripped of broad autonomy by Mr. Milosevic in 1989.

"I would agree that Ambassador Holbrooke should go to Belgrade with an ultimatum, but this is not a new ultimatum," said Bujar Bukoshi, the prime minister of the shadow government of ethnic Albanians in Kosovo, who is also a member of the delegation to the peace talks.

Mr. Holbrooke, whose traveling party includes Lieut. Gen. Edward Anderson and Greg Schulte, a National Security Council specialist on the Balkans, will be preceded in Belgrade by the three negotiators from the Paris peace talks.

According to one of the negotiators, Ambassador Wolfgang Petritsch, the Austrian envoy to Belgrade, the trio—Mr. Petritsch, the United States Ambassador, Christopher R. Hill, and the Russian Ambassador, Boris Mayorsky—will meet Mr. Milosevic Monday afternoon.

"It's important to put everything on the table with Mr. Milosevic," Mr. Petritsch said. "We want to make it clear to him what is in the accord—there has been such a propaganda war against the accord in Belgrade, people won't give credit to what is in the agreement."

Mr. Petritsch said he would stress that the accord allows Kosovo to stay within Serbia as an autonomous region and that it gives the Serbian minority protection.

To stress NATO unity, President Clinton spoke today about the situation with President Jacques Chirac of France, Prime Minister Tony Blair of Britain and Chancellor Gerhard Schroder of Germany, a White House spokesman said.

Administration officials also said that the planned visit to Washington by Prime Minister Yevgeny M. Primakov of Russia would not affect the timing of possible NATO action. Mr. Primakov, who opposes the bombing by NATO, begins meeting with Administration officials on Tuesday.

Mr. Berger, questioned on whether the Administration would ask Mr. Primakov to postpone his visit, said, "No, I think that would be his decision to make if it came to that."

*   *   *

March 24, 1999

MILOSEVIC-HOLBROOKE: NEVER A SMOOTH MIX

By ROGER COHEN

BERLIN, March 23—When Slobodan Milosevic and Richard C. Holbrooke first met in August 1995, an onlooker remarked of their prolonged and animated exchange, "The two egos danced all night."

From that encounter in Belgrade through many desperate sessions at the Bosnia peace talks in Dayton to the fruitless talks in the Yugoslav capital today, a particularly charged chemistry has existed between the Serbian leader and Washington's Balkan envoy: a web of repulsion, rancor and grudging respect.

Through its highs and lows, its tantrums and its truces, the relationship has brought results—most conspicuously, a belated peace in Bosnia that was forged in Ohio in November 1995 and has held ever since. But today, it seems, nothing could be conjured from the old ties, not even a diplomatic phrase.

The situation in the Balkans is "the bleakest since we began this effort almost four years ago," Mr. Holbrooke told CNN, adding that Mr. Milosevic was not even ready to enter serious talks on the deployment of NATO peacekeepers in Kosovo.

These words, bereft of any hint of compromise, appeared to open the way for the United States and its allies to reverse course and bomb the country led by the man they rehabilitated and turned into their de facto ally at Dayton just three years ago.

It has been a long road for Mr. Holbrooke. The observer who watched and recorded the egos dancing that first night in Belgrade was Robert C. Frasure, a seasoned State Department official who was killed five days later in Bosnia.

In a sense, as Mr. Holbrooke knows, it was Mr. Milosevic who sent Mr. Frasure and two other senior American officials to their deaths on Aug. 19, 1995, by refusing to provide security guarantees for a flight from Belgrade to Sarajevo and so obliging the officials to take a dangerous mountain road where their vehicle crashed.

Ever since that accident, on a mission he was leading, Mr. Holbrooke has been obsessed by the memory of his fallen colleagues.

Even for a man seldom lacking in energy or drive, the loss has added an overwhelming personal determination to somehow wrestle Mr. Milosevic to the floor and bring an end to the wars of Yugoslavia's slow destruction that began in 1991.

Another memory has also colored Mr. Holbrooke's relationship with Mr. Milosevic, whose 12 years in power have coincided with an almost uninterrupted cycle of killing. That memory is of the start of the Bosnian war in 1992, when Mr. Holbrooke was a direct witness to the Serbian rampage against the Muslims that marked the first six months of the conflict.

In Banja Luka, at the heart of the horror, a Muslim survivor of a Serbian concentration camp handed Mr. Holbrooke a wooden carving of man with head bowed. Asked once if he thought of that carving when speaking to Mr. Milosevic, he replied, "No, it's not that linear." He added: "But I understand the connection. I'm sure we all do."

The connection, of course, is the one between Mr. Milosevic and the killings for which he has so often denied responsibility. It is a chain that links the Serbian leader's quashing of Kosovo's autonomy in the late 1980's, his relentless whipping of the Serbs into a fury of nationalist indignation, and his arming of the marauding Serbian militias of 1992 that hounded Muslim civilians into packed camps in Bosnia.

Mr. Holbrooke has never had any illusions about this; he would not argue with the notion that he has been talking to an unusually destructive man. But when he began his diplomacy in 1995, he found Mr. Milosevic anxious to end a Bosnian war that was turning against the Serbs. There lay the seeds of a bond of sorts.

There were other elements to the initial success of the relationship. Mr. Milosevic's dismissal of detail—referred to, in his broken English, as "mere technology"—suited Mr. Holbrooke, who likes the big picture.

The Serbian leader's extraordinary power—he gave away Sarajevo with a wave of the hand at Dayton—was also useful to the American envoy: in effect, Mr. Holbrooke was able to move fast because he had to deal with only one man.

Shouting, cajoling, laughing, raging, the two men gradually learned how to deal with each other. Each understood that the other had a deep respect for force. Mr. Milosevic has made a habit, as in Kosovo today, of applying military might even as he talks. Mr. Holbrooke was convinced by the NATO bombing of Bosnia in 1995 that Balkan diplomacy unbacked by force is dithering.

In his memoir of Balkan diplomacy, "To End a War," Mr. Holbrooke held back from an in-depth portrait of his Serbian interlocutor, no doubt because, as events have proved, he knew he had unfinished business.

But at one point Mr. Holbrooke wrote, "Watching Milosevic turn on the charm, someone observed that had fate dealt him a different birthplace and education, he would have been a successful politician in a democratic system."

That "charm" has not been much in evidence of late, and it seems clear that the intensity, even the thrill, of the two men's initial jousting has gradually given way to a battle marked by sourness and mistrust.

After his Kosovo diplomacy last October, which brought a short truce, Mr. Holbrooke expressed only exasperation with Mr. Milosevic, saying he would be happy if he never had to return to Belgrade again.

But events have brought this most forceful of American diplomats back to the scene of his first meeting with Mr. Milosevic, only in changed circumstances. Kosovo, of course, is not Bosnia. It is still seen by many Serbs as the womb of their civilization.

Moreover, the question of placing foreign troops on Serbian soil is as explosive as any can be in Belgrade. Having fought, for much of the last 200 years, for the territory it now controls, Serbia is passionately, irrationally and often destructively attached to every inch of it.

How, in these circumstances, Mr. Holbrooke thought he could sway the Serbian leader—squeeze out one last waltz in the long dance—remains unclear. Today the envoy expressed indignation at how American plans were being "grossly mischaracterized" by Serbian politicians and suggested that their comments revealed "a lot of history" and misunderstanding.

But there is nothing new about this state of affairs. A lot of history and a lot of misunderstanding have accompanied Serbia's destructive implosion for more than a decade. What is new is that Mr. Holbrooke seems unable to use Mr. Milosevic to bully his way past the Serbian bravura.

Perhaps this time America's patience with the Serbian leader has simply run out.

*   *   *

March 25, 1999

NATO OPENS BROAD BARRAGE AGAINST SERBS AS CLINTON DENOUNCES YUGOSLAV PRESIDENT

By FRANCIS X. CLINES

WASHINGTON, March 24—The forces of NATO opened an assault on Serbia with cruise missiles and bombs today as President Clinton denounced the Yugoslav President, Slobodan Milosevic, for feeding the "flames of ethnic and religious division" in Kosovo and endangering neighboring countries.

The missiles began striking Serbian targets within minutes of Mr. Clinton's midday announcement that the long-threatened attack was under way. It was expected to be a broad, sustained barrage intended to stun the Yugoslav leader and punish the military for its yearlong onslaught against the ethnic Albanian separatists of Kosovo.

"Ending this tragedy is a moral imperative," Mr. Clinton declared in an address to the nation tonight from the Oval Office. "It is also important to America's national interests."

He spoke several hours after the first explosions of incoming missiles erupted in the night skies of Pristina, Kosovo's capital. The Yugoslav news agency Tanjug said the city's main commercial and military airport had been hit.

At 5:24 A.M. Thursday (11:24 P.M. Wednesday, Eastern time), all-clear sirens sounded in Belgrade, indicating the end of the raids, Agence France-Presse reported.

The biggest allied military assault in Europe since World War II occurred after a day in which Serbian forces maintained their military pressure against the ethnic Albanian majority in Kosovo. Steady streams of alarmed residents fled toward Kosovo's borders.

Sirens sounded, and the flash and thunder of explosions cut through the night sky of Belgrade and other scattered targets, including Novi Sad, in northern Serbia, and the main airport in the Yugoslav coastal republic of Montenegro. One explosion was reported near Batajnica, the main Serbian airport and military base near Belgrade.

As he explained the NATO attack—an attempt to solve a problem that Serbia considers purely internal—Mr. Clinton sought to reassure the United States against a commitment to any large-scale ground war.

"I don't intend to put our troops in Kosovo to fight a war," he emphasized. He denounced Mr. Milosevic as a dictator "who has done nothing since the cold war ended but start new wars and pour gasoline on the flames of ethnic and religious division."

"We act to prevent a wider war, to defuse a powder keg at the heart of Europe that has exploded twice before in this century with catastrophic results," the President said gravely of the military attack by the 19-member NATO alliance.

In his afternoon announcement of the military attack, Mr. Clinton said, "President Milosevic, who over the past decade started the terrible wars against Croatia and Bosnia, has again chosen aggression over peace."

Flames lit up the Belgrade skyline yesterday after NATO missiles and planes punished Yugoslavia for not signing a peace agreement for Kosovo.

A defiant Mr. Milosevic called for defense of his nation "by all means possible," terming Kosovo "only the door intended to allow foreign troops to come in and steal away our freedom."

The Belgrade Government, in denouncing what it called neo-Nazism, called upon the United Nations Security Council to condemn "NATO's criminal, terrorist, underhanded and cowardly attack."

American defense officials said their targets included missile batteries, radar installations and military communication sites in Kosovo, Belgrade and other key areas. Some air-to-air combat was reported by Pentagon officials, who said all NATO planes had returned safely.

President Boris N. Yeltsin of Russia, which has longstanding ties to the Serbs, angrily denounced the American-led raids as "open aggression." Mr. Clinton had tried to justify the military action today in a 35-minute phone call with Mr. Yeltsin. But the Russian leader recalled his chief military envoy to NATO.

After months of threats, NATO finally resorted to military action as Mr. Milosevic, far from heeding peace overtures, stepped up his latest offensive against ethnic Albanian villages and rebels of the Kosovo Liberation Army.

Since violence began intensifying a year ago, more than 400,000 ethnic Albanians have fled their homes as Serbian forces have torched and bombarded villages, massacring civil-

ians in some raids. In recent decades ethnic Albanians have come to outnumber Serbs by 9-to-1 in Kosovo, which Serbs long have revered as the birthplace of Serbian nationhood.

The ultimate fear about the mounting violence in Kosovo, the southernmost province of Serbia, is that it might reignite the ethnic and religious wars in the Balkans that NATO earlier worked to resolve in Bosnia with the commitment of troops.

Critics who until now accused the Administration of equivocating in facing Mr. Milosevic's assault fear that Albania and Macedonia could be drawn into a larger war or even break up if the Serbs are not prevented from an "ethnic cleansing" of the Albanian majority in Kosovo. Even beyond that, it is feared that Turkey and Greece, two NATO members, might take opposite sides.

Trent Lott, the Senate majority leader, voiced qualified support for the NATO attack. "Whatever reservations about the President's actions in the Balkans," the Mississippi Republican said, "let no one doubt that the Congress and the American people stand united behind our men and women who are bravely heeding the call of duty."

The attack was the first uninvited offensive against a sovereign nation by NATO, the alliance founded 50 years ago as the European bulwark against the cold war military power of the Soviet Union. NATO's 17 days of air strikes against Serbian forces in Bosnia in 1995 were conducted at the request of the embattled Bosnian Government against military targets of the Bosnian Serbs.

No detailed casualty reports were immediately available. But scores of Serbian military bases and depots, aircraft and munitions factories were expected to be hit by NATO forces equipped with more than 400 bomber aircraft from European bases, and missile weaponry aboard a half dozen warships in the Adriatic region. The operation marked the first combat use of the B-2 "stealth" bomber designed to elude radar, according to Pentagon officials who said two B-2's had journeyed from Whiteman Air Force Base in Missouri on a mission to drop satellite-guided bombs.

"Clear responsibility for the air strikes lies with President Milosevic, who has refused to stop his violent action in Kosovo and has refused to negotiate in good faith," said NATO's Secretary General, Javier Solana.

The attack began after Mr. Milosevic rebuffed a final peace plea from the United States intended to restore the autonomy that Mr. Milosevic had stripped from Kosovo and its ethnic Albanian majority 10 years ago. Under diplomatic prodding, he signed a peace agreement in October but then reneged. The proposed peace plan would include the deployment of thousands of NATO peacekeeping troops in Kosovo.

Denouncing Mr. Milosevic for ethnic violence and atrocity, Mr. Clinton conceded that NATO forces risked casualties against Mr. Milosevic's modernized military. But he warned: "The dangers of acting now are clearly outweighed by the risks of failing to act: the risks that many more innocent people will die or be driven from their homes by the tens of thousands; the risks that the conflict will involve and destabilize neighboring nations."

The NATO attack was authorized after Mr. Clinton's envoy, Richard C. Holbrooke, paid an 11th-hour visit to Mr. Milosevic and failed to persuade him to join the peace proposal accepted by the ethnic Albanians. The military task then was placed in the hands of NATO's Supreme Commander, Gen. Wesley K. Clark of the United States, with orders to deal with Mr. Milosevic's authoritarian assault on the Kosovo majority.

"It's the right decision, and we have to see it through all the way," said Prime Minister Tony Blair of Britain.

Mr. Clinton said the action had three objectives: "to demonstrate the seriousness of NATO's opposition to aggression," to deter Mr. Milosevic from "continuing and escalating his attacks on helpless civilians by imposing a price for those attacks" and "if necessary, to damage Serbia's capacity to wage war against Kosovo in the future by seriously diminishing its military capabilities."

While Congressional Republican leaders' support of the NATO attack was qualified, Senator John H. Chafee, a Rhode Island Republican, declared, "The danger of inaction in Kosovo—of doing nothing—greatly exceeds the dangers of the action begun today."

Representative John P. Murtha, a ranking Democrat and ex-Marine from Pennsylvania with close ties to the Pentagon's

senior commanders, predicted a prolonged air war against dug-in Serbian forces. "I think it could go on for a month," he said.

Elizabeth Dole, former American Red Cross president and Republican Presidential aspirant, endorsed the NATO attack. "Because I believe this action can be instrumental in forging a peaceful solution to a dangerous, escalating military conflict, I support it," she said. "The atrocities carried out by Serbian nationalists must be halted."

Commenting on alternatives if the air strikes fail, Senator Mitch McConnell, Republican of Kentucky, said, "Arming the Kosovars would be a lot cheaper, less dangerous to American troops and wouldn't put us in the middle of a civil war."

Mr. Clinton, however, maintained that the stakes were far higher than a Yugoslav civil war.

"At the end of the 20th century, after two world wars and a cold war," he said, "we and our allies have a chance to leave our children a Europe that is free, peaceful and stable. But we must, we must, act now to do that, because if the Balkans once again become a place of brutal killing and massive refugee flights, it will be impossible to achieve."

*   *   *

March 27, 1999

MR. MILOSEVIC'S CAMPAIGN OF TERROR

By ANTHONY LEWIS

BOSTON—For three days now, on Slobodan Milosevic's orders, Serbian policemen, soldiers and paramilitary thugs have been spreading terror across Kosovo. They have burned and shelled villages, driven thousands of ethnic Albanians from their homes and carried out dozens of assassinations.

The scale of the terror campaign has not fully registered in the outside world because Mr. Milosevic has expelled Western journalists and cut off television links. But enough details have got through to make clear that a human disaster is taking place.

One example: On Thursday a respected source saw many thousands of civilians making a forced march from the town of Qirez. Serbian tanks were behind a column, a mile or more long, of men, women and children. What happened to them is not known.

A second example: At 1:10 A.M. on Thursday armed men in black uniforms with Serbian police insignia broke into the Pristina home of a leading Kosovo Albanian human rights lawyer, Bajram Kelmendi. His wife said they shouted, "You have five seconds to come out of your rooms."

The policemen ransacked the house, beat Mr. Kelmendi and took him and his two sons away. At daybreak Mrs. Kelmendi went to police headquarters, where she was told to take her troubles to NATO and the Kosovo Liberation Army. Yesterday Mr. Kelmendi and his sons were found shot dead a few miles from Pristina.

A third: Serbian police shot the elderly doorman at the last Albanian-language newspaper in Kosovo, Koha Ditore, as they shut the paper down. The publisher, Veton Surroi, went into hiding.

Mr. Milosevic has targeted for kidnapping and assassination the top Albanian editors, lawyers, doctors and educators. The idea is to decapitate the leadership—exactly what his killers set out to do in Bosnia seven years ago.

The Milosevic terror campaign mocks one of the main purposes given by President Clinton and others for the NATO operation. In the President's words, that is "to deter an even bloodier offensive against innocent civilians in Kosovo."

If we and our allies did not act, Mr. Clinton said, "President Milosevic would read our hesitation as a license to kill. There would be many more massacres—tens of thousands more refugees, more victims crying out for revenge."

Mr. Milosevic has, rather, made the NATO operation a license to kill. The massacres are occurring, and there are tens of thousands of new refugees. That puts a heavy responsibility on President Clinton. He faces a humanitarian debacle. What should he do?

First, he should support the NATO Supreme Commander, Gen. Wesley Clark, in his desire to intensify the air attacks. The scale of the operation so far has been nowhere near large enough to make Mr. Milosevic believe we mean business—much less to destroy his military power.

Second, NATO must begin using in Kosovo the aircraft that operate against tanks and artillery: attack helicopters and A-10 Warthogs. They have been held back because they fly lower and slower, and hence are more vulnerable to anti-aircraft weapons. But not using them means giving a free hand to Mr. Milosevic in his Kosovo terror campaign.

Third, the United States has compelling evidence of what Mr. Milosevic is doing in Kosovo: high-resolution photographs from satellites that show burning villages and shattered houses. We should publish those pictures to counter Mr. Milosevic's tactic of shutting out the world.

Finally, NATO has to face the fact that more than air power may be needed to save the people of Kosovo. Mr. Clinton and the Europeans have said that no ground forces would go in unless Mr. Milosevic agreed. But we are beyond that now. We have to think about a protection force on the ground.

It is not easy, and it never was going to be. But caving in to Slobodan Milosevic would be inestimably worse. He is using the tactics of the Gestapo. His regime increasingly has the smell of the first fascist state in post-cold-war Europe.

What will NATO celebrate at its 50th anniversary party next month if it has allowed Kosovo to become a graveyard? What will become of the humanitarian ideal, of what President Clinton called "a moral imperative"? One former diplomat said: "If they don't get serious, Kosovo will be the humanitarian Bay of Pigs."

*   *   *

March 27, 1999

WHO WILL CRACK FIRST?

By CRAIG R. WHITNEY

BRUSSELS, March 26—The allied military strategy for stopping Serbian attacks against ethnic Albanian rebels in Kosovo rests largely on the hope that Serbian military commanders will seek an end to the intense NATO bombing before it destroys their army and air defenses.

The hope, allied officers and diplomats say, is that the strikes that began on Wednesday will cause so much damage that the Yugoslav high command will put pressure on President Slobodan Milosevic to back down and accept allied terms before the military loses everything.

Asked what basis there was for such a hope, one senior NATO diplomat said, "There have been signs that the army was reluctant to get involved in Kosovo, and that it was forced by Milosevic to engage."

"His strategy is retaining power," this official said. "The longer NATO action continues, the more he is in danger of losing his grip."

But the Balkans have often demonstrated a logic of their own. From Mr. Milosevic's point of view, there may be good reason to hope that the longer the bombing continues, the greater the chance that fissures will develop within the alliance—a hope that may be as illusory as NATO's own about dissension in the Serb ranks.

In recent months Mr. Milosevic moved to strengthen his control. He replaced the army's longtime commander, Gen. Momcilo Perisic, an architect of the war in Bosnia, after the general publicly criticized him for letting Yugoslavia become a pariah state. He also removed the head of the air force, the chief of the internal security service, along with a dozen of the service's top operational officers, and the deputy leader of the governing political party.

And Mr. Milosevic's popularity seems to be soaring, not plummeting, say Western reporters who were expelled from Belgrade this week, as Serbs rally around him in defiance of the allied bombing.

Nevertheless, the allies are counting on the intensity of the bombing to convince Mr. Milosevic that his best course is to call off his operations in Kosovo.

Today, alliance officials said, Yugoslavia lost two more of its supersonic MIG-29 fighter-bombers. It had 15 of the MIG's at the start of the bombing and lost 3 in earlier dogfights. The NATO spokesman, Jamie P. Shea, said two of the planes had flown to Bosnia today with the apparent intention of attacking the NATO peacekeeping force there. The alliance's planes shot them down and its troops were searching for the pilots, he said.

"We want to be in a situation where eventually it will become clear to the leadership that the price of this campaign is too high," Mr. Shea said.

Whether the peace agreement that the Serbs refused to sign in France a week ago will still be on the table if it takes weeks to bring Mr. Milosevic around is unclear. "If we said we would continue bombing Milosevic until he signs the

Rambouillet agreement, we could be bombing for years," one diplomat said.

The bombing continued for a third day today after allied warplanes attacked more than 50 targets during the first two days, military commanders said. The allied command said almost all of those sites were either command centers for the Yugoslav Army and the internal security police who have been rounding up suspected rebels and burning Albanians out of their homes in Kosovo, or air defense radar, missile and antiaircraft sites that the allies need to eliminate before they can do anything else.

Clearing out the antiaircraft batteries should take a few more days, officials said. At that point, there would probably be a pause while NATO's Secretary General, Javier Solana, consults with allied leaders to see whether they still agreed that warplanes should start directly striking the tank bases, arms arsenals, fuel depots and artillery bases that the army and Interior Ministry police forces in Kosovo have been using in their campaign against the Albanians.

But even Gen. Wesley K. Clark, the American who is NATO's top military commander in Europe, said today that the bombing, however long it lasted and however intense it was, could not stop all Serbian assaults against civilians on the ground.

"It was always understood from the outset that there was no way we were going to stop these paramilitary forces from going into these villages and attacking," General Clark said.

But allied attacks against those forces and their support systems, he and other officials said, would leave Serbian forces much less capable of carrying out big sweeps like the ones that have sent tens of thousands more ethnic Albanians fleeing for their lives in the last week.

Unless Mr. Milosevic does back down, that kind of bombing could go on for weeks or months, with periodic air attacks against Serb mobile antiaircraft gun and missile sites when they turned on their radars and threatened allied planes—much like the pinprick war of attrition that the forces General Clark commands in Turkey have been waging against air defenses in Iraq.

The European allies, some of their representatives here say, are just as prepared as the United States is to see the bombing continue for many days, if not weeks, if it takes that long to get Serbia's leader to back down.

But their resolve might not survive the pressure that would come if allied planes were shot down and pilots taken prisoner, or if misfired allied bombs caused heavy civilian casualties in Serbia.

"Everybody in NATO would like to see the bombing stop as soon as possible," Mr. Shea said. Greece is probably the NATO ally with the most reservations about the attacks. But even Italy, the country from which most of the 400 allied missions have been launched against Serbia, would like to take advantage of a pause in the bombing to restart diplomatic efforts, Prime Minister Massimo D'Alema said today.

Diplomats from several European countries said no allied ambassadors here had dissented from the consensus supporting the bombing. The 19 countries in the alliance, Mr. Solana said today, were as one—at least in daily meetings of its North Atlantic Council here—in support for continuing the bombing in the hope it would lead Mr. Milosevic to end the violence in Kosovo.

As for an exit strategy for the allies, the sooner the Yugoslav President backs down, the better for them. The longer the bombing continues, the harder they predict it will be to revive the peace negotiations and send a NATO-led international military force into Kosovo to police the peace.

Another question is whether the allies, who have insisted so far that they have no intention of becoming the air force of the Kosovo Liberation Army, will consider providing support for the rebels if the Serbs do not back down.

"If this goes on, we may have to reassess some aspects of our basic policy," a senior diplomat said, "but we are still a long way from that."

Negotiators for the rebels signed the peace accord in Paris on March 18 under which Kosovo and its ethnic Albanian majority would regain their autonomy within Yugoslavia and an international peacekeeping force would be deployed in the province.

But like many of his compatriots, Mr. Milosevic regards Kosovo as sacred Serbian ground, on which Orthodox Christian Serbs fell as martyrs to Islamic Turkish invaders six centuries ago, and has rejected any international military presence.

Mr. Milosevic has also complained to Western mediators that in his view the proposed peace agreement and the peacekeeping force it envisions would just provide international cover for the secession of the province, with a referendum on independence at the end of a three-year transition period.

"Milosevic cannot destroy the Kosovo Liberation Army with the military option," a senior official said. It remains to be seen whether NATO's military option can end Mr. Milosevic's defiance.

*   *   *

March 28, 1999

U.S. STEALTH FIGHTER IS DOWN IN YUGOSLAVIA AS NATO ORDERS ATTACK ON SERB ARMY UNITS

By JOHN M. BRODER

WASHINGTON, March 27—An American F-117 stealth fighter went down in Yugoslavia tonight, the first allied loss in the four-day Balkan conflict, even as NATO officials announced a broad new phase of the air assault on Serbian targets.

The pilot of the F-117 was rescued by an American military search-and-rescue team six hours after his plane went down, according to Administration officials.

Authorities in Belgrade claimed that Serbian air defenses had shot down the radar-evading stealth aircraft, one of the most advanced weapons in the American arsenal. There was hostile missile activity in the area where the plane was operating, one Pentagon official said tonight, but there was no independent confirmation that the plane was brought down by Serbian fire.

The official Tanjug news agency in Yugoslavia said the F-117 was brought down late today near Budjenovci, 35 miles northwest of Belgrade.

Although pictures of the fiery wreckage were shown on Serbian and American television for hours tonight, Administration officials did not confirm the loss of the aircraft until the pilot was safely out of Serbian air space. The Pentagon would not discuss why the plane went down.

President Clinton tonight expressed relief that the pilot, who was not identified, was safely snatched from Serbian territory only hours after his plane went down. He said that the United States and NATO were broadening the goals of the four-day-old military operation in Yugoslavia to include attacks on equipment and troops of the Serbian army and police forces.

"As I've said from the outset," Mr. Clinton said in a statement released by the White House late tonight, "this military operation entails real risks. However, the continued brutality and repression of the Serb forces further underscores the necessity for NATO forces to persevere."

Reports of the loss of the American aircraft stunned White House officials, who had spent most of the day consulting with European leaders about expanding the military mission in Yugoslavia. Appalled by numerous reports of atrocities in Kosovo, including mass executions, deportations and forced marches, NATO and United States officials accelerated a decision to attack Serbian forces in the field, officials here and in Europe said.

The loss of the F-117 was a propaganda coup for the Serbians, who have absorbed four days of heavy pounding from American and NATO bombs and missiles and the loss of at least five MIG fighters in air-to-air combat. It was the first time one of the $43 million F-117's had gone down in hostile action. They performed flawlessly in hundreds of missions over Iraq in 1991.

Serbian television broadcast images of the burning wreckage of an aircraft that bore the distinctive markings of the F-117 Nighthawk, with tail numbers indicating it was from the 8th Fighter Squadron at Holloman Air Force Base, N.M.

Besides the loss of the plane in Serbia, the United States faces a loss of the secret technology that allows the F-117 to evade detection. That technology includes the composite materials used for the outer surface of the plane, which absorbs radar instead of reflecting it back to defensive missile sites.

Any secrets lost to the Serbs could find their way to the Russians, who have been supporting Serbia.

The expansion of the allied air strikes announced today marked a new phase in the four-day-old campaign against the Yugoslav military. Until now, air strikes had chiefly targeted air defenses and military infrastructure, not Yugoslav troops and armor that could be used to kill ethnic Albanians in Kosovo.

Images from Yugoslav TV via Associated Press

A television image shows what the Yugoslav Government says is the wreckage of an American F-117 stealth fighter shot down west of Belgrade.

This week, when the United States and NATO initiated the attacks, President Clinton said the West had a "moral imperative" to try to halt the slaughter of civilians in Kosovo. Mr. Clinton warned Slobodan Milosevic, the Yugoslav president, that if he did not cease the repression in Kosovo, NATO would "seriously damage" Serbia's capacity to make war.

Today, NATO and the United States moved to make good on that threat, setting plans for attacks by allied warplanes that would take aim at supply depots, communications facilities and troop concentrations located south of the 44th parallel in Yugoslavia. The area includes all of Kosovo and a substantial portion of Serbia south of Belgrade.

"Our aim is to strike at heavy weapons, which are of course what are used to bombard villages and kill people," said Jamie Shea, a NATO spokesman in Brussels.

But officials in Washington said that NATO is not yet sending low-flying combat ground-attack planes or helicopters to hit Serbian troops in Kosovo. While there are signs that NATO attacks have weakened some Serbian air defense systems, low-flying aircraft would still remain vulnerable to Serb ground fire, and the current weather in the Balkans has been too poor to permit such operations, officials said.

And while the cause of the downing of the F-117 is not yet known, allied war planners likely will treat Serbian air defenses with more respect in coming days.

The White House and NATO officials in Brussels announced the escalation of the air war and the shift in strategy this afternoon after a series of conversations among President Clinton, Prime Minister Tony Blair of Britain, President Jacques Chirac of France, Chancellor Gerhard Schroder of Germany and Prime Minister Massimo D'Alema of Italy. Later, Mr. Chirac also contacted the Russian Government in an attempt to restart talks with the Serbs toward a diplomatic settlement of the conflict.

"There was total unity that the campaign was moving as planned and that it was important to move to a new phase of the air campaign, including focusing on forces in the field," said David C. Leavy, a White House spokesman.

"President Clinton believes that Slobodan Milosevic's continued repression and continued intransigence remain an obstacle to resolving this crisis and thus it was necessary to move forward in broadening the scope of the air assault," Mr. Leavy said. Mr. Milosevic is the President of Yugoslavia, of which Serbia is the dominant part.

A senior Clinton Administration official said that the reports of Serbian violence were numerous and credible and had triggered the intensified air campaign.

"The continuing brutality made it an easy call to broaden and deepen the attack," the official said.

Another official said that the decision to go ahead with the second phase of the air war was moved up by several days because the humanitarian disaster unfolding in Kosovo is far worse than any previous campaign against ethnic Albanians by Serbian forces.

"The Serbs have been torching villages," the British Defense Minister, George Robertson, said in London. "There are reports that the Serbs are bombing villages to the point of obliteration. There are clear signs now that an all-out Serb offensive against the Albanian population has started."

Mr. Robertson accused Mr. Milosevic of being a "serial ethnic cleanser."

Mr. Shea cited reports that large groups of Kosovo Albanians—conspicuously lacking adult men—have been spotted under the guard of Serbian forces. "Dark things are happening," he said.

Despite the alarming reports and the pleas from some in Kosovo for more forceful intervention, Administration officials insisted that they were not planning to use American or NATO ground troops to halt any killings and punish Mr. Milosevic's forces.

"There is no consideration by NATO or any of the allies for the introduction of ground troops," Vice President Al Gore said in response to a question while campaigning in New Hampshire. "I believe that we can achieve our objectives with the use of air power."

In Belgrade, for the first time, people heard large explosions before air-raid sirens sounded, suggesting that Yugoslavia's air defense system has been damaged around the capital, as NATO has said it was.

Early in the day, Belgrade television broadcast images showing the city almost deserted by shoppers today after heavy overnight missile raids aimed at military targets on the outskirts of the city.

Stinging chemical fumes wafted over parts of the city today after allied warplanes bombed a rocket fuel depot in the Ibarska Magistrala area in the southern suburbs.

The air campaign has been conducted until now using cruise missiles and precision-guided bombs dropped from high-altitude aircraft. Any serious effort to destroy tanks, artillery pieces, trucks and mobile ground forces would require lower-flying aircraft like the tank-killing A-10 Warthog and ground-attack helicopters.

But United States officials indicated that they were not yet prepared to employ such weapons in the new phase of the air combat because of their increased vulnerability to ground fire and surface-to-air missiles. Instead, aircraft already involved in the campaign—F-16's and F-15E's—will be used to attack the new set of targets in southern Yugoslavia.

Earlier today, a White House spokesman said that NATO had begun to attack ground units of the Yugoslav army. But Pentagon officials said later that the flights had not yet occurred because of concerns over weather and Serbian air defense systems.

President Clinton said in his weekly radio address today that Mr. Milosevic was conducting a "brutal military offensive" against civilians and that allied forces must "stay the course" to prevent the war in Kosovo from spreading.

"Serb troops have continued attacks on unarmed men, women and children," Mr. Clinton said. "We must, and we will, continue until Serbia's leader, Slobodan Milosevic, accepts peace or we have seriously damaged his capacity to make war."

But there were no visible signs Mr. Milosevic was backing off. Serbian television broadcast programs with patriotic themes along with coverage of NATO attacks and news of protests against them in Greece and Russia.

In the Serbian province of Kosovo, the center of the conflict that led to the attacks that began on Wednesday, Serbian troops continued their rampage against the ethnic Albanians, burning homes and villages and rounding up ethnic Albanian men.

"This is not happening because of NATO," Mr. Robertson, the British minister, said. "This violence was going on before we began."

The allies planned to continue bombing airfields, industrial sites and anti-aircraft defenses throughout Yugoslavia today, officials said.

"The weather is not very good," Air Commodore David Wilby of Britain said in a Brussels briefing early today. In operations that ended before dawn today, he said, "some of the airplanes turned back because of the weather, but manned aircraft did get through to their targets last night."

In all, 249 allied planes took to the air between Friday and early today, he said. Bombs dropped from aircraft and the warheads of unpiloted cruise missiles struck military targets around Belgrade and the southeastern Serbian city of Nis, and in six areas in and around Kosovo, officials said.

NATO officials have given only sketchy accounts of damage from the air raids because they say it will take time to analyze photographs taken after the attacks. And without people on the ground, they say, it is impossible to provide accurate estimates of casualties.

Mr. Robertson and other officials warned Mr. Milosevic today not to try to retaliate by attacking international peacekeepers in neighboring Bosnia or Macedonia. About 12,000 allied soldiers in Macedonia are preparing for missions to enforce a peace agreement in Kosovo if, as the allies hope, the bombing forces Mr. Milosevic to accept one.

The allies, he added, will do their best to see that Serbian authorities who may be responsible for atrocities against civilians are prosecuted for them by the international criminal tribunal in The Hague.

* * *

March 29, 1999

FOR FIRST TIME IN WAR, E-MAIL PLAYS A VITAL ROLE

By NEIL MacFARQUHAR

The E-mail messages from Yugoslavia spill forth by the thousands, each freighted with a miniature etching of life under the bombs.

"It's as big as a house—the peasants had gone into the hole and were looking around," a woman wrote from near the town of Sabac, in southern Serbia, describing a bomb crater to Dr. Krinka Petrov, a literature professor at the University of Pittsburgh.

"Someone said it was made by a bomb launched from one of those invisible airplanes because it was so big. The man whose cornfield this was said he was going to charge tickets for those who wanted to see the hole."

This is the first instance of warfare where a small but significant slice of the population has Internet access. The Yugoslavs, a technically savvy group for decades, have used the Web to create an entire news network consisting of E-mail exchanges, chat rooms and bulletin boards—where no rumor is too small to dissect at length and almost no hamlet too remote to mention.

Members of the diaspora community, not sated by 24-hour cable television news, catch themselves hunched over their computer screens for five, six, seven hours a day, trolling for reports from home.

"Sometimes if I log on in the middle of the night, the people over there are giving me a play-by-play thing," said Momir Milinovich, a 27-year-old law student at the University of Illinois at Urbana. "They type things like 'The bombs are flying right over our heads.' "

Those living through the bombing in Serbia often find E-mail better than uneven international telephone lines as a means to reassure loved ones that they are O.K. It is also a way for them to get around their state-controlled news media if they do not have access to satellite television.

But the Internet's power to reassure equals its ability to spread unease. Many Web correspondents who had been communicating with ethnic Albanians in the Serbian province of Kosovo find that their previous E-mail correspondents have fallen ominously silent.

"The feeling is that we are participating in this war in a strange way because of the Internet," said Aleksander Slavkovic, 32, a computer engineer in Pittsburgh. "You feel like you have access to the information firsthand."

Serbian chat room participants said that before the bombing began, maybe 250 people would be logged on at once. Now as many as 1,500 people clog the chat rooms simultaneously. Each usually jumps right in with an urgent appeal for news from his or her hometown.

Someone named Clo recently signed onto one of the chat rooms by asking "Is there anyone from Kraljevo? Have they hit the airport? Please tell me, my house is VERY close by."

Mr. Milinovich was frantic when he logged on last week. He had tried calling his grandfather's house in the tiny Montenegran coastal village of Morinj unsuccessfully for days. A cousin in New York had heard that the town barracks was hit in the first NATO air strikes.

When the law student posted a question in the chat room at Montecafe.com, he got an instant answer. Dragan, a 20-year-old college student, was tapping away in Risan, a town just four miles down the road from Mr. Milinovich's family.

(Most of the people interviewed for this article insisted that at most the first names of their correspondents be used, in case the Yugoslav Government cracks down on them.) Dragan told him that the nearest bombing was across the bay and no civilian targets had been struck. He talked to Mr. Milinovich's family and got back on line to assure him that they were fine and had shelter if the bombing got close.

The Web often serves as a greater source of innuendo and political screed than hard facts. But the attacks on President Slobodan Milosevic of Yugoslavia have almost entirely evaporated as Serbs feel obligated to back their Government during a war. But nothing spreads rumors faster than having thousands of people chattering around the globe.

Despite the uneven quality of the information, those on line say the Web tends to have more detailed reports of what towns were hit and suffered civilian casualties.

Predrag Tosic, a 29-year-old graduate student in computer science at the University of Illinois, left his computer behind during a weekend trip to Milwaukee. "I felt bad because in the hotel room I had to rely on CNN for several days," he said.

Inside Yugoslavia, CNN and other international all-news television stations are available via satellite, but the Government has shut down B92, the main independent radio station broadcasting from Belgrade.

Real Networks, a Seattle-based company that specializes in distributing broadcasts over the Web has since put it on line. Mark Hall, a general manager for the company, said the site gets about 30,000 to 40,000 hits daily.

But information coming from the ethnic Albanians in Kosovo has dropped precipitously. Illyria, an Albanian-American newspaper based in the Bronx, used to receive 250 E-mails a day from various residents of Kosovo or from the bulletin boards to which it subscribed.

On Thursday, with widespread reports that the Serbians were carrying out reprisal attacks in Kosovo, the newspaper got just two E-mail messages. "It is very frustrating to not know if your family is alive or not," said Isuf Hajrizi, the editor.

For those sitting under the NATO bombs in Serbia, the Internet is a welcome distraction.

It is reassuring to be able to communicate with the outside world, wrote Deana Srajber, a 29-year-old Web designer, in response to an E-mail query from a newspaper reporter. "With the Internet we have the means of telling the world about how we feel about all this," she wrote. "The frustrating part is that the world seems not to care how we feel."

*   *   *

April 2, 1999

REFUGEES TELL OF METHODICAL EMPTYING OF PRISTINA

By JOHN KIFNER

KUKES, Albania, April 1—In a chilling display of force, Serb gunmen are systematically emptying Kosovo's capital city, Pristina, marching its ethnic Albanians out through gauntlets of masked, heavily armed Serbs, refugees crossing the border today said.

More than 10,000 Kosovars arrived here today, stretching at times more than a dozen miles back into Serbia in a heartrending line of farm tractors, frail old people being pushed in wheelbarrows and weeping village women on foot clutching their children and sometimes a blanket or a plastic bag with a few clothes. An elderly man died of exhaustion crossing the border this morning.

They were the people of Pristina, once an urbane center with a university, coffee houses, cinemas and newspapers. And they told in almost identical accounts—as other refugees have in previous days—of the latest Serbian tactics.

This is what they said.

In homes throughout the ethnic Albanian neighborhoods that comprised most of the city there was a knock on the door yesterday afternoon. Sometimes it was only one gunman— from the special police or paramilitary—with a black ski mask over his face.

Leave now, they were told. Many were quickly and roughly thrown out of their houses. They were robbed of their money in the process.

Once in the street, they joined their neighbors in a forced march between lines of masked, uniformed Serbs draped in weaponry. At one point the Serbs videotaped the march. Two days ago, Serbian state television broadcast just such a forced march in Pristina.

They were split into two groups, one taken to the city's railroad station, the other to a soccer stadium. It was difficult to estimate from the refugees' accounts exactly how many people were involved, but they clearly numbered tens of thousands. One trainload was sent to the Macedonian border. At least three babies were born last night in the railroad station.

During the night, the refugees said, the Serbs brought in fleets of buses and large trucks, including freezer trucks of the kind used to transport sides of beef. Many refugees spent hours packed into the buses and trucks until they were driven south past burning villages early in the morning and dumped out at the last village, Szhur, to walk the final few miles to the border.

"You cannot imagine what happened," wailed Suzana Krusnigi, collapsing in tears a few steps over the border with her elderly parents.

"I was watching television, Sky News, and I walked out into the garden and there were three people with black masks and big guns," she said.

"They wanted to kill my mommy," she said. "They said you give me money or I will kill her. I had 550 Deutsche marks hidden in my sock and I gave it to him.

"They were not policemen. They were criminals Milosevic let out of jail. It is not easy to earn money. But I don't care about the money. They wanted to kill my parents.

"In every house they broke the doors," she said, crying. "When we went out everyone was in the street walking between men with black masks and big weapons."

She described the forced march and a sleepless night at the railroad station.

"All Pristina is empty today," she said. "No Albanians. Only Serbs with guns, they all have guns. Can the world see what they are doing?"

The long lines of silent, shaken refugees, many crying, stretched all around her. Among the seemingly endless procession of people atop carts pulled by tractors was 98-year-old Shahin Jhabani, stretched motionless on a wheelbarrow, his feet in maroon socks dangling over the wheel. Tucked around him were a few family possessions: a blanket, a pair of women's high heels and a bright child's jacket.

By 7 o'clock tonight, some 13,000 people had crossed over the border, a process made painfully slow for much of the day by the Albanian authorities' insistence on a new procedure for registering the refugees.

What they were registering mostly were the refugees' automobiles—which had been stripped of license plates by the Serbs—and they issued mimeographed pieces of paper good for a month.

Late in the afternoon, after pressure from European aid officials and the flood of people on foot, the system quickened somewhat. But in the darkness there were still thousands of people waiting to cross the border, backed up in a line nearly 10 miles into the Serbian territory. And even as it inched forward, the line lengthened, with people from Pristina and areas to the north.

"They exploded something at the main door of our house," said one, Ruzhid Morina, 56. "Four police with masks came in. Their first demand was money. The children were frightened and started to cry.

"We took only the things we had at hand, two blankets for the kids and a plastic sheet in case it rains," he said. "All this happened in just five minutes, and we were made to leave the house. On both sides of the street were long lines of Serb police in masks and we had to walk between them to the train station."

As the procession passed a movie theater, he said, police officers in a white Opel Cadet cruised alongside, videotaping him.

After the march and the long night in the train station, Arsim Rahmani, 26, said, he could see from the windows of

Thousands of people boarded trains in Pristina yesterday. At the Albanian border, many refugees said that Serbs had herded them either to the train station or to the soccer stadium.

the bus that there were no ethnic Albanians. "Our shops were looted," he said. "There were only Serbs, driving our cars."

At the border, many refugees seemed shattered at the thought of all that they had lost. And yet many also experienced a certain relief, like Mr. Rahmani and his wife, Aferdita, who was three months pregnant.

"It is not important that now we are poor people," she said, leaning close to her husband. "What is important is now I am not afraid."

* * *

April 5, 1999

MISERY AND DISEASE SWEEP MACEDONIAN CAMP

By CARLOTTA GALL

BLACE, Macedonia, April 4—Every few minutes stretcher-bearers struggled through the crowd today, slipping and falling on their way up the muddy slope in their haste to get another patient to the medical tent. Others charged the hill with children in their arms.

They were among the very few who were allowed through the police cordon. Macedonian soldiers and police in riot gear have formed a human barrier around the thousands of Kosovo Albanian refugees camping here on a small patch of land at the border, beating back anyone who tries to pass.

As the tide of refugees has swelled the miserable crowd to 30,000, conditions have deteriorated alarmingly. Death and disease are becoming commonplace.

Aid agencies said 11 people died Friday night, and another 14 died Saturday night—mostly the old and very young—many of them suffering from exposure. Local journalists reported that several babies had been born in the camp too, and that a mother died in childbirth Saturday.

The temperature fell to 39 degrees tonight. Hepatitis and pneumonia are already raging through the sprawling camp, where people are sleeping in the open under the rain, or beneath makeshift shelters of blankets and plastic. There are no toilets, and people have been using the nearby river for washing and drinking.

Stephen Tomlin, a vice president of the International Medical Corps said: "When you have a large number of people and the sanitation is poor, there is a high risk of diarrhea and disease. And with children, measles. The priority now is water and sanitation. Water must be piped in quickly because of dehydration."

Mr. Tomlin said that even with the cold weather, diarrhea and the resulting dehydration are big problems and that preventing these problems must take priority now. People had been rationed a few liters of water a day. This will not be enough, Mr. Tomlin said.

International aid agencies have been barred from working in the camp for several days now, apparently to discourage more refugees from coming here, though the Government has not given its reason. And the local Red Cross, which is permitted to enter, is not prepared to handle an emergency situation of this scope.

The scene of thousands of people camped on the hillside and across the fields is a messy and noisy jumble. Smoke drifts from hundreds of fires. Men squat beside their plastic shelters, and others crush together around the single white tent registering refugees. The occasional person who tries to slip out is shoved back hard by police officers or soldiers.

There is a growing sense of desperation in the sodden encampment. Many refugees appear to be in severe shock from their ordeal in Kosovo. Expelled at gunpoint and herded into railroad cars, many of the refugees have arrived with only the clothes they were wearing.

One family held up a huge sign made out of cardboard. They had written the simple message in English: "Help."

More are trapped on the other side of the border, unable to pass since Macedonian authorities effectively closed the border. A long trail of cars snaked back up the road into the embattled province today. Many refugees have abandoned their cars and stand massed by the immigration booths waiting to come through.

They face Macedonian police, who on Friday used batons to keep the crowd back. The Macedonian Government denies closing the border, but is adamant that it cannot absorb any more refugees for reasons of both economic and political stability.

A 20-year-old mechanic, Gazmend Kumnova, said his aunt died three days ago on the Serbian side of the border. "It was impossible to get food to them," he said. "It was only when she died that they let the family through," he said. They buried her the next day in the nearby Macedonian capital, Skopje.

With the foreign aid organizations barred from the camp, local aid workers have been driving into the camp on tractors, laden with food and drink. They stop at intervals and throw provisions into the crowd in random fashion.

Foreign aid organizations have a single overflowing medical tent alongside the camp to care for the sick. Patients, mostly old people unable to move on their own, lie and sit around on the ground outside.

The authorities have begun transferring refugees to other camps, piling them into buses in haphazard fashion. One busload was taken to the refugee camp of Ragushe.

Surrounded by wire fencing and guarded by Macedonian police, the refugees are confused and fearful. "We thought we were moving away from an aggressor and we find something very similar to the Serb police," said Hazen Dakaj, a 52-year-old refugee. He stood by the wire fence, greeting family members stuck inside the camp.

In the chaos of boarding the buses in the middle of the night, 3 of the 14 members of his family had been separated and lost. "They brought us in buses here when they saw people dying. They did not care if we were together or not," he said.

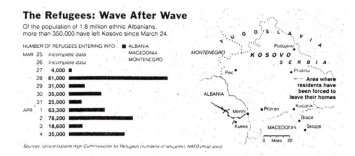

The Refugees: Wave After Wave
Of the population of 1.8 million ethnic Albanians, more than 350,000 have left Kosovo since March 24.

NUMBER OF REFUGEES ENTERING INTO ☐ ALBANIA / ■ MACEDONIA / MONTENEGRO

MAR 25	Incomplete data	
26	Incomplete data	
27	4,000	
28	61,000	
29	31,000	
30	35,000	
31	25,000	
APR 1	63,300	
2	78,200	
3	18,600	
4	35,000	

Sources: United Nations High Commissioner for Refugees (numbers of refugees), NATO (map area)

In the face of Macedonia's reluctance to take in the refugees, NATO and other countries today were gearing up to take over responsibility for them. The United States, Canada, Turkey, Germany, Norway and Austria have pledged to take in 101,000 refugees between them.

Flights began to arrive with supplies for the refugees today and flew out the first few loads of refugees.

Meanwhile, just down the road from the border, NATO troops were constructing a large transit camp with military tents and showers. The NATO camp was in stark contrast to the chaos by the border, and the first refugees were being moved there tonight. The refugees will be given food and water, medical treatment and washing facilities while they are registered and will then be sent on, either to other camps or abroad.

* * *

April 11, 1999

UNEASINESS SHADOWING ORTHODOX EASTER RITE

By CELESTINE BOHLEN

MOSCOW, April 10—As Orthodox Christians from Moscow to Belgrade and from Athens to Bucharest start celebrating Easter at midnight services tonight, the usual joy of this most sacred of holidays has been tinged with feelings of unease, grief, fear and anger over the continuing conflict in Yugoslavia, home of their Orthodox brethren the Serbs.

Not only church leaders, but also politicians from predominantly Orthodox countries have appealed for an Easter cease-fire, on the ground and from the air. The latest was a telephone call made Friday night to the NATO Secretary General, Javier Solana, by the Romanian President, Emil Constantinescu, a supporter of NATO policy who asked that NATO war planes stop their bombing on a day of "great spiritual significance" for Orthodox Christians.

In Athens on Friday, anti-NATO demonstrators joined traditional Good Friday processions, with vociferous calls for a halt to the bombing. And in Russia, Aleksei II, the Patriarch of Moscow and All Russia, recently questioned the morality of those who would continue to bomb on Easter Day.

"If they carry on bombing over Orthodox Easter, what kind of Christians are they?" he asked in a statement aired on the Voice of Russia radio station on Tuesday. "They are not Christians, they are barbarians."

In a televised address on Friday night, the Patriarch called on both NATO and Yugoslav leaders to end "the vicious cycle of violence" and appealed for calm in Russia itself, where the war in the Balkans has added a note of belligerence to the national political debate.

For many Orthodox Christians, the latest war in Yugoslavia has posed a deep moral dilemma, as they struggle between concern for their fellow Orthodox Serbs now living under NATO attack and disgust with Serbian policies in the predominantly Albanian province of Kosovo.

"It has to affect the joy of the day," said the Rev. Daniel Hubiak, an American parish priest at an Orthodox church in Moscow. "All of this only points to the message in one of our readings today. 'Do not put your trust in princes, in sons of men.' Christ is our only hope, and in the final analysis, He is the one who is going to judge all of this."

Almost all Orthodox church leaders have joined in calls to end the violence in Yugoslavia, just as Pope John Paul II and other Christian leaders led an appeal for a cease-fire last Sunday, when the rest of the Christian world celebrated Easter.

"Clearly the religious leadership of the Christian churches, without covert or overt coordination, has been calling for roughly the same thing, for a cessation of the violence, not just a pause," said the Rev. Leonid Kiskovsky, ecumenical officer of the Orthodox Church in America.

In Bulgaria, where the Orthodox church has been split by a dispute between rival Patriarchs, the church's voice has been relatively muted. But in a newspaper aligned with the Bulgarian Socialist Party, a recent front page showed a picture of Christ on the cross under attack by stealth bombers, beneath a headline that read "Their Easter."

In Greece, a NATO member with an overwhelmingly Orthodox population, the Government of Prime Minister Costas Simitis has also appealed for an Easter cease-fire, most recently during a visit to Athens by a top State Department official, Strobe Talbott. With the Greek Orthodox Church in the lead, Greek popular opinion has been generally critical of NATO, fueled in part by sympathy for the Serbs and by lingering resentments toward the United States.

In a traditional Easter message distributed by the Serbian Orthodox Church, the theological message of Christ's resurrection was followed by a paragraph accusing NATO of causing the catastrophe that has sent hundreds of thousands of people fleeing their homes.

In an unusual move that reflected the unusual circumstances of this Easter, Gen. Dragoljub Ojdanic, the Yugoslav chief of staff, joined Yugoslav political leaders in issuing a message to mark the Easter holiday. General Ojdanic stressed that the Army expects, "in this difficult and fateful historic moment," to be able to count on the Serbian Orthodox Church for national unity, defense and "love towards the homeland."

In his separate message, published in all daily newspapers, President Slobodan Milosevic made no mention of the NATO bombing campaign. In a departure from previous years, however, he addressed his message to all Yugoslavs, rather than to the Serbian Orthodox Church.

The mood in one Belgrade church this morning was one of unease and anger, said Deacon Radomir Rakic in a telephone interview. "We would not like this Easter to be like the Easter of 1941, when the Nazis bombed Belgrade, or Easter 1944, when the Allies bombed at the end of the war," he said.

"We were celebrating the liturgy this morning when believe me or not, as I was reading the Gospel at about 9:25, just when I was reading the Easter Greeting of the Angel at the Tomb, 'Rejoice, He is not here,' at that very same moment, we could hear the air raid siren," said Father Rakic. "And I thought, my good God, we are listening to the happiness of these words, and to the alarm, at the same time. But when the all-clear signal was sounded, we didn't hear it because we were deep in prayer."

*   *   *

April 18, 1999

HOW A PRESIDENT, DISTRACTED BY SCANDAL, ENTERED BALKAN WAR

By ELAINE SCIOLINO and ETHAN BRONNER

On Jan. 19, President Clinton's top aides met in the Situation Room in the White House basement to hear a fateful new plan for an autonomous Kosovo from Madeleine K. Albright, the Secretary of State. NATO, she urged, should use the threat of air strikes on Yugoslavia to force a peace agreement to be monitored by the alliance's ground troops.

The President, who had other matters on his mind, was not there. His lawyers were starting their arguments on the Senate floor against his removal from office. That night he was to deliver his State of the Union address.

Nearly 5,000 miles away, in Belgrade, Gen. Wesley K. Clark, the NATO commander, and Gen. Klaus Naumann, chairman of the NATO military council, were sitting with President Slobodan Milosevic of Yugoslavia. They came brandishing a plastic portfolio of color photographs documenting a massacre of Albanians three days earlier by Serbian security forces in the Kosovo town of Racak. They also came with threats of NATO air strikes.

This was far from their first encounter with the Serbian leader, but this time, they recalled, they found a newly hardened man with a bunker mentality.

"This was not a massacre," Mr. Milosevic shouted. "This was staged. These people are terrorists."

When General Clark warned him that NATO would "start telling me to move aircraft," Mr. Milosevic appeared infuriated by the prospect of bombings. He called the general a war criminal.

Jan. 19 is already seen as a pivotal day in the Clinton Presidency. But it may turn out to be so less for the Senate impeachment hearings and State of the Union address than for the moves toward war over Kosovo.

Kosovo would have presented a daunting foreign policy challenge even to a President whose powers of persuasion and moral authority had not been damaged by a year of sex scandal and impeachment.

It is unclear whether the President's decisions on Kosovo would have been any different if he had not been distracted by his own political and legal problems. But it is clear that his troubles gave him less maneuvering room to make his decisions. Diplomacy that came to rely heavily on military threats reduced the wiggle room even further.

Over the previous year, sharp criticism and questioning of Mr. Clinton's motives arose each time he did take military action, as with the strikes in December against Iraq when the House was poised to vote on his impeachment.

Now, Mr. Clinton is facing mounting criticism for not having acted earlier or more decisively on Kosovo. His critics say that had he done so, Mr. Milosevic would not have been able to move troops and equipment into Kosovo and carry out the massive "ethnic cleansing" of the past four weeks.

As the President viewed the situation, there were only "a bunch of bad options" confronting him, he said earlier this month.

Throughout, the NATO allies hoped, even assumed, that they were dealing with the Milosevic who negotiated the Bosnian peace at Dayton, Ohio, the man who lied and manipulated and ranted in all-night, Scotch-laden negotiations and then cut a deal in the morning when he saw that it was in his interest. Instead they were dealing with the Milosevic of Belgrade, who was willing to employ mass murder to assure his continued dominance of Serbia.

George J. Tenet, the Director of Central Intelligence, predicted in Congressional testimony in February that there would be a major spring offensive by the Serbs in Kosovo and huge refugee flows. But intelligence assessments presented to Mr. Clinton about how Mr. Milosevic would respond to NATO threats of military force were vague. These reports included speculation that the Yugoslav leader would back down in the face of air strikes.

One interagency intelligence report coordinated by the C.I.A. in January 1999, for example, concluded that "Milosevic doesn't want a war he can't win."

"After enough of a defense to sustain his honor and assuage his backers he will quickly sue for peace," the assessment went on. Another interagency report in February stated, "He doesn't believe NATO is going to bomb."

Prodded by such assessments and his advisers, the President pressed ahead with a strategy of threats coupled with negotiations, gambling that Mr. Milosevic would back down. These threats quickly became a test of NATO's credibility, with the added onus of the alliance's looming 50th anniversary, which is to be observed next weekend.

Last September, former Senator Bob Dole went to Kosovo to gather facts for an international refugee group of which he is chairman. On his return, he reported his findings to Mr. Clinton. Afterward Mr. Clinton sat with him alone in the Oval Office and asked for his help in lobbying his former Senate colleagues to vote against conviction in the impeachment trial.

In an interview, Mr. Dole said he thought "a lot of attention was diverted" from Yugoslavia and other foreign policy issues by the impeachment. It was "all consuming," he added, and Kosovo "may have been one of the casualties."

The Dangers: A Balkan Firestorm That Slowly Spread

From the moment Yugoslavia fell apart in 1991, Kosovo—with its 90 percent ethnic Albanian population, and a Serbian minority that held its land sacred—was viewed as a place from which a wider war could erupt. The Bush Administration, which had adopted a hands-off policy on the killings in Croatia and Bosnia, warned Mr. Milosevic on Dec. 29, 1992, that the United States was prepared to take unilateral military action if the Serbs sparked a conflict in Kosovo.

The Clinton Administration reiterated the warning weeks after the inauguration. Three years later, when the Administration convened the conference in Dayton to end the Bosnia war, Kosovo was not on the agenda.

"Bosnia was then the emergency, and it had to be stopped," said Richard C. Holbrooke, the American envoy who negotiated the agreement at Dayton, in an interview. "Otherwise there would have been a real risk that Bosnia would merge with Kosovo into a huge firestorm that would destabilize the whole region." Over the next two years, younger, more confrontational ethnic Albanians began to build a ragtag army, supplied with weapons from neighboring Albania and financed largely by the Albanian diaspora in Europe and the United States.

They faced serious obstacles. Mr. Milosevic, who had risen to power on the cause of protecting Kosovo's minority Serbs, took away Kosovo's broad autonomy in 1989 and was unlikely to give it back without a fight.

The killing in Kosovo began in earnest in February 1998, when the Serbs retaliated for rebel attacks on policemen with brutal operations of their own in the Drenica area. Members of the Kosovo Liberation Army and their families were slain.

The Administration sent Robert S. Gelbard, its envoy to the region, to confront Mr. Milosevic with horrific photographs of death and mutilation. A veteran State Department official respected for his tenacity but known for his temper, Mr. Gelbard had experience in Bosnia and Croatia. But he did not have much of a personal relationship with the Serbian leader, whom he castigated in unusually blunt language.

The Drenica killings, Mr. Gelbard felt, were the kind of ruthless act that would further radicalize the restive Albanian population and lead to an explosion that could affect the entire region.

"You have done more than anyone to increase the membership of the K.L.A.," Mr. Gelbard told Mr. Milosevic. "You are acting as if you were their secret membership chairman."

The meeting ended badly, American officials said. Mr. Milosevic was infuriated and would eventually refuse to meet with Mr. Gelbard at all.

The Distractions: Foreign Policy Crisis Comes at a Bad Time

The eruption of violence in Kosovo in early 1998 could not have come at a more inopportune moment for the Clinton Administration.

The President and his aides were consumed by the Lewinsky affair. The Clinton foreign policy team was focused on Presidential visits to China and Africa and on Russia's economic implosion. Legislative electoral politics, especially with an incendiary sex scandal enveloping the White House, was never far from the President's concerns. And Kosovo did not register in any public opinion polls.

One of the President's political advisers said in an interview: "I hardly remember Kosovo in political discussions. It was all impeachment, impeachment, impeachment. There was nothing else."

Nonetheless, the spring of 1998 posed a question: Would the Administration, which had reaffirmed Mr. Bush's Christmas warning, take any action?

Weighing their options, officials said, they quickly ruled out unilateral military strikes, the very response Mr. Bush had promised. If anything was to be done, it would be in concert with the NATO allies, who along with America had troops on the ground as part of the international force in Bosnia. The United States could not start bombing while its allies were exposed in a neighboring country.

From then on, everything about Kosovo was subject to decisions by an alliance that worked by consensus and was soon to grow from 16 to 19 members.

Senior Administration officials who had lived through the years of delay and inaction in Bosnia believed they had learned a few things about how to deal with Mr. Milosevic. Diplomacy could work, but only if it was linked to the credible threat of force.

Ms. Albright began making the case for military action. At one key meeting in May, Mr. Gelbard argued that the time had come for air strikes.

Officials say Samuel R. Berger, the national security adviser, was opposed. The United States could not threaten without being prepared to follow up with a specific action.

Mr. Gelbard replied that he had already worked out some bombing targets with the NATO commander, General Clark. But Mr. Berger rejected the plan and no one else in the room supported Mr. Gelbard, who declined to discuss his role, saying only, "When I had the lead role on Kosovo issues I had complete support from the President and the Secretary of State."

The Administration then turned to Mr. Holbrooke. He pressed the Kosovo Albanians' main political leader, Ibrahim Rugova, who was becoming increasingly marginalized in his own camp, to meet with Mr. Milosevic. The payoff for Mr. Rugova was a meeting with Mr. Clinton in the Oval Office on May 27.

In a brief conversation with the President and Vice President Al Gore, Mr. Rugova warned that without direct American intervention, Kosovo was headed for all-out war. He pleaded for urgent American action and an increased American presence to halt the escalating violence.

"We will not allow another Bosnia to happen in Kosovo," a senior Administration official quoted Mr. Clinton as telling Mr. Rugova. The assurances were largely theoretical. Nothing concrete was promised.

After Mr. Rugova presented the President with a gift of a large piece of quartz mined from Kosovo, Mr. Clinton spent part of their time together telling him about similar minerals in his home state of Arkansas.

The two men posed for a photo. The meeting received little press coverage.

The Options: From Cruise Missiles to a Force of 200,000

There was plenty of other news in Washington that spring. Kenneth W. Starr's sex-and-lies inquiry was still preoccupying the White House. There were drawn-out court battles between the President's lawyers and Mr. Starr over whether senior Administration aides, a few of whom were involved in foreign policy issues, should be forced to testify before Mr. Starr's grand jury.

In June, with the six-nation Contact Group on the Balkans warning Mr. Milosevic that he could not count on the West's dithering on Kosovo as it had on Bosnia, NATO was ordered to draw up plans for military action. Mr. Milosevic promised concessions.

The American strategy seemed to be working.

The situation on the ground, however, was far from stable. The Albanian guerrillas used the early summer to take control of some 40 percent of Kosovo, and Mr. Milosevic responded with a major offensive.

NATO's military planners began weighing their options. These ranged from an attack involving only the firing of cruise missiles to a phased air campaign to deployment of peacekeeping troops as part of a negotiated or imposed settlement. The planners also looked at what it would take to invade Yugoslavia. Western officials said the numbers were staggering: As many as 200,000 soldiers would be needed for a ground war.

In a few months in the spring and summer of 1992, Bosnian Serb forces expelled hundreds of thousands of non-Serbs from their homes in Bosnia. In 1995, the Croats in Croatia drove more than 100,000 Serbs from their homes in just a few days.

Seven years later, officials said, no one planned for the tactic of population expulsion that has been the currency of Balkan wars for more than a century and that Mr. Milosevic adopted in Kosovo: the expulsion, this time within weeks, of hundreds of thousands of people.

"There were a lot of Milosevic watchers who said a few bombs might do it," a senior NATO official said. "What was not assumed, and not postulated, was that he would try to empty the country of its ethnic majority."

NATO officials were wrestling with several legal and political hurdles, officials disclosed. Some NATO members were worried about imposing a peace without the approval of the United Nations Security Council.

Alexander Vershbow, the United States representative to NATO and a former National Security Council aide who had been deeply involved in Bosnia policy, suggested an answer in a classified cable titled "Kosovo: Time for Another Endgame Strategy."

Mr. Vershbow's plan, officials said, arrived with a heavy political price tag: The possible dispatch of NATO soldiers just before a midterm election and in the midst of the impeachment fight.

The cable spelled out a plan to impose a political settlement in Kosovo with the cooperation of the Russians, longtime allies of the Serbs. Moscow and Washington would then go together to the Security Council.

"Kosovo endgame initiative could become a model of NATO-Russian cooperation," Mr. Vershbow wrote. "No kidding."

The proposed deal called for creation of an international protectorate in Kosovo. The settlement would be policed by an international military presence, or ground force. If a peace settlement was negotiated in advance, as many as 30,000 troops might be required to enforce it. But Mr. Vershbow also left open the possibility that NATO might have to impose a settlement without Belgrade's consent, requiring 60,000 troops. To help sell the idea in Congress, Mr. Vershbow said, the American contribution could be limited.

"Sooner or later we are going to face the issue of deploying ground forces in Kosovo," he wrote in his cable. "We have too much at stake in the political stability of the south Balkans to permit the conflict to fester much longer."

Beyond concerns about the American ground troops in Bosnia, there were fears that a Kosovo war could spread, and even engulf Greece and Turkey, both NATO members.

The cable landed in Washington on Aug. 7, the day bombs exploded outside the American Embassies in Kenya and Tanzania. It was circulated as Mr. Clinton was preparing for his pivotal appearance before the grand jury investigating the Lewinsky affair and the White House was planning the cruise missile attack against Sudan and the Afghan bases of Osama bin Laden, the Saudi exile suspected of directing the attacks.

The plan generated some interest among midlevel officials in Washington. Senior officials agreed that it underscored the need to come up with a comprehensive strategy. In the end nothing came of it.

Mr. Clinton was under attack for his grand jury testimony and faced questions about whether his military decisions were motivated by domestic politics.

Jokes about the movie "Wag the Dog" became commonplace. Fittingly, the President in the movie seeking to distract attention from a sex scandal stages an ersatz conflict in, of all places, Albania.

The Politics: No Will for Troops On Eve of Election

In Washington, impeachment was on Mr. Clinton's mind. Returning from a September visit to the region, Mr. Dole stopped in to see Mr. Clinton and Mr. Berger.

"The President listened carefully," Mr. Dole said in the interview. "I don't recall him saying a great deal. He agreed it

was terrible. Sandy Berger didn't say much, either." Then Mr. Berger left the room. "We discussed impeachment," Mr. Dole said. "This was a critical time in the Monica events."

Midterm elections were also at hand, and the Democrats were perceived to be on the run. Republicans fired another shot across Mr. Clinton's bow, warning against bombing Serbia.

"The Serbians have done what they wanted," Senator Trent Lott, the majority leader, said in an interview broadcast Oct. 4. "Now they're pulling back and now, only now what appears to be—will be—three weeks before an election, we're going to go in and bomb."

Senate Democrats were warning at the same time that they had little appetite for military involvement of any kind in Kosovo.

Senator Joseph R. Biden, the Delaware Democrat who favored action on Kosovo, said then that several Democratic colleagues approached him at a party caucus on Oct. 6 and said, "Don't count me in, Joe, don't count me in."

At the White House, the Democrats' leading Presidential contender for 2000, Vice President Gore, was keeping an eye on his own political future.

Officials say he supported air strikes in Kosovo but was careful to say little in meetings attended by large numbers of officials. His national security adviser, Leon Fuerth, prodded intelligence officials to scour the files for evidence that might implicate Mr. Milosevic in war crimes.

In October, the President outlined the plan for NATO air strikes in a letter to leading senators. The attacks, he said, would start out strong and "progressively expand in their scale and scope," especially if Mr. Milosevic and his forces remained in Kosovo.

"There will be no pinprick strikes," the President said in the letter.

NATO had agreed to the approach in a meeting of defense ministers in late September, in Vilamoura, Portugal. At the private meeting, William S. Cohen challenged his colleagues to embrace a new role for the alliance. If NATO could not muster a threat to Mr. Milosevic under these circumstances, he asked, what was the point of the alliance?

The Defense Secretary's toughened stance was striking. During the Bosnia crisis, he had assured his Congressional colleagues that American troops would be out of the region within 18 months.

There were limits. As Mr. Cohen made clear this week in Congressional testimony, his commitment was to air power, not the deployment of American soldiers on the battlefield. Questioned by the Senate Armed Services Committee as to why the United States did not field a credible ground threat last fall, he replied:

"At that time, you may recall there was great discontent up here on Capitol Hill. If I had come to you at that time and requested authorization to put a ground force in—U.S., unilaterally, acting alone—I can imagine the nature of the questions I would have received. You'd say, 'Well, No. 1, where are our allies? And No. 2, who's going to appropriate the money? No 3, how long do you intend to be there? How many? How long? How much? And what's the exit strategy?' "

The Secretary concluded, "And that would have been the extent of the debate and probably would have received an overwhelming rejection from the committee."

The First Deal: Bargain on Monitors Averts an Air Strike

Despite the harsh words and warning to Mr. Milosevic in the fall of 1998, no one, either in the Administration or in NATO, was eager to use force against the Serbs. So the White House turned again to Mr. Holbrooke to broker a deal that would push the issue into the next year.

It was a tall order.

For Dayton, Mr. Holbrooke had softened up Mr. Milosevic for months in advance and had sensed that the Serbian leader wanted a deal. In Ohio, Mr. Milosevic gave up territory in Bosnia, which was a separate country, and ended a war that was costing Belgrade huge sums of money.

When it came to Kosovo, the American envoy was pushing Mr. Milosevic to loosen his grip on land in his own country, a hallowed battlefield on which Serbian soldiers died trying to repel a Turkish invasion six centuries ago.

His only inducement was the threat of air strikes.

Mr. Milosevic and Mr. Holbrooke talked for nine days, and when it was over, the Serbian leader had made some concessions, perhaps significant, but they were only loosely outlined.

He agreed to withdraw the bulk of his forces from Kosovo. He said he would permit 1,800 unarmed international inspectors to monitor the deal and would allow overflights by NATO spy planes.

A token number of Yugoslav officers were to be sent to the NATO air base at Vicenza, Italy, with an equally small number of NATO officers stationed inside Serbia's Defense Ministry.

There was a catch. Mr. Milosevic wanted the lifting of the NATO order that gave authority to launch strikes immediately. Mr. Holbrooke made no promises. But he headed to Brussels, where he summoned NATO representatives to a meeting to report that a deal was nearly clinched.

The representatives voted to suspend the order, not remove it, angering Mr. Milosevic.

In Belgrade the next day, Mr. Milosevic told Mr. Holbrooke he was enraged that the order had not been entirely lifted. "He considered it a declaration of war," said one American involved in the discussions.

President Clinton praised the deal as a triumph of force-backed diplomacy, saying it was the basis for a lasting peace. Mr. Milosevic, he said, has "agreed to internationally supervised democratic elections in Kosovo, substantial self-government and a local police—in short, rights the Kosovars have been demanding since Mr. Milosevic stripped their autonomy a decade ago."

Within days, there were strong hints that Mr. Milosevic was not cowed. At a meeting in Belgrade to discuss imple-

menting the agreement, General Clark asked him why some of the security forces covered by the agreement had not been withdrawn from Kosovo.

"That was not agreed," Mr. Milosevic shot back, according to an American official familiar with the conversation. "You call Holbrooke. He'll tell you what we agreed."

"No, I won't do that," replied General Clark, a veteran of hours of negotiations with Mr. Milosevic in Dayton. The general walked to a map to point out the locations of the brigades and battalions he wanted removed.

"We have no extra forces," Mr. Milosevic said. "NATO must do what it must do."

And then General Clark moved bluntly to the alliance's bottom line.

"Mr. President, get real," General Clark replied. "You don't really want to be bombed by NATO."

The Standoff: Deal With Milosevic Is Quickly Unhinged

The October agreement quickly fell apart, and Western officials now acknowledge that the Serbs' preparations for a purge of Kosovo were evident in what they did and what they said.

According to NATO officials, the Serbs began infiltrating reinforcements and equipment in violation of the deal. Serbian officers bluntly told General Clark in October that they were just two weeks away from eliminating the Kosovo Liberation Army.

In January, the commander of the main military unit in Kosovo, Lieut. Gen. Dusan S. Smardzic, told local reporters that they could look forward to a "hot spring" in which the problems in the province would finally be resolved.

The Kosovo Albanian rebels were pushing ahead with their own war aims. Sensing that the deal essentially placed the world's most powerful military alliance on their side—despite NATO's continued assurances that it did not want to become the guerrilla army's "air force"—the rebels quickly reclaimed territory abandoned by the Serbian forces and mounted a continuous series of small-scale attacks. American intelligence officials warned Congress that the rebels were buying weapons, improving their training and becoming a more formidable force.

The unarmed observers, caught in the middle, could do little. William S. Walker, the American diplomat who headed the observer group, was threatened at one point by a belligerent drunken Serb wielding a gun and a hand grenade. Mr. Walker pleaded privately with old friends at the State Department for some security. The State Department was sympathetic but was struggling to cope with the aftermath of the embassy bombings.

American intelligence analysts struggled to read Mr. Milosevic's intentions. Was he playing for time or preparing for war? Were the troop movements in October a prelude to a major offensive in which the population would be displaced so that the Serbs could more easily root out the Albanian guerrillas?

"The October agreement," read a highly classified National Intelligence Estimate dated November 1998, "indicates

Milosevic is susceptible to outside pressure." The estimate is a lengthy formal report drafted by the C.I.A. and vetted by all Government intelligence agencies.

It suggested that Mr. Milosevic "could accept a number of outcomes from autonomy to provisional status, with the final resolution to be determined, as long as he remained the undisputed leader in Belgrade."

Mr. Milosevic, this assessment added, would only accept "new status" for Kosovo "if he thinks he is in danger because the West is threatening to use sustained and decisive military power against his forces."

About the same time, NATO intelligence detected signs of a Serbian military buildup around Kosovo. Western intelligence officials, particularly the Germans, believed that these troops could form the backbone of a military operation to push hundreds of thousands of Albanians out of Kosovo.

Its code name was Potkova—in Serbian, Horseshoe.

American officials agree that Jan. 16 of this year was a turning point. On that day, the bodies of at least 45 peasant farmers and their children were found on hillsides and courtyards in the village of Racak.

Most had been shot at close range in the head or neck with a single bullet, according to American officials. Some had been mutilated.

Witnesses said a small group of hooded men dressed in black and wearing gloves had carried out the killings. Mr. Walker arrived on the scene within hours, and accused the Serbian security forces of committing "a crime very much against humanity."

The Serbian Government declared him persona non grata and fiercely protested its innocence. The killings galvanized public opinion in the United States and Europe.

Three days after the bodies were discovered, Ms. Albright presented her new plan at a White House meeting.

It again threatened bombing if Mr. Milosevic did not go along with the West. But, for the first time, it demanded that he accept NATO troops in his own country to enforce a deal under which he would withdraw almost all his security forces and grant Kosovo broad autonomy.

Until then, the goal had been to stick to an agreement that had come to be known as "October plus"—the accord reached by Mr. Holbrooke plus some sort of protection for the observers. Mr. Berger was skeptical of going beyond that.

Mr. Cohen and Gen. Hugh Shelton, Chairman of the Joint Chiefs of Staff, had even greater reservations. They had wanted at all costs to avoid a troop presence that would require Americans.

But in the end the advisers embraced Ms. Albright's approach and sent it to the President, who accepted it.

Two days later, President Clinton was on the phone to Prime Minister Tony Blair of Britain describing the new approach.

The two leaders agreed that there were two options: to initiate an immediate bombing campaign in reprisal for Racak, or to fashion a diplomatic solution that included ground troops as peacekeepers in Kosovo, according to a White House aide who listened in on the conversation.

"Blair said that ground troops could not be used to fight a war, but only as part of a political strategy," the official said. "The President said, 'I completely agree with you on that. If we sent in a ground force without some sort of agreement beforehand, sooner or later they're sitting ducks for either side who is willing to provoke something.' "

Mr. Clinton said he would instruct his aides to try to bring Mr. Milosevic and the Kosovo Albanians to the bargaining table. "I will try to get Congress to go along with me," he promised Mr. Blair.

Meanwhile, General Clark and General Naumann were confronting Mr. Milosevic.

The two generals refused food and drink. This was to be a serious negotiating session in which they told Mr. Milosevic he was violating the October agreement.

"We figured we'd starve him out," General Clark told colleagues afterward.

Mr. Milosevic was, as General Clark later told reporters, "determined to go his own way."

His face red, his voice cracking, the Serbian leader described the Racak incident as provocation.

"This was not a massacre," Mr. Milosevic insisted, according to a NATO official familiar with the meeting. "It was staged. These people were terrorists. They do these things to people."

Mr. Clark warned that NATO is "going to start telling me to move aircraft" if Serbia did not live up to its agreement.

"You are a war criminal to be threatening Serbia," Mr. Milosevic replied.

Unquestionably, the meeting had gone badly. But General Clark, perhaps because he had lived through the stormy Dayton peace talks, reported to his superiors that he still saw some flexibility.

Two days after General Clark's meeting, two State Department veterans of the Dayton talks, James Pardew and Christopher Hill, delivered a similar message to the Yugoslav President.

This time Mr. Milosevic said that the killings had resulted from a firefight between rebels and the Serbian security forces.

The rebels, he continued, rearranged the bodies and dressed them to make them look like peasants and farmers, shooting the bodies through the heads and necks to make the incident look like a massacre.

Mr. Milosevic's behavior raised a crucial question for Western officials: What were his intentions? Were the troop movements into Kosovo saber-rattling, or preparations for war?

American intelligence agencies governmentwide were utterly divided on how to read the Serbian leader, classified reports show.

"Confronted with a take-it-or-leave-it deal, Milosevic may opt to risk a NATO bombing campaign rather than surrender control over Kosovo," read one late January report, according to a Government official. "He may assume he can absorb a limited attack and the allies will not support a long campaign."

A week later the prediction was the opposite. "Milosevic will seek to give just enough to avoid NATO bombing."

The day the bombing began, March 24, an intelligence report said Mr. Milosevic "would interrupt the offensive and sign the peace plan if he suffers or expects to suffer substantial damage to his armed forces and national level infrastructure from a bombing campaign."

Two days later, the analysts had changed their minds. "Air attacks," they wrote, "will not suffice to shake Milosevic's confidence."

In addition, while it was widely expected that NATO bombing would prompt retaliation against the Kosovo Albanians, officials said there had been no predictions that Mr. Milosevic would try to empty the province of them, as he has done.

After the Racak killings in January, some American officials favored air strikes. But there remained the delicate matter of NATO unity.

On Jan. 28, the NATO allies warned that they were ready to use force immediately, and Britain and France said they were prepared to send in ground troops to enforce a peace settlement. Two days later, after Kofi Annan, the United Nations Secretary General, said that the threat of force was justified to get the Serbs to the bargaining table, the allies decided they had justification enough under international law to authorize air strikes against Yugoslavia if it did not agree to negotiate a settlement.

To try to strike that deal, the Europeans wanted a conference that would be their equivalent of Dayton, Ms. Albright said in an interview on Friday.

The Negotiations: Talks at a Castle Set Stage for War

But the gathering at Rambouillet, a former royal hunting lodge near Paris, was no Dayton.

The Americans approached the negotiations hoping to impose a solution on the Serbs and the Kosovo Albanians, but that attempt quickly broke down. Mr. Milosevic, who was a central figure at Dayton, did not even attend the meetings. The Albanians were balky, too, refusing to accept a three-year autonomy deal offered by NATO because it carried no guarantee of eventual independence.

If Dayton was a diplomatic triumph for the Clinton Administration and Mr. Holbrooke, Rambouillet was a debacle for Secretary Albright. She told friends it was one of the worst experiences of her career.

With the two-week deadline set for the talks almost expired, Ms. Albright went to Rambouillet and implored the Albanians to sign on to the deal. Ms. Albright failed to convince the hardliners, the representatives of the Kosovo Liberation Army, who insisted on inserting language that held out promise of a referendum on independence after the three years of autonomy. But they also insisted that they needed a two-week pause to sell even that deal to their supporters.

That set the stage for the ultimate failure of diplomacy. By refusing to sign the deal, the Kosovo Albanians had taken the pressure off the Serbs, leaving NATO with no reason to order air strikes at that point. "If this fails because both sides say 'No,' there will be no bombing of Serbia," Ms. Albright said on Feb. 21, as the Rambouillet talks wound down.

Mr. Milosevic, for his part, concluded that there was not enough incentive for him to deal. While Ms. Albright had inserted language to satisfy the Albanian rebels, apparently none of the parties were negotiating any changes that the Serbs might have sought—particularly changes related to the deployment of NATO ground troops. Two days after Rambouillet ended, said the European Union envoy to the talks, Wolfgang Petritsch, the Yugoslav President decided that he was not going to accept NATO troops—and mustered his own forces and propaganda to prepare for the military showdown.

The standoff over Kosovo was growing more dire as President Clinton's political fortunes were rising and as the crisis drew more of his focus and energy. On Feb. 12, he was acquitted by the Senate. Only a few days later, on a trip to Mexico with Senator Biden, the President wanted to talk about the Kosovo crisis.

"All the way down on the plane I was reading a book about the Balkans and he saw me reading it," Mr. Biden recalled in an interview.

The book was "History of the Balkans," by Barbara Jelavich (Cambridge University Press). "And you know how he is," Mr. Biden added. "He asked me to give it to him to read. And I said, 'No, get your own copy.' And I'll lay odds that he eventually got it and read it."

President Clinton believed war could still be averted, though he was prepared to undertake a short burst of bombings, if necessary.

In a meeting with Italy's new Prime Minister, Massimo D'Alema, in the Oval Office on March 5, Mr. Clinton said Mr. Milosevic had "accepted almost everything," according to Italian officials in Europe.

Mr. D'Alema, a rough-around-the-edges former Communist, was skeptical. He asked the President what the plan was if there was no deal and NATO air strikes failed to subdue the Serbian leader. The result, Mr. D'Alema said, would be 300,000 to 400,000 refugees passing into Albania and crossing the Adriatic into Italy.

"What will happen then?" Mr. D'Alema wanted to know, according to Italian officials.

Mr. Clinton looked to Mr. Berger for guidance. NATO will keep bombing, Mr. Berger replied.

After Rambouillet fell apart, a followup conference was called in Paris three weeks later. While the world waited, Mr. Milosevic continued to build up his forces in and around Kosovo.

A defining moment came on March 18 at the International Conference Center on the Avenue Kleber in Paris. To polite applause, four ethnic Albanian delegates signed the peace plan that would give their people broad autonomy for a three-year interim period. The Serbs did not sign. That paved the way to air strikes.

Even though the United States and its NATO allies were now committed to war, three European Foreign Ministers—Robin Cook of Britain, Hubert Vedrine of France and Joschka Fischer of Germany—began murmuring about making a final appeal to Mr. Milosevic in Belgrade. Ms. Albright persuaded them to allow Mr. Holbrooke to go instead. But even as Mr. Holbrooke was en route to Belgrade, the situation grew more hopeless.

"The racial hatred was unleashed," said one senior Administration official. "Albanians began to kill Serbs; Serbs were shooting up villages."

Mr. Holbrooke has described his last meeting with Mr. Milosevic in Belgrade's Beli Dvor—White House—on March 22 as "unreal." Mr. Milosevic accused the Americans of "sitting at the Albanian side of the table" at Rambouillet.

He insisted that there was no war in Kosovo, just a few terrorists who needed to be rooted out once and for all. Mr. Holbrooke later described parts of his conversation with Mr. Milosevic. "I said to him, 'Look, are you absolutely clear in your own mind what will happen when I get up and walk out of this palace that we're now sitting in?' "

"And he said, 'You're going to bomb us.' "

"And I said, 'That's right.' "

In the end it was Mr. Milosevic who was left to decide whether his country and NATO would go to war. "It was Milosevic who deliberately and consciously chose to trigger the bombing of his own country," Mr. Holbrooke said.

Ms. Albright said that setting up a deal signed by only one side was a crucial step forward. "Signing Rambouillet was crucial in getting the Europeans two things." she said. "Getting them to agree to the use of force and getting the Albanians on the side of this kind of a settlement."

The Serbs had already begun their offensive, she added, and if the signing had not been forced at that time, "we would be negotiating while they were carrying out their 'village a day keeps NATO away.' "

At 12:30 on the morning of March 25, hours after the first bombs fell, the President was wide awake. He had called his key counterparts in NATO and monitored the beginning of the air war that day. His foreign policy team had gone home and there was nothing left to do.

But the President apparently needed to assure and be reassured. So he called his Secretary of State and woke her up.

The President said, "We're doing the right thing here," Ms. Albright recalled. "We've got a long way to go. This is not going to be over quickly and we're all in this. I feel we've explored every option, that we're doing the right thing."

The Secretary said she replied: "I feel the same way. Nobody should ever think that we had gone into this without our eyes wide open."

* * *

April 19, 1999

REDRAW THE MAP, STOP THE KILLING

By JOHN J. MEARSHEIMER and STEPHEN VAN EVERA

President Clinton is still clinging to his position that NATO should accept nothing less than a settlement giving autonomy to the Albanian Kosovars inside Serb-dominated Yugoslavia. But this goal is not only unattainable, it's also undesirable. Does anyone seriously believe the Albanian Kosovars and Serbs can live together again?

Instead, NATO should pursue a settlement that partitions the province, creating an independent Albanian Kosovar state. This state would control most of current Kosovo, while the Serbs would retain part of northeastern Kosovo. It could remain independent or unite with Albania if it chose.

Autonomy is a dead letter because the Serbs have shown their attitude toward cohabitation by their savage ethnic cleansing of Albanians in Kosovo. Moreover, the 600,000 refugees who have fled Kosovo since mid-March will hardly be willing to return to a province inside Serbia, whether autonomous or not, after the cruelty they just suffered.

Finally, the United States would have to station sizable forces in Kosovo indefinitely to help NATO police any autonomy agreement. But we cannot afford to tie our military down doing such police work. The world is full of civil wars, and the whole American military would soon be committed to peacekeeping.

The history of Yugoslavia since 1991 shows that ethnic separation breeds peace, while failure to separate breeds war. Slovenia seceded from Yugoslavia with little violence in 1991 and has since been at peace with itself and its neighbors. The key is its homogeneity: 91 percent of the people are Slovenes; less than 3 percent are Serbs. Croatia fought a bloody war of secession from 1991 to 1995, finally resolved when it expelled most of its sizable Serb minority at gunpoint. This expulsion set a poor example for how groups should separate, but it did bring an end to the Serb-Croat conflict. Separation did not end the deep hatred between Croats and Serbs, but it did stop the violence between them.

Bosnia saw fierce fighting among Croats, Muslims and Serbs from 1992 to 1995, then an uneasy truce under the Dayton accords. Dayton created a confederated Bosnia in which the three groups were supposed to live together. This has failed, quietly but quite completely. Few Bosnian refugees have returned to their homes, and Bosnia still has no functioning central government. If the large NATO peacekeeping force in Bosnia were withdrawn, fighting would soon explode again.

Now Kosovo is consumed by a war that stems from hatreds born of the great cruelties that Albanians and Serbs have inflicted on each other in the past. This war could have been avoided if they had been separated by political partition at some earlier point, when Slobodan Milosevic might have been more amenable to the idea.

Under what circumstances would the Serbs accept such a partition today? The NATO bombing since March 24 has fired Serb nationalism to a fever pitch, stiffening Serb resistance to any compromise. And the bombing campaign alone gives NATO too little coercive leverage to compel the Serbs to accept partition, since bombing by itself cannot defeat Serb forces in Kosovo. Serbia always has the option of hunkering down and absorbing NATO bombing until NATO publics tire of it.

But Serbia may accept partition if NATO offers it carrots as well as the stick. To entice the Serbs, NATO should offer a "grand bargain" that partitions Bosnia as well as Kosovo—moving Serbia toward its dream of a homogeneous greater Serbia.

Under this grand bargain Serbia would concede most of Kosovo to the Albanians. In return, the Serbs would be compensated with a portion of northeast Kosovo that includes many Serbian historical sites. Serbia would also get the eastern portion of Bosnia, which is now populated mainly by Serbs. The rest of Bosnia would be transformed into an independent Bosnian Muslim state, save for the Herzegovina region, which would become part of Croatia. Finally, NATO would lift all economic sanctions against Yugoslavia if the Serbs took the deal.

NATO would also need to put heavy pressure on the Serbs to get them to accept the breakup of Kosovo. In addition to bombing, NATO must also arm and train the Kosovo Liberation Army, so the Serbs are faced with the prospect of unending warfare in Kosovo unless they accept partition.

This is not a perfect solution by any means, but it solves several important problems. First, it provides the Albanian Kosovars with their own homeland, where they can live free of Serbian terror. Second, it solves the refugee problem. Third, it requires no American troops in Kosovo, since the Albanians and Serbs would be living separate lives, and the Albanians would have guns to protect themselves. Fourth, partitioning Bosnia would allow the United States to pull its troops out of Bosnia, thus removing that albatross of permanent occupation from around America's neck.

Some warn that an independent Kosovo would spark secessionist violence among Albanians living next door in Macedonia. But an independent Kosovo would more likely dampen than spark violence in Macedonia. The main trigger for war in Macedonia will be the presence of a large, radicalized Albanian refugee population there.

The solution is to achieve a settlement that returns the Albanian Kosovar refugees to their homes. Only a partition offers such a settlement, and hence is more likely to pacify Macedonia than to inflame it.

Still, it may be that peace cannot be maintained in Macedonia. Macedonia's Slavic majority discriminates against the large Albanian minority, which makes up 30 percent of the population. If the Slavs refuse to share more equally with the Albanians, violence is inevitable. To forestall this, NATO should consider calling for a plebiscite to determine whether the Albanians want to remain in Macedonia. If not, Macedonia should also be partitioned. This is feasible because the Albanians of Macedonia are concentrated in western Macedonia, next to Kosovo and Albania.

Partition is an ugly formula for ending wars. It destroys communities and violates individual rights. It forces minorities that are trapped behind new borders to leave their homes. But there are only two other options in Kosovo: endless ethnic war or allowing the Serbs to win the war and cleanse Kosovo of Albanians permanently. Partition is clearly better than these unacceptable choices. If we shrink from it, then we merely make the catastrophe in the Balkans even more devastating.

John J. Mearsheimer and Stephen Van Evera teach political science at the University of Chicago and the Massachusetts Institute of Technology, respectively.

* * *

April 20, 1999

NATO ADMITS PILOT BOMBED 2D CONVOY ON KOSOVO ROAD

By MICHAEL R. GORDON

BRUSSELS, April 19—NATO acknowledged for the first time today that it had bombed two separate groups of vehicles last week near a Kosovo town, Djakovica, and might have killed civilians.

Until now, NATO has only acknowledged that its planes accidentally bombed a tractor northwest of Djakovica. But Serbian authorities and Kosovar refugees have insistently reported allied hits along the road southeast of Djakovica, putting NATO credibility to a severe test.

Providing its first comprehensive briefing on the attacks, in which the Serbs claim that 74 civilians were killed, NATO officers said their pilots, flying at high altitude, had been convinced they were striking only military vehicles.

But as the raids proceeded, allied officers at a command post in Italy became concerned that fleeing refugees might be in the second group, a huge convoy of more than 100 vehicles southeast of the town. Their suspicions were aroused after NATO intelligence experts warned that Serbian forces do not generally travel in such long columns.

A pair of OA-10 observation planes were quickly dispatched. Using binoculars, the pilots reported that civilian vehicles appeared to be interspersed with the military ones, and the attacks were halted.

"What we know from the debris that the Serbs showed is that some civilians died there and that there is the possibility that NATO aircraft were the cause," said Brig. Gen. Daniel Leaf, the American commander of an air wing at Aviano, Italy, who led the official NATO inquiry into the episode.

Today's briefing demonstrated the difficulties of identifying targets from high altitude over a region where Serbian army and police forces have been driving civilians from their homes and often herding them down roads. Allied planes have spotted Serbian tanks concealed next to ruined homes, and Serbian soldiers have reportedly used tractors and other vehicles as well as military equipment.

Today's assessment was also an important political test for the alliance. Since the air strikes against the convoys, on April 14, and the reports of civilian casualties, NATO spokesmen have been on the defensive.

This was a result not only of the insistent Yugoslav charges, which Belgrade sought to reinforce by organizing visits to the scene by reporters; it was also a result of contradictory statements by the NATO Commander, Gen. Wesley K. Clark, and conflicting accounts of the raid by the Pentagon and the alliance. The Yugoslavs continue to accuse NATO of killing civilians in places NATO said it did not bomb.

NATO sought to answer its critics today by releasing a flood of information about aircraft patrols, laser-guided bombs and even conversations between the pilots and airborne controllers. NATO officials said information was not released sooner because they had to interview pilots, gather intelligence information and analyze television broadcasts to determine what had happened.

An excerpt was drawn from a conversation between an airborne command post, referred to in military parlance as AB-triple-C, and an F-16 pilot attacking the convoy.

"We just received word that this is a VJ convoy," the command post told the F-16 patrols, using the acronym for the Yugoslav Army.

After weeks of bad weather and frustrating attempts to uncover hidden Serbian armor, the pilots thought they had stumbled on a bonanza.

"Great!" responded one of the pilots. "AB-triple-C, I want as many fighters as I can get, now."

Important questions still remain, however. One is how many civilians were killed; General Leaf said reporters taken to the site saw only about 20 victims.

Another is whether they were killed by allied planes or by Serbian artillery or even Serbian aircraft.

And another is whether the allies can reduce the risk of hitting civilians without hampering their attacks on Serbian forces. There is also the question whether it is possible to dependably distinguish civilian from military targets at an altitude of 15,000 feet.

General Leaf said the episode began about 12:30 P.M. local time when a pair of United States F-16's saw Albanian villages being set on fire north of Djakovica. Their call sign was Bear 21. The episode was first documented last week at NATO.

A pilot in Bear 21 saw people running from a house that burst into flames and jumping onto a vehicle, which NATO officials said may have been a tractor. Believing that they had set the house on fire, he attacked the vehicle with a laser-guided bomb, destroying it.

NATO officials added today that in addition to the Bear 21 attack, another bomb was later dropped north of the town in an attack by a different group of F-16's, Bear 41. Serbian television later showed destroyed tractors at that site, raising the possibility of civilian casualties.

NATO's principal disclosure today, however, was of the later attack southeast of the town on a convoy of more than 100 vehicles. That raid involved several sets of aircraft, including F-16's, French Jaguars, OA-10 observer planes and a flying airborne command and control aircraft, the AB-triple-C.

Another important link was NATO's command center in Vicenza, Italy, the Combined Air Operations Center, which coordinates the raids.

The raids on the second column began when two F-16's, Bear 31, saw the convoy. From the start, the pilots were worried about the possibility of civilian casualties. With many villages aflame there was reason to think that many refugees might be on the road.

General Leaf said the pilots in Bear 31 had an "extensive discussion" with the command plane about whether the convoy was a civilian or military target.

It was not easy for the pilots to identify the vehicles from their altitude, and while F-16's carry advanced military technology, these systems have their limits. Potential targets are shown in the F-16 cockpit on a special display, which is about 4.5 inches wide and 4.5 inches high. The targets are not shown in color, but in shades of green.

An F-16 pilot has to look out the cockpit to see the color of the vehicles below him, an important factor since military vehicles are often painted dark green. He cannot use binoculars because the cockpit is too small, a military official said.

As was the case of the Bear 21 patrol north of Djakovica, the Bear 31 F-16's were flying air controllers, whose mission was not only to carry out strikes but also to coordinate attacks by other allied planes.

Despite worries about refugees on the road, a number of factors led the Bear 31 pilots to conclude they had spotted a military column: The 20 or so vehicles at the front appeared to be traveling in formation, with a set distance between them, and they were moving quickly, leading the pilots to believe they were not tractors.

Further, the command and control plane told the F-16 pilots that the convoy was made up of Yugoslav military vehicles.

The two F-16's in Bear 31 attacked the convoy, destroying one vehicle and missing one. They called in strikes by two French Jacguar planes, who missed the convoy.

The F-16's ran low on fuel and were replaced by another pair, Bear 41, who came under Serbian antiaircraft fire.

Suddenly there was an ominous warning. After twenty minutes of bombing the convoy, the command center in Italy wanted the planes to check the targets again and make sure that they were military. Military intelligence experts at the command center were dubious that Serbian forces would be driving down an open road in such a long convoy.

To get a better look Bear 41 asked for help from a pair of OA-10's, known as Cubs. The pilots reported that military vehicles had been struck, but that civilian vehicles also seemed to be present. By then eight laser-guided bombs had been aimed at a convoy south of Djakovica, though not all of them hit their mark.

General Leaf, while insisting that some military vehicles were hit, says other targets destroyed appeared to be tractors.

"As we watch these videos in the comfort of this room and on a large display, it appears possible the vehicles are tractors or tractor-type vehicles," he said. "As I reviewed the tapes with the pilots, they agreed. However they were emphatic that from the attack altitude, to the naked eye, they appeared to be military vehicles."

General Leaf acknowledged that British Harrier pilots had seen a convoy in the area and had identified it as containing refugees. This happened at about the same time as the attacks on the convoy were being carried out, but General Leaf said the Harriers were "not in communication with the aircraft in question."

A senior allied officer said the episode has led NATO commanders to re-examine procedures for finding and identifying targets. But worried also about antiaircraft fire, the alliance appears intent on continuing high-altitude strikes for now.

* * *

April 22, 1999

AT NATO'S BIRTHDAY PARTY, CHILLING SPECTER OF KOSOVO

By FRANCIS X. CLINES

WASHINGTON, April 21—The word "gala" still appears on some official schedules of NATO's 50th anniversary celebration. But the word rings unseemly now as the bombs continue to fall on Yugoslavia from NATO warplanes.

As workmen hammered and vacuumed and United States marines stood guard at the celebration hall today, the grimmer reality of that uncertain war already was in the air of the anniversary setting, like crepe where bunting was once intended.

Two days before the opening ceremony of welcome to 44 summit delegations, the schedule of events has been discreetly altered to allow for shifts in tone and emphasis in the face of the open-ended aerial assaults that, far from being a crowning anniversary success, have called NATO's very future into question.

For one thing, the bombing briefing by NATO's now familiar spokesmen on the war will be held right here at the commemoration's media center as a kind of Orwellian prelude to the day's speeches and events. For another, the planned outdoor opening ceremony, replete with a thundering flyover of NATO warplanes as a heavyweight television anchor waxed historic, has been scrapped. Instead, there will be a three-hour jubilation-free indoor working meeting on the harrowing snares of NATO's confrontation of Slobodan Milosevic.

Black-tie formal wear has been ruled out at the two White House dinners in favor of the more sober imagery of business attire. And officials said there is a likelihood that the three-day gathering will offer an added agenda item—the catastrophic refugee sufferings of Kosovo's ethnic Albanians—as the heart of its final working session Sunday and thus the parting image of its commemoration.

"Five months ago when we were planning this, it was going to be much more of an occasion to look at the successes of the past and to try to put a matrix around the challenges of the future," said Richard Socarides, the special assistant to President Clinton who is the NATO summit's chief operating officer. "Now, of course, the weekend will be much more oriented to the present. The foreign policy challenges are being played out in real time."

Attempts to screen out suggestions of global junketeering in the historic commemoration have not been entirely successful. This afternoon, the fact sheet handed out to some of the more than 2,000 workers of the world news media arriving to cover the event began with the question: "How do I get into the press party on Thursday night?" ("To get three free drinks, you must have the Media Reception card," the answer emphasized.)

With security ultratight and no events accessible to the public, NATO will be presenting a hermetic television event. The images of diplomacy and the speeches of resolve—all 19 NATO heads of state are expected to give opening speeches—will vie with the daily feeds from the air war that, NATO officials emphasize, will be going on even as they talk.

"The mood will be serious, dignified and focused," declared Mr. Socarides, who said the President was receiving lengthy briefings and was looking forward to the summit meeting as an opportunity to rally the alliance.

The working sessions will be held in what is now called Andrew Mellon Auditorium, formerly Departmental Auditorium, where the NATO alliance was signed into being on April 4, 1949, as the bulwark against the Soviet Union after World War II. The hall, which faces the National Museum of American History across Constitution Avenue, had previously served as the site of the Selective Service draft when American troops last fought in Europe.

Fifty years ago, President Harry S. Truman and the other signers presided over what was then the first event of its kind to be broadcast live in its entirety to the nation in a display of NATO's determination to protect the world. Delegates sat in gold colored chairs. These have been reupholstered for the 50th anniversary gathering where tiny Kosovo, not global Communism, is the haunting theme.

Months ago, planners were polishing an ambitious, optimistic agenda emphasizing the need for closer cooperation with Russia and for a decision on theoretical questions about the future role of NATO and whether and how it might ever have to enter combat beyond the borders of its member nations. That question has since been put to the test in Kosovo to the considerable fury of Russia, which, even as the first delegates were arriving with hopes of possible Kremlin mediation, declined to attend.

The ultimate question lurking about the commemoration is whether NATO might cross the Balkan Rubicon and send ground troops into the costly, inconclusive fray. In the passing crowds outside the NATO hall today, before a cocoon of security closed off the downtown heart of the capital, fit young NATO soldiers behaved like tourists, stopping to snap photographs against a backdrop of history.

*   *   *

April 23, 1999

NATO STRIKES SERB STATE TV; CASUALTIES SEEN

By STEVEN ERLANGER

BELGRADE, Serbia, Friday, April 23—NATO knocked Serbian state television off the air in the middle of a newscast early this morning, leaving the building that housed the main Government propaganda arm in flames, with reports of many casualties.

The attack on the television building followed a more surprising strike at President Slobodan Milosevic, when three NATO missiles devastated his residence—an elegant villa in the wealthy Dedinje district at 15 Uzicka Street—the most famous address in Belgrade.

NATO had been debating for weeks whether or not to destroy state television, and warnings had gone out earlier this week to American television correspondents to stay out of the a complex at 10 Takovska Street, in the heart of the city and surrounded by residential and commercial buildings.

State television has been the main source of immediate news and film footage for Western television correspondents. With the damage, CNN and other networks were also unable to transmit pictures from Belgrade.

Senior state television journalists have said they have alternative transmission installations and expected to be able to get back on the air, at least in some parts of the country, if NATO blew up the main studios and transmission center.

Witnesses told Studio B, the Belgrade city channel that is in a different building and remains on the air, that ambulances and firefighters were at the scene and that the wounded were being taken out of the building, which houses Serbian Radio and Television. Studio B is controlled by the relatively liberal Serbian Renewal Movement, and it has been less rigid and has sometimes provided more information than state television in its coverage of events here.

Although NATO sent a missile into Mr. Milosevic's bedroom, officials insisted that it was nothing personal. The residence, an eclectic two-story building of white stucco, with columns and rounded windows described by its original owner as a little inspired by Hollywood, the villa was built as a private house and finished in 1936.

Tito appropriated half the house for himself in 1944, as he took power in Belgrade, and it came to be thought of as the official residence of Yugoslavia's President.

Today, it is a charred ruin. One entire side wall of the structure is blown away, all the windows are broken, and many trees in the surrounding parkland have been uprooted.

There are gaping holes where the missiles pierced the walls, flares of soot shoot from the arches of the empty window frames, and chunks of concrete and broken glass are scattered over the lavish grounds.

NATO may have intended its missiles as a message to Mr. Milosevic, who has not been sleeping at the house in recent weeks.

Tito, who is most associated with the house, is buried in a sort of mausoleum 200 yards away in what is known as the House of Flowers. That glassed-in structure was apparently not damaged in the attack, which truly marked the death of the Yugoslavia Tito built—the country that deftly wove a path between Soviet East and American West, borrowing from, yet independent of and even admired by both cold war foes.

Yugoslav officials were livid in the name of Mr. Milosevic, and of the past represented by his villa. They accused NATO of trying to assassinate the leader of a sovereign state, and said the other missiles, which hit at about 3:15 A.M., had struck the living and dining rooms.

Mr. Milosevic has been avoiding the house ever since a little-reported missile attack on a nearby building housing his presidential guard, in which as many as 30 people are reported to have been killed, Serbian officials said on Thursday.

NATO, for its part, claimed that the building was a vital link in the military command system of Yugoslavia and that the strike had nothing to do with Mr. Milosevic or its symbolic importance to the nation.

But the building was no radar station, and some Serbs reacted with anger and incredulity.

A Serbian photographer said: "This is simply demagoguery. Whether one likes Milosevic or not, this is outrageous."

A senior Serbian journalist with the magazine Vreme said: "This building is part of our cultural heritage. Yesterday Tito lived there, and today Milosevic does, but tomorrow it will be Pera Peric." That is the Serbian form of John Doe.

"If NATO wants to pretend now that it's hit at the heart of the repressive regime and not the Serbian nation, it's not true, because they've only done this after a month of hitting civilian targets," the journalist said.

Nearby, the old royal palace, the Beli Dvor, or White Palace, is a ceremonial residence, where Mr. Milosevic, like Tito before him, normally greets guests, but does not live.

NATO has put the Beli Dvor off-limits as a target, in part because a Rembrandt borrowed from the National Museum is on the first floor. But the residence destroyed on Thursday is also a listed building, on the Yugoslav register of protected cultural sites.

Goran Matic, a Serbian government minister of the Yugoslav United Left party led by Mr. Milosevic's wife, Mirjana Markovic, was scathing in a news conference. "NATO committed a criminal act without precedence—an assassination attempt against the President of a sovereign state," Mr. Matic said.

NATO and other Western officials called the building a presidential command post and legitimate military target.

Pool Photo by Reuters

The President's residence after the bombing. Neither Slobodan Milosevic nor his family were home when the building was bombed yesterday.

"Milosevic himself is not a target," said the White House spokesman, Joe Lockhart. "The command and control center is."

But the Yugoslav Foreign Ministry spokesman, Nebojsa Vujovic, said the building had no military utility, and he challenged NATO to find "one wire or one button." He asked, "Are their next targets child-care centers?"

About 24 hours earlier, NATO destroyed a building housing the offices of Mr. Milosevic's party and that of his wife's, as well as the radio and television studios and transmitters of stations belonging to their daughter, Marija, and their friends.

In the town of Krusevac, some 125 miles south of Belgrade, Zivadinka Damjanovic, the director of an old-age home, was furious about the attack on the residence.

"NATO showed its real position when they destroyed the President's house," she said to a small group of reporters visiting the town. "This was not his house, but an official one, and it was built long before him."

The attack gave the lie to NATO's stated war aims, she said. "The point is destruction, and not any kind of humanitarian protection or intervention. It's very obvious they want to occupy us and destroy us as a people."

Aleksandar Acovic, a wealthy engineer, built the villa. His nephew, Dragomir Acovic, is currently the president of the Serbian Heraldic Society and something of a monarchist.

According to Mr. Acovic, the Nazis seized the house in 1941 when they occupied the country. Tito confiscated half of it in 1944, when he came to Belgrade, forcing the elder Mr. Acovic to sell the rest to the state in 1946.

The building is said to have one of the best air raid shelters in Belgrade, which was apparently part of the original design. Dragomir Acovic has said that on April 6, 1941, when the city was bombed by the Nazis, the Government held a Cabinet meeting in the shelter.

Serbian state television led its evening news on Thursday with the building's destruction. A commentator called the attack "the drop that spills the glass of condemnation by the largest part of justice-loving humanity."

It also cited the former Russian Prime Minister, Viktor S. Chernomyrdin, for his disapproval of the attack and "the barbaric destruction of a country."

*   *   *

April 25, 1999

NATO BOMBING TEARS AT GREEK LOYALTIES, REAWAKENING ANTI-AMERICANISM

By ALESSANDRA STANLEY

ATHENS, April 23—Anti-American demonstrations, like dinner, start late in Athens. But for some Greek teen-agers, too young to remember similar riots of the 1960's and 1970's, protesting against the United States is still novel.

Hours before protesters and riot policemen clashed in front of the American Embassy on Thursday night, two sisters, Eleni and Constantina Vafiadou, sat by a fountain in Constitution Square expectantly ready to register their anger over the NATO bombing of Yugoslavia.

"It's ludicrous to say the bombing is to help humanity," Eleni, 18, said over the rally's amplified Serbian music—the soundtrack to "Underground," a popular Serbian film. "It's about the U.S. pursuing its own expansionist strategic interests."

Her 16-year-old sister explained the film's allegorical anti-war message her own way.

"It's like what Ashley told Scarlett," Constantina said, referring to characters in "Gone With the Wind." "After all the war and destruction, nobody remembers what they were fighting about in the first place."

Sympathy for the Serbs—and a cultural affinity with the United States—is deeply rooted in Greece. But the latter sentiment is being sharply tested. More than any other country in NATO, Greece has been struggling between loyalty to the Western alliance and outrage over the bombing nearby.

While Prime Minister Costas Simitis is attending the NATO anniversary summit meeting in Washington this weekend and has restated Greece's support, back home Greeks of every age and political conviction are voicing fierce opposition to what they view as an unjust war.

Some of the wrath stems from Greek ties to Serbia, a historically and key trading partner that shares the Orthodox Christian faith. Much of it is caused by anxiety over what a new war in the region could do to Greece's fragile economy and uneasy borders. But it is fueled by a revival of anti-American sentiment that, though dormant, has never really died.

Greece, which has been steering toward full integration with Europe, now finds itself pulled back into a tragic Balkan history, and into feelings that the United States played a pivotal role in Greek suffering. Greeks blame the United States for supporting the military dictatorship and for failing to prevent the Turkish invasion of Cyprus in 1974. The bombing has not only created new fears but has also resurrected old grievances.

"America, way on the other side of the world, keeps interfering in something that is not their business, and that will not affect them," Margaret Liaveris, 25, a civil servant, said. "I find it so annoying when Clinton says, 'Our children need a free Europe.' Most of their children never even come here."

Her views, among them a fear that the conflict could destabilize the region and reignite tension with Turkey, are widely shared. A recent poll published by Greece's largest daily newspaper, Ta Nea, indicated that more than 95 percent of Greeks oppose the bombing. Some 63.5 percent of those polled expressed a favorable view of President Slobodan Milosevic of Yugoslavia. And 94.4 percent said they had a negative view of President Clinton.

Greek newspapers and television have fanned public discontent, stressing the suffering of Serbian civilians over the plight of Albanian refugees from Kosovo. And that has alarmed the country's 500,000 Albanian immigrants, who mostly work illegally, and are viewed with suspicion by many Greeks.

"I ask myself, why is Greece supporting Serbia; aren't they in NATO?" a 52-year-old unemployed immigrant said, adding that he relied on the Albanian-language service of Voice of America.

Some Greek journalists agree that there is an imbalance. "Greek television shows the exact opposite of what Americans see," Stelios Koulogrou, a well-known television documentary filmmaker, explained. "On CNN you see 80 percent refugees and 20 percent Serbs. On our channels it is the reverse."

Coverage of American news, meanwhile, is newly shaded by the war.

To the newspaper Ethnos, a center-left daily, the mass killings at a high school in Colorado this week had a direct link to NATO bombings. "The violence that Pentagon hawks are using in their foreign policy has boomeranged on social life in the U.S.," a front-page headline said on Thursday. "The evidence is overwhelming: 10,000 assaults in American schools each year."

A Greek naval officer who was given a two-and-a-half-year sentence this week for refusing to serve on a destroyer set to join NATO forces in the Adriatic has become a hero of left- and right-wing groups, as well as many in the Greek Orthodox clergy. Archbishop Christodoulos Paraskevaidis has described the bombers as "pawns of Satan."

Greeks have not taken their anger out on their Government, which has given NATO access to two air bases and its land routes into Macedonia, and is seeking a cautious balance between loyalty to NATO and support for a cease-fire. Since the crisis broke out, Mr. Simitis's ratings have risen.

"There is a silent majority that feels that Greece has no choice but to be prudent, prudent, prudent," said Thanos Veremis, who runs a foreign policy research institute in Athens. "We are a small, weak country and people feel that poor Simitis has no choice for now." He added, "But that of course could change."

Relations between Turkey and Greece have been relatively free of strain since the bombing began on March 24, but many Greeks nevertheless worry that the war will reignite that conflict.

"Thrace," a 25-year-old engineering student replied when asked about his opposition to the war. He was referring to the small Muslim minority in Thrace, whose rights are yet another sore point between Greece and Turkey, which is largely Muslim.

"Turks could use Kosovo as a precedent," he said. "As an excuse to demand autonomy for Muslims in Thrace."

He, like many others, complained that NATO was applying a double standard on human rights in the Balkans. As Eleni Vafiadou put it: "Albanians had some rights in Kosovo, but the Kurds in Turkey don't have any. Why hasn't the United States bombed Istanbul?"

The anxiety over the war is free-floating. The Greek stock market has fallen, some tourism agencies are reporting cancellations and Greek investment in Serbia, worth more than $1 billion, is at obvious risk.

Greek political leaders and voters speak passionately about the need to protect borders, fearing that any redrawing of the map of Kosovo could infect Macedonia or spawn Muslim aspirations of a "Greater Albania" including northern parts of Greece.

And there is growing talk of sinister American goals in the Balkans that have little to do with defending an oppressed minority.

"I think America is threatened by an independent Europe," said Leon B. Karapanayotis, editor in chief of Ta Nea, "and it is no accident that now the euro is falling against the dollar. The U.S. is asserting itself in Europe, and Europe is now considerably weaker. I suspect the U.S. has no reason to feel unhappy about this."

* * *

April 29, 1999

INSIDE AN ACCIDENT OF WAR: SIRENS. BLAST. GRIEF

By STEVEN ERLANGER

SURDULICA, Serbia, April 28—"We grew up together," said Momir Andjelkovic, his eyes veined and red, staring fixedly at the green, encircling hills. "He was my finest friend."

Mr. Andjelkovic stopped, dropping his clouded eyes to the mounded rubble across narrow Zmaj Jovina Street, where Aleksandar Milic, 37, died on Tuesday. Mr. Milic's wife, Vesna, 35, also died. So did his mother and his two children, Miljana, 15, and Vladimir, 11—all of them killed about noon when an errant NATO bomb obliterated their new house and the cellar in which they were sheltering.

"We lived together here for 32 years, for good and bad," Mr. Andjelkovic said. "He was a great man, a great friend."

He sobbed once, briefly. "This was a completely new house, three stories, with completely new furniture," he said, still astonished at the jagged pile of refuse where it used to stand. "It had a large basement. Everyone felt safe there. But the whole family died."

Dying with them were at least two cousins: Stanica Rasic, 21, and Dragan Manoluv, 18. Altogether, Yugoslav officials said, 20 civilians, half of them children, died in Surdulica, this small town of 11,000 people 200 miles south of Belgrade, near the Bulgarian border. At least six houses were destroyed and another 20 or so had significant damage.

A short distance from Mr. Milic's house, his father, Vojislav, head bent, sat on a broken bit of wall, cupping an unlit cigarette in his palm.

He was in shock. Two women hovered, arms around his shoulders, squeezing them through his black jacket as if he might otherwise fall over. They urged him in steady whispers to stand up, to eat something, to drink some water.

Mr. Milic rocked silently, oblivious, his head bobbing up and down with the even beat of a human heart.

NATO officials in Brussels said that this was yet another accident of war. At least one laser-guided bomb, they said, fell 200 or 300 yards from its intended target—an army barracks and military depot previously bombed on April 6.

The barracks is at least 500 yards away. Only after Western journalists saw another large crater a half-mile from Mr. Milic's house did NATO officials concede that they "could not exclude" that another bomb might have gone astray. NATO did not say what might have caused either to do so, though they have said in the past that weather and other factors can throw the weapons off.

The other crater—a nearly perfect scoop in the earth, 30 feet across and 20 feet deep—had blasted three houses away on muddy Beogradska Street. The hole, slowly filling with ground water, was scattered with the debris of human life: filthy clothes, exploded sofa cushions, pill boxes, the back of an oven, the cracked circuit board from a television set.

No one died here, officials said, although at least five people were wounded.

"Death can be a blessing, too," said Borica Novkovic. The house of her son, Stanko, 35, was obliterated. He, his wife, Tatjana, and their 8-month-old daughter, Andrijana, were not in the house. "My son is not here," Mrs. Novkovic said, with pride. "Stanko is in the army now."

The noise was indescribable, she said: "The sound was like a huge blow on my head. Everything turned over and rolled down the hill.

"Radica was screaming, screaming, when we came to help her," Mrs. Novkovic added, bending to pull up her coarse woolen stocking.

Radica Rastic's house was closest to the impact. "She was taken from the house all twisted and bent over," Mrs. Novkovic said. "She was shaking and shaking, her hands were pressed tight over her ears."

Perica Jovanovic, a 44-year-old economist at the Narodni Bank, said: "I'll never forget the strange voice of the bomb. When the plane is flying and drops the bomb the noise changes. It's awful. It's like the static on the radio but so loud, and then there is this awful crash and pressure and everything moves and boils up."

Mr. Jovanovic was outside with his two children, Biljana, 13, and Nemanje, 8. "Somehow we stayed alive," he said quietly, with care. "But I think these NATO bastards will come back."

He stopped and glared.

"You should pass through that," he said. "Americans should have this experience."

He softened then, to say: "People think I'm very calm, but I'm not, I'm very upset. Here you have 11,000 people who are crazy, nervous. People died here and what was the aim? There is nothing around here."

He threw up his hands. "We were very brave for 34 days, but we've moved now," he said. "I've moved the family now to a lake in the hills."

About 200 yards from the crater, a half-finished house was badly damaged. Over the door was a handpainted sign: "Kuca na prodaju"—house for sale—"Tel: 85-552."

On Zmaj Jovina Street, Slobodan Milosevic, 48, the bearer of a common Serbian name, stood covered with dust in the ruins of his own house, across the street from Mr. Milic's. Photographers had scrambled up to the second floor, easily visible from the street because the entire front of Mr. Milosevic's house had been ripped away.

"This house is a ruin," he said. "To build it I worked four years in Africa—two in Tunisia and two in Algeria." He laughed sourly. "Now I'll have to go there again."

Mr. Milosevic, a civil engineer, was out visiting relatives with his wife, Sladjana, 45, son Sasa, 25, and daughter Suzana, 22, when the bomb hit his street.

"My first thought when I saw it all was that we were very lucky not to be in the house, because we would have died," he said. "We're alive, so we will build another house."

He said he was sure that NATO had aimed for the houses. "It's impossible for the pilot to make this mistake," he said. "The sky was clear. He couldn't miss. The barracks isn't even that close."

Asked about his neighbor, Mr. Milic, Mr. Milosevic said he worked in a small factory, PES, that made components for Zastava, the huge car and munitions factory in Kragujevac that NATO destroyed. Mr. Milic also owned two small convenience stores in town, and it seemed he was returning home for lunch when the air raid sirens sounded and he and his family and neighbors went down to the basement of his fine new house. "But Momir," he said, "was really his friend."

Mr. Andjelkovic described how he went down to his own basement with his parents and emerged to see what had happened.

"I couldn't understand what was going on," he said. "There was dust everywhere, and the houses existing two minutes before—right in front of my house—were just gone. I heard people screaming, and one of the people down there was my uncle. We tried to dig with our hands, I made him a small hole to breathe until first aid could come."

The uncle, Stojanka Petkovic, 65, "was the only one to survive this house." He pointed to the elder Mr. Milic, still sitting frozen on the wall. "He came from somewhere else," Mr. Andjelkovic said. "He lost everyone."

Asked quietly if he thought that keeping foreign troops out of Kosovo was worth this kind of price, Mr. Andjelkovic looked up, stunned. "I don't understand the question," he said. "You shouldn't ask me that now—we can talk about that in 10 or 15 days."

He shook his head. "We haven't buried these people and you want to ask me that?"

* * *

April 30, 1999

NATO MISSILE GOES ASTRAY AND HITS HOUSE IN BULGARIAN CAPITAL

By CRAIG R. WHITNEY

BRUSSELS, April 29—A straying NATO missile fell on the outskirts of Bulgaria's capital, Sofia, on Wednesday night, going through the roof of a house without exploding.

NATO, which hopes to get permission from Bulgaria to use its airspace for bombing attacks against Yugoslavia, today expressed regrets about the incident.

It was the fourth time an allied missile had strayed into Bulgaria, according to allied officers. None of the errant missiles, including the latest, has killed anybody.

The latest missile was fired by an allied plane on Wednesday night after a Yugoslav antiaircraft missile radar system locked onto the jet. The missile kept flying 40 miles east after the radar was turned off and landed without exploding on a two-story house in the suburb of Gorna Banya, an allied spokesman said.

Bulgaria's President, Petar Stoyanov, visited the area to inspect the damage and kept his representative in Brussels on the telephone to the alliance most of Wednesday night to find out what had happened, NATO officials said.

Allied warplanes also carried out the heaviest attacks of the war on Wednesday and today on Montenegro, a part of Yugoslavia whose elected government is opposed to President Slobodan Milosevic and his war against the ethnic Albanians of Kosovo. Montenegro's population of 600,000 includes a sizable minority of Serbs and Albanians.

The alliance spokesman, Jamie P. Shea, said NATO had had "no choice" but to attack Yugoslav military planes that were using the airport at Podgorica, the capital of Montenegro, and posed a threat to allied soldiers based not far away in Albania.

The AGM-88 Harm missile that landed on a house near Sofia is fitted on a variety of allied planes from various countries, seeks out radar signals after being launched but is essentially unguided if it cannot find any. The warhead automatically disables itself when the missile nears the end of its range, up to 50 miles, allied officers said.

"In operations yesterday, a NATO aircraft was illuminated by a Serbian surface-to-air missile radar and fired a missile," Mr. Shea said. "After the radar was turned off, the missile strayed and landed in Bulgaria."

"Thankfully, there were no casualties," he said. "We regret any damage." He added that the alliance would try to clarify what happened and to minimize the chances of its happening again.

Bulgaria is also a leading applicant for membership in the alliance. But there is powerful opposition in the Bulgarian Parliament, which is expected to vote soon on whether to give permission to NATO to fly over Bulgaria in the course of air operations against Yugoslavia.

Reports from Bulgaria on Thursday said the Bulgarian Army had detected an unidentified plane in violation of the country's airspace about 30 miles north of Sofia shortly before the missile landed.

It was the second mistake the allies have had to acknowledge this week. On Wednesday, the allied command acknowledged that at least one laser-guided bomb had missed its intended target and gone off in a neighborhood of civilian houses in southern Serbia on Tuesday afternoon. Serbian officials said at least 20 people had been killed.

The bombing of Serbian military targets in Kosovo and beyond continued into a 37th day today, command spokesmen said, after pounding the airfield at Podgorica overnight with almost 30 strikes.

The allies had previously avoided striking targets in Montenegro, except for Yugoslav antiaircraft defenses there, because its government under President Milo Djukanovic has distanced itself from Yugoslavia's war against the ethnic Albanian civilian population in Kosovo.

"While we would have preferred not to have attacked sites in Montenegro, Podgorica airfield is becoming an important operating location for the Federal Republic of Yugoslavia Air Force," said Brig. Gen. Giuseppe Marani, the allied military spokesman.

"Aircraft driven from their main bases by NATO attacks are using the airfield as a dispersal base," he said. Only a few dozen miles away from the nearly 10,000 allied troops in Albania, aircraft based at Podgorica could also pose a significant threat to those soldiers, General Marani said. "Thus we see our attack as prudent self-defense," he said.

The strikes were aimed at military hangars, fuel tanks, air defense radars and single-engine Yugoslav-made Super Galeb aircraft parked on runway aprons or in protected shelters, General Marani said.

Mr. Shea said some military planes had been destroyed in the attacks. Serbian news media had reported bombing on Wednesday night near the main Montenegrin port, Bar, but General Marani said allied planes had not made any attacks on port sites.

Central Belgrade Hit Again

BELGRADE, Serbia, Friday, April 30 (Reuters)—NATO hit the main Yugoslav Army headquarters, the Defense

A house on the outskirts of Sofia yesterday after it was hit by a missile that went through its roof without exploding. The missile, fired by a NATO plane, kept flying east after it lost its radar target in Yugoslavia.

Ministry and a police building in central Belgrade on the 37th night of air raids against Yugoslavia early this morning, residents said.

They said a series of loud explosions rocked the Yugoslav capital at around 2:30 A.M.

NATO hit a Belgrade television transmitter, knocking Serbian state television off the air, and attacked the Kosovo provincial capital, Pristina, and a Serbian oil refinery earlier, official news media said.

*   *   *

May 8, 1999

NATO RAID HITS CHINA EMBASSY; BEIJING CITES 'BARBARIAN ACT'; ALLIES ADMIT STRIKING HOSPITAL

By STEVEN LEE MYERS

WASHINGTON, May 7—NATO forces that were pounding the center of Belgrade struck and badly damaged the Chinese Embassy tonight during an attack that knocked out electricity across much of Yugoslavia and battered targets at the very heart of President Slobodan Milosevic's power.

Yugoslav authorities immediately reported injuries inside and outside the embassy, where, they said, 26 people were at the time. China said two of its citizens were killed and two more were missing.

China quickly denounced the attack and tonight called an emergency meeting of the United Nations Security Council, which convened just before midnight. "We are greatly shocked by the reports of NATO's bombing of the Chinese Embassy," the Chinese representative at the United Nations, Qin Huasun, said. "NATO's barbarian act is a violation of the U.N. Charter."

In a statement released late tonight, NATO said it had conducted its "most concentrated attack to date" against Yugoslavia's capital since the air war began on March 24. It also acknowledged mistakenly bombing a hospital complex and marketplace in Nis, an attack which the Yugoslav Government said had killed 15 people.

Among the targets in Belgrade was another of Mr. Milosevic's residences, beneath which was a major bunker complex that NATO described as the wartime political and military headquarters for the Yugoslav Government.

"NATO has information that suggests this is now the center of Mr. Milosevic's high command, following the destruction and damage done to other command facilities," NATO's statement said.

NATO said it did not mean to hit the Chinese Embassy. "NATO regrets any damage to the embassy or injuries to Chinese diplomatic personnel," the statement said.

Although NATO and American officials offered no explanation for how NATO could have hit the embassy, NATO did target the Hotel Yugoslavia, which is close by. The officials said that this hotel has been taken over as a headquarters and barracks for the special paramilitary police, headed by Zeljko Raznjatovic, who is known as Arkan.

A senior Pentagon official declined to say whether NATO's barrage was intended to kill him or any other Yugoslav leaders, including Mr. Milosevic, but NATO's statement could be read as implying as much. "These strikes were planned to disrupt the national leadership of military and special police operations," the statement said.

The barrage tonight came after a day in which NATO faced new questions about the consequences of its air war. Moments before reports of the midnight strike against the embassy, NATO officials acknowledged that cluster bombs dropped from an F-16 fighter jet had extensively damaged a

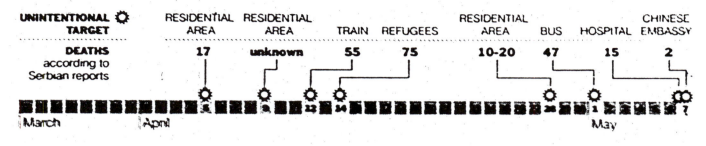

As War Continues, Errors Mount

NATO's unintentional bombing of the Chinese Embassy in Belgrade is the eighth such error since the bombing began on March 24.

UNINTENTIONAL ☼ TARGET	RESIDENTIAL AREA	RESIDENTIAL AREA	TRAIN	REFUGEES	RESIDENTIAL AREA	BUS	HOSPITAL	CHINESE EMBASSY
DEATHS according to Serbian reports	17	unknown	55	75	10-20	47	15	2

March   April   May

hospital complex and marketplace in Nis, the third largest city in Yugoslavia. The Yugoslav Government said 15 people died.

Yugoslav officials, who escorted journalists to the scene in Nis, reported that an additional 60 to 70 people had been wounded. Dismembered bodies lay on a nearby street around yellow casings from the cluster bombs. The bombs, after detonating, cover a target with smaller bomblets that float to the ground with small parachutes.

The damage to the embassy, which is in the new section of Belgrade, west of the Sava River, is certain to add tumult to the strained relations between the United States and China, which has been sharply critical of the NATO air campaign.

As a permanent member of the United Nations Security Council, China has veto power over any settlement that would have the international body's imprimatur.

On Thursday, the Foreign Ministry of China called on NATO to halt the bombing, saying that it had caused "great civilian casualties." Tonight, Mr. Qin, the representative to the United Nations, said, "We call on NATO to stop immediately its military actions, so as to avoid further humanitarian disasters."

The White House immediately reached out to the Chinese Embassy in Washington to inform it about the strike, an Administration official said. Later, the American Ambassador to China, James Sasser, spoke with officials in Beijing, the Washington official said.

The United Nations Secretary General, Kofi Annan, was "shocked and distressed" at the report of the strike, his spokesman said.

Despite the questions about casualties, officials vowed to press ahead with the air war and predicted a heavy night of bombardment was expected across the country.

The strikes began as evening fell in Yugoslavia and allied planes attacked four electrical transformers in and around Belgrade, once again darkening the capital and much of the rest of the country, officials said.

In its statement, NATO also reported striking numerous Government and military buildings in the center of the city, including the Army's General Staff building, two Ministry of Defense buildings, the Federal paramilitary police head-

quarters and two other buildings linked to Yugoslavia's weapons procurement.

The barrage followed a three-day lull in strikes against the capital that coincided with diplomatic efforts to end the air campaign, even though NATO officials insisted that there was no correlation. The strike at the embassy occurred after a second powerful series of explosions rocked the capital. A Yugoslav official reported that the building was evacuated and that some people had been taken to hospitals.

"Now I would like to see how NATO will justify this," a Yugoslav Cabinet Minister, Goran Matic, said, according to The Associated Press. "It was a deliberate targeting of the Chinese Embassy. It's high time to end this madness."

Even as diplomats from Washington to Moscow shuttled from capital to capital, carrying the outlines of a possible peace settlement, the United States and NATO pledged to intensify the attacks, which continued for the 45th day today.

A consequence of the intensified assault has been growing numbers of misfires and civilian deaths, which the alliance has repeatedly said it hoped to avoid. For the fifth time, a stray missile landed in Bulgaria. No one was hurt.

NATO's errant bombing in Nis was far graver. NATO and Pentagon officials reported a major attack by allied planes against the airfield in Nis, as well as a radio tower, but at least one bomb fell short of its target, for reasons that remained unclear.

"Unfortunately, it is highly probable that a weapon went astray and hit civilian buildings," a statement released tonight at NATO headquarters in Brussels said. "There was no intent to harm civilians during this strike."

From the start, NATO has emphasized that civilian deaths were always a possibility in warfare. The Yugoslav Government has used the deaths to portray the attacks as indiscriminate acts of barbarity.

To counter what many officials here consider disproportionate attention to NATO's mistakes, the Pentagon today provided a compilation of reports of atrocities attributed to Mr. Milosevic's campaign of "ethnic cleansing" in Kosovo.

The Pentagon's compilation detailed more than 20 towns or cities in Kosovo where more than 100 people have been reported killed or more than 1,000 people have been displaced.

In Washington today, the Army commander of the three American soldiers captured along the Macedonian border six weeks ago said that NATO had closed its posts there. Maj. Gen. David Grange said NATO had kept the observation posts open throughout March despite the attacks on the United States Embassy in the Macedonian capital, Skopje, and the rising tensions along the border. It only decided to close the posts after the three soldiers were held.

During a briefing on the nearly completed military investigation of the soldiers' monthlong captivity, General Grange insisted that the three soldiers were more than one mile inside Macedonia when they were captured on March 31.

*   *   *

May 9, 1999

POPE JOINS PATRIARCH IN PLEA FOR PEACE IN BALKANS

By ALESSANDRA STANLEY

BUCHAREST, Romania, May 8—Pooling their moral authority, Pope John Paul II and Patriarch Teoctist of the Romanian Orthodox Church today jointly requested an immediate end to the fighting in Kosovo.

It was the first communal appeal for peace between leaders of the long estranged Roman Catholic and Orthodox churches since the violence in Kosovo began.

The two expressed support for victims on both sides of the conflict. Without referring to either by name, they elliptically suggested that both NATO and the Serbian government were to blame for the suffering.

"We want to appeal in the name of God to all those who, in one way or another, are responsible for the current tragedy, that they may have the courage to resume dialogue and find the right conditions to bring about a just and lasting peace," they said in a joint statement.

Pope John Paul II, who is the first Pope to visit a predominantly Orthodox Christian country, is in Romania to mend relations with the Eastern church. He is also seeking to use his presence at the edge of the Balkans to allay age-old Orthodox mistrust of the Vatican that has only been heightened by the war next door.

The Vatican has denounced the NATO bombing and the expulsion of ethnic Albanians from Kosovo many times. Prominent Orthodox leaders have mostly focused on the killing of civilians in Serbia, though Patriarch Aleksy II of the Russian Orthodox Church mentioned the plight of ethnic Albanian refugees when he met with the Yugoslav President, Slobodan Milosevic, in Belgrade. For the Romanian Patriarch, however, it was one of the fullest acknowledgments to date of the suffering Serbs are inflicting on ethnic Albanians.

"We want to express our human and spiritual solidarity toward those who have been chased from their homes, their lands and separated from their loved ones, as well as the victims of murderous bombings," the statement said. "In the name of God and of all mankind, we ask all parties engaged in the conflict to permanently put down their arms."

The statement did not mention the bombing of the Chinese Embassy in Belgrade overnight.

Serbs, who share a border with Romanians, are also mostly of the Orthodox faith, and many of them view the NATO campaign as an assault by the West on their nation and religion. In Bucharest, some Romanians said they viewed the papal visit as part of a Western plot to keep the Bulgarian Government on NATO's side, evidently unaware that the Pope has been highly critical of the alliance's bombing campaign.

The Pope's dream of full reconciliation with the Orthodox faith before the beginning of the third millennium, which he first laid out 20 years ago, is further complicated by deep tensions between Orthodox Romanians and the Catholic minority here, many of whom belong to the Greek Catholic Church, which follows Eastern rites but is loyal to the Pope.

Some of the deepest conflicts between the two faiths date back to the Communist era in Eastern Europe.

This morning, the Pope prayed at a cemetery at the tombs of several Greek Catholic bishops who were persecuted under Communism.

When the Communists took power in 1948, they persecuted the Orthodox Church and forced its leaders to collaborate. Catholics, who were viewed as less compliant, were treated even more mercilessly. Bishops and priests were executed and Catholic churches were turned over to the Orthodox Church. The Orthodox church has only returned about 100 of some 2,000 properties that once belonged to the Greek Catholic church.

The Pope today asked Orthodox bishops to end the conflict. "The end of persecution has given back freedom, but the problem of churches still awaits a definitive solution," he said in a meeting at the Patriarchy. "Let dialogue be the means to healing still open wounds and to resolve remaining difficulties."

Earlier, at a Greek Catholic mass at the Cathedral of St. Joseph, the Pope also asked his Romanian followers to forgive old grievances.

"A painful wound was inflicted on our fellowship with our brothers and sisters in the Orthodox Church," the Pope said in his homily, "even though many of them shared your suffering in persecution.

"Let common suffering generate, not separation, but the miracle of reconciliation."

Hundreds of thousands of Catholics from all over Romania today poured into the capital and lined the streets around the Cathedral for a glimpse of the Pope.

The Orthodox Church did not allow the Pope to travel to heavily Catholic regions like Transylvania, where religious tensions are high.

"The fact that the Pope chose to come anyway is a sign that he is willing to go the extra mile for reconciliation," said John Michael Botean, Bishop of St. George in Canton, a Greek Catholic diocese in Canton, Ohio, who was in Bucharest to greet the Pope. Monsignor Botean said he told American congressmen last month, "Castro couldn't do in Cuba what is being done here, restricting the Pope to one city."

But the Bishop noted that sacrifices in the name of reconciliation were necessary, nevertheless.

"The fact that the Pope would come under these circumstances sets an example for Catholics in Romania and elsewhere," he said. "It has to happen. The only thing that keeps our churches apart are the same things that divided them 1,000 years ago, human pride and stubbornness."

* * *

May 9, 1999

NATO SAYS IT THOUGHT EMBASSY WAS ARMS AGENCY

By MICHAEL R. GORDON

BRUSSELS, May 8—A NATO aircraft bombed the Chinese Embassy in Belgrade on Friday night because the military command mistakenly believed that it was a headquarters for a Yugoslav arms agency, allied officials said today.

The plane carried out its mission correctly and struck its assigned building. But the aircraft was given faulty target information, the officials explained.

NATO officials said that the Central Intelligence Agency had picked the target, but stressed that the episode is being investigated. One possibility, they said, is that intelligence officials used out-of-date maps, although the site of the embassy building was well known in the Yugoslav capital.

"We hit what we were aiming for," a NATO official said. "But we did not mean to hit the Chinese Embassy."

A military spokesman for NATO said a single aircraft was involved and three bombs were dropped. While allied officials declined to provide further details, the air raid may have been carried out by a United States B-2 "stealth" bomber.

The accidental bombing of the Chinese Embassy, which killed at least 3 people and wounded about 20, has stirred up a political storm for NATO, which has been anxious to secure China's cooperation in fashioning a peace settlement for Kosovo.

Javier Solana, NATO's Secretary General, insisted today, however, that air strikes would not end until President Slobodan Milosevic of Yugoslavia stopped his attacks on ethnic Albanians and agreed to NATO's terms. "The attacks will continue," Mr. Solana said.

The accidental attack comes on the heels of other notable mistakes in the alliance's air campaign, including the bombing of a hospital complex this week.

Given that the alliance has launched more than 5,000 bombing missions and used more than 15,000 missiles and bombs, its mistakes have been relatively few. But they have been politically costly, and now there is a risk that they will interfere with diplomatic efforts on Kosovo.

The latest accident revealed a glaring limitation of high-technology warfare. Even in an age of precision-guided

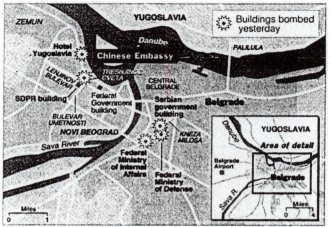

The New York Times

China's embassy in Belgrade appeared to have been hit from two sides.

bombs, an air campaign, which the alliance has relied on exclusively, can be no better than the intelligence on which it is based.

Before Friday's strike against the Chinese Embassy, NATO's accidents stemmed from mistakes by the pilots, weapons failures and, sometimes, plain bad luck.

In the attack on the hospital, for example, an F-16 was trying to drop an unguided cluster bomb on an airfield a mile away. A NATO official said it was not clear if the pilot dropped the bomb too soon or if there was a technical problem.

The embassy episode was different. In this case the pilot successfully hit the target he was told to strike.

People in Belgrade said that it was difficult to confuse the Chinese Embassy with the intended target, the Federal Directorate for Supply and Procurement. The Chinese Embassy is a marble structure with blue mirrored glass and flies the Chinese flag. It is one of the few embassies in Belgrade that houses some staff members and other Chinese residents.

The directorate, which coordinates Yugoslavia's weapons imports and exports, is housed in a white office building. That building is several hundred yards away, on the other side of a major thoroughfare, Lenjinov Bulevar. Both structures are several years old.

The accidental bombing of the embassy recalled the American strike on the Al Firdos bunker in Baghdad during the Persian Gulf war in 1991.

In that case the pilot also accurately carried out his instructions. He bombed an underground bunker used by Iraqi intelligence officers. But as a result of an intelligence failure, the C.I.A. had overlooked indications that civilians were also using the shelter.

The uproar over the Al Firdos attack prompted Gen. Colin L. Powell, then the Chairman of the Joint Chiefs of Staff, to restrict attacks against targets in downtown Baghdad.

Since NATO's air strikes more than six weeks ago, allied officials have made extensive use of laser-guided bombs and

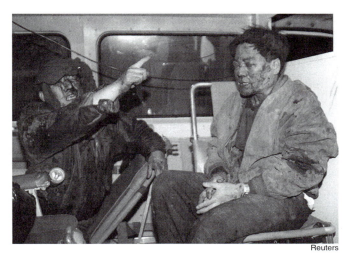

Reuters

NATO air strike on Belgrade hit China's Embassy overnight Friday, killing at least three people and injuring about 20. Two men wounded there sat in an ambulance outside the building early yesterday.

satellite-guided munitions. A major aim has been to take the war home to the Yugoslav leadership in Belgrade while avoiding civilian casualties.

The strike against the Chinese Embassy was part of a broader series of high-technology attacks against the Yugoslav capital. Friday's strikes in Belgrade, in fact, were the heaviest so far.

They included strikes against the Dobanovci Command Complex, a residence of the Yugoslav President, Slobodan Milosevic, which includes a bunker for his high command.

The Hotel Yugoslavia was also pounded. Allied officials say it houses a barracks and command center for Zeljko Raznjatovic, the paramilitary leader knows as Arkan who has been charged with war crimes for his attacks in Bosnia. His gang, "Arkan's Tigers," has been accused of attacking ethnic Albanians in Kosovo.

Other targets struck in Belgrade include various Defense Ministry buildings, an Interior Ministry headquarters and a building used by the Yugoslav general staff, which has a satellite antenna for military communications.

Electrical transformers in Belgrade and Obrenovac were also attacked. Along with additional attacks today, the strikes disrupted Serb's command and control, NATO spokesman insisted.

Still, the bombing was a major political setback for NATO, particularly since China has been a sharp critic of the bombing attacks and holds a veto on the United Nations Security Council.

The alliance has agreed to seek the Security Council's approval for a settlement in Kosovo and the dispatch of a security force there to protect returning refugees.

At the same time, NATO believes that it needs to keep up the military pressure to achieve a diplomatic settlement.

Its air commanders have sought not just to pummel Serbian troops. By targeting military ministries, command posts and communications center in and around Belgrade, they

have also sought to compel Mr. Milosevic to withdraw his troops from Kosovo and meet other allied demands.

But in pursuing their goals, NATO officials have made strenuous efforts to limit civilian casualties. It is not just a moral concern. Allied officials have been concerned that public support in the West would be undermined if too many civilians are killed or hurt.

"NATO did not intentionally target the Chinese Embassy in Belgrade last night, " said the NATO spokesman, Jamie Shea. "The wrong building was attacked. This was a terrible accident. NATO deeply regrets the loss of life, and injuries to Chinese diplomatic personnel or to any other civilians in the Embassy at the time."

*   *   *

May 27, 1999

TRIBUNAL IS SAID TO CITE MILOSEVIC FOR WAR CRIMES

By ROGER COHEN

BRUSSELS, May 26—The international tribunal in The Hague has decided to indict Slobodan Milosevic, the Yugoslav President, for war crimes and will formally announce the action on Thursday, Western officials said today.

Reuters

Slobodan Milosevic of Yugoslavia is to be charged with war crimes.

The officials, who spoke on condition of anonymity, declined to specify the charges for which Mr. Milosevic is to be indicted. But Louise Arbour, the chief prosecutor of the tribunal, began an investigation into responsibility for war crimes in Kosovo last year, and has intensified her inquiries in recent weeks.

The indictment of Mr. Milosevic, whose almost 12 years in power in Serbia have coincided with wave after wave of violence in the Balkans, is certain to pose added difficulties for the diplomatic quest to end the war in Kosovo.

Mr. Milosevic has been the object of steadily harsher condemnation from NATO leaders, who have recently dropped all diplomatic niceties in referring to him. But he has remained the sole interlocutor in Belgrade for Russian-led efforts that have been broadly supported by the United States and its allies to end the war.

"In effect, this decision has pulled out the rug from under the negotiating process," said one court official. Viktor S. Chernomyrdin, the Russian envoy to the Balkans, is due to visit Belgrade on Thursday for a meeting with Mr. Milosevic.

Paul Risley, a spokesman for the tribunal, said there would be a news conference Thursday at 2 P.M. at which the court's decision would be announced. He declined to provide any further details.

If the past is any precedent, Western governments may now find themselves under intense pressure to shun Mr. Milosevic, who has always denied any responsibility for Serbian war crimes in Bosnia and Kosovo that have been largely consistent in nature.

When the Bosnian Serb leader, Radovan Karadzic, and his top military officer, Gen. Ratko Mladic, were indicted for war crimes in Bosnia by the tribunal in 1995, Western leaders took the view that all official contacts with them should cease.

Although the indictment will formally oblige Western governments and other authorities to seek the arrest of Mr. Milosevic, it is unclear whether they will energetically pursue that aim. Mr. Karadzic and Mr. Mladic were indicted four years ago and their whereabouts are well-known to the NATO troops stationed in Bosnia, but neither man has been arrested. Unlike those two men, Mr. Milosevic is a head of state, which may make any attempt to detain him even more complicated.

If Western governments now determine that they can no longer do any business with Mr. Milosevic, the only alternative would appear to be his defeat and removal from office. But NATO has said repeatedly that this is not one of its war aims.

"The tribunal is an independent body, and we respect its decision," said Michael Steiner, the chief diplomatic adviser to Gerhard Schroder, the German Chancellor. "There is no point complaining or applauding. Now we will just have to see how the whole legal, military and diplomatic cocktail works."

It is just four years since Mr. Milosevic was invited to the United States to participate in the Dayton peace conference and became the Balkan politician around whom the Clinton Administration built a tenuous peace accord.

But the brutality of the Serbian campaign that has expelled about one million ethnic Albanians from Kosovo since NATO bombing of Yugoslavia began two months ago appears to have convinced President Clinton and many Western leaders that stability in the Balkans is incompatible with his rule.

Ms. Arbour, who only two months ago was complaining about the degree of cooperation from Western governments, has received extensive assistance from Western intelligence agencies in recent weeks, notably during visits to London, Bonn and Washington, officials said.

This information has complemented the research of court investigators, who have been questioning ethnic Albanian refugees in Kosovo and Macedonia. A month ago, Ms. Arbour said that her aim was to establish the responsibility for war crimes in Kosovo in "something close to real time."

Certainly, the slow-moving investigation into Mr. Milosevic's responsibilities for crimes in Bosnia and Kosovo—an inquiry that was started shortly after the special court was established in 1993—has accelerated dramatically in recent weeks.

What precisely Mr. Milosevic will be charged with is unclear. Several Western politicians—including the British Prime Minister, Tony Blair, and the German Defense Minister, Rudolf Scharping—have called the crimes in Kosovo "genocide." It is possible, but by no means definite, that the Yugoslav leader could be charged with genocide.

If Mr. Milosevic is ever brought to trial in The Hague, it appears certain that the primary difficulty of the investigators will be in establishing a credible link between him and the killing, looting, rape and other crimes that appear to have been committed by the Serbian forces marauding through Kosovo since NATO began bombing on March 24.

The Yugoslav President has argued that Albanians have been fleeing Kosovo as a result of the NATO bombing, which his Government has described as an act of "genocide" by Western governments.

Mr. Milosevic has long honed the art of "plausible deniability"—setting foot in Bosnia only once during the war, claiming ignorance of the actions of his army commanders, and avoiding written communication that has his name on it.

For example, he has long maintained the fiction that Bosnian Serb forces had no link to the Yugoslav Army during the Bosnian war, although all the officers were on the Yugoslav Army payroll. Similarly, he dismissed the Serbian-run prison camps for Muslims in Bosnia as "Muslim propaganda."

Although the tribunal is avowedly apolitical, its decision to indict Mr. Milosevic comes at a time when a sea change has occurred in the attitude of Western governments toward the Serbian leader.

Until the events of the last two months, Western leaders refrained from direct criticism of a man who had been the linchpin of the Dayton agreement.

This approach was consistent with the attitude that enabled Mr. Milosevic to be invited to the London peace conference on Yugoslavia in 1992 just weeks after an archipelago of brutal Serbian camps in Bosnia had been discovered. Similarly, three years later, he was invited to Dayton just months after the massacre of Bosnian Muslims at Srebrenica occurred.

But in recent weeks, Robin Cook, the British Foreign Secretary, has threatened Mr. Milosevic with extraordinary directness. "We know who you are," he said. "We know what your troops are doing. There will be no hiding place."

At the same time, Jacques Chirac, the French President, has started calling Mr. Milosevic "le dictateur"—an extraordinary departure from Gallic formality in addressing an elected head of state, albeit one heading a notoriously repressive system.

And Mr. Clinton has not hidden his radical rethinking of the Balkan conflict, apologizing for past statements in which he attributed the killing to "ancient tribal rivalries" and addressing Mr. Milosevic's responsibilities with a new and punishing directness.

The Serbian acts in Kosovo, in so far as it has been possible to determine them up to now, appear to bear a striking resemblance to actions in Bosnia, where over 750,000 Muslims were driven from their homes between April and September 1992.

But seven years later, a Western readiness to confront these methods through judicial means and the use of force appears to have emerged after a long period of uncertainty. How—if at all—these methods can be combined with diplomacy involving Mr. Milosevic remains unclear.

"If you are just looking at a tactical, day-by-day approach, this may look like a setback," said Mr. Steiner, the German diplomat. "But perhaps in terms of long-term strategy, it will not prove to be a setback after all."

*   *   *

May 28, 1999

SERBS DISMISS INDICTMENT AS JUST ANOTHER ENEMY TACTIC

By STEVEN ERLANGER

BELGRADE, Serbia, May 27—The Yugoslav Government scornfully dismissed the indictment today of President Slobodan Milosevic and four other top leaders on war crimes charges in Kosovo and repeated its desire to solve the conflict through negotiation.

Goran Matic, a Yugoslav Minister Without Portfolio, called the indictment a political event directed by Washington and designed to step up pressure on the Belgrade Government to agree to a less favorable deal over Kosovo. He said the tribunal had no standing to indict the officials because his country was not engaged in war, but in an internal police action.

He also said that Belgrade was concentrating on the visit planned for Friday by the Russian peace envoy, Viktor S. Chernomyrdin, who will be bringing a more detailed draft of a possible settlement to end the war. In an interview, Mr. Matic said he hoped that NATO remained serious about negotiating a deal.

Mr. Matic accused Washington officials of using the international war crimes tribunal in The Hague to go after those who disagreed with them. "The Hague tribunal belongs to the sort of inquisition used by the U. S. to annul sovereignty and legal order in other countries which they dislike," he said at an earlier news conference.

"If they cannot kill them when they hit their residences, they can ask for their exclusion from the international community in the countries which they control via NATO," he said. He was referring to a NATO missile that hit Mr. Milosevic's bedroom last month, two nights after he had last slept there.

Mr. Milosevic himself made no comment on the indictment, nor would he, said senior Yugoslav officials. He met the former Greek Prime Minister, Constantine Mitsotakis, who said Mr. Milosevic seemed unruffled by the indictment.

"It appeared that he did not care," Mr. Mitsotakis said. "I believe that this decision will strengthen his position in the same way that the NATO bombings did."

In an official statement issued by the state news agency, Tanjug, the indictment was called "just another way of stopping diplomatic attempts to solve the crisis through peaceful political negotiations."

Describing the tribunal's chief prosecutor, Louise Arbour, as "a puppet in the hands of the masters of war," the statement called the indictment "another attempt to mislead the world community in order to conceal who is really responsible for the genocide against the Yugoslav people."

Mr. Milosevic told Tanjug that Yugoslavia wanted peace, "which means an early solution of problems should be transferred from the military to the political sphere."

And Mr. Mitsotakis insisted that "the Yugoslav leadership is ready to take a constructive approach to the proposals of NATO and the international community that are going to be presented" by Mr. Chernomyrdin.

"There are still problems, but the Yugoslav leadership is ready to contribute for their solution," he said. "NATO must contribute as well."

There were few details available here of what proposals Mr. Chernomyrdin might be bringing as a result of his discussions in Russia with the Deputy Secretary of State, Strobe Talbott, who flew on to Bonn with the Finnish President, Martti Ahtisaari.

But the makeup of an international force to police a Kosovo settlement is a key issue, and Mr. Chernomyrdin is said to be concentrating on non-American troops, like German and Italian ones, as the core of a NATO contingent.

The official state radio and television led their broadcasts with the Mitsotakis visit, showing Mr. Milosevic appearing confident and healthy.

The indictment was given broad coverage, though the concentration was on Russian, Greek, Chinese and other criticism of its validity and timing. There was also a series of interviews with ordinary, unnamed Serbs on the street, who generally said that the indictment would backfire against NATO, that Mr. Milosevic represented the country and that he should pay no attention to what the "aggressors" did.

Later this evening, NATO strikes again took out electricity in Belgrade, another attack on essentially civilian services that most people here regard as a cruel and inhumane form of collective punishment.

Even Serbia's democratic opposition parties were critical today of the timing of the indictment, suggesting that it put Mr. Milosevic into a corner and would reduce his willingness to make a serious compromise for peace.

The spokesman for the Democratic Party, Slobodan Vuksanovic, called the indictment "a disaster for democrats and for the nation in general."

"It seems to be a signal sent by the international community and NATO that they don't want to stop the attacks," he said.

Mr. Vuksanovic said: "There was hope yesterday. Today there is not. We think the accusation from The Hague comes at the wrong moment."

His party is led by Zoran Djindjic, who has fled to Serbia's sister republic, Montenegro, where he said the most important priority was to end the war.

Asked today if any Serb believed that Ms. Arbour and the international tribunal were acting independently of NATO and Washington, Mr. Matic, the Yugoslav minister, said: "Maybe Zoran Djindjic. Maybe."

The president of the Serbian Civic Alliance of opposition parties, Goran Svilanovic, accurately predicted that the state-run news media would portray the indictment as an attack on the Serbian people, not on Mr. Milosevic and the Government, and said it would further strengthen the President's hold on power.

Aleksa Djilas, a historian, said it would be better for all concerned if Mr. Milosevic "dies a peaceful death in his bed."

If NATO kills him "or puts him on trial in The Hague, he will be a martyr and a hero to most Serbs," Mr. Djilas said. "And he will then in this way rule Serbia from his grave or from his prison cell."

One Serbian analyst who requested anonymity saw the indictment as an invitation to a coup against Mr. Milosevic, but then pointed out that anyone in a position to mount such a coup had also been indicted today.

In general, ordinary Serbs regard the actions of their security forces in Kosovo as a war against the insurgent Kosovo Liberation Army, which is fighting to separate the Serbian province and make it independent. They consider the expulsion or flight of ethnic Albanians to be a regrettable aspect of that war against a popular, village-based insurgency. And they consider a large part of the charges by NATO and the tribunal to be unproved or propaganda.

Ivica Dacic, the spokesman for Mr. Milosevic's Socialist Party, said that Serbs and Mr. Milosevic were simply defending their country against outside aggression.

"This is a precedent in world history," he said, "when someone defending his country is accused of war crimes."

Mr. Dacic called the indictments "just a show directed by NATO criminals who are trying to throw dust into the eyes of their publics and the world in order to hide their own crimes."

But Belgrade's position on a settlement remains the same, he said.

"We support the continuation of the political process, with the aim to find a peaceful solution through diplomatic means on the principles of sovereignty and territorial integrity of Serbia and Yugoslavia, and equal status for all national communities in Kosovo."

*   *   *

May 29, 1999

THE RAVAGING OF KOSOVO, A SPECIAL REPORT

How Serb Forces Purged One Million Albanians

By JOHN KIFNER

On the night of March 24, as NATO bombs began falling over Yugoslavia, Hani Hoxha said he saw black-masked Serbs swaggering through Djakovica, shooting, cutting throats and burning houses.

At 3:30 in the morning, about nine miles east, a tank pulled up and parked in front of Isuf Zhenigi's farmhouse in the village of Bela Crkva. At daybreak the slaughter began there.

That day, in Pec, 22 miles to the northwest, and Prizren, 15 miles southeast, Serbian forces began firing wildly and burning Albanian-owned shops.

Meanwhile, in Pristina, about 44 miles to the northeast, Serbian operatives driving military jeeps and private cars set fire to Albanian-owned cafes, clinics and the printing presses of Kosova Sot, an independent Albanian newspaper.

These were the opening assaults in what quickly became a drive to empty the city, the provincial and intellectual center of Kosovo.

As it began, the Serbs' purge of more than one million ethnic Albanians from Kosovo seemed from the outside to be a random kaleidoscope of violence. But a reconstruction of the early days of the operation—based on interviews with scores of refugees, and with senior officials in Washington and NATO, as well as on a computer analysis of reported horrors from many sources—shows that it was meticulously organized and aimed, from the outset, at expelling huge numbers of people.

From this reporting over the last nine weeks, it is possible to see the design behind the roster of atrocities cited by the United Nations war crimes tribunal in The Hague in its indictment on Thursday of President Slobodan Milosevic of Yugoslavia and four of his top officials for crimes against humanity.

With specific charges including the wave of killings in Djakovica and its surrounding villages and the forced expulsion of Albanians from Pristina, the indictment charged the Serbian forces with a "campaign of terror" that "intentionally created an atmosphere of fear and oppression through the use of force, threats of force and acts of violence" in order to drive out Kosovo's majority Albanians.

The Serbs have insisted in recent months that most of the refugees fled Kosovo because of NATO's bombing. Western officials, however, say the plans were drawn up by the Yugoslav Army and the Interior Ministry of the Serbian Republic and carried out, under a single command, by a variety of Serbian forces acting in concert: regular soldiers, the blue-uniformed Special Police of the Interior Ministry and the dreaded private armies of ultra-nationalist warlords who had achieved a reputation for blood lust and looting in Bosnia and Croatia.

The plan was a harsh refinement of a campaign last summer by Interior Ministry forces that failed to crush Albanian rebels. It was put into effect after a mounting campaign of terrorism on both sides, including the ambushing of Serbian police patrols and officials by the Albanians and several instances of the kidnapping and killing of Serbian civilians.

But in retrospect, it seems evident that the operation had at least two major goals from its inception: crushing the rebel Kosovo Liberation Army and permanently changing the ethnic balance of Kosovo by driving out as many Albanians as possible.

Hounding more than a million Albanians from their homes accomplished two purposes for the Serbs.

First, it removed the guerrillas' base of support and cover, in effect, drying up the sea in which the guerrilla fish swam. With the Serbs controlling the borders and scorched earth along the highways, they could isolate and mop up the Kosovo Liberation Army in the forests and mountains. Young men viewed as potential rebel recruits were singled out and either killed or removed to an unknown fate.

In the longer run, depopulating Kosovo defused a demographic time bomb for the Serbs: Albanians already made up 90 percent of the population and were reproducing at a far higher rate than the Serbs.

Although killing and torching were plentiful, the Serbs' most potent weapon was fear. The seemingly random, flamboyantly public killings of the first few days meant that as the campaign progressed, all it took was a handful of armed, masked Serbs to drive thousands of people from their homes, rob them and send them off in caravans, their houses in flames.

Independent accounts indicate that there have been mass killings of from a dozen to roughly 100 people in more than 40 places. The State Department now puts the death toll at 4,600, a number only likely to increase as time goes on and more is known. But even that horrifying statistic indicates a goal of depopulation rather than extermination; it is low by comparison with the ethnic cleansing of Bosnia, where in one massacre alone, at Srebrenica, the Serbs were accused of killing 7,000 people.

To amplify the effect of the killings in Kosovo, Serbs gunned down Albanians in the streets and in their homes, sometimes at random, sometimes from target lists. Bodies have been mutilated, with ears cut off, eyes gouged out or a cross, a Serbian symbol, carved into foreheads or chests.

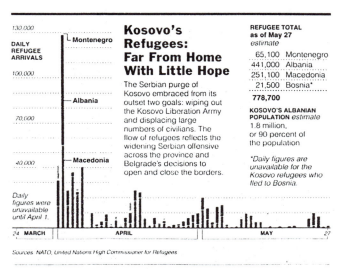

Sources: NATO, United Nations High Commissioner for Refugees

In many places the Serbs compounded the fear with humiliation. Older men were beaten for wearing the white conical hats of the Albanian mountains or forced to make the Serbian Orthodox three-fingered sign. One refugee convoy passed row on row of white conical hats set atop fence posts.

Two months into the campaign now, the terror has been devastatingly effective and virtually unhampered by NATO's bombing campaign, judging by accounts from refugees, relief workers and officials from international agencies, NATO and the United States Government.

By early May, 90 percent of all ethnic Albanians in Kosovo had been expelled from their homes, the State Department says, 900,000 driven across the province's borders and 500,000 more displaced inside Kosovo. Most of those remaining have been chased into hiding in forests and mountains, huddled together in villages penned in by snipers waiting to be allowed to flee, or captured, their fate unknown.

More than 500 villages have been emptied and burned, the State Department said.

And there was another element to the pattern: The Serbs made every effort to insure that those who fled abroad would not come back. Almost universally, refugees reported that they had been not only robbed but also systematically stripped of all identity papers, rendering them, in effect, stateless nonpersons, at least in the eyes of the Serbian government, and making it difficult for them ever to return home. Even the license plates of their cars—the Serbs kept the good ones—were methodically unscrewed at the borders.

"This is not your land—you will never see it again," the refugees were told. "Go to your NATO—go to your Clinton."

Djakovica: Emptying a City Of All but Bodies

The Serbs began attacking Kosovo Liberation Army strongholds on March 19, but their attack kicked into high gear on March 24, the night NATO began bombing Yugoslavia.

Djakovica was one of the Serbs' first major targets.

A look at a map explains the strategic significance of this city of 60,000, which was populated almost entirely by Albanians. The city and its surrounding chain of villages, stretching between Junik and Prizren, lie in the shadow of the Accursed Mountains, a remote, rugged range running along the border between Albania and Kosovo.

The Kosovo Liberation Army maintains its camps and staging areas on the Albanian side of the mountains. A Western military officer, sketching out a map, slashed a series of lines down the mountains into the valleys around Djakovica, indicating rebel infiltration routes. Clearly, he said, the Serbs want to empty the area of ethnic Albanians, fortify and control it to block the rebels.

Those who survived it say they will never forget the focused fury of the Serbian forces who attacked Djakovica in the hundreds hours after the first NATO bombs fell.

"A group of six men with masks came, and they took the women and children out of the houses, and they burned the houses," said Mehdi Halilaj, a 27-year-old economist, recalling that first night. "The first night they burned 50 or more shops and about 35 houses. They were helped by the police."

"They took 11 men and killed them, and some they cut up their bodies," he continued, speaking in English. "They left their bodies in the street for everybody to see, and nobody dared take them away. The city was very scared from Wednesday on."

A woman called Ardina, who asked that her family name not be used, said: "The second night we saw their lights, cars, trucks, an armored vehicle. They started shooting like I have never heard in my life. I thought everyone was dead."

"We were lucky," she said, speaking in English. "All the houses around us were burned and people killed. That night killed two brothers were, a man about 40 burned in his house and my sister-in-law with Down syndrome, they burned her in her house. She is dead. There was a body on the street, nobody could touch that body all day long."

As in many places, the Serbs were guided to the most affluent and influential families, the people who helped give the Albanian community its cohesion. It is not known whether this was on instruction, or perhaps motivated by the greed, or grudges, of individual attackers, but one effect may be to damage Albanian prospects for rebuilding their communities.

"In this block, they burned a lot of houses," Ardina said. "They were the best houses in town, the rich people," she said. "There was a Serb from the city guiding them. He told them: 'Burn this house. Kill this one.' Everyone in Djakovica knows him. They killed a large number of intellectuals, especially doctors. They shot a prominent surgeon, Dr. Izet Hima. They went for the rich people, to steal their television sets or whatever they see, burn their houses and kill them."

From the first days, the speed and scale of the Serbian campaign were stunning, even by the violent standards of Balkan wars as waves of paramilitary thugs, special policemen, regular soldiers and armed Serbian civilians swept through region after region of Kosovo, acting in concert.

The burning and killing in the center of Djakovica went on for three weeks beginning in the narrow streets and small Ottoman-style houses of the Old Town, and then moved on to the newer high-rise buildings in the more modern section. "In the beginning they were just burning at night," Ardina said. "But after a week they were burning all day long, starting at 9 o'clock in the morning."

"There were selected homes burned in the beginning, after that it was all the buildings," Dr. Flori Bakalli said, in English. "There were special police, local police, paramilitaries, and some of them civilians, armed. They were burning the houses and they started to scream like a wolf—'woo, woo'—and they shot people in the back. Near my house there were five of them I saw myself."

Ethnic Albanians moved from house to house and apartment to apartment, fleeing and moving in with relatives and friends, they said, to stay ahead of the advancing Serbs. In the old town, where many of the dwellings were built close together, Albanians broke holes through the walls so they could run from one home to another to escape if the Serbs knocked on the door.

Everybody, children included, slept fitfully in their clothes and shoes, ready to run. Someone had to be always awake, peering through a window or the peepholes of steel gates to see if the Serbs were coming.

Mr. Hoxha, a dignified white-haired man, took a reporter's notebook to sketch his family's compound and their futile attempts to elude Serbian attackers as they killed and burned their way through the neighborhood.

"We moved from one house to another and finally to my older daughter Tringa's house," he said. "That night I saw an old man, about 80, killed and burned and a 15-year-old boy as well. We stayed there for four nights, and the fifth night the Serbs came."

"It was around 12 o'clock, and we didn't have any electricity, when they came, about 30 people, paramilitary, V.J. and Serbs from Djakovica who had been given uniforms and guns," Mr. Hoxha said, using the initials by which the Yugoslav Army is known. "We were sleeping. My son-in-law was watching through the hole in the steel gate and came and told us to wake up."

They had parked a car sideways across the gate to block it, but the Serbs pushed through with a heavier vehicle. Thinking that the Serbs were looking only for men of military age, Mr. Hoxha and two other men climbed out a second-story window, dropped onto a wall and escaped.

He spent the next seven hours hiding in the narrow space between two buildings, squeezed between the concrete walls, listening to shouts and screams and gunshots.

In the morning he came back to the compound and found the bodies of everyone who had been left behind, some of the bodies burned. Later he said he had learned that the Serbs had first shot his 15-year-old daughter, Flaka, in front of her mother, then the older daughter, Tringa. His wife pleaded with them not to kill the children, but then they killed her. One of his granddaughters, Shihana, a spunky girl of 6, ran away and tried to hide in a closet, but they killed her there and set fire to the closet.

After he explained all this, he put his head in his hands and cried.

Next door, in the Caka family house, 20 people were hiding in the basement, when the Serbian forces broke in. They shot 18 people in the back of the head. A 10-year-old boy, Dren Caka, was somehow only wounded in the left arm, and escaped by pretending to be dead, and later gave his account to reporters at the medical tent set up at the Morini border crossing. After the Serbs left, he said, he managed to slip out a window, but he could not take his 2-year-old sister with him and she was burned alive when the Serbs torched the house. It was he who witnessed the killing of Mr. Hoxha's family.

Over the course of the assault, more than 100 boys—presumably regarded as potential Kosovo Liberation Army recruits—were captured, refugees said, and taken to a sports center. No one knows what has happened to them.

In just seven days, March 30 to April 5, some 51,880 people were herded on foot, according to records of the United Nations High Commissioner for Refugees, from Djakovica to a tiny remote border crossing in the mountains called Qafar-e-Prushit. The way looks like a road on a map, but it really becomes just a muddy footpath up the steep climb, which can be traveled only on foot because vehicles would set off the mines the Serbs had planted. They were city people in city shoes, and they pushed the sick and elderly along with them in wheelbarrows.

As Djakovica suffered, other Serbs were at work nearby purging a wide area they regarded as a rebel highway.

In a rare account by a Serb, a captured soldier described to NATO interrogators how his infantry battalion was sent without explanation to Pec.

On March 27, the soldier said, his commander gathered about 100 men outside an elementary school and outlined their mission: expelling Albanians from their homes. The time had come, he said, to drive the Albanians out of Serbia, according to an American official familiar with the account.

The troops were to move through the city house by house, he said, ordering residents to dress in a few minutes, pack one small bag and leave in the direction of Decani, a city to the south. The soldiers looted jewelry, torched homes. At day's end, many were driving new cars.

An artillery and armoured unit deployed to the nearby village of Ljubenic used rougher tactics. The soldier said a friend in the unit had told him they had killed 80 men while expelling the women, children and elderly.

In another of the region's villages, Bela Crkva (Bellacrkva in Albanian), on March 25, soldiers and special policemen torched the homes and farm buildings and killed at least 62 people, most of them gunned down with automatic weapons in a stream bend.

"They just started shooting," Mr. Zheniqi, a survivor, said in an interview. "The dead bodies behind me pushed me over a cliff and into the stream. I was lucky because all the dead bodies fell on top of me."

It was one of a series of mass killings over the next few days along a seven-mile stretch of villages in the rolling hills,

Heidi Bradner for The New York Times

HANI HOXHA, DJAKOVICA: Wedged in hiding between two buildings, he could hear gunshots and screams as Serbian irregulars stormed into his daughter's home and killed his wife, two daughters and other relatives. Only his three grandchildren are left.

including Celina, Pirane, Krush-e-Vogel (called Mala Krusa in Serbian) and Krush-e-Mahde (Velika Krusa), where Bekim Duraku remembered, life was so "beautiful, if someone offered to take me to the United States, I wouldn't have gone."

On March 26, the third day of the NATO bombing, the idyllic life ended in one of the best-documented of the mass killings, including an amateur videotape of the bodies. Serbian forces stormed through the village shooting down people in several areas, burning some bodies, digging a mass grave with a backhoe for others and leaving some lying in piles on the ground.

Villages: Expelling Refugees For a Relief Crisis

The violent emptying of the Djakovica region had a specific military purpose: cutting off the Kosovo Liberation Army supply lines. The Serbs followed it up by planting more mines, strengthening their forces along the border and mounting raids into Albania.

But in a long stretch of villages, towns and cities across Kosovo—places either close to the border or on main transportation routes—there were similar, if less intensely concentrated, outbursts of killing and burning in those same days with another aim: driving out the majority Albanian population.

How it worked is readily discerned by comparing the refugee figures kept at the Albanian, Macedonian and Montenegrin borders with a map of Kosovo. What the comparison shows is how areas close to the border were cleared first, often by wild bursts of killings that served as an example. This cleared transportation routes that facilitated the hounding out of people from other villages, who gathered in the main town of a region, and from the cities.

Sweeping his hands over a map in broad arcs across the major roadways, Fron Nazi, an Albanian-American scholar heading up a major human rights study and in touch with both refugees and the rebels, demonstrated how the Serbian strategy was apparent: first to empty the population centers and control that scorched earth, then to isolate the rebel fighters in the forests where they could be contained, squeezed and even starved out.

Forcing the refugees over the borders, NATO intelligence experts believe, served another purpose: overwhelming NATO troops stationed in Macedonia with an unmanageable relief crisis, calculating that the task of feeding, housing and caring for hundreds of thousands of refugees would consume the alliance's energies and divert it from preparing a military campaign.

"It was the first use of a weapon like this in modern warfare," a NATO intelligence officer said. "It was like sending the cattle against the Indians."

The refugees accounts in their thousands bear a striking sameness as they tell of Serbian gunmen bursting into their homes, threatening to kill if the Albanians do not give up jewelry, of seeing relatives or neighbors killed. Almost every Albanian interviewed begins by telling the exact time the Serbs arrived. But after days of hiding or plodding along in refugee columns, they often could not remember what day it was.

In many accounts, it is possible to discern a division of labor among the Serbian attackers.

Typically the Yugoslav Army, usually the Pristina Corps of the Third Army, surrounded an area, shelling it with tanks, artillery or Katyusha rockets. Then the police, local Serbs who were sometimes reservists, and the paramilitaries moved in for the close-in dirty work, going block by block, house by house, pounding on doors, demanding money, and often shooting people on the spot.

After the door-to-door terror, the military moved in to herd the people out, either on foot or tractor, or sometimes on trains and buses, the refugee accounts agree.

The Pristina Corps, in close conjunction with the blue-uniformed Serbian Interior Ministry troops, cleared transit routes. As the flow of refugees accelerated, regular soldiers in green camouflage were deployed at key intersections to control movement.

By all accounts, it was a tightly ordered, coordinated campaign, from the artillery that shelled villages, to the masked gunmen who killed, looted and spread terror, to the armored cars and lines of troops who chased people hiding in the woods to corral them in larger central towns for eventual expulsion. In some cases, human rights workers interviewing refugees say, different groups of gunmen were distinguished by different colored armbands or headbands.

Even the wild-appearing masked irregulars—Arkan's Tigers, the White Eagles and others—were under tight control, NATO experts said, and reported to the intelligence arm of the Serbian Interior Ministry.

"They were in there with Belgrade's blessing," a NATO intelligence official said. "What they would be allowed to do is up to the local commander."

The level of violence varied widely, depending on the whim of the local Serbian official in charge, or even individual gunmen. An international official visited a woman of about 50 in a hospital with both of her nipples hacked off.

"All she wanted was to tell her brother in Srbica what happened," he said, referring to a town in north-central Kosovo. "How could I tell her Srbica doesn't exist any more."

Some people were clearly targeted, particularly men age 15 to 50, suspected or potential rebel fighters, and those who worked for or rented space to the observer teams from the Office of Cooperation and Security in Europe. One key political activist who was a bridge between Kosovar factions, Fehmi Agani, was pulled off a train outside Pristina by the Serbian police and killed. There were reports by human rights groups that doctors had been singled out.

Evidence on the incidence of rape is less complete. President Clinton and other Western leaders often charge that there has been organized rape. But while it is clear that there have been rapes, accounts that are available do not resolve whether they were systematic. Rape was not mentioned in the indictment by the war crimes tribunal.

But for all the signs of a logic behind the purge of Kosovo, many of the individual episodes—including the gunning down of women and children—seem inexplicable in military terms, except that the very unpredictability of the savagery added the powerful fear that drove the exodus.

"That's what so terrifying—there are no rules," said an official in close touch with the international war crimes investigation in The Hague. "It's so random. One set of people might be spared, and the people next door do the same thing and are all killed. There was a man who gave the police 10 marks and they let go, and another who gave them 250, so they thought he must have more and killed him."

By the time, three weeks into the campaign, that the Serbs came to drive the ethnic Albanians out of the north-central city of Mitrovica, said Jacques Franquin, a United Nations official, it was enough for them to gun down an old woman and a teen-age girl in one neighborhood for everyone around to quietly board buses and be directed out of town through traffic control points.

Pristina: 'In Every House They Broke the Doors'

In Pristina, the knock on Bajram Kelmendi's door came at 1 o'clock in the morning of the night NATO started bombing.

"We will kill you if you do not open in five seconds," the Serbian police shouted, his wife, Nedima, recalled. Five uniformed policemen burst in, forced the family to lie on the floor and demanded money, one warning, "If you are lying, I will kill the little children."

They took away Mr. Kelmendi, a well-known human rights lawyer, and his two sons, age 30 and 16. They told the elder son, Kastriut, "Kiss your wife and two children because this will be the last time you see them," the elder Mrs. Kelmendi said.

The family found the three bodies by the side of the road two days later.

Brutal, too, but Pristina was different.

In the Djakovica region, the Serbs had a clear military goal: to cut off the Kosovo Liberation Army. But Pristina, like the other cities the Serbs emptied, was not a rebel stronghold. Indeed, in previous outbursts of fighting in Kosovo, villagers often went to stay in the city until things calmed down.

Born in the Drenica valley, the Kosovo Liberation Army was largely a rural movement and tied in with the traditional clans, although it did begin to pick up urban sympathy with a Serbian crackdown in March 1998.

Within the divided Kosovar society, Pristina was the base of the nonviolent leader Ibrahim Rugova and his Democratic League of Kosovo, whose tactics won the praise of Western leaders—mainly because they did not cause trouble. Among the city's educated elite, there had been suspicion and criticism of the Kosovo Liberation Army.

In Pristina, the Serbian aim appears to have been depopulation.

And from some of the targets chosen, like Mr. Kelmendi and Mr. Agani, the activist pulled from a train and killed, it also seems clear that the Serbs set out to destroy the Albanian political class and its institutions.

The office of Mr. Rugova's Democratic League was burned down on March 24, and a guard was shot and killed by the police at the newspaper Koha Ditore, whose publisher, Veton Surroi, had been a delegate at the talks in Rambouillet, France, early this year. The next night, the warehouse of the largest Kosovar charity, the Mother Teresa Society, was burned. On March 28, the house of Rexhep Qosja, a prominent academic, head of the Albanian Democratic Movement and another member of the Rambouillet delegation, was torched.

The first few days of the NATO bombing were marked in Pristina by nightly arson and bomb attacks on Albanian homes, shops and businesses, refugees recall. Police cars raced through the night, amid explosions and gunfire that terrified the Albanian residents. Some people began fleeing, mostly middle-class residents who had cars.

"At first, while the telephone was working, friends were calling and telling us this house was burning, or they arrested this guy and so on," said Ali Muriqi, 34, of the engineering faculty at Pristina University. "They were talking about intellectuals. Then at 6:30 in the evening, the electricity went off. Then the movement started, the police going around with weapons." Mr. Muriqi fled Pristina by car on March 29.

On March 30, in a chilling display of force, the Serbs began systematically emptying Pristina's neighborhoods—Vranjevci, Tashlixhe, Dardania, Dragodan—marching the Albanians along streets lined with gauntlets of masked gunmen draped with weaponry, refugees said.

By the tens of thousands—in an operation that required extensive advance logistical preparations—they were herded into the city's railroad station overnight. At dawn some were packed aboard trains—one refugee said he was among 28 people in a compartment meant for eight—bound for Macedonia. Others were loaded on buses and even a refrigerator truck that normally transports sides of beef and dumped near the Albanian border to leave the country on foot.

"I walked out into the garden, and there were three people with black masks and big guns," said Suzana Krusniqi, collapsing in tears as she crossed the Albanian border with her elderly parents the next day.

"In every house they broke the doors," she said, speaking in English. When we went out, everyone was in the street walking between men with black masks and big guns."

The forced exodus of Pristina gathered momentum in April. When the Serbs marched Ramadan Osmani and his family from their home to the railroad station in early April, he said, it was so crowded they had to wait 12 hours for a train to Macedonia, where they slept in a field for six days before finding a space at the Bojane refugee camp.

Some ethnic Albanians tried to stay in Pristina. Many lived a cat-and-mouse existence after eluding the first wave of Serbian looting and expulsions, hiding in other people's homes or fleeing to nearby villages. Fearing discovery, they left always by back doors, made little noise, lit candles only in rooms where heavy blankets covered the windows, and sent old people out to buy food.

Hafiz Berisha and his family evaded being expelled from Pristina for two months, hiding in five homes. But last Sunday, the 70-year-old retired policeman was standing in line to buy bread when Serbian policemen walked up and pulled his cousin and a neighbor, both men under 30, out of the line and hustled them away. Mr. Berisha said he had seen two people gunned down in front of him and 40 bodies in a mass grave, but the sight of the helpless men being led away was too much. "You can't even buy bread," he said. He fled the next day.

Luljeta Jarina, 19, and her father, Ramiz, who had worked in the personnel department of a mining company, were among those who went into hiding. Once when she ventured into the garden behind her home out of boredom, a Serbian sniper shot at her, she recalled. And each night, Serbian soldiers and policemen cruised the streets of the city, firing their Kalashnikovs wildly into the air. Just this Wednesday, the Serbs rounded up 18 men, including her father, at gunpoint. All but her father and two others were taken away, to an unknown fate, she said.

"We waited two months, hoping something would happen," she said.

On Sunday, they found a Serb cruising the city in a bus—a new entrepreneur driving refugees to the border for 20 to 100 German marks apiece, about $10 to $55—and fled their native land.

Michael R. Gordon, Thom Shanker, Carlotta Gall, David Rohde, Anthony DePalma, Barry Bearak, Josh Barbanel and Ford Fessenden contributed reporting to this article.

*   *   *

June 9, 1999

MOSCOW AND WEST AGREE ON KOSOVO; PLAN GIVEN TO U.N.

By R. W. APPLE Jr.

WASHINGTON, June 8—An end to the war in Kosovo crept closer today with agreement among the United States, six allies and Russia on a plan to send peacekeepers into the shattered Yugoslav province, perhaps in a week.

Shortly after the Russians, who had resisted certain provisions of the plan, dropped their objections at a conference in Cologne, Germany, NATO and Yugoslav generals reopened crucial negotiations at a remote site in Macedonia on detailed provisions for a withdrawal of Serbian troops from Kosovo. Negotiations on that subject, which had broken down over the weekend, continued into Macedonia's dawn.

In Washington, the Pentagon said there were signs that Serbian troops were already preparing to withdraw, although none had begun to do so.

Robin Cook, the British Foreign Secretary, said in Cologne that a Serbian withdrawal and a suspension of the NATO bombing campaign could take place "in the next few days." Joschka Fischer, the German Foreign Minister, said the Cologne agreement represented "a very decisive step toward peace."

Secretary of State Madeleine K. Albright was more guarded in public, but she told officials in Washington that she had "had a very good day."

Nonetheless, important questions remain to be resolved.

Among the most important was what an American diplomat tonight termed "a double Catch-22." The Yugoslavs were still insisting that they would not agree to withdrawal procedures until the United Nations Security Council had acted upon the Cologne agreement, which is in the form of a draft United Nations resolution that could be adopted as early as Wednesday.

The Russians and the Chinese, both with vetoes, do not want the Security Council to act until a bombing pause is in effect, and the United States and its NATO partners want to verify that a phased Serbian withdrawal is underway, in accordance with a detailed understanding with the Yugoslav military, before agreeing to a pause.

"It is not at all clear how we are going to untie that knot," a senior American official said, "but we're reasonably sure we can manage it."

For the second straight day, President Clinton telephoned President Boris N. Yeltsin of Russia in an effort to push the peace plan forward, and he also sent Deputy Secretary of State Strobe Talbott, a Russian expert, back to Moscow.

In addition to the sequence of agreements, votes and withdrawal, Mr. Talbott has another problem to resolve: the role of Russian troops in the peacekeeping force and who will command them. NATO is eager, as ever, to have a unified command-and-control system, with a single man in charge; the United States is particularly wary of any ambiguity, given its unhappy experience in a United Nations force in Somalia.

Russia, on the other hand, would like to have its troops under United Nations rather than NATO control, and has suggested placing them along Kosovo's northern border, with the rest of the peacekeeping force to the south. This has raised serious apprehensions in the West of a de facto partition of Kosovo.

Mr. Clinton said today that he did not expect Russian troops to fall directly under NATO control, but hoped that "there will be an acceptable level of coordination the way we worked it out in Bosnia." He added, "I think it's very important for the Russians to be involved in this"—at least in part, presumably, because of long-standing Russian ties to the Serbs.

The President continued to sound what he called "some note of caution" despite the day's developments, emphasizing that arrangements were not yet in place that would guarantee the safe repatriation of the refugees.

Missing from today's agreement at Cologne, which in most other respects replicated an accord signed by President Slobodan Milosevic of Yugoslavia last week, was a footnote in the earlier agreement specifying that the peacekeeping force would have "NATO at the core." Also missing was language stating that a unified NATO chain of command would be under the political control of the NATO nations, "in consultation with non-NATO force contributors."

Some American officials said the absence of that language signified nothing, but others said it could present serious problems down the road.

Another problem centers on Serbian insistence that, since the peace framework recognizes Yugoslav sovereignty in Kosovo, Serbian officials should be present at the border when ethnic Albanians begin to cross back into the province. NATO opposes that, on the ground that it could only intimidate the ethnic Albanians who have been driven from their homes in recent months.

"The place to come back is through border crossings," said Nebojsa Vujovic, the Foreign Ministry spokesman in Belgrade, referring to posts manned in part by Serbian officials. "There should be border crossings and customs officials to make sure there are not Albanian people who might be fishing in the mud and terrorists who might come over the mountains chasing Serbs."

Many refugees have no papers, their Serbian enemies having destroyed them, and it is not clear how it would be possible to tell ethnic Albanians from Albanian nationals, for example. But Kenneth H. Bacon, the Pentagon spokesman, said he did not foresee any problem, and other American officials said they were determined to deny the Serbs a role at the border.

Another Administration official said that regardless of what the Serbs want, the peacekeeping force eventually would control the borders and the United Nations High Commissioner for Refugees would oversee the resettlement of hundreds of thousands of refugees. The refugees' lack of papers, he said, should not complicate their return. The bigger challenge, he said, is to create conditions, including food, shelter, sanitation and security, that will permit their safe return.

Over the horizon, but perhaps only by a week or 10 days, is an even larger question that has not been addressed, that of a civilian representative in Kosovo after the peacekeepers enter. That has been a significant problem in Bosnia. While it is obvious that the representative would have broad powers—something like those of a proconsul, perhaps on the pattern of John J. McCloy as high commissioner in occupied Germany—many other things remain to be decided.

The exact job description, the chain of command and who will fill the post are all up in the air.

Britain, Canada, France, Germany, Italy, Japan and the United States—the G-7 countries—all signed the Cologne agreement, along with Russia. But after the Russian Foreign Minister, Igor S. Ivanov, affixed his signature, he said that the participation of Russian peacekeepers was not yet assured.

Mr. Bacon, the Pentagon spokesman, said the American contingent would include 1,900 marines from the 26th Marine Expeditionary Force now on board ships in the Aegean Sea as well as 1,700 Army personnel, including an aviation unit with at least eight Apache attack helicopters now in Albania.

Eventually, the force could number as many as 55,000 troops, including 7,000 Americans. The Russians might contribute as many as 10,000. Already, there are 17,000 British, French, German and other troops in Macedonia, and they would presumably form the vanguard of the international force.

At his daily briefing, Mr. Bacon said that United States intelligence had picked up signs that the Serbs were mobilizing heavy transport vehicles in Kosovo, which he described as a sign that Serbian forces were preparing to pull out. There are an estimated 40,000 Serbian army, police and paramilitary forces in Kosovo at present.

But until they start moving, in keeping with an agreed timetable, Mr. Bacon and his NATO counterpart, Jamie P. Shea, made clear that NATO air strikes would continue. Most of the 222 bombing strikes overnight Monday, Mr. Shea said in Brussels, were directed at Serbian forces near the Albanian border. B-52 bombers hit suspected Serbian troop concentrations there again today.

And tonight, while the peacekeeping force commander, Lieut. Gen. Sir Michael Jackson of the British Army, was meeting with Yugoslav generals in Macedonia, NATO strike aircraft attacked again, on the 77th day of the air war.

"We are not going to prematurely surrender the pressure of air operations and wait for President Milosevic to move," Mr. Shea declared.

*   *   *

June 10, 1999

SERB MILITARY ACCEPTS ACCORD, CLEARING WAY TO HALT BOMBING

By STEVEN LEE MYERS

KUMANOVO, Macedonia, June 9—The Yugoslav military tonight acceded to an agreement that will permit a military force commanded by a NATO general with sweeping powers to occupy Kosovo, clearing the way to an end to the Western alliance's first war.

The agreement, signed at a French helicopter base here not far from the border of Kosovo, was immediately approved by NATO leaders meeting in Brussels. The agreement gave the alliance's Secretary General, Javier Solana, the authority to suspend bombing once NATO verifies that the Serbian-dominated army, police and paramilitary units had begun to withdraw.

NATO and Pentagon officials have already reported detecting preparations for a withdrawal after 11 weeks of bombing, and the air campaign could be suspended as soon as late Thursday or Friday morning, an official here said, as long as the Serbs keep their pledges and begin to pull out.

The first of nearly 50,000 NATO troops will then move into Kosovo, replacing the retreating Serbian forces as they abandon their positions and head north. The Serbs will have 11 days to fully pull out or face a resumption of bombing. Under the plan, the province will be ringed by a five-kilometer buffer zone (about three miles) and divided into five sectors, each under the charge of a major power. NATO is to provide for the safe return of hundreds of thousands of Albanians who have either fled the country or been driven from their homes and are hiding in Kosovo.

Lieut. Gen. Sir Michael Jackson, the British officer who led the negotiations here, will command the peacekeepers, with the power to use whatever force he deems necessary to enforce the peace, insure the Serbian withdrawal, and keep President Slobodan Milosevic's troops from returning to Kosovo en masse.

"It is tragic that intransigence has made it necessary for the international community to resort to air strikes in order to reach a settlement," General Jackson said after emerging from a camouflage tent at the base here at 9:45 P.M. "However, NATO's resolve in conducting a sustained air campaign has finally achieved this agreement, and now is the time to look ahead," he added.

The agreement on the military details of Yugoslavia's withdrawal from its southern province, cherished as a symbol of Serbian history and culture, came a week after the Government of Mr. Milosevic agreed in broad terms to all of NATO's demands. Those included the withdrawal of all Serbian forces, the intervention of a NATO-led peacekeeping force and the return of the Kosovo Albanians who fled their homes.

In a compromise resolving one of the last, most nettlesome disputes in the talks here, NATO agreed on the 11-day period to complete the withdrawal of nearly 40,000 soldiers and police officers from the province, even though Mr. Milosevic's Government agreed last week to do so in only a week. The Yugoslav delegation here had asked for 17 days.

Secretary of Defense William S. Cohen warned tonight that if Mr. Milosevic orders his commanders to drag their feet or otherwise violate the accord, the air campaign will resume in full ferocity.

"In the event there's any reversal of their activities, in the event there's any evidence that they intend to simply try to bog this down in some other way, then we made it very clear, the document makes it very clear, the pause will no longer be in effect," Mr. Cohen said.

In Washington, President Clinton responded cautiously, perhaps mindful of the weeklong delay in nailing down the terms of the withdrawal.

"The agreement reached today by NATO and Serbian military officials is another important step toward achieving our objectives in Kosovo," he said. "It lays out the details to meet the essential conditions for peace: the rapid, orderly withdrawal of all Serb forces from Kosovo and the deployment of an international security force, called KFOR, with NATO at its core, which means a unified NATO chain of command so the Kosovars can return home safely."

But how long that will take—along with myriad questions about the future of the Kosovar Albanian rebel organization, the Kosovo Liberation Army, and its armed struggle for independence—remained unclear in spite of tonight's agreement.

Although the return of refugees has become one of NATO's fundamental objectives in the wake of the bombing campaign, NATO hopes to hold off a rush of returning refugees until its forces have made it safer. In addition to land mines and booby traps left behind, a major concern of NATO commanders is the possibility that at least some Serbian soldiers and police officers will simply shed their uniforms and remain in Kosovo with weapons, ready to harass NATO troops or returning refugees, the official here said.

The accord specifies that to establish a stable peace, no Yugoslav or Serbian forces may "enter into, re-enter or remain within the territory of Kosovo."

Although the six-page agreement signed here tonight explicitly authorizes a resumption of the bombing if the Serbs violate the timetable for withdrawal, it is not clear how NATO could respond to low-level menacing of its troops.

Another major concern is the willingness of the rebels to abide by the agreement, which calls for them to disband as an organized force and turn over their heavy weapons. Mr. Clinton said the alliance had contacted members of the rebel force and received assurances that they would not attack retreating Serbian forces or try to seize the territory they abandon.

"This will not be an easy operation and it will take time," General Jackson said. "I fully understand the wishes of the refugees to return home quickly, and I promise that KFOR will do its utmost to insure this is done as soon and as safely as possible."

Tonight's agreement came after a final 24 hours of talks that came perilously close to collapse once again. At one

Source: Defense Department

The New York Times

Deadlines in the Withdrawal Agreement

TODAY	JUNE 12	JUNE 15	JUNE 18	JUNE 20
Serbian forces in zone 3 must begin to withdraw through designated exit points. No Serbian aircraft may fly in the air safety zone.	All aircraft and air-defense systems must be removed from the air safety zone.	All Serbian forces must be withdrawn from zone 1.	All Serbian forces must be withdrawn from zone 2.	All Serbian forces must be withdrawn from Kosovo, and outside the ground safety zone.

The New York Times

point, they appeared to break down completely, when the Yugoslav delegation, led by Col. Gen. Svetozar Marjanovic, abruptly left the helicopter base here late this afternoon, saying they needed to consult with authorities in Belgrade.

The delegation, however, made it only as far as a border post north of here, in Serbia itself. After telephone discussions with authorities in Belgrade, the delegation returned to the base an hour after they left, and the talks resumed.

Tonight, General Jackson and General Marjanovic signed the agreement in what one official described as a subdued, unceremonious end to five days of wrangling. They did not shake hands.

Eager to avoid the appearance of capitulating to NATO's demands, the Yugoslav delegation had insisted that a withdrawal not begin until the United Nations Security Council, with Russia and China wielding veto power, had given the peacekeeping force its formal approval.

But when it became clear to the Yugoslav delegates today that the Security Council would not force NATO to halt its bombing before a withdrawal and would authorize the peacekeepers under the chapter of the United Nations Charter that permits the use of force, they relented, according to a NATO official who attended the talks.

NATO officials, who have described these talks not as negotiations, but rather as the ironing out of the details of last week's agreement, said the final document reflected refinements that the foreign ministers of seven industrial nations, along with Russia, had agreed to in Germany on Tuesday. It also put the NATO-led peacekeepers under the auspices of the United Nations, giving them what General Jackson called "a clear legal basis" for the peacekeeping force. Not only the Serbs, but also some NATO allies had insisted on United Nations leadership.

Significantly for the Serbs, the document does not mention NATO explicitly. Neither did General Marjanovic when he appeared before a scrum of television journalists to announce the signing tonight. "It means that the war has ended," General Marjanovic said. "It also means that the policy of peace prevailed."

However, the NATO official who attended the talks said the mood was far from celebratory, indicating that the alliance remained wary of Mr. Milosevic and his intentions.

"It's not what he says," the official said. "It's not what he signs. It's what he does."

In the meantime, NATO continued to amass forces here in Macedonia for the operation in Kosovo. On Thursday morning, the Unites States Army plans to send in a wave of helicopters, including Apache gunships, along with 1,700 soldiers, who sat out the air war in Albania.

*   *   *

June 11, 1999

BOMBING ENDS AS SERBS BEGIN PULLOUT

By CRAIG R. WHITNEY

BRUSSELS, June 10—NATO suspended its bombing of Yugoslavia today after Serbian troops began withdrawing from Kosovo, halting an assault that rained 23,000 bombs and missiles on Serbia without losing the life of a single NATO fighter.

The halt in the bombing after 78 days set the stage for the United Nations Security Council's swift approval of a resolution that permits 50,000 international peacekeepers to move in to help more than a million Albanian refugees driven out of Kosovo to try to return.

NATO's Secretary General, Javier Solana, announced the suspension of the bombing in midafternoon European time, morning in the United States.

"I would urge all parties to the conflict to seize this opportunity for peace," he said, adding that the moment was a result of allied determination and intense diplomacy by many countries, including Russia.

Allied leaders on both sides of the Atlantic were restrained in claiming victory in NATO's first war, a fight that took a toll not only on the Serbs and Kosovars, but also at times on the allies themselves. The war challenged the alliance, leaving it transformed and helping to determine its course in the coming century.

"We have to finish the job and build the peace," President Clinton said today, while Prime Minister Tony Blair of Britain said, "I feel no sense of triumph now, only the knowledge that our cause was just and rightly upheld."

President Jacques Chirac of France said, "A page has been turned in the conflict."

Stephen Crowley/The New York Times

An Army helicopter transporting members of the 82d Airborne Division arriving at an American base outside of Skopje, Macedonia.

With their approval and that of other allied leaders, Mr. Solana halted the bombing after Gen. Wesley K. Clark, the Supreme Allied Commander in Europe, confirmed that the withdrawal of 40,000 Serbian soldiers, police officers and paramilitary units had begun at midday.

Several hundred Yugoslav Army military trucks bearing soldiers clogged the road north from Pristina, the capital of Kosovo, today, more than 12 hours after Yugoslav military commanders agreed to allied terms with the commander of the peacekeeping force in Macedonia on Wednesday night. Allied commanders swore vigilance to make sure the Serbian forces lived up to the agreement.

President Slobodan Milosevic of Yugoslavia, in his first address to his people regarding the conflict with NATO, did not claim victory for the Government today, but instead thanked ordinary citizens for their contributions and sacrifices. In the televised address, he said, "The aggression is over, happy peace to us all."

The first deployment of NATO peacekeeping troops had been scheduled for Friday. But it will probably be delayed until Saturday because Serbian forces have encountered dif-

Goran Tomasevic/Reuters

Yugoslav army withdrawing near Podujevo. The allies confirmed 40,000 Serbian troops had begun to pull out.

ficulties in carrying out their withdrawal, Western officials said.

"The Serbs are having trouble getting their equipment out," a senior Western official said. "Their equipment is broken and out of fuel" and they need more time to clear the road of mines. The official said the Serbs were wary of moving at night because they fear the Kosovo Liberation Army.

Once bombs were no longer falling—a condition Russia, China and France had set for a Security Council vote—the Council reconvened in New York City today and quickly approved a resolution that had been worked out earlier this week in Cologne by the European allies, the United States, Russia, Canada and Japan.

The vote this morning, 14 to 0 with one abstention, China's, put Kosovo under international civilian control and placed the peacekeeping force under United Nations authority.

Lieut. Gen. Sir Michael Jackson of Britain, the force commander, was set to start leading the 18,500 European and American soldiers in Macedonia into Kosovo. NATO ambassadors met again tonight and approved an operation order clearing the way for the move, which is expected eventually to involve a total of around 50,000 troops, mostly Europeans from allied and other countries, with about 7,000 Americans.

Russian troops, expected to number about 2,500, could also join if Deputy Secretary of State Strobe Talbott and American military negotiators who met Russian officers in Moscow today can work out command arrangements for them. Russia was vehemently opposed to the NATO bombing and says it will not put its troops under the alliance's orders.

Allied warplanes flew their last 82 strike missions Wednesday, the allied command said, but will continue flying reconnaissance missions to monitor the Serbian withdrawal, which is to be completed within 11 days.

"Violence or noncompliance by any party will not be tolerated," Mr. Solana warned. But he said that the alliance and other international organizations would now try to help all the ethnic groups of Kosovo, including the Serbs, to build a society free of the repression that had spawned the conflict in the first place.

The bombing campaign sorely tested and profoundly changed the 50-year-old alliance, which never fired a shot in anger during the cold war.

It surmounted objections to the use of force to make peace in Kosovo, but at the price of a strategy that retired generals from San Diego to Vladivostok said would never succeed, using air power alone to try to prevent and then reverse the expulsion of the ethnic Albanian majority living in hallowed Serbian territory in Kosovo.

In the end it was diplomacy, by Western powers and by Russia, that tipped the balance, convincing President

Milosevic that he had no choice but to accede to international demands and make peace in Kosovo. Now the alliance has taken on the challenge of keeping the peace, a challenge that may prove even more difficult than waging the air war.

Preserving unity among 19 allies during more than two months of a bombing campaign was a formidable task, one that allied diplomats from several countries today said Mr. Solana had handled with diplomatic skill.

From Britain, which alone among the allies argued for preparations for an invasion of Kosovo with troops on the ground to force Mr. Milosevic to accept their will, to Greece, where opposition was strong against using force against a fellow Orthodox Christian nation, the allies constantly questioned the air war strategy, but never could agree on anything better.

In the end, Mr. Solana always insisted, NATO's air war was about human values, about 21st-century Europe not tolerating the throwback to 20th-century totalitarian brutality that the allies said Mr. Milosevic's "ethnic cleansing" in Kosovo represented. In this, NATO had public opinion behind it on most of the Continent.

"What Milosevic didn't reckon with," said a European diplomat at NATO, "was the effect on public opinion of seeing all those hundreds of thousands of refugees streaming out of Kosovo. It reminded all Europeans of the scenes they had seen during World War II and caused immediate and long-lasting revulsion."

NATO's bombing took the highest toll on Serbia, where President Milosevic, in his address today, called for unity to rebuild the country.

Led by Germany's Chancellor, Gerhard Schroder, foreign ministers of the world's seven largest industrial democracies plus Russia met with Balkans leaders in Cologne today and agreed to commit money and effort to a stability pact.

The "Schroder Plan," which European leaders say could cost $5 billion to $6 billion a year for many years, aims at raising all the Balkans to the economic and social level of the rest of Europe, in an effort to make another war there after a decade of ethnic conflict as unthinkable as it is now in France, Britain or Germany.

"Europe cannot be fully secure unless its southeast corner is free from strife," Secretary of State Madeleine K. Albright said in Cologne today, warning Mr. Milosevic against putting political or military pressure on Montenegro, another constituent republic of Yugoslavia whose leaders did not support his attacks in Kosovo.

Now NATO hopes its relationship with Russia can slowly begin to recover from the damage it suffered from the bombing campaign. Russian officials have refused to attend regular meetings at the alliance headquarters since the bombing began on March 24.

*　　*　　*

June 22, 1999

NATO'S PEACEKEEPING FORCE, DEFIED BY BOTH SIDES, STRUGGLES TO KEEP ORDER

By DAVID ROHDE

MITROVICA, Kosovo, June 21—For the third consecutive day, several dozen Serbs in civilian dress who call themselves "warrior citizens" prevented ethnic Albanians from entering the predominantly Serbian sector of this northern Kosovo industrial town today, jeering and threatening any Albanian who dared to enter.

In a direct challenge to NATO authority, the Serbs are declaring their neighborhood, about a third of the city, and the predominantly Serbian towns to the north a "Serbian zone." The area stretches the width of a valley 30 or so miles from here to the border with Serbia.

NATO officials say that for now their strategy is to avoid confronting the Serbs and to hope that the situation will calm over time.

"The important thing is to reduce tensions through maintaining a physical presence there," Lieut. Gen. Sir Michael Jackson, the commander of NATO forces in Kosovo, said at a news conference today. "The principal goal is to lower tensions."

French troops continued to provide escorts for Kosovo Albanians and Serbs wishing to enter either part of the city. But they also continued to allow small crowds of Serbs in civilian dress to stand at the ends of the two bridges dividing the neighborhoods and to berate any Albanian who tried to enter.

At dusk today, tensions appeared higher than on Sunday, and the de facto partitioning of the city only seemed to be hardening. Serbs were fleeing into the Serbian section of town while few Albanians dared to enter that area. The Serbs made it clear that partition was their goal.

"This is going to be like Beirut," said George Petrovic, a member of the Serbian group blocking Albanians. "This is going to be the green line."

How NATO chooses to respond to initial challenges is likely to set a tone for the entire mission and could prove crucial in determining its authority and effectiveness here. The incidents, particularly the standoff here in Mitrovica, reflect on a thorny problem that confronted NATO troops in Bosnia and faces them again here.

The issue is how heavily armed NATO troops should respond to civilian crimes. NATO commanders in Bosnia, fearing that it would go beyond the scope of their mission, generally have not responded to crimes like looting, declaring them the responsibility of civilian police.

The standoff in Mitrovica is the latest in a series of incidents in which French troops appear to be acting less aggressively or responding more slowly than other NATO troops. In Srbica, the largest city in the Drenica region in central Kosovo, French soldiers allowed the rebel Kosovo Liberation Army soldiers to take over the town last week and to carry their weapons during an initial grace period. And on Sunday and again today, French forces were slow to respond to looting by Kosovo Albanian civilians in the abandoned Serbian village of Grace, 20 miles south of here.

In general, British and American troops have been more aggressive than other NATO forces in stripping the Kosovo Liberation Army of weapons. And British soldiers responded first to looting in Grace today and on Sunday, even though it was two miles outside their area of responsibility here.

French officers contend that they are being aggressive, but are handicapped because their entire force has not yet arrived in Kosovo.

General Jackson made clear today that he wanted to establish an atmosphere that would not tolerate looting. But as he spoke, abandoned Serbian houses in Grace were on the verge of being set aflame.

By 1:30 this afternoon, half a dozen Serbian homes were burning in Grace. Dozens of local Albanians were streaming out of the town in tractors loaded with windows and roof tiles that appeared to have come from the homes, as well as fences, stoves, bureaus, water heaters, clothes, television antennas and scores of other items. Some looters ignored a reporter's questions, but others grinned and waved as they went about their work.

"We burn the houses so they won't have a way to come back," said a young Albanian. "We cannot live with them. They leave or we leave."

A half hour later, a British battle tank and dozens of French Foreign Legionnaires swept into the town, sending the looters quickly to their tractors. In a reflection of NATO's continuing confusion about how to handle such situations, French officers at first allowed the Albanians simply to leave with their tractors and the goods. One French jeep even helped tow an apparent looter's jeep from a ditch after it became stuck.

But British forces who arrived at the scene sealed off the three entrances to the village, catching about 40 tractors inside. Then the French commanders called in French military policeman to investigate the looters. The Albanians, surrounded by NATO troops they see as liberators, expressed more confusion and surprise.

"I don't agree with all that is going on," said Ibrahim Hajrudinaj, one of the looters. "I think it's primitive. But I need something to live with. I'm taking some things that are mine and some things that are not mine to bake some bread."

The show of force apparently did not impress all the Albanians. As the group waited for French military police to arrive, at least seven Albanian men slipped back into the village and began lighting fires in more abandoned Serbs' homes. They were arrested by French troops and were being held for questioning last night. Looters were allowed to keep perishable food but were forced to return other items, NATO officials said.

In Mitrovica, where the Serbs were making their own challenge to NATO authority, they stood beside a spot where a small mosque was destroyed during the NATO bombing. The Serbs cursed, jeered and shouted ethnic slurs at Albanians who tried to enter the neighborhood, calling them "terrorist" members of the Kosovo Liberation Army.

This afternoon, the French said they had reached an agreement with the Serbs to allow women and children to pass. But when one Albanian woman tried to cross, the Serbs kicked and spat on her as French soldiers struggled to control the crowd. She was finally allowed to enter when a Serb she knew stepped forward and escorted her.

Another four Albanian women tried to cross later this afternoon, but the Serbs jeered and taunted them. French soldiers told the Serbs to quiet down, but at that point the Albanian women were so frightened they refused to enter the area.

One shooting incident occurred in the Serbian area this afternoon when French troops reported a shot fired over their heads. Three Kosovo Albanian men were detained at dusk, but they insisted that they were not involved.

By the end of the day three French police officers, the first of 135 to be sent here, quickly walked through the area. They said they hope to handle such disputes in the future, but they had little immediate impact yesterday.

As the sun began to set, Serbs said they were determined to keep the de facto partition in place. "This river and this bridge, they are a natural border," said Nikola Kabasic, one of the men there, who said he was a municipal judge. "We want to keep it that way."

* * *

June 29, 1999

U.N. SENDS REFUGEES BACK ON FIRST BUSES

By The Associated Press

PRISTINA, Kosovo, June 28—After two weeks of watching ethnic Albanian refugees travel home on their own, refugees returned to Kosovo from Macedonia today in the first bus convoy organized by the United Nations.

Seven buses with 335 refugees, escorted by representatives of the United Nations High Commissioner for Refugees, left the Stenkovec 1 camp. Dozens of other refugees were picked up at Stenkovec 2 for the trip to Pristina.

Less than three hours later, the buses arrived in the capital, where each refugee received rations.

"I am very happy we came back to a free Kosovo," said Luljeta Sherifi, 20, on arriving.

Hundreds of thousands of refugees have ignored pleas to delay their returns until mines can be cleared.

* * *

July 24, 1999

NATO PATROL FINDS BODIES OF 14 SERBS NEAR PRISTINA

By The Associated Press

PRIZREN, Kosovo, Saturday, July 24—The bodies of 14 men, apparently Serbs, were found on a farm road in central Kosovo about 10 P.M. Friday, after a NATO patrol heard shots in the area, a spokesman for the peacekeeping force said early today.

NATO said a patrol heard shots near the mixed Serb and ethnic Albanian village of Gracko, about 20 miles southeast south of Pristina, at 9:30 P.M.

Thirteen males were found shot dead near a combine harvester about a mile outside of the village. Another body was found about 150 yards away on a tractor, NATO said.

The peacekeepers sealed off the area and military police were investigating.

Maj. Louis Garneau, a NATO spokesman, said all of the victims were believed to be Serbs.

"KFOR condemns this despicable act and calls upon the leaders of all communities in Kosovo to do the same," NATO said in a statement, referring to the peacekeeping force by a widely used nickname.

The killings were one of the worst single acts of violence in Kosovo since NATO peacekeepers entered the province in mid-June.

Peacekeepers have been struggling to curb attacks by Albanians on Serbs across the province, mostly believed to be revenge attacks by ethnic Albanians.

Tens of thousands of Serbs have fled Kosovo in the face of revenge attacks by returning ethnic Albanians, many of whom were infuriated to find their property destroyed and relatives dead or missing after the Serbian crackdown.

The report of the 14 killings came a day after the German Chancellor, Gerhard Schroder, in the first visit to Kosovo by a Western government leader, pledged moral and material aid to ethnic Albanians and Serbs but told them democracy was the key to their future.

"Without the democratization of Yugoslavia, there will be no Western support for reconstruction," Mr. Schroder said.

Meeting separately with ethnic Albanian political leaders and Serb religious figures, Mr. Schroder said he sought assurances that they would work together to build a democratic society where the two groups can live together in peace.

"All political leaders, including the Albanian side, accepted that this should be a multi-ethnic Kosovo, and that Serbs have a right to live freely and peacefully in Kosovo," he said.

*   *   *

July 30, 1999

REBUILDING THE BALKANS

President Clinton's meeting with more than 30 other national leaders in Sarajevo today offers a chance to get the postwar reconstruction of Southeastern Europe off to a sound start. Billions of dollars have already been pledged to help rebuild Kosovo and several neighboring countries. But a lot of this could be wasted unless Washington, the European Union and the United Nations show they have learned from their only partly successful efforts in Bosnia. This time, more must be done to build new locally based economic and political institutions so that international relief can give way to long-term recovery.

The Sarajevo meeting launches the Balkan Stability Pact, an international relief and recovery plan intended to help the Balkan region overcome its history of conflict and ethnic strife and speed its integration into democratic Europe. The main beneficiaries will be Kosovo, Albania, Macedonia and Montenegro, which like Kosovo is formally part of Yugoslavia. Help will also be available for Romania and Bulgaria.

So long as Slobodan Milosevic remains in power, most international reconstruction aid will rightly bypass Serbia. The point is not to punish the Serbs but to hasten Mr. Milosevic's downfall. Once he is gone, building a more democratic and prosperous Serbia will help cement regional stability.

Bosnia shows that it is best to avoid building big, overlapping international bureaucracies that attract corruption and crowd out local political and economic initiatives. Western intervention brought desperately needed peace to Bosnia. But unemployment remains devastatingly high, foreign investment minuscule and politics dominated by ethnic nationalist parties.

In Kosovo, international administrators need to make sure moderates and independents get a fair chance to compete politically with the activists of the Kosovo Liberation Army. The K.L.A. has begun forcibly taking over political institutions and businesses while the U.N. administration is still getting organized. Once U.N. officials take charge, they should set a reasonable target date for local elections to begin the process of establishing self-government. A degree of economic self-sufficiency can be attained relatively quickly by assisting local farmers in getting back on their feet. They need modern equipment and lower trade barriers for their exports.

President Clinton helped to free Kosovo from brutal Serbian rule and enable its refugees to return home. Now he must help consolidate a wider Balkan peace.

*   *   *

November 15, 1999

ELECTION TAKES MACEDONIA ANOTHER STEP TOWARD DEMOCRACY

By CARLOTTA GALL

SKOPJE, Macedonia, Nov. 14—The weather was dull, the streets in the capital quiet. And yet today's presidential election represented a landmark in the often authoritarian and violent politics in the countries of the former Yugoslavia, because Macedonia is the first to have a president step down and make way for new politicians.

President Kiro Gligorov, 82, who steered Macedonia to independence from Belgrade in 1991, avoided bloodshed and kept his fragile state together despite its volatile mix of Slavs and Albanians and its historic frictions with neighbors, will leave office this week.

"The important thing is that there is no vacuum of power without a president, and that a new president is elected democratically," Mr. Gligorov told reporters after casting his ballot. Badly scarred in an assassination attempt four years ago, President Gligorov has played an increasingly distant role in the last few years.

He is credited with guiding Macedonia's peaceful transition to independence and leaves this country of two million people as something of an example in its progress toward democracy, international election observers said.

Two men were contesting the runoff for the presidency today: Tito Petkovski, 54, a former speaker of Parliament and the chosen candidate of the Social Democratic Alliance, the former Communist Party, and Boris Trajkovski, 43, a Methodist preacher trained in Kentucky and deputy foreign minister for the last 10 months, who represents the VMRO party, which leads the coalition government.

Several hours after polling stations closed, Mr. Trajkovski's party claimed victory, but Mr. Petkovski's camp did not accept defeat. The final count was expected overnight. The votes of Macedonia's sizable Albanian minority—between a quarter and a third of the total population—were expected to play an important role in a vote overshadowed by calls for a boycott from some first-round losers. Mr. Trajkovski, unusually a Methodist member of the heavily Orthodox Slav majority, was expected to attract most of the Albanian vote.

Turnout appeared to have reached the necessary 50 percent plus one vote, election officials said.

The two contenders, both lawyers by training, waged lackluster campaigns. Mr. Petkovski, a sober, white-haired man, is seen as left-wing and more of a Macedonian nationalist appealing to older Macedonians and the small Serb minority. He has been attacked by his opponents as a Communist, whose party oversaw a period of sharp economic decline during their eight years in power until 1998.

Mr. Trajkovski's center-right party won a significant victory last year in parliamentary elections, but has already lost much popular support with the continuing economic decline in this landlocked country and the aggravations caused by the war in neighboring Kosovo.

The leader of the main Albanian party, Arben Xhaferi, has warned that Mr. Petkovski's politics are intolerant and dangerous.

"They say without scruple that they do not need the votes of Albanians and send a message to Macedonians not to allow Albanians to decide who can be the next president," Mr. Xhaferi said.

"Mr. Trajkovski is more human and more democratic," he said.

The Macedonian president does not exercise significant power under the Constitution, yet can block the passage of legislation and exercises a certain moral influence.

Both men are expected to continue pursuing the path set by Mr. Gligorov toward membership in NATO and the European Union.

Macedonia, which is host to some 5,000 NATO troops supporting the peacekeeping operation in neighboring Kosovo, is in a potentially precarious situation geopolitically. To the south, Greece imposed a complete blockade on Macedonia because of its claim to the name of Greece's northern province, lifting it only after a compromise was forged by United Nations mediation in 1995. Relations have been improving, and Greece is now a major investor in the country.

Bulgaria claims the Macedonian language as its own, Serbia disagrees about its borders with Macedonia, and Albania and Kosovo are perceived as threatening to Macedonian sovereignty because of their influence on the large Albanian community in northwestern Macedonia.

* * *

November 23, 1999

A GRATEFUL CLINTON OFFERS ENCOURAGEMENT TO BULGARIA

By MARC LACEY

SOFIA, Bulgaria, Nov. 22—President Clinton thanked Bulgaria today for supporting the NATO campaign against Slobodan Milosevic in nearby Yugoslavia and urged the struggling nation to stay the course of economic reform.

More than 10,000 people packed the central square under the glittering Cathedral of St. Alexander Nevsky—the same spot where mass rallies 10 years earlier led to the overthrow of the Communist government—and celebrated the visit with music and fireworks.

"I am very proud to be the first American president to visit Bulgaria—a free Bulgaria," Mr. Clinton told the crowd in a 45-minute speech at dusk. "I am proud to stand in this place where voices were silenced for too long."

He arrived late on Sunday, a week into his European tour, which will end with a trip to Kosovo on Tuesday. The visit here was intended to reward Bulgaria for letting NATO planes use its air space in the Kosovo campaign last spring, to offer some encouragement, and to send a message to the Serbs only 30 miles away.

"I am told that during the recent war you could actually hear some of the bombs falling in Serbia from this square," Mr. Clinton said. "Tonight, I hope the people of Serbia can hear our voices when we say if you choose as Bulgaria has chosen, you will regain the rightful place in Europe Mr. Milosevic has stolen from you, and America will support you too."

The crowd of people—most of whom were taught at an early age of the evils of America's imperialist ways—roared with approval and shouted Mr. Clinton's name.

"It used to be dangerous to talk to foreigners," said Kiril Manov, 70, a retired lawyer who was bundled up against the chilly evening air. "We used to learn about the evils of America. Never did we think an American president would stand here."

During his visit today, Mr. Clinton laid a wreath at a soldiers' memorial, spoke with a small group of college students over a lunch of tabbouleh and skewered chicken, and slipped out to a jazz club with President Petar Stoyanov.

During his visit to Kosovo, his first trip there, Mr. Clinton is to meet military commanders, opposition leaders and American troops, and is expected to urge the Albanians of Kosovo to set aside revenge as they rebuild after the war.

"I think it's very important that Kosovo, in effect, not become the mirror image of Serbia," he told the Bulgarians.

During his speech, the president held out the possibility of NATO membership for Bulgaria in the coming years and thanked the nation for allowing the alliance's jets to streak over Sofia during the air campaign in Kosovo. "You stood with NATO," he said. "I know it was very hard for you to do."

But most of all, Mr. Clinton's visit was intended to leave a measure of hope to a country still struggling with the difficult transition from dictatorship to democracy.

"I ask you to remember what you left behind," he said. "A police state with no room for disappointment, because there was no hope for improvement. When nobody felt left behind because no one was allowed to get ahead. When there were no dreams and some Bulgarians were even robbed of their very identities, forced to change their names."

The border with Serbia lies just 30 miles to the east of Sofia, the Bulgaria capital, so close that a handful of NATO bombs that veered off course actually landed here. The sanctions against Yugoslavia, a onetime trading partner, have had a crippling effect on Bulgaria's economy, which already suffered from a steep drop in living standards and high inflation that followed the Soviet era, a period when Bulgaria was one of the most Stalinist of the East Bloc countries.

American support is considered important to the people here, where jobs are difficult to come by, salaries are low, and gray concrete-block architecture stands as a reminder of a Communist system that left little room for initiative. Mr. Clinton arrived without bringing any big offers of aid, but he talked of a continued partnership with Bulgaria.

"Most of the people living here are desperate with the economic situation," said Ognyan Minchev, the director of the Institute for Regional and International Studies in Sofia. "This visit is a sign of hope."

That is how Snezhana Popova saw it. She stood in the back of the crowd with two tiny flags in her hand, one from the United States and one from Bulgaria. Mr. Clinton's visit, she said, just had to help make things better.

"It's very difficult to get a well-paying job here," she said.

The remark that most encouraged her came midway through Mr. Clinton's speech when he talked of plans to encourage more United States companies to do business in Bulgaria.

Bulgaria is making a push for entry into the European Union, which Mr. Clinton said ought to happen one day. In closed meetings with President Stoyanov and Prime Minister Ivan Kostov, he discussed Bulgaria's effort to reduce and modernize its Soviet-era military, among other issues.

As he encouraged Bulgarians to continue their reform efforts, the president reminded them that democracy has been a long road for the United States. He said it has taken America more than two centuries "to overcome slavery and civil war, depressions and world wars, discrimination against women and ethnic and religious minorities."

Bulgaria was allied with the Germans in both world wars, but it came to the aid of its Jews when the Nazis sought to send them to concentration camps. Today, the country has a legacy of religious and ethnic tolerance that Mr. Clinton praised.

"We must help all of southeastern Europe choose freedom and tolerance and community," he said. "We must give all the people in this region a unifying magnet that is stronger than the pull of old hatreds that has threatened to tear them apart over and over again."

*   *   *

December 23, 1999

10 YEARS AFTER REVOLT, LITTLE GLEE IN ROMANIA

By DONALD G. McNEIL Jr.

BUCHAREST, Romania, Dec. 22—Iona Berbelescu wasn't going to let the young man whose life she saved 10 years ago be forgotten. But she was upset at how few other Romanians cared. There were 20 fat wreaths from political parties leaning against the stone crosses in University Square, but precious few of what she had brought—a single red carnation.

In the chill wind blowing over the puddles where a wet snowstorm had been stamped into slush, it took her five minutes to light her candle, and then it guttered out against a wreath.

Ten years ago, on the night of Dec. 21, this square had been jammed with students demanding an end to the dictatorship of Nicolae Ceausescu, waving the blue-yellow-red flags of Romania with circular holes where the Communist Party emblem had been cut out.

After darkness fell, armored cars had raced through the plaza, then doubled back and opened fire. Red tracer bullets zipped into some students; others were simply run down. A boy named Marius had seen a friend nearly beheaded by a soldier swinging his trench shovel; he had panicked and run to a girlfriend's house nearby. She wouldn't let him in. Mrs. Berbelescu, a single mother with a 12-year-old daughter at home, had.

"If Ceausescu were still alive, I'd be in prison now," she said, by way of explaining why she'd returned.

Today, the police had closed Magheru Boulevard to permit big ceremonies at the crosses, which are on a traffic divider. Someone had placed hundreds of candles in red jars along the center lane dividers. They hardly needed to have bothered.

The 1 p.m. wreath-laying ceremony had drawn fewer than 100 people. The rest of the day saw a trickle of people like Mrs. Berbelescu.

At 12:08 p.m. today, exactly 10 years from the moment when the presidential helicopter snatched Mr. Ceausescu off the roof of the Communist Party headquarters as a mob of 100,000 was surging through its doors to lynch him, nothing much was happening. The square outside was full of parked cars.

Upstairs, Ion Iliescu, Romania's president from 1989 to 1996 and leading in the polls for next year's vote, was alone in his office. Ten years ago, he had pulled together the National Salvation Front that took over after Mr. Ceausescu fled and that executed the dictator and his wife three days later.

Mr. Iliescu had spent the morning visiting the crucial spots of Dec. 22, 1989, with his comrades of those days: this building itself, with the balcony from which Mr. Ceausescu had retreated from the booing crowd; Studio 4 of the national television station, where Mr. Iliescu had first told the nation, "The dictator has fled"; the TV conference room where the National Salvation Front was drawing up a new constitution when bullets began crashing in.

Only one reporter was there to walk with him. When he entered Studio 4 to reminisce with the staff for half an hour, a monitor in the corner showed what the station was broadcasting just then: a movie about a giant squid.

Live television hasn't been Romania's forte since the revolt, when it galvanized the nation but also poured forth rumors that knotted the country in chaos: that Libyan terrorists were fighting to save the Ceausescus, that the tapwater was poisoned, that the Soviets were invading.

Drawing a reporter along by the arm, Mr. Iliescu pointed out the bullet holes in the window frames and broadcast equipment. The trajectories showed that, as he said, some had been fired from a helicopter. He pointed out the radiator the fledgling government had huddled behind, and the glass bridge between buildings they had crawled across, cut by flying glass but missed by the bullets. He described the man in the parking lot who drew a pistol as he approached, but was clubbed on the arm by a soldier and ran off in the dark.

Even now, no one knows who started the shooting that evening, which went on for five nights and faded only after the Ceausescus' corpses were shown on television. The assumption is that it was small, loyal sniper squads trying to create panic, which they did.

"It's still a problem," he said. "Over 1,000 people were questioned, but it was never concretized—who fired from here, who organized this attack. Aren't there questions left over from your Civil War? Look how long you investigated who shot Kennedy, and it was only one man—or maybe two."

Lingering mysteries aside, he was asked, why aren't average citizens part of this anniversary? Why can't the nine political parties—including those that defeated him in 1996—get together and celebrate just for a day?

"We did have speeches in Parliament about the revolution two days ago," he answered. "But the people are disappointed, generally dissatisfied with life that is worse than it was in 1989. And the people in power now are not those who were connected with the revolution."

To be fair, private TV stations and newspapers have made an effort, using old pictures and new interviews with the principals. But the coverage is largely mournful and angry: it concentrates on those maimed, widowed or left childless. It describes their poverty now, and their angry belief that their sacrifices were betrayed by politicians, including Mr. Iliescu.

The mood is not celebratory. Some Romanians say the government fears riots, since a third of the country lives on less than $2 a day and blames the government. The current president was shouted down during a Dec. 1 speech and his prime minister was forced to resign this month. The new government was sworn in today.

Tonight a street party that echoed 1989—it had two armored cars parked beneath a screen with clips of the fighting and this time artificial fireworks—drew only about 1,200 people to the same square that held 100,000 a decade ago.

But it started well behind schedule—as someone there pointed out, "It's much colder than it was that night."

* * *

October 6, 2000

YUGOSLAVS CLAIM BELGRADE FOR NEW LEADER

By STEVEN ERLANGER

BELGRADE, Serbia, Oct. 5—As the federal Parliament burned and tear gas wafted through chaotic streets, vast throngs of Serbs wrested their capital and key levers of power away from Slobodan Milosevic today, bringing his 13-year reign to the edge of collapse.

Vojislav Kostunica, the opposition leader who claimed victory in the presidential election on Sept. 24, moved through an ecstatic crowd of several hundred thousand and proclaimed, "Good evening, dear liberated Serbia!"

The crowd shouted his name, and he shouted back: "Big, beautiful Serbia has risen up just so one man, Slobodan Milosevic, will leave."

Behind the crowds, smoke from the burning Parliament building mingled with the blacker smoke from the burning

Against a backdrop of smoke from the Parliament building mingling with smoke from the TV and radio center in Belgrade, thousands of Serbs demanded that Slobodan Milosevic leave power. With the outpouring in the streets, important bastions of state power defected to the opposition.

state television and radio center—bombed by NATO during last year's war over Kosovo—and tear gas, all set loose as hundreds of thousands of Serbs roamed through the city to demand the exit of a leader who had brought them years of ethnic conflict, isolation and international contempt.

The whereabouts of Mr. Milosevic and his family was unknown, though he was believed to be in Serbia. Two main pillars of his regime, the state news media and many of his police, were gone. But though the army stayed out of the fray, the chiefs of the security forces had yet to formally shift their allegiance to Mr. Kostunica, and Mr. Milosevic had not relinquished power.

While the Belgrade police did not take serious action against the protesters and many joined them, Mr. Milosevic's interior minister, Vlajko Stoiljkovic, refused to meet Mr. Kostunica's representatives, instead asking them, "What have you done to Belgrade?"

Opposition leaders, including Momcilo Perisic, the chief of staff whom Mr. Milosevic fired in October 1998, were reportedly talking to the army to persuade them to recognize Mr. Kostunica as president.

For the time being, there were no contacts between Mr. Milosevic and Mr. Kostunica. The opposition leader told the crowd not to march on Mr. Milosevic's home and office in Dedinje, a suburb, saying: "Answer their violence with non-violence. Answer their lies with the truth."

As Mr. Kostunica tried to call the new federal Parliament and city government into session, the mood was boisterous, ecstatic and proud. "All of us have simply had enough," said Petr Radosavljevic, a mechanical engineer. "All we want is a normal country, where there is a future for young people."

Damir Strahinjic, 25, waving his arm over the crowd, said: "This should be enough to see the end of him. But you never know in this country, with this guy." His fears were echoed by a senior member of Mr. Kostunica's staff tonight, who said, "I'm thinking Milosevic has one more trick up his sleeve."

Earlier, Mr. Milosevic's ruling Socialist Party attacked the opposition for causing unrest and violence and vowed to fight back with "all means to secure peaceful life." But faced with an uprising that has spread throughout much of Serbia, Mr. Milosevic may have run out of moves. Party members were talking to opposition leaders and even human rights lawyers.

The United States and European governments threw their support behind Mr. Kostunica. In Washington, President Clinton declared: "The people of Serbia have made their opinion clear. They did it when they voted peacefully and quietly, and now they're doing it in the streets."

With the massive outpouring in the streets, major bastions of state power defected to Mr. Kostunica. The state news agency Tanjug began referring to him as "the elected president of Yugoslavia" in a report signed, "Journalists of Liberated Tanjug." The state newspaper Politika, founded in 1904 and deeply degraded under the Milosevic regime, went over to the opposition. And on state television, a new slide appeared: "This is the new Radio Television Serbia broadcasting."

At 11:30 tonight, Mr. Kostunica appeared on the "liberated" state television, urging reconciliation on a nation used to a steady diet of government propaganda.

Speaking of the burning buildings and clashes, Mr. Kostunica said: "We hope that these sad incidents are behind us. My first hours started with pleasure, that a vision of Serbia I had all these years has started to be fulfilled." He promised that state television would remain "open to all views and all voices," including those of the coalition that has run this country.

He called for the lifting of international sanctions against Yugoslavia, which he said the European Union tonight promised him it would do as early as Monday. While he said "we cannot forget what some countries did to us last year during the NATO bombing, we can't live against the grain," and he promised normal relations with the world.

As thousands of people pressed into Belgrade from opposition strongholds, some were spoiling for a fight. They pushed aside police barricades on the roads to Belgrade, and some stripped police officers of their shields and weapons. Some were equipped with sticks and rocks, and they led the taking of the federal Parliament building, which was heavily guarded by police.

The building was soon on fire, its windows broken, and some demonstrators began to loot it for souvenirs, including chairs, hatracks and leather briefcases used by Parliament members. Portraits of Mr. Milosevic and ballot papers for the Sept. 24 elections were dumped from the second floor, all of them already circled to vote for Mr. Milosevic.

The police were lavish with their use of tear gas, which filled downtown Belgrade, but they did not charge the crowd. They used batons and stun grenades, but those who did were overwhelmed by the crowd, and some young men marched happily with their trophies: plastic police riot shields and helmets.

When crowds approached the back entrance of Radio Television Serbia, the police started to come out with their hands raised. The crowd greeted them with "plavi, plavi," or blue, the color of their uniforms, and gave them opposition badges.

As people entered the building, some workers came out the side, including television anchors and personalities like Staka Novakovic, Simo Gajin and Tanja Lenard, who is a senior member of the Yugoslav United Left party of Mr. Milosevic's wife. The crowd began to spit on them, and Ms. Lenard found refuge behind some garbage containers.

The crowd then looted the building.

There was a similar scene at a police station in nearby Majke Jevrosime Street. When the police left the building, some in the crowd gave them civilian clothes. But the building was then looted—with weapons taken—and was set afire with gasoline bombs.

In the skirmishing, at least one person died and 100 were injured today, according to independent radio B2-92, which also returned to its old frequency in Belgrade when its own headquarters were taken. The station had been seized by the government twice, and had been broadcasting by satellite. Belgrade Studio B television was also taken back from political control, and private stations affiliated with the Milosevic regime, like TV Palma and TV Pink, stopped broadcasting and put up slides that read, "This program is canceled because of the current situation in the country."

The day's vast uprising was the culmination of a campaign to defend Mr. Kostunica's victory in the presidential elections that Mr. Milosevic called in an effort to restore his own tattered legitimacy. It was a tactical mistake of the first order, because Serbs took the election as a referendum on Mr. Milosevic's 13 years of rule and misrule.

According to the opposition, Mr. Kostunica won at least 51.33 percent of the vote against four other candidates, an outright victory. But with electoral fraud, the Federal Election Commission reduced his percentage to just under 50 percent and called a runoff.

Mr. Kostunica called it theft and vowed that he would not accept a runoff for an election he had won. Strikes and protests on his behalf began to spread through Serbia this week.

The key moment may have come on Wednesday, when Mr. Milosevic's police failed to break a strike at a key coal mine in Kolubara. The workers, who had struck Friday to support Mr. Kostunica, refused to leave and called for help. Some 20,000 relatives and ordinary citizens from surrounding towns came to their aid, and the police let them go through, refusing to attack. Tonight, the police withdrew entirely from the mine.

Later Wednesday night, Tanjug reported that the highest court had ruled that the presidential election was invalid because of irregularities. But the court's judgment, supposed to be published today, did not come, and Mr. Kostunica made it clear tonight that it was simply too late to think about any compromise over the election with the authorities.

* * *

October 6, 2000

SERBIA'S RELUCTANT REVOLUTIONARY CALMLY LOOKS BEYOND THE CHAOS

By STEVEN ERLANGER

BELGRADE, Serbia, Oct. 5—Vojislav Kostunica had just made a rousing speech from the balcony of City Hall to several hundred thousand roaring supporters, who had just made him a revolution, and as he slouched in a leather chair, as aides and politicians rushed about, he had trouble believing that it was really his own life that was being transformed.

"I could never have imagined this for myself," he said quietly in an interview, as those below shouted his name. "First, to be in party politics and then suddenly elected to the highest position in the land, and also," he stopped, then laughed, "to be in a way a very mild revolutionary."

Then he hardened a bit, leaning forward. "I didn't want it this way. But there was no other way to defend democratic institutions and the people's will. There was no other possibility; we tried in every other way to get Slobodan Milosevic to recognize his defeat."

The smell of the burned and looted federal Parliament hung in the air across the park. "At one moment, I feel sorry seeing all that is happening," he said. "And on the other hand, we are coming closer to the end of our suffering."

Mr. Kostunica (pronounced kosh-TOON-eet-zah), in his trademark gray suit, rumpled white shirt and simple tie, is 56 years old, a constitutional lawyer who spent much of his career in academic institutes.

He was chosen by a fragile coalition of 18 opposition parties to run against Mr. Milosevic because of his polling figures: he is perceived by Serbs as one of their own—a Serb from the heart of Serbia, unlike Mr. Milosevic, whose father hailed from Montenegro—and he seems honest, uncorrupted and has an abiding and even mystical sense of Serbian nationhood.

As important, he had never served in a Milosevic government or—unlike other leaders of the Serbian opposition—even talked with him.

But Mr. Kostunica, who was reluctant until the very last moment to accept the opposition's nomination for the presidential elections on Sept. 24, has developed an extraordinary serenity and sense of mission over these past weeks of campaigning and quiet, but determined struggle.

"What makes me calm," he said tonight, "is that the people here trust in me, and those on the other side, in the Socialist Party, know I'm the safest option for them."

Mr. Kostunica has pledged no revenge against those who served the old regime. He said tonight that he had no intention of arresting Mr. Milosevic, who was indicted for war crimes last year over the action of his security forces in Kosovo. When some in the crowd shouted, "to Dedinje!" the Belgrade suburb where Mr. Milosevic lives, he told them: "No one is marching to Dedinje."

Mr. Kostunica expected Mr. Milosevic to take one of the legal opportunities the opposition provided him to concede the momentous election held 11 days ago—the first ballot in which Mr. Milosevic had stood for direct election since 1992.

Despite some private wavering among his staff, Mr. Kostunica stuck to his principles, and refused to let Mr. Milosevic require a second-round runoff through vote stealing. But Mr. Kostunica also shied away from street confrontations, feeling grave responsibility for sending people against the police, said Zarko Korac, another opposition leader.

But Mr. Korac, a psychologist, insisted in a private meeting with opposition leaders this week that the responsibility

Reuters

Vojislav Kostunica, the opposition leader, waving to crowd last night.

would rest with Mr. Milosevic for his election fraud, not with Mr. Kostunica. Still, Mr. Kostunica said, he did not expect today to turn into a revolt.

Asked if today was a revolution, the man now broadly hailed as president of Yugoslavia hesitated. "It's a democratic revolution," he finally said. "When I always thought of what would be the revolution in this country, it was Tocqueville and his democratic revolution. That's what I had in mind. But I suppose this is a revolutionary way of defending the will of the people."

He said that he had made many efforts to establish contact with Mr. Milosevic, without success. But with the rage of the people today, the silence of the regime, its manipulation of the courts to annul the election result and the burning of the Parliament, legal compromise ran out of time, he said. "Now too many steps have been taken to retreat, that's for sure," he said.

"Milosevic tried his old tactics from 1996," when he delayed as protests built for three months, then finally gave in to the opposition's victory in local elections, saving his power. "But now it's too late," Mr. Kostunica said, a touch wearily. "He doesn't command matters here anymore."

His aides were beckoning. Other political leaders were waiting. He rose up, listening to whispers. He was told that the state media, television and the newspaper Politika, long a mouthpiece for Mr. Milosevic, now belonged to the opposition. He made arrangements to go to state television, to speak to the nation.

Then he said, "Politika is very important to us—so go prepare the next edition of Politika." Aides dispersed, carrying out his orders. Only he seemed surprised.

* * *

October 7, 2000

MILOSEVIC CONCEDES HIS DEFEAT; YUGOSLAVS CELEBRATE NEW ERA

By STEVEN ERLANGER

BELGRADE, Serbia, Oct. 6—Bowing to a vast popular revolt against him, a pale Slobodan Milosevic resigned tonight as Yugoslavia's president, ending 13 years of rule that have brought his country four wars, international isolation, a NATO bombing campaign and his own indictment on war crimes charges.

Vojislav Kostunica, a 56-year-old constitutional lawyer of quiet habits and a firm belief in a future for Yugoslavia as a normal country within Europe, is expected to be inaugurated as president on Saturday.

An already exuberant and chaotic Belgrade, celebrating its extraordinary day of revolution on Thursday, exploded with noise as the news of Mr. Milosevic's resignation, made in a short speech on television, quickly spread. Cars blasted their horns; people banged on pots and pans from balconies, blew whistles and danced in the street.

Mr. Milosevic appeared on television about 11:20 p.m.—shortly after Mr. Kostunica announced, on a television phone-in program, that he had met Mr. Milosevic and the army chief of staff, Gen. Nebojsa Pavkovic, this evening, and that both had congratulated him on his election victory on Sept. 24.

The resignation deal was helped along by Foreign Minister Igor S. Ivanov of Russia, who met with Mr. Kostunica and Mr. Milosevic today. Mr. Ivanov was carrying assurances that if Mr. Milosevic gave up power now, the world would not press for his extradition to face war crimes charges in The Hague, senior Western officials said tonight.

"I've just received official information that Vojislav Kostunica won the elections," Mr. Milosevic said in his television address. "This decision was made by the body that was authorized to do so under the Constitution, and I consider that it has to be respected."

Mr. Milosevic spoke with a straight face after an extraordinary set of manipulations on his part—of the Federal Election Commission and the highest court in the land—to deny Mr. Kostunica outright victory.

Speaking of how important it is for political parties to strengthen themselves in opposition, Mr. Milosevic said he intended to continue as leader of the Socialist Party of Serbia after taking a break "to spend more time with my family, especially my grandson, Marko."

Despite his brave words, it is unlikely that the Socialist Party, with its own future to consider, will keep Mr. Milosevic as its leader for long. The remarks seemed part of a deal to save him a little bit of face.

There is deep resentment in this semi-reformed Communist Party—Serbia's largest and best organized, in power since World War II—of Mr. Milosevic's indulgence of his wife, Mirjana Markovic, who began her own party, the Yugoslav United Left. Ruling in coalition, the Socialists saw more and more of their positions, powers and benefits going to the United Left.

The reaction in Belgrade was immediate and loud.

Tanja Radovic, a 23-year-old student blowing her whistle furiously on Knez Mihailova Street, said: "He's gone. It's finally true. We had too much of him, it's enough. This is the end of him and all these thieves."

Dragana Kovac, 31, said: "I'm happy, and not just because of him, but because of her. He should have spent more time with his family starting 10 years ago."

Ilija Bobic said: "I wish all my family were alive to see this. My father used to say that the Communists would finish quickly. He was wrong, but it came true, finally."

Mr. Bobic stopped, then said: "We all know it won't be better quickly here. But now you can talk. You're not afraid of the phone, of being an enemy inside, of having to join the party to have a job."

The United States and Europe have promised a quick lifting of international sanctions against Yugoslavia, as well as aid, once Mr. Milosevic goes. The sanctions include a toothless oil embargo and a flight ban, currently suspended. But financial sanctions and a visa ban aimed at the Milosevic government are likely to remain in place for now.

The United States and Britain have urged that Mr. Milosevic be handed over to the war crimes tribunal, and continued to do so publicly today. But Mr. Kostunica, who considers the tribunal a political instrument of Washington and not a neutral legal body, has made it clear that he will not arrest Mr. Milosevic or extradite him.

Mr. Kostunica's vow was also intended to give Mr. Milosevic the security to leave office, so that an electoral concession did not have to mean, as Mr. Kostunica said, "a matter of life or death."

Foreign Minister Ivanov came here today to deliver a similar message, Western officials said tonight.

If Mr. Milosevic conceded and renounced power, even after the pillars of his rule collapsed this week, he and his family would be allowed to remain in Serbia, they said. But no Western country would say so publicly, given the United Nations tribunal's indictment.

Mr. Kostunica has pointed out that if democratic and international stability is at stake, the requirement to pursue those indicted is secondary under international law.

The collapse of Mr. Milosevic's position came soon after Mr. Ivanov met him this morning in Belgrade. This afternoon, the Constitutional Court suddenly issued its ruling approving Mr. Kostunica's appeal of the election results.

The official press agency Tanjug said on Wednesday night that the court had decided to annul the main part of the Sept. 24 presidential vote, implying a repeat of the election. But then the court said that in fact Mr. Kostunica had won the first round outright, with more than 50 percent of the vote, precisely as he has insisted. It was another example of Mr. Milosevic's manipulation, but this time to others' ends.

Then the speaker of the Serbian Parliament, Dragan Tomic, one of Mr. Milosevic's closest allies, announced that he would convene that body on Monday to recognize Mr. Kostunica's election as federal president. He addressed a letter to Mr. Kostunica this way: "To the president of the Federal Republic of Yugoslavia."

The election of Mr. Kostunica—carried to power first by the votes of a majority of Serbs, and then by an uprising by even more of them—will present difficulties and opportunities for Montenegro and Kosovo, both parts of Yugoslavia.

The Western-leaning president of Montenegro, Milo Djukanovic, will find himself offered a new deal within Yugoslavia that will be aimed at blunting the effort toward independence. That may quickly undermine Mr. Djukanovic's governing coalition in Montenegro, which contains parties firmly backing independence.

Mr. Djukanovic boycotted the federal elections, allowing Milosevic allies to win all of Montenegro's seats in the federal Parliament. Those allies are now likely to make a deal with Mr. Kostunica, abandoning Mr. Milosevic, and leaving Mr. Djukanovic in effect powerless in a Belgrade that could quickly become the center for democratic life in the Balkans.

Mr. Kostunica will also offer Kosovo a high degree of autonomy. While outside powers recognizes Yugoslav sovereignty over Kosovo, Mr. Milosevic was a perfect foil for Kosovo Albanian desires for independence, which have only grown stronger since NATO intervened on the Albanians' behalf in the 1999 bombing war.

Mr. Kostunica says he will live within United Nations Security Council Resolution 1244, governing Kosovo, but will insist on the return of Serbs who fled during the war.

In his television appearance, Mr. Milosevic thanked those who voted for him and even those who voted against him, "because they lifted from my soul a heavy burden I have borne for 10 years," he said. He also said a time in opposition would be good for the left coalition, to allow them to purge those who got into the party "to feed some personal interest," an extraordinary comment for a leader who allowed a form of state-sanctioned mafia to develop.

"I congratulate Mr. Kostunica on his election victory and wish for all citizens of Yugoslavia great success during the new presidency," he concluded.

In his own television appearance, Mr. Kostunica described his meeting with Mr. Milosevic. "It was ordinary communication, and it's good that we met, because there was a lot of fear over the peaceful transfer of power, especially last night," Mr. Kostunica said.

"This is the first time for many years in this country that power has been transferred normally, in a civilized manner," he said.

And he said he pointed out a lesson to Mr. Milosevic: "I talked about how power, once lost, is not power lost forever. You can regain it. This is something that all my experience taught me. The other side couldn't even imagine something like this, but now the other side has accepted this, and it is getting used to this lesson."

* * *

October 11, 2000

EUROPEAN UNION MOVES TO EMBRACE YUGOSLAV LEADERSHIP

By STEVEN ERLANGER

BELGRADE, Serbia, Oct. 10—The world began to embrace the new Yugoslavia and its new president, Vojislav Kostunica, in earnest today, with the visit here of the French foreign minister, Hubert Vedrine, representing the European Union.

Praising the ousting of Slobodan Milosevic, Mr. Vedrine said: "I have come here to express my admiration to Mr. Kostunica and the Serbian people. Together they have written a huge page in the democratic history of Europe."

Mr. Vedrine arrived the day after the European Union lifted some major sanctions against Yugoslavia and promised $2 billion in aid. Mr. Kostunica will attend a European Union summit meeting in Biarritz, France, probably on Friday.

Though his own domestic politics remained unsettled, with a good deal of political jockeying, Mr. Kostunica also moved to improve relations with the United States, whose policies he has often criticized, not least NATO's bombing of Yugoslavia over Kosovo. James C. O'Brien, the chief Balkan adviser to President Clinton and Secretary of State Madeleine K. Albright, is expected here Thursday.

The United States is eager to restore diplomatic relations with Yugoslavia after Mr. Milosevic's departure and to build a relationship with Mr. Kostunica.

In a telephone interview, Mr. O'Brien said he "looks forward to a good discussion" with Mr. Kostunica, hoping "to begin to create a normal relationship" and offer help, if wanted, to build democratic institutions after 13 years of Mr. Milosevic's rule.

Mr. Vedrine has kept close touch with Mr. Kostunica, who regards improving relations with Europe as more important and less harmful to Serbia's interests than warming ties with the United States. Still, Mr. Kostunica describes himself as by no means anti-American, but wary of a superpower that, as the guarantor of the 1995 Dayton agreement, kept Mr. Milosevic in power much longer than necessary.

Mr. Kostunica said today that the European Union's decision to lift sanctions against Yugoslavia will "enable us to move closer to what always has been our natural environment—Europe." The United States is also expected to lift most sanctions, but the process is more cumbersome legally.

The situation remained muddled with the government of Serbia, the dominant republic in Yugoslavia. Mr. Kostunica and his allies in the 18-party coalition that supported his candidacy continued trying to assert control over the powerful government of Serbia and its Parliament, which was not up for election on Sept. 24. But they found new resistance from Mr. Milosevic's Socialist Party and the Radical Party of the ultranationalist Vojislav Seselj.

The Serbian Parliament will be disbanded for new elections on Dec. 17, but there is bitter fighting over ministries in the temporary government that is supposed to rule until then.

Both the Socialists and the Radicals said they were suspending talks on a new, provisional, all-party Serbian government until "the end of riots, violence and lawlessness in cities and against the citizens of Serbia."

The complaint is seen as a bit disingenuous, given the pattern of Mr. Milosevic's rule, and seems a cover for bargaining about jobs—in particular the Interior Ministry, which controls the police. Mr. Seselj wants that job for his party, and the Socialists want it for themselves, but Mr. Kostunica's allies insist that they must have it to protect their victory over Mr. Milosevic.

Some Kostunica allies warned tonight that they would bring more popular protest and pressure to bear on the Serbian Parliament if it did not stop obstructing the new order. Velimir Ilic, the mayor of Cacak, a center of the opposition to Mr. Milosevic, said today, "Serbs are so eager to see changes, and I do not know who will protect Socialists, and how, if they continue to drag their feet."

But the way Mr. Kostunica's more revolutionary allies have moved to assert control over the police, customs operations and some state-owned companies, sometimes with the aid of armed men, has caused wider complaints.

Major banks, ministries, university faculties and important companies and factories were being taken over, but often by employees who are trying to restore rights, like university autonomy, stripped from them by the Milosevic government. Often, too, companies are removing managers imposed on them by the ruling parties, often the Yugoslav United Left party of Mr. Milosevic's wife, Mirjana Markovic.

There is concern among the Kostunica group, too. A statement from his economic and policy advisers today appealed to "all employees and those in managing positions in institutions and companies to protect property and prevent various abuses."

Today, for example, former Prime Minister Milan Panic, a Serbian-American, regained control of a pharmaceutical plant that had belonged to his ICN Pharmaceuticals and was taken over by the Serbian government last year. The government failed to pay the factory for its goods and then took it over. This evening, after a visit and calls by Mr. Panic, shareholders of the Galenika factory met at the request of workers and agreed to return majority ownership to ICN.

An important member of the coalition that backed Mr. Kostunica, Zoran Djindjic, complained today that the Socialists and their allies were also meddling with the police. State Security, led by a Milosevic ally, Rade Markovic, "is still closed to us," Mr. Djindjic said, warning that telephone tapping had resumed after a break of a few days.

"There are attempts of consolidation within Secret Service," Mr. Djindjic said. "We have warned them we do not want conflicts. We expect that the people from that service realize that the situation has changed."

Mr. Kostunica is also trying to mend fences with Serbia's smaller sister republic, Montenegro, and its president, Milo Djukanovic, who wants a new constitutional arrangement with Serbia in a Yugoslavia that would look more like a confederation.

Mr. Kostunica, as federal president, is chairman of the Supreme Defense Council, which consists of the Serbian and Montenegrin presidents. He announced that the council would meet on Wednesday—the first time it has met in years and the first time Mr. Djukanovic has attended since he broke away from Mr. Milosevic in 1998. But the meeting has been delayed because Mr. Djukanovic is recovering from a minor road accident.

After meeting Mr. Kostunica, Mr. Vedrine and his wife took a walk in central Belgrade and discovered the ambivalence felt by many here toward the NATO countries that bombed Yugoslavia last year over Kosovo.

France and Serbia have traditionally warm relations, and Mr. Vedrine began his walk at a large monument to the two countries' alliance in World War I.

One man said, "Vive la France!" and others clapped. But another man shouted: "Aren't you ashamed to show your face here? I have my children here. You bombed them."

* * *

October 30, 2000

ALBANIAN MODERATES CLAIM KOSOVO VICTORY

By CARLOTTA GALL

PRISTINA, Kosovo, Oct. 29—The moderate Kosovo Albanian leader, Ibrahim Rugova, claimed victory for his party today in Kosovo's first postwar elections, saying that unofficial results from the election on Saturday showed that the party had won more than 60 percent of the vote in municipalities across the province.

The more militant parties, formed by members of the armed rebel force, the Kosovo Liberation Army, appeared to have fared poorly except in a few areas. If the results hold, it is a sign that Kosovo Albanians have opted for peace and stability and largely rejected the thuggery of some of the people who assumed power after the war last year.

Votes were still being counted through the day, and official results were not expected until Monday. But political parties and independent monitoring groups disclosed their calculations. The results from an independent monitoring group, as well as from Mr. Rugova's party, the Democratic League of Kosovo, indicated that the party had won broadly, in particular in all the major towns.

"Based on preliminary results," he said at a news conference in Pristina, the province's capital, his party won "60 percent of the vote throughout Kosovo."

Mr. Rugova declared his determination to lead Kosovo to independence, but also said his party would protect minorities in Kosovo, a reference to the Serbian population, as well as to Gypsies and Muslim Slavs, who have been subject to attacks and killings in the last year, since NATO-led peacekeeping troops maintained control of the province.

Kosovo remains a province of Serbia, the dominant republic in Yugoslavia. Albanians have long made up the preponderance of Kosovo residents, and they had a substantial degree of autonomy in the Communist era. That was withdrawn in 1989 after Slobodan Milosevic became the Serbian leader, and by the late 1990's the Albanians mounted an armed rebellion for independence. After Mr. Milosevic failed to halt what the West called horrific atrocities by his security forces, NATO bombed Yugoslavia for 78 days until Mr. Milosevic agreed to withdraw his troops. Since then, the United Nations has been trying to re-establish civilian government.

The small remaining population of Serbs in Kosovo overwhelmingly boycotted the elections. Today they said the vote was illegal because only the Albanians voted.

Vojislav Kostunica, who took Mr. Milosevic's place as Yugoslav president earlier this month, issued a statement today saying that "Yugoslavia cannot recognize the results of local elections." According to Agence France-Presse, he urged international bodies to carry out the United Nations Security Council resolution that governs the foreign presence in the province, and foresees that Kosovo's future will be determined in talks between provincial leaders and Belgrade.

Mr. Rugova's party said its calculations showed that it won 60 to 70 percent of the vote in all of Kosovo's main towns, including Pristina, and it called for parliamentary and presidential elections to be held next June.

An independent monitoring group, the Kosovo Action for Civic Initiative, released similar figures, showing an overall victory for the Democratic League of Kosovo.

Mr. Rugova's party acknowledged losing several areas in central Kosovo to its main rival, the Democratic Party of Kosovo, led by Hashim Thaci, a former leader of the Kosovo Liberation Army.

Mr. Thaci has played a prominent role in Kosovo, and his supporters and associates acquired influential positions of power after Serbian forces withdrew in June last year. But voters appear to have rejected the roughness and criminality associated with the former guerrilla fighters.

Mr. Thaci declined to talk to reporters today. He emerged only briefly from a meeting in his offices dressed in casual clothes and looking pensive. The mood of supporters at his party headquarters in Pristina today was subdued.

*   *   *

November 26, 2000

LONG-SUFFERING ROMANIANS TO VOTE FOR A LEADER TODAY

By DONALD G. McNEIL Jr.

CRAIOVA, Romania, Nov. 25—Broken promises made in fading industrial cities like this are causing both the left and right to surge in Romanian politics.

In the presidential election on Sunday, Ion Iliescu, the 70-year-old former Communist who was president from 1990 to 1996. is expected to make a comeback with about 40 percent of the vote, then face a runoff on Dec. 10.

More surprising to political analysts, polls show Corneliu Vadim Tudor, whose brand of nationalism is just beginning to go out of style in neighboring Yugoslavia, headed for second place. Mr. Tudor is shoving aside the coalition of centrists who have run this devastated country since 1996 but failed to fix the economy because of bickering and now cannot unite behind one candidate.

Mr. Tudor is a senator, poet and magazine owner who has written anti-Hungarian, anti-Semitic and anti-Gypsy tracts, and talked of ending corruption "with a Kalashnikov" and of uniting "Greater Romania."

There is little suggestion that voters endorse such right-wing ideas. But Romanians are monumentally frustrated. Eleven years after the collapse of Communism and the personality cult of Nicolae Ceausescu, they live in the second biggest country in eastern Europe after Poland, but are virtually last in line to join the European Union. Living standards are edging toward those of India or Africa: 40 percent of the population lives on less than $35 a month.

The lei, which was 21 to the dollar when Mr. Ceausescu was executed, is now 25,000 to the dollar. In a population of 23 million, there are 6 million retirees and only 4.3 million registered workers supporting them. Between 25 and 40 percent of the economy goes untaxed. The young flee west.

Here in Craiova, the Heavy Machine Tool Factory has laid off 6,200 of the 7,000 who used to work inside. Other factories making train engines, agricultural vehicles and Daewoo cars are suffering similar fates. The afternoon shift change disgorged a trickle of workers.

"It's become very tough," said Dumitru Popa, 40. "We don't have much work to do, and we're doing more starving than eating."

From the politicians, he said, "it's all lies."

"But Iliescu," he said, "is probably the most popular because he's more charismatic."

Mr. Iliescu, 70, cheerful and sometimes teased by his nickname "Granny," still draws crowds of elderly women who kiss his car and workers who like his pledges of better pensions and no more layoffs. He was a popular first-term president, the head of the National Salvation Front, which assumed power during the confused street fighting that drove out the Ceausescus.

But he could never bring himself to close the dying state-owned factories or sell failing banks.

A center-right coalition led by Emil Constantinescu, a university professor, ousted him, promising to do just that and push for European Union integration. But it fell apart.

Corruption, a perennial problem, appears to have been the main undoing of Mr. Constantinescu. In July, he refused to seek a second term, saying he was disgusted at the greed that blocked his reforms. Last week, he got specific: 30,000 tons of fuel oil was illegally shipped to neighboring Yugoslavia in breach of the international embargo with the connivance of the border police and transport ministry, he said. Embezzlement of public funds was as routine as cigarette and coffee smuggling.

"If we continue to break laws and if theft, crime and lies continue to proliferate, then any investments or support through international programs are in vain," he said.

Haphazard privatizations have hurt consumers: phone bills soared after a Greek telephone company bought Romania's and a private monopoly replaced a public one.

That anger has opened the way for Mr. Tudor. His older ideas about taking back lands that now lie outside Romania's borders—Moldavia and Bessarabia—excite few and only lunatics want war with Hungary over Transylvania, which for centuries was part of the Hungarian Empire and still houses a substantial Hungarian minority. But Mr. Tudor's plans to recentralize the economy, establish price controls and "liquidate the business Mafia" do strike chords.

He is also quick-witted—in the last presidential debate, his arguments with a pompous moderator stole the show. A showman with a sense of history, he dismissed Sweden's $3 billion unpaid-loan claim, a debate point, by saying Romania fed a lost Swedish army for five years after it was trounced by Russia in 1729, which should cancel the debt.

Mr. Iliescu skipped the last debate, as if he had already won.

The centrist candidates, Prime Minister Mugur Isarescu, Foreign Minister Petre Roman, former Prime Minister Theodor Stolojan, and former Foreign Minister Teodor Melescanu, are all respected—but indistinguishable—political leaders.

Dorel Sandor, a political analyst, said that Mr. Roman, for example, is respected by intellectuals and the young; his fluency in English, French and Spanish help make him Romania's best-known political face abroad. But like the other centrist technocrats, Mr. Sandor said, "he appears not to be credible in his concern about poor people—and they are the majority."

Mr. Iliescu appeals to 15 million struggling voters because he is still a populist, Mr. Tudor because he is a nationalist who has tempered his anti-NATO, anti-Europe stance. "It's an antidemocratic trend, but the poor have to live," Mr. Sandor said.

The top issues in the election, said Alin Teodorescu, a market survey specialist, are inflation, sinking standards of living, corruption, and health and education. The issues on the mind of the West—polluted rivers and European Union standards—are well down the list.

Transitions Online, a web magazine covering eastern Europe, predicted a comeback by Mr. Iliescu last week and used as a title the response a schoolboy once had to give to each stroke of the cane: "Thank you, sir. May I have another?"

*   *   *

December 11, 2000

FORMER CHIEF OF ROMANIA RETAKES OFFICE OVER RIGHTIST

By DONALD G. McNEIL Jr.

BUCHAREST, Romania, Dec. 10—In what experts called a showing of political maturity, Romanians today gave former President Ion Iliescu another term in office, rejecting an ultranationalist by a large margin.

Exit polls indicated that Mr. Iliescu had won 70 percent of the vote in his runoff against Corneliu Vadim Tudor, who had run on a promise that he would "liquidate the mafia" that has drained the economy but is infamous for his magazines' screeds against Jews, Hungarians and Gypsies. The final vote will not be known for a day or two, but recent exit polls have been accurate here.

Minutes after the polls closed, an angry Mr. Tudor charged that the vote was "the biggest fraud in the history of Romania" and claimed that pollsters had been paid $150,000 to invent data, bribe election monitors and sabotage vote-tallying computers.

"How can Mr. Iliescu have won the whole pot?" he demanded, wondering if the likely winning party and election officials "really think we are so stupid?" He said he would complain to an international human rights court and called the results "a victory of the Antichrist."

Television commentators refused even to discuss his charges. Emil Hurezeanu, who covers Romania for German radio, called the statement "delirium and self-parody"; and Cornel Nistorescu, editor of Evenimentul Zilei, a national daily, said: "We have more important things to discuss tonight."

When he voted at noon today, Mr. Tudor made an impromptu speech that accused his opponents of "crucifying" him and conducting a "lynching campaign." He said he

The ex-president of Romania, Ion Iliescu, won another term yesterday. Newspapers reported exit polls showing he won 70 percent of the vote.

was the victim of "a huge electoral fraud perpetrated by a former K.G.B. agent"—Mr. Iliescu—who is also "an atheist free-thinker with the blood of the people on his hands" as well as a tool of Moscow "since it lost Yugoslavia and now wants to get to the Balkans through Romania.

"Inside every child born is another Vadim Tudor, who will know what to do to protect this country," Mr. Tudor added. He said repeatedly that he is not a vengeful man and, borrowing Jesus' dying words, added: "Forgive them, God, for they know not what they do."

Mr. Iliescu said later that Mr. Tudor's failure to concede and his claims "show him for what he is: not qualified to be president or even a politician."

Mr. Iliescu's own victory speech, delivered seconds after the polls closed at 9 p.m., was a promise "to reform a suffocated economy in order to fight poverty, starvation and misery," to pursue integration with the European Union, membership in NATO and a partnership with the United States; to enforce laws against "those who have stolen our national property" and to pursue "dialogue, tolerance and cooperation."

During Mr. Iliescu's last presidency, from 1990 to 1996, he was seen as at heart a socialist who could not bring himself to close dying factories or shrink a bloated bureaucracy. Asked tonight if he had become a convert to Western-style market economics, he answered: "Life forces us to change. Those who don't are eliminated."

Despite intense interest in the race outside Romania, turnout appeared to be even lower than for the first round of voting two weeks ago, when it was less than 60 percent.

Exit polls suggested that Mr. Iliescu had picked up most of the votes for the four centrists and a moderate ethnic Hungarian candidate, who were eliminated in the first round. Many young voters, who heavily backed Mr. Tudor in the first round, apparently came over to Mr. Iliescu's side. One poll suggested that 15 percent of voters who picked Mr. Tudor the first time switched to Mr. Iliescu, while only 4 percent switched the other way.

Neither side conducted a get-out-the-vote campaign, as is routine in American elections.

Ilie Neacsu, secretary of Mr. Tudor's Greater Romania Party, said the idea was not even discussed because it "would be taken as electoral campaigning, or as propaganda." Under Romanian law, campaigning is illegal in the last 48 hours before an election.

Lucia Ceuca, a spokeswoman for Mr. Iliescu's Party of Social Democracy, said there was no voter-turnout plan, but mayors from her party were authorized to prod people to vote if turnout seemed low. In the 1996 election, she said, the party tried something like a get-out-the-vote effort. It hired political science students, some of them educated in the United States, to telephone voters, "but we received negative publicity—people said these were poisoned phone calls."

This year, confident of victory, they did not repeat the effort.

Political experts repeated their frustration that the center-right coalition that may have begun an economic turnaround last year had been unable to pick a single candidate and had knocked itself out of running in the first round, allowing an extremist to get close to the presidency.

Dorel Sandor, a political analyst, said that the world had seen "a rational vote in the second round" and that the new government "can rely on that maturity."

SUBJECT INDEX

BYLINE INDEX